Hotel Asset Management

Principles & Practices

EDUCATIONAL INSTITUTE BOOKS

UNIFORM SYSTEM OF ACCOUNTS FOR THE LODGING INDUSTRY
Eleventh Revised Edition

PLANNING AND CONTROL FOR FOOD AND BEVERAGE OPERATIONS
Ninth Edition
Jack D. Ninemeier

UNDERSTANDING HOSPITALITY LAW
Fifth Edition
Jack P. Jefferies/Banks Brown

SUPERVISION IN THE HOSPITALITY INDUSTRY
Sixth Edition
Jack D. Ninemeier

MANAGEMENT OF FOOD AND BEVERAGE OPERATIONS
Seventh Edition
Jack D. Ninemeier/David K. Hayes

MANAGING FRONT OFFICE OPERATIONS
Eleventh Edition
Michael L. Kasavana

MANAGING SERVICE IN FOOD AND BEVERAGE OPERATIONS
Fifth Edition
Ronald F. Cichy/Philip J. Hickey, Jr.

THE LODGING AND FOOD SERVICE INDUSTRY
Eighth Edition
Gerald W. Lattin/Thomas W. Lattin/James E. Lattin

SECURITY AND LOSS PREVENTION MANAGEMENT
Third Edition
David M. Stipanuk/Raymond C. Ellis, Jr.

HOSPITALITY INDUSTRY MANAGERIAL ACCOUNTING
Ninth Edition
Raymond S. Schmidgall/Agnes L. DeFranco

MANAGING TECHNOLOGY IN THE HOSPITALITY INDUSTRY
Seventh Edition
Michael L. Kasavana

HOTEL AND RESTAURANT ACCOUNTING
Eighth Edition
Raymond Cote

ACCOUNTING FOR HOSPITALITY MANAGERS
Fifth Edition
Raymond Cote

CONVENTION MANAGEMENT AND SERVICE
Ninth Edition
James R. Abbey

HOSPITALITY SALES AND MARKETING
Sixth Edition
James R. Abbey

MANAGING HOUSEKEEPING OPERATIONS
Revised Third Edition
Aleta A. Nitschke/William D. Frye

HOSPITALITY TODAY: AN INTRODUCTION
Ninth Edition
Rocco M. Angelo

HOSPITALITY FACILITIES MANAGEMENT AND DESIGN
Fourth Edition
David M. Stipanuk

MANAGING HOSPITALITY HUMAN RESOURCES
Sixth Edition
Robert H. Woods, William Werner, Seonghee Cho, and Misty M. Johanson

RETAIL MANAGEMENT FOR SPAS

HOSPITALITY INDUSTRY FINANCIAL ACCOUNTING
Fourth Edition
Raymond S. Schmidgall/James W. Damitio

HOTEL INVESTMENTS: ISSUES & PERSPECTIVES
Fifth Edition
Edited by Lori E. Raleigh and Rachel J. Roginsky

LEADERSHIP AND MANAGEMENT IN THE HOSPITALITY INDUSTRY
Third Edition
Robert H. Woods/Judy Z. King

CONTEMPORARY CLUB MANAGEMENT
Third Edition
Edited by Joe Perdue and Jason Koenigsfeld for the Club Managers Association of America

HOTEL ASSET MANAGEMENT: PRINCIPLES & PRACTICES
Third Edition
Edited by Rich Musgrove, Lori E. Raleigh, and A. J. Singh

MANAGING BEVERAGE OPERATIONS
Second Edition
Ronald F. Cichy/Lendal H. Kotschevar

FOOD SAFETY AND QUALITY MANAGEMENT
Third Edition
Ronald F. Cichy and JaeMin Cha

SPA: A COMPREHENSIVE INTRODUCTION
Elizabeth M. Johnson/Bridgette M. Redman

REVENUE MANAGEMENT: MAXIMIZING REVENUE IN HOSPITALITY OPERATIONS
Second Edition
Gabor Forgacs

FINANCIAL MANAGEMENT FOR SPAS
Raymond S. Schmidgall/John R. Korpi

09/06/23

Hotel Asset Management

Principles & Practices

Third Edition

Edited by

Rich Musgrove, CHAM, CHA, CPM, CCIM, RPA

Lori E. Raleigh

A. J. Singh, Ph.D.

Disclaimer

ISBN: 978-0-86612-507-9 (print version)
ISBN: 978-0-86612-516-1 (e-book version)

Printed in the USA

Contents

Preface

THE FIRST EDITION of *Hotel Asset Management: Principles & Practices* was published in 2004 with the intention of creating a resource guide for asset managers.

The second edition was published in 2009 to help practicing asset managers advance their knowledge of the profession by providing the latest thinking on topics relevant to asset management. Given the breadth of topics covered, the second edition appealed to a much broader audience including students and faculty along with hotel industry executives recognizing the importance of the asset management profession in value creation in the hospitality industry.

We are now pleased to present this third edition, which provides the most comprehensive coverage of the principles and practice of asset management to date. The book is divided into four sections that focus on important facets of asset management as they relate to hospitality real estate.

Part I, "The Foundations and Processes of Asset Management," begins by profiling the current state of the profession. It goes on to cover the asset management cycle, the development of the asset management plan, the evaluation of franchise and chain affiliation programs, the use of benchmarking and financial analysis tools, and the need for effective channel management.

Part II, "Real Estate and the Physical Asset," offers chapters on hotel development, managing capital expenditures, insurance and risk management, sustainability, and technology.

Part III, "Contracts and Legal Aspects of Asset Management," addresses hotel management contracts, franchise and license agreements, key legal issues that all hotel asset managers should be familiar with in managing hotel investments, and risk vs. return from the lender's perspective.

Part IV, "Planning and Executing the Hotel Investment," presents chapters covering principles of hotel investment ventures, the art of the capital structure, hospitality REITs and the evolution of ownership in the lodging industry, hotel valuation techniques, and the hotel investment buy, hold, sell decision-making process, and the hotel as an investment alternative.

Hotel Asset Management: Principles & Practices represents the collaborative work of thirty-seven industry professionals—experts in their respective specialty areas—all of whom contributed their time and expertise without remuneration. We are very fortunate that this distinguished group of men and women agreed to contribute their expertise to this book, and we are deeply appreciative of the time and effort involved to make this third edition possible.

Richard Musgrove
Lori Raleigh
A. J. Singh

Part I

The Foundations and Processes of Asset Management

1

A Current Profile of the Hotel Asset Management Profession

By Robert D. Kline and A. J. Singh

***Robert D. Kline** is the CEO and Co-Founder of the Chartres Lodging Group, LLC, a private equity investment firm focused on the lodging sector, and Co-Chairman of Kokua Hospitality, LLC, a property management firm specializing in turnarounds. Mr. Kline is recognized as a proactive investor and a leading asset manager in the lodging sector. He has been an early cyclical investor in meetings hotels, urban turnaround hotels and destination resorts. Mr. Kline was among the first investors to evolve an institutionally recognized program of asset management systems and procedures and is a Founding Director of the Hospitality Asset Managers Association. He began his career in 1984 upon graduating from Cornell University's School of Hotel Administration and has since led more than $11 billion of transactional activity. He pioneered the establishment of a preeminent lodging investment and asset management advisory practice under The Yarmouth Group/Lend Lease, and conducted extensive business throughout the U.S., Asia, Mexico and Europe. Mr. Kline previously served as the initial Head of Acquisitions for Strategic Hotel Capital during its formative years where he oversaw their purchase of $2 billion of luxury hotels across three countries. In 1998, he began investing directly as a principal and has successfully invested over $6 billion of capital on his own behalf and a select group of private investors and institutional funds. Mr. Kline sits on Cornell University's Real Estate Finance Advisory Committee and serves on the Dean's Advisory Board for the institution's School of Hotel Administration, as well as ULI's Hotel Development Council where he created the Lodging Confidence Meter.*

Since his formation of Chartres Lodging with Maki Nakamura Bara in 2002, Chartres Lodging has developed into the lodging investment manager of choice among private funds, pension funds, and sovereign wealth funds. The firm is headquartered in San Francisco and operates from additional offices in Los Angeles, New York, Chicago, Denver, Scottsdale, St. Louis, and Tokyo.

***A. J. Singh, Ph.D.,** is a professor in* The *School of Hospitality Business at Michigan State University and focuses on International Lodging, Finance, and Real Estate. He is Director of the Hospitality Business Real Estate Investment Management Minor. Dr. Singh earned his undergraduate degree from the University of Delhi in India, his M.S. in Hotel, Restaurant, and Institutional Management from Purdue University, and his Ph.D. in Park, Recreation, and Tourism is from Michigan State University. He is an active member of Hospitality Asset Managers Association, Council of Hotel, Restaurant and Institutional Education, the Association of Hospitality Financial Management Educators, the International Society of Hospitality Consultants, and the Urban Land Institute.*

In the second edition of this book, Greg Denton described the historical context of the hotel industry and evolution of hotel ownership, which helped us gain an appreciation of the increasing complexity of hotel assets and of the investment needs and expectations of hotel owners. To bridge the gap between ownership and management, asset management as a discipline emerged in the 1980s, initially as performed by work-out specialists. It later evolved to include detailed oversight of operations and physical asset enhancements and, more recently, a strategic emphasis on managing the investment with an eye to value creation and, ultimately, value monetization.

It is important to capture the essence of a discipline or practice by establishing definitions. However, during rapidly evolving times, definitions also rapidly evolve. Rather than defining asset management as a discipline, this chapter presents it as a profession and attempts to explain why people seek this profession. While the characteristics of a profession are also dynamic, it is easier to track those changes if we study the professionals who make up that profession.

Hospitality Asset Management Association: The Emergence of a Profession

A profession arises when any trade or occupation transforms itself through "the development of formal qualifications based upon education and examinations, the emergence of regulatory bodies with powers to admit and discipline members, and some degree of monopoly rights."[1] The process by which a profession arises from a trade or occupation is often termed *professionalization* and has been described as one starting with the establishment of the activity as a full-time occupation, progressing through the establishment of training schools and university links, the formation of a professional organization, the struggle to gain legal support for exclusion, and the formation of a formal code of ethics.

The Hospitality Asset Managers Association (HAMA) was formed in 1991 with the principal objective of creating a unified voice for hotel owners frustrated with management companies and contracts that heavily favored the operator. The organization, which started with six founding members, now consists of 204 domestic members. Owners represented in HAMA have approximately 3,200 hotels and 760,000 hotel rooms. These figures represent five-year increases of 60 and 52 percent, respectively. During this recent time period, HAMA has also expanded internationally with chapters representing Japan, Asia Pacific, Europe, and China comprising 200 additional members. Its current mission statement signifies its evolution from a loose-knit group of owner's representatives to a global professional organization representing an emerging and vitally important profession:

> The Hospitality Asset Managers Association is the preeminent organization of professionals representing hotel ownership worldwide. Our mission is the enhancement of hospitality asset values, through education, advancement of the profession, and serving as the collective voice of ownership.

Profile of the Hotel Asset Manager Today

In order to understand the makeup of hotel asset managers and the profession of hotel asset management, we conducted a comprehensive survey of HAMA members in 2009 and again in 2015 with a modified format. Our primary purpose was to develop a current profile of the hotel asset management profession and to note how it is evolving. Specifically, the objectives of the survey were to develop an academic and professional profile of hotel asset managers, identify specific functions and activities of asset managers, and summarize their opinions about issues related to the current profession. The survey questionnaires were developed with the assistance of the co-editors of this text and feedback at HAMA meetings. They were mailed to all HAMA members in the U.S. using a web survey.[2] Participants were given an opportunity to respond over a three-week period followed by three reminder e-mails. The 2009 data was tabulated based on 86 responses, which represented a 57 percent response rate; while the 2015 data was based on 112 responses out of 187 invites representing a 60 percent rate. In the 2009 survey, 68 percent of the respondents were vice presidents or senior vice presidents and approximately 23 percent were presidents, principals, or partners. The balance (less than 10 percent) had the title of director or asset manager. The participants were similar in the 2015 survey, with almost 96 percent having achieved undergraduate and/or graduate degrees. In presenting the results of the survey in this chapter, we have divided it into four segments.

1. Profile of hotel asset management practice
2. Academic and professional profile of the hotel asset manager
3. Functions of the hotel asset manager and measures of performance
4. State of the hotel asset management profession

The chapter concludes with our attempt to determine why professionals choose to be hotel asset managers.

Hotel Asset Management Practices

Asset management companies may be broadly divided into three types of practices (see Exhibit 1). Approximately 28 percent of the asset managers work for private ownership groups. Institutional owners constitute 47 percent of asset management practices, while 22 percent of asset managers are independent advisors. Private ownership groups comprise private equity investors, opportunity funds, sovereign funds, wealthy individuals, property development firms and companies whose ownership of hotels is incidental to their primary business function. Institutional owners are broadly characterized by pension funds, endowment investors, life insurers, banks and publicly traded companies. Independent advisors operate as third party asset managers hired by private investors or institutional owners. A few asset managers (3 percent) work for lenders. Interestingly, as noted below, there has been a significant increase of independent advisors and asset managers working for institutional owners.

Exhibit 1 Profile of Asset Management Practices

Asset Management Practice	2009 Survey		2015 Survey	
	N	Percentage	N	Percentage
Private owner	36	37%	31	28%
Institutional owner	35	37	52	47
Independent advisor	16	17	22	21
Other, please specify	4	4	1	1
Lender	5	5	3	3
Total Responses	96	100%	109	100%

Academic and Professional Profile

Educational Qualifications. As outlined in Exhibit 2 it is clear that asset managers are a highly educated professional group with 96 percent having at least a bachelor's degree. Forty-four percent of the 2015 survey respondents have received either a master's degree or a juris doctor, which is a significant increase from the 2009 survey result of 33 percent. While asset managers are achieving higher education than ever before, it is interesting to note that none of the managers surveyed has earned a Ph.D. This speaks to the opportunity of HAMA to work with educational institutions in developing curriculum specific to the profession.

Career Progression. In the 2009 survey, we asked the respondents to indicate the progression of professional careers on their path to becoming a hotel asset manager. As the question was asked in an open-ended format, we categorized their professional careers into hotel general management (P1), consulting (P2), hotel

Exhibit 2 Academic Education Profile

Academic Degree	2009		2015	
	N	Percentage	N	Percentage
Ph.D.	0	0%	0	0%
Juris Doctor	1	1	1	1
Master's Degree	27	32	48	43
Bachelor's Degree	52	62	58	52
Associate Degree	2	2	3	3
Other, Specify	2	2	1	1
Total Responses	84	100%	111	100%

development (P3), asset management (P4), accounting (P5), and other (P6). Exhibit 3 tabulates these results in a bi-directional grid and reveals an interesting career profile for hotel asset managers. When reading the table from the top row moving right, you notice that most asset managers had their first jobs in hotel general management (56 percent), while 18 and 16 percent started in consulting and accounting careers, respectively.

You may also read the table vertically. Only 4 percent of the respondents stated their first job was asset management, while 50 percent said it was their third job and 54 percent said that it was their fourth job.

The last row is the weighted mean of all the responses and is indicative of the proportion of respondents who had worked in various positions leading to the time this survey was done. From the 254 responses, we know that 28 percent had held hotel management positions over the course of their careers, 15 percent held consulting jobs, 13 percent held hotel development jobs, 25 percent held asset management jobs, and 18 percent held accounting jobs.

A further analysis of the open-ended responses reveals the depth, breadth, and mix of experience that hotel asset managers have had before becoming asset managers. The open-ended responses, listed below, illustrate the types of jobs respondents held on their path to becoming an asset manager.

1. Hotel operations—hotel management—hotel corporate—asset management
2. Restaurant management—accounting—operational accounting—hotel consulting—asset management
3. F&B operations—hotel management—consulting—asset management with REIT
4. Hotel management—corporate level management—development officer—asset management

Exhibit 3 Career Progression of Hotel Asset Managers (2009 Survey)

	P1	P2	P3	P4	P5	P6	Total
First Job (N = 84)	56%	18%	6%	4%	16%	1%	100%
Second Job (N = 74)	23%	20%	19%	16%	22%	0%	100%
Third Job (N = 56)	11%	7%	13%	50%	20%	0%	100%
Fourth Job (N = 26)	0%	12%	15%	54%	15%	4%	100%
Fifth Job (N = 10)	20%	0%	30%	40%	10%	0%	100%
Sixth Job (N = 4)	0%	0%	0%	75%	0%	25%	100%
Weighted Mean** (N = 254)	28%	15%	13%	25%	18%	1%	100%

P1 = Hotel General Management; P2 = Consulting and Investment Advisory; P3 = Hotel Development (Real Estate and Brand); P4= Asset Management; P5 = Accounting; P6 = Other (list___)

5. Hotel feasibility—acquisitions/development—asset management
6. Appraisal/consulting—analyst—director acquisitions—asset management
7. Consulting—development—consulting—asset management
8. Consulting—development planning—equity research—asset management
9. Accounting—hotel operations—regional hotel operations—asset management
10. Assistant controller—controller—asset management

Firms that Launched Asset Management Careers. In our attempt to develop a profile of hotel asset managers, we wanted to know the type of firms that launched asset management careers. In our 2015 survey, we asked the respondents to write the name of the firm where they were first employed as an asset manager and to indicate the type of firm. The responses summarized in Exhibit 4 clearly indicate that firms most influential in launching asset management careers were private equity, private investment groups, real estate investment trusts, advisory firms, and hotel ownership and development companies. Jointly, they contributed to 92 percent of the asset management career launches. A sampling of the private firms represented in this segment of the industry includes Kingdom Holdings, The Chartres Lodging Group, Thayer Lodging, HEI Hotels & Resorts, Rockbridge, Hyatt Development, Colony Capital, Maritz, Wolff & Co., and CTF Hotels & Resorts. These respondents represented 64 percent of the 2015 survey, up from 49 percent in the 2009 survey. This is a meaningful increase which indicates private firms are exercising a more direct level of involvement in overseeing their lodging investments by engaging in asset management.

REITs (such as Host Hotels & Resorts, Apple Hospitality, MeriStar Hospitality, and Highland Hospitality) and consulting and asset management firms (such as Laventhol & Horwath, Geller & Co., hotelAVE, CHM, Warnick + Company [the latter two recently merging to form CHMWarnick], SCS Advisors Inc., and The

Exhibit 4 Type of Firm that Launched Asset Management Career

Type of Firm	2009		2015	
	N	%	N	%
Private Equity and Private Investment Groups	20	25%	31	28%
Hotel Ownership and Development	20	25	40	36
REIT/Consulting-Investment Advisory-Asset Management	30	37	31	28
Institutional	6	7	8	7
Management Company	3	4	1	1
Lender	2	2	0	0
Total	81	100%	111	100%

Yarmouth Group) were responsible for the launch of 28 percent of asset management careers. Eight asset managers started their asset management careers with institutional investors such as Prudential, Mass Mutual, and John Hancock. It is notable that asset management careers launched by REITs and consultancy firms declined from 37 percent in the 2009 survey to 28 percent in 2015. This may reflect the increased sophistication of the asset management programs in these firms and their reliance upon professionals with higher levels of experience.

Chronology of Asset Management Hiring Practices. To further understand the evolution of the asset management profession, we drilled deeper into the 2009 sample survey data to identify when firms hired asset managers during the past nearly forty years. Exhibit 5 provides a summary of this analysis. During the late 1970s to mid-1980s, there were few asset managers. This started to change around 1986–1992. The hotel industry at that time was overbuilt and unprofitable due to the abundance of easy credit in the early 1980s, tax-driven investing, and an overabundance of supply additions as brands segmented into specific focus customer groups. As a result, many syndicates failed and hotels went into receivership, which increased the demand for asset managers. During this time, private equity firms and institutional investors hired asset managers. The big boost to the profession came during 1993–1997 when the industry was recovering. Most hires during this time period were at private equity, asset management, or consulting firms and were driven by new owners seeking to maximize investment returns through renovations, rebranding, and repositioning strategies. It was also during this time that owners successfully challenged the control property managers had enjoyed during the previous decades. Through high profile legal judgments, operators were determined to have a fiduciary responsibility to hotel owners. As the separation of ownership and management had become entrenched into the business of hotels, the profession of asset management became an integral part of the business model.

As the industry continued to recover and grew profitable from 1993–2007 (excluding the short-lived anomaly caused by September 11, 2001, attacks), new

Exhibit 5 Historical Analysis of Firms and Hiring Trends (2009 Survey)

Year Hired	Private Equity	Hotel Owner Developer	REIT	Consulting Asset Management	Institutional	Management Company
1978–1985	1	1		1	1	
1986–1992	3	1		2	3	
1993–1997	8	1	2	5	1	
1998–2007	8	17	15	5	1	3
Total*	20	20	17	13	6	3

* Sample based on results of the survey.

ownership entities such as real estate investment trusts further increased the number of asset managers hired. The availability of debt and equity capital during this time resulted in the growth of hotel development firms, private equity, and private investment companies. They in turn increased the number of asset managers needed to oversee their growing portfolio of assets and to manage complex relationships with the growing number of brands and property managers. The Great Recession of 2007–2009 led to even greater emphasis on the relevancy of asset management oversight. The following years of recovery in property-level operating fundamentals attracted new and traditional investors looking to integrate asset management into their investment strategies.

Training and Education. We asked asset managers where they learned their asset management skills. Results from the 2009 and 2015 surveys are presented in Exhibit 6. The "Other" category included experience in corporate offices of hotel companies, reading trade and research publications, investment courses, and work experience in multiple companies and positions such as brands, lending institutions, acquisitions, development, brokerage, and accounting firms.

While the survey did not specifically ask about the nature of the training and education received, we may surmise that it followed a building block pattern. As they progressed through their careers, they built on their general learning (college and hotel operations), which they brought into sharper focus and sophistication at an asset management firm.

We further analyzed the data to cross tabulate the first job and source of asset management skills. This is summarized in Exhibit 7. If hotel asset managers started their career in hotels, that became the most likely training ground for asset management skills. For those who started in consulting or hotel development, the training ground was most likely in a real estate advisory firm. The logical conclusion of this analysis may be that asset managers that started in hotel operations will bring a strong set of operational analysis skills to their position as asset man-

Exhibit 6 Source of Asset Management Training and Education

Training and Education Source	2009		2015	
	N	Percentage	N	Percentage
Training in Hotel Operations	55	30%	75	31%
Training in an Asset Management Firm	36	20	61	25
Training in a Real Estate Advisory Firm	29	16	46	19
College	23	13	23	9
Other, please specify	20	11	14	6
Professional Education Courses	18	10	25	10
Total Responses	181	100%	244	100%

Exhibit 7 First Job and Source of Training and Education

	Career Progression: First Job						
Training and Education Source	P1	P2	P3	P4	P5	P6	Total
Training in Hotel Operations (N = 55)	40%	15%	15%	0%	31%	0%	30%
Training in an Asset Management Firm (N = 36)	20%	21%	23%	33%	15%	0%	20%
Training in a Real Estate Advisory Firm (N = 29)	11%	29%	31%	17%	12%	0%	16%
College (N = 23)	12%	12%	15%	17%	15%	0%	13%
Other, please specify (N = 20)	9%	12%	15%	17%	12%	100%	11%
Professional Education Courses (N = 18)	9%	12%	0%	17%	15%	0%	10%
Totals (N)	101	34	13	6	26	1	181

P1 = Hotel General Management; P2 = Consulting and Investment Advisory; P3 = Hotel Development (Real Estate and Brand); P4= Asset Management; P5 = Accounting; P6 = Other

agers, compared with those who started in consulting and development. The latter are more likely to be stronger in their real estate and investment analysis skills.

Professional Experience. Based on survey results, Exhibits 8 and 9 summarize the experience level of hotel asset managers. Forty-three percent of the sample has greater than ten years of asset management experience, which is up from 35 percent of the 2009 sample. A full 83 percent have greater than five years of experience, which was 71 percent in the 2009 sample. Not surprisingly, as the profession matures and demand increases for expertise, a greater number of asset managers are staying longer in the profession. (Note that Exhibit 9 presents 2009 survey

Exhibit 8 Hotel Asset Managers: Experience Levels

Years of Experience	**2009 Survey**		**2015 Survey**	
	N	%	N	%
≤ 5 years	24	29	19	17
6–10 years	30	36	45	40
11–15 years	17	20	23	21
16–20 years	7	8	17	15
21–25 years	4	5	4	4
> 25 years	2	2	3	3
Total	84	100	111	100

Exhibit 9 Hotel Asset Managers: Years of Experience by Position

Position/Title in Company	Mean	SD*	Min	Max
President, CEO, COO, MD	13.2	4.6	4.0	20.0
Vice President	9.3	6.7	2.0	30.0
Senior Vice President	9.2	4.1	3.5	19.0
Principal Partner	9.4	5.4	4.0	20.0
Director	6.3	1.5	5.0	8.0
Asset Manager	5.0	0	5.0	5.0
Hold Various titles	22.0	0	22.0	22.0
Not Practicing now	23.0	0	23.0	23.0
Total	9.9	6	2.0	30.0

* SD = Standard Deviation

data; HAMA did not collect this information in recent years, so updated figures are not available.)

Accreditation. Professional designations exist for various professions, such as MAI (Member of Appraisal Institute) for real estate valuation professionals, CPA (Certified Public Accountant) for auditors, CHAE (Certified Hospitality Account Executive) for hotel controllers, and CFA (Certified Financial Analyst) for financial analysts. It is generally recognized that professionals with these designations have learned a common body of professional knowledge and demonstrated their competency through a combination of tests and work experience. Professional organizations offering these designations use them to systematize and codify professional knowledge, create a path to the earned designation, and provide assurance that the professional has the necessary competency.

In 2012, HAMA spearheaded the creation of an asset management accreditation program with assistance from a certification committee chair, a committee that included asset managers, academicians, and AH&LA's Educational Institute. HAMA describes this newly established designation as follows:

> The Certified Hotel Asset Manager (CHAM) designation is the world's only advanced certification available to accomplished hotel asset management professionals. CHAM designees represent an elite group of senior hospitality professionals whose advanced knowledge in all facets of hotel ownership and operations was developed over a significant number of years serving in the role of "lead" asset manager. Their knowledge base is further validated by achieving a passing score on the comprehensive CHAM exam in addition to satisfying other designation requirements.

The requirements to become recognized with the CHAM accreditation are a stringent combination of direct experience, knowledge of industry practice, and peer group recognition. The applicants are required to sign a CHAM ethics policy, and recertification is required every five years. An on-line assistance tool has been developed and is further supported by on-campus academic courses. These requirements are detailed in Exhibit 10. As of the writing of this book, eighteen professionals have passed these requirements and have received the CHAM designation. While all members who meet the minimum criteria are encouraged to apply for the coveted designation, we expect the CHAM designation to grow slowly because of its rigorous testing and experience requirements.

Exhibit 10 Accreditation Requirements for Certified Hotel Asset Managers

Accreditation Requirements	Combined Responses by Hotel Asset Managers
Peer Group Recommendations	Two letters of recommendation, preferably including one from a current or prior employer/supervisor and one from an "end-user" of the hotel asset management profession (i.e., capital partner, client, lender, etc.).
Years of Practice	Seven years of *lead* hotel asset management experience.
Examination and Tests	The CHAM exam consists of 200 multiple-choice questions that must be answered within a four-hour time period. All test questions are designed to test the candidate's mastery of various competencies derived from six key areas of knowledge in combination with the minimum years of *lead* hotel asset management experience. The exam will test knowledge in the following areas of core competency: • The Asset Management Process • Hotel Operations • Real Estate and the Physical Asset • Contracts and Legal Aspects • Financial Analysis and Benchmarking • The Investment Decision
Logistics of Implementation	HAMA has partnered with AH&LA's Educational Institute to offer an online exam option for interested candidates. All online exams require that examinations be administered under the supervision of a CHAM designee serving as proctor. Approved candidates for CHAM can test their readiness for the CHAM exam with the online CHAM Assessment Tool available through AH&LA's Educational Institute.
Additional Information	Website: http://www.hamagroup.org/cham.php#prerequisites Email: certification@hamagroup.org

Functions of the Hotel Asset Manager and Measures of Performance

Time Allocation. In order to determine the amount of time asset managers spend on typical asset management activities, we identified ten activities and asked the respondents to rank order these activities based on the amount of time spent on each activity in the past year. Rank 1 represents the most time spent and rank 10 is the least time spent. We summarized the results into three categories: most time, average time, and least time. As noted in Exhibit 11, asset managers allocated the most amount of time to monitoring the asset's financial performance, with 81 percent of the respondents choosing rank 1. About 58 percent of the respondents said they spend significant time on capital expenditures, while 55 percent indicated significant time spent on revenue management and 52 percent on operational reviews. About 38 and 35 percent spent significant time advising ownership on investment strategies and management issues, respectively. In the past year, asset managers did not spend much time with loan compliance, contracts, or franchise affiliation activities. Less time spent on loan compliance issues may be explained by a generally strong asset performance environment in 2014. In general, when asset performance is strong, less attention is paid to management contract and franchise performance issues.

The percentages under the Most Time column in Exhibit 11 have changed quite a bit since the 2009 survey. As Exhibit 12 evidences, asset managers are shifting a significant amount of their focus onto revenue management, capital expenditures and ownership advice on investment strategies. This may be explained by the rising importance of the revenue management function, its impact on overall

Exhibit 11 Distribution of Time Allocated to Asset Management Activities (2015 Survey)

Asset Management Activity	Rank 1–3: Most Time	Rank 4–7: Average Time	Rank 8–10: Least Time
Monitor the financial performance	81%	17%	2%
Capital expenditures	58%	35%	6%
Revenue management	55%	36%	9%
Operational reviews	52%	45%	3%
Advise ownership on investment strategies	38%	33%	29%
Advise ownership on management issues	35%	50%	15%
Contracts	15%	57%	28%
Monitor investment community	9%	32%	59%
Loan compliance	5%	27%	68%
Franchise affiliations	2%	36%	62%

Exhibit 12 Time Allocation Changes from the 2009 to 2015 Surveys

Asset Management Activity	Rank 1–3
Revenue management	72%
Capital expenditures	49%
Advise ownership on investment strategies	31%
Advise ownership on management issues	21%
Operational reviews	18%
Monitor the financial performance	14%
Contracts	-25%
Monitor investment community	-47%
Loan compliance	-76%
Franchise affiliations	-85%

asset value, and the desire to increase asset competitiveness in a rising market through capital reinvestment. Also likely at play is the rise in private ownership, which tends to drive greater frequency in asset trading once value creation has been achieved, as opposed to longer term investors like REITs and institutional investors.

The Need for External Expertise. Based on the preceding discussion, a profile emerging of the hotel asset manager is that of a highly qualified and experienced executive with a wide range of operational, financial, and investment management skills. However, the growing complexity and scale of the hotel business require that they periodically tap into outside expertise to assist with their asset monitoring and management activities. In our survey we asked asset managers to identify outside expertise they have hired on an ad hoc basis in the past year. Exhibit 13 summarizes their responses. Legal and property tax consultants dominate the list. Other important areas include risk management, purchasing, and labor management.

Most interesting is that substantial increase of usage since 2009 of experts in the areas of service standards, revenue management, and information technology. This meaningful shift reflects several key trends among hotel asset managers. First, it is apparent that these professionals are getting far more involved in day-to-day property management functions, procedures, and strategies of revenue management, Internet accessibility, and social media. Second, as these professionals continue gaining industry experience, we expect that their knowledge will translate into deeper oversight of the property manager's activities. Finally, with an increase in private owners driving for speed to transaction (i.e., return monetization), higher demands are being placed on asset managers to drive property revenues and value.

Exhibit 13 External Expertise and Consultants (2015 Survey)

External Expertise	2015 Survey		2009 Survey
	N	Percentage	Percentage
Other (please specify)	96	87	6
Service standards	10	9	1
Revenue management	41	37	6
Information technology	40	36	6
Labor management	36	32	7
Purchasing	35	32	8
Food and beverage cost reduction	19	17	5
Property taxes	81	73	21
Green operations and development	16	14	4
Legal issues	91	82	26
Risk management	37	33	11

Some of the other outside consultants listed by asset managers were primarily renovation-related consultants such as project managers, designers, and architects, but they also included utility advisors, appraisers, telephone, parking, design, sales and marketing, and brokers.

Performance Measurement and Benchmarks. The quality of any performance management system is directly related to the objectivity of its measurement. A common understanding of quantitative and qualitative performance metrics is critical for the objective assessment of an asset manager's performance. In our study, it was important to understand the measures and benchmarks used to assess asset managers' effectiveness. The survey asked, "What are the performance measures used to evaluate your effectiveness as an asset manager?" As the question was open ended, we have collated the results into five quantitative and two qualitative measures, along with metrics associated with the quantitative performance measures and performance benchmarks (see Exhibit 14).

The first qualitative measure is associated with developing or maintaining relationships with stakeholders such as operators, brands, lenders and owners. The second measure is associated with quality and measured through various quality, satisfaction, and property condition scores. We were not able to identify benchmarks for either of the qualitative measures from the response results.

One respondent indicated the use of a balance scorecard performance measurement system, which combines qualitative and quantitative measures into an integrated, cause-effect system of measurement. It was interesting to note that no

Exhibit 14 Measures and Benchmarks Used to Assess Hotel Asset Manager Performance

Performance Measures and Benchmarks	Quantitative	Qualitative
Value creation measures: Market value of asset **Value creation benchmarks:** Increased value, comparison to investment objectives set at acquisition	X	
Financial performance measures: Revenue, rental income, GOP, net profit, EBITDA, IRR, ROI, underwriting returns, maximizing debt coverage ratio **Financial performance benchmarks:** Returns compared to NCREIF, EBITDA compared to public REITs, returns compared to asset potential, incremental income associated with tenant growth, compared to underwriting, budget	X	
Operating measures: Occupancy, RevPAR, ADR, comp set, market share, operating efficiency **Operating benchmarks:** Comparison to budget and competitive set, RevPAR Index	X	
Asset utilization measures: Capital expenditure **Asset utilization benchmarks:** Capital plan implementation, capital expenditure budget	X	
Growth measures: NOIPAR, change in asset market value, operational efficiency improvement, forecast variance analysis, ability to find investment opportunities, RevPAR growth index, incremental market share **Growth benchmarks:** Year over year	X	
Relationship measures: With operator, franchise relations, long term relationship with owners, consistent ability to meet loan compliance tests **Relationship benchmarks:** None identified		X
Quality measures: Property condition scores, guest satisfaction/quality scores **Quality benchmarks:** None identified		X

response identified sustainable development measures or green metrics as benchmarks to evaluate performance.

Essential Knowledge, Skills, and Experiences. To identify the knowledge, skills, and experiences necessary for effective asset manager performance, our survey asked, "What are the critical knowledge, skills, and experiences that help you achieve and exceed these performance benchmarks?" As the question was open-ended, we have collated the results into categories (see Exhibit 15). Effective hotel asset managers need a wide range of knowledge, skills, and abilities. Most responses pointed to strong operational experience and a particular understanding of the drivers of revenue, costs, and intangibles such as service management and guest satisfaction. A few asset managers stated that experience with franchise and management companies is valuable. Finally, with regard to experience, a few stated that a wide range of experiences between operations and investment analysis is the best recipe for success.

State of the Hotel Asset Management Profession

Finally, we surveyed the HAMA membership with two sets of issues confronting the industry. The first set of questions mirrored the questions we queried in 2009. We asked the respondents in 2009 and again in 2015 to state their agreement or disagreement with these eight matters. The 2015 responses are summarized in Exhibit 16. Exhibit 17 shows how the sentiments of the respondents have shifted between 2009 and 2015. Of those responding to the survey, 65 percent felt that the balance of power with property managers favors ownership, which is significantly up from the 2009 survey with 50 percent of the respondents feeling similarly.

Exhibit 15 Knowledge and Skills Important for Asset Manager Performance

Knowledge	Skills
Real Estate Finance and Valuation	Investment Skills: Understanding market investment cycles, supply demand and competitive analysis, ability to model discounted cash flow analyses, valuations and hold/sale analyses
Economics, Financial Management, and Investment Analysis	Financial Skills: Reading and analyzing financial statements, capital expenditure analysis, forecasting and budgeting
Management Contracts	Soft Skills: Negotiating skills, analytical skills, judgment, interpersonal relations, critical thinking, persuasion, and empathy
Marketing	Planning Skills: Revenue management, strategic planning, market positioning forecasting and budgeting
Basic Engineering, Building Construction, and Project Management	People Management Skills: Leadership, communication and motivation, teamwork, basic understanding for technical skills
Law and Legal Systems	

Exhibit 16 Hotel Asset Manager Opinion on Select Issues Related to the Profession (2015 Survey)

Note: top number is the count of respondents. Bottom number is percentage of respondents.	Strongly Agree	Agree	Somewhat Agree	Somewhat Disagree	Strongly Disagree	Don't Know
The balance of power today favors ownership versus management.	11	30	31	30	9	0
	10%	27%	28%	27%	8%	0%
Goals of ownership and management are relatively aligned now.	0	19	51	32	9	0
	0%	17%	46%	29%	8%	0%
In general, ownership has become more demanding of asset managers today.	40	51	16	1	1	2
	36%	46%	14%	1%	1%	2%
Most asset management compensation is tied to value enhancement.	14	36	32	19	5	5
	13%	32%	29%	17%	5%	5%
The asset manager's role has shifted from day-to-day monitoring to strategic investment advisory.	13	30	39	21	7	1
	12%	27%	35%	19%	6%	1%
The best asset managers in the future will have a strong grounding in real estate investments.	34	37	21	14	5	0
	31%	33%	19%	13%	3%	0%
The best asset managers in the future will have a strong grounding in hotel operations.	24	49	25	10	2	0
	22%	44%	23%	9%	3%	0%
Current coursework at universities adequately prepare asset managers to enter the profession.	0	8	24	36	16	27
	0%	7%	22%	32%	14%	24%

Notably, more than one-third of the respondents felt that management companies still hold sway over ownership.

The traditional misalignment between the goals of ownership and management appears to continue based on survey results, as only 17 percent fully agreed with the statement that the goals of management and ownership are aligned. Asset managers strongly believed that ownership has become more demanding in the performance of asset manager, as over 82 percent fully agreed with this statement and another 14 percent somewhat agreed. However, linking compensation of asset managers to value enhancement was fully confirmed by only 45 percent, while

Exhibit 17 Opinion Shift from 2009 to 2015 on Select Issues Related to the Profession

	2009 Survey Agree	2015 Survey Agree	% Change	2009 Survey Disagree	2015 Survey Disagree	% Change
The balance of power today favors ownership versus management.	50%	65%	30%	49%	35%	-29%
Goals of ownership and management are relatively aligned now.	57%	63%	11%	43%	37%	-14%
In general, ownership has become more demanding of asset managers today.	96%	96%	0%	4%	2%	-50%
Most asset management compensation is tied to revenue/value enhancement.	69%	74%	7%	26%	22%	-15%
The asset manager's role has shifted from day-to-day monitoring to strategic investment advisory.	64%	74%	16%	36%	25%	-31%
The best asset managers in the future will have a strong grounding in real estate investments.	84%	83%	-1%	15%	17%	13%
The best asset managers in the future will have a strong grounding in hotel operations.	88%	88%	0%	13%	12%	-8%
Current coursework at universities adequately prepare asset managers to enter the profession.	21%	29%	38%	51%	47%	-8%

29 percent only somewhat agreed and 22 percent disagreed that compensation is linked to value enhancement.

Nearly three-fourths of the respondents felt that the role of the hotel asset manager has shifted toward investment advisory, with 39 percent in agreement and 35 percent somewhat agreeing with the statement. However, it is clear from the open-ended responses that a regular monitoring of the asset is still an important part of an asset manager's job. This is further supported by their responses to the next two questions, which asked them to decide between real estate investments versus hotel operations for their initial grounding and training. Their responses show that they felt that a grounding in real estate investments and operations were equally important. This was further elaborated in the open-ended responses to this question. Forty-six percent of hotel asset managers felt that current coursework as universities and colleges does not adequately prepare people to enter the profession. However, there was an increase in respondents in 2015 who agreed that current coursework at universities prepared asset managers (from 21 to 29 percent).

The second "state of the industry" survey we conducted in 2015 queried participants on six more "prickly" matters and concerns. These topics and the respondents' answers are detailed below in Exhibit 18. When taken in context, the results reveal a most interesting portrait as to the current state of mind of the collective body of asset managers. Seventy-three percent of the respondents believe access to multiple levels of data benchmarking performance is very important, and nearly as many agreed that brand transparency and having influence over hotel operating decisions is very important. And 96 percent of the respondents expressed desire to have control over rate-setting decisions and marketing/distribution choices. Interestingly, while a little over one-third of the respondents agree that the hotel management agreement should be terminable, 49 percent think it of only somewhat importance and 8 percent believe it to be unimportant. Hotel asset managers heretofore have not been known as political activists, although this survey revealed that 85 percent believe increased lobbying to influence gov-

Exhibit 18 Key Issues Relevant to Achieving Greater Asset Manager Effectiveness

Note: top number is the count of respondents. Bottom number is the percentage of respondents.	Very Important	Somewhat Important	Not Important	Don't Know
Access to multi-dimensional benchmark data	81	29	1	0
	73%	26%	1%	0%
Brand transparency	76	31	2	0
	70%	28%	2%	0%
Influence on property level operating decisions	71	37	2	0
	65%	34%	2%	0%
Control over rate setting and Internet marketing/distribution	45	61	4	1
	41%	55%	4%	1%
Termination of hotel management agreement	40	53	9	7
	37%	49%	8%	6%
Soliciting influence on government policies, spending and regulations	33	61	16	0
	30%	55%	15%	0%

ernment policies, spending, and regulations is necessary to meaningfully enhance their effectiveness.

Today's asset managers are more educated, have greater levels of experience, and have backgrounds that are well balanced in both hotel operations and real estate finance. Today's asset managers are passionate about the details and analytics, are driven by a deep understanding of how the hotel operator's performance has a stark impact on property values, and possess perhaps a dash of our neurosis that the operator is not fully aligned with their fiduciary obligations. We are harmoniously strategically minded with a hefty orientation toward value creation and monetization. Asset managers are demanding more data and greater activity and are getting more involved in key hotel operating decisions typically earmarked for the hotel manager. While this activism may consequentially risk blurring the lines between owner and operator, it speaks to the drive of today's asset manager to minimize risk and maximize control over variables that influence value.

Why Do People Choose To Become Hotel Asset Managers?

Having now thoroughly defined the profile of today's asset manager, the question that begs to be explored is, "Why do we do it?" Why do we subject ourselves to the tsunami of resistance from the property managers and to the cries of doubters who question the economic benefit of piling asset management fees on top of already high property management fees? Why do we go on to fight the good fight in the face of the torrential downpour of obstacles brought on by the inevitable cyclical turns in capital liquidity and global economic health, which have an uncanny way of turning downward just as the industry's developers are delivering record amounts of new hotel rooms? And why do we battle the seemingly oft occurring rogue waves such as the negative impact of wars and terrorist attacks, significant tax increases (real estate, sales, occupancy) instituted by cash starved governments, union strikes, spikes in energy, insurance and health care costs, the ubiquitous enhancement to brand standards driving owners to divert precious capital funds, airline bankruptcies, and the disastrous effects wrought by ill-fated acts of God such as flooding, fires, and wind storms? Many asset managers, like most other property managers, were initially attracted to the hospitality industry by its glamour and promise of perpetually "feel good" times. Are asset managers the product of the industry's disgruntled outcast seeking to play out an unrequited desire to be general managers? Are we frustrated developers/designers, or are we perhaps just masochists?

Quite to the contrary! Rather, as professionals, we have discovered the perfect stage on which to orchestrate a dynamic combination of talents, experiences, and skills toward achieving the central objective of protecting and maximizing investment value. We sit in the basement poring over financial and economic data, market research, customer surveys, and property condition reports; we reflect upon hours of discussions with property managers, revenue managers, owners, lenders, lawyers, accountants, tax specialists, lobbyists, insurers, brokers, buyers, sellers, architects, designers, demand generators, customers, partners, vendors, economists, and researchers; and we carefully assess the risks of known and unknown factors that may or may not occur over the coming years. We emerge from our think tank with a thoughtfully developed strategic plan detailing the steps necessary to maximize revenues, contain expenses, and get the most value out of the real estate. As we exit our bunker, we are confronted by our "Mt. Everest"—the seemingly impossible task of convincing everyone else to align behind the implementation of this plan. To achieve this Herculean task, we must rely heavily on our abilities as communicators, motivators, nurturers, negotiators, diplomats, coaches, and leaders. We must exercise patience, remain willing to bend and sway, but maintain a laser-like focus. We walk over coals and dance through fires to trumpet a vision for the asset. We scream, we cajole, we charm, and we sometimes even beg.

And, like committed parents, we watch the result of our actions evolve over a period of years. We understand that value emerges over time, but we prepare ourselves to react quickly when the capital market avails itself, if ever so briefly, allowing us to monetize the value that's been created. Asset managers have a distinctive understanding of both the real estate and operational fundamentals of hotel investing, and we revel in our special role as a bridge between Main Street (hotel operators, guests) and Wall Street (investors). While reporting performance is a grinding requirement of the role, asset managers delight in knowing they serve the more meaningful purpose as catalysts of change. They challenge the status quo and strive to stay ahead of the market and their competitors. While they are often unheralded for their visionary triumph, asset managers relish the successful result of the foundations they laid years and years before.

Why do hotel asset managers do what we do? Because creating value is fun, monetization is the goal, and the journey is the reward.

Endnotes

1. Alan Bullock and Stephen Trombley, *The New Fontana Dictionary of Modern Thought* (London: Harper-Collins, 1999), p. 689.
2. Note that, although HAMA has added international members since the 2009 survey, the 2015 survey was sent only to U.S. members to maintain comparative relevancy with the 2009 survey of U.S. membership.

Chapter Appendix: Summary of Open-Ended Responses about the State of the Hotel Asset Management Profession

Balance of Power: Owner vs. Management Company	Goal Alignment: Ownership and Management	Ownership Demands	Link: Asset Management Compensation - Value Creation	Role of Asset Manager: Monitor to Strategic Advisory	Future of Asset Manager: (Real Estate)	Future of Asset Manager: (Operations)	University Coursework Adequacy
I give the edge to owners only because over time the concentration of owners has migrated from diverse to concentrate among entities who specialize in owning hotel assets.	The management will always focus on developing their brands in most markets (long term). Owner looks for fast return on investment and increased real estate value (short term).	This may depend on the incentive structure negotiated for the Manager (if it exists).	Not if you work for a publicly traded company.	Asset managers only provide strategic investment advice during certain portions of the asset management cycle: during underwriting, during the capital investment phase and when it is time to sell.	The sooner people recognize this fact and stop believing that a lengthy operations background is necessary the better off the industry will be.	You need both operation and real estate finance background.	Current coursework does not provide adequate preparation for an Asset Manager, but it should provide more.
Ownership has dramatically more relative power than 5–10 years ago, nevertheless management executes which inherently gives them power—to succeed or fail.	Not in all cases. There remain several brand management companies who will place their "brand standards" ahead of the owner and operators desire to optimize profits.	Demands seem to flex with the economy and results.	Not in our shop.	Both are equally important.	They need some knowledge, but not at the expense of hotel ops.	A myth — most hotel operations people have no idea how to calculate EBITDA or calculate an IRR or understand value multiples.	I disagree only because the coursework needs to be complemented by actual experience.

Strong brands do have leverage but ownership, for the most part, has the power.	Management is more concerned with top line revenue as they are provided incentives to do so compared to GOPPAR (GOP Per Available Room) where management companies should also be responsible.	To a large extent, asset management reflects ownerships intent or requirements for an asset and that can vary widely.	Most is tied to performance of the properties.	Depends on the individual company structure and whether the AM is a consultant or employee.	This should be the case, but owners want monitoring and influence on operations.	This is very helpful but essentials can be picked up quickly.	University coursework, while valuable, cannot replace industry experience in an individual's preparation to become an asset manager.
Power is still with the brand managers.	Management continues to focus harder on revenue than profit.	Depending on owner type.	Again, as previous. Value enhancement can come in many forms not just gains from operations.	Strategic investment advisory has always been part of asset management. No change.	I think an effective asset manager needs to be very good in many different areas of overall hotel real estate, operational issues, market/revenue management and the list goes on.	Depending on ownership and management structure, this could vary. Operations skill should be strong but not absolutely necessary.	I'm only familiar w/ Cornell hotel school curriculum—there is only one asset management course, elective, offered half year. More courses need to incorporate asset management principles.
Depends on the deal, one cannot generalize.	Brands appear to be more conciliatory these days but to say the goals are aligned 100% is a dream.	Asset managers are the voice of ownership, the AM's are more demanding of operators.	Varies dependent on Asset Manager's role.	Very much so, but the monitoring remains important.	Essential for those dealing with acquisitions and capital improvements—less so for those dealing with day to day monitoring.	It really is a combination of operations and real estate consulting/investments. One needs to understand the macro economic environment (real estate) as well as the micro environment (hotel operations) to be effective.	Need to teach more Real Estate Principles.

This very much depends on the manager and type of asset: larger, full service/luxury assets are still primarily controlled by the operator/brand.	Much better than it was, but brands still have their own goals, which often conflict with those of owners.	An asset manager, particularly a 3rd party like myself, has to add and prove value or they won't remain engaged.	Incentive fees—yes.	Still a requirement for hands-on involvement, but shifting to a strategic focus.	Hotel asset managers must also have an appreciation for the human/operating side of the business as well.	Especially understanding technology applications.	
Larger ownership companies benchmarking has led to greater accountability of management companies.	Depends on how strong your GM is.	Pressure increases as performance declines.	Bonus is tied directly to property performance or value-enhancement activity.	Yes...but the period-to-period review is still critical. Too much AM activity can be monopolized with the strategic vision and related efforts with the core blocking and tackling missed.	Sort of. I am one of those (real estate folks that learned the operational side) but I recognize my operational weaknesses. Of course, hotel operations isn't rocket science (nor is real estate) but a solid understanding on the concept of valuation will be helpful.	They should have some working knowledge.	

M/C's are always too long and to the manager's favor.	Alignment is better, but the economics remain materially different for the parties, at least in most cases where the manager has no interest in the real estate.	Especially so in a down market—preserve market share and NOI.			I think it is important to understand both the asset and RE and business components or operations!	I think the best asset managers are former controllers as they understand the financial aspects of the operation/some of the people issues with operations/ and likely have the aptitude to learn the real estate side. Generally speaking, former general managers tend to have more challenges than controllers with the basics of the job.	
There needs to be a level of respect that goes both ways, or there will always be an us versus them mentality, which is not productive and will impact the overall performance of the asset.	CapEx versus operational expenses ongoing debate					Experience in hotel operations, in my opinion, is the key to a successful asset manager.	
Consolidation has given power back to brands.	However, they can be if the proper incentives are negotiated with management.					Valuation metrics are inextricably tied to operational quality. If the asset manager is not grounded in operations, he doesn't have all the tools necessary to perform most effectively.	

Management continues to flex significant power particularly in the face of owners.	Structuring of incentive fees to owner's minimum priority return have helped.						
The pendulum has swung to ownership groups but management companies continue to flex muscles where possible. Of course, if ownership groups are overly authoritarian, that will result in damaged relationship for both. The truly profitable partnerships are those with relatively equal balances of power.	As management companies downsize their real estate holdings, they will have less in common overall. Contracts with strong incentive fees will keep both parties honest.						
Based on agreements in place, current market economics and brands available in markets the pendulum swings back and forth.	Until Management companies are paid on the bottom line vs revenues, it will never fully align.						
Depends upon when the management contract was drafted and by whom as well. It also depends upon the owners existing portfolio (leverage) and the quality of asset under consideration.	Management companies will never have the sense of urgency that ownership has to have to deliver results to their investors.						

I am not sure if this is the right question. Often we are in a triangular relationship and not a linear relationship. Brand leverage is increasing relative to ownership and management.	As brands become more active in management, the divide increases. The alignment of ownership and management is a function of the thoughtfulness of the Management Agreement.						
We inherited long term Mgt Agreements drawn up in the 80's. Capex in the form of technology updates has been a drain on financial resources.	Operator is top line focused as it links up with the Mgt fee, but the growth is not reflected in the bottom line.						
Particularly where franchisor is the manager. Brands control product and trade areas.	Brands totally have their own agenda. Management Companies are better aligned with Ownership.						

2

The Asset Management Cycle and the Development of the Asset Management Plan

By Rich Niedbala and Bill Robinson

Rich Niedbala *is Senior Vice President—Asset Management, Lodging Capital Partners LLC. His career has spanned a broad spectrum of opportunities related to hotel investment. Mr. Niedbala has held analyst positions with Laventhol & Horwath and Holiday Corporation, gaining critical experience in market and operations analysis as well as hotel valuation. From these positions, Mr. Niedbala moved into hotel asset management with Lincoln Life, Boykin Lodging, and Lend Lease Real Estate Advisors. After a period with The Plasencia Group on the investment advisory side, Mr. Niedbala came into his present position.*

Over the course of his asset management career, Mr. Niedbala has worked with more than sixty hotels ranging from distressed select-service properties to major brand luxury hotels to boutique resorts throughout the United States. His experience with ownership entities has ranged from life companies to pension advisors, hotel REITs, and private equity investors. Mr. Niedbala has been instrumental in the disposition of almost $2 billion worth of assets and loans as well as approximately $50 million in renovations.

Mr. Niedbala has also served as an adjunct instructor for several hospitality programs and is active with The *Hospitality Management School at Michigan State University, his alma mater, where he serves on the school's Real Estate Advisory Council and teaches a section of the school's asset management course. Mr. Niedbala has been a long-time active member of the Hospitality Asset Managers Association, having served on its board and as president. Mr. Niedbala received the Certified Hotel Asset Manager designation in 2013.*

Bill Robinson *is Principal of Robinson Asset Management Group. Through his firm, he works as a third-party asset manager, currently providing asset management and operational advisory services primarily to one client, Rockwood Capital. In his role with Rockwood, Mr. Robinson provides asset management oversight across a portfolio of eighteen hotels located along the east coast of the U.S. and in the Caribbean. Mr. Robinson has also provided a wide-ranging variety of consulting services to other investment organizations including Allbridge Investments, The Beal Companies, Brentwood Hotels, The Donohoe Companies, and Urbana Realty Advisors.*

Prior to forming the Robinson Asset Management Group in mid-2007, Mr. Robinson was an asset manager with an affiliate company of Olympus Real Estate Partners (WMC Management), a position he held from mid-2002 to 2007. At Olympus, Mr. Robinson participated in the acquisition, repositioning, asset management, and dispositions of up to forty-five hotels throughout the United States. From 2001 to 2002, Mr. Robinson was a sell-side equity research analyst with Lehman Brothers, where he focused primarily on providing coverage of publicly traded C-corporations in the hospitality sector. Mr. Robinson's work included valuation analysis as well as various other proprietary research related to Lehman Brothers' coverage universe. From 1995 to 2001, Mr. Robinson was a member of Marriott International's Development Planning and Feasibility department, where he participated in the underwriting of well over one hundred development, acquisition, and conversion projects throughout the United States and Canada.

Mr. Robinson received a Bachelor of Arts in Economics from Hobart College and a Master of Professional Studies in Hotel Management from Cornell University. He is a member of HAMA and achieved the CHAM designation in 2013.

THE ASSET MANAGEMENT CYCLE is a continuous process of evaluation, planning, and implementation. Just as a hotel operates continuously, so must the asset management process keep revolving around the key objectives of ownership, principally the creation of value. The asset management plan is where ownership's objectives are identified and quantified and the path is projected for the hotel asset. The asset management cycle is, therefore, the execution of the asset management plan.

This chapter will identify and discuss how ownership objectives are varied and how they must be accurately identified. The asset management plan is developed to address ownership's objectives. Therefore, one can understand how critical it is to completely understand what the owner wants to accomplish.

Ownership always expects a return from its investment. That return is measured as a return on (actual value creation) and a return of (preserving the ability of the property to create value) capital. From picking the appropriate affiliation for the hotel, to evaluating the return on investment for additions to the asset, to monitoring the ongoing operations of the hotel, to systematically planning for the repair and replacement of the actual physical components of the hotel, an asset manager must be cognizant of the spectrum of unique opportunities that exist to improve the value and performance of any hotel asset.

Finally, this chapter will discuss how to put together an asset management plan. Elements of the plan include research, analysis, and planning how and when to spend additional capital, as well as when to consider selling the asset, if that is part of ownership's objectives.

The Asset Management Cycle

The asset management cycle has four primary phases:

- Determining the owner's objectives
- Acquiring and absorbing the asset
- Unlocking value and monitoring performance
- Disposing of the asset

The asset management cycle is an iterative process primarily between determining the owner's objectives and unlocking and monitoring performance. As ownership evaluates the current and prospective performance of the hotel, its objectives will evolve and react to new information. Additionally, time will present more opportunities to the asset manager to take action to either create or preserve value.

The acquisition and disposition of a hotel asset are specific events, the beginning and end of the asset's life cycle under a specific ownership. The initial evaluation by ownership to acquire the hotel is a critical, strategic decision by ownership when considering its options regarding where it will invest its capital. Equally critical is the decision to dispose of, or sell, the asset. The asset manager must assist the ownership in identifying whether all of the practical value has been harvested from the asset at returns acceptable to ownership. Further, the asset manager must help identify whether transaction market conditions are optimal for ownership to put its hotel asset up for sale.

Ownership Objectives

Hotels, often to the surprise of most people outside of the industry, are generally not owned by the various brands that consumers are familiar with from advertising and marketing campaigns. A wide variety of entities and individuals own hotels with an equally varied number of objectives. While we do not get into a detailed overview of all types of owners in this chapter, we do focus on the types of ownership that typically employ and rely on the asset management function either as employees or from a third-party perspective.

There are as many types of owners of hotels as there are motivations for owning hotels. Historically, hotels were owned by individuals or companies that viewed the operation of a hotel, the actual accommodation of guests, as their business model. From this type of ownership, hotel brands began, which in turn led to the franchising of hotels. This expanded the types of owners into corporate, management-oriented types as well as individuals owning both branded and independent hotels.

Over time, as the sophistication of real estate investment increased, non-typical owners emerged. Rather than day-to-day operators, these owners were more investment-oriented entities, such as large insurance companies, pension funds, banks, etc. They saw hotels as a way to further diversify their portfolios to achieve their varied financial objectives. Beginning in the late 1960s, these large institutions became more active in the actual ownership of hotels. Previously, an institution may have come by ownership of a hotel through foreclosure or similar loan collateral transfer. Often they ended up with what at first glance appeared to be real estate, but which ultimately became an operating nightmare for some.

As these institutions took ownership of the hotel assets, they most often hired brands to manage the hotels for them. This was a rather lucrative opportunity for the brands as they were able to subject the ownership to long-term management contracts. Furthermore, no one at the institutions was typically experienced enough in hotel operations to fully understand whether or not the hotel managers were running the hotels efficiently or "maximizing value." As a result, beginning in the 1970s, these institutions began to hire individuals with backgrounds in hotel operations to focus on the performance of their hotel assets. The need for this expertise has continued and expanded through to today, thus creating the framework for the current hospitality asset management industry.

Today, a broad spectrum of hotel ownership types exists. Some owners are long-term investors looking to ensure a consistent, increasing cash flow from operations. Others are looking at the investment as an opportunity to increase value quickly and to take advantage of market swings to reap a high, shorter-tem return. Additionally, there are still troubled properties that have been taken back by lenders who need direction on how to optimize the hotels' dispositions.

Asset managers must be fully aware of owners' expectations and ultimate goals. These expectations and goals must be established immediately and initially in the asset management process and should be reviewed regularly to identify any changes throughout the hold period.

Asset Acquisition

As the acquisition process is initiated and due diligence has begun, the owner's tolerance for risk and investment horizon will begin to emerge, as will the tools the asset manager has at hand to realize those objectives. Enormous amounts of information are processed during the acquisition process and the asset manager should have access to all of it. The better and more complete the information gleaned during due diligence, the better and more accurate the asset manager's actions and recommendations will be to ownership.

Once it appears likely the asset will be acquired, there exists a brief window of opportunity to (1) reevaluate any previously made recommendations based on newly acquired information and knowledge and (2) identify other opportunities that may have not been apparent at the outset of the acquisition analysis. Effective asset managers know the phases in which an asset is acquired and sold represent small fractions of the ownership cycle. The effort to unlock the asset's full value comprises the greatest portion of the cycle. That phase where the asset manager is regularly evaluating the performance of the hotel in light of the changing market dynamics and opportunities constitutes the greatest risk for ownership and, subsequently, the asset manager.

At this point, it is critical to reassess the elements discovered during the due diligence process as they relate to the owner's objectives. The asset manager must compare the original underwriting assumptions to the new and current data to determine whether the original objectives and expectations are still valid or, if the new and current data change the underwriting results, whether pursuit of the acquisition is still supported.

Components of the underwriting that are critical to determine and verify include the prospective hold period for the asset, whether the risk/reward parameters established by ownership will be met by investing in the asset, and finally if there is enough capital (equity and debt) available to support not only the initial investment in the hotel, but also future projects intended to enhance the value of the project.

In the brief discussion of different ownership types from earlier in this chapter, it is obvious that how long investors hold on to assets is a critical component of their investment objectives. Cash flow investors prefer assets that will deliver a consistently increasing distribution of cash from the operation of the asset, suggesting they are looking for a long hold period. Conversely, value investors are looking to maximize the return of the investment, often measured as the internal rate of return (IRR) of the asset. The greatest IRR returns are most often achieved in a shorter time period, usually within a three- to five-year hold period. Therefore, an asset manager must assess if any information was gleaned from the market that would have an effect on a hold period. Items that could affect a hold period include, but are not limited to, the following:

- Local zoning regulations or building codes that may affect the ability to implement any physical changes to the hotel
- New supply coming in that was not identified before the due diligence that could affect future performance of the subject hotel
- Changes in local convention activity, whether or not a local convention center will be expanding, and the implication of completing any renovation or expansion work in relation to ownership's time frame
- Business accommodated by the asset that turns out to be short-term in nature and will not be at the hotel after acquisition
- New demand generators entering the market during the prospective hold period

Ownership places value on assets by the assets' ability to achieve the types of returns the owners are targeting. They are willing to accept risk in a project if it will achieve a minimum threshold of return. The return is ultimately measured by the amount of cash flow a hotel can produce relative to the risk of acquiring that hotel, which is measured in the cost to buy the hotel versus an alternative investment. Any disruptions or enhancements to the anticipated cash flow based on new data need to be factored into the return equation.

The examples identified above for hold period evaluations also hold true for risk/return measure. Those above were generally macro issues, issues affecting the broader market area. Following are several more micro-oriented issues that also apply in these considerations.

- Any changes in fees associated with hiring a management company; the return would be in generating incremental cash flow that more than compensates for any increase in fees associated with the new manager.
- Individual ROI projects, such as adding guestrooms or meeting space, enhancing existing facilities or outlets, or purchasing new equipment.
- Changes in brand affiliation; much like changing management companies, the increase in cash flow must be greater than any costs associated with the change, such as required improvements, installation of new systems, or additional payroll costs.

Upon the transfer of the hotel to new ownership, the asset manager must coordinate the takeover of the asset. This is not as simple of a process as with most other types of real estate. Issues include the transfer of the employees from one employer to another, legal issues such as liquor licenses, sales tax licenses, checking and replenishing inventories, and transfer of bank accounts to name a few. The asset manager must be able to handle relationships with the operator, attorneys, the seller, the lender, and the brand, if applicable.

And finally, as all of this is occurring, the asset manager must always keep focused on the longer term goals of the owner and continuously identify opportunities as they appear and refine the owner's goals.

Identifying Value and Monitoring Operating Performance

Identifying value and monitoring the operating performance are concurrent activities. As Exhibit 1 illustrates, this stage of the ownership period is iterative in nature and will be repeated continuously throughout the hold period of the asset. As the asset matures in its holding period and market conditions fluctuate, the continual

Exhibit 1 Unlock Value/Monitor Performance

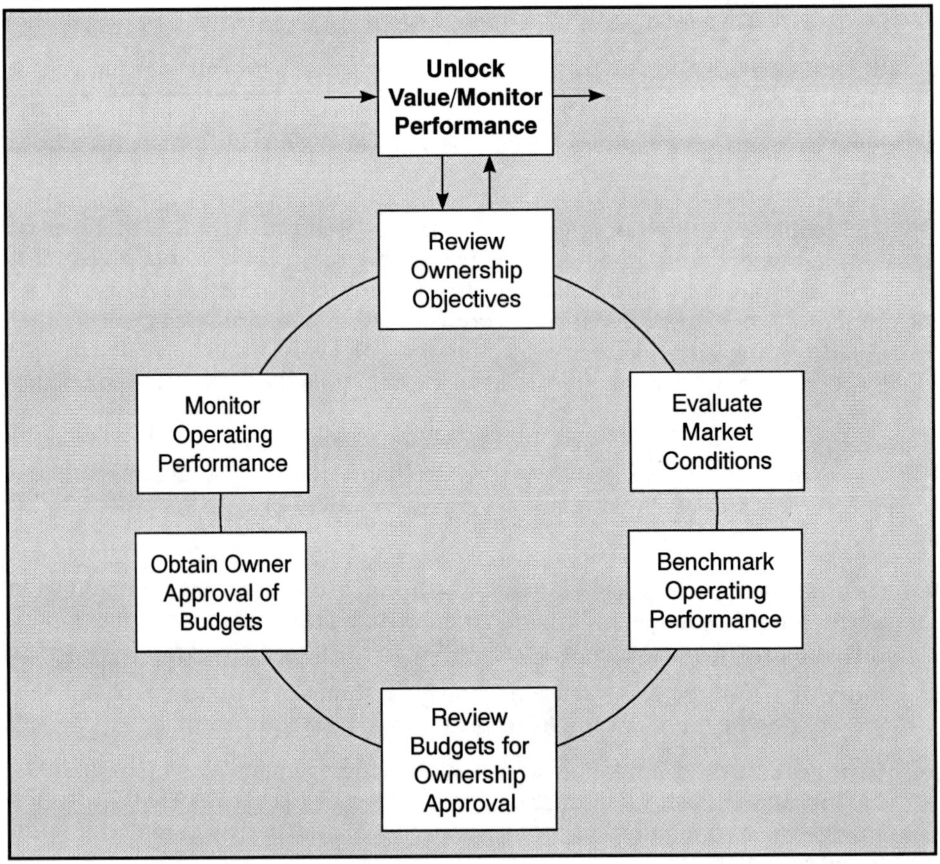

evaluation of the performance of the asset can identify value creation opportunities, shortcomings in the execution of the asset management plan, or a significant change in the asset management plan itself.

It is up to the asset manager to initiate the plans to achieve the goals established at the outset of the acquisition. The initial steps toward creating value are typically queued up and ready to be initiated. As discussed previously, this is the time to make the significant changes to reposition the hotel, such as renovation or changing brand and/or management. Other steps to be initiated can include closing under-performing outlets and evaluating personnel and staffing levels.

Other efforts that can lead to immediate returns include implementing new insurance coverage, appealing the real estate taxes, directing management to raise prices in the outlets, or adding service charges where customary. During the takeover and absorption of the asset, other opportunities may become evident. Perhaps there are some contracts or leases coming up for renewal that may have been below market and can be improved through a new marketing or negotiation process.

The implementation of specific initiatives can be the exciting part of the asset management process. Major improvements can be realized in a short amount of time, but the asset manager should not lose focus on the ongoing process of monitoring the operating performance of the hotel. There are several key processes the asset manager must establish in order to be as efficient as possible in this aspect of the assignment.

Asset managers must regularly visit the asset to make sure it is being taken care of in the manner expected and reasonable, in accordance with the plan. The asset is a tangible piece of property that can deteriorate if not cared for appropriately. Property visits should be scheduled as often as the asset manager feels is necessary, as approved by ownership. Typically, these visits are conducted monthly or quarterly, depending on the complexity of the asset and the scope of the asset management engagement. Additionally, regular calls with the management team can keep an asset manager fully aware of all current actions and events affecting a hotel's performance.

In conjunction with the regular visits to the property and contact with the management team, the asset manager will review reports and data about the performance of the hotel, generally prepared by management. While receiving monthly financial reports is helpful and important, these reports detail historic information about the hotel's performance. It is critical to also monitor ongoing and future business. Evaluating leading indicators such as booking pace, market pace, future room rate levels, and competitor movements is also important so the asset manager can question strategy and offer insights. Additionally, if significant changes to business levels are becoming apparent, the asset manager can take action to adjust plans to either take advantage of better than expected business levels or adjust expectations if business levels begin to slip.

It is therefore evident that one of the key components of effective asset management is the asset manager's ability to review, interpret, and apply and act upon information regarding the performance of the hotel. The breadth of this information can be as basic as reading the monthly financial statements to reviewing other management reports such as the daily flash report, booking pace, revenue management reports, guest comment cards, engineering reports, lost business reports, etc. Information is widely available, but how does an asset manager judge the relative success of a hotel's performance? There are various and plentiful sources of information that can be used to guide the asset manager in evaluating the performance of the asset.

Data regarding operating measures for each department, practically each line, of the profit and loss statement is available. Traditional accounting measures can be applied to the balance sheet. The abundant amount of historical property performance can be evaluated and summarized.

Competitive market data can be gleaned from an equally varied number of sources. Broader economic and demographic indicators are easily available from local sources to national indices. Our purpose here is not to list every conceivable source of data, but rather to suggest that any and all of this data can and should be used to establish performance benchmarks for the hotel. A discussion of specific information sources may be found in the chapter on benchmarking and financial analysis.

Establishing benchmarks will make the asset manager's job more efficient as critical performance indicators will have already been identified and targets established. The asset manager can either prepare a report as the information is available, or have it prepared, for evaluation of the performance of the hotel. Measured variances against the targets can quickly flag unacceptable or concerning patterns of operation. Additionally, property trends consistently surpassing positive performance standards can alert the asset manager to reevaluate the benchmark to more realistic expectations.

Another critical component of monitoring operating performance is the occasional execution of ad hoc analysis. This type of analysis usually arises as trends emerge from the regular measure and evaluation of the hotel's performance against its benchmarks. Alternatively, new market information or even industry advancements are identified and the asset manager would like to explore further the potential for value creation stemming from one or more of these observations.

Suppose you, as an asset manager, have been tracking a decline in weekend business. Perhaps a dynamic of the market has changed, a new hotel has opened, or a local banquet venue that used to generate wedding and other demand for the hotel on weekends has closed. Additionally, the hotel has historically received inquiries from airlines to contract for guestrooms on a daily basis for its flight crews. In the past, you and your management team may have judged the opportunity to accommodate this business not profitable enough for you to consider. However, now may be a time to consider this business. Ultimately, you would need to know if the reward (profit) for accepting this business is worth the risk (associated costs). To determine this, you will have to work with your management team to identify all of the elements of revenue and expense in taking on such a contract and properly calculating the results. At the end of the analysis, you may decide there is no profit to be gained by taking on such a contract, but you as the owner's representative can be secure in your decision as a result of conducting this one-time analysis.

Finally, keeping in mind the primary objective of an asset manager—that is, to assist an owner in achieving its objectives—the asset manager must also regularly review these objectives. In reviewing these objectives, the asset manager must evaluate her or his success in implementing the owner's plans. This will require the periodic completion of a "hold-sell" analysis.

The hold-sell analysis combines an updated projection of the future performance of the hotel with an estimation of the present value of the hotel compared to the potential future value of the property. This analysis must take into account the likely income levels of the hotel over the next several years and the potential value of the hotel at these times. Furthermore, factors such as necessary future capital investment, changes in the investor markets, and potential changes in the competitive dynamics of the hotel's market must all be considered.

Upon completion of the analysis, the hotel's value and potential future value can be compared with the owner's original expectation. If the current value exceeds the original underwriting, perhaps consideration should be given to taking the hotel to market. Or, will holding onto the hotel for one or more years yield an even greater risk adjusted return for ownership? This consideration should be presented to ownership so a fully-informed decision can be made and a possible change in ownership objectives should be implemented.

Asset Disposition

Inevitably, ownership will make a decision to sell the hotel. (Exhibit 2 provides a brief overview of the process.) By this time, the asset manager likely has been involved in making numerous decisions as well as reporting to ownership on market conditions and factors regarding the optimum time to sell the asset. The value enhancement strategies set forth and implemented at the outset of the investment, the continual monitoring of the hotel's performance and ongoing market conditions, and the strategic implementation of new opportunities have all come to fruition as ownership has decided it is time to bring the asset to market.

Exhibit 2 The Disposition Process

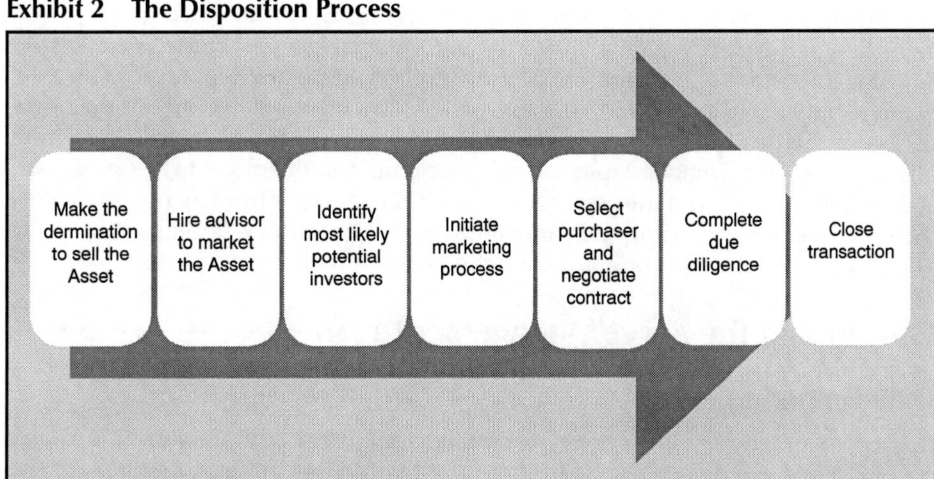

But is the decision to sell as simple as meeting the inflection point of the asset's current market value compared to the underwriting assumption of potential future value? Again, it depends on the owner.

Profit is a typical motivation to sell, but other factors peculiar to different types of ownership can influence the timing of asset disposition. For instance, perhaps the hotel owner is a larger institution with its property ownership tied to established funds. Occasionally, the portfolio managers responsible for the decisions driving a fund's investments may have determined that their desired asset types no longer include hotels, or their outlook for hotel investment is not positive and they fear the fund will have an unacceptable exposure by continuing to invest in and hold lodging properties. The issues could also have nothing directly to do with broader investment markets, but rather in decisions specific to their holdings, such as unexpected capital requirements, or a fund liquidation event. In the latter case, the subject property may be one of the last assets and the investors may be more interested in cashing out and moving onto other opportunities rather than waiting out a maximum value strategy.

Suppose the ownership is a public company, specifically a REIT. While a REIT's motivation for owning property is a bit different from many other institutional investors, it is still compelled to evaluate its holdings continuously. Perhaps the REIT has identified one or several properties where the income from those assets is no longer accretive relative to the likely ongoing capital requirements. The senior management of the REIT may decide to sell several or all of their underperforming assets and redeploy the cash into more accretive investments or actions that provide more benefit to the REIT overall by way of reducing debt, improving share value, or providing capital to purchase other assets.

These scenarios have been examined to illustrate the need for an asset manager to thoroughly understand ownership's objectives and motivations as well as possess the ability to be flexible in response to an owner's needs.

In addition to helping ownership arrive at the decision to sell the asset, the asset manager most likely will play a significant role in assisting ownership through the disposition process. At the very least, the asset manager will likely be the one individual with the most working knowledge of the history of the ownership period regarding performance, capital invested, and the management of the hotel.

It is important to note that no transaction is closed until it is closed. The asset manager must continue to look out for ownership's interests not only in the negotiation of the deal points but also to ensure the hotel is taken care of from both physical and performance aspects. Sometimes transactions do not close and ownership continues to hold the asset for some period of time. The asset manager must then be prepared to pick up and move forward with little to no impact from the sale process affecting the ongoing operation of the hotel.

Developing the Asset Management Plan

Data Gathering

Regardless of whether it is a heavy, formal document or a summary outline of proposed actions and objectives, there should always an asset management plan. The plan should be prepared with the end-user in mind. As investors' experience level with hospitality assets can vary significantly, the plan should include sufficient content that someone unfamiliar with lodging projects can read it and understand the asset and investment direction described in the document.

Developing an effective plan requires accumulating and evaluating large amounts of data. This data can come from a wide variety of places. Reports developed during the due diligence process are usually good sources for information about the hotel, including, but not limited to, the property condition assessment, appraisal, management agreement, historic operating statements and budgets, business plans, market performance reports, leases, and local governmental business reports. Furthermore, interviews with management, competitors, and local government representatives can add insight and perspective into the market information gathered.

Developing an effective plan also requires fully evaluating the large amount of data gathered. Summarizing the physical characteristics of the property, explaining the various aspects of the competitive hotel market, identifying prevailing trends within the market and the strategies that could be implemented are essential components of the plan. Processing all of this information facilitates development of the action steps necessary to achieve ownership's objectives. The rationale behind developing these steps will comprise much of the discussion within the plan.

Property Summary. Starting with the basics is the easiest approach. A hotel is a physical asset with specific and unique physical characteristics. Creating a summary of the physical components of the property is essential to the plan. This provides a handy reference for owners and the asset manager regarding questions that could come up with respect to real estate tax appeals, pricing renovations, or having the hotel valued.

Furthermore, a detailed inventory of major building systems will also be critical for capital planning purposes. During the due diligence process when the hotel was purchased, prudent investors will have an assessment completed of the condition of building systems. Tying this analysis into the summary of the buildings components will provide a map for future capital expenditures.

A listing of the important agreements that affect the property should be compiled and summarized. Appropriate contracts and documents would include such items as ground leases, franchise agreements, management agreements, significant retail or space leases and employment contracts for key employees. Information should be immediately available concerning term, rent, scheduled increases or escalations, fees (both base and incentive), renewals, terminations, space definitions, and similar information.

Finally, the onsite property management team should be evaluated. It will be necessary to make some value judgments about the quality of the team. While this part of the information collection effort will be somewhat subjective, it is important to evaluate the team's ability to support ownership's objective for the hotel.

Market Overview. Critical to the plan is the asset manager's ability to understand the broader economic marketplace in which the hotel operates. Collecting information on the aspects of the local economy that affect hotel market performance will help identify opportunities hotel management can exploit. Information such as flight/passenger activity, local job growth, infrastructure expansion or repair, visitor counts from local attractions, and local office and industrial leasing trends can be considered, individually and in aggregate, to develop opinions regarding the vitality of the local marketplace.

For instance, hotel demand for properties near a major airport will likely be influenced by travel indicators such as enplanements and deplanements, changes in the number of flights into and out of the airport, any expansions of service by existing carriers, or any new carriers beginning service to an airport. Highway demand factors typically include traffic counts, concentration of services at the property's exit, and local development. While identifying the statistics and information that are most appropriate to consider for the asset manager's hotel is important, the more imperative action is to understand why the statistics may change over time and what has driven those changes. Looking at the enplanement statistics, perhaps they demonstrate a consistent growth over the past five years. That would at first pass indicate a level of stability in the market. But looking deeper into the statistics, perhaps the number of flights has actually increased at a greater rate than the passenger activity has increased. Could this mean there is a trend of fewer passengers per flight? Is this significant? Maybe in gateway markets that rely on international travel to be a primary source of demand, this would be significant. A change like this could indicate that fewer large jets are originating from Europe and the passenger activity that is actually growing is increasingly domestic, perhaps even regional. How might this conclusion affect the hotel's performance going forward?

Many of the specific economic factors that affect the broader demand aspects of an asset manager's hotel can generally be identified through review of the hotel's sales and marketing plan. This document presents management's view of where business comes from and against whom the hotel competes. Key demand generators will be identified in a properly prepared sales and marketing plan. These can range from specific companies or associations to annual events, local attractions, city-wide convention demand, or leisure-driven sources. The information compiled within the sales and marketing plan, while generally reliable, should at least initially be verified by the asset manager.

Ultimately, the asset manager will use this data, in conjunction with the information developed during the competitive supply overview, to begin to identify the relative advantages the subject hotel will have over its competitive set as well as the property's competitive deficiencies. As these aspects become more apparent, they will be aggregated with other data developed in other sections of the asset management plan to lead the rationale of the initiatives for value creation.

Competitive Supply Overview. By this point, the asset manager has begun to develop a view of the hotel and how it appears to be positioned in the market. The asset manager should understand the business the hotel is accommodating as well as the various market pressures that can affect this business demand. The next step is to scrutinize the hotel's competitive set and take stock of the relative advantages or deficiencies that exist across the market.

The starting point is to collect all of the available physical data on each of the existing competitors as well as others that may be considered competitive once ownership initiates its plans for the hotel. Collection of this information will lead to comparative information of how the facilities at the asset manager's hotel stack up against the competition.

Most property information can be found on hotel and brand websites as well as through direct inquiry at the hotels. Generally, asset managers collect this information in a simple table that includes the following information:

- Name of hotel
- Year open, including additions and most recent renovation
- Address/phone number
- Brand and management information
- Number of guestrooms
- Mix of guestrooms by type
- Average size of guestrooms
- Restaurant and lounge information (number, seats, hours of operation, etc.)
- Total meeting space by square feet, number of rooms, number of configurations
- Summary of other physical facilities (spa, retail, swimming pool, etc.)
- Summary of guestroom amenities

While this list is not exhaustive, the items described are typically what are collected. Other information, of course, can be added based on market specifics. For instance, distances from primary demand generators, access to public or private beaches, or the availability of golf might be meaningful.

In addition to collecting the physical data of the competitive set, the asset manager must actually visit each of the competitive hotels. Walking around the hotels and gaining familiarity with the level of finish, the functionality of the space, and the quality and consistency of the service offered will help the asset manager understand his or her hotel's competitive position within the market.

While collecting the data and touring the competitive set of hotels, the asset manager should meet and interview management at the competitive properties. Conversations with these operators will help the asset manager develop a complete perspective of the market. Operators are usually willing to discuss their views on the competitive market and to give their thoughts about the subject hotel. Additionally, the asset manager will likely get some further detail regarding future renovations or additions to the competitive hotel. By comparing the information collected during this fieldwork to what the asset manager has gleaned from management of the subject hotel, the asset manager can begin to evaluate how reasonable is the management team's view of the market as well as how well they understand and react to the competition's efforts.

After the physical information of the competitive hotels has been collected and interviews completed, market performance statistics should be compiled. Ideally, during the operator interviews, the general managers and directors of sales will have disclosed pertinent current and historic operating information including occupancy, average daily rate, demand segmentation, proportion of room sales to the balance of the hotel's revenue, and other bits of information that can lead the asset manager to a more precise understanding of the subject hotel's market position and how it may have evolved over time.

Most likely, though, historic market operating statistics will be derived from data services such as STR, specifically the STAR Report. STR reports provide an aggregate snapshot of the competitive set's occupancy, average daily rate, and mix of demand in daily, weekly, monthly and annual reports. Reports such as the STAR Report are very useful for the ongoing monitoring of the performance of the asset manager's hotel. They provide a reliable and industry-accepted barometer for how a specific hotel matches up to its competitive set.

In markets where neither the STAR Report nor any other comparable resources are available, the asset manager may very well have to rely on old school methods such as conducting periodic interviews of the competitors. While this information may not be as objective as the STAR Report, over a period of time it will provide reliable order of magnitude benchmarks against which trends can be observed. Another source, which may not be the most precise, is lodging tax information. This information is typically available to the general public for individual properties. With a little bit of effort, the asset manager can create a legitimate summary of the competitive set's performance using these statistics.

Performance Overview. Asset managers must have a thorough understanding of their hotels' operating performance in order to make the best judgments and decisions to meet the goals and objectives of ownership. It is imperative that the asset manager recognize the critical aspects of the financial performance of the asset. Several approaches, none of them mutually exclusive, but rather additive in nature, will be discussed in this section.

The most obvious place to start is with information prepared by management of the subject hotel. Every year, management is compelled to prepare a business plan. While this document is an all-encompassing presentation of how management had arrived at their proposed budget for the following year, there should be a comprehensive analysis of the hotel's financial performance.

This analysis will present details ranging from occupancy and average daily rate by month to hours per cover for the restaurant operation. The level of detail can be astounding. A good asset manager will understand all of these statistics and will be knowledgeable enough to understand how they are calculated. Furthermore, the astute asset manager will be able to recognize trends in particular indicators as well as aberrations that may flag a challenge.

Even the best asset managers are sometimes challenged by a property that presents operating characteristics with which the asset manager may not be thoroughly familiar. What proves to be the most helpful in these instances is the review of data from comparable operations. This usually takes the form of P&L statements from other hotels, either in the market or not, that operate within similar physical and market dynamics. Evaluating similar operations can help the asset manager begin to develop benchmarks for the subject hotel. Furthermore, as with the STAR Report, there are several data services that provide comparable operating data across the spectrum of hotels in the United States and around the world. Through the aggregation of data from a number of sources, consistent performance marks are developed that can reasonably be compared to the same performance markers at the subject hotel. By measuring the variance, positive and negative, of the subject hotel's performance against these benchmarks, the asset manager can build a strong case for challenging, and ultimately changing, the direction management is taking in operating the hotel.

The greatest expense in nearly every hotel is its payroll expense. This expense includes not only the salaries and wages of the management and staff of the hotel, but also associated costs, often referred to as the "load," such as payroll taxes, employee benefits, bonuses, and accrued vacation and other time off. Being able to understand the staffing of the hotel versus the necessary staffing is a critical component to controlling management and creating value. Most management companies use payroll scheduling models to schedule staff based on the forecast for the upcoming week. Asset managers must become familiar with management's process so they can monitor and check management's practices.

Another key area in which asset managers must be fully versed is understanding the relative costs of different sources of demand. Historically, costs associated with booking guestrooms were rather homogeneous—commissions paid to travel agents and reservation costs paid to the brand or reservation system provider. These costs were consistent and predictable primarily because the sources for bookings were few.

Presently, the proliferation of on-line booking sites and third-party meeting planners has created very broad and expensive sources of demand for lodging properties. Tracking the costs associated with all of the sources is critical, as these costs have a direct and significant impact on the hotel's profit margins. The asset manager will have to work closely with management as this information is not always available on site. Many of the contracts with these third-parties are negotiated at the brand level and the bills are paid at the brand level and charged back to the individual hotels. The array of booking channel options continues to evolve and likely will remain in a state of flux for the foreseeable future. By recognizing the impact of these demand sources on the asset manager's hotel and establishing a reliable method for tracking this information, the asset manager will at least be able to keep pace with the changes.

On the P&L, property management generally maintains control of revenues and expenses through the Gross Operating Profit line. After this line item, the remaining items are referred to historically as Fixed Charges and as Non-Operating Income and Expenses with the adoption of the Eleventh Revised Edition of the *Uniform System of Accounts for the Lodging Industry*. Ownership tends to maintain almost exclusive control over these costs and revenues. These costs, including insurance and real estate taxes, can create significant value-enhancing opportunities. Ownership typically places the insurance coverage on its asset. By virtue of ownership's buying power or the lack of buying power by the previous ownership, substantial savings can be found. Likewise with the real estate taxes, ownership is in control of this cost by virtue of the fact that the owner is responsible for paying these taxes. By employing consultants and legal counsel, owners may be able to determine that the amount of taxes being charged on the asset is inconsistent with the balance of the market. Ownership may have the opportunity to appeal the taxes according to local law, resulting in reducing the annual tax bill and, possibly, receiving a refund for overpayment. The asset manager should plan to regularly review both of these expenses and make recommendations to ownership as to whether an opportunity exists to reduce either item.

Capital Analysis. This component of the plan is among the most critical to ownership because it determines how the asset manager's time will be directed and how the owner's capital will be deployed over the holding period. There are four components that make up the overall capital plan:

- Life safety/ADA compliance
- Asset protection/preservation
- Brand compliance/guest impact
- Value creation/ROI

These elements of the capital analysis are identified in different ways throughout the acquisition process. Life safety issues and asset protection recommendations are generally noted within the property condition assessment performed before acquisition. This important document summarizes the condition of the building, site improvements, and major systems. A Phase I environmental site assessment should also be generated during acquisition, which may identify conditions such as the existence of asbestos, underground storage tanks, and other potential hazardous situations. Additionally, these reports will present an estimated schedule of when significant areas or systems of the hotel will need to be repaired, updated or replaced, and what the repairs and replacements will likely cost.

Information regarding any life safety issues should be immediately prioritized and initiated once new ownership takes possession. Generally these issues reflect local jurisdiction permit violations, outdated alarm systems, new code requirements, etc. Hotel management will often be a key source for this information, though issues can also be disclosed through the property condition assessment. Any life safety issues should be summarized with a specific disposition plan and a timeline for completion. Though these items can generally be resolved by the hotel's engineering team, sometimes more complicated issues will require hiring a consultant and an outside contractor.

The asset protection portion of the capital analysis is critical to the return of capital component of ownership's expectation of return. It is counter-intuitive to not take care of the physical asset of the ownership. While it is an appealing, though unrealistic, thought to not spend money on the asset to maximize the investment's return, it would be equivalent to killing the goose that laid the golden egg. A poorly maintained asset quickly undermines the ability of management to adequately attract business.

From the property condition assessment, a schedule for repair/replacement of the following systems should be prepared:

- Roofs
- HVAC systems
- Driveway and parking lots

- Window system/façade systems
- Elevators and other vertical transportation systems
- Telephone equipment
- Major IT equipment

Ideally, the schedule should lay out timing of the projects to match the availability of funding from the FF&E reserve. If there are serious physical deficiencies, the timing should be scheduled immediately and the funding should be included within the underwriting of the transaction as additional owner funding.

Brand compliance and guest impact projects are usually identified through a brand's product improvement plan (PIP) or within current capital plans prepared by property management. Depending on the particular affiliation, brand representatives will inspect the hotel before acquisition and evaluate the condition of the hotel in light of the brand's current standards. Often this document is made a condition of maintaining the franchise or management agreement for the hotel by the brand. If a PIP is not completed, there will generally still be ongoing requests from the brand to update the condition and offerings of the property.

The PIP often calls for some level of renovation, from a simple guestroom soft goods refresh to a complete refurbishment of the entire facility. The items called out in the PIP may coincide with ownership's plan for repositioning the hotel; however, PIP requirements are often directed at maintaining the hotel's brand identity rather than exploiting any specific opportunities apparent within the market. Ownership should negotiate with the brand regarding specific aspects of what is called out in the PIP as well as the timing required for completion of the items. An owner's objective is to minimize the cost of completing the PIP requirements so more capital can be used for renovations and projects that have an identifiable return on investment.

Value creation is the most important level of capital deployment. This type of capital expenditure is the part of the overall investment that should produce the incremental increases in the value of the property envisioned when the investment was undertaken, thus contributing to the return on capital component of ownership's return. Opportunities identified during due diligence that were of a physical nature, such as adding meeting space, adding a coffee shop or building an entire addition, are intended to generate increased revenues contributing to an increase in the hotel's value. Additionally, major projects intended to decrease expenses and costs, such as upgrading or replacing HVAC components, installing new plumbing fixtures designed to reduce water use, or retrofitting lighting for energy savings, are also considered to be value enhancing investment.

Final decisions relating to value creation projects will come from the review of market feasibility analysis and ROI analysis. Proposals for changing the market position of the hotel from its present market status will need to include a critical view of how the owner's hotel compares to competitive hotels within the market as well as comparable hotels of which the owner and asset manager may be aware. Examining the offerings of the subject hotel against current trends in the industry as well as obvious shortcomings compared to the market will help the asset manager identify a direction to take the property and to prepare his recommendations.

After identifying the market potential of the considered course of action, the asset manager must measure the ROI of such action. He or she will have to identify as accurately as possible the likely costs of the project. These costs can be determined from a variety of sources. Typically, the asset manager or owner has completed similar projects. By applying estimates from these other projects, a reasonable cost assumption can be developed for the subject project.

Next, the asset manager must forecast either the new revenue or the savings that will occur. When determining the improvement in income from cost savings, the estimation of the ROI is simply the calculation of the savings subtracted from the projected costs. This ROI is often expressed with the payback period measure, which presents how long it would take to pay back the cost of the project with the savings generated. This payback period is often expressed in months or years. Every owner has its own threshold to determine a reasonable amount of time, but generally, a project that has a payback period of three years or less is considered attractive.

For revenue-generating projects, a much more complicated and technical analysis must take place. It is critical not to equate revenues with cash flow. Expense savings are accounted for below the revenue line on the P&L and thus are already incorporated into the cash flow equation. Revenues are the measure of the cash that is handed to the hotel in return for the service provided. The important part to the owner is how much of this revenue it gets to keep.

To evaluate this, the asset manager must identify all of the costs associated with collecting the new revenue. For instance, if this incremental revenue were the result of increased room sales, the asset manager would need to assess if there were any incremental costs created to capture this revenue. If it was due to selling more rooms, there are direct costs associated with selling every single room, such as cleaning the room and replacing bathroom and other guestroom amenities. Furthermore, there are fees tied to the new revenue, including but not necessarily limited to:

- Management fees
- Franchise royalty fees
- Brand reservation fees
- Travel agent commissions
- Credit card commissions
- Allowance for FF&E

Additionally, the asset manager must take into account the potential for business disruption and temporary loss of income during the construction period. If the project consists of simply switching out pieces of HVAC equipment, the disruption will likely be minimal. However, if the scope of the renovation encompasses guestroom renovation, converting existing space from one use to another, upgrading the pool area, etc., the potential for interruption is significant. The asset manager must work with property management to estimate the impact on cash flow during the renovation and this must be incorporated into the ROI analysis as an additional cost of the project. Working with the manager to determine the optimal timing of a disruptive project is a critical component of planning, so as to fit the project into a seasonally lower period of demand.

The final part of the analysis is calculating the likely return generated by the investment. This will incorporate all of the information on project cost and incremental income generated over time. The time line is typically the prospective holding period considered in the initial underwriting, though it is not unusual to present different time periods to reflect periodic return measures. The typical calculation used is the IRR. This calculation takes into account not only the impact of the upfront costs and additional cash flow, but also the reversionary value of that cash flow upon a sale of the asset.

Upon ownership approval, the asset manager will initiate the plan by assembling a project team. For major capital investment, the asset manager will put together a team to prepare a plan for the overall project. This team can consist of the following members:

- Project manager
- Contractor
- Interior designer
- Architect
- Purchasing agent
- Project accountant (generally for very large projects)
- Various sub-consultants as needed

Often, owners will blend together fulfillment of PIP requirements with the initiation of the value creation projects. Elements of this plan include preparing a budget for the project, finalizing the design of new elements for the hotel as well as new or improved spaces, and determining the timing of the project—that is, how much time it will take to complete the work, including allowances for necessary approvals and manufacturing and shipping of materials, as well as when the renovation work should occur in order to minimize the impact on the hotel's business levels.

Typically, the design portion of the plan must be submitted to the brand for approval. This can involve some level of negotiation as ownership may not want to complete certain aspects of the PIP given the relative cost versus potential benefit. However, ownership can make the case it will exceed the PIP requirements in other areas that will be more beneficial not only to the owner, but to the brand as well.

Upon completion and acceptance of the design by both the brand and the owner, the asset manager and project manager will prepare a budget finalizing the cost of completing the project. Ownership will have the final approval of the costs. This approval process will likely require some changes to the design to possibly reduce the costs to a level more in line with the initial expectations.

Upon final approval of the budget and the scope of work, the asset manager and project manager must prepare a schedule that will reasonably represent the timing to complete the project. Regular meetings with the team to update adherence to schedule as well as to budget are critical. Any deviations should be reported to ownership as soon as possible and implications to the budget or operations must be assessed.

A final exercise outside of the execution of the capital plan will be completed when the time has come to consider taking the asset to market. When the time comes to sell the hotel, the asset manager will need to have good knowledge regarding any looming capital requirements of the hotel. The asset manager will need to identify the capital exposure of the property in terms of both necessary projects and the related costs. These projects should not be confused with what a potential purchaser may want to do to reposition the hotel, but rather the condition of the building components such as the roof, parking garage, building exterior, etc. These are critical considerations to how the market will value the hotel and ownership must have an accurate status of these areas.

Preparing the Asset Management Plan

All of the quantitative and qualitative information required to prepare the asset management plan should now be compiled. There is no reason to include every bit of information in the plan as it would yield a document far too cumbersome to be of any value to anyone wishing to review or refer to the information. As stated, the purpose of the plan is so ownership or any other interested party can easily and without confusion understand the specific attributes of the asset and the historic and current dynamics of the hotel's performance, as well as that of the competitive set and the broader economic market area. Of utmost importance, the plan will concisely spell out the roadmap to create value, the costs expected to be incurred, and the ultimate disposition and exit from the investment.

While the plan itself can take on whatever format is appropriate for the owner's use, the following elements should be incorporated into the plan:

- Summary of key product facts
- Executive summary
- Strengths, weaknesses, opportunities, and threats (SWOT) analysis
- Plans and actions
- Exit strategy
- Key data summary

Summary of Key Product Facts. This section can be tabular. The objective is to summarize, in an easy to interpret manner, the key facts about the hotel. If not completed during the data gathering effort, a table listing such items as dates opened and renovated, number of rooms, rooms by type, amount and configuration of meeting space, summary of the food and beverage and retail outlets, list of amenities, etc., should be presented. This summary will give a reader a quick but thorough understanding of the physical attributes of the hotel and an idea of some of its potential uses of space.

Executive Summary. This piece of the document should concisely present the current status of the hotel and the key steps to creating value over ownership's holding period. The purpose of this section is to provide the plan in succinct portions whereby readers can easily interpret the purpose of the investment. If additional information is needed, it should be available to anyone from the source information from which the summary was developed.

To start, the hotel's current market position should be clearly stated. This will provide the baseline for where the asset management plan will ultimately take the hotel from a competitive perspective and will help define the success of the plan. The statement should summarize the asset's value from a real estate perspective, property condition, accommodated demand, strength of brand/identity, and how the property will fit the objectives of ownership's plan.

The subject hotel's unique advantages and challenges should be highlighted. Discussion points summarizing such items as the barriers to entry into the market, proximity to major demand sources, and the ability of the asset to change brands and/or management easily are some of the key advantages a hotel could possess that make it an intriguing investment. On the other hand, challenges such as major capital requirements to bring the hotel into compliance with brand or local requirements or changes in competitive supply that could affect the subject hotel's current market position, are risk factors that need to be identified.

After highlighting the key motivators and potential impediments to the deal, the key actions proposed to be taken to achieve ownership's goals need to be laid out. These can be presented in a step-by-step sequence along the critical path that may be necessary, depending on whether certain actions must be completed before commencing with other elements of the program. Alternatively, if the plan includes rather complex strategies to achieve ownership objectives, these may need to be presented in a level of detail sufficient for the reader's understanding, yet concise enough to fit with the intent of an executive summary.

After presenting the steps proposed to complete the plan successfully, summarize any particular risks that will be incurred by implementing the plan. Some risks are relatively self-evident, such as costs associated with capital improvements. However, not only is the amount of money required a risk, but also the potential availability of the capital. Questions such as whether or not the money will need to be borrowed and on what terms will need to be addressed. If the owner is an investment fund, another risk associated with required capital could be whether spending that capital could put the fund into any kind of default or risk of default relative to any covenants or restrictions by which the fund must abide.

Other risks may include local code considerations. Will any proposed increases to the meeting space or restaurant trigger a need for additional parking? Will there be land available to use for additional parking or must ownership seek a variance from the local municipality? Perhaps there are timing risks involved regarding significant retail tenant lease rollovers relative to the optimum timing for the sale of the hotel at the end of the projected holding period. All significant risks must be identified.

Finally, the holding period for the asset must be discussed. This will identify the prospective timing of completing the specific value-enhancing actions, as well as any local market conditions that influence ownership's holding period and expected investment market conditions. The exit plan should also list who the likely purchasers will be and why other types of investors may not be attracted to this asset. As part of this discussion, appropriate investment data should also be summarized. Various return measures should be summarized, such as IRR, equity multiples, cash-on-cash return, etc. Each owner will require a different measure or combination of several measures. If ownership is a partnership, a presentation of the distributions to the partners should be presented in accordance with the terms of the partnership agreement.

SWOT Analysis. The SWOT analysis will serve as a presentation basis of the detailed advantages and challenges of the subject hotel which have been considered in the investment underwriting. A sample table format typically used to present the SWOT findings is shown in Exhibit 3. This format is helpful as it presents the corresponding elements of the analysis adjacent to each other. Within the analysis, Strengths and Weaknesses are generally aspects of the subject hotel and its operations that are inherent to the hotel itself. Note in Exhibit 3 that the strengths of the hotel describe the hotel specifically with respect to its location and level of service. Weaknesses are also specific to the hotel, such as the condition of the asset and the turnover in the sales department.

Exhibit 3 SWOT Analysis Format

SWOT Analysis for Subject Hotel	
Strengths	**Weaknesses**
• Closest property to Widget, Inc.	• Hotel has not been renovated in seven years
• Most meeting space in competitive market	• High turnover in sales department
• Consistently strong guest service scores	• Small pool facility; limited recreational amenities
Opportunities	**Threats**
• Convention center will expand next year	• Local airport losing one of its carriers
• Competitive hotel under same brand umbrella changing flags to new affiliation	• Three new competitive hotels will be opening over next two years
• Widget, Inc. just purchased Gaggle	• Highway exits closest to the market will be under construction over the summer

Opportunities generally are factors that present themselves as positive market developments, such as a convention center expansion or economic news such as a local employer possibly expanding. Similarly, threats are often from outside of the hotel and have to do with potentially negative changes in the market, such as additions to supply, renovation of existing competitors, or economic news such as losing an air carrier/service or a major demand generator.

The plans and actions should adequately address any of the items identified in your SWOT analysis.

Plans and Actions. This section presents the narrative of the actions that were summarized in the executive summary. An expansion of the description of the plans must be presented in this part of the document. Specific plans need to be addressed for both operations and capital improvement. An example of possible plans and actions is presented below:

Plans for Operations	Proposed Capital Improvements
• Change in Brand or Management	• Major Renovation to the Hotel
• Staffing Changes	• Addition of Meeting Space
• Closing Outlets; Changing Operating Hours	• New HVAC Systems
• Reduce Cost of Insurance	• New Roof
• Appeal Property Tax Assessment	

Changes in operations are generally straightforward with respect to creating additional profit. Capital improvements, as discussed previously, will not necessarily always lead to increased profits or value. Some of these actions may be for asset preservation, some may be to comply with local or federal regulations, and some may be to comply with a new brand standard. It is important to identify under which category of capital investment a proposed plan will fall.

This section is more detailed than the executive summary. This detail must thoroughly identify the plans and the rationale for implementing the plans. Cost, timing, expected outcomes, and returns are all necessary in this section. Additionally, all risks must be presented, as well as what will mitigate specific risks.

Critical to this section is a sources and uses analysis detailing the source(s) of funding for the project as well as any costs associated with acquiring the funding. Capital improvements ideally will be funded through the FF&E reserve; however, if a very large project is proposed for the property and the existing FF&E reserve plus what it is likely to accumulate over the course of the project will be insufficient, or if the proposed investment is inconsistent with debt covenants or contractual restrictions on the FF&E reserve, additional owner equity or debt funding may be required.

The deal underwriting is also presented in this section to demonstrate how the expected returns will be achieved. Often included with this presentation is a sensitivity analysis that may show several different projections with different variables in the underlying assumptions changed to reflect the impact from the identified risks associated with the deal. This sensitivity information will help ownership understand just how susceptible the project is to various outcomes. Inherent in this portion of the plans and actions is the discussion of ownership's holding period for the asset.

Exit Strategy. The final component of the asset management plan is a review of the exit strategy for the investment. The type of owner will greatly influence this part of the plan. Is the owner a value investor looking to create value quickly and divest as soon as possible to attain the greatest level of return possible, or is the owner a public company or institution with a longer-term view relying upon the income generated by the property? The criteria used to develop the exit strategy should be clearly defined.

How will the property be presented to the market? Most likely a formal marketing process will be initiated and bids will be solicited. Also, it is necessary to identify the anticipated bidders and to explain why other types of investors may not be interested in the asset.

Finally, any projection of where the investment market will be at the time of disposition is pertinent. Presumably this foresight will have been considered in the formation of the holding period, but a review of current market value trends and transactions will be helpful at this juncture.

Key Data Summary. In addition to the summary of key product facts, where specific information about the physical nature of the hotel was presented, other critical data should be compiled and included in the asset management plan. This information will help not only the owner but also potential investors. If the asset manager changes, this section of the document in particular will be very helpful to the new asset manager during the transition of the property. In addition, when this information is prepared up front, it can be used in developing performance benchmarks or best practices.

Each property is typically subject to a myriad of legal agreements and requirements. Items such as identification of the management and franchise companies and key terms of the contracts, whether or not the hotel is subject to a ground lease or operating lease, debt and lender information, and any other major agreements affecting the ownership or operation of the property should be noted in summary form. Critical information that should be highlighted includes: any dates tied to the termination of major agreements, such as management contracts or franchise agreements; loan maturity dates; due dates for completion of obligations, such as PIPs; and required reporting schedules, such as reporting periodic financial results to lenders or other parties requiring this information.

Summaries of comparative historical performance, as well as an historical summation of capital projects completed including timing and the associated costs, are essential to this section. A tracking of the relative success of historical ROI capital projects would also be very helpful.

As a rule of thumb, if the information was a significant part of the underwriting assumptions, it should be included in this section.

Conclusion

The asset manager role covers a broad spectrum of responsibility. Ownership will rely on the asset manager to know the physical asset inside and out and to understand its operation well enough to quickly identify new opportunities to exploit or threats to contain. The asset manager must be able to interpret historical facts and trends from both the subject hotel operation and the market area within which the hotel operates. Furthermore, the asset manager must be astute enough to look forward and help management anticipate changes. Asset management assignments are both strategic and tactical.

The iterative nature of the asset management cycle can be tedious, but it is when the tedium breaks ever so slightly that the asset manager has an opportunity to create or preserve value for the owner. Constantly measuring, reviewing, asking questions, and then reporting the pertinent information to ownership with recommendations is the essence of asset management.

Much of the asset manager's baseline for measurement is provided by the asset management plan. This plan, compiled at the outset of the investment, lays out the initial course of action to achieve ownership's goals. While the asset manager is charged with executing the plan through the asset management process, the plan should constantly be reviewed, evaluated, and updated to account for the inevitable changes to the original assumptions that will occur as time passes and new information is gathered. It is through that critical process that the asset manager becomes indispensable to the owner.

Chapter Appendix

A Narrative Example of the Asset Management Process

Overview

At the peak of the last lodging transaction cycle, a mid-size private equity investor, NextGen Capital, acquired a portfolio of twenty-five hotels, a mix of independent, full-service, select service, resort, and business-oriented properties. Due to the frothy market at the time, NextGen acquired more hotels as part of this portfolio acquisition than it otherwise would have liked, in order to win the deal. At the time of the acquisition, NextGen's Managing Director in charge of lodging assets devised a business plan aimed at bifurcating the properties into two buckets. The first bucket comprised the true targets of the acquisition, ten hotels in high-barrier-to-entry, high-profile resort locations. This group of hotels was considered the core holdings of the portfolio acquisition and slated for a long-term hold. The second bucket comprised a hodge-podge of assets carrying miscellaneous brands in mixed locations. These assets were considered to be candidates for a shorter term hold with a disposition targeted after completion of change of ownership property improvement plans (PIPs), selective conversions to new brands, other value add initiatives, and post investment ramp-up.

Conversion/Repositioning/Value-Add Analysis Summary

	Pre Conversion Proforma	%	Year 1 Proforma	%	Year 2 Proforma	%	Year 3 Proforma	%
Rooms Available:	62,050		62,050		62,050		62,050	
Rooms Sold:	48,957		42,752		44,738		45,731	
Occupancy:	78.9%		68.9%		72.1%		73.7%	
ADR:	$77.49		$110.30		$124.44		$126.04	
Rooms RevPAR:	$61.14		$76.00		$89.72		$92.89	
Rooms RevPAR Growth:			24.3%		18.1%		3.5%	
Total RevPAR:	$102.63		$86.25		$100.36		$103.78	
Total RevPAR Growth:			-16.0%		16.4%		3.4%	
Market Occupancy:	63.4%		76.5%		78.4%		78.4%	
Market ADR:	$105.80		$85.71		$94.22		$97.52	
Market Rooms RevPAR:	$67.08		$65.57		$73.87		$76.45	
Market Rooms RevPAR Growth:			-2.2%		12.7%		3.5%	
Property RevPAR Index:	91.1%		115.9%		121.5%		121.5%	
Operating Revenue								
Rooms	3,793,713	59.6%	4,715,595	88.1%	5,567,203	89.4%	5,763,916	89.5%
Food & Beverage	2,214,835	34.8%	559,202	10.4%	569,963	9.2%	583,068	9.1%
Other Operated Departments	344,660	5.4%	74,389	1.4%	77,844	1.3%	79,572	1.2%
Miscellaneous Income	14,687	0.2%	2,565	0.0%	12,527	0.2%	13,189	0.2%
Total Operating Revenue	6,367,896	100.0%	5,351,752	100.0%	6,227,537	100.0%	6,439,745	100.0%
Departmental Expenses								
Rooms	1,172,041	30.9%	1,094,035	23.2%	1,244,613	22.4%	1,230,160	21.3%
Food & Beverage	2,135,101	96.4%	492,266	88.0%	501,567	88.0%	513,100	88.0%
Other Operated Departments	165,437	48.0%	51,329	69.0%	53,713	69.0%	54,904	69.0%
Other	-	0.0%	-	0.0%	-	0.0%	-	0.0%
Total Departmental Expenses	3,472,579	54.5%	1,637,629	30.6%	1,799,892	28.9%	1,798,164	27.9%
Departmental Profit								
Rooms	2,621,671	69.1%	3,621,560	76.8%	4,322,590	77.6%	4,533,756	78.7%
Food & Beverage	79,734	3.6%	66,936	12.0%	68,396	12.0%	69,968	12.0%
Other Operated Departments	179,223	52.0%	23,061	31.0%	24,132	31.0%	24,667	31.0%
Miscellaneous Income	14,687	100.0%	2,565	100.0%	12,527	100.0%	13,189	100.0%
Total Departmental Profit	2,895,316	45.5%	3,714,122	69.4%	4,427,644	71.1%	4,641,581	72.1%

Undistributed Operating Expenses								
Administration & General	321,864	5.1%	224,715	4.2%	221,193	3.6%	256,541	4.0%
Information & Telecom Systems	114,793	1.8%	118,236	2.2%	121,783	2.0%	125,437	1.9%
Sales & Marketing	151,556	2.4%	138,075	2.6%	147,593	2.4%	150,690	2.3%
Franchise Fees	356,230	5.6%	514,943	9.6%	609,052	9.8%	628,267	9.8%
Property Operation & Maintenance	374,269	5.9%	256,729	4.8%	303,713	4.9%	313,037	4.9%
Utilities	377,532	5.9%	225,910	4.2%	268,664	4.3%	271,590	4.2%
Total Undistributed Expenses	1,696,243	26.6%	1,478,608	27.6%	1,671,998	26.8%	1,745,562	27.1%
Gross Operating Profit	1,199,074	18.8%	2,235,514	41.8%	2,755,647	44.2%	2,896,019	45.0%
Base Management Fees	191,037	3.0%	160,553	3.0%	186,826	3.0%	193,192	3.0%
Income Before Non-Oper Inc and Exp	1,008,037	15.8%	2,074,962	38.8%	2,568,821	41.2%	2,702,826	42.0%
Non-Operating Income and Expenses								
Rent	-	0.0%	-	0.0%	-	0.0%	(180,000)	-2.8%
Property, Insurance & Other	322,320	5.1%	439,110	8.2%	452,283	7.3%	465,852	7.2%
Total Non-Operating Inc & Expenses	322,320	5.1%	439,110	8.2%	452,283	7.3%	285,852	4.4%
Earnings Before Interest, Taxes, Depreciation and Amortization	685,717	10.8%	1,635,852	30.6%	2,116,537	34.0%	2,416,975	37.5%
Replacement Reserve	254,716	4.0%	214,070	4.0%	249,101	4.0%	257,590	4.0%
EBITDA Less Replacement Reserve	$431,001	6.8%	$1,421,782	26.6%	$1,867,436	30.0%	$2,159,385	33.5%
Capitalization Rate In-Place NOI	10.0%		9.0%		9.0%		8.6%	
Implied Value	4,310,009		15,797,573		20,749,287		24,993,164	
Renovation/Value Add Capital	-		6,800,000		6,800,000		7,200,000	
Cash on Cash Yield on Incremental Investment			15%		21%		24%	
	$431,001	6.8%	$1,421,782	26.6%	$1,867,436	30.0%	$2,159,385	33.5%

Challenge

The majority of the hotels in the second bucket of assets were branded with one of the well-known select service brands of a major national lodging company, MillINNium Hotels, a brand highly in favor with larger, sophisticated institutional investors. However, there were a handful of older assets that were branded with an older midscale brand with full-service food and beverage offerings, BoomerINN. The BoomerINN brand had been created and seen its heyday in the 1960s and 1970s. However, with an aging inventory and the accelerating obsolescence of many of its hotels, the brand was no longer attractive to institutional investors by the 2000s. An additional challenge with the portfolio as a whole, and for the BoomerINN hotels in particular, was that they were, and would remain, encumbered by third-party management with prohibitively high termination costs for the foreseeable future. NextGen's hotel team and its investment advisors and brokers all felt that the most logical buyers for the BoomerINN properties would be smaller, regional "owner-operators," but given the management encumbrance, this buyer pool would not be interested. The challenge with the second bucket of hotel assets, therefore, was how to maximize the return for NextGen and execute a smooth disposition of these assets.

Alternatives

There appeared to be two viable alternatives that NextGen could choose from with respect to the eventual disposition of the second, non-core portfolio of hotels. Perhaps the easier route would be to assume the existing franchise affiliations of all fifteen hotels, execute the change of ownership PIP, hopefully prove out a marginal return on those invested PIP dollars, and try to sell this sub-portfolio as-is after a moderate post-renovation ramp-up. The drawbacks to this approach were at least two-fold, one being that the post-renovation "pop" would likely not produce meaningful incremental profit or returns for this segment of the portfolio, and two as discussed above, the presence of the BoomerINN properties in this portfolio would decrease the interest of larger institutional buyers, thus depressing pricing. The second alternative that NextGen investigated, and eventually pursued, was to convert the four BoomerINN hotels to the MillINNium Hotel brand, thus creating upside in operating performance, broadening the appeal of the portfolio for institutional investors, creating an easier financing environment, and perhaps most importantly, with an increased scale of portfolio transaction, the larger institutional investors would be amenable to retaining the third party manager (which would not be the case with the owner-operator population). In addition to the core strategy of changing brands, NextGen's asset management team would seek out other value add opportunities directly related to the brand change (different market mix, segmentation, etc.), as well as organic opportunities such as additional lease revenue.

Solution

In the year-plus following its initial portfolio acquisition, NextGen successfully converted the four BoomerINN hotels to the MillINNium Hotel brand and commenced the ramp-up process. With the conversions complete, the non-core hotel portfolio comprised fifteen hotels all within the same national brand company's family, which theoretically improved its appeal to the larger institutional investor. Once all properties were operating under the new brand, asset management commenced upon the next step in the process toward an eventual disposition that would achieve NextGen's investment goals.

Execution

The four hotels were converted to the MillINNium Hotel brand for approximately $40,000 per room. Upon reopening, the hotels ramped up to levels commensurate with MillINNium Hotel's chainwide average RevPAR and typical penetration levels versus their competitive sets. For ease of example, we will follow the cycle of one of the four hotels from pre-conversion to post-conversion, to ramp-up and execution of additional value add opportunities.

The newly converted MillINNium Hotel located in Boca Vista, Florida, was proximate to a major airport and, prior to conversion to the MillINNium brand, had accommodated significant airline crew demand at low rates. In its last year of operation under the BoomerINN affiliation, the hotel had operated at an occupancy premium to its competitive set of over 124 percent, but with an average daily rate so far below the competitive set that its RevPAR index was only 91 percent. In addition to low rates, the airline crew business brought with it other related expenses, such as required transportation to and from the airport. Further, pre-conversion the hotel had been required to operate a three-meal-a-day restaurant. The food and beverage operation had been relatively popular and generated over $2.2 million per year in revenue, but with expenses of over $2.1 million, profitability was challenging.

Converting to the MillINNium brand brought enough incremental business and higher end demand that management decided to move forward without the airline crew business. Although demand shifted as the airline crews were displaced to the competition and the MillINNium Hotel's occupancy index declined from the 124 percent pre-conversion level to a stabilized level of 94 percent, the hotel's RevPAR index improved from 91 percent to 121.5 percent upon stabilization. Additionally, the need to provide transportation and other services for the airline crew business was negated, leading to an improvement in Rooms department profit margin from 69.1 percent pre-conversion to 78.7 percent upon stabilization. Further, the MillINNium brand standard for food and beverage consisted of a limited menu grab-and-go concept, only required to be open for breakfast and lunch. This hotel was located in a community with a healthy retail and restaurant population, so there were plenty of full-service restaurants for the hotel guest to choose from outside of the hotel. As such, while food and beverage revenues declined from $2.2 million to a level in the mid-$500,000s, absolute food and beverage profit dropped only marginally. Overall, EBITDA after replacement reserve improved from a pre-conversion level of 6.8 percent to a post-conversion level better than 30 percent.

During the second year of post-conversion ramp-up, ownership decided that after stabilization in the third year it would market the portfolio of select service hotels for sale, now all flagged under the MillINNium brand. To best position the portfolio for sale, ownership tasked the operations and asset management teams with continuing to improve operating margins and profitability, while asset management was further tasked with an additional goal of finding other opportunities from which to generate additional revenue from the underlying real estate within the portfolio. At the Boca Vista property, a parking study was commissioned that revealed that by converting the former three-meal restaurant to the new grab-and-go concept, far fewer parking spaces were required than had been the case when the property was first developed. It was determined that a stand-alone restaurant pad/outparcel could be developed on the property, which could be leased to a trendy, upscale casual restaurant chain. This was completed during year two of the ramp-up, and with the restaurant opening at year end, lease revenue of $150,000 per year was in place at the beginning of the third year of ramp-up. Also during year two, asset management reached out to several cellular telecommunications providers for potential rooftop antennae lease agreement. The asset manager moved forward with the highest bidder, which added another $30,000 annually to the low-cost commercial leasing revenue stream at the hotel.

By way of the conversion and the other repositioning and value add moves by the owner, asset manager, and operator, not only did the underlying EBITDA of the property improve, but the marketability of the asset at the time it was put up for sale had improved markedly as well. Most hotel brokers and advisors indicated that the move from the BoomerINN brand to MillINNium brand would lower the exit capitalization rate by a full 100 basis points, from 10 percent to 9 percent. Additionally, it was advised that net lease revenue streams frequently enjoy capitalization rates of 5 percent to 6 percent, which when taken as a weighted average with the EBITDA of the hotel, brought down the expected exit capitalization rate to 8.6 percent. Due to all these efforts, the implied sale value from pre-conversion to post-repositioning increased from $4.3 million to $25.0 million. These value improvements did not come without a cost—as discussed the conversion cost $40,000 per room, or $6.8 million, and the landlord's work to gain approval and provide a shovel-ready restaurant pad cost $400,000—but clearly the cash on cash yields from these investments were incrementally positive, as would be the anticipated final sales proceeds.

3

Evaluating Franchise and Chain Affiliation Programs

By John McCarthy and Lori Raleigh

John McCarthy *is a Principal of Wright Street Hospitality, a real estate investment and hospitality advisory firm. Before founding the company, he was the President of Liberty Hospitality Group, a subsidiary of Liberty Mutual. While at Liberty, he managed Liberty's investment in Sanibel Harbour Resort & Spa and participated in numerous real estate transactions, including a portfolio of Resolution Trust Corporation assets as well as a large portfolio of Residence Inn by Marriott hotel assets.*

Mr. McCarthy completed Marriott's Management Training Program and held management positions in pre-opening operations, sales and marketing, food and beverage, general management and regional management for full service and extended stay hotels.

He is a former board member and Chairman of the National System Marketing Fund Committee for RIBM. He has served on the board of the Hospitality Asset Managers Association and the FGCU Resort and Hospitality Management Advisory Board. He has spoken at numerous industry events including the Americas Lodging Investment Summit, Hospitality Design Expo, and Hotel Investment Conference. Mr. McCarthy is a graduate of Ithaca College.

Lori E. Raleigh *is President of The Travers Group, a hotel investment and asset management advisory firm. Before founding The Travers Group, she headed up the Hotel Asset Management Group at Liberty Real Estate, a subsidiary of Liberty Mutual. For many years, she served as the Executive Director of the International Society of Hospitality Consultants.*

Ms. Raleigh has spoken at numerous industry conferences and her work has appeared in many prominent hotel, finance, and real estate publications. She is co-author and co-editor of Hotel Investments: Issues & Perspectives.

Ms. Raleigh currently serves on the Michigan State Hospitality Business Real Estate Investment Management Advisory Council. She has also served on the board of directors of Residence Inn by Marriott, the American Hotel & Lodging Association, the Tisch Center for Hospitality & Tourism Advisory Board, Real Estate Forum's Hotel Industry Advisory Board, and the by-invitation-only Industry Real Estate Finance Advisory Council.

Ms. Raleigh is a longtime member and past President of the Hotel Asset Managers Association. She is a graduate of Emmanuel College with a degree in Economics and holds an MBA from Boston College.

WE ARE VERY PLEASED to have an opportunity once again to serve as contributing authors to *Hotel Asset Management: Principles & Practices.* In this edition, we will discuss the following topics:

- What's new? What has changed since the prior edition of the book in 2008?
- Franchise and brand affiliation programs: perspectives
- Evaluating franchise and brand affiliation programs
- The independent alternative—when going it alone makes sense
- A forward look: some important issues to keep in mind

What's New?

In updating this chapter, we found it very interesting to note what has and has not changed since the last edition of the book was written in 2008. Here are a few summary observations for you.

Continued Dramatic Growth in Online Reservations. Internet bookings increased from 10 percent of reservations in 2002 to 40 percent in 2008; in 2014, they represented approximately 57 percent of all bookings. Industry expert John Burns estimates that for smaller boutique hotels, as many as 75 percent of all reservations are made online. The dramatic increase in the role of the Internet understandably has had a tremendous impact on the marketing, promotion, and the distribution of hotel room inventory. Online marketing expenditures were expected to increase another 18 percent to $5 billion in 2015.

Migration to Mobile. An estimated 26 million travelers made a purchase via a mobile device in 2014. Mobile is expected to account for 25 percent of online bookings in the U.S. in 2015 and 20 percent of online bookings in Europe. It has been predicted that by 2017, 50 percent of online bookings in the U.S. will be made via mobile devices.

Brand Proliferation. The number of brands continues to escalate. In 2008, it was estimated that there were approximately 300 brand and affiliation alternatives with 38 brands having been introduced in the prior 38 months alone. Today, according to the most recent summary on Hospitalitynet.com, there are 479 brands globally and 254 brands in the United States alone.

Fair Franchising. The Asian American Hotel Owners Association (AAHOA) published its inaugural fair franchising report in mid-2008. The report examined the business practices of five major hotel chains relative to AAHOA's twelve points of fair franchising. While there has been significant progress in many areas, exit terms and impact continue to represent points of contention. One of the major issues of concern involves liquidated damages and a franchisee's ability to exit a franchise system if his or her property is not performing adequately without having to pay an exorbitant fee to do so.

Points of Brand Differentiation. "Lifestyle" features, product and design enhancements, and numerous technology initiatives have emerged during the past several years as important points of differentiation.

Dramatic Escalation in Customer Acquisition Costs. In 2014, HAMA sponsored a white paper study on customer acquisition costs. According to the study, the rapid growth in customer acquisition costs can be linked to an escalation in brand allocation and commission expenses. Based on the study, brand allocation and commission expenses exceeded revenue growth for several of the major brands.

Introduction of Programs to Promote Direct Bookings. Two major brands have recently announced special incentives for customers to book via direct channels to potentially lower customer acquisition/reservation expenses. In October 2014, Best Western offered a special 20 percent discount incentive to motivate customers to book direct. Also in late 2014, Marriott announced that, effective in mid-January of 2015, the company would be offering free Wi-Fi at full-service hotels for Marriott's 47 million rewards/loyalty members who book directly through Marriott channels. On a supplemental note, Marriott's announcement was not well received by the travel agent community.

Some brands have taken a different approach. Rather than offer incentives to book direct, they have withheld rewards/loyalty points for customers that book on-line via OTAs.

"Soft" Brands. In recent years, we have seen the emergence of several new soft brands including Starwood's Tribute Portfolio, Marriott's Autograph Collection, IHG's Alliance Program, Best Western's Premier Collection, the Ascend Hotel Collection by Choice Hotels International, and more recently the Curio Collection by Hilton and the introduction of a soft brand by National Geographic. Soft brands provide an opportunity for hotel owners to retain their "independent" status while also having an opportunity to participate in the sales and marketing programs of the brand companies, including access to their frequent guest/customer loyalty programs.

Alternative Accommodations. While the company faces legal challenges in various communities—New York and California, in particular—Airbnb has emerged as a very formidable competitor. In 2014, the market capitalization of Airbnb was greater than two of the largest leading hotel companies and by midyear 2015 Airbnb was one of the first companies to reach the one million "rooms/accommodations" milestone. And VBRO, while still a bit under the hospitality industry's radar screen, continues to expand its inventory.

Expanding Role of "Influencers" in Hotel Selection Decision-Making. A recent study conducted by TrustYou and Donna Quadri-Felitti, Director of and Associate Professor in the School of Hospitality Management at Penn State University, concluded that guest reviews have a significant impact on hotel conversion rates as well as the rates that travelers are willing to pay.

Franchise and Brand Affiliation Programs: Perspectives

Top- versus Bottom-Line Impact. In light of the dollars involved in purchasing, implementing, and maintaining a franchise or affiliation, the decision to be a franchise or chain-affiliated property is one of the most critical decisions affecting the value of a hotel investment. For many hotels, franchise and related fees represent the second largest expense category of a hotel. With the ongoing cost (including annual franchise royalty or chain affiliation and marketing fees) of a typical franchise or chain affiliation program representing 7 to 9 percent of revenue and given that the hotel industry in the U.S. in general is bringing approximately 25 cents of a revenue dollar to the net income line, franchise or chain affiliation and marketing fees (alone, i.e., not including reservation, IT, and other various fees) can potentially account for the equivalent of 28 to 36 percent of a hotel's bottom line.

The Landscape: Branded versus Independent Hotels. In the U.S. today, it is estimated that approximately 66 percent of all hotels are branded and 34 percent are independent. From an international perspective, however, a much higher percentage of hotels are independent. Following is a summary from STR of the percentage breakout of branded versus independent hotels in the U.S., South America, Europe, and Asia.

	Branded	Independent
United States	66%	34%
South America	40%	60%
Europe	39%	61%
Asia	45%	55%

Historical Perspective. For many hotels, affiliation can represent the difference between financial viability and failure. However, affiliation does not ensure successful investment performance. Moreover, certain types of hotels, depending upon their market positioning and segmentation, perform better as independents.

Historically, affiliation decisions have often been driven by financing considerations. Lenders and institutional investors stressed the importance of a property's access to a reservation system and the need for many hotels to tie into national marketing and promotional programs. Since these services were not readily available on a stand-alone basis, a franchise or affiliation was often routinely required as a prerequisite for financing. Today, however, there are numerous cost-effective options available for purchasing reservation system support, direct sales and trade show representation services, advertising and public relations expertise, and other services on a stand-alone basis.

Additionally, the Internet has had a dramatic impact on both the marketing of hotels and the manner in which hotel rooms are booked. In 2014, nearly 60 percent of all hotel bookings were via the Internet through brand websites, individual hotel websites, OTAs, etc. This is versus 40 percent in 2008 and less than 10 percent of bookings via the Internet in 2002. Industry sources say that a substantial number of offline hotel bookings are also influenced by the Internet.

Franchise and Brand Affiliation Program Alternatives. As stated earlier, there are nearly 500 different brand and affiliation alternatives globally, each offering various brand identification, marketing, promotional, and distribution opportunities. This is a 60 percent increase in brand and affiliation programs since the prior edition of this book was written in 2008.

Franchise or affiliation program alternatives include:

- Franchise agreement executed directly with hotel owner/operator
- Management contract with a branded operator
- Management contract with an unbranded third-party operator, coupled with a franchise agreement
- Strategic marketing alliance/affiliation
- Soft branding

It is important to keep in mind that different affiliation programs have the potential to generate different types and volumes of business. The cost of a franchise or affiliation can also vary substantially depending on the scope of services and benefits provided. According to the HVS 2014 franchise fee guide, *total costs* for various programs may range from approximately 3 to 15 percent of rooms revenue.

Evaluating Franchise and Brand Affiliation Programs

Although there are some rules of thumb to consider, essentially *there is no single best approach or established criteria for evaluating affiliation alternatives*. Affiliation options should be evaluated based on the strategic objectives and specific marketing needs of a given hotel (while mindful of the overall profitability of the business generated!). Following are some criteria to consider in evaluating affiliation alternatives:

- Analyzing the business mix
- Assessing the potential benefits of affiliation
- Determining the costs of affiliation
- Evaluating the costs versus the benefits of affiliation
- Evaluating potential conflicts of interest

Analyzing the Business Mix

Evaluating the merits of a franchise or affiliation should begin with an in-depth analysis of both the existing and potential market segmentation for the subject hotel. Hotels do not compete with all other hotels for all types of business. Rather, a particular hotel competes with certain hotels for specific types of business. The size, location, level and scope of services, ambience or character, physical characteristics, and condition of a hotel along with guest recognition and loyalty programs are all factors that will affect the market segments the hotel may potentially attract. Various market segments typically require very different marketing strategies, as well as different sales and promotional programs.

For example, an extended-stay hotel generally captures a very large percentage of its business from demand generators located within a 10–15 mile radius. At the opposite extreme, a destination resort will typically realize a small percentage of its business from within the local community. A typical extended-stay hotel will have property-level sales managers focusing on direct sales efforts targeting local companies. At a destination resort, the sales and marketing efforts are broader-based and require many sources of distribution, including a much larger property-level sales force and regional, national, and international sales representation. In addition to this more complex sales structure, destination resorts also require dedicated marketing, public relations, and advertising campaigns at the local, regional, national, and international levels.

Moreover, some types of business can be significantly more profitable for a hotel than others. Accordingly, given the specific attributes and positioning of a particular hotel, there may be a more desirable business mix and distribution channel strategy for optimizing the property's financial performance. This strategic business mix along with distribution channel considerations will determine the marketing and promotional programs and distribution systems needed for an individual hotel. An analysis of a property's business mix should begin with answers to fundamental questions, such as:

- What type of business is the hotel targeting?
- Why are guests staying at the hotel?
- Where is the business coming from?
- Who is booking the business?
- How is the business being booked?
- What is the cost to acquire business?

What Type of Business Is the Hotel Targeting? The market segmentation or business mix can vary significantly by hotel. Business travelers represent a large percentage of the bookings for airport, suburban, and downtown hotels. Group business and leisure travelers are typically the predominant market segments attracted to convention hotels and resorts. Additionally, certain hotels are better positioned than others to capture international or non-U.S. business. Non-U.S. visitors have represented a significant potential source of business for some hotels in key city markets.

The reality is that some franchise and affiliation companies are better at promoting certain types of business than others. Understanding what type of business a hotel is best positioned to capture and which mix or combination of business from the various segments is potentially the most profitable is essential to evaluating the ability for a franchise or affiliation to meet the specific marketing, sales and promotional and ultimately the return on investment objectives of a hotel owner.

Why Are Guests Staying at the Hotel? While seemingly simple, this is one of the most difficult questions to answer. Are current guests attracted to the property because of its location, service, reputation, cleanliness, price-value relationship, or other factors? Why are they staying at this particular hotel and not at a competitor's property? To what extent is the brand name or affiliation of the hotel or a hotel's loyalty or guest recognition program a factor in the guest's decision?

There have been many studies conducted over the years on hotel selection criteria—always with interesting results. Exhibit 1 summarizes key hotel selection criteria from three recent studies, one conducted by PhoCusWright, another by Market Metrix, and a third by MMGY Global. It is very interesting to note that several of the selection criteria identified in these surveys such as price, location, amenities, service, and so forth are property-specific versus brand or affiliation based. A property does not necessarily require an affiliation to deliver on these key decision criteria.

Where Is the Business Coming From? Various market segments have different origination patterns. Understanding where the business comes from and identifying the distribution channels that provide the best opportunities and the most cost-effective means of generating and/or capturing a particular type of clientele

Exhibit 1 Hotel Selection Criteria

Factors Influencing Last Hotel Decision*	Global Results: American, European and Asian Travelers**	Top Influencers for Selecting a Hotel/ Resort (Millennials)***
1. Price	1. Location	1. Value for the price
2. Location of hotel/property	2. Price	2. Location of the hotel/ resort
3. Previous experience	3. Past experience	3. Room rate
4. Hotel brand	4. Someone else's choice	4. Previous experience with the hotel/resort
5. Amenities	5. Recommendation by friend or colleague	5. Previous experience with the chain
6. Special offer/discount	6. Reputation hotel or brand	6. Reputation of the hotel/resort
7. Positive hotel reviews	7. Special promotion	7. Reputation of the chain
8. Pictures/photos	8. Convention or event location	8. Free Internet access from guest rooms
9. Class/star rating hotel	9. Loyalty program points/ rewards	9. Free breakfast included
10. Loyalty membership	10. Other	

* PhoCusWright Sept 2014 White Paper figure 13.
** Market Metrix Blog 2013 study.
*** MMGY Global Portrait of American Travelers.

are fundamental to evaluating the merits of various franchise and affiliation programs. In addition to evaluating where the business is coming from, as market dynamics shift, it is equally important to assess where the business could otherwise be coming from.

Who Is Booking the Business? It is also important to understand the source of business, and the cost of generating business by booking channel. How much business is being booked online, directly by on-site staff, and by the regional or national staff of the franchise or chain organization? Are customers booking directly through an individual hotel site, or via brand website, or by a third-party website and so forth. For direct sales programs, it is important to assess whether the business booked by regional or national staff could have been booked directly—and potentially more profitably—by on-site staff. If business is booked through other intermediaries, such as travel agents or wholesalers, it is important to understand if the travel agent and wholesaler relationships are property-based or franchise-based.

How Is the Business Booked? It is important to identify and understand how business is booked because the cost to the hotel of different reservation/booking alternatives varies significantly. The analysis should include a review of the room nights and revenue booked by market segment by channel, including online reservations with a further breakdown of business booked directly via the hotel's website, via the individual brand's website, via the parent company/brand website (for hotel companies with more than one brand) or through third-party websites (e.g., Expedia, Hotels.com, Travelocity). The analysis should also include a review of the volume and revenue of business booked through the franchisor's or chain's central reservation system (CRS) as well as business booked through global distribution systems (GDS). Finally, the analysis should include a review of how much business is being booked directly by the hotel including through the property's website and via sales staff or through an on-site toll-free telephone number.

What Is the Cost to Acquire the Business: Profit Contribution Analysis. All rooms revenue dollars are not created equal. The cost of generating business can vary dramatically by source of booking—from 1 to 2 percent for a repeat piece of business booked directly by the hotel to 35 percent or more for an OTA booking involving frequent guest points. Thus, the profit contribution can also vary dramatically, ranging from less than 65 percent to nearly 99 percent for a repeat booking. It is important to understand the cost of generating various types of business by distribution channel to potentially maximize a property's overall profitability.

Assessing the Potential Benefits of Affiliation

Most franchise or chain affiliations offer reservations, sales, marketing, an online presence and various promotional programs. Many also offer additional services, including training, purchasing programs, technical assistance (for design and development), operating policies and procedures, technology programs and support, revenue management systems, and inspection and quality assurance programs. Many hotel companies also offer various guest loyalty and recognition and/or frequent stay programs.

The decision to affiliate is a financial one and the cost versus benefits need to make economic sense. Once the hotel has developed an understanding of its book of business, the next step in evaluating the merits of a franchise or affiliation is to assess the potential of a particular brand or affiliation program/system to generate room nights from the various market segments (e.g., association, incentive, leisure, corporate, international, and so forth) the hotel is targeting to meet its strategic business-mix objectives. *Here one needs to evaluate the potential of a particular brand or affiliation to generate incremental business—business the hotel could not otherwise capture—or business the hotel might capture at a higher average rate or more cost effectively.* It is also important for the hotel to evaluate the cost-effectiveness of a particular franchise or affiliation program in comparison with other franchise and affiliation program options and also versus the option of remaining independent and purchasing various services on a stand-alone basis.

Exhibit 2 details various potential sources of business and distribution channels for generating different types of business. Promotional programs and distribution channels typically available through a franchise or chain affiliation are highlighted. There are many sources of business and potential distribution channel alternatives for generating different types of business. For example, potential sources of group business include the Internet, direct sales programs, advertising, directory listings, public relations, trade shows, word-of-mouth referrals, etc. Although most franchises and affiliations offer certain key programs to promote group business (e.g., via regional, national, and/or global sales programs, the Internet, advertising, trade show representation), there are also numerous options available to a hotel to generate group business on its own (e.g., the hotel's website and online presence, on-site sales staff, representation firms, trade show attendance, relationships with local CVBs).

Determining the Cost of Affiliation

The next step in evaluating a franchise or brand affiliation program is to determine the likely costs involved in acquiring, implementing, and maintaining the franchise or brand affiliation. According to the HVS 2014 U.S. hotel franchise fee guide, based on their review of 65 brand/affiliation programs, the median franchise cost (including royalty fees, marketing fees, reservation fees, honored/frequent guest program fees, and miscellaneous fees, including required PMS system–related expenses) in 2014 was 11.8 percent of rooms revenue.

Keep in mind, however, that the cost of one franchise or affiliation program versus another can vary substantially depending upon the perceived value of the brand and the scope of services and programs provided. Based on the HVS study, in 2014, franchise and related fees ranged from 3.3 to 14.7 percent of rooms revenue. For some hotels, the total costs can be substantially higher depending upon the various additional fees for services and/or costs involved to support franchise and brand standards, technology platforms, amenity upgrades, and the mix/source of hotel reservations.

Traditionally, the cost of a franchise or affiliation has been thought of as comprising four components: initial, royalty, marketing, and reservation fees. However, the expenses involved in implementing and maintaining the affiliation (e.g.,

Exhibit 2 Business Segmentation and Source of Business/Distribution Channel Alternatives

XYZ Hotel/Resort				
Group	**Social**	**Corporate**	**Wholesale**	**Discount Programs**
• Direct Sales (via on-site staff) Program • Internet -hotel website -brand website -CVB/Destination -on-line travel agent sites -Intermediaries websites • Representation Firms • Alliance Partners • Franchise/Affiliation Company -regional sales staff -national sales staff -global sales • Advertising (print/digital) -property-specific/generated -franchise/affiliation-based • Public Relations -property-specific/generated -chain/franchise program • Trade Shows • Directory Listings (print/ digital) • Direct Mail/electronic communication • Word of Mouth Referral • Repeat Business	• Internet -hotel website -brand/chain website -on-line travel agent sites -intermediaries/third party websites • 800# -franchise/affiliation -on site -independent res service • Travel Agent (retail) -direct sales -via 800# (franchise/ affiliation) -via 800# (on site) -via 800# (independent service) -incentive/reward programs • OTAs • Advertising: print/digital -property-specific/generated -franchise/affiliation-based • Public Relations -property-specific/generated -affiliation-based • Walk In/Drive By • Directory Listings • Direct Mail/electronic • Word of Mouth Referral • Repeat Business • Tourism Dev Councils Chamber of Commerce • 800# (franchise/ affiliation) -800# (on site) -800# (independent serv)	• Internet -hotel website -brand/chain website -on-line travel sites -third party websites • 800# -franchise/affiliation -on site -independent service • Travel Agent -800# booking (via franchise/ affiliation) -800# booking (via indepen-dent service) -direct booking • Direct Sales • Recognition/Reward Programs -franchise/affiliation -property specific • Directory Listing -individual property -franchise/affiliation • Direct Mail • Word of Mouth Referral • Repeat Business • Meeting Planner referrals • Affinity programs • Advertising -property-specific/generated -franchise/affiliation-based • Public Relations -property-specific/generated -franchise/affiliation-based	• Direct Sales to Intermediaries -wholesalers -tour operators -via on-site staff -independent representatives -franchise/affiliation • Trade Shows • Directory/Publication Listings • Advertising • -property-specific/ generated -franchise/affiliation-based • Direct Mail • Public Relations -property-specific/ generated -franchise/affiliation-based • Online Wholesalers-Global Travel	• Internet -hotel website -brand/chain website -On-line Travel Sites -third party websites • Direct solicitation offers -via on line communication -direct sales -via mail • Industry/Target Audience Publication Listings print/ digital • Advertising -property-specific/generated -franchise/affiliation-based • Public Relations -property-specific/generated -franchise/affiliation-based • Word of Mouth Referral • Repeat Business • Special offer of the Day Websites

signage, upgrading to comply with system standards, providing amenities), participating in honored or frequent guest programs, and meeting technology standards should also be accounted for in estimating the total costs. Following is a brief overview of the various fees and expenses.

Initial Fees. Most franchisors charge an initial fee as the price of admission to their systems. Initial fees may be established as a minimum dollar amount, as a variable payment based on the property's room count, or as a fixed payment coupled with a per-room assessment. Initial fees can vary from $5,000 to over $100,000 from one chain/brand to another. On occasion, some franchisors have considered waiving or reducing their initial fees to secure more business.

Royalty Fees. Royalty fees reflect the ongoing charge by a franchisor for the right to use the brand and to participate in the system. Most royalty fees are based on a percentage of revenue (rooms revenue and/or a combination of rooms and F&B revenue), and they range from approximately 1.5 to 7 percent. Royalty fees for a few chains/brands are based on a fixed fee per room basis.

Management Fees. Major branded hotel operators incorporate the right to use their brand name and to access their chain marketing and promotional services into their management contract agreements. The fee structure for this arrangement differs significantly from that of the traditional franchise relationship. The cost associated with the right to use the name and the chain's system is effectively built into the management fee structure.

Representation and Soft Brand Affiliation Fees. Some programs (including Preferred Hotels and Leading Hotels of the World, among others) provide an opportunity on a fee basis for a hotel to affiliate with a recognized name but also retain the character and identity of their individual properties. In recent years, we have seen the emergence of several new soft brands introduced by major hotel brand companies. Soft brands provide an opportunity for hotel owners to retain their independent status while having an opportunity to participate in the sales and marketing programs of the brand companies, including access to their frequent guest/customer loyalty programs.

Marketing and Promotional Fees. Many franchisors and chain organizations assess properties in their systems for marketing and promotion services. There are various alternative fee structures including fixed fees per room, fixed fees per property, and fees calculated on a percentage of rooms revenue basis (which is the predominant fee structure). Fees for these services currently range from 1 to 5 percent of revenues.

Sales Representation Fees. These fees support regional, national, and international direct sales programs. In some franchise systems, the costs associated with direct sales programs are covered by assessments for marketing and promotional services. In other systems, affiliated properties may be charged an additional amount, based on the actual volume of bookings generated by a franchisor's or chain's direct sales programs.

Reservations Fees. Although some franchise and affiliation programs provide for the cost of reservation services in their marketing fees, most chains charge a separate reservations fee. Methods of charging for reservation services include a fee per reservation, a fixed percentage of rooms revenue, and a fixed amount per room plus a fee per reservation booked. For many companies, the fees vary depending upon whether a reservation is made online, via the GDS and or via a call center. For example, for one major chain, the costs for an online reservation, a voice reservation, and a booking via the GDS are $3.50, $11.50, and $9.75, respectively.

Complying with System Standards. In evaluating the costs of affiliation, a hotel owner must consider the expense of complying with system-wide standards. Franchisors and chain organizations implement programs and impose standards that meet system needs and make economic sense at a national or international level. However, system-wide programs and standards may not always meet the needs or make economic sense for an individual property in the system. For example, F&B requirements (e.g., hours of operation, availability of room service, menu offerings) or levels of service (e.g., turn-down service, amenity offerings, etc.) may not be necessary given a particular hotel's positioning, customer profile, or competitive market. FF&E requirements, landscaping standards, and staffing guidelines are other areas where system standards may not always meet the needs or make economic sense for an individual property.

Technology. Brand-mandated investments in technology along with system support fees can vary greatly from one franchise/brand affiliation program to another and can represent a significant cost to an owner.

Guest Loyalty Programs. Many hotel chains have implemented guest recognition and/or honored or frequent guest programs to promote brand loyalty. Offerings range from basic recognition programs (in which a frequent guest receives upgraded accommodations, a welcome gift, or other premium) to complex reward programs that permit customers to earn points and mileage redeemable for hotel room nights, airline travel, car rentals, and myriad other products and services.

The cost of customer loyalty programs can vary from less than 2 percent to as much as 6 percent of loyalty customer–related revenue. Therefore, assess the potential costs versus benefits of the guest recognition and reward programs offered by different franchise or chain organizations. Note also that some hotels within a franchise system or brand affiliation program may experience a disproportionate amount of redemption of such rewards, which may potentially increase associated costs.

Termination Fees and Liquidated Damages. The fees payable on termination of a contract with a brand can vary substantially. From an owner's perspective, an exit strategy from a hotel asset is as important as the acquisition decision, so a clearly defined and reasonable termination provision is a critical component of a franchise or affiliation agreement.

Evaluating the Costs versus the Benefits of Affiliation

It is difficult to conduct a cost-benefit analysis for a franchise or affiliation because there is no single approach or standard set of evaluation criteria. Not only is it challenging to evaluate the merits of an individual franchise or affiliation, it is also difficult to evaluate the merits and performance of one franchise or affiliation program over another.

Traditionally, metrics for evaluating a franchisor's or chain affiliation's performance have included the volume or percentage of business/revenue generated by the brand online, through traditional reservations systems, national/global sales programs, and/or by loyalty program customers.

Various franchisors and chain organizations indicate that their reservation systems are the source of anywhere from 15 to more than 40 percent of a property's business. However, it is difficult to make performance comparisons between affiliation alternatives because franchisors and chain organizations have different ways of accounting for reservation activity.

Also, it is often difficult to determine the total cost of generating reservations. For example, the total cost might include expenditures associated with frequent or honored guest programs, print and/or online or other digital marketing and promotional costs, in addition to the costs involved in booking.

In some instances, it is not clear whether all reservations/ bookings attributed to the brand or chain represent incremental business. For example, group business represents a major market segment for many hotels. Although a group meeting may be booked directly by the on-site hotel sales staff, reservations for meeting attendees are frequently included in brand reservation-system counts, especially in situations where attendees are responsible for making their own reservations (the typical case for association group business). Many hotels are utilizing Passkey, an online booking system that can be customized on a brand or hotel basis to allow for individual attendees (at group meetings) to make their reservations on line. It is not clear, however, if these reservations are included in brand business volume/booking performance numbers.

In light of the difficulties inherent in evaluating a franchisor's or chain's reservations and revenue performance, it is important to identify alternative ways of evaluating the costs versus the benefits of the available franchises and affiliations. Some alternative approaches include:

- Assessing the bottom-line versus the top-line impact of franchise or affiliation fees
- Estimating the net effective cost of business generated by a franchise or affiliation
- Estimating a breakeven point that suggests the volume of business needed to support the cost of a specific franchise or affiliation

Assessing Bottom-Line Versus Top-Line Impact. The cost of a franchise or affiliation has traditionally been measured in terms of its top-line impact expressed as a percentage of revenue. While this ratio is a reasonable approach for comparing the nominal costs of one franchise or affiliation program to another, it does not take into account the fact that the profitability of different types of hotels can vary significantly. The impact of franchise or affiliation fees can change dramatically when evaluated from a bottom-line perspective.

According to STR, in 2014 hotels on average generated approximately 25 cents in profit or net income (or EBITDA equivalent) for every revenue dollar. This ratio, however, varies significantly by property, depending upon the economics of running a particular hotel. The potential EBITDA of a hotel can vary substantially, depending upon the revenue per available room (RevPAR) generated, the mix of total revenues (e.g., rooms revenue versus F&B revenue), margin performance, and the degree of operating leverage, or the ratio of fixed to variable costs. At the upper end of performance, some hotels are yielding over 40 cents on the average revenue dollar at the net income or EBITDA line. Other hotels struggle to make a profit.

Exhibit 3 presents a comparative matrix highlighting the relationship between fees as a percentage of top-line revenue and the impact on bottom-line profits. For purposes of example, we have not adjusted the numbers to account for the mix of rooms versus other sources of revenue. The leftmost column in the matrix lists levels of franchise or affiliation fees, ranging from 3 to 14 percent of revenue. The topmost row lists varying levels of net income (or EBITDA) expressed as a percentage of revenue. The matrix shows the relationships between various franchise or affiliation fees versus alternative net income (or EBITDA) performance levels. For purposes of illustration, 7 percent of revenue is highlighted as a representative cost for a franchise or affiliation. In this case, the ratio of franchise or affiliation fees to bottom-line performance could potentially range from 15.6 percent for a hotel with a 45 percent net income ratio to 70 percent for a hotel with a 10 percent net income ratio.

Exhibit 3 Franchise/Affiliation Fees: Bottom-Line Versus Top-Line Impact

	EBITDA or Net Operating Income Percentage							
	10.0%	**15.0%**	**20.0%**	**25.0%**	**30.0%**	**35.0%**	**40.0%**	**45.0%**
3.0%	30.0%	20.0%	15.0%	12.0%	10.0%	8.6%	7.5%	6.7%
4.0%	40.0%	26.7%	20.0%	16.0%	13.3%	11.4%	10.0%	8.9%
5.0%	50.0%	33.3%	25.0%	20.0%	16.7%	14.3%	12.5%	11.1%
6.0%	60.0%	40.0%	30.0%	24.0%	20.0%	17.1%	15.0%	13.3%
7.0%	70.0%	46.7%	35.0%	28.0%	23.3%	20.0%	17.5%	15.6%
8.0%	80.0%	53.3%	40.0%	32.0%	26.7%	22.9%	20.0%	17.8%
9.0%	90.0%	60.0%	45.0%	36.0%	30.0%	25.7%	22.5%	20.0%
10.0%	100.0%	66.7%	50.0%	40.0%	33.3%	28.5%	25.0%	22.2%
11.0%		73.3%	55.0%	44.0%	36.7%	31.4%	27.5%	24.4%
12.0%		80.0%	60.0%	48.0%	40.0%	34.3%	30.0%	26.7%
13.0%		86.7%	65.0%	52.0%	43.3%	37.1%	32.5%	28.9%
14.0%		93.3%	70.0%	56.0%	46.7%	40.0%	35.0%	31.1%

Estimating the Net Effective Cost. Another method of evaluating the costs versus the benefits of a franchise or affiliation program is to determine the net effective cost of business generated by the franchise or chain organization. The net effective cost can be defined as the ratio of franchise fees to the revenue contribution of the brand.

Exhibit 4 highlights the net effective cost by showing the ratios of franchise or affiliation fees, expressed as a percentage of revenue, to the percentages of business generated by the franchise or chain affiliation. For purposes of illustration, 7 percent of revenue is again highlighted as a representative cost for a franchise or affiliation and a range of from 15 to 45 percent has been used for the revenue contribution of a brand. In this case, the net effective cost of the business generated by a brand or affiliation would range from 15.5 percent when 45 percent of the hotel's revenue is attributable to a brand to 46.7 percent if only 15 percent of the hotel's business is attributable to the brand or affiliation.

Estimating a Breakeven Point. Another useful tool for evaluating the financial contribution of a franchise or affiliation program is to estimate the incremental volume of business needed to break even, or just cover the cost of a franchise or affiliation. To determine the additional volume of business necessary, the estimated cost of the franchise or affiliation should be divided by the departmental profit per room sold. For example, assume that the annual cost of a franchise or affiliation would be $200,000 for a hotel of 120 rooms. And if, for example, the

Exhibit 4 Net Effective Cost of Business Generated by a Franchise or Affiliation

	15.0%	20.0%	25.0%	30.0%	35.0%	40.0%	45.0%
3.0%	20.0%	15.0%	12.0%	10.0%	8.6%	7.5%	6.6%
4.0%	26.6%	20.0%	16.0%	13.3%	11.4%	10.0%	8.8%
5.0%	33.3%	25.0%	20.0%	16.7%	14.3%	12.5%	11.1%
6.0%	40.0%	30.0%	24.0%	20.0%	17.1%	15.0%	13.3%
7.0%	46.7%	35.0%	28.0%	23.3%	20.0%	17.5%	15.5%
8.0%	53.3%	40.0%	32.0%	26.7%	22.9%	20.0%	17.8%
9.0%	60.0%	45.0%	36.0%	30.0%	25.7%	22.5%	20.0%
10.0%	66.7%	50.0%	40.0%	33.3%	28.5%	25.0%	22.2%
11.0%	73.3%	55.0%	44.0%	36.6%	31.4%	27.5%	24.4%
12.0%	80.0%	60.0%	48.0%	40.0%	34.2%	30.0%	26.6%
13.0%	86.7%	65.0%	52.0%	43.3%	37.0%	32.5%	28.8%
14.0%	93.3%	70.0%	56.0%	46.6%	40.0%	35.0%	31.1%

average daily rate for the hotel is $80 and the departmental profit from rooms is 75 percent, it would require over 3,300 additional room nights ($200,000/$60 contribution margin per room sold) specifically attributable to the franchise or affiliation to reach the breakeven point. This equates to an additional 7.5 occupancy points required to cover the costs of the franchise or affiliation (365 × 120 rooms = 43,800 annual available room nights; 3,300/43,800 = 7.5 percent incremental occupancy).

Identifying and Evaluating Potential Conflicts of Interest

In making the decision to become a franchisee or chain-affiliated property, the investor must consider potential conflicts of interest between the franchisee or licensee and a franchisor or chain. Conflicts might arise between competing properties bearing the same brand or among properties of different brands within systems with multiple brands.

The interests of the brand and its affiliates are not always aligned. The brand's room count, revenue, and profit growth objectives are not necessarily always in harmony with the best interests of its franchisees. AAHOA published its inaugural Fair Franchising Report in mid-2008. The report examined the business practices of several major chains relative to AAHOA's 12 points of fair franchising. AAHOA continues to monitor performance in key areas on an ongoing basis. Exit strategies, liquidated damages, and impact issues continue to represent areas of contention between franchisors and franchisees.

Brands will inevitably seek growth. Therefore, it is important that a hotel owner understand a franchise or chain system's growth strategy and how anticipated system growth might affect the future performance of their investment. It is also beneficial to evaluate past practices to determine the likelihood of a licensor's reasonably resolving such conflicts, should they emerge.

Potential Conflicts of Interest within a Brand. Conflicts within a specific brand include those that might arise from radius-clause or impact issues, regional, national, and global sales, marketing and promotional programs, and quality control and image concerns.

Radius-cause or impact issues. Radius-clause and impact conflicts typically arise when there is overlap in competitive market(s) or in potential customers for which two or more hotels with the same brand or affiliation compete. When evaluating the potential for conflicts in this area, it is important to define clearly the market segments the subject hotel competes for, the market areas its customer base is drawn from, and the competitor properties that vie with the subject hotel for specific types of business.

Regional, national, and global sales programs. While the primary objective of regional, national, and global sales programs is to generate as much business as possible for properties within the system, the degree to which an individual hotel might actually benefit from these programs can vary dramatically. Regional, national, and global sales programs must be evaluated in relation to the specific needs and objectives of a hotel. The hotel investor should also ensure that there are no conflicts of interest in the way the programs are administered. Factors to consider include how leads are generated, how bookings are handled (for example, how does the sales staff determine the business allocated to properties within the system?), what types of information are exchanged with other properties, and how the sales staff is compensated.

System-wide marketing and promotional programs. Although system-wide marketing and promotional programs can be expected to enhance the overall performance of a franchise or chain system, it is difficult for a brand to develop strategies and programs to meet the specific needs of *all* properties within the system. System-wide programs tend to address the broad goals and objectives of the brand, such as increasing weekend occupancy or promoting family business. The benefits of these programs for an individual hotel in the system may vary substantially.

Digital marketing: online presence. Many hotel companies spend a lot to support their brand websites. Some, however, have implemented restrictions on the ability of hotels within their systems to develop their own websites to promote their individual hotels. While brand websites are important for developing brand awareness and capturing certain types of business, individual hotel websites represent a potential untapped source of business opportunities for many hotels.

Quality control and image concerns. A guest's favorable experience at one hotel can positively influence that customer's perception of other hotels within the brand. Conversely, a guest's unsatisfactory experience at another hotel within the system can negatively influence that individual's overall perception of the brand and other properties in the system. For some older brands, the quality of product can vary dramatically from one hotel to another; maintaining product consistency can represent a huge challenge. When selecting a franchise or affiliation, it is important to review the system's quality assurance and control requirements, as well as its compliance policies and procedures to ensure consistency in the quality and standards across the properties within the system.

Potential Conflicts of Interest among Brands. When chains have more than one brand, the franchisee/licensee should ensure that there are no conflicts in the way that the various brands are marketed and promoted. Potential problem areas include positioning conflicts among brands in the marketplace, multi-brand sales and promotional programs, and multi-brand reservation systems.

Positioning conflicts. As the number of brands has proliferated, the demarcation lines separating brands have blurred for many hotel product types. As a result, it is often difficult for a franchisor or chain organization to position one brand without overlapping with its other brands. Moreover, on the consumer side, the reality is that frequently there is overlap in the customer base of different brands in a multi-brand chain. To minimize the potential conflict in this area, it is important for the prospective franchisee/licensee to identify early in the decision process the likely overlap in customer bases among the franchisor's various brands and to try to quantify the impact on the franchisee's hotel.

Multi-brand sales and promotion programs. The primary objective of multi-brand sales and promotion programs is to maximize overall revenues for all properties within the chain. However, the extent to which such programs affect different brands in a company's array of flags and specific hotels in the system can vary greatly. These programs should be closely monitored and evaluated to ensure that they contribute to—rather than undermine—the financial performance of a hotel.

Multi-brand joint reservation systems. For companies with more than one brand, it is important to understand the search methodology for displaying hotels online. Reservation agents can also affect bookings for one brand versus another, as well as for one hotel within a brand versus another. In instances where a franchisor's or chain's reservations center sells more than one product or hotel brand, it is important to understand and evaluate how the different brands are promoted and sold.

Proprietary Systems: Ownership of Information. Many brands have developed proprietary systems, some of which (typically including property management systems, reservations systems, etc.) franchisees are required to use, while others (e.g., revenue management systems) are offered à la carte. It is important that franchisees and owners of hotels managed by brands or participating in various affiliation programs give thought at the front end to addressing the critical issues of the "ownership" of customer and operational data and the rights (of a franchisor or affiliation or brand management company) to use this information.

Assessing the Independent Alternative

The decision to align a property with a particular franchise or affiliation is often arrived at by evaluating the merits of one system or program versus another. However, the decision-making process should also include an evaluation of the merits of various franchise and affiliation programs in comparison with operating as an independent hotel.

What Types of Hotels Potentially Perform Better as Independents

An interesting way to think of hotel products is to place them on a continuum. At one end are hotels with little opportunity to differentiate themselves from similar types of properties. At the other end are those hotels and resorts that are considered to be one-of-a-kind properties. Affiliation alternatives and the merits of affiliation differ substantially, depending upon where a hotel is situated on this continuum.

Certain limited-service and highway properties have few ways of differentiating themselves from their competitors. For these hotels, a franchise or brand affiliation often is critical to financial success. For hotels at the other end of the continuum—e.g., specialty properties with unique locations, high-end resorts, four- and five-star or -diamond properties—a franchise or affiliation may not be necessary. For these hotels, a franchise or brand affiliation could potentially have an adverse impact and undermine their ability to attract certain market segments and clientele, possibly including millennials, high-end social and corporate business travelers, certain types of group business, incentive meeting business, etc. Often, these types of guests prefer to stay at a unique property rather than at a franchise or chain-affiliated hotel or resort. The purpose/occasion of travel can also potentially affect a customer's hotel selection—for example, Ms. Smith may stay at a brand-affiliated hotel while on business and/or to attend a conference, yet prefer to stay at an independent hotel when traveling for leisure.

As mentioned earlier, the location of a hotel is an important consideration. Hotels in major cities or in unique locations, where the market area or location is the destination, can also potentially perform better as independent versus branded hotels.

Marketing, Promotion, and Reservations Systems Support

Several years ago, there were limited opportunities for independent hotels to tie into a global reservations system or into national or global marketing, sales, and promotional programs. Programs that were available tended to be expensive when sold on a stand-alone basis, making it more cost-effective to purchase sales, marketing, and reservation support services through a franchise or chain affiliation.

Today, however, many firms specialize in providing services in these areas. Many options are available for purchasing reservation system support, direct sales and trade show representation services, digital marketing, advertising and public relations expertise, etc. Depending upon the needs of an individual hotel, the cost of purchasing such services on a stand-alone basis can be significantly less than the cost associated with a franchise or chain affiliation.

Digital Marketing Channels Level the Playing Field

The Internet and digital marketing opportunities have had a dramatic impact on the marketing and promotion of hotels and customer booking patterns. One can argue that they have substantially leveled the playing field for independent hotels.

For example, although brand websites can offer potential advantages over hotel-specific websites—in particular given their greater potential customer reach—there are many other avenues to locate hotels online other than via Brand.com websites. For group business, convention and visitor bureau websites are often an important source for information in planning meetings. Vacationers frequently visit destination websites to hone in on accommodation alternatives. Social media also represents an excellent opportunity for independent hotels to engage directly with customers.

PhoCusWright recently published a white paper entitled "Online Travel Agencies: More than a Distribution Channel." According to PhoCusWright, OTAs are playing a pivotal and expanding role in the travel landscape. They currently represent 38 percent of the global online market and 13 percent of the total market. PhoCusWright further notes that while customers over 55 typically chose to book a hotel via a supplier website when booking online, millennials clearly prefer booking via an OTA website. The expanding global reach of OTAs along with millennial booking preferences represent opportunities for certain independent hotels.

Opportunity to Customize Positioning, Promotional and Pricing Strategies

It is difficult for chains to develop and implement positioning, pricing, and promotional strategies and programs that meet the specific needs of all properties within their systems. The absence of a brand can afford an owner greater flexibility in positioning a specific hotel against its competition. As an independent hotel, the property has the opportunity to explore its strengths and special points of differentiation from the competition, especially in terms of location, size, character, ambience, and level of service.

Independent positioning also allows for greater flexibility in establishing rates and more control over rate integrity. As a member of a chain, a hotel must use a pricing strategy consistent with the positioning and perception of the chain. Rate integrity, inventory control and allocations to intermediaries, and transparent versus opaque pricing have emerged as major issues and challenges, particularly in light of the dramatic increase in online bookings.

Financial Performance: A Comparative Review of Chain-Affiliated versus Independent Hotels

In reviewing STR hotel industry performance numbers for 2013 (published in *2014 HOST Almanac Report*), it is interesting to note based on the sample properties included in the summary of U.S. hotels that independent hotels outperformed chain-affiliated hotels. As noted in Exhibit 5, chain-affiliated hotels on average had substantially higher occupancies, but independent hotels commanded a significant rate premium; overall, the RevPAR for independent hotels was 15.8 percent higher in 2013. While expenses for independent hotels were substantially higher than for chain-affiliated hotels (rooms expenses in particular), the overall bottom-line performance for independent hotels was $1,165 (more than 7 percent) higher—$17,010 per available room for independent hotels versus $15,845 for chain-affiliated hotels.

These numbers reflect averages. Individual hotel performance can vary dramatically from industry averages.

Exhibit 5 Financial Comparison of Chain-Affiliated and Independent Hotels

	Chain-Affiliated	Independent	Variance Indep. vs. Chain-Affiliated	% Variance
Occupancy	72.6%	66.5%	(6.1% pts)	(9%)
ADR	$146.23	$184.85	$38.62	26.4%
RevPAR	$38,749	$44,863	$6,114	15.8%
Rooms Expense	26%	29.9%	3.9% pts	15% higher
NOI % of TR	28.5%	23.2%	(5.3% pts)	(18.6%)
NOI Dollars PAR	$15,845	$17,010	$1,165	7.35%

Source: STR Analytics *2014 HOST Almanac Report*.

A Forward Look

Looking to the future, following are thoughts to share regarding some important issues to keep an eye on:

- Greater flexibility in franchise and affiliation contracts
- Standardization of brand performance criteria
- Expanded and evolving role of digital marketing programs
- Escalating cost of customer acquisition: profit contribution analysis
- Incentives to book via less expensive distribution channels
- Need for better analytics
- Continued growth of soft brands
- Disruptors?
- National Labor Relations Board joint employer decision (McDonald's Case)
- Exit strategy and transition planning
- Enhancing brand value from the owner/investor perspective

Greater Flexibility in Franchise and Affiliation Contracts. Many contracts in effect today are geared to protecting a franchisor's interests and objectives. These contracts often provide little opportunity for a franchisee or affiliation member to address and resolve problems or conflicts should they arise. Going forward, we might expect that contracts will provide for stricter franchisor default covenants and will address some of the conflicts of interest (e.g., adverse impact, multi-brand conflicts) that exist, as well as providing franchisees with more flexible termination provisions. In brief, if a hotel is not performing at a level that makes economic sense and/or a conflict of interest should arise that cannot be resolved, it is in the best interest of both parties to reasonably "wind down" the relationship.

Standardization of Brand Performance Criteria. Given the inherent challenges in evaluating brand performance, ideally in the future we will see more transparent, better standardized benchmarks for evaluating brand performance.

Many brands continue to cite reservation and/or revenue contribution/delivery as primary indicators of performance—despite the shortcomings of these approaches. These indicators do not account for the cost of acquiring business or the different approaches hotel brands use to account for reservation delivery.

The number and percentage of customers participating in guest loyalty programs is also cited as an indicator of brand performance. Customers participating in guest loyalty programs account for a very large percentage—from 40–60 percent—of business for several of the leading hotel brands.

The cost from an owner's perspective of participating in guest loyalty programs and their contribution to profit varies by brand; thus, these numbers do not necessarily provide a meaningful way to compare the performance of different brands.

Expanding and Evolving Role of Digital Marketing Programs. As stated earlier, Internet bookings have increased dramatically during the past few years. There has clearly been a migration to mobile. In 2014, an estimated 26 million travelers made a purchase via a mobile device. Mobile is expected to account for 25 percent of online bookings in the U.S. in 2015 and 20 percent of online bookings in Europe. It has been predicted that, by 2017, 50 percent of online bookings in the U.S. will be made via mobile devices. It is important to understand how the customer is using mobile. For some users, mobile is used only to search; then they call the hotel directly to book. And for customers using last-minute booking sites like hoteltonight.com, mobile is the new walk-in.

It is not clear how these trends will ultimately play out for branded and affiliated versus independent hotels, but it is something to keep an eye on.

Escalating Cost of Customer Acquisition: Profit Contribution Analysis. In 2014, a white paper was prepared for HAMA. For the first time, the issue of the dramatic escalation in the cost of customer acquisition received industry-wide attention. We can anticipate that this will be an area of keen focus going forward.

Many hotel companies have implemented sophisticated revenue management systems. Most of these programs, however, focus on revenue only and do not take into account the cost of generating the business. As we've already pointed out, the cost of generating business can vary dramatically. According to The Travers Group, we can anticipate that hotels will increasingly focus on the profit contribution of various types of business by distribution channel versus focusing on revenue only.

Incentives to Book via Less Expensive Distribution Channels. With the dramatic escalation in the cost of customer acquisition, hotel companies are motivated to encourage customers to book through lower cost distribution channels. Two major hotel companies have recently introduced programs to encourage customers to book via direct channels because direct channels typically represent the most cost-effective distribution program. Direct booking program incentives, however, are not without controversy.

In a recent *HotelNewsNow* article, it was suggested that 2015 may well have presented the perfect opportunity for hoteliers to return to the era of rate disparity or at least selective rate disparity as part of an overall channel conversion strategy to drive more direct bookings.

While we can anticipate that more hotel companies will explore and implement programs to encourage bookings via direct channels, they will need to be careful to not alienate industry travel partners.

Need for Better Analytics. Historically, it has been challenging to isolate and account for the total costs of customer acquisition and determine the profit contribution by market segment by distribution channel. As noted by Cindy Estis Green of Kalibri Labs, "You can only manage what you measure. The industry knows how to manage operating and labor costs and now it's time to put a maniacal focus on [measuring and managing] acquisition costs." Kalibri Labs has recently introduced an analytics platform to assist hotels with this analysis.

In mid-2014, the AH&LA introduced a new edition of the *Uniform System of Accounts for the Lodging Industry (USALI)* with changes that became effective as of January 1, 2015. It is important for readers to become familiar with the new Eleventh Revised Edition because the revisions affect the definitions of revenue, net income, the accounting for sales and marketing–related technology expenses, and other account categories.

Continued Growth in Soft Brands. Several soft brands have emerged in recent years. They are attractive from an owner's perspective for they provide an opportunity for a hotel to retain its independent status while also having an opportunity to participate in the sales and marketing programs of the brand companies, including access to their frequent guest/customer loyalty programs. From a franchise and brand company perspective, "creating soft brands has been a way for hotel companies to grow without having to compromise the standards of their traditional brands and at the same time generate additional revenue" according to Bjorn Hanson, with NYU's Tisch Center for Hospitality & Tourism. This trend is certainly one to keep an eye on.

Disruptors? How Will these Issues and Trends Play Out?

- *New distribution platform alternatives for independent hotels.* AccorHotels.com is available to independent hotels. According to Chairman Sebastien Bazin, Accor is transforming its distribution platform into an open marketplace and placing its powerful digital tools at the service of independent hoteliers. This will represent a potential excellent affiliation opportunity for some independent hotels.
- *Inflexibility of legacy systems.* Historically, legacy systems have provided a competitive advantage for some major brands. However, according to Jeffrey Katz, Managing Partner of KA Holdings and founding chairman of Orbitz, "The inflexibility of legacy systems is a growing constraint." And Tim Harvey, CEO of Core Ideas LLC, suggests that "information will be the biggest disruptive factor in our industry."
- *Alternative accommodations.* Airbnb's rooms/accommodation count reached the 1 million milestone in 2015. Although still a bit under the radar screen, HomeAway/VBRO inventory is also expanding. According to *TravelWeekly*, travel agents are tapping into private home rentals and industry analyst Henry Harteveldt forecasts that "for some, staying in a hotel will become an unusual experience, and staying in a home will be the norm." Some issues to think about include whether these customers represent incremental demand? Or are these customers that would otherwise be staying at a hotel? And if so, would they normally be staying at a franchise or an independent hotel?
- *Expanded role of TripAdvisor*. TripAdvisor recently introduced instant booking functionality. While some brands are participating on a limited basis, the program is specifically targeted to independents.
- *Google as OTA.* What will be the impact of Google's potentially becoming the world's biggest OTA? How will this play out for independent versus branded and affiliated hotels?

- *Where is the cost of customer acquisition headed?* According to Kalibri Labs, the cost of customer acquisition is 5–10 percent for the airlines, 4–6 percent for car rental companies, and 15–25 percent for the hotel industry. According to Cindy Estis Green, "Legacy sales and marketing infrastructure [in the hotel industry] is due for a fresh evaluation."
- *Amazon entering the hotel space.* Donna Quadri-Felitti, with the School of Hospitality Management at Penn State University, noted that "Amazon has proven itself to be a customer-centric culture that studies, tests, and adapts to consumer preferences, needs, and expectations. Their entry into online hotel sales should prove to teach legacy brands in distribution another approach to the travel landscape."

National Labor Relations Board Joint Employer Decision. It will be important to closely monitor the next steps in the NLRB's McDonald's ruling. The initial decision ruled against McDonald's and could pose a major threat to the traditional franchise model in the hotel industry by potentially including the parent company as a joint employer of franchisees, thus making the franchisor liable for the acts of its franchisees.

Exit Strategy and Transition Planning. It is important to address exit strategy and transition issues up front as part of the negotiation process. With the expiration of a contract and/or if for whatever reason a particular franchise or affiliation is terminated prior to expiration, it can be difficult to wind down the relationship without major disruption to the hotel's operations and financial performance.

Some important issues to think about at the front end when evaluating various franchise and affiliation programs and negotiating contract terms—in particular when the franchisor is also the manager—are:

- the ownership of the "customer" and customer data.
- ownership access and control of financial and other important books and records, etc.
- a transition plan for the use of the brand logo and how to wind down/replace various brand legacy and proprietary systems.

Enhancing Brand Value from the Owner/Investor Perspective. Some of the major brands have tended to focus on enhancing value from a shareholder versus the owner/investor perspective. The cost of customer acquisition has escalated dramatically due in large part to increases in brand allocations and commissions expenses. Major brands are keenly focused on increasing participation in brand loyalty programs—but it is important to ensure that the economics make sense from the owner's perspective. In the future, we anticipate that some brands will need to tweak/rethink the value proposition from the owner/investor perspective and focus more on profitability than revenue and potentially reducing capital reinvestment exposure through improved capital asset preservation programs and insuring that the return on investment of PIPs makes financial sense from the owner/investor perspective.

4

Benchmarking and Financial Analysis

By Michelle Russo and Scott Legel

***Michelle Russo,** CHAM, MAI, CHA, is Founder and CEO of Hotel Asset Value Enhancement, LLC (hotelAVE), one of the nation's largest independent hotel real estate advisory firms, specializing in asset management and hotel real estate consulting for hospitality owners. Her firm has over 135 assets and $8 billion of hotel assets under management and advises on an additional $4 billion of hotel real estate annually for clients, including many of the world's largest banks and investment funds. Ms. Russo previously managed a $500 million portfolio for John Hancock Mutual Life Insurance, where she improved the profitability and efficiently repositioned the portfolio to achieve 20 percent cash-on-cash returns.*

Prior to her asset management experience, Ms. Russo spent 10 years conducting real estate appraisals and feasibility studies for more than 500 hotels throughout the United States. She garnered capital markets experience while on Wall Street as a stock analyst. Ms. Russo has appeared as an industry expert on CNN and CNBC, and authored the widely followed Top 15 Urban Market Report while at Deutsche Bank. She has also published in The Real Estate Finance Journal *and* Real Estate Review. *She is a guest speaker at numerous industry conferences such as NYU, ALIS, ULI, Boston University, Distressed Hotel Summit, and Hunter Hotel Conference and was a five-year board member and two-term President of the Hospitality Asset Managers Association. Ms. Russo is also a member of ULI's Hotel Council, Marriott's Distribution Strategy Advisory Committee, the AHLA's Financial Management Committee, Morgans Hotel Group's Board of Directors, and the Pillsbury Institute for Hospitality Entrepreneurship Advisory Board at Cornell University. Ms. Russo is a graduate of Cornell University's School of Hotel Administration and is a frequent guest lecturer as well as a former professor of the school's hospitality asset management course.*

***Scott Legel,** CHA, is currently a Senior Director of asset management at hotelAVE. He is actively involved in the asset management of multiple assets and is responsible for monitoring portfolio performance to budget and owner objectives while identifying value enhancement opportunities through market research. His other responsibilities include operational reviews, management contract consulting, pro-forma underwritings, industry research, capital oversight, and strategic planning.*

Before joining hotelAVE, Mr. Legel was an operations task force manager for Marriott International. He is a graduate of Cornell University's School of Hotel Administration. He also maintains the Certified Hotel Administrator (CHA) designation through the Educational Institute of the AH&LA.

ONE OF THE PRIMARY GOALS of an asset manager is to enhance an asset's market value, which, in the hospitality industry, is typically a function of a property's profitability. In practice, this involves evaluating a property's performance and working with the hotel's management staff, regional representatives, and other involved parties to develop strategies for revenue enhancement and expense reduction consistent with the quality and market-orientation of the asset. These actions include:

- Identifying a property's competitive strengths and weaknesses.
- Developing and implementing strategies for increasing market penetration.
- Reviewing expense control measures and increasing profitability.
- Implementing short- and long-term strategic capital plans.
- Analyzing the management contracts and other agreements to identify further a scope for owner benefit.

Determining achievable revenue and expense targets can prove a difficult task, mostly owing to the extensive number of factors that affect a hotel's ability to generate revenue and manage expenses. When faced with the challenge of enhancing a property's overall performance, how does an asset manager determine whether the hotel is properly positioned in the marketplace? How can an asset manager be confident that revenue and expense levels are reasonable? And what profitability ratios indicate an efficient operation versus one that needs further improvement?

Fortunately, there are a number of data sources available to the lodging industry, with reports that include recurring datasets of weekly, monthly, and annual schedules that are available to asset managers. There are a myriad of industry benchmarks designed to assist asset managers in understanding the relative or potential performance of a hotel asset, and the availability of these data can be ascertained through third-party market research reports. These reports include a variety of STR, PKF Benchmarker, HotStats, and TravelClick Hotelligence reports (such as Demand360, Agency360, etc.). Other third-party organizations, such as Cvent and Expedia, offer operators and owners benchmarking type reports to assist in their use with that company. Historically, consultants and asset managers have had to rely primarily on interviews, industry contacts, and data estimation.

While benchmarking is commonly referred to as assessing an existing property's performance and enhancing its profitability, the benchmarking process can also be applied to a number of aspects of the asset management process. This chapter's focus is primarily on revenue and expense benchmarking, but comparable analyses are applicable across all things measurable. For hotel purposes, these include underwriting a proposed hotel, valuation (comparative or "comp" sales), management contract negotiations, e-commerce/web analytic data, guest satisfaction, real estate tax assessment comparisons, and physical condition assessments.

The first part of this chapter outlines useful revenue and expense benchmarking tools available to asset managers in the hospitality industry today. These tools can provide the basis from which an asset manager can analyze a hotel's performance. Another section covers alternative opportunities to apply benchmarking as part of the asset management process. Chapter Appendix 1 lists specific questions an asset manager would ask property management in an effort to identify opportunities for increasing a given property's profitability and value.

Framework for Analysis of Hotel Performance

The goal of every owner is to increase the value of an asset. An asset manager contributes to this goal by completing two fundamental exercises:

- Determining a hotel's proper market position, based on external, market-based factors
- Increasing the hotel's net income, which involves identifying areas for additional revenue, and areas for expense control improvement based on internal, property-specific determinants

These steps can be initiated using two analysis techniques known individually as *comparative analysis* and *variance analysis*. These techniques are defined in Exhibit 1.

A hotel's performance may be benchmarked against other properties, either in a region or on an industry-wide basis. In general, a hotel's revenue performance is benchmarked against other hotels in its immediate competitive set or within the hotel's region. On the expense side, the hotel can be benchmarked against the overall industry and within a given service tier; area hotels with similar size, segmentation, class, etc., should also be included. Exhibit 2 outlines these concepts in greater detail.

There are exceptions to this rule, however. For example, sometimes it may be reasonable to compare a hotel's individual revenue performance with the revenue of all similar hotels within the same brand (such as comparing performance of all Ritz-Carltons in Florida). Similarly, it is most appropriate to compare utility expenses to comparable hotels in the same region because utility rates are determined at a local level. Whenever possible, using local, market-specific comparative revenue figures is preferable, because they will reflect any peculiar trends of the area in which a property competes.

Exhibit 1 Comparative and Variance Analysis Defined

Comparative Analysis—review of a hotel's performance relative to other hotels or the market, using industry data or standards. For example, an asset manager might compare the hotel's occupancy in January 2015 against that of its competitive set during the same month.

Variance Analysis—review of a hotel's performance relative to its budgeted or prior results in a similar period. For example, an asset manager might compare a hotel's January 2015 linen expense to what was spent in January 2014.

Source: hotelAVE, Inc., Providence, RI.

Exhibit 2 Data Benchmarking Value Comparison

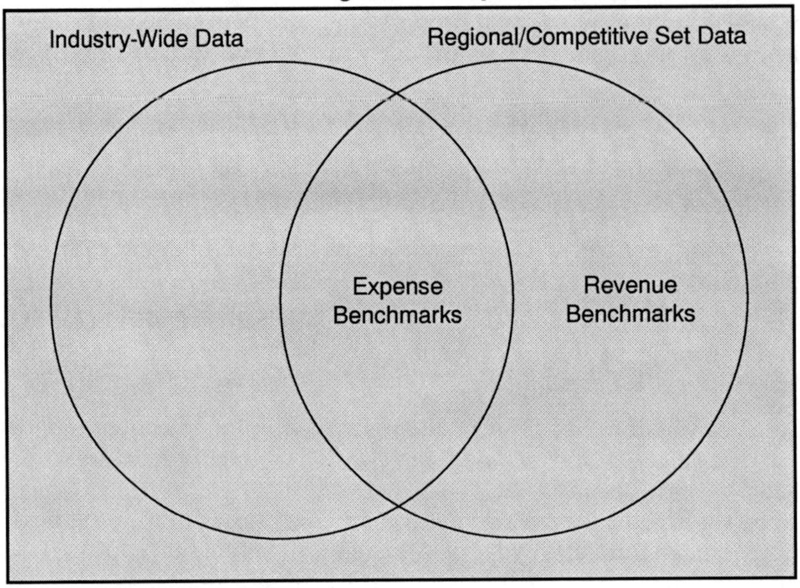

Industry-Wide Data
Regional/Competitive Set Data
Expense Benchmarks
Revenue Benchmarks

Source: hotelAVE, Inc., Providence, RI.

Comparative Analysis Techniques

Because of the possibility of extreme variations in monetary amounts of revenues and expenses from one hotel to the next or from one reporting period to the next, it is preferable to convert line items from an income statement to more useful metrics that facilitate comparisons. In general, hotel financial statement line items are expressed in terms of three measures:

- Percentage of revenue: percentage of total sales or applicable departmental revenue
- PAR: amounts per available room
- POR: amounts per occupied room

Formulas demonstrating the calculation of these three fundamental metrics commonly used to express hotel operating statistics appear in Exhibit 3 and are evident in the sample benchmarking reports from the various data sources later in this chapter.

Certain metrics are more appropriate to the analysis of individual line items, depending on the factors affecting the revenue or expense. For example, line items that are a function of guest use (e.g., telephone revenues, rooms department labor cost, etc.) are generally measured on a POR basis. Line items that are affected primarily by the size of the hotel (e.g., most undistributed operating expenses) are measured on a PAR basis. Costs that are mostly variable and dependent on revenue levels—for example, contractual items like base management fees or franchise royalty fees—are measured as a percentage of total revenue.

Exhibit 3 Metrics for Converting Line Items

$$\text{Percentage of Revenue} = \frac{\text{Total Monetary Amount of Line Item} \times 100}{\text{Total Revenue or Total Departmental Revenue}}$$

$$\text{Amount Per Available Room (PAR)} = \frac{\text{Total Monetary Amount of Line Item}}{\text{Total Daily Available Rooms at the Hotel}}$$

$$\text{Amount Per Occupied Room (POR)} = \frac{\text{Total Monetary Amount of Line Item}}{\text{Total Occupied Rooms at Hotel in That Period}}$$

It is not unusual to mix the metrics used to analyze line items, even within the same department. For example, unless there is significant local demand for a hotel's food and beverage outlet(s), a hotel's food and beverage departmental revenue is generally a function of how many guests are staying at the hotel, so the most meaningful measure of departmental sales performance is expressed as revenue per occupied room-night. Food and beverage expenses, however, are typically a function of departmental revenue, since most of the department's costs vary with sales volume.

Exhibit 4 lists various line items from a standard hotel operating statement and identifies primary and secondary metrics generally used to analyze them.

There are also other methods that are a take-off of these three primary measures. For example, in order to evaluate the efficiency of F&B sales, the following additional metrics can be analyzed, assuming availability of the benchmarking data. They include evaluating:

- Banquet & Catering sales per square foot of meeting space and per occupied group room (POGR)
- Outlet revenue per seat and outlet covers as a percentage of total guests

Section III (Financial Ratios and Operating Metrics) of the Eleventh Revised Edition of the *Uniform System of Accounts for the Lodging Industry (USALI),* published by the American Hotel & Lodging Association (www.ahla.com), provides additional details about ratio analysis that can also be used for benchmarking. The limitations or availability of the additional data required to complete the benchmarks (whether it is market mix, occupied group rooms, number of seats, etc.) will determine the extent of the benchmarking analysis.

Sample Line-Item Comparative Analysis

Comparative analysis reviews how the subject hotel has performed relative to comparable data. Exhibit 5 demonstrates how these data might be organized for a subject hotel when analyzing the energy line item. In this example, we have used data drawn from an STR *HOST Report* (discussed later in this chapter) on five

Exhibit 4 Basis for Analysis of Line Items

	% of Total Revenue	POR	PAR	% of Rooms Revenue
Revenue				
Rooms		X		
Food*		X		
Beverage*		X		
Other Operated Departments		X		#
Miscellaneous Income		#	X	
Departmental Expenses				
Rooms		X		#
Food & Beverage**	X			
Other Operated Departments**	X			
Undistributed Operating Expenses				
Administrative & General	#		X	
Information & Telecommunications Systems	#		X	
Sales & Marketing	#		X	
Franchise Fee				X
Property Operations & Maintenance	#		X	
Utilities	#	#	X	
Management Fees	X			
Income Before Non-Operating Income & Expenses				
Property Taxes			X	
Insurance	#		X	
Rent			X	
Other	X			
EBITDA				
FF&E Reserve	X			

*Note: * Food & Beverage revenue might also be analyzed on a per-cover or per-guest basis.*
*** Measured as a percentage of departmental revenue*

Legend: X = primary metric. # = secondary metric.

Source: hotelAVE, Inc., Providence, RI.

Exhibit 5 Example of Line Item Comparative Analysis

Energy Expense Analysis				
	Keys	***% of Revenue***	***POR***	***PAR***
Subject Hotel	**275**	**4.5%**	**$11.30**	**$2,409**
HOST Average	*300*	*4.6%*	*$11.69*	*$2,917*
Comparable Properties	***Keys***	***% of Revenue***	***POR***	***PAR***
Hotel A	200–250	5.8%	$11.50	$2,795
Hotel B	250–300	4.8%	$10.75	$2,952
Hotel C	300–350	3.9%	$8.50	$1,506
Hotel D	200–250	4.2%	$10.25	$1,965
Hotel E	300–350	4.8%	$13.72	$3,248
Average of Comps	250–300	4.7%	$10.94	$2,493

Source: hotelAVE, Inc., Providence, RI.

hotels (A–E) that we determined to be operationally comparable to the subject property.

As shown, the subject property's energy expense seems to be in line with the comparables' average expenditure for energy. The subject property's energy expense was $2,409 PAR, which is in the mid-range of the comparable properties, and lower than the average dollar amount PAR. Assuming that the comparables presented are operationally and physically similar to the subject property, it is reasonable to conclude that the subject's annualized energy expense is within the industry range. However, two comparable properties are achieving lower energy expenses on a PAR basis and three are lower on a POR basis, indicating that there may be an opportunity to decrease the subject property's energy expense. It may, in fact, be worth evaluating the practices of Hotel C to determine if the subject hotel might achieve similar energy costs per room. However, Hotel C's physical plant and age should be taken into consideration when analyzing the numbers, as these factors may be the drivers of its energy efficiency. If that is the case, the subject hotel's expense could be determined to be appropriate.

Sample Line-Item Variance Analysis

In addition to the comparative analysis just discussed, the asset manager should also scrutinize the subject property's performance relative to budgeted and prior years' performance. This review, known as variance analysis, is typically completed on a monthly basis against the budget and the prior year and on an annual basis as part of the budget process.

A detailed variance analysis of the subject property permits the asset manager to understand recent trends and the impact of operational decisions at the hotel. Asset managers generally complete a variance analysis on a monthly basis, comparing the property's month-over-month performance with the same time period of the preceding year, the current year budget, and/or the most recent property reforecast. Particular attention should be given to significant variances in the property's year-over-year performance or against budgeted performance.

In Exhibit 6, we present data on energy expense from the same subject hotel discussed in Exhibit 5. However, in this example, we omit data from its comparable set and look instead at historical data for the subject property. As seen in Exhibit 6, the subject property's management has budgeted for an increase in energy expenses in 2015 on an actual dollar basis (as measured by dollars PAR), but budgeted a decline in expense POR. On a percent-of-revenue basis, it is flat to last year. The budgeted decline in energy expense POR may have been the result of energy initiatives implemented by the hotel and/or the expectation of more moderate temperatures, especially since energy expense has been increasing above inflation for the past several years. The benchmarking may also suggest that this may be an unreasonable budget.

The asset manager should conduct parallel variance analyses of each line item on a monthly basis to ensure that revenues and expenses are in line with the plan for the period. In the event that a substantial variance has occurred, an explanation of what led to the variance should be requested from the property. Once details have been uncovered and reported, the asset manager and hotel team should discuss, depending on the line item and cause of the variance, if there are adjustments that can be made to bring the line item closer to the plan going forward. In some instances, there may be a variance due to changes in the operation since the plan was made.

Increasing the Property's Efficiency and Profitability

The exercise of completing comparative and variance analyses provides insights into a property's efficiency and profitability, but only by reviewing operational aspects of the hotel can the asset manager uncover opportunities for improvement. Thus, a financial analysis generally results in a lengthy list of questions regarding

Exhibit 6 Historical Line Item Variance Analysis

Energy Expense Analysis (2)					
Historical Financials	***% of Revenue***	***POR***	***% Change POR***	***PAR***	***% Change PAR***
2011	4.2%	$8.37		$2,033	
2012	4.3%	$8.75	4.5%	$2,150	5.8%
2013	4.5%	$10.63	21.5%	$2,350	9.3%
2014	4.5%	$11.30	6.3%	$2,409	2.5%
Budget 2015	**4.6%**	**$11.15**	**-1.3%**	**$2,600**	**7.9%**
YTD 2014	4.4%	$11.25			
YTD 2015	4.4%	$11.06	-1.7%		

Source: hotelAVE, Inc, Providence, RI.

the hotel's operation. Chapter Appendix 1 to this chapter presents questions in the left column that asset managers might pose to property managers. In the right column are action steps and suggestions to improve the hotel's profitability. The list presented in the appendix is by no means exhaustive, but rather a sampling of questions to ask the management team as the asset manager works to enhance the value of a hotel asset.

Benchmarking Rooms Revenue

A hotel and its competitive market are generally analyzed using three key metrics: average occupancy percentage, average daily rate (ADR), and revenue per available room (RevPAR). The formulas for calculating these ratios appear in Exhibit 7. The purpose of revenue benchmarking is to determine a hotel's appropriate occupancy and average rate potential or positioning, as indicated by comparing the hotel's performance relative to its competitive market.

Competitive Lodging Supply and Demand

A critical component of benchmarking a hotel's revenue is defining a set of competitive properties whose performance serves as a standard of comparison. The importance of selecting an appropriate competitive set cannot be overstated, as it will serve as an asset manager's starting point and provide the basis of analysis. The asset manager, in turn, must review data from:

- Management personnel at the subject property.
- Recent marketing plans for the subject property. These plans will provide an asset manager with an overview of the hotel's positioning and market strat-

Exhibit 7 Calculations for Revenue Analysis

$$\text{Average Occupancy Percentage} = \frac{\text{Occupied Rooms* } \times 100}{\text{Total Available Rooms Over Same Time Period}}$$

$$\text{Average Daily Rate (ADR)} = \frac{\text{Total Rooms Revenue for a Period}}{\text{Total Occupied Rooms for the Same Period}}$$

$$\text{Revenue Per Available Room (RevPAR)} = \text{ADR} \times \text{Occupancy} \quad \textit{or} \quad \frac{\text{Rooms Revenue for a Period}}{\text{Total Available Rooms for the Same Time Period}}$$

* Note: occupied rooms do not include complimentary rooms based on *USALI*, Eleventh Revised Edition.

egy and describe the relative strengths and weaknesses of the hotel and its competition as understood by the management team.

- Primary market research, including the asset manager's tours of competing properties, discussions with market contacts, local operator and demand-generator interviews, local government agencies, convention and visitor bureau, and regional economic development offices, and real estate brokers.
- Market representatives (e.g., Expedia or Travelocity representatives).
- Existing feasibility studies, appraisals, and other market reports for the subject property.

Whenever possible, the asset manager should complete primary market research, including interviews with local operators as well as an on-ground tour of the local market to understand the property's proximity to demand generators and their degree of access to the subject property. Before accepting that a competitive set proposed or used by the hotel manager is optimal, the asset manager must independently compile and analyze the aforementioned information to validate and determine the most appropriate (or correct) competitive set, as an improper set will skew the fundamental benchmarks upon which the hotel's performance will be evaluated. The industry rule of thumb is that a competitive set is not appropriate if a hotel's stabilized RevPAR index (defined later) is less than 80 percent or more than 130 percent.

To determine what hotels compete most directly with the subject property, an asset manager must collect and evaluate the following data relative to the subject hotel (keep in mind these data sets comprise both quantitative and qualitative factors):

- Number of rooms
- Published rates
- Physical characteristics: year built, condition, most recent renovation
- Quality level (as defined by AAA, Forbes and/or TripAdvisor or Expedia)
- Franchise affiliation
- Ratio of meeting space per guestroom
- Amenities, e.g., indoor/outdoor pool, food and beverage offerings, gift shop, health club, business center, etc.
- Fees associated with amenities
- Location, as gauged by proximity to major demand generators
- Prior operating history (occupancy and ADR statistics)
- Market segmentation (commercial, group, leisure)
- Management: brand or third-party

Exhibit 8 presents a sample of a competitive profile benchmark. Generally, hotels that share similar physical attributes, proximity to demand generators, and mix of market segments will form the subject hotel's competitive set.

Exhibit 8 Sample of a Competitive Profile Benchmark

	Subject Hotel	Hotel 2	Hotel3	Hotel4	Hotel5	Hotel6	Hotel 7
Address	Anytown	Anytown	Different Town	Your Town	Our Town	Anytown	Another Town
Location	Here	5mi from Here	3.4mi from Here	2.6mi from Here	3mi from Here	5.1mi from Here	12.4 mi from Here
Opening Year	19XX	19XX	19XX	19XX	19XX	19XX	19XX
Affiliation Management Company Ownership	Brand Hotel Company	Brand Hotel Company	Big Brand Hotel Company	Any Brand Hotel Co	XXL Hotel Company	6 Hotel Company	Brand X Hotel Company
AAA Diamonds	3	3	3	3	3	3	
Last Refurbishment	19XX	19XX	19XX	19XX	19XX	19XX	19XX
Number of Rooms	320	290	371	300	267	334	259
% Suites	2%	8%	3%	3%	100%	2%	
Facilities/Amenities Restaurants Lounges	Café Hotel Lounge Coffee Shop	Trattoria Coffee Shop	Coffee Shop Restaurant W	 Café Lounge	 Steakhouse	Bistro Lounge	Restaurant (leased out) Lounge
Total Meeting Space (sq. ft.) Largest Room/Ballroom (sq. ft.) Square Fee/Guest Room	13,244 7,505 34.0	12,389 5,418 38.6	15,739 6,720 50.6	10,266 5,280 35.4	7,068 5,206 25.5	11,550 8,400 38	10,552 7,760 41.7
Swimming Pool Exercise Room Business Center Gift Shop	Yes Yes Yes Yes	Yes Yes Yes Yes	Yes Yes Yes Yes	Yes Yes Yes Yes	Yes Yes Yes Yes	Yes Yes Yes Yes	Yes Yes Yes Yes
Parking	Complimentary	Valet ($15) or Self ($12)	Complimentary	Onsite ($14) or Valet ($14)	Complimentary	Complimentary	Complimentary
Other Amenities/Services	Complimentary Internet, Club Level	Complimentary Internet, Club Level	Complimentary Internet, Club Level	Complimentary Internet, Club Level	Complimentary Internet, Complimentary Breakfast, Mgrs Reception	Club Level, Complimentary Internet	Club Level, Complimentary Internet

Source: hotelAVE, Inc., Providence, RI.

The asset manager should also collect information from local planning or zoning offices regarding any planned or proposed hotel construction in the competitive lodging market; this is often disclosed in a hotel's marketing plan and/or is known by local-market hotel consultants or appraisers. The impact of a new hotel in the market, and the degree to which it will compete with the subject property, should be estimated by the standard supply-and-demand analysis techniques used when preparing lodging feasibility studies.

In addition to supply research, an asset manager should determine the major demand generators in a market through interviews with the general managers and sales directors in the competitive market and an analysis of key accounts from the TravelClick reports (described later). Demand generators typically include major companies, convention centers, colleges and universities, and leisure attractions (such as theme parks). Demand generators can also include special events, such as music festivals, large sporting events (such as a Super Bowl), city events, etc. Direct interviews with these demand generators will provide a valuable understanding of their hotel preferences and the characteristics of their demand (both current and projected), and will help an asset manager to identify a proper competitive set and market positioning for the subject hotel. Taken together, these interviews will help an astute asset manager uncover:

- Number of annual room nights generated in the competitive market.
- Seasonality of demand by day of week and month of year.
- Purpose of travel for incoming guests.
- Negotiated corporate rates with area hotels.
- Selection criteria by market segment.
- Special leisure rates negotiated with area hotels.
- Preferred or required amenities or services.
- Demand for meeting facilities.

Positioning the Subject Property

Using the preceding data, an asset manager can determine which hotels are likely to be most competitive with the subject property, estimate how well the subject property is positioned to capture demand within its competitive market, and identify potential opportunities to improve the asset's market positioning. Local research like this enables asset managers to rank the competitive properties' anticipated success based on individual property characteristics. For example, it is likely that a newly renovated hotel will command a higher rate than an aging, dated hotel, and a hotel situated nearby to a major demand generator will capture more of that generator's demand than a hotel located five miles away. These assessments and others can only be brought about through the analytical framework afforded by a well-researched competitive set.

A property's market positioning is generally gauged by its *penetration ratio*, which compares a property's performance to the performance of its market. A penetration ratio is calculated by dividing the property's performance on a given metric by the same performance metric of the overall market. Exhibit 9 presents some standard penetration ratios that asset managers use. Penetration ratios are expressed as a percentage; therefore, ratios in excess of 100 percent indicate that the hotel is out-performing the market.

For example, let us assume a hotel's annual RevPAR is $70.00 (an occupancy of 70 percent and an average rate of $100) and that the RevPAR of its competitive set is $73.44 (an occupancy of 68 percent and average rate of $108). Based on this data, the hotel's RevPAR index would be 95.3 percent, which is $70.00 divided by $73.44. The same principle would be applied to calculate occupancy and average rate indices, which would be 102.9 percent and 92.6 percent, respectively (occupancy index = 70 percent ÷ 68 percent; average rate index = $100 ÷ $108). In aggregate, these three ratios indicate that for this particular time period, the hotel outperformed the market (102.9 percent) in occupancy but achieved less than its fair share of average rate (92.6 percent) resulting in a RevPAR index ($70.00 ÷ $73.44) of 95.3 percent, or 4.7 percent below the average for its competitive set.

But how does an asset manager determine the appropriate RevPAR position for the subject hotel? In theory, if a hotel's competitive set consists exclusively of purely competitive properties, the hotel should consistently strive to achieve above 100 percent RevPAR penetration. However, in reality, lodging markets consist of such a wide array of properties that defining a perfect competitive set within a local market may not be achievable. Data availability can be a factor should a competitor choose not share its data with industry publications like STR. Consider a subject hotel that is an independent property in fair condition with no meeting space and serving primarily a transient market. Further assume that the properties within the competitive market are in relatively good condition, contain adequate meeting space, and are flagged with nationally recognized hotel brands. Assuming that there is a base of group-demand in the market that seeks branded, high-quality hotel accommodations, it would be rather difficult for the subject hotel to achieve an overall RevPAR penetration in excess of 100 percent under competitive circumstances. On the other hand, it may exceed 100 percent of the transient RevPAR for the market.

Exhibit 9 Penetration Ratio Calculations

$$\text{ADR Penetration Index} = \frac{\text{Property ADR}}{\text{Market ADR}} \times 100$$

$$\text{Occupancy Index} = \frac{\text{Property Occupancy}}{\text{Market Occupancy}} \times 100$$

$$\text{RevPAR Index} = \frac{\text{Property RevPAR}}{\text{Market RevPAR}} \times 100$$

$$\text{Transient Demand Index} = \frac{\text{Property Transient Demand}}{\text{Market Transient Demand}} \times 100$$

It is clearly unreasonable (and mathematically impossible) to expect every hotel to achieve a RevPAR penetration in excess of 100 percent given a competitive market. Moreover, RevPAR positioning is an admittedly subjective matter. For example, positioning expectations may be user biased and other market and economic factors may prevent the subject property from achieving a desired status. But, in considering and defining the goals for the hotel, the asset manager should work with the property management to analyze:

- The subject hotel's competitive advantages and disadvantages relative to the hotels in its competitive set and therefore the appropriate RevPAR penetration relative to fair share. Note that an appropriate stabilized RevPAR penetration may be above or below 100 percent depending upon the selection of competitors used.
- Recent trends in RevPAR at the subject property and in its market, including the subject's historical RevPAR penetration.

In simple terms, a reasonable goal for a hotel might simply be to improve its penetration levels on an incremental basis and then achieve specific stabilized target level over a period of time. Using the previous example, if a hotel achieved a RevPAR penetration of 95.3 percent last year, it may be challenged to achieve 97.0 percent this year and 98.0 percent next year.

Data Sources—Revenues

Once the competitive market and anticipated positioning of the subject hotel are defined, the asset manager should review industry publications that provide industry-wide or market-specific competitive set statistics for revenue performance. In addition to collecting data from national lodging consulting companies and speaking with area hospitality consultants, an asset manager must also collect reports used by the hotel's management team to measure the property's performance. Two commonly used sources of competitive data are STR (www.str.com) and TravelClick, Inc. (www.travelclick.net).

Specifically, STR reports are primarily used to measure a property's occupancy, average rate, and RevPAR relative to the market. STR will also generate specialized reports, including RevPAR Positioning Matrix (RPM), Bandwidth (used to measure spread and positioning in the competitive landscape), and Food & Beverage STR reports. TravelClick offers services such as the Hotelligence360 business intelligence platform (including Rate360, Demand360, and Agency360), used collectively to analyze a hotel's capture of the demand generated by global distribution systems (GDSs). GDSs generally represent 20–30 percent of net transient demand in a given market and are over-weighted to negotiated corporate demand, travel agencies, and consortia accounts. We will review other benefits of these reports later in this chapter, such as marketing strategies for corporate demand in the market.

STR's database includes total supply, demand, and revenue data for all major hotel chains and management companies, as well as many under independent management. STR collects data from over 50,000 properties representing some 6.4 million rooms globally, and the company's reports are based on actual total demand as reported by individual properties, management companies, and major hotel chains. Some of their reports include:

- *The STAR Report:* This monthly report provides performance measurements (occupancy, ADR, RevPAR, and market share) for an individual hotel and the comparative averages for the aggregate market area, alongside one or more user-defined competitive sets.
- *STR Weekly STAR Report:* This report provides daily performance statistics on a weekly basis. It is e-mailed to participant properties weekly. The data is collected at the property level versus the corporate level and thus slight variations may exist between the monthly and weekly reports.
- *STR Bandwidth Report:* This report displays graph-based evaluation metrics of a property's position against a range of performance indicators across the entirety of its competitive set, illustrating the minimum and maximum daily performance for the set.
- *STR RevPAR Positioning Matrix "RPM":* This report visualizes the relative relationship between performance indicators for each individual hotel in the competitive set.
- *STR Pulse Report:* This report diagnoses a hotel's complete "performance health" using new metrics that look beyond just the RevPAR index.
- *STR F&B STAR:* This report benchmarks a selected hotel property against competitive food and beverage revenue streams including banquet & catering, outlets, and in-room dining.

These reports include separate tabs outlining market segmentation (transient, group, or contract) and the market segment's occupancy, average rate, and RevPAR for both the subject and competitive set, if reported. The report also includes tabs outlining occupancy and ADR by segment and by day of week for the current month and year-to-date. These many tabs provide additional details behind the drivers for the overall performance and are very helpful in isolating opportunities for the subject property. In addition to segmentation analyses are tabs outlining additional revenue per room sold and per rooms available for both the subject and competitive set, again assuming the source data is reported. Additional revenue includes rooms, food and beverage, and other. "Other" revenue is defined in the STR report as all hotel revenue other than room and food and beverage revenue. Exhibit 10 provides an example of a standard monthly STAR report worksheet for a hotel that participates in STR's program. Generally, an asset manager receives STR reports from the hotel manager, who in turn will receive these reports for a fee, provided the manager's hotel contributes its data to the STR system.

The STAR report page shown in Exhibit 10 shows three sections that detail the performance and penetration indices of occupancy, ADR, and RevPAR. STAR reports are useful in that they can provide weekly or monthly data to help an asset manager and others demonstrate a property's historical performance relative to the market. The reports also include the relative ranking of the subject property compared to the competitive set in multiple metric comparables. In addition to the sample report page shown in Exhibit 10, a STAR report can include segmenta-

Exhibit 10 Sample STAR Report

Tab 4 - Competitive Set Report

Property Information
STR # 0000 ChainID: NA MgtCo: None Owner: None
For the Month of: October 2014 Date Created: November 18, 2014 Monthly Competitive Set Data Excludes Subject Property

Monthly Indexes

RevPAR Percent Change

Occupancy (%)	2013 May	Jun	Jul	Aug	Sep	Oct	Nov	Dec	2014 Jan	Feb	Mar	Apr	May	Jun	Jul	Aug	Sep	Oct
My Property	[illegible]	[illegible]	[illegible]	[illegible]	[illegible]	[illegible]	[illegible]	[illegible]	[illegible]	[illegible]	[illegible]	[illegible]	[illegible]	[illegible]	[illegible]	[illegible]	[illegible]	[illegible]
Competitive Set	[illegible]	[illegible]	[illegible]	[illegible]	[illegible]	[illegible]	[illegible]	[illegible]	[illegible]	[illegible]	[illegible]	[illegible]	[illegible]	[illegible]	[illegible]	[illegible]	[illegible]	[illegible]
Index (MPI)	[illegible]	[illegible]	[illegible]	[illegible]	[illegible]	[illegible]	[illegible]	[illegible]	[illegible]	[illegible]	[illegible]	[illegible]	[illegible]	[illegible]	[illegible]	[illegible]	[illegible]	[illegible]
Rank	[illegible]	[illegible]	[illegible]	[illegible]	[illegible]	[illegible]	[illegible]	[illegible]	[illegible]	[illegible]	[illegible]	[illegible]	[illegible]	[illegible]	[illegible]	[illegible]	[illegible]	[illegible]
% Chg																		
My Property	[illegible]	[illegible]	[illegible]	[illegible]	[illegible]	[illegible]	[illegible]	[illegible]	[illegible]	[illegible]	[illegible]	[illegible]	[illegible]	[illegible]	[illegible]	[illegible]	[illegible]	[illegible]
Competitive Set	[illegible]	[illegible]	[illegible]	[illegible]	[illegible]	[illegible]	[illegible]	[illegible]	[illegible]	[illegible]	[illegible]	[illegible]	[illegible]	[illegible]	[illegible]	[illegible]	[illegible]	[illegible]
Index (MPI)	[illegible]	[illegible]	[illegible]	[illegible]	[illegible]	[illegible]	[illegible]	[illegible]	[illegible]	[illegible]	[illegible]	[illegible]	[illegible]	[illegible]	[illegible]	[illegible]	[illegible]	[illegible]
Rank	[illegible]	[illegible]	[illegible]	[illegible]	[illegible]	[illegible]	[illegible]	[illegible]	[illegible]	[illegible]	[illegible]	[illegible]	[illegible]	[illegible]	[illegible]	[illegible]	[illegible]	[illegible]

Occupancy (%)	Year To Date 2012	2013	2014	Running 3 Month 2012	2013	2014	Running 12 Month 2012	2013	2014
My Property	[illegible]	[illegible]	[illegible]	[illegible]	[illegible]	[illegible]	[illegible]	[illegible]	[illegible]
Competitive Set	[illegible]	[illegible]	[illegible]	[illegible]	[illegible]	[illegible]	[illegible]	[illegible]	[illegible]
Index (MPI)	[illegible]	[illegible]	[illegible]	[illegible]	[illegible]	[illegible]	[illegible]	[illegible]	[illegible]
Rank	[illegible]	[illegible]	[illegible]	[illegible]	[illegible]	[illegible]	[illegible]	[illegible]	[illegible]
% Chg									
My Property	[illegible]	[illegible]	[illegible]	[illegible]	[illegible]	[illegible]	[illegible]	[illegible]	[illegible]
Competitive Set	[illegible]	[illegible]	[illegible]	[illegible]	[illegible]	[illegible]	[illegible]	[illegible]	[illegible]
Index (MPI)	[illegible]	[illegible]	[illegible]	[illegible]	[illegible]	[illegible]	[illegible]	[illegible]	[illegible]
Rank	[illegible]	[illegible]	[illegible]	[illegible]	[illegible]	[illegible]	[illegible]	[illegible]	[illegible]

ADR	2013 May	Jun	Jul	Aug	Sep	Oct	Nov	Dec	2014 Jan	Feb	Mar	Apr	May	Jun	Jul	Aug	Sep	Oct
My Property	[illegible]	[illegible]	[illegible]	[illegible]	[illegible]	[illegible]	[illegible]	[illegible]	[illegible]	[illegible]	[illegible]	[illegible]	[illegible]	[illegible]	[illegible]	[illegible]	[illegible]	[illegible]
Competitive Set	[illegible]	[illegible]	[illegible]	[illegible]	[illegible]	[illegible]	[illegible]	[illegible]	[illegible]	[illegible]	[illegible]	[illegible]	[illegible]	[illegible]	[illegible]	[illegible]	[illegible]	[illegible]
Index (ARI)	[illegible]	[illegible]	[illegible]	[illegible]	[illegible]	[illegible]	[illegible]	[illegible]	[illegible]	[illegible]	[illegible]	[illegible]	[illegible]	[illegible]	[illegible]	[illegible]	[illegible]	[illegible]
Rank	[illegible]	[illegible]	[illegible]	[illegible]	[illegible]	[illegible]	[illegible]	[illegible]	[illegible]	[illegible]	[illegible]	[illegible]	[illegible]	[illegible]	[illegible]	[illegible]	[illegible]	[illegible]
% Chg																		
My Property	[illegible]	[illegible]	[illegible]	[illegible]	[illegible]	[illegible]	[illegible]	[illegible]	[illegible]	[illegible]	[illegible]	[illegible]	[illegible]	[illegible]	[illegible]	[illegible]	[illegible]	[illegible]
Competitive Set	[illegible]	[illegible]	[illegible]	[illegible]	[illegible]	[illegible]	[illegible]	[illegible]	[illegible]	[illegible]	[illegible]	[illegible]	[illegible]	[illegible]	[illegible]	[illegible]	[illegible]	[illegible]
Index (ARI)	[illegible]	[illegible]	[illegible]	[illegible]	[illegible]	[illegible]	[illegible]	[illegible]	[illegible]	[illegible]	[illegible]	[illegible]	[illegible]	[illegible]	[illegible]	[illegible]	[illegible]	[illegible]
Rank	[illegible]	[illegible]	[illegible]	[illegible]	[illegible]	[illegible]	[illegible]	[illegible]	[illegible]	[illegible]	[illegible]	[illegible]	[illegible]	[illegible]	[illegible]	[illegible]	[illegible]	[illegible]

ADR	Year To Date 2012	2013	2014	Running 3 Month 2012	2013	2014	Running 12 Month 2012	2013	2014
My Property	[illegible]	[illegible]	[illegible]	[illegible]	[illegible]	[illegible]	[illegible]	[illegible]	[illegible]
Competitive Set	[illegible]	[illegible]	[illegible]	[illegible]	[illegible]	[illegible]	[illegible]	[illegible]	[illegible]
Index (ARI)	[illegible]	[illegible]	[illegible]	[illegible]	[illegible]	[illegible]	[illegible]	[illegible]	[illegible]
Rank	[illegible]	[illegible]	[illegible]	[illegible]	[illegible]	[illegible]	[illegible]	[illegible]	[illegible]
% Chg									
My Property	[illegible]	[illegible]	[illegible]	[illegible]	[illegible]	[illegible]	[illegible]	[illegible]	[illegible]
Competitive Set	[illegible]	[illegible]	[illegible]	[illegible]	[illegible]	[illegible]	[illegible]	[illegible]	[illegible]
Index (ARI)	[illegible]	[illegible]	[illegible]	[illegible]	[illegible]	[illegible]	[illegible]	[illegible]	[illegible]
Rank	[illegible]	[illegible]	[illegible]	[illegible]	[illegible]	[illegible]	[illegible]	[illegible]	[illegible]

RevPAR	2013 May	Jun	Jul	Aug	Sep	Oct	Nov	Dec	2014 Jan	Feb	Mar	Apr	May	Jun	Jul	Aug	Sep	Oct
My Property	[illegible]	[illegible]	[illegible]	[illegible]	[illegible]	[illegible]	[illegible]	[illegible]	[illegible]	[illegible]	[illegible]	[illegible]	[illegible]	[illegible]	[illegible]	[illegible]	[illegible]	[illegible]
Competitive Set	[illegible]	[illegible]	[illegible]	[illegible]	[illegible]	[illegible]	[illegible]	[illegible]	[illegible]	[illegible]	[illegible]	[illegible]	[illegible]	[illegible]	[illegible]	[illegible]	[illegible]	[illegible]
Index (RGI)	[illegible]	[illegible]	[illegible]	[illegible]	[illegible]	[illegible]	[illegible]	[illegible]	[illegible]	[illegible]	[illegible]	[illegible]	[illegible]	[illegible]	[illegible]	[illegible]	[illegible]	[illegible]
Rank	[illegible]	[illegible]	[illegible]	[illegible]	[illegible]	[illegible]	[illegible]	[illegible]	[illegible]	[illegible]	[illegible]	[illegible]	[illegible]	[illegible]	[illegible]	[illegible]	[illegible]	[illegible]
% Chg																		
My Property	[illegible]	[illegible]	[illegible]	[illegible]	[illegible]	[illegible]	[illegible]	[illegible]	[illegible]	[illegible]	[illegible]	[illegible]	[illegible]	[illegible]	[illegible]	[illegible]	[illegible]	[illegible]
Competitive Set	[illegible]	[illegible]	[illegible]	[illegible]	[illegible]	[illegible]	[illegible]	[illegible]	[illegible]	[illegible]	[illegible]	[illegible]	[illegible]	[illegible]	[illegible]	[illegible]	[illegible]	[illegible]
Index (RGI)	[illegible]	[illegible]	[illegible]	[illegible]	[illegible]	[illegible]	[illegible]	[illegible]	[illegible]	[illegible]	[illegible]	[illegible]	[illegible]	[illegible]	[illegible]	[illegible]	[illegible]	[illegible]
Rank	[illegible]	[illegible]	[illegible]	[illegible]	[illegible]	[illegible]	[illegible]	[illegible]	[illegible]	[illegible]	[illegible]	[illegible]	[illegible]	[illegible]	[illegible]	[illegible]	[illegible]	[illegible]

RevPAR	Year To Date 2012	2013	2014	Running 3 Month 2012	2013	2014	Running 12 Month 2012	2013	2014
My Property	[illegible]	[illegible]	[illegible]	[illegible]	[illegible]	[illegible]	[illegible]	[illegible]	[illegible]
Competitive Set	[illegible]	[illegible]	[illegible]	[illegible]	[illegible]	[illegible]	[illegible]	[illegible]	[illegible]
Index (RGI)	[illegible]	[illegible]	[illegible]	[illegible]	[illegible]	[illegible]	[illegible]	[illegible]	[illegible]
Rank	[illegible]	[illegible]	[illegible]	[illegible]	[illegible]	[illegible]	[illegible]	[illegible]	[illegible]
% Chg									
My Property	[illegible]	[illegible]	[illegible]	[illegible]	[illegible]	[illegible]	[illegible]	[illegible]	[illegible]
Competitive Set	[illegible]	[illegible]	[illegible]	[illegible]	[illegible]	[illegible]	[illegible]	[illegible]	[illegible]
Index (RGI)	[illegible]	[illegible]	[illegible]	[illegible]	[illegible]	[illegible]	[illegible]	[illegible]	[illegible]
Rank	[illegible]	[illegible]	[illegible]	[illegible]	[illegible]	[illegible]	[illegible]	[illegible]	[illegible]

STR, Inc.

Source: STR, Inc.

tion comparisons (transient, group, and contract) along with additional revenue comparisons (food and beverage and other) if the subject hotel and a significant enough share of the competitive set reports the data. Additionally, there are sections of the report that provide a comparison of these metrics by day of week. Complete sample reports can be found on the STR website or by contacting STR directly.

When looking to create a STAR competitive set, asset managers can request a list of participating hotels by market, room count, published ADR, etc., directly from STR or through the STR website, select the type of report they would like to order, and view the hotels that participate and provide data. From there, one can determine the appropriate set among the hotels that submit data. There are guidelines to which STR adheres with regard to its data extraction and transparency, so as not to compromise the confidentiality of an individual property's data, and these guidelines can be provided by STR upon request. STR's website offers a tool to determine if a proposed competitive set meets the proper confidentiality criteria. STR also offers a report known as the Trend Report that reports the monthly occupancy percentage, ADR, RevPAR, room revenue, room supply, and room demand aggregated for a competitive set of hotels for six or more years. This report does not calculate the penetration data for the subject hotel as compared to its competitors, but is available to anyone (even non-participating hotels).

HotStats offers a RevPAR Plus Report that includes monthly volume mix and average rate by six different segments of an aggregated set of comparable hotels. As of this publication, this data source is currently only available for hotels located in the UK, Europe, and Middle East (EMEA).

TravelClick's comprehensive database is the exclusive source of hotel industry electronic distribution data from the Amadeus, Galileo, Sabre, and Worldspan GDSs, which collectively are used by 98 percent of travel agents worldwide. TravelClick's reports are particularly useful for transient-oriented hotels, while group-oriented properties are less likely to benefit from these data. However, with the introduction of Demand 360, the market group forecast and total demand picture is relevant to all hotels.

TravelClick's data is significantly different from STR's data in that the firm reports only actual demand data from the GDSs, which is primarily generated by travel agents, versus total demand from all sources, as reflected on STR reports. Based on TravelClick estimates, GDS-related transactions are 20–30 percent of total transient lodging demand nationwide. TravelClick also produces eMonitor, a quarterly newsletter that provides a snapshot of electronic distribution performance worldwide.

Reports available from TravelClick include:

- *Agency360:* This tool (see Exhibit 11) aggregates data of bookings through the GDSs. It is a useful application to compare hotel demand to production in the competitive set and the report provides a GDS penetration calculation (similar to how RevPAR penetration is calculated); it also provides a relative ranking versus each hotel in its set. The aggregate data is broken down by each individual account (categorized by an International Air Transport Association code used for booking) while also indicating the demand source

Exhibit 11 Sample Agency360 Report

Top 25 Agencies By Comp Set Revenue for All Rate Types (YTD through 14 Jan 2015)

*A maximum of 150 Agencies will be retrieved. (Click here to get More Agency Information...)

▲	Agency	Penetration			Subscriber					Comp Set				
		Surplus / (Opportunity)	Revenue Penetration	Variance	Revenue	Variance	Room Nights	Variance	ADR	Revenue	Variance	Room Nights	Variance	ADR
1	AMERICAN EXPRESS (Z8B0)	$13,109	191	46	$27,465	$8,325	69	18	$398	$104,261	$2,394	240	(4)	$434
2	Best Travel Elk Grove (AN41V)	($1,607)	0		$0	$0	0	0		$14,744	$8,261	47	25	$314
3	BCD Ubs (27SU1V)	($1,445)	0		$0	$0	0	0		$13,262	$5,092	59	18	$225
4	BCD No Citadel Investments (1U8B)	($1,313)	0		$0	$0	0	0		$12,043	$4,663	40	14	$301
5	Bmo Ca (2E7D1V)	($1,239)	0		$0	$0	0	0		$11,373	$11,373	51	51	$223
6	American Express (UH72)	$1,769	211	145	$3,365	$2,735	9	7	$374	$11,280	$3,140	24	7	$470
7	AEGBT (1R9U1V)	$1,657	223	65	$3,010	$1,505	14	7	$215	$9,402	$2,142	34	1	$277
8	Amex Btc Mexico Patriotismo (2T57)	($984)	0		$0	$0	0	0		$9,028	$8,208	22	20	$410
9	AMERICAN EXPRESS (7UWF)	($978)	0		$0	$0	0	0		$8,975	($4,794)	37	(25)	$243
10	Ovation Travel Group Soros (18SB)	($939)	0	(180)	$0	($885)	0	(3)		$8,620	$4,990	30	17	$287
11	Magellan Vacations (8O7B)	($74)	93	(19)	$945	($1,030)	3	(2)	$315	$8,401	($5,767)	28	(21)	$300
12	CWT Jpmc (9BL1V)	($772)	0	(105)	$0	($1,320)	0	(4)		$7,088	($3,175)	34	(17)	$208
13	Corporate Travel Oak Brook (B6G0)	($760)	0		$0	$0	0	0		$6,972	$5,307	25	19	$279
14	Carlson Wagonlit Travel (2BJ11V)	($656)	0		$0	$0	0	0		$6,018	$3,738	30	18	$201
15	AEGBT (S7Q0)	($370)	46	46	$315	$315	1	1	$315	$5,971	$71	23	(1)	$260

Source: TravelClick, Inc.

(name of company or travel agency) that booked those rooms. The data is on a cloud-based platform and can be manipulated in many ways including account ranking by amount of room night production, length of stay, ADR consideration, and production volume, among others.

- *Rate360:* This tool collects data from the subject property and competitors through their property management systems to give a snapshot of historical and future ADR. The tool provides the asset manager with benchmark rates against competitors by comparing booking channels, length of stay, and room inclusions.
- *Demand360:* This application is used to understand the future booking pace of competitors. It is useful to measure a hotel's future GDS penetration index and is therefore a useful revenue management tool. It is vital for sales team members to use tools like Demand360 to understand and react to latent demand in a given market or a fall-off of demand from a key account, and to respond by both deploying and adjusting strategies, such as pricing and mix development.

In evaluating sample report data, the Sample Dashboard Report (Exhibit 12) indicates that the property is outperforming its competitive set within GDS systems by capturing 107 percent of its fair share, but it has lost share from last year (when its penetration was 116 percent).

USALI Eleventh Revised Edition Uniform Market Segments

The most recent version of the *USALI* was made effective January 1, 2015. The update was needed to continue the mission of financial and operational reporting parity among the hotels in today's marketplace. Key changes affecting benchmarking include updating the definition of revenue and the methods with which revenue is reported on financial statements as well as third-party benchmarking resources such as the aforementioned STR and TravelClick.

The revenue-based revisions identified below are paramount to standardizing the hotel financial report mechanism:

- This edition defines transient segments (retail, discount, negotiated, qualified, and wholesale) and group (corporate, association/convention, government, tour/wholesale and SMERF) to be used uniformly throughout the industry. (SMERF refers to social, military, educational, religious, and fraternal groups.)

Exhibit 12 Sample Hotelligence Dashboard

Your Revenue Penetration

MTD Jan 2015 Rank	*YTD 2015 Rank*
3 of 6	3 of 6

	MTD Jan 2015	YTD 2015
Revenue Penetration	107	107
Last Year	116	116
Variance vs. Last Year	(9)	(9)
Revenue Surplus/(Opportunity)	$5,241	$5,241

Your Performance for MTD Jan 2015 vs. MTD Jan 2014

	Revenue			Room Nights			ADR		
	Current	Last Year	Growth	Current	Last Year	Growth	Current	Last Year	Growth
Subscriber	$80,194	$75,534	6.2%	240	244	(1.6%)	$334	$310	7.9%
Competitive Set	$607,539	$523,524	16.0%	1,958	1,739	12.6%	$310	$301	3.1%
Chicago	$12,641,544	$9,783,664	29.2%	92,807	74,901	23.9%	$136	$131	4.3%

Key Alerts and Warnings

Source: TravelClick, Inc.

- Room revenue no longer includes resort fees as part of the ADR calculation.
- Package allocation is given defined language regarding retail cost, which was ambiguous in the previous addition.
- Rebates or group subsidies are no longer considered expenses; rather, they are considered contra-revenue in normal accounting practice.

A clear articulation of these rooms revenue changes is important to the benchmarking process because different hotel operators report revenue in different ways or in different segments, which can skew the results and negatively affect the benchmarking comparison. Communicating and maintaining standardized reporting parameters, therefore, is a critical condition for reliable analysis.

Net RevPAR: Demand Sources

The growing impact of third-party demand sources, such as Expedia or Cvent, is having a significant effect on the net profitability of revenue generated through those channels. As a result, the cost to acquire hotel guests/customers through them is rising. It is therefore important for asset managers to understand how booking channels and third-party vendor costs affect the profitability of an asset; some vendors net the cost before delivering the revenue (and thus the ADR) to the hotel, while others deliver all of the revenue and charge a commission that is booked as a rooms expense. Kalibri Labs is pioneering the research into customer acquisition cost and benchmarking net revenue trends.

For example, Exhibit 13 displays the total amount a customer has paid (*gross revenue*), *P&L revenue* (net of contra revenue commissions), *net reservation revenue* (net of reservation expense, commissions, transaction fees), and *net of all customer*

Exhibit 13 Historical Customer Acquisition Cost

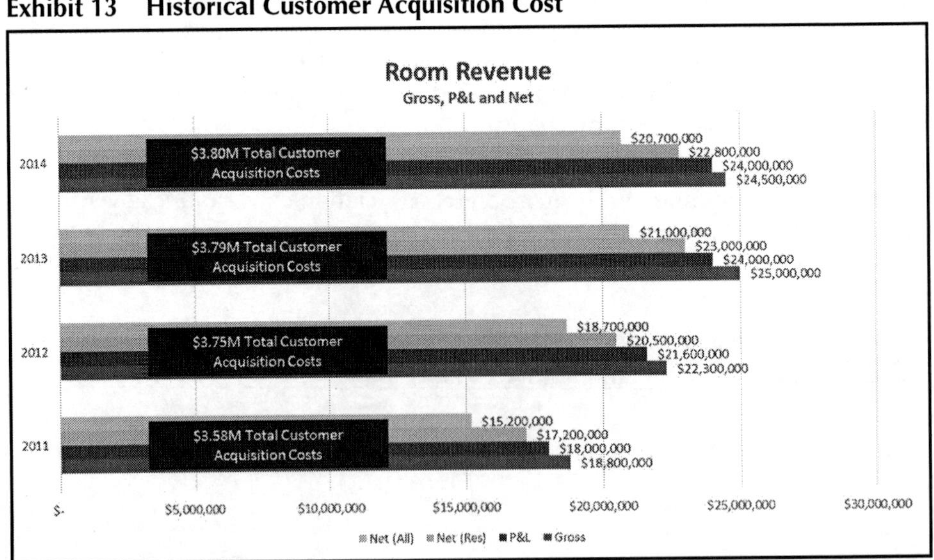

Source: Kalibri Labs, LLC.

acquisition costs revenue (additional sales and marketing costs). This chart illustrates why the asset manager must track occupancy by source of demand and the corresponding cost of those sources as each has a different cost of acquisition and therefore profitability.

Detailed differently in Exhibit 14, the chart benchmarks the RevPAR capture by booking channel along with the profitability of those sources. As indicated, each segment differs in its profitability contribution due to the cost associated with the channel. Asset managers must be aware of these variable costs and ensure that their assets do not receive a disproportionate amount of revenue from lower profitability sources.

The graph in Exhibit 15 is an example of the benchmarking process one would use to assess channel demand and determine an appropriate source allocation mix. This chart illustrates the performance of the subject hotel's channel mix demand compared to a similar type of hotel (extended stay, resort, inventory size, similar market) and to a hotel with a similar online travel agent (OTA) demand percentage.

Summary: Revenue Benchmarking

As the hotel industry moves toward greater methods of standardization, as illustrated by the updated *USALI*, revenue benchmarking will become increasingly important as a tool for asset evaluation and management.

An asset manager can contribute to the achievement of revenue goals by working with management to create appropriate revenue management strategies and employ efficient, targeted marketing strategies. This might include reviewing local demand generator production via TravelClick reports to ensure that important sources of room nights have not been overlooked and are appropriately priced, employing best practices regarding Internet advertising and pricing, redeploying sales and marketing funds, and, in the case of group-oriented hotels, increasing the property's marketing exposure through contacts with meeting planners, direct marketing efforts, and the use of familiarization trips. Moreover, with the rise of

Exhibit 14 RevPAR Capture by Booking Channel

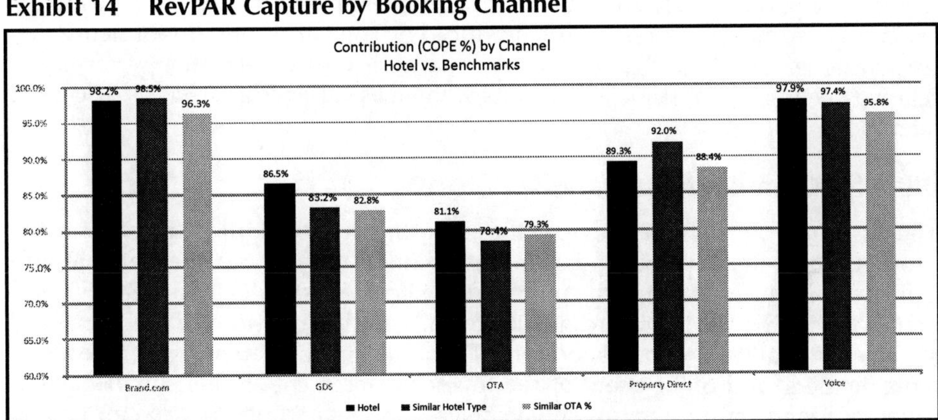

Source: Kalibri Labs, LLC.

Exhibit 15 Booking Channel Mix Benchmarking

Channel Mix Demand by Room Nights

	Brand.com	GDS	OTA	Property Direct	Voice
Hotel	27%	17%	22%	9%	25%
Similar Hotel Type	22%	20%	25%	13%	20%
Similar OTA %	18%	22%	23%	15%	22%

Source: Kalibri Labs, LLC.

acquisition costs, it is important for the asset manager to benchmark and monitor channel distribution and demand sources.

The goal of revenue benchmarking is to allow the asset manager, using a host of industry tools and analytical techniques, to review both the historical revenue performance of the hotel and its future rate positioning and to design strategies for increasing the property's overall revenue.

Benchmarking Expenses and Non-Rooms Revenue

Data permitting the benchmarking of expenses and non-rooms revenue are also abundant, with several reliable sources providing a framework for comparative analysis. Typically, the asset manager completes an analysis during the budgeting season, comparing a property's performance to comparable hotels or assessing it against aggregate data from reports produced by consulting and investment advisory firms serving the lodging industry. Analysis of the hotel's own performance relative to budgeted or prior year results, known as variance analysis, is discussed later in the chapter.

Basis for Comparative Analysis

The asset manager should review the departmental schedules supporting the property's summary profit and loss statement to understand the revenue and expense items included in each summary line item. Most hotel management companies follow the *USALI* to provide uniformity in the reporting of their financial statements relative to other operators. This uniformity enables owners, consultants, lenders, and other users of the financial statements to benchmark across different brands and operators. Nonetheless, understanding the account coding system of each property's management company is critical to validating an appropriate comparative analysis, as minor adjustments to financial statements of different brands and third-party managers may be required to ensure an "apples-to-apples" comparison.

Adjustments to the presentation of the subject hotel's results might be required to maintain comparability. For example, profit and loss statements prepared by some management companies identify credit card commissions as a separate expense, while under the *USALI* format, they are typically included in the administrative and general (A&G) area. For true comparability, the A&G expense in this example must be adjusted to include credit card commissions. Similarly, independent management companies operating franchised hotels might include all fees associated with the franchise (reservation expense, frequent guest program fees, franchise royalty fees, and national marketing fees) in a property's franchise-fee line item. This would clearly present a significantly higher franchise expense than that reported by other hotels following the *USALI* convention of coding reservation costs as an expense of the rooms department, while frequent-guest-program costs and national marketing fees are coded as marketing expenses. Also, for a resort property, it may be more useful to itemize "other operated departments," given the greater significance and variability of amenities (and, thus, revenue) from resort to resort, including golf and spa revenue. If an asset manager is not cognizant of such financial reporting nuances, the reliability of the comparative analysis may be compromised.

Numerous investment advisory and consulting firms gather data and operating statements from various hotels nationwide. These reports include industry-wide survey reports and more focused reports that can be customized to provide data from a selection of hotels defined according to a narrower set of attributes.

Choosing the Right Comparable Hotels for Expense Benchmarking

When conducting an analysis of the operating expenses, it is important for the asset manager to rely on data derived from comparables that are similar to the subject hotel in terms of operational characteristics. Therefore, it is not critical that the comparables used be properties in the same competitive set used to determine the most appropriate RevPAR positioning.

Why? Total rooms department expense at a subject hotel would be affected most by service staffing levels, complexity of guestrooms (e.g., all-suite versus standard room mix), the level of the amenities package, and the overall market orientation of the hotel. Similarly, food and beverage total departmental expense will be a function in part of the department's sales mix; higher proportions of beverage and banquet revenues, for example, will typically yield lower costs as a percentage of overall food and beverage revenue. Thus, for these line items, the asset manager would want to focus attention on comparables that are physically and operationally most like the subject hotel, not necessarily those located in the same competitive market or region.

Alternatively, for some fixed charges, it may be helpful for the asset manager to rely on regional or market-area statistics to determine the most reasonable expense levels. For example, the per-room property tax liability should be relatively comparable for hotels within the same legal jurisdiction. Similarly, a subject hotel's energy expenses should track closely with statistics for local hotels, as factors affecting energy costs will affect all hotels similarly in a competitive market.

The following factors should be considered when selecting comparables, whether from industry-wide databases or from the asset manager's ad hoc sources:

- Number of guestrooms
- Market mix (e.g., proportion of group to transient business)
- Mix of rooms revenue to total revenue
- Occupancy percentage and ADR, or RevPAR positioning
- Branding or franchise affiliation
- Operation (corporate- or brand-managed or third-party hotel manager)
- Physical plant layout (single tower, atrium, or spread throughout a property) and amount of meeting space
- Collective bargaining agreements (are employees union or non-union?)
- Location within a certain region and whether urban, suburban, or resort

The data sources outlined below will provide the asset manager with a list of hotels in their database to allow the asset manager to select the best comparables. While the asset manager may not have access to comparable hotels' occupancy, ADR or RevPAR positioning or mix of revenue, all of the other aforementioned data is publicly available and should be analyzed when selecting comparables. The asset manager can also request that the data source eliminate any comparables selected by the asset manager that vary too much in terms of occupancy, ADR or RevPAR. For example, the comparable set selected for the PKF Benchmarker Report in Exhibit 16 reflects hotels containing 275 to 375 rooms (and averaging 340) versus the subject hotel with 316 rooms, in the Southeast Region with an average RevPAR of $90.23 versus the subject hotel at $90.82.

As mentioned previously, it is important to ensure that the data being compared is "apples-to-apples" by using the *USALI* or an alternative standard as a guide.

It should be further noted that when looking at comparable profit and loss statements (P&Ls), it is preferable to have the P&L data be from the same year as the subject property—if it is not, it should be adjusted for inflation. One method of inflating the data for comparison purposes is by using the Consumer Price Index (CPI). To inflate the data using the CPI, the asset manager would take the CPI for the year of the subject property's P&L and divide it by the CPI from the year of the comparable property's P&L and then multiply the comparable property's P&L line items by that amount. For example, let's assume the subject property's data is from 2014 and the comparable P&L is from 2013; further assume that the CPI in 2014 was 105.0 compared to 103.0 in 2013. In our calculation, 105.0 divided by 103.0 equals 1.02 and indicates a roughly 2.0 percent growth in the CPI from 2013 to 2014. The comparable hotel's P&L line items would then be multiplied by 1.02 to inflate them to 2014 levels.

Exhibit 16 PKF Benchmarker Income Statement

BENCHMARKER INCOME STATEMENT

PKF HOSPITALITY RESEARCH A CBRE COMPANY

SUMMARY

REVENUES AND EXPENSES	Comparative Set - Average of 4 Properties: Year End 2011 Average $	Ratio To Revenue	$ Per Available Room/Year	$ Per Occupied Room/Day	Subject Property: Year End 2011 Total $	Var-iance	Ratio To Revenue	Var-iance*	$ Per Available Room/Year	Var-iance	$ Per Occupied Room/Day	Var-iance
Revenues												
Rooms	$ 11,189,245	69.5	$ 32,934	$ 129.34	$ 10,475,355	-6.4%	73.1	3.6%	$ 33,150	0.7%	$ 128.97	-0.3%
Food and Beverage	3,897,976	24.2	11,473	45.06	3,755,759	-3.6%	26.2	2.0%	11,885	3.6%	46.24	2.6%
Other Operated Departments	907,244	5.6	2,670	10.49	84,184	-90.7%	0.6	-5.0%	266	-90.0%	1.04	-90.1%
Rentals and Other Income	99,908	0.6	294	1.15	17,702	-82.3%	0.1	-0.5%	56	-80.9%	0.22	-81.1%
Total Revenues	$ 16,094,373	100.0	$ 47,371	$ 186.04	$ 14,333,001	-10.9%	100.0	0.0%	$ 45,358	-4.3%	$ 176.47	-5.1%
Departmental Costs and Expenses**												
Rooms	$ 2,504,081	22.4	$ 7,370	$ 28.95	$ 2,442,160	-2.5%	23.3	0.9%	$ 7,728	4.9%	$ 30.07	3.9%
Food and Beverage	2,962,285	76.0	8,719	34.24	2,335,463	-21.2%	62.2	-13.8%	7,391	-15.2%	28.75	-16.0%
Other Operated Departments	682,114	75.2	2,008	7.88	120,956	-82.3%	143.7	68.5%	383	-80.9%	1.49	-81.1%
Total Costs and Expenses	$ 6,148,481	38.2	$ 18,097	$ 71.07	$ 4,898,579	-20.3%	34.2	-4.0%	$ 15,502	-14.3%	$ 60.31	-15.1%
Total Operated Departmental Income	$ 9,945,893	61.8	$ 29,274	$ 114.97	$ 9,434,422	-5.1%	65.8	4.0%	$ 29,856	2.0%	$ 116.16	1.0%
Undistributed Operating Expenses												
Administrative and General	$ 1,474,427	9.2	$ 4,340	$ 17.04	$ 859,016	-41.7%	6.0	-3.2%	$ 2,718	-37.4%	$ 10.58	-37.9%
Marketing (Includes Franchise Fees)	1,758,369	10.9	5,175	20.33	1,719,462	-2.2%	12.0	1.1%	5,441	5.1%	21.17	4.2%
Property Operation and Maintenance	730,335	4.5	2,150	8.44	495,433	-32.2%	3.5	-1.1%	1,568	-27.1%	6.10	-27.7%
Utility Costs	691,692	4.3	2,036	8.00	490,265	-29.1%	3.4	-0.9%	1,551	-23.8%	6.04	-24.5%
Total Undistributed Expenses	$ 4,654,821	28.9	$ 13,701	$ 53.81	$ 3,564,176	-23.4%	24.9	-4.1%	$ 11,279	-17.7%	$ 43.88	-18.4%
Gross Operating Profit	$ 5,291,072	32.9	$ 15,573	$ 61.16	$ 5,870,246	10.9%	41.0	8.1%	$ 18,577	19.3%	$ 72.27	18.2%
Management Fees	$ 520,049	3.2	$ 1,531	$ 6.01	$ 715,552	37.6%	5.0	1.8%	$ 2,264	47.9%	$ 8.81	46.5%
Income Before Fixed Charges	$ 4,771,023	29.6	$ 14,043	$ 55.15	$ 5,154,694	8.0%	36.0	6.3%	$ 16,312	16.2%	$ 53.46	15.1%
Fixed Charges												
Property Taxes and Other Municipal Charges	$ 540,236	3.4	$ 1,590	$ 6.24	$ 576,480	6.7%	4.0	0.7%	$ 1,824	14.7%	$ 7.10	13.7%
Insurance	87,242	0.5	257	1.01	88,398	1.3%	0.6	0.1%	280	8.9%	1.09	7.9%
Total Fixed Charges	$ 627,478	3.9	$ 1,847	$ 7.25	$ 664,879	6.0%	4.6	0.7%	$ 2,104	13.9%	$ 8.19	12.9%
Net Operating Income***	$ 4,143,545	25.7	$ 12,196	$ 47.90	$ 4,489,815	8.4%	31.3	5.6%	$ 14,208	16.5%	$ 55.28	15.4%

ROOM STATISTICS

Comparative Set - Average of 4 Properties

4	Number of Properties in Comparative Set
340	Average Number of Rooms
69.8%	Average Occupancy
$129.34	Average ADR
$90.23	Average RevPAR

ROOM STATISTICS

Subject Property

1	Number of Properties in Subject Set
316	Number of Rooms
70.4%	Occupancy
$128.97	ADR
$90.82	RevPAR

.... Columns with dotted lines do not total

* Ratio to revenue shown as a percentage of corresponding departmental revenue

** Before deductions for rent, capital reserve, interest, income taxes, depreciation, and amortization

NC - Not Comparable

*Expressed as percentage points difference

Source: PKF Hospitality, a CBRE Company.

Data Sources: Expenses

Companies that currently provide industry-wide survey data include STR (www.str.com), PKF Consulting (www.pkfc.com), and HotStats (www.hotstats.com). Each offers reports for purchase that include consolidated data for a set of comparable hotels from their extensive databases of operating financials. The major benefit of using these companies' databases is that the asset manager can define the competitive set based on relevant attributes, including location, region, property size, and rate tier and all of the statements entered into their databases are adjusted to conform to the *USALI* to the best of their ability.

Please note that the sample reports included herein are presented in compliance with the Tenth Revised Edition of the *USALI* as they reflect 2014 or prior data, before the Eleventh Revised Edition went into effect.

PKF Hospitality Research, a CBRE Company, offers three types of Benchmarker Reports that provide summary statistics derived by averaging data from a comparable set of properties selected by the asset manager. PKF's database contains nearly 6,000 full- and limited-service properties' detailed financial statistics. PKF is able to provide more detailed data on revenue and expense line items appearing on the summary income statement.

The three main reports contained in the PKF Benchmarker report include:

1. Summary income statement reports (similar to STR's Custom HOST and HOST P&L Profitability Scorecard reports combined)
2. Departmental labor costs statistic reports, including salaries, wages, and employee benefits for each department, but no full-time equivalent (FTE) labor data
3. Detailed departmental statistics reports for the following departments: Rooms, A&G, F&B, Marketing, Property Maintenance, and Utilities

Exhibit 16 shows a sample Benchmarker Income Statement report. A distinct advantage of the format of PKF's income statement (similar to the STR Custom Report) is that it reports the percentage variance from the competitive set's average value for each metric. For example, the subject hotel depicted in Exhibit 16 achieved a total gross operating profit that is 8.1 percentage points higher than its competitive set when expressed as a percentage of revenue and 19.3 percent higher when compared on a per-available-room basis.

The Benchmarker Labor Cost tab of the report is a valuable tool, as labor is the largest operating cost of lodging properties. PKF provides labor in the greatest detail of all of the data sources by separating the cost between salaries, wages and bonuses, and payroll-related expenses. Exhibit 17 shows a sample labor cost report comparing the subject hotel's performance to its competitive set. As can be seen, the report shows the total payroll and related expenses for various revenue and cost centers in the hotel, further categorized into (1) wages including overtime and bonuses and (2) benefits and payroll taxes. For example, the subject hotel's labor cost in the A&G department is 2.8 percent of revenue, which is lower than the labor cost of 4.7 percent of revenue reported by the four hotels in the comparative set. The hotel expends almost half as much than the comparative set on sala-

Exhibit 17 Benchmarker Labor Cost Analysis

BENCHMARKER SUMMARY

PKF HOSPITALITY RESEARCH A CBRE COMPANY

LABOR COST ANALYSIS

EXPENSES	Comparative Set - Average of 4 Properties: Year End 2011 Average $	Ratio To Hotel Revenue	$ Per Available Room/Year	$ Per Occupied Room/Day	Subject Property: Year End 2011 Total $	Var-iance	Ratio To Hotel Revenue	Var-iance*	$ Per Available Room/Year	Var-iance	$ Per Occupied Room/Day	Var-iance
Rooms Department												
Salaries, Wages, and Bonuses	$ 1,185,212	7.4	$ 3,488	$ 13.70	$ 1,145,230	-3.4%	8.0	0.6%	$ 3,624	3.9%	$ 14.10	2.9%
Payroll-Related Expenses	347,572	2.2	1,023	4.02	367,135	5.6%	2.6	0.4%	1,162	13.6%	4.52	12.5%
Total Payroll and Related Expenses	$ 1,532,784	9.5	$ 4,512	$ 17.72	$ 1,512,365	-1.3%	10.6	1.0%	$ 4,786	6.1%	$ 18.62	5.1%
Food and Beverage Department												
Salaries, Wages, and Bonuses	$ 1,158,765	7.2	$ 3,411	$ 13.39	$ 984,116	-15.1%	6.9	-0.3%	$ 3,114	-8.7%	$ 12.12	-9.5%
Payroll-Related Expenses	450,388	2.8	1,326	5.21	333,091	-26.0%	2.3	-0.5%	1,054	-20.5%	4.10	-21.2%
Total Payroll and Related Expenses	$ 1,609,153	10.0	$ 4,736	$ 18.60	$ 1,317,207	-18.1%	9.2	-0.8%	$ 4,168	-12.0%	$ 16.22	-12.8%
Other Operated Department												
Salaries, Wages, and Bonuses	$ 106,130	0.7	$ 312	$ 1.23	$ -	NC	0.0	NC	$ -	NC	$ -	NC
Payroll-Related Expenses	32,255	0.2	95	0.37	0	NC	0.0	NC	0	NC	0.00	NC
Total Payroll & Related Expenses	$ 138,385	0.9	$ 407	$ 1.60	$ -	NC	0.0	NC	$ -	NC	$ -	NC
Administrative and General Department												
Salaries, Wages, and Bonuses	$ 571,749	3.6	$ 1,683	$ 6.61	$ 296,972	-48.1%	2.1	-1.5%	$ 940	-44.2%	$ 3.66	-44.7%
Payroll-Related Expenses	178,208	1.1	525	2.06	107,637	-39.6%	0.8	-0.4%	341	-35.1%	1.33	-35.7%
Total Payroll and Related Expenses	$ 749,957	4.7	$ 2,207	$ 8.67	$ 404,608	-46.0%	2.8	-1.8%	$ 1,280	-42.0%	$ 4.98	-42.5%
Marketing Department												
Salaries, Wages, and Bonuses	$ 533,403	3.3	$ 1,570	$ 6.17	$ 439,802	-17.5%	3.1	-0.2%	$ 1,392	-11.4%	$ 5.41	-12.2%
Payroll-Related Expenses	167,034	1.0	492	1.93	167,283	0.1%	1.2	0.1%	529	7.7%	2.06	6.7%
Total Payroll and Related Expenses	$ 700,437	4.4	$ 2,062	$ 8.10	$ 607,084	-13.3%	4.2	-0.1%	$ 1,921	-6.8%	$ 7.47	-7.7%
Property Maintenance Department												
Salaries, Wages, and Bonuses	$ 231,791	1.4	$ 682	$ 2.68	$ 205,953	-11.1%	1.4	0.0%	$ 652	-4.5%	$ 2.54	-5.4%
Payroll-Related Expenses	72,720	0.5	214	0.84	66,505	-8.5%	0.5	0.0%	210	-1.7%	0.82	-2.6%
Total Payroll and Related Expenses	$ 304,511	1.9	$ 896	$ 3.52	$ 272,458	-10.5%	1.9	0.0%	$ 862	-3.8%	$ 3.35	-4.7%
Total Overall Payroll & Related Expenses												
Salaries, Wages, and Bonuses	$ 3,787,050	23.5	$ 11,147	$ 43.78	$ 3,072,073	-18.9%	21.4	-2.1%	$ 9,722	-12.8%	$ 37.82	-13.6%
Payroll-Related Expenses	1,248,176	7.8	$ 3,674	$ 14.43	1,041,651	-16.5%	7.3	-0.5%	$ 3,296	-10.3%	$ 12.82	-11.1%
Total Overall Payroll and Related Expenses	$ 5,035,226	31.3	$ 14,820	$ 58.21	$ 4,113,724	-18.3%	28.7	-2.6%	$ 13,018	-12.2%	$ 50.65	-13.0%

ROOM STATISTICS

Comparative Set - Average of 4 Properties

4	Number of Properties in Comparative Set
340	Average Number of Rooms
69.8%	Average Occupancy
$129.34	Average ADR
$90.23	Average RevPAR

ROOM STATISTICS

Subject Property

1	Number of Properties in Subject Set
316	Number of Rooms
70.4%	Occupancy
$128.97	ADR
$90.82	RevPAR

NC - Not Comparable

*Expressed as percentage points difference

Source: PKF Hospitality, a CBRE Company.

ries, wages, and bonuses, but more for benefits and payroll taxes (when calculated as a percentage of salaries, wages, and bonuses).

STR compiles summary and detailed financial operating data from nearly 6,000 full-service and limited-service properties through its Hotel Operating Statistics (HOST) program. Individual hotel data is gathered on revenues, operating expenses, and fixed charges from major chains, management companies, and independent hotels. The *HOST Almanac* is published annually and offers broad categories of comparability, including a summary report by full-service or limited-service, geographic region, location type (airport, city center, etc.), and class. The annual *HOST Almanac* is a relatively inexpensive industry resource and a good starting point for expense analysis.

To benchmark non-rooms revenue and expenses, STR offers the following reports:

1. Custom HOST Report (similar to PKF's Benchmarker Report)
2. Individualized HOST Report (includes five or more actual but masked individual P&L statements)
3. HOST P&L Profitability Scorecard (similar to PKF's Benchmarker Report from a comparative analysis standpoint but also providing a relative ranking versus each individual comp via a percentile ranking)
4. Monthly F&B STR Report

Exhibit 18 shows a sample custom HOST report. Similar to how the PKF tool is used, the asset manager can select the hotels from a database of contributor hotels maintained by STR. Similar to the STAR report, there are criteria that must be complied with to ensure the confidentiality of any individual hotel's performance among a consolidated set of data. Narrowing the list of hotels to those most similar to the subject hotel will result in a better comparison versus the broader, annual report. STR averages the data for each property and provides a consolidated and departmental profit and loss statement for two years, which the asset manager can use to compare to the subject hotel's historical performance.

Note that the three units of comparison on which the data is reported are percent of revenue/ratio to sales, per occupied room, and per available room. These metrics will be explained in further detail later in the chapter.

While the report does not provide the comparative analysis to the subject property (like the PKF Benchmarker report), it is similarly delivered in Excel, enabling the asset manager to create his/her own analysis.

One of the unique attributes of the STR Custom Report is a tab that provides a detailed revenue breakdown by department. For example, the report outlines F&B revenue by outlets, in-room dining, banquet and catering, mini-bar, and other. It can also provide breakdowns of other department revenue (golf, spa, and other), which is especially useful when benchmarking a resort property. For example, the report revenue shows spa revenue separately between treatment, salon, retail, and other revenue.

The table in Exhibit 19 shows a sample HOST P&L Individualized Report. The advantage of this report is that the asset manager receives data from each comp

Exhibit 18 STR Custom Report

STR ANALYTICS STR GLOBAL

STR Analytics & STR Global
2014 Custom HOST Report
Summary

	2014	2013
Props:	8	8
Rooms:	2,776	2,776
Occupancy:	70.5%	69.7%
ADR:	$157.62	$151.78
RevPAR:	$111.11	$105.73
TrevPAR:	$185.24	$179.11
GOPPAR:	$70.07	$64.46

Currency: *USD*

	2014			2013			Variance %	
	Ratio to Sales[1]	Amount Per Available Room	Amount Per Occupied Room Night	Ratio to Sales[1]	Amount Per Available Room	Amount Per Occupied Room Night	Amount Per Available Room	Amount Per Occupied Room Night
REVENUE	%	$	$	%	$	$	%	%
Food	22.8	15,398	59.98	23.0	15,010	59.14	2.6	1.4
Other Food & Beverage	5.6	3,793	14.77	5.6	3,679	14.50	3.1	1.9
Rentals & Other Income	1.6	1,091	4.25	1.8	1,247	4.91	(12.5)	(13.4)
TOTAL REVENUE	100.0 %	$ 67,614	$ 263.39	100.0 %	$ 65,376	$ 257.60	3.4 %	2.2 %
DEPARTMENTAL EXPENSES								
Food & Beverage	65.7	15,318	59.67	67.1	15,116	59.56	1.3	0.2
TOTAL DEPARTMENTAL EXPENSES	39.8 %	$ 26,514	$ 103.29	41.2 %	$ 26,516	$ 104.48	(0.0) %	(1.1) %
DEPARTMENTAL PROFITS								
Rooms	75.8 %	$ 30,690	$ 119.55	75.2 %	$ 28,980	$ 114.19	5.9 %	4.7 %
Other Operated Departments	41.6	1,322	5.14	31.9	1,231	4.85	7.4	6.0
TOTAL DEPARTMENTAL PROFITS	60.2 %	$ 41,100	$ 160.10	58.8 %	$ 38,860	$ 153.12	5.8 %	4.6 %
UNDISTRIBUTED OPERATING EXPENSES								
Marketing (*excluding Franchise Fees*)	7.2	4,885	19.03	7.6	4,968	19.58	(1.7)	(2.8)
Utility Costs	3.1	2,088	8.13	3.2	2,094	8.25	(0.3)	(1.5)
TOTAL UNDISTRIBUTED OPERATING EXPENSES	23.0	$ 15,524	$ 60.46	23.4	$ 15,333	$ 60.42	1.2 %	0.1 %
GROSS OPERATING PROFIT	37.2 %	$ 25,576	$ 99.64	35.4 %	$ 23,526	$ 92.70	8.7 %	7.5 %
Base Management Fees	2.4	$ 1,596	$ 6.22	2.6	$ 1,689	$ 6.65	(5.5)	(6.5)
INCOME BEFORE FIXED CHARGES	34.7 %	$ 23,941	$ 93.27	32.6 %	$ 21,710	$ 85.55	10.3 %	9.0 %
SELECTED FIXED CHARGES								
Rent	0.5 %	$ 309	$ 1.20	0.6 %	$ 361	$ 1.42	(14.5) %	(15.5) %
Insurance	0.6	412	1.61	0.6	392	1.55	5.1	3.9
EBITDA / NET OPERATING INCOME	29.3 %	$ 20,284	$ 79.02	27.4 %	$ 18,340	$ 72.27	10.6 %	9.3 %
SUPPLEMENTAL PAYROLL ANALYSIS[3]								
Rooms	13.1 %	$ 5,305	$ 20.67	13.3 %	$ 5,106	$ 20.12	3.9 %	2.7 %
Other Operated Departments	35.2	1,355	5.31	44.7	1,900	7.52	(28.7)	(29.4)
Marketing	2.9	1,986	7.74	3.0	1,936	7.63	2.6	1.4
TOTAL PAYROLL & RELATED EXPENSES	94.8 %	$ 21,385	$ 83.37	106.9 %	$ 21,784	$ 85.88	(1.8) %	(2.9) %
SUPPLEMENTAL FOOD & BEVERAGE INFORMATION[3]								
Cost of Food Sales	23.6 %	$ 3,536	$ 13.89	22.9 %	$ 3,350	$ 13.21	5.5 %	5.1 %
Total Cost of F&B Sales	18.5 %	$ 4,355	$ 17.10	18.3 %	$ 4,094	$ 16.14	6.4 %	5.9 %
Food & Beverage Payroll	38.0 %	$ 8,851	$ 34.48	40.0 %	$ 9,011	$ 35.51	(1.8) %	(2.9) %
Food & Beverage Other Expenses	11.9 %	$ 2,783	$ 10.84	10.6 %	$ 2,395	$ 9.44	16.2 %	14.8 %

[1] *Ratio to Sales for departmental expenses and profits are based on their respective departmental revenues. All other expense ratios are based on total revenue.*
[2] *EBITDA does not include Depreciation and Amortization, Interest, nor Income Taxes*
[3] *Payroll and Costs of Sales are included in expenses. Amounts shown here are for additional detail only. Not all participants provide detailed data on payroll and F&B costs; therefore, the following supplemental analyses provide the ratios for only those hotels in the samples that reported detailed information. Consequently, the amounts may not tie to the departmental figures provided.*

Source: STR, Inc.

rather than in aggregate. The asset manager is then able to evaluate best and worst performance metrics as well as median performance.

The report shows each of the five comparable (albeit masked) hotels' P&L data. Rooms expenses range from $23.67 to $31.21 with the majority falling between $25.67 and $27.35. Assuming that the asset manager has a general understanding of each of the comparables, (s)he can infer whether the mix of guestroom types and complexity of the subject guestroom justifies a cost structure at the low, high, or midpoint of the comparables.

The HOST Profitability Scorecard allows the asset manager to perform comparative benchmarking between the subject hotel and an aggregated set of similar hotels, and illustrates the property's percentile for each revenue and expense cate-

Exhibit 19 Individualized HOST Report

STR ANALYTICS

STR Analytics
2014 HOST P&L Individualized Report
Summary

2013		Comp 1	Comp 2	Comp 3	Comp 4	Comp 5
	Rooms:	200 - 400	200 - 400	200 - 400	200 - 400	200 - 400
	Occupancy:	70.0%	70.0%	70.0%	80.0%	70.0%
	ADR:	$140.00	$120.00	$120.00	$130.00	$140.00
	RevPAR:	$100.00	$90.00	$90.00	$110.00	$100.00

2013 Data

	Ratio to Sales					Amount Per Available Room					Amount Per Occupied Roomnight				
	Comp 1	Comp 2	Comp 3	Comp 4	Comp 5	Comp 1	Comp 2	Comp 3	Comp 4	Comp 5	Comp 1	Comp 2	Comp 3	Comp 4	Comp 5
	%	%	%	%	%	$	$	$	$	$	$	$	$	$	$
REVENUE															
Rooms	70.2 %	68.1 %	81.6 %	71.6 %	67.7 %	$34,946	$32,243	$27,310	$40,183	$35,587	$138.34	$122.51	$121.41	$134.51	$142.28
Food	21.5	25.9	14.2	20.0	24.2	10,695	12,257	4,738	11,241	12,720	42.33	46.57	21.06	37.63	50.86
Beverage	7.0	3.5	3.2	5.5	7.4	3,466	1,654	1,083	3,094	3,867	13.72	6.28	4.81	10.36	15.46
Telecommunications	0.6	0.6	0.1	0.3	0.4	301	292	34	193	223	1.19	1.11	0.15	0.65	0.89
Other Operated Departments	0.4	0.9	0.9	1.3	0.2	189	428	309	726	101	0.75	1.63	1.38	2.43	0.41
Rentals & Other Income	0.3	0.9	-	1.3	0.2	151	441	-	719	85	0.60	1.68	-	2.41	0.34
TOTAL REVENUE	100.0 %	100.0 %	100.0 %	100.0 %	100.0 %	100	100	100	100	100	100.00	100.00	100.00	100.00	100.00
DEPARTMENTAL EXPENSES															
Rooms	18.6 %	19.3 %	22.1 %	23.2 %	19.2 %	6,484	6,229	6,025	9,325	6,842	25.67	23.67	26.79	31.21	27.35
Food & Beverage	65.8	60.8	79.7	50.8	58.2	9,315	8,456	4,639	7,279	9,662	36.87	32.13	20.62	24.37	38.63
Telecommunications	153.4	103.5	114.1	126.1	99.4	462	302	39	243	222	1.83	1.15	0.17	0.81	0.89
Rental Income	-	-	-	-	-	-	-	-	-	-	-	-	-	-	-
Other Expenses	47.3	53.7	54.3	31.2	53.4	89	230	168	226	54	0.35	0.87	0.75	0.76	0.22
TOTAL DEPARTMENTAL EXPENSES	32.9 %	32.2 %	32.5 %	30.4 %	31.9 %	18,350	15,218	10,871	17,073	16,779	64.72	57.82	48.33	57.15	67.06
DEPARTMENTAL PROFITS															
Rooms	81.4 %	80.7 %	77.9 %	76.8 %	80.8 %	28,464	26,014	21,285	30,858	28,746	112.67	98.84	94.63	103.30	114.93
Food & Beverage	34.2	39.2	20.3	49.2	41.8	4,846	5,455	1,181	7,056	6,925	19.18	20.73	5.25	23.62	27.69
Telecommunications	(53.4)	(3.5)	(14.1)	(26.1)	0.6	(161)	(10)	(5)	(50)	1	(0.64)	(0.04)	(0.02)	(0.17)	0.01
Rental Income	100.0	100.0	100.0	100.0	100.0	151	441	-	719	85	0.60	1.68	-	2.41	0.34
Other Expenses	52.7	46.3	45.7	68.8	46.6	99	198	142	499	47	0.39	0.75	0.63	1.67	0.19
TOTAL DEPARTMENTAL PROFITS	67.1 %	67.8 %	67.5 %	69.6 %	68.1 %	33,399	32,098	22,603	39,082	35,805	132.21	121.96	100.49	130.83	143.15
UNDISTRIBUTED OPERATING EXPENSES															
Administrative & General	6.5 %	8.3 %	9.4 %	7.7 %	6.7 %	3,231	3,933	3,137	4,326	3,541	12.79	14.94	13.94	14.48	14.16
Marketing	8.1	11.4	6.2	7.5	9.2	4,051	5,385	2,079	4,205	4,823	16.04	20.46	9.24	14.08	19.28
Utility Costs	3.3	2.8	3.9	2.7	2.6	1,662	1,338	1,308	1,506	1,361	6.58	5.09	5.82	5.04	5.44
Property Operation & Maintenance	3.6	5.2	4.0	3.1	3.2	1,792	2,444	1,341	1,723	1,693	7.09	9.29	5.96	5.77	6.77
TOTAL UNDISTRIBUTED OPERATING EXPENSES	3.3 %	2.8 %	3.9 %	3.7 %	2.6 %	1,662	1,338	1,308	1,506	1,361	6.58	5.09	5.82	5.04	5.44
GROSS OPERATING PROFIT	45.6 %	40.0 %	44.0 %	48.6 %	46.5 %	22,662	18,996	14,736	27,322	24,387	89.71	72.16	65.52	91.46	97.50
Franchise Fees (Royalty)	3.5	3.4	3.0	5.1	5.0	1,747	1,612	997	2,875	2,620	6.92	6.13	4.43	9.62	10.47
Management Fees	3.5	1.0	3.0	3.0	3.5	1,747	470	1,008	1,687	1,855	6.91	1.79	4.48	5.65	7.42
INCOME BEFORE FIXED CHARGES	36.5 %	35.7 %	36.0 %	40.5 %	37.9 %	19,168	16,914	12,734	22,760	19,912	75.88	64.27	56.61	76.19	79.61
SELECTED FIXED CHARGES															
Taxes	- %	3.5 %	3.1 %	4.7 %	5.0 %	0	1,652	1,039	2,622	2,643	0.00	6.28	4.62	8.78	10.57
Insurance	0.6	0.7	1.0	0.6	0.6	278	332	350	343	291	1.10	1.26	1.56	1.15	1.16
Reserve For Capital Replacement	-	-	-	-	-	-	-	-	-	-	-	-	-	-	-
AMOUNT AVAILABLE FOR DEBT SERVICE & OTHER FIXED CHARGES [2]	37.9 %	31.5 %	33.9 %	34.4 %	32.3 %	18,890	32	11,345	34	34	74.78	31.50	50.44	34.40	34.40
SUPPLEMENTAL PAYROLL ANALYSIS [3]															
Rooms	33.0 %	4.9 %	- %	6.3 %	2.0 %	16,433	2,296	-	3,547	1,073	65.05	8.72	-	11.87	4.29
Total Food and Beverage	68.6	2.7	-	-	-	34,117	1,282	-	-	-	135.05	4.87	-	-	-
Telecommunications	2.8	-	-	-	-	1,401	-	-	-	-	5.54	-	-	-	-
Other Operated Departments	1.5	-	-	-	-	729	-	-	-	-	2.89	-	-	-	-
Administrative & General	13.4	2.1	-	1.6	0.7	6,655	990	-	897	373	26.34	3.76	-	3.00	1.49
Marketing	9.4	1.0	-	1.8	-	4,689	451	-	986	-	18.56	1.71	-	3.30	-
Property Operations & Maintenance	10.6	1.0	-	1.2	-	5,289	469	-	661	-	20.94	1.78	-	2.21	-
TOTAL PAYROLL & RELATED EXPENSES	139.3 %	11.6 %	- %	10.8 %	2.7 %	69,312	5,488	-	6,091	1,446	274.37	20.85	-	20.39	5.78

[1] *Ratio to Sales for departmental expenses and profits are based on their respective departmental revenues. All other expense ratios are based on total revenue.*
[2] *Other Fixed Charges include Depreciation and Amortization, Interest, Rent, and Equipment Leases.*
[3] *Payroll is included in expenses. Amounts shown here are for additional detail only. Not all participants provide detailed data on payroll; therefore, the following supplemental analyses provide the ratios for only these hotels in the samples that reported detailed information. Consequently, the amounts may not tie to the departmental figures provided.*

Source: STR, Inc.

gory. This report also provides similar labor data breakdown to the Benchmarker report, but not in a single tab. As can be seen in Exhibit 20, the report shows the subject hotel ranking in the 82nd percentile in terms of rooms revenue per available room, which is positive, but in only the 41st percentile for food revenue, suggesting an opportunity to improve food revenue (presuming the comparables all have similar outlet size and meeting space). The report also shows that the subject hotel's rooms expense of $40.67 is not only below the comp set average of $34.34, but ranks in the 1st quartile for cost, implying that 80 percent of the comp hotels selected outperform the subject hotel in rooms expense.

HotStats offers monthly profit and loss benchmarking for hotels located in the UK, Europe, and Middle East. The reports contain 100 performance metric comparisons. The HotStats database comprises operating data from 1,650 hotels representing 360,000 rooms. While there are many similarities between HotStats Classic Report and the PKF Benchmarker report, HotStats includes an aggregated comp data in annual summary and monthly data to enable analysis of seasonality trends, collects six rooms revenue market segmentation details, calculates banquet and catering revenue per square meter of meeting space, and breaks out credit card commissions from A&G—all of which are unique to this company.

HotStats is also beta-testing two additional reports:

1. HotStats KPI Report: a monthly report of key performance indicators of an aggregated set of comparable hotels that the asset manager can personally customize.
2. Hotel Market Profitability Forecast Report: a report prepared in conjunction with e-forecasting.com that projects changes in RevPAR and GOP for a market over a 36-month period.

Each of the HOST, Benchmarker, and HotStats reports are valuable because they offer the asset manager the ability to compare the subject property's performance with the results achieved by a set of similar hotels chosen based on specific criteria, including number of rooms, region, or RevPAR. There are several reasons why a hotel might operate differently from comparable properties, but looking at a representative sample of similar hotels' performance data can provide a reliable standard, forming a basis for asking important questions about the subject property's overall operation. It is important to reiterate that these tools should only be used to focus the asset manager's attention to certain areas and raise questions. An expense that seems out of line when compared to these industry reports may in fact be justified, so it is important to have a thorough understanding of the property and business.

Labor Expense Benchmarking: FTE/Productivity Metrics

In addition to the methodology detailed in the PKF labor benchmarking tool earlier in this chapter, labor can also be analyzed using other metrics besides POR/PAR. For example, two other metrics hotel asset managers use to analyze labor for their properties are full-time equivalents (FTEs) and efficiency/productivity.

FTEs are typically grouped into two categories, management and non-management. Management FTE counts usually comprise salaried (exempt) employ-

Exhibit 20 STR Profitability Scorecard

STR ANALYTICS

2013		Subject	Selected Set	Variance	Percentile
	Props:	1	98		
	Rooms:	390	315	23.8%	76%
	Occupancy:	73.8%	71.2%	3.7%	69%
	ADR:	$162.02	$137.19	18.1%	77%
	RevPAR:	$119.55	$99.21	20.5%	82%

Overall Grade	B+
	70

STR Analytics
2014 HOST P&L Profitability Scorecard
Summary

2013 Data

	Ratio to Sales				Amount Per Available Room				Amount Per Occupied Roomnight			
	Subject	Selected Set	Variance	Percentile	Subject	Selected Set	Variance	Percentile	Subject	Selected Set	Variance	Percentile
	%	%	%	%	$	$	%	%	$	$	%	%
REVENUE												
Rooms	70.0 %	67.4 %	3.9 %	58 %	43,634	36,211	20.5 %	82 %	$ 162.02	137.19	18.1 %	77 %
Food	13.9	19.3	-27.9	24	8,663	9,441	-8.0	41	32.24	36.31	-11.2	37
Beverage	2.4	3.9	-39.1	16	1,466	2,475	-40.8	38	5.44	7.87	-29.1	23
Other Food & Beverage	8.5	4.1	108.0	81	5,277	2,129	147.9	88	19.59	8.82	122.2	88
Telecommunications	0.7	0.4	71.9	78	439	218	101.4	82	1.63	0.85	91.1	81
Other Operated Departments	-	2.9	-100.0	-	-	1,735	-100.0	-	-	6.85	-100.0	-
Rentals & Other Income	3.7	0.5	638.6	98	2,332	240	871.7	98	8.66	0.94	818.1	98
Cancellation Fee	0.8	0.3	129.8	94	472	172	173.9	97	1.75	0.66	163.9	94
TOTAL REVENUE	100.0 %	100.0 %	0.0 %	100 %	62,303	52,626	18.4 %	89 %	$ 231.34	207.06	11.7 %	71 %
DEPARTMENTAL EXPENSES												
Rooms	25.1 %	24.7 %	1.8 %	44 %	10,953	8,735	25.4 %	17 %	$ 40.67	34.34	18.4 %	21 %
Food & Beverage	65.9	68.1	-3.1	64	10,172	9,976	2.0	48	37.77	36.95	2.2	48
Telecommunications	151.0	205.1	-26.4	68	663	479	38.4	21	2.46	1.86	32.5	25
Rental Income	-	53.0	-100.0	100	-	107	-100.0	100	-	0.38	-100.0	100
Other Expenses	-	40.0	-100.0	100	-	389	-100.0	100	-	1.65	-100.0	100
TOTAL DEPARTMENTAL EXPENSES	35.0 %	38.0 %	-7.9 %	68 %	21,788	20,032	8.6 %	37 %	$ 80.90	75.89	6.6 %	40 %
DEPARTMENTAL PROFITS												
Rooms	74.9 %	75.3 %	-0.6 %	44 %	32,682	27,218	20.1 %	81 %	$ 121.35	103.21	17.6 %	75 %
Food & Beverage	34.1	31.9	6.6	64	5,254	4,575	14.8	63	19.51	17.53	11.3	61
Telecommunications	(51.0)	(103.2)	-50.6	67	(224)	(181)	24.0	35	(0.83)	(0.68)	22.6	41
Rental Income	100.0	79.9	25.2	59	2,803	209	1243.8	99	10.41	0.87	1097.3	99
Other Expenses	-	81.6	-100.0	8	-	797	-100.0	9	-	3.28	-100.0	9
TOTAL DEPARTMENTAL PROFITS	65.0 %	62.0 %	4.9 %	68 %	40,515	32,656	24.1 %	75 %	$ 150.44	126.61	18.8 %	75 %
UNDISTRIBUTED OPERATING EXPENSES												
Administrative & General	9.4 %	8.7 %	7.7 %	37 %	5,833	4,623	26.2 %	23 %	$ 21.66	17.70	22.4 %	27 %
Marketing	6.5	8.3	-21.4	85	4,074	4,403	-7.5	64	15.13	17.16	-11.8	74
Utility Costs	4.5	4.1	9.0	41	2,802	2,236	25.3	20	10.40	8.45	23.1	25
Property Operation & Maintenance	4.9	4.6	5.2	42	3,048	2,497	22.1	24	11.32	9.52	18.8	30
TOTAL UNDISTRIBUTED OPERATING EXPENSES	25.3	26.1	-3.3	58	15,757	14,105	11.7	27	$ 58.51	55.01	6.4	33
GROSS OPERATING PROFIT	39.7 %	35.9 %	10.8 %	70 %	24,757	18,880	31.1 %	77 %	$ 91.93	73.00	25.9 %	78 %
Franchise Fees (Royalty)	-	4.0	-100.0	100	-	1,954	-100.0	100	-	7.26	-100.0	100
Management Fees	3.9	3.0	31.9	6	2,442	1,410	73.3	6	9.07	5.41	67.5	9
INCOME BEFORE FIXED CHARGES	36.8 %	30.7 %	16.8 %	71 %	22,315	16,451	35.6 %	78 %	$ 82.86	63.44	30.6 %	75 %
SELECTED FIXED CHARGES												
Taxes	3.2 %	2.9 %	8.8 %	45 %	1,982	1,674	18.4 %	35 %	$ 7.36	6.55	12.4 %	40 %
Insurance	0.8	0.7	19.6	38	528	364	45.2	30	1.96	1.41	39.8	35
Reserve For Capital Replacement	2.9	5.0	-41.2	3	1,832	2,515	-27.2	6	6.80	9.32	-27.0	6
AMOUNT AVAILABLE FOR DEBT SERVICE & OTHER FIXED CHARGES [2]	28.8 %	25.7 %	12.1 %	82 %	17,973	12,966	38.6 %	76 %	$ 66.74	51.22	30.3 %	75 %
SUPPLEMENTAL PAYROLL ANALYSIS [3]												
Rooms	14.9 %	14.6 %	2.2 %	42 %	6,507	5,086	27.9 %	15 %	$ 24.16	19.06	26.7 %	19 %
Total Food and Beverage	42.5	40.8	4.2	38	6,556	5,864	11.8	41	24.34	22.65	7.5	39
Telecommunications	82.0	121.9	-32.8	73	360	362	-0.6	52	1.34	1.42	-5.7	55
Other Operated Departments	-	29.8	-100.0	100	-	423	-100.0	100	-	1.73	-100.0	100
Administrative & General	4.3	4.4	-3.7	56	2,668	2,382	12.0	40	9.91	9.31	6.4	44
Marketing	2.9	3.1	-5.3	59	1,817	1,610	12.9	40	6.75	6.06	11.3	41
Property Operations & Maintenance	2.5	2.1	17.1	33	1,560	1,143	36.5	23	5.79	4.42	31.1	27
TOTAL PAYROLL & RELATED EXPENSES	31.2 %	31.6 %	-1.2 %	53 %	19,468	16,935	15.0 %	29 %	$ 72.29	64.82	11.5 %	34 %
SUPPLEMENTAL FOOD & BEVERAGE INFORMATION [3]												
Cost of Food Sales	21.5 %	24.2 %	-11.1 %	76 %	1,865	2,300	-18.9 %	66 %	$ 6.93	9.23	-24.9 %	72 %
Cost of Beverage Sales	20.9	21.3	-1.6	56	307	424	-27.6	67	1.14	1.61	-29.2	70
Total Cost of F&B Sales	14.1 %	19.9 %	-29.2 %	98 %	2,172	2,809	-22.7 %	70 %	$ 8.07	10.83	-25.5 %	73 %
Food & Beverage Payroll	42.5 %	40.8 %	4.2 %	38 %	6,556	5,864	11.8 %	41 %	$ 24.34	22.65	7.5 %	39 %
Food & Beverage Other Expenses	9.4 %	7.1 %	31.4 %	25 %	1,444	960	50.3 %	30 %	$ 5.36	3.74	43.3 %	30 %

[1] *Ratio to Sales for departmental expenses and profits are based on their respective departmental revenues. All other expense ratios are based on total revenue.*

[2] *Other Fixed Charges include Depreciation and Amortization, Interest, Rent, and Equipment Leases.*

[3] *Payroll and Costs of Sales are included in expenses. Amounts shown here are for additional detail only. Not all participants provide detailed data on payroll and F&B costs; therefore, the following supplemental analyses provide the ratios for only these hotels in the samples that reported detailed information. Consequently, the amounts may not tie to the departmental figures provided.*

Source: STR, Inc.

ees and are benchmarked against hotels with similar sizes/number of keys. Conversely, non-management FTEs usually include hourly paid associates who fall under certain federally mandated working conditions such as overtime regulations and break recording. Obviously, hotels with higher service standards such as luxury resorts will have more FTEs than limited-service hotels with similar key counts. Also, properties that are not encumbered by a collective bargaining agreement generally will have greater efficiencies and more flexibility in staffing.

- Management FTEs: Property operations require a base level of managers/department heads. As hotels grow in size and complexity, more managers are required to successfully operate the hotel. Theoretically, a hotel with 500 keys and 25,000 square feet of meeting space should have more management FTEs than a 100-key select-service hotel with limited meeting space. A productive management FTE benchmarking exercise would use a similar size/type of hotel to get the most accurate comparison of hotels operations.
- Non-management FTEs: These FTEs are usually positions that can be flexed and more actively managed in terms of productivity. As a result, occupancy levels, footprint of asset, operational service standards and labor agreements should all be considered in the selection of benchmarking opportunities.

Labor efficiency measurement is vital in determining the effectiveness of a particular operation. For example, in the rooms department, efficiency in housekeeping is usually measured in how many minutes it takes to clean an occupied room (MPOR). This number is typically measured as an aggregate of the amount of time to clean check-outs and stay-overs. Many factors determine the impact on efficiency for any given hotel:

- Size of guestroom: Larger guestrooms with more items to clean (such as a five-fixture bathroom) will require more time than smaller, less complicated products.
- Type of guest: Guestrooms occupied by families with more occupants per guestroom will typically require more attention in the cleaning process than a prototypical solo business traveler.
- Stay pattern: Longer stay patterns result in more stay-over rooms that require less attention and time to clean.
- Collective bargaining agreement: Some properties have agreements that dictate the number of rooms/credits housekeepers must clean on a daily basis. As a result, it may be more difficult to enhance productivity.
- Employee turnover: Properties with high turnover struggle to keep productivity up due to the constant training of new associates to perform the job at a high level.
- Cleaning systems: Many hotels have implemented third-party cleaning systems such as the PDQ Steps Program. These programs require an investment by the property/owner and give specific tools and cleaning guidelines to help improve productivity.

When benchmarking labor productivity in housekeeping, asset managers should be sure to account for the above factors when selecting appropriate comparables.

Calculating Flow Through and Flex

One way to determine the efficiency and financial agility of a hotel operation is to look at its flow through/flex in relation to the desired profitability benchmark (usually GOP or EBITDA). Flow through and flex can be calculated based on actual results relative to budget, actual results relative to last year, or budget projections relative to last year.

Flow through is the rate at which incremental revenue relative a comparable time period (usually budget or prior year) filters down to the bottom line of a property's P&L. *Flex* is used when revenues decrease relative to budget or last year and can be defined as the amount of profit that is saved as revenue declines.

When revenue increases, flow through is calculated as follows:

$$\text{Flow through} = \frac{\text{Actual GOP} - \text{Baseline GOP}}{\text{Actual Revenue} - \text{Baseline Revenue}}$$

When revenues decrease, expense flex is calculated as follows:

$$\text{Expense flex} = 1 - \frac{(\text{Actual GOP} - \text{Baseline GOP})}{\text{Actual Revenue} - \text{Baseline Revenue}}$$

The standard goal for flow through or flex is typically 50 percent; however, it will vary depending on what is driving the revenue increase or decline as well as other outside factors. For example, if a revenue increase is rate driven, we would expect the flow through to be higher, given there are few additional variable expenses that would need to be added to generate the additional revenue.

Revenue flow through and expense flex can be calculated for individual departments as well as on a GOP and EBITDA level. Sample calculations of flow through and expense flex for the different scenarios are included in Chapter Appendix 2.

Other Sources of Comparable Hotel Data

In addition to industry-wide databases and custom reports derived from them, various publications can be useful. These are most commonly written by regional hotel real estate brokerages and consulting or accounting firms that provide local benchmarking data, from the *Pinnacle Report* that provides occupancy and ADR benchmarking for hotels in Massachusetts to the *Hospitality Benchmark Report* published by KPMG providing revenue, expense, and labor details about hotels in the Netherlands. The asset manager should research regional as well as the national data sources to most effectively benchmark.

To the extent possible, the asset manager should also collect individual operating statements from properties similar to the subject hotel. These comparables may be shared with the asset manager by consultants and other hospitality real estate professionals, or the asset manager may use internal data from a portfolio of managed assets to develop comparable operating statements. In addition, to the extent available, the asset manager should request copies of operating statements of comparable hotels currently operated by the management company of the hotel or ask the hotel to compile an average of these statements. This will allow the asset manager to benchmark how the hotel operates relative to other hotels in the management company's portfolio and help identify areas of opportunity where the management company may be able to implement best practices or other successful strategies from hotels within its portfolio.

Balance Sheet Benchmarking

There are certain key metrics that asset managers can use to benchmark a property's internal balance sheet. When done properly, asset managers can glean the health and performance of specific operations with significant granularity. For example, the beverage inventory in a fine dining restaurant is typically a function of the restaurant's wine selection. If an asset manager compares inventory of similar venues and finds a large variance in the wine inventory between the two properties, then this discrepancy may provide an analytical direction, and investigating the cause of the difference may prove prudent. Upon further investigation, an asset manager may find an accumulated stock of wine that is nearing its "turning" or deterioration point, or may find that the inventory contains a surfeit of underperforming products, and purchasing changes may need to be made. These insights and many others are possible through a combination of investigative accounting methods and process-based analysis.

Moreover, benchmarking against industry standard ratios is a useful tool in the asset manager's arsenal. For example, a property's food inventory should typically constitute about 25 percent of the monthly food cost. This benchmark can be applied across many restaurant and F&B operations without the necessity of the detailed information of other operations.

Other items that can be benchmarked and analyzed within the balance sheet include:

- Cash reserves, usually on a per-key or per-guestroom basis
- Receivables, typically using standard aging metrics
- Inventory (e.g., food, beverage, guest supplies, retail, etc.), based on a percentage of revenues, expenses, or other standard operating metrics
- Insurance, using accrual procedures
- Working capital, usually on a per-key basis
- Vacation, using accrual procedures
- Incentive compensation, using accrual procedures

Additional Benchmarking Opportunities

Benchmarking can also be used in other areas of the asset management arena. These include valuation, management contract negotiation, guest satisfaction, capital expenditures, and web analytics:

1. *Valuation:* Comparable sales can be gathered through industry resources to aid in determining a market value for the property. Just as in the revenue and expense benchmarking process, it is important to gather data from sales of properties with similar characteristics to the subject hotel. Typically, sales are compared on a per-key basis as well as a cap rate basis.
2. *Management contract negotiation:* In some instances, the asset manager will be called upon to negotiate a new management agreement for a property or to amend an outdated agreement. In this process, term sheets or draft management agreements can be benchmarked against existing management agreements to the extent that these documents are available. This will help an asset manager determine the appropriate market terms for contracts and where there may be opportunities to negotiate a more favorable deal to have an impact on the asset's overall value. In management contract benchmarking, it is common to compare contracts from the same management company. It is also important to use recently negotiated contracts, as management contract terms tend to change over time, and older contract terms and provisions may no longer be relevant.
3. *Guest satisfaction:* A majority of hotel management companies have some form of guest satisfaction survey that is given to guests following their stay. This data is typically compiled into a report format for review. In most instances, the report benchmarks the subject hotel to the average for the entire brand or management company. This benchmarking can help identify recurring guest issues that need to be addressed. Moreover, this presents an opportunity to tweak processes and implement practices from higher-performing hotels.
4. *CapEx spending:* Benchmarking can also be used as part of the capital decision-making process. When reviewing proposed capital projects throughout the year, the asset manager can compare proposed pricing with the amounts spent on other projects at other properties, which allows the asset manager to determine whether an opportunity to reduce the amount spent on a specific project might exist. In addition, from a local market standpoint, the asset manager should benchmark the subject hotel against its competitive set from an amenities or product quality standpoint and determine if additional capital must be invested in the property.
5. *Web analytics:* As the majority of marketing expenses are now digital and measurable, the importance of monitoring and comparing results of online marketing, search engine results, website productivity, revenue-sourcing, and demand flow becomes increasingly important. For example, benchmarking the return on investment of marketing campaigns through brand resources such as Hilton's EDGE program is vital in strategic planning of marketing spend. As with the other techniques discussed, benchmarking the digital metrics of a property's competitive set will offer asset managers insight into the practices and weaknesses of the property's overall online strategy.

Some hotels, specifically upscale and luxury properties, have begun using other benchmarking tools to help them maximize revenue and profitability, such as revenue per available customer (RevPAC) and gross operating profit per available customer (GOPAC). These statistics can help hotels identify their most profitable customers, which the hotels can then use to create products and marketing strategies tailored to attract them. While not as widely used as other benchmarking metrics, RevPAC and GOPAC are additional examples of how benchmarking can be used.

Conclusion

Several resources are available to asset managers for benchmarking the performance of lodging assets. In addition to industry-wide databases, a hotel asset manager can rely on user-defined compilations of data to evaluate a hotel's relative performance. These industry data sources provide powerful tools for understanding a hotel's current performance in comparison to competitors' results and for identifying the hotel's potential.

The asset manager's review of a property's revenue and expense performance must be timely—at a minimum, on a monthly basis. The majority of statistical data is available from the lodging industry's research and advisory firms on a weekly or monthly basis, permitting virtually continuous benchmarking of a property's current performance. Studying a wide range of data and publications provides the asset manager with a strong framework for analysis and decision-making.

Variance and comparative analyses of financial performance using reliable industry norms can reveal opportunities to increase operational efficiency and profitability. Improved operating performance validates the asset management function, enhancing a property's market value and protecting the owner's equity interest in the investment. Again, though, it is very important to note that all of these tools, while extremely useful, are merely tools; it is in the evaluation of the resources where the asset manager adds value to ownership. Variance analysis and comparative analysis are best at raising questions or flagging areas for further inquiry, but it is dangerous to draw conclusions from these analyses without discussing them with management and fully understanding the property. Asset managers can also use benchmarking beyond just the financial area. We have briefly touched on some of these additional areas, which include valuation, management contract negotiation, guest satisfaction analysis, the CapEx process, and web analytics. In almost every case when benchmarking is used in these additional areas, it is important to make sure that the items being compared are as similar as possible.

Chapter Appendix 1

Asset Management Value-Enhancing Questions

Rooms Division Questions	***Asset Management Suggestions***
• How many rooms do room attendants clean each day? • Is the property offering more services and amenities than the brand standards dictate? • How much does the hotel spend on linen, towels, and in-room guest amenities on a POR basis? • What is the efficiency of the laundry operation, as measured in number of pounds of laundry cleaned per labor hour?	• Review labor productivity. Consider front of house cross training and implementation of incentive programs. • Consider cleaning standards, both checkout vs. stay-over, and evaluate specialized cleaning training programs and tools to improve efficiency. • Consider revising amenities package, club floor offerings, and operating supplies to reduce costs (but not at the expense of guest experience or brand standard). • Implement a green program. • Consider outsourcing laundry.
Food & Beverage Division Questions	***Asset Management Suggestions***
• What is the breakdown of outlet revenue vs. banquet and catering revenue? (Catering tends to be more profitable than outlet revenues.) • Is the hotel's banquet service charge at market price? • What is the catering and banquet revenue per occupied group room? • What is the food and beverage capture ratio by meal period? (i.e., how many of the in-house guests are eating meals at the hotel?) • Has a departmental organizational chart been reviewed and critically evaluated? • Have food, beverage and labor cost percentages been evaluated using comparative analysis?	• Evaluate pricing and menu mix at restaurants via benchmarking of prices at other area restaurants. • Evaluate opportunity to increase capture of food and beverage demand from local residents. • Determine catering goals for the sales staff, including group food and beverage requirements. • Brainstorm off-site catering opportunities. • Evaluate possibility of increasing audio visual profitability by renegotiating the contract. • Ensure management is regularly bidding its food and beverage purveyors. • Check pour control mechanisms, beverage mix and policy on free drinks if beverage cost seems high. • Consider closing outlets during slower meal periods to reduce labor hours. • Consider decreasing overall complexity or service level of menu/outlets to decrease kitchen labor cost. • Evaluate ROI on live entertainment.

<table>
<tr>
<td>

Other Revenue Questions

- What do competitors charge for overnight parking, health spa services, resort fee, and exercise facility access?
- Are guests of the property charged for Internet access capabilities, fax service at the front desk, additional amenities, or minibar service?
- What is the hotel's policy on cancellations?

</td>
<td>

Asset Management Suggestions

- Consider selling parking to non-guests.
- Determine whether exercise, spa or other hotel amenities are of a caliber and size that the hotel could solicit outside memberships.
- Identify and evaluate opportunity to lease space at the hotel to a third party retail tenant.
- Evaluate adjusting compensation for spa massage therapists.

</td>
</tr>
<tr>
<td>

Administrative and General Questions

- Has a departmental organizational chart been reviewed and critically evaluated?
- What travel-related and training expenses are being charged to the hotel?
- What corporate management charges are being allocated to the property for human resource or financial reporting services, and how are they being allocated?
- Is accounting done on-site or at a corporate office?
- What is the hotel's program for ensuring guest and employee safety and thereby reducing accidents?
- Is security performed in-house or outsourced to a third party?
- How does the property attract talent?

</td>
<td>

Asset Management Suggestions

- Evaluate staffing and opportunity to reduce management or administrative support positions.
- Solicit bids on general liability insurance and understand why premiums are at current levels. Determine if increasing the hotel's deductible would help reduce insurance expense.
- Renegotiate credit card agreements.
- Evaluate the use of executive/employee search firms.
- Evaluate time management software.
- Consider cluster positions (HR).
- Reduce printing/licensing electronics.
- Audit centralized charges.

</td>
</tr>
<tr>
<td>

Information & Telecommunications Questions

- What are the current contract commitments for the property?
- How is IT staffed?
- What telecommunications services does the hotel provide?
- How secure is the property's credit card and guest information data?

</td>
<td>

Asset Management Suggestions

- Evaluate scope and price of maintenance contracts.
- Consider outsourcing the IT function.
- Reduce software licenses per application.
- Evaluate and audit the sensitive data system security and ensure appropriate insurance protection is in place.

</td>
</tr>
</table>

Sales & Marketing Questions	***Asset Management Suggestions***
• Have the property's market plan and departmental organizational chart been reviewed and critically evaluated? • How are corporate marketing/advertising fees and frequent guest charge fees calculated and allocated? • How does the on-site team work with the brand's national sales force to generate business? • What is the current pay-per-click budget and strategy? • What is the sales department deployment or breakdown of employee responsibility (i.e., are sales managers assigned specific regions or market segments)? • How is the marketing budget, particularly for travel, trade shows and entertainment, determined? It is zero-based? What control mechanisms are in place? • How is the revenue management team structured?	• Ensure that revenue goals are defined and tracked for each employee in the sales department. • Evaluate employees' salaries vs. revenue goals for reasonableness/appropriate ROI. • Evaluate ROI on pay-per-click. • Evaluate profitability of market segments by allocating resources costs to capture. • Evaluate benefit/detriment of shared/clustered revenue management services. • Review marketing budget and allocations to ensure dollars are not wasted on fruitless campaigns.
Property Operations & Maintenance Questions	***Asset Management Suggestions***
• Does the hotel have a scheduled preventive maintenance program for all equipment and guest rooms? How is it monitored and tracked? • How many contracted serviced are utilized? • Is aged equipment creating excessive labor or parts expense?	• Review all contracts for services and labor, including elevator, trash removal, and snow removal, and bid each contract out annually or upon expiration/opportunity to terminate. • Review the preventative maintenance process, including communication with housekeeping—evaluate ROI of service optimization software. • Prepare ROI for aged equipment (replacement cost vs. maintenance expense).

Utilities Questions	***Asset Management Suggestions***
• Has the hotel taken advantage of any available energy deregulation opportunities? • Does the hotel have a building or energy management system (BMS/EMS)? If so, how effectively is it being used? • Are the domestic waters set at the most effective temperature (typically 115-125 degrees Fahrenheit)? • Does the property have incandescent lighting which can be replaced with more energy efficient alternatives? • Does the property utilize water saving "low flow" plumbing fixtures or control apparatuses? • Does the property have (and follow) guestroom temperature SOP's/protocols for housekeeping?	• Consider completing an energy audit to determine opportunities to decrease cost (some local utilities will provide them free of charge). • Complete ROI analysis of installing an energy management system. • Ensure that the hotel solicits competitive bids for deregulated utilities—evaluate usefulness of multi-year contracts. • Evaluate ROI for LED and other energy efficient lighting (including potential utility rebates for conversion). • Evaluate installing low flow plumbing fixtures.
Insurance Questions	***Asset Management Suggestions***
• Does the hotel solicit competitive bids for insurance? • How are replacement cost and deductibles determined? Do they conform with management contract and lender requirements? • What risk factors (flood zone, seismic, windstorm, etc.) impact the property's insurance rates and what efforts have been taken to mitigate? • If the manager procures insurance, how are premiums allocated across the portfolio and are allocations reasonable for the property?	• Study potential reasonableness of increasing the deductible to reduce expense. • Determine the property's eligibility for premium discounts based on its management/ franchise affiliation or claim history. • Conduct a risk management audit to identify opportunities. • Complete ROI analyses on risk mitigation measures.
Real Estate and Personal Property Tax Questions	***Asset Management Suggestions***
• How does the per room building assessment of the hotel compare to other hotels in the same municipality? • Is the assessment income-based? How has the hotel's income changed in recent years? • Does the hotel employ a tax consultant?	• Consider engagement of a property tax consultant and contesting the real estate tax assessment as possible by jurisdiction.

Management/Franchise Fee Questions	***Asset Management Suggestions***
• Is the hotel being charged the proper base and incentive management fee? • What are the calculations for the hotel's franchise royalty and other franchise related fees?	• Review and discuss contracted fees; understand calculations for allocated management and franchise related costs. • Compare fees being charged to management and franchise agreements. Make sure hotel is receiving the negotiated services for the fees.
General Labor Questions	***Asset Management Suggestions***
• Has an organizational chart for the hotel been reviewed? It should include all management positions by department. • Are the hotel's employees unionized? • Are the salaries and wages of the hotel's employees at competitive levels? • Do employees pay for meals?	• Identify and evaluate opportunities to cross-train associates within and among departments. • Consider replacing overtime hours with contracted labor. • Identify and evaluate opportunities to reduce supervisors, middle management staffing or number of full time employees per shift. • Consider purchasing/upgrading the property's labor management system.

Chapter Appendix 2

Examples of Revenue Flow Through and Expense Flex Scenarios

EXPECTATIONS FOR REVENUE FLOW THROUGH SCENARIOS will vary depending on the cause of the incremental revenue. For example, when rooms revenue increases are driven by incremental room rate, the incremental rate does not entail incremental operating cost, and thus should be highly profitable. The only additional costs associated with this incremental revenue are expenses tied to revenue, such as management fees, franchise fees, marketing and other fees based on revenue, credit card commissions, and FF&E reserve. These associated costs typically combine to average 10 percent. Therefore, ninety cents of every incremental dollar of rate would be expected to flow to the bottom line in this scenario.

On the other hand, when rooms revenue increases are driven by increased occupancy, the incremental occupied rooms do entail incremental operating costs. These costs include labor (housekeeping, front office, engineering, F&B), guest supplies, laundry, and utilities as well as the revenue-related expenses, among others. Since profit margin expectations should be tempered relative to rate-driven growth, flow through expectations in this scenario typically would be closer to 50–60 percent.

When revenues increase, profits may increase or decrease. Exhibits A-1 and A-2 present sample calculations for these two situations, respectively.

Similarly, flex expense scenarios result from different causes that can lead to different expectations. For example, when rooms revenue falls short of baseline because of an occupancy shortfall, some expenses may also decline because less labor, supplies, utilities, etc., are needed to execute operations. Fewer guests checking in means shifts can be reduced at the front desk, housekeepers are not cleaning as many rooms and it may be possible to eliminate shifts, F&B staff won't have as many potential customers, and utility costs will be modestly reduced because fewer guests are using the electricity and water in the rooms. The key to maximize flexing opportunities is accurate forecasting.

On the other hand, if an F&B revenue shortfall is caused by a decline in banquet and catering revenue, flexing overall F&B department expenses is much harder to do. Outlets generally run at a significantly lower profit margin than banquet and catering, since most outlet meals are à la carte preparations requiring more individualized service, while banquet and catering functions have broader service requirements and food is usually prepared buffet style or pre-planned with limited option plating. Again, accurate forecasting by the catering team and banquet events manager is critical for staffing the banquet and catering functions to make them as efficient and profitable as possible.

When revenues decrease, profits may increase or decrease. Exhibits A-3 and A-4 present sample calculations for these two situations, respectively.

EXHIBIT A-1

Flow Through—Revenues Increase and Profits Increase

hotelAVE

	ACTUAL		BUDGET		*VARIANCE*	
Number of Rooms	350		350		-	
Available Rooms	127,750		127,750		-	
Occupied Rooms	91,980		89,425		2,555	
Occupancy	***72.0%***		***70.0%***		***2.0%***	
ADR	***$160.00***		***$150.00***		***$10.00***	
RevPAR	***$115.20***		***$105.00***		***$10.20***	
Operating Revenue	**Amount $**	**%**	**Amount $**	**%**	**Amount $**	**%**
Rooms	14,716,800	63.1%	13,413,750	61.6%	1,303,050	82.8%
F&B	8,200,000	35.1%	8,000,000	36.8%	200,000	12.7%
Other Operated Departments	300,000	1.3%	250,000	1.1%	50,000	3.2%
Miscellaneous Income	120,000	0.5%	100,000	0.5%	20,000	1.3%
Total Revenue	**23,336,800**	**100.0%**	**21,763,750**	**100.0%**	**1,573,050**	**100.0%**
						Flex/Flow
Operating Profit						
Rooms	10,450,000	71.0%	9,400,000	70.1%	1,050,000	80.6%
F&B	2,600,000	31.7%	2,500,000	31.3%	100,000	50.0%
Other Operated Departments	125,000	41.7%	100,000	40.0%	25,000	50.0%
Miscellaneous Income	120,000	100.0%	100,000	100.0%	20,000	100.0%
Total Departmental Profit	**13,295,000**	**57.0%**	**12,100,000**	**55.6%**	**1,195,000**	**76.0%**
Total Undistributed	**5,200,000**	**22.3%**	**5,035,000**	**23.1%**	**165,000**	**10.5%**
Gross Operating Profit	**8,095,000**	**34.7%**	**7,065,000**	**32.5%**	**1,030,000**	**65.5%**
GOP Flex/Flow			FLOW --->		**65%**	

EXHIBIT A-2

Flow Through—Revenues Increase and Profits Decrease

hotelAVE

	ACTUAL		BUDGET		VARIANCE	
Number of Rooms	350		350		-	
Available Rooms	127,750		127,750		-	
Occupied Rooms	91,980		89,425		2,555	
Occupancy	*72.0%*		*70.0%*		*2.0%*	
ADR	*$160.00*		*$150.00*		*$10.00*	
RevPAR	*$115.20*		*$105.00*		*$10.20*	
Operating Revenue	**Amount $**	**%**	**Amount $**	**%**	**Amount $**	**%**
Rooms	14,716,800	63.1%	13,413,750	61.6%	1,303,050	82.8%
F&B	8,200,000	35.1%	8,000,000	36.8%	200,000	12.7%
Other Operated Departments	300,000	1.3%	250,000	1.1%	50,000	3.2%
Miscellaneous Income	120,000	0.5%	100,000	0.5%	20,000	1.3%
Total Revenue	**23,336,800**	**100.0%**	**21,763,750**	**100.0%**	**1,573,050**	**100.0%**
						Flex/Flow
Operating Profit						
Rooms	9,650,000	65.6%	9,400,000	70.1%	250,000	19.2%
F&B	2,275,000	27.7%	2,500,000	31.3%	(225,000)	-112.5%
Other Operated Departments	125,000	41.7%	100,000	40.0%	25,000	50.0%
Miscellaneous Income	120,000	100.0%	100,000	100.0%	20,000	100.0%
Total Departmental Profit	**12,170,000**	**52.1%**	**12,100,000**	**55.6%**	**70,000**	**4.4%**
Total Undistributed	**5,200,000**	**22.3%**	**5,035,000**	**23.1%**	**165,000**	**10.5%**
Gross Operating Profit	**6,970,000**	**29.9%**	**7,065,000**	**32.5%**	**(95,000)**	**-6.0%**
GOP Flex/Flow			FLOW --->		**-6%**	

EXHIBIT A-3

Expense Flex—Revenues Decrease and Profits Decrease

hotelAVE

	ACTUAL		BUDGET		*VARIANCE*	
Number of Rooms	350		350		-	
Available Rooms	127,750		127,750		-	
Occupied Rooms	83,038		89,425		(6,388)	
Occupancy	***65.0%***		***70.0%***		***-5.0%***	
ADR	***$150.00***		***$150.00***		***$0.00***	
RevPAR	***$97.50***		***$105.00***		***-$7.50***	
Operating Revenue	**Amount $**	**%**	**Amount $**	**%**	**Amount $**	**%**
Rooms	12,455,625	60.2%	13,413,750	61.6%	(958,125)	88.5%
F&B	7,800,000	37.7%	8,000,000	36.8%	(200,000)	18.5%
Other Operated Departments	300,000	1.5%	250,000	1.1%	50,000	-4.6%
Miscellaneous Income	125,000	0.6%	100,000	0.5%	25,000	-2.3%
Total Revenue	**20,680,625**	**100.0%**	**21,763,750**	**100.0%**	**(1,083,125)**	**100.0%**
Operating Profit						*Dept. Flex/Flow*
Rooms	8,700,000	69.8%	9,400,000	70.1%	(700,000)	26.9%
F&B	2,320,000	29.7%	2,500,000	31.3%	(180,000)	10.0%
Other Operated Departments	120,000	40.0%	100,000	40.0%	20,000	40.0%
Miscellaneous Income	125,000	100.0%	100,000	100.0%	25,000	100.0%
Total Departmental Profit	**11,265,000**	**54.5%**	**12,100,000**	**55.6%**	**(835,000)**	**22.9%**
					-	
Total Undistributed	**4,900,000**	**23.7%**	**5,000,000**	**23.0%**	**(100,000)**	**90.8%**
					-	
Gross Operating Profit	**6,365,000**	**30.8%**	**7,100,000**	**32.6%**	**(735,000)**	**32.1%**
GOP Flex/Flow			FLEX --->		**32%**	

EXHIBIT A-4

Expense Flex—Revenues Decrease and Profits Increase

hotelAVE

	ACTUAL		BUDGET		VARIANCE	
Number of Rooms	350		350		-	
Available Rooms	127,750		127,750		-	
Occupied Rooms	83,038		89,425		(6,388)	
Occupancy	***65.0%***		***70.0%***		***-5.0%***	
ADR	***$150.00***		***$150.00***		***$0.00***	
RevPAR	***$97.50***		***$105.00***		***-$7.50***	
Operating Revenue	**Amount $**	**%**	**Amount $**	**%**	**Amount $**	**%**
Rooms	12,455,625	60.2%	13,413,750	61.6%	(958,125)	88.5%
F&B	7,800,000	37.7%	8,000,000	36.8%	(200,000)	18.5%
Other Operated Departments	300,000	1.5%	250,000	1.1%	50,000	-4.6%
Miscellaneous Income	125,000	0.6%	100,000	0.5%	25,000	-2.3%
Total Revenue	**20,680,625**	**100.0%**	**21,763,750**	**100.0%**	**(1,083,125)**	**100.0%**
						Dept. Flex/Flow
Operating Profit						
Rooms	9,500,000	76.3%	9,400,000	70.1%	100,000	110.4%
F&B	2,320,000	29.7%	2,500,000	31.3%	(180,000)	10.0%
Other Operated Departments	120,000	40.0%	100,000	40.0%	20,000	40.0%
Miscellaneous Income	125,000	100.0%	100,000	100.0%	25,000	100.0%
Total Departmental Profit	**12,065,000**	**58.3%**	**12,100,000**	**55.6%**	**(35,000)**	**96.8%**
					-	
Total Undistributed	**4,900,000**	**23.7%**	**5,000,000**	**23.0%**	**(100,000)**	**90.8%**
					-	
Gross Operating Profit	**7,165,000**	**34.6%**	**7,100,000**	**32.6%**	**65,000**	**106.0%**
GOP Flex/Flow			FLEX --->		**106%**	

Chapter Appendix 3 Summary of *USALI* Changes

hotelAVE hotelAVE

USALI 11th Edition – Key Changes and P&L Implications

Asset Management • Loan Surveillance • Lender Support • Receivership • Acquisition Due Diligence • Manager & Franchise Selection • Development & Repositioning Services • Project Management • Property Management

Fees, Performance Test & Incentive Fee Implications:

CHANGE	IMPACT
RevPAR (but not likely RevPAR penetration)	
Rooms Revenue excludes Resort Fee (p 82)	Reduce RevPAR but not penetration if uniform for all hotels.
Package Revenue Accounting Clarification (p 13)	Unknown. Allocation of revenue is based on retail pricing. Previously non-rooms revenue allocations were more arbitrary.
Package Revenue Breakage (p 82)	Reduce RevPAR if included in Rooms previously. Clearly now in Miscellaneous.
Rebates or Subsidies to Group (p 10)	Reduce RevPAR. No longer expense; contra-revenue.
Surcharges and Service Charges (p 10)	Included in hotel ADR if meet Gross (vs. Net) test. No change from 10th Edition. Risk is if Operators try to change Resort Fee to Surcharge or Service Charge. (Many management contracts already exclude service charges from definition of revenue).
Rooms sold to Wholesalers and OTAs (p 15)	No change from 10th Edition. Revenue recorded at net rate received by hotel.
Mixed-Ownership (p 15)	Unknown. Excluded from rooms revenue if lease is short term (only in inventory for part of the year). Impact will depend upon past practice.
Total Operating Revenue	
Non-Operating Income (incl. CAM, cost recovery, interest income & other income generated by hotel not associated with operations such as antenna leases and billboards & retail space) (p 120)	Reduce. Total Operating Revenue "replaces" Total Revenue. Total Operating Revenue excludes Non-Operating Income. (Note: many contracts use term "Gross Revenue").
Excludes Cost Recovery (p 121)	Reduce. Cost Recovery Income is revenue per GAAP. Cost Recovery Income and Expense is now in Non - Operating Income and Expense (Eg: CAM reimbursement or reimbursement of a portion of GM salary from mixed-use facility).
Excludes Interest Income (p 121)	Reduce. Now in Non-Operating Income, below GOP.
GOP ($)	
Owner driven Income is not in Operating Revenue (p 120)	Reduce. Moved to Non-Operating Income & Expense below GOP.
GOP Margin	
Removal of Non-Operating Income from Operating Revenue (p 120)	Likely to lower as these line items are highly profitable.
Improved guidance of gross vs net causing change in revenue reporting (p 342)	Likely to increase as net revenue is 100% profit.
EBITDA Less Replacement Reserve	
Name Change	Shoul. EBITDA replaces NOI. Net Income now defined (on Owner P&L) as EBITDA less interest, depreciation and amortization and income taxes. Replacement Reserve is not a deduction to calculate Net Income. It is still a deduction on "Operators" P&L.

Major Changes Affecting the Income Statement:

- Revised Summary Operating Statement.
- Definition changes. Total Revenue and NOI are gone.
- New Non-Operating Income & Expense Schedule.
- New uniform descriptions of Rooms revenue market segmentation (with detail beyond transient and group).
- Addressed forfeited deposits or unused Gift Certificate Revenue .
- Fixed language to comply with GAAP - Rebates & Subsidies to Groups is Misc. not Rooms revenue.
- Package Revenue breakage from Rooms to Misc.
- Labor Cost "replaces" Payroll Cost; clarification of service charges and outsourced labor.
- Expanded labor reporting for each department to include sub-categories (such as housekeeping and laundry).
- Cluster Services is a new line item.
- Improved guidance to address revenue as gross vs net (particularly relevant to AV & parking agreements).
- New IT Dept. Schedule / Telephone Dept. Schedule is gone.
- New mixed ownership revenue guidance.
- New language to address employee housing.
- Revenue Manager and Catering Sales moved to S&M from Rooms & F&B expense, respectively.

Issues affecting Existing HMAs:

Definition changes	Gone: Total Revenue, NOI New: Operating Revenue, EBITDA Definition change: Net Income
Fee & Performance Tests	Revisit how 11th Edition affects calculation.
Obligation to comply with current edition of USALI	Defined terms versus USALI compliance. Inconsistency will cause interpretation issue.
Defining whether lease income is Misc. Revenue or Non-Operating Income	Depends on "operator involvement".

Key Reads in the 11th Edition:

	Pages:
Summary of changes from 10th Edition	xv-xviii
Summary Operating Statement	3-4
Rooms Revenue	12-17
Non-Operating Income & Expense	120
Gross vs. Net	342-350

3 Accounting Clarifications:

- Gross vs. Net (banquet gratuity, AV, Parking, Mixed Use)
- Package Revenue (Allocation Methodology)
- Group Rebates & Commissions (Now Misc. Not Rooms)

Owner Concerns that need to be addressed in Future HMAs (b/c not addressed with GAAP or in 11th Edition):

Operating Revenue	Fees should be based on operating revenue. Gross revenue term never existed in USALI.
Define Revenue Exclusions	Exclude service charges, surcharges and cost recovery which are all revenue per GAAP as well as Non-Operating Income.
Define Hotel Premise Exclusions	Exclude "owner controlled" spaces such as roof, parking, F&B or other retail spaces.
	Ideally owner right to change use of spaces to convert to leased spaces.
Parking and AV Agreements	Owner should have approval rights on all agreements where revenue could be categorized as gross versus net.

 Hotel Asset Value Enhancement, Inc. | 333 Westminster St - #3 | Providence, RI 02903 | p. 401.865.6900 | f. 401.865.6999

hotelAVE

USALI 11th Edition – Key Changes and P&L Implications

Asset Management • Loan Surveillance • Lender Support • Receivership • Acquisition Due Diligence • Manager & Franchise Selection • Development & Repositioning Services • Project Management • Property Management

SUMMARY OPERATING STATEMENT

10th Edition	11th Edition - Operators	11th Edition - Owners
Rooms Available	Rooms Available	Rooms Available
Rooms Sold	Rooms Sold	Rooms Sold
Occupancy	Occupancy	Occupancy
ADR	ADR	ADR
RevPAR	Rooms RevPAR	Rooms RevPAR
	Total RevPAR	Total RevPAR
REVENUE	OPERATING REVENUE	OPERATING REVENUE
Rooms	Rooms	Rooms
Food & Beverage	Food & Beverage	Food & Beverage
Other Operated Departments	Other Operated Departments	Other Operated Departments
Rentals and Other Income	Misc. Income	Misc. Income
TOTAL REVENUE	TOTAL OPERATING REVENUE	TOTAL OPERATING REVENUE
DEPARTMENTAL EXPENSES	DEPARTMENTAL EXPENSES	DEPARTMENTAL EXPENSES
Rooms	Rooms	Rooms
Food & Beverage	Food & Beverage	Food & Beverage
Other Operated Departments	Other Operated Departments	Other Operated Departments
TOTAL DEPARTMENTAL EXPENSES	TOTAL DEPARTMENTAL EXPENSES	TOTAL DEPARTMENTAL EXPENSES
TOTAL DEPARTMENTAL INCOME	TOTAL DEPARTMENTAL INCOME	TOTAL DEPARTMENTAL INCOME
UNDISTRIBUTED OPERATING EXPENSES	UNDISTRIBUTED OPERATING EXPENSES	UNDISTRIBUTED OPERATING EXPENSES
Administrative and General	Administrative and General	Administrative and General
	Information & Telecomm Systems	Information & Telecomm Systems
Sales and Marketing	Sales and Marketing	Sales and Marketing
Property Operation and Maintenance	Property Operation and Maintenance	Property Operation and Maintenance
Utilities	Utilities	Utilities
TOTAL UNDISTRIBUTED EXPENSES	TOTAL UNDISTRIBUTED EXPENSES	TOTAL UNDISTRIBUTED EXPENSES
GROSS OPERATING PROFIT	GROSS OPERATING PROFIT	GROSS OPERATING PROFIT
MANAGEMENT FEES	MANAGEMENT FEES	MANAGEMENT FEES
INCOME BEFORE FIXED CHARGES	INCOME BEFORE NON-OPERATING INCOME & EXPENSES	INCOME BEFORE NON-OPERATING INCOME & EXPENSES
FIXED CHARGES	NON-OPERATING INCOME & EXPENSES	NON-OPERATING INCOME & EXPENSES
	Income	Income
Rent	Rent	Rent
Property and Other Taxes	Property and Other Taxes	Property and Other Taxes
Insurance	Insurance	Insurance
	Other	Other
TOTAL FIXED CHARGES	TOTAL NON-OPERATING INCOME & EXPENSES	TOTAL NON-OPERATING INCOME & EXPENSES
NET OPERATING INCOME	EBITDA	EBITDA
REPLACEMENT RESERVES	REPLACEMENT RESERVE	
ADJUSTED NET OPERATING INCOME	EBITDA LESS REPLACEMENT RESERVE	
		INTEREST, DEPRECIATION & AMORTIZATION
		Interest
		Depreciation
		Amortization
		TOTAL INTEREST, DEPRECIATION & AMORTIZATION
		INCOME BEFORE INCOME TAXES
		Income Taxes
		NET INCOME

5

Channel Management, OTAs, and Rising Cost of Customer Acquisition

By Cindy Estis Green (with Kristi White) and Marco Benvenuti (with Eric Stoessel)

Cindy Estis Green, *CEO and Co-founder, Kalibri Labs, LLC, began her career in corporate marketing and senior operations roles for Hilton International. After starting up the data mining consultancy Driving Revenue and selling it to Pegasus Solutions, she spent twelve years as managing partner of The Estis Group providing strategic marketing consulting to the hospitality industry. Co-author of the 2012* Distribution Channel Analysis: A Guide for Hotels *and many other industry publications on the topic of marketing technology, Estis Green has been honored as one of the 25 Extraordinary Minds in Sales and Marketing, was inducted into the prestigious Hospitality Technology Hall of Fame, and named as one of Cornell University's 90 Influential Hoteliers. She is currently a member of the HITEC Advisory Council and the HSMAI Foundation Board of Trustees, she leads the AH&LA Consumer Innovation Forum and the HSMAI Resort Best Practices Initiative and holds a board seat for The Knowland Group. She launched Kalibri Labs in 2012 offering the hospitality industry data analytics to evaluate net revenue performance and manage the rising cost of customer acquisition. Estis Green holds a B.S. from Cornell University and an MBA from The American University.*

Marco Benvenuti, *Duetto Chief Analytics and Product Officer and Co-Founder, directs product vision, direction, and implementation. He was formerly Executive Director at Wynn and Encore where he founded and managed the Enterprise Strategy Group, leading revenue management, data analytics, direct marketing and online channels. Prior to Wynn, Marco worked for Caesars Entertainment, Expedia, and Four Seasons. Marco has patented two unique inventions: the Pricing Engine for one-to-one dynamic pricing and the Enterprise Value Algorithm for calculating the value of every customer. He holds a Master of Management in Hospitality from Cornell University, where he currently serves on the Board of the Center for Hospitality Research, and a Bachelor in Hotel Administration from UNLV.*

THE DIGITAL MARKETPLACE is ever changing with constant disruption. Newspapers, digital photography, retailers, and financial services have undergone massive changes as a result of consumer behavior. The hotel industry is no exception. Hotel selection happens much deeper in the sales process because consumers are gathering travel information on aggregator sites like online travel agencies (OTAs), Google, and TripAdvisor well before narrowing down to a short list. By the time consumers decide to make a hotel purchase, they may have touched seven to ten sites[1] and been directed or diverted by the search or information site based on which hotel(s) have a more prominent listing or a higher ranking for the destination.

Managing Acquisition Costs—the Marketplace

The bifurcation of brands in hospitality into "booking brands" and "stay brands" (see Exhibit 1) has been a driving force behind the escalation of customer acquisition costs. Hotel operators and corporate and regional teams have to navigate the digital marketplace with a new imperative to modify the way revenue performance is evaluated. Supplementing the traditional methods of tracking operating margins and market share, managing gross margins (revenue minus cost of sales)

Exhibit 1 Booking and Stay Brands

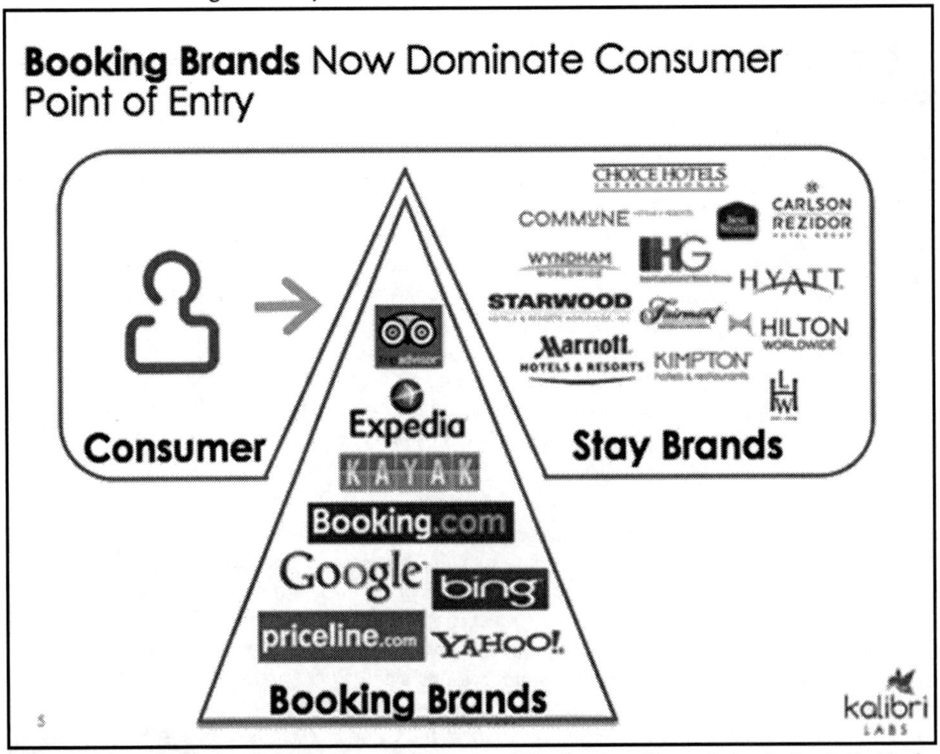

Source: Cindy Estis Green and Mark Lomanno, *Distribution Channel Analysis: A Guide for Hotels*, HSMAI Foundation and AH&LA, 2012.

may prove to be a key to success in a dynamic and turbulent online arena. What does this mean for hotels going forward? Some argue third-party aggregators and search engines will ultimately control the consumer path and that hotels are going to be commoditized, passive recipients of business as they pay third parties for traffic and then pay again to compete with each other on the stay experience.

The first industry study examining customer acquisition costs was completed in 2014 for the Hotel Asset Managers Association (HAMA) by Kalibri Labs. HAMA provided data from almost 500 member hotels for the period from 2009 to 2012 and found that *commission costs for the hotels were rising at two times the rate of revenue growth* (see Exhibit 2). A Kalibri Labs study conducted on 2012 data in New York City indicated the estimated acquisition costs (retail and wholesale commissions, transaction fees, and sales/marketing expenses) in the North American market ranged from 15 to 25 percent of revenues.

By contrast, the airlines have what Tom O'Toole (CMO, United Airlines; ex-CMO, Hyatt), speaking recently at an industry conference, called a "maniacal" focus on distribution costs; if they spend $1, they feel that is $1 too much (not figuratively, literally). Tom shared the anecdote that "the airlines are like the guy who had two near-fatal heart attacks and decided to start exercising and completely alter his diet," and by comparison, "hotels are like the guy who casually decides

Exhibit 2 Commission Cost and Revenue Growth, 2009–2012

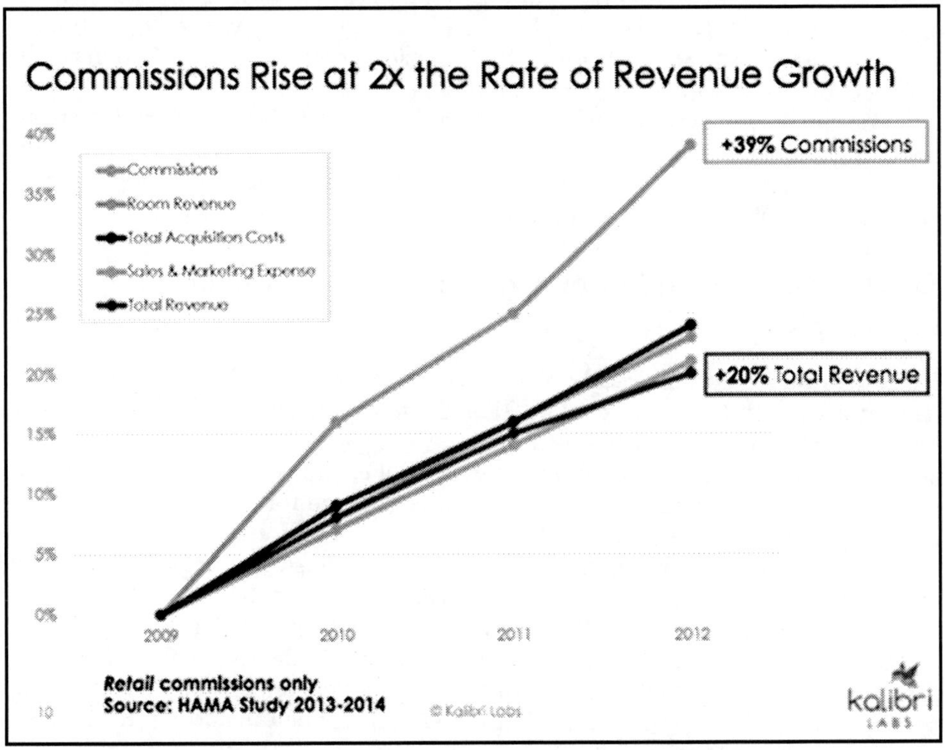

Source: Kalibri Labs Hotel Asset Managers Association study, 2013–2014.

to make a new year's resolution to try to go to the gym a little more and cut back on potato chips and French fries."

The hotel industry's triple threat for increased dependence on third parties is: (1) brand dilution through commoditization of hotel rooms, (2) increased costs with little control over the shopping and buying process, and (3) a diminished relationship with the customer. Brands have a dual challenge: to generate demand for their hotels without duplicating third-party costs, while at the same time managing to differentiate the brand booking and/or stay experience in the eyes of their consumers.

Beyond brand strategy, there are tactical issues in the world of rising acquisition costs. Many would like to think they can "price optimize" their way out of higher acquisition costs. While rate and inventory levers are important, a successful hotel will have to do more; it will have to find ways to efficiently deploy resources to achieve an optimal channel mix—not just investing in brand.com (including mobile) but also business triggers (including social and meta-search) that can be tapped to influence not only brand.com, but also voice and other direct channels. Conversion, retention, and ancillary revenue will also play into a hotel's results, as well as closely managing traditional wholesalers.

What changes are needed? Legacy sales and marketing infrastructure are due for a fresh evaluation. Piling on incremental new opportunities, however compelling, may push costs to a level that is unsustainable. What can be eliminated without diminishing the foundation of any given hotel's demand? Establishing a cap on acquisition costs will be essential and will vary based on the hotel's position in its marketplace, including factors such as physical condition, brand (large, small, or independent), the intensity of competition, and location.

You can only manage what you measure. The industry knows how to manage operating and labor costs and now it's time to put a maniacal focus on acquisition costs. It's time to face down the risks in this new territory we call the digital marketplace and pursue the opportunities.

The Rise of the Metamediaries and the Implications for Hotels

Hotel distribution continues to evolve as consumers tap more kinds of online content on their path to a hotel booking. For the ten years starting just before 2000, there were two primary online venues—travel agencies and hotel brand sites—and that is where marketing resources were applied. Since 2012, there has been a wave of development responding to consumer demand for a more refined search process and better intelligence on the travel and hotel options.

Google Hotel Finder emerged as a hotel-specific search engine and had a companion in the Google Flight Search tool, all part of what has been called travel "meta-search." The notably inefficient process for consumers to visit seven or eight (or more) sites in the run-up to a hotel booking[2] flies in the face of Google's goals for search. Honing in on the need to streamline and enhance the travel shopping process, Google has systematically improved their content including the acquisition of Frommer's Travel Guide.

Google's entrance sparked many others to come onto the scene, ranging from 2010 startup Hipmunk to the well-established TripAdvisor, which in mid-2013 declared itself to be a meta-search engine. Even Facebook, in its showdown with arch-rival Google, is morphing into a mobile-based app built around "social graph search" with travel established in late 2012 as one of their seven primary industry verticals. It wants to connect hotels to those who have interacted with them on a Facebook fan page using algorithms that point to products and services similar to what a consumer's Facebook friends (and their extended network) "like."

In response to this disruptive phenomenon, the OTAs have been highly motivated to improve search as they compete with the meta-search sites to simplify the traveler's shopping experience. The original OTA product was a type of search engine offering a wide range of hotels in any given destination, but it is being quickly supplanted by the meta-search model and they are scrambling to offer compelling alternatives. After all, the consumer will often reach a search engine before they get to an OTA and if the traveler's needs are met, many will no longer need to make that OTA visit. In the space of a few months in 2013, Priceline announced the acquisition of Kayak while Expedia acquired European-based Trivago. By early 2015, Expedia had gobbled up Travelocity and Orbitz. Further, Priceline announced it was offering website development and property management system services, heralding the start of tech companies offering a full service distribution platform to hotel owners and operators.

All of these developments happened while mobile growth was skyrocketing. Everyone with a website online (and even some without a traditional website) is now diving into mobile to tap the unquenchable thirst of consumers who can't get enough use out of mobile devices—smartphones, tablets, and all the hybrids in between. In the last year, Apple's site has begun deployment of the first phases in its iTravel patent which, when fully loaded, may include a full-service travel app that allows the user to make all types of travel reservations, manage confirmations, check-in, and control the in-room or on-flight experience. With the massive adoption of Apple mobile products, this app could be popular with consumers who will find the all-in-one, end-to-end nature of it a great convenience. What is not clear is how Apple will tap into hotel content such as inventory and rates to facilitate the hotel room shopping experience and how their monetization of the app will affect hotel distribution costs. No doubt Apple will charge for all this convenience and hotel suppliers will be more likely to pay rather than the consumer.

We are now in an era in hotel distribution where some of the giants in technology and media have decided to enter the travel industry, establishing a new form of intermediary built on the meta-search model and therefore nicknamed "metamediaries." Few emerging vendors want to be transaction-based sites; there is little interest in building out new OTAs in the traditional model. The preferred role is to pass along the consumer to the supplier site, whether it's a hotel brand or an OTA, and to charge a small fee for their efforts. The metamediaries will serve as the gatekeepers, and those with the strongest consumer power will have the upper hand on determining the fees.

Hotel brands, individual hotels, and OTAs have been pushed deeper into the shopping and buying process with greatest consumer adoption at the device or app level, typified by consumer giants Google, Facebook, and Apple. Mobile users are after convenience and are likely to prefer generic applications that offer multi-brand airline, hotel, or car rental companies. It is a great time saver to have one go-to app that stores travel documents, allows the traveler to shop and buy and even to check in, buy services and get local information about dining, transportation and/or attractions while on the road. Many of the mobile apps are entering the market with last minute deals such as the popular Hotel Tonight. This model is essentially training consumers to believe that reservations are not necessary and there is always a deal to be had up to the day of travel. When millions of consumers are engaged, the network effect will push even more suppliers onto the path of the most popular mobile apps, and these companies' market capitalizations will be strengthened. As for the hotels, there is a limit to how much a hotel can pay to acquire a customer. Commissions, transaction fees, and media costs will dominate marketing budgets going forward. The crucial decisions made by hotels and hotel companies will be about how much to spend and where.

The new reality in a marketplace dominated by mobile apps and devices, controlled largely outside of traditional travel companies, calls for an urgency to integrate a financial discipline that will address multi-channel revenue planning with a focus on business acquisition costs and an eye to sustainable profit.

Revenue Strategy—At the Intersection of Marketing and Finance

Who are the revenue strategists in the hospitality industry? Is it the marketing director who enhances the content in the website and runs an aggressive multi-channel campaign for a specific promotion? Is it the revenue manager who carefully adjusts rates when anticipated demand looks promising? Is it the sales manager who designs and executes a blitz against big Pharma in its feeder markets knowing they are meeting more often in local hotels?

Revenue strategy calls for the integration of the disciplines that drive the highest quality revenue mix while accounting for the costs of business acquisition. In contrast to the short-term tactics that deliver maximum daily revenue, revenue strategy is about *actively identifying, planning for, and tapping an optimal blend of sustainable revenue streams and making the needed resource trade-offs to enable margin growth*. Some simple trade-offs might be to reduce direct sales by one staffer and put more funds into point-of-sale initiatives in the call center; or to invest in targeted online intermediary promotions and reduce mass-market print advertising. These trade-offs require a view into the business that predicts the nature of demand, selects which revenue levers can best capture the expected demand, incorporates corresponding costs, and manages a hotel on the basis of net revenue (i.e., revenue net of business acquisition costs). After all, in this new marketplace with its skyrocketing costs, brands, owners, and managers will have a more meaningful gauge of performance when they evaluate the revenue that remains after the acquisition costs are removed.

It's Not Simply Channel Shift

When the lament is that distribution costs are too high, the perennial response is to work on channel shift, which, more specifically, usually means to reduce the OTA channel and increase the brand.com channel. However, that is a response from a bygone era. It's not about a simple two-channel shift; it's about a broad evaluation of the production and *margins* by channel, and making trade-offs that put a premium on recurring revenue streams that can be acquired at a cost that sustains an acceptable profit level. The new metamediaries will offer media models that will add costs to brand.com, while the OTA costs may in fact start to decline due to intense competition from the search engines. The analysis will not be a simple choice of one channel over another. There will be more factors that enter into evaluation of each channel. The margins may vary by segment, day of week, lead time, length of stay, or season of the year. It will take vigilance to frequently review all the combinations so a hotel can stay on top of the way these costs play into the revenue stream of each hotel and what they can ultimately claim as net revenue.

Already high, the cost of business acquisition continues to climb. In New York City, Kalibri Labs gathered data from more than fifty brands and found that commissions/transaction fees ranged from 10 to 20 percent of room revenue; when sales/marketing costs were added, total business acquisition costs generally doubled. The industry cannot sustain these costs and remain healthy. As owners and management learn to measure and manage these costs, they will find ways to lower them. But beyond the cost factor, some third-party channels undermine the value of the brand in other ways by diverting control over the consumers away from the hotel as they shop, buy, and even when they interact with the hotel on-site.

Business acquisition costs have to be measured so they can be managed, or they will continue to grow; the only place all of the costs come together is at the hotel itself, and responsible management will impose tight controls on them by tracking margins carefully. A proactive revenue strategy laser-focused on the "true north" of net revenue will enable each hotel to leverage its advantage in this dynamic and costly marketplace.

Conducting a Revenue Audit: What Can a Hotel GM Do about These Costs?

Whoever has responsibility for managing the profit of the hotel will want to track their business acquisition costs. Those with responsibility for profit will orchestrate a revenue strategy while managing its associated costs with the support team (whether in-house or regional) to take the actions that move the needle. In some hotels, the GM monitors the metrics and a regional team digs into the details to assemble an action plan that improves the hotel's position. In smaller chains and independent hotels, the internal management team does it all: sets objectives, takes the actions, and monitors results. No matter how the tasks are assigned, it is critical to have an agreed set of metrics and a clearly documented set of objectives and actions that can be articulated both internally and externally to owners and other constituents.

Someone has to take responsibility for efficiently generating revenue. The leaders must be identified and then the rest of the team members support the plan. In Exhibit 3, black diamonds indicate direct responsibility and hollow diamonds indicate indirect responsibility. There are many separate teams that support a hotel's operations and ensure the highest value for the hotel as an asset. Optimal results will ensue for those that are coordinated and focus on the margins. Net revenue as a metric creates a laser focus on the margins.

You may find the net contribution is too low; gross revenue could be too low or the reservations or sales/marketing expense could be too high. In Exhibit 4, the left column includes the "levers" you can use and the right column lists the type of tactical actions. There are many actions that may be taken by many different groups in an organization. This is no longer the simplistic and perennial decision to "lower OTA and raise brand.com volume"—there are dozens of other actions that can be taken. Optimizing prices is only one of many actions that can be taken to improve the situation. The traditional role of revenue (or yield) management has to merge with the rest of revenue strategy to change the outcomes.

It is a complex ecosystem that supports a hotel. Many actions have to happen and a coordinated plan is needed to achieve results. The guidepost is the set of metrics that drive the program so the disparate team that may be scattered across disciplines and at corporate, regional, and hotel levels all point their efforts to

Exhibit 3 Responsibility Grid

Who is responsible...

for *net revenue* (net of business acquisition costs)?

	HOTEL MGT TEAMS	REGIONAL TEAMS (digital, RM, sales/mktg)	CORP TEAMS (digital, RM, sales/mktg)	FINANCE	ASSET MGT AND OWNERSHIP
SET TARGETS	◆	◆		◇	◇
MONITOR RESULTS	◆	◆	◆	◆	◆
BUILD ACTION PLANS	◆	◆	◇		
REFINE PLANS WITH RATE/INVTY LENS	◆	◆			
FEEDBACK LOOP FOR REGIONAL &/OR CORP INITIATIVES	◇	◆	◆	◇	◇

Source: Kalibri Labs, LLC.

Exhibit 4 Revenue Strategy Levers and Actions

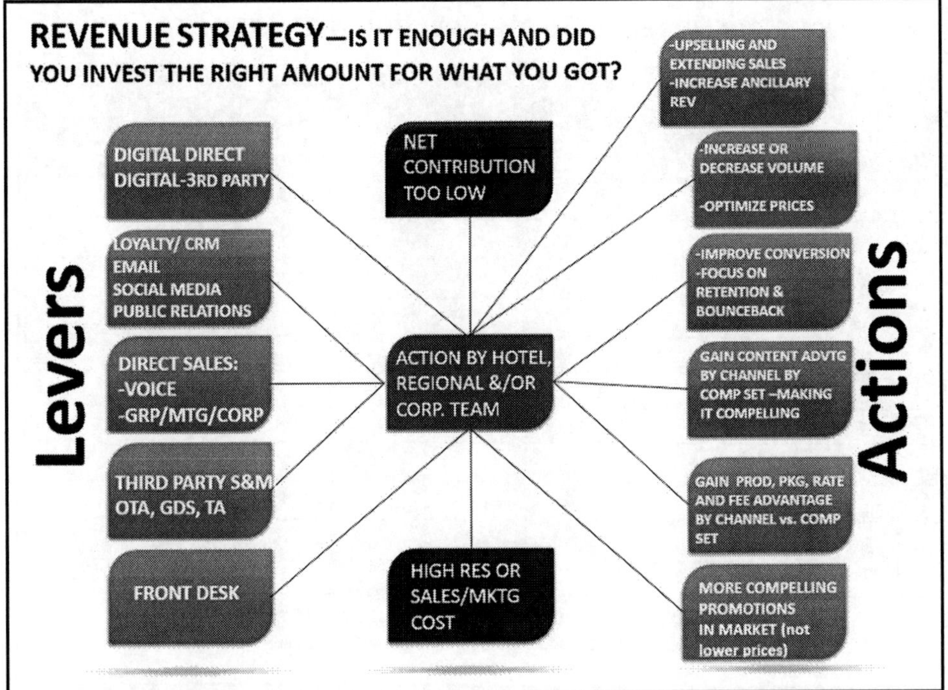

Source: Kalibri Labs, LLC.

"true north" which is net revenue growth. Once again, the plan generally has to extend well beyond the price optimization function of revenue management to achieve meaningful improvement in net revenue. Who coordinates it all? Who orchestrates all of these actions? Exhibit 5 illustrates the functions that fall under the revenue strategist; black diamonds indicate directly responsibility, while hollow diamonds represent indirect responsibility.

Managing a revenue strategy that generates optimal revenue for market conditions and does it cost effectively requires different intelligence than one that only seeks optimal revenue; measuring return on investment (ROI) on business acquisition spend is a critical addition to management's toolkit, particularly in a marketplace where these costs are growing so rapidly and are difficult to quantify. Tracking ROI is valuable; being able to compare to a benchmark group of similar hotels adds even more power to the metrics. These metrics serve as the guidepost at the hotel, regional, and corporate levels since there are so many members of the team involved in various aspects of the revenue strategy.

The goal is to improve net revenue contribution, a metric that will resonate strongly with ownership, management, and brands. If the industry focuses on increasing it, it will enable added investment by brands and owners to retain greater control of direct channels triggering a continued positive cycle of growth in net revenue, which empowers further investment by owners.

Exhibit 5 Functions of the Revenue Strategist

What does the Revenue Strategy action plan look like*? kalibri LABS

ACTION MATRIX	Upsell	Incr or Decr Volume	Grow Ancillary Rev Extend Sales	Improve Conversion	Improve Retention	Gain Content Advantage	Product Mix, Rate & Fee Advantage	Price Optimization	Gain Promo Advantage
Digital Direct	◆	◆	◆	◆	◆	◆	◆	◆	◆
Digital-3rd party		◆		◆		◆	◆	◆	◆
Loyalty-CRM	◆	◆	◆	◆	◆		◆		◆
Social Media PR	◆	◆	◆	◆	◆	◆			◆
Email	◆	◆	◆	◆	◆				◆
Voice	◆	◆	◆	◆	◆	◆	◆	◆	◆
Group Sales	◆	◆	◆	◆	◆		◆	◆	◆
OTA marketing		◆		◆		◇	◆	◇	◇
GDS marketing		◆		◆		◆	◆	◆	◆
TA marketing	◆	◆	◆	◆	◆	◆	◆	◆	◆
Front Desk	◆	◆	◆	◆	◆			◆	◆

BUSINESS ACQUISITION COSTS INCLUDE SALES, DIGITAL, LOYALTY, MARKETING, RM, COMMISSIONS AND TRANSACTION FEES
***to improve net revenue**

40

Source: Kalibri Labs, LLC.

With the significant investment that has been made in each brand by its owners and management, allowing rooms to be sold mainly based on price will quickly undermine that brand value and train consumers to think of hotel rooms as a commodity. This reduces the opportunity to engage with customers. And finally, simply looking at the cumulative cost of third-party channels is enough to give pause. Most hotels cannot sustain reservation costs of 20 percent of room revenue and still have enough funding available to spend on additional business acquisition efforts through sales and marketing.

After all, the combination of commissions, transaction fees, and total sales/marketing spend is the sum total of a hotel's customer acquisition efforts and should be looked at holistically. The consumer's point of entry will be through many new metamediary channels; however, the consumers are then passed to brand.com to book directly. This still calls for careful tracking of the various media costs incurred to shepherd travelers along the shopping path to the hotel website, and it may mean fees on multiple sites along that path. Once the travelers book directly, the chances of seeing them again go up dramatically. This supports the concept of a sustainable revenue stream, revenue that has a high chance of recurring with carefully managed margins that yield a corresponding growth in profits.

No More One Size Fits All

How often do the e-commerce or finance teams complain about the high cost of wholesalers and then the sales department turns around and pays incentives to the staffers who produce the most revenue from these same accounts? This diversion of funds and management attention is what happens without a focus on profit contribution and margins and a lockstep integration between customer acquisition/revenue disciplines. A "one size fits all" approach will not work in today's marketplace for direct sales or for digital initiatives; hotels have to build acquisition strategies around segmentation by customer type and geographic market, with margins tracked by channel, segment, and even down to account. If you sift through business opportunities by margin, it will drive priorities to work in a more targeted manner, yielding more efficient outcomes.

We have spent many years in hospitality optimizing revenue and we achieved broad revenue goals. With growing challenges imposed by the high cost of business acquisition, we have to shift our focus to profit contribution and the way to accomplish that will be to manage by margin, a discipline that means optimizing *net revenue.*

Net Revenue Performance Evaluation and Acquisition Costs by Channel

Hotels have a variety of costs related to customer acquisition. Customers only book in one channel, but they shop in many. The costs that support the shopping experience (maintaining a presence for a hotel or brand in the sales path) have to be considered in addition to those directly related to the transaction or the buying costs. Exhibits 6 and 7 provide examples of some of the different types of costs incurred to acquire customers. By managing the contribution by channel, a hotel can better target and manage its net revenue.

Using the channel mix listed in Exhibit 8 combined with the example in Exhibit 7 illustrating costs, it is easy to calculate what these shifts in mix ultimately cost the hotel. The example in Exhibit 9 illustrates how a hotel's net revenue varies based upon the management of channel mix by the hotel. The property experienced a channel shift by losing ground in brand.com, property direct, and voice while increasing share in the OTA channel. The left columns in Exhibit 9 show the calculation of gross revenue (revenue paid by the customer) by channel by year.

Exhibit 6 Sample Costs Associated with the Sales Process and Transactions

Costs that Support the Sales Process	Costs Associated with the Transaction
Sales & Marketing Payroll	Channel Costs (CRS or Booking Engine Fees)
Website Design and Maintenance	Travel Agent Commissions
Pay Per Click Advertising (PPC, CPC, CPA, CPI, etc.)	OTA Margin Fees
Meta Agency Participation Fees	Pass Through Fees (e.g., GDS)
Marketing Coop Funds	Transaction Cost (Switch Related)
Social Media	Consortia Program Fees

Exhibit 7 Sample Costs by Hotel Reservation Scenario

Reservation Scenario	Amount Paid by Customer	Channel Cost CRS Fee	Travel Agent/OTA Commission	Pass Through Fee	Net Revenue for Hotel	Acquisition Cost
Two night reservation made in the GDS by travel agent	$300	$10	$30	$8	$252	16.00%
Two night reservation made on an OTA by guest	$300	$10	$75	$4	$211	29.70%
Two night reservation made on hotel's website by guest	$300	$10	$0	$0	$290	3.30%
Two night reservation made via the call center by a guest	$300	$15	$0	$0	$285	5.00%
Two night reservation made at the hotel by a guest	$300	$15	$0	$0	$285	5.00%

Exhibit 8 Sample Hotel Channel Mix

Channel	2013	2014
Brand.com	19.1%	18.5%
GDS	4.2%	4.3%
OTA	12.2%	15.6%
Property Direct	54.1%	52.7%
Voice	10.3%	8.9%

Exhibit 9 Sample Hotel Customer and Net Revenue by Channel

	Customer Revenue			Hotel Net Revenue		
	2013	2014	Variance	2013	2014	Variance
Brand.com	$1,914,176	$1,851,347	-$62,829	$1,851,008	$1,790,253	-$60,755
GDS	$420,060	$431,877	$11,817	$352,850	$362,777	$9,927
OTA	$1,224,066	$1,561,463	$337,397	$860,518	$1,097,708	$237,190
Property Direct	$5,413,796	$5,269,163	-$144,633	$5,143,107	$5,005,705	-$137,401
Voice	$1,027,902	$886,149	-$141,753	$976,507	$841,842	-$134,665
Total	**$10,000,000**	**$10,000,000**	**$0**	**$9,183,990**	**$9,098,285**	**-$85,705**

The right columns show the net revenue the hotel would keep after acquisition costs are paid. In both examples, revenue was calculated at $10 million annually and costs were kept the same across each year. The only change made was the change in channel mix. Note that the minor shifts in mix cost the hotel more than $85,000 in net revenue. These revenue shifts become more apparent as revenue increases or the shifts become even more pronounced. Properties must manage their channel mix with a laser focus. The optimal mix will vary by season, month, and day of week. Each hotel must determine the optimal mix and then use all of its energies in managing to this measure. These metrics should be incorporated into the forecasting methodology of the hotel. Understanding the costs (both selling and buying) allows hotels to better understand how they can manage those costs in order to reap the highest Net Revenue.

Media Channels vs. Transaction Channels

There is a blurring of lines between channels that convey messages and those that process transactions. Travelers shop in many channels but they only buy in one. The many channels used for the consumer shopping experience provide the opportunity for "shelf space" to hotel marketers so consumers can view their options. The transaction channels are the places where consumers can actually make a hotel booking and consummate a transaction.

Hotels pay for both the presence in the *shopping* channels and for the direct transaction fees in the *booking* channels. Both are necessary. There are many business models that drive the way hotels pay for that online presence.

When consumers shop and click through various elements within a website, there are charges for those clicks and the model is called "CPC" or cost-per-click. This model asks the hotel to pay for the traffic to provide visibility on a website. When the hotel is charged for a booking, the fees are set up in a "CPA" model; this refers to a cost-per-acquisition. The hotel is charged only after the booking occurs. Another common media model is a "CPI" or cost per impression, which means an advertiser pays every time a media message is displayed based on an estimated number of visitors to the site. The costs may include media (CPA, CPC, CPI), commissions, and marketing position (e.g., pay for position, directory listings).

Introduction to Revenue Performance Evaluation Metrics

Historically, to evaluate revenue performance, a hotel would typically include a look at P&L Revenue and P&L RevPAR (revenue per available room). Given the skyrocketing costs of customer acquisition, hotels would benefit from evaluating their revenue performance based on net revenue (net of acquisition costs). The primary metrics that evaluate net revenue are:

- *Net RevPAR:* quantifies the net revenue per available room (after the cost of acquisition is removed from the P&L revenue). Equals P&L revenue – (commissions/transaction fees + total sales/marketing costs)/available rooms.
- *RevPAR Capture:* indicates what percentage of revenue is retained by the hotel out of the amount the customers spend for the room, including wholesale markups. Equals Net RevPAR/Gross RevPAR.

- *Contribution Percentage (COPE or Contribution to Operating Profit and Expense Percentage):* indicates how much revenue remains after direct commissions and transaction fees are removed from each channel. Equals (P&L revenue for the channel – commissions/transaction fees)/gross revenue
- *Net Sales and Marketing Efficiency:* conveys how much net revenue is generated for every $1 spent in Sales and Marketing. Equals (P&L revenue – commissions/transaction fees)/total sales and marketing costs

Tactical Execution by Channel

Within a hotel there are five distinct channels from which hotels acquire business:

- *Brand.com:* The hotel's booking engine from its proprietary website. This is one of the most direct and profitable ways for a hotel to acquire a reservation.
- *GDS (Global Distribution System):* The system used by travel agents to make reservations for customers.
- *OTA (Online Travel Agencies):* Aggregator digital sites used by consumers to shop and purchase rooms indirectly from hotels.
- *Voice:* Reservations made via a call center or hotel reservation office.
- *Property Direct:* Reservations made with the property. These are typically via the sales office or walk-ins.

Each channel has different methodology and opportunities for merchandising and marketing. Every hotel will employ a mix of tactics to achieve its net revenue objectives.

Brand.Com. This is one of the most important channels for both merchandising and selling direct to consumers. While branded hotels do not have quite the freedom for the look and feel of the website, they benefit from overarching marketing strategies the brand has in place. Independents may have full control over their websites but this comes with a cost. Within either scenario, the hotel can benefit from conducting a full audit of its website:

- Is the site easily navigable and intuitive for consumers?
- Can consumers easily determine how to book on your website?
- Is the content up-to-date?
- Is photography indicative of the caliber of the property?
- Are room types compelling?
- Are room types and rate codes sequenced to encourage the sale of the right product to the right customer?

Understanding and managing the way the property is merchandised will assist marketing efforts in driving business to the site.

There are multiple levers hotels can pull to help drive traffic to their sites.

- *Online marketing* (e.g., pay-per-click, retargeting). This investment helps capture customers earlier in the shopping process. By placing the hotel higher in the generic search, potentially placing the website higher in search rankings, the hotel can bring more shoppers to the website.

- *Email campaigns*. These campaigns can be foster awareness or may be tactical with the intention to target specific need periods.
- *Search engine optimization*. Although the majority of search rankings are now pay-for-position, to the extent that a hotel may appear in a desirable non-paid position, the hotel can use relevant content to improve their ranking.

Hotels can do a variety of things to increase volume to their sites. However, if they don't have a clear understanding of why and how customers choose to transact on their site, they are looking at only half of the puzzle. On a monthly basis, properties evaluate all of the following metrics:

- Traffic to website.
- Number of visitors who click through to the booking engine. It is important to understand the gap between these two metrics. Are customers truly shopping to buy on a hotel website or shopping to gain information, then transacting elsewhere? The higher the gap is, the more likely there is a weakness within in the website.
- Last page visited before abandonment or clicking through to the website. This will often help a hotel understand what is factoring into the purchase decision for the consumer.

A hotel digital marketer needs to understand the key metrics. Some basic examples are shown in Exhibit 10.

GDS. This technology is built on a legacy platform and has significant constraints. Properties must work within the confines of character limitations, minimal merchandising opportunities and limited visual appeal of the systems. However, there are ways hotels can optimize what and how they display their inventory and rate offerings. Additionally, there are paid marketing opportunities the hotel can take advantage of to improve its merchandising.

Exhibit 10 Hotel Digital Marketer Issue and Resolution Examples

Issue	Resolution
Too little traffic to site	Increase direct spending on PPC, SEO, e-mail marketing.
Significant decline in number of guests who click through from website to booking engine	Audit website for navigability. Determine where precisely guests are abandoning process. When was website last refreshed?
Declining or low conversions	Pinpoint booking engine abandonment to determine if the process is relative to merchandising issues, price issues or inventory issues.

Hotels should always start by reviewing their long descriptions for room types within the GDS. The hotel will need to work with their brand and/or CRS provider to view these and adjust. There are character limitations for each of these descriptions. Within these limitations, the property should make the descriptions as compelling as possible. These descriptions are the tools travel agents use when selling the property to consumers. The hotel should be as concise as possible.

Consider the following description:

> Redesigned residential guestroom--wine hour with one king bed--flat screen TV and iHome

This description does not provide enough detail for the agent to create a compelling picture. Being a redesigned room may not tell the agent much and a guest room is inherently residential. Wine hour is not a room amenity. Flat screen TV is also unnecessary, as it is assumed in most hotels these days. Better would be as follows:

> 450 SQ FT room one king bed Stand up shower with separate bath. Aveda amenities, 60 inch flat screen television

An agent can build a strong narrative around the revised description. Room size should only be used where it is a competitive advantage, such as dense urban markets. In the example below from Sabre, the property has done a better job providing a description the agent can use to tell a story to the customer.

> The cozy 300-square-foot traditional room features a four-poster king-size bed or two twin-size beds, hand-crafted furnishings and a gas-lit kiva fireplace.

In addition to the description limitations, in an initial search, hotels will only return fifteen to twenty room type/rate combinations. As a result, properties must be cautious about which inventory and rates are displayed. Properties will want to sequence their room type and rate offerings in the most effective fashion. Primary sequencing should always be done against room type. Least expensive room types can typically be sequenced first, stair stepping up to more expensive room types.

Secondary sequencing should be against rate types. The property should always choose a top position for rates with no fences or hurdles the customer must meet to book. Best Available Rate (BAR) is often most effective for the property. As a GDS is largely used to book corporate accounts, placing "fenced" rates such as advance purchase or member rates would not be as attractive to business travelers' needs as the lead time tends to be shorter and decisions around business trips are not always discretionary. If agents want to find qualified rates, they will search for them.

Beyond merchandising, there are other programs in which hotels can participate to help drive placement and the number of times they show up in searches (see Exhibit 11).

OTA. Most of the opportunity for this channel is related to placement. Approximately 80 percent of all bookings via OTAs occur on the first page. Hotels must balance the ability to be on the first page against their need to balance healthy profit contribution from an optimal channel mix. Typically, hotels that provide the

Exhibit 11 Hotel GDS Issue and Resolution Examples

Issue	Resolution
Improve Placement	Paid participation in placement programs such as Sabre Spotlight or Amadeus Instant Preference. Each of these programs guarantee placement in the first 20 returns on standard city searches within the GDS. They are annual purchases. The costs vary dependent on the market.
Access to More Agents	Participate in the Consortia Programs available for your hotel. Costs vary dependent on market, size of hotel and often the program.
Travel Agent Advertising	Need-based advertising that lets hotels target specific need dates to attract travel agents searching for stays during those dates.

most inventory combined with the lowest rates receive preferential treatment on placement. Some hotels make a conscious decision to avoid the best placement in order to limit the volume through this typically low profit channel.

Merchandising opportunities are very similar to those on brand.com. Hotels will want to decide what content (e.g., photography and room descriptions) they want used to merchandise their property. Sequencing room types low to high with logical upselling for premium room types helps customers work through the upsell process if they are receptive to higher value offerings.

There is the ability to drive more volume within the channel by participating in promotions. Hotels offering OTA promotions are given preferential treatment in terms of page placement. Again, if a hotel wants to constrain volume through this channel, then promotions (typically deep rate discounts) may be less attractive to achieve a hotel's net revenue objectives.

Voice. The call or contact center is a frequently overlooked channel that has high potential for improving net revenue and profit contribution. Additionally, efforts to improve conversions and sell strategies within this channel adjusted be made very quickly. Hotels have the ability to control how inventory and rates are presented to customers as well as what the sales strategy is when the customer is resistant. The order and the way this is presented directly affects how calls convert. Many hotels have conversion rates between 25 and 35 percent. Conversion improvement of even 1 percent can result in hundreds more bookings for the hotel and a substantial spike in net revenue.

Evaluation may include these questions:

- Are the sales scripts appropriate to fit the trip purpose for the customer's visit?
- Are the reservation sales agents asking qualifying questions so they can present the best offer to the customer early in the call?

- Do the agents understand the product/service they are selling? Can they effectively sell each rate category, room type, etc., so the guest understands the value of the offer? Are they sales personnel?
- Does the hotel have upsell incentives in place for reservation agents?

Voice is not a channel where one size fits all. What a hotel says to a leisure traveler should differ from what it says to a corporate traveler. Trying to fit all aspects of a hotel into the same script will serve only to frustrate the customer and potentially lead to lower conversion rates.

Key metrics hotels need to monitor to determine the health of the voice channel include:

- Call volumes by month
- Revenue per call
- Conversions by month
- Denials and regrets by date (if this is tracked effectively)

Understanding how these numbers change based upon seasonality is important for hotels. If conversions stay relatively flat but call volumes go down, what has been done differently which might be causing volumes to go down? If call volumes remain consistent (or go up) while conversions fall, what has changed in the sell process that might be negatively affecting performance?

Managing call performance can be vital for hotels. The higher rated the hotel is, the more likely it is to receive higher contribution via the voice channel. Hotels wanting to improve performance via the channel and potentially increase mix contribution have a few opportunities:

- Training of reservation agents to make sure they understand all sell strategies across all market segments.
- Regularly test selling strategies to ensure they are current with revenue goals for the hotel. These will shift over time as hotels update its marketing plans and changing needs.
- Targeted email campaigns of past guests. Campaigns can be built as offers which are specific to phone campaigns and followed up by sales agents.

Property Direct. A component of property direct for many hotels is walk-in business converted via the front desk or upselling upon check-in for those guests booking through any channel.

- Does the hotel have understanding, by day of week, of how many walk-ins it averages?
- Is there a strategy to capture walk-in business (e.g., sell strategy, fallback options, training for staff)?
- Is there a strategy to upsell at the front desk (e.g., premium room types, ancillary services, add on nights)?

Taking advantage of business that literally walks through the door and having a definitive plan can help a hotel close out those dates where there are only a few remaining rooms to sell. Yielding higher revenue from front desk sales by offering value-added benefits to guests who are receptive can result in happier guests and higher net revenue.

Price Optimization and Yield Management

When Marriott introduced yield management to the hotel industry in the 1980s, the Internet barely existed and most hotel bookings came from phone calls. Today, the Internet dominates the shopping and booking experience. The increasing costs and complexities of this evolving distribution landscape require hoteliers to embrace a more comprehensive revenue strategy that includes the latest tools and technologies if they hope to remain as profitable as in years past.

Revenue management—sometimes known as price optimization or yield management—is the art and science of predicting real-time customer demand and optimizing the price and availability of products to match that demand. It's more commonly known as selling the right hotel room at the right price to the right customer at the right time, and in today's world of increasing customer-acquisition costs, the definition must also include selling that room using the right distribution channel.

Although not written specifically for the hotel industry, an article in *The McKinsey Quarterly* a dozen years ago introduced the idea of improving profitability through transaction pricing. "The most effective path is to get prices right for one customer, one transaction at a time, and to capture more of the price that you already, in theory, charge," the authors wrote. They went on to add, "The game of transaction pricing is won or lost in hundreds, sometimes thousands, of individual decisions each day."[3]

To do this effectively today, the hotel industry needs new tools and strategies. Revenue management practices centered on best available rate (BAR) are no longer effective in a world with hundreds of channels, intermediaries, and new players like Google and Facebook, all taking some cut of the action.

A new approach called *open pricing* has emerged, which moves beyond BAR and into pricing all room types, channels, and dates independently of each other to maximize revenue without ever having to close any off. Rates across different channels are no longer linked to BAR; they are instead yielded independently based on their price elasticity. Room types aren't locked in with fixed modifiers, but are instead priced independently. This new strategy allows hoteliers to maximize value one transaction at a time, while also not frustrating guests who may be confused as to why a hotel is often open on some channels, but closed on others.

With acquisition costs rising faster than revenue and no slowdown in sight, hotel owners must regain control of their bottom line. Understanding how much revenue is kept from each transaction is paramount to maintaining profits. Moving beyond BAR pricing and the basics of revenue management and into a revenue strategy that embraces this idea and new consumer-centric data is more critical than ever.

Disconnect from BAR

Until recently, most revenue management practices have started and ended with the benchmark best available rate. Once BAR is set, all other rates across all other channels are adjusted not on forecasted demand, but by pre-determined and fixed percentages off of BAR. The reason for this fixed-tier approach has been its simplicity. Hotels can easily implement and manage this strategy based on the price elasticity of BAR, but true dynamic pricing is not being achieved and profits are not being optimized.

With fixed-tier pricing, revenue managers set the BAR, typically the lowest public price available on the hotel's website and other OTAs in parity, and all other rates adjust accordingly, usually based on a fixed percentage difference from BAR. For example, if BAR is set at $100 for any given day, the AAA rate might be 10 percent less, the loyalty rate 15 percent less, OTA package rate 35 percent less, all the way down to opaque channels like Hotwire that might be discounted 45 percent. If BAR goes up or down, the other rates all move in lockstep.

Revenue managers set one price and everything derives from that, usually through a revenue management software system that helps facilitate rate changes across different segments and channels. Clearly the benefit of this methodology is its simplicity, but the disadvantage is the loss of potential revenue. Look at the basic demand curve in Exhibit 12, showing the relationship between price and quantity sold. The six blocks represent revenue captured from tiered pricing, but the static price points limit a hotel's opportunity to capture everything in between (the triangles where there are no price points). The more price points that are available for demand, the more opportunity exists to capture revenue.

This detriment of a fixed-tier strategy is worsened by hotels managing other segments (OTAs, loyalty members, groups, opaque channels, etc.) as percentages tied to BAR. The hotel misses the opportunity to use differentiated pricing with each transaction to better match demand. Should an OTA booking always be priced 35 percent less than BAR? Or would 25 percent or even 10 percent be the right price in many circumstances?

On a date with compression, revenue managers sometimes close down discount channels to yield more profitable bookings, but then customers shopping those discount sites see no availability, and potential revenue that could have come from a customer booking a stay for multiple days is lost. Rather than closing channels, another workaround has been adding complicated length-of-stay restrictions, but then consumers looking for one night are forced to consider buying something they really don't want.

These fixed-tier strategies aren't consumer or hotel friendly. To capture as much money as possible, hotels should be determining the right rate for all the different segments of their business every day.

Open to a New Way

Instead of prices moving up and down in lockstep across numerous channels and hotels shutting off discounts they no longer want to take, revenue managers can use an open pricing strategy to yield all room types across all channels based on the actual demand within each of these individual buckets. This strategy goes beyond

Exhibit 12 Basic Demand Curve

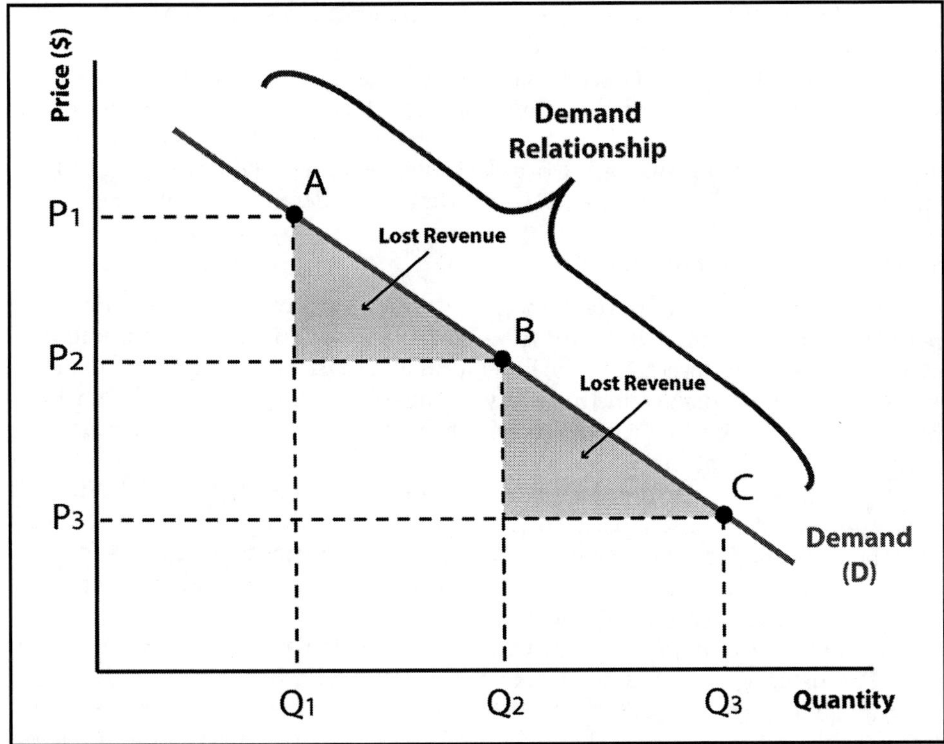

Source: Duetto.

what the hotel industry has understood as dynamic pricing, which is typically the fixed-tier pricing described above or length-of-stay restrictions that ultimately either close the doors on customers or keep them from booking what they want.

Instead of choosing between a 10 percent discount for the AAA rate, a 35 percent discount for the OTA package rate or closing channels completely, hotels should be able to price those channels dynamically based on actual demand within those rate codes. On a compressed date, the AAA rate could be priced 5 percent less than BAR, or 3 percent, or not reduced at all, depending on demand, but the channel would remain open so customers shopping that rate would still see availability.

Advances in technology are making this possible. With better integration among property management, central reservation, revenue strategy, and channel management systems, rates can automatically be updated and pushed across all outlets. Revenue management no longer needs to be simplified, centered on BAR, and should instead evolve into a revenue strategy utilizing open pricing and the ability to yield rooms by channel, segment, and even room type.

Like the standard AAA rate discounted 10 percent, most hotels also don't fluctuate prices between room types. A king suite is usually priced the same amount more than the basic queen without regard for demand and availability. If the queen room were $200, the king suite might be $250. If the queen were $300, the suite would be $350. With open pricing, the modifier doesn't always have to be the same and rates flex based on demand.

Open pricing is about never closing the door on potential revenue or a guest who wants to book a specific hotel on a specific date. Discount channels can be yielded up rather than shut off. Room types can be priced independently so suites are always available for the high-worth last-minute traveler who is willing to pay a premium. Revenue and profits can be maximized one transaction at a time.

Forecasting Is the Foundation

Forecasting is the most important and most difficult job of the revenue management function at any hotel. It is impossible to make smart pricing decisions without an accurate demand forecast. In the hotel industry, revenue managers are dealing with significant complexity and volatility because they are tasked with forecasting the behavior of individual customers who base their decisions on numerous and many unknown variables.

The simplest type of forecast totals the number of rooms that will be occupied by day and summarizes the performance of the hotel as a whole. However, almost every hotel breaks down its forecast by channel or customer segment. It is easy to track a handful of channels and it is important to divide the demand based on how customers book and what rate they pay.

A constrained forecast caps demand at the available room inventory of the hotel. For instance, a constrained forecast for a hotel with 200 rooms would never show demand exceeding 200 rooms. This makes sense because managers know that even on the busiest days they will not be able to accommodate more guests than the fixed capacity of the property. A forecast like this is perfect for operating departments that need to know how much to staff and is adequate for a financial analyst building a budget, but it has serious shortcomings for revenue managers.

An example will demonstrate the dilemma faced by revenue managers making pricing decisions from a constrained forecast. Imagine you are managing the same 200-room hotel and are looking at two days that are approximately two months in the future. Both days are projected to be sold out so the forecast shows 100 percent forecasted occupancy; however, you notice that one day has 100 rooms on the books and the other already has 140 rooms sold due to a recent spike in bookings. Are these two days really the same?

An unconstrained forecast provides a much better representation of the intensity of demand by day. The forecast extrapolates from what has already been booked and the pace of bookings to determine how many room nights would be consumed if the current pricing and distribution strategies were continued. In the example above, the first day may be pacing to occupancy of 205 rooms while the other day may be pacing to 287 rooms. Therefore, the first day has unconstrained demand of five rooms and the second day has 87 rooms of unconstrained demand, which is much more useful information to have when determining appropriate pricing and distribution than to simply note both days will sell out.

New Indicators of Demand

The first step of any forecast is assembling the data. Until recent years, the bedrock of any demand forecast has been historical booking information from the property management system and the pace of bookings leading up to an arrival date. From this, revenue managers have forecasted demand and priced rooms.

Unfortunately, this approach has only ever been about unconstrained purchases and inward looking data. In recent years, advances in data science and technology have given way to better information. Instead of looking only at past and ongoing booking information, new customer-centric data sets like online reviews and ratings, weather, airlift and web shopping data are being used to forecast unconstrained demand. Instead of looking only at consumers actually making purchasing decisions, the insight gleaned from those shopping, as well as other factors, can be much more valuable.

These new data sets provide visibility into future demand and lead to better pricing decisions. By looking at airline data, such as arrivals into a specific airport on a given date, hoteliers can better predict room night demand. If there are 500 arrivals one day compared to 100 another day, which one is likely to lead to more hotel bookings?

Weather can work in a similar fashion. If hot and dry weather is forecast for the weekend, an ocean resort is likely to be far busier than a ski resort with a similar forecast. Social reviews and ratings are also becoming part of demand forecasts as properties with a surge in positive reviews are able to attract more business and ultimately a higher rate. A property with poor reviews obviously faces stiffer challenges in driving bookings and rate.

Web shopping data — looking at consumers browsing and comparing rooms online rather than just those who are booking — gives hoteliers the clearest vision of true demand. By tracking shopping behavior and whether consumers are looking or booking, revenue managers can see how their pricing influences customers' decisions. If two separate dates both received three bookings, but one had 30 consumers shopping the website and another had 100, which date had more demand? By tracking and analyzing data like this, revenue managers can gain a far better understanding of price elasticity.

The math behind revenue management hasn't evolved much over time, but what has changed is the amount of data giving visibility to future demand and the technology allowing hoteliers to take full advantage of it with advanced revenue strategies and systems. The goal of always selling the right room at the right price to the right customer at the right time and on the right distribution channel is now becoming a reality, and so are increased profits.

A Brief Example

The James New York SOHO, a 114-room boutique property in Lower Manhattan, was looking to grow its revenue in an extremely competitive luxury market. In January 2014, it implemented a cloud-based revenue strategy application that provided easy access to competitor intelligence, more accurate forecasting, price recommendations and historical data comparisons.

The improved forecasting combined with more flexible and more dynamic pricing paid immediate dividends. In the first six months of implementation, The James New York saw a 2.3 percent increase in ADR (average daily rate) Index and an impressive 6.2 percent increase in RevPAR Index. The hotel operated by Denihan Hospitality Group grew revenue while the rest of the market dipped. In April alone, The James experienced a 10.1 percent growth in RevPAR Index. Hanna Weller, Director of Revenue Management, The James New York, states, "The solution gives us the information and confidence to optimize our rates to ever-changing demand. It's given us a distinct competitive advantage in a hotel market where you need it—Lower Manhattan. We have been delighted to see strong results immediately."

Conclusion

Revenue strategy will give a hotel the tools to integrate all revenue levers and examine revenue performance based on the revenue net of customer acquisition costs. When a hotel wants to manage the flow of demand with a set of tactical tools, it will turn to price optimization and yield management for these daily activities. By integrating revenue strategy with price optimization and yield management, a hotel will be able to forecast more accurately, implement tactical initiatives, and ultimately improve its net revenue.

What can a hotel do to improve its net revenue and manage its channels best? First, it should establish an optimal channel mix target for the hotel. Every hotel has an optimal channel mix. It will differ based on its location, physical condition, room types, meeting room size and configuration (if applicable), local demand generators, and competitive climate. In spite of a desire to achieve a particular revenue target, management should maintain a realistic perspective about the mix and rates that are possible given the constraints in play.

The hotel should also test different scenarios by channel looking at room night and rate combinations. In order to establish an optimal channel mix, hotel management can examine combinations of demand and rate by channel, applying the associated direct cost with that channel and adding sales and marketing expense to those costs to determine a total customer acquisition cost and establish the net revenue objectives.

The hotel should also examine opportunities by day of week and work on price optimization. The price optimization efforts may be undertaken to match the rates charged with the demand streams that are available on a daily basis. Examining lost business, unconstrained demand, and disconnecting rate decisions from BAR are all techniques that will prove effective in a highly competitive, digitally driven market.

The hotel should also monitor revenue performance metrics to manage to the hotel's optimal channel mix objectives. Like managing labor costs, a hotel has to manage its acquisition costs and be held accountable to a net revenue objective. Tracking Net RevPAR, RevPAR Capture, Contribution by Channel (COPE Percentage), and Net Sales and Marketing Efficiency on a weekly or monthly basis will enable management to contain costs, find opportunities, and respond to threats by having an early warning system to guide their decisions.

Endnotes

1. Cindy Estis Green and Mark Lomanno, *Distribution Channel Analysis: A Guide for Hotels* (Lansing, Mich.: HSMAI Foundation and AH&LA, 2012).
2. Estis Green and Lomanno, p. 133.
3. Michael V. Marn, Eric V. Roegner, and Craig C. Zawada, "The Power of Pricing," *The McKinsey Quarterly*, Number 1, 2003, Pages 26–36.

Glossary of Definitions

Definitions of Distribution Channels

Call or Contact Center. Most hotels have an in-house or outsourced call center to handle telephone or click-to-chat/click-to-call inquiries for reservations or information requests. Most large hotel companies operate their own call centers, and many independent hotels contract with third parties to provide this service. These call centers may handle calls for routine individual reservations, small groups, loyalty program questions, wholesale or travel agent needs, and complaints or problem management.

Complementary Partner (e.g., airlines, car). Many hotels work with airlines or car rental companies so they can sell hotel rooms. They provide rates and inventory to them so they can sell them either as rooms only or packaged with air and/or car rental services.

GDS. The global distribution systems are technology platforms for travel agents to book air, car, and hotel reservations. There are three primary GDS companies: Sabre, Travelport (Galileo and Worldspan), and Amadeus. These legacy systems were originally in widespread use as airline reservation systems and expanded to allow for car bookings before they were spun off from the airlines. Although the GDS can book any type of travel, the majority of users of the GDS are travel agencies focused on servicing corporate accounts who have negotiated rates with hotels for business travel and who want the agencies to provide booking and other travel management services to control travel and entertainment expenses.

OTAs. Online travel agencies are technology-based companies that sell travel products including hotel rooms directly to consumers. They negotiate commissions with hotel suppliers and resell rooms, earning money on the markup. There are three primary business models used by OTAs: merchant, retail, and opaque.

The *merchant model* is a common one in the U.S. market. The consumer pays the OTA and then the OTA passes on a previously agreed net rate and retains the difference as the commission. Under the *retail model,* the consumer pays the hotel a rate and the hotel later pays out a commission based on an agreed percentage of the room rate (traditional travel agent model). The *opaque model* is one in which the OTA offers a deeply discounted rate without disclosing the name of the hotel. The consumer either accepts the posted rate or "names their own price" and bids for a room at a lower rate which the OTA has the discretion to accept or reject. The consumer pre-pays the OTA and later finds out the precise hotel that was booked. The OTA passes on an agreed amount to the hotel and keeps the difference as a commission. Online travel agencies operate largely as wholesalers, but they do not make any commitment to sell any particular amount of inventory. However, many have requirements with hotels that as long as there is a room left to sell that the hotel is contractually obligated to make that room available for sale through their site. This condition is typically called "last room availability" or LRA.

Meta-search. There are search engines that are purpose-built to handle travel transactions. Some are designed just for hotels, others for flights and some can accommodate all travel types. These search engines are intermediaries that attract consumers looking for hotels. They are sometimes called "meta-mediaries" for this reason.

Mobile. Mobile is a general term to refer to applications that enable a consumer to interact with a hotel using a mobile device such as a smartphone, tablet, or other technology. This interaction may be for the shopping or buying of a hotel room or it may be for a part of the arrival or stay experience such as check in, arrival notification in a destination, local restaurant or attraction information, or making arrangements for spa appointments or in room dining orders.

Peer to Peer. A new class of vendors emerged and started to gain traction in the 2014–15 timeframe. These are vendors offering to connect consumers to each other for the provision of services. Companies such as Uber for transportation services as an alternative to taxis or limos, or Airbnb for accommodations with consumers as "host" to other consumers offering everything from spare bedrooms to entire condos or villas that may have previously been a traditional rental property. These sites may be mobile only or may evolve to become a next generation type of online travel agency. They generally have a heavy dependence on consumer reviews to provide insight on the expectation for the experience and provide confidence that the service provider is legitimate and safe.

Travel Inspiration. There are many websites used by travelers to provide inspiration for travel ideas. Lonely Planet, Travel and Leisure, and other magazine or publication-based sites are some that consumers use for travel inspiration. Many travel inspiration sites will tap inventory from OTAs if they want to enable booking from their site.

Wholesalers. Many traditional wholesalers operate in the hospitality industry and have done so for decades without a direct technology link to the hotel companies. The wholesalers are given discounted room rates that they combine with air, car, or other travel services and sell as a package. The discounted rates they are given are contingent on the agreement that they will only be sold as part of a bundled package, not as a room-only offer. Many traditional wholesalers are now moving to having direct connections with hotel companies to enable more efficient inventory, rate status, and the relay of reservations.

Definitions of Connectivity Types

One of the key components for a hotel in distributing its inventory is the technology platform that deliver the reservations. Technology platforms connect the hotel to all of the major distribution channels. Due to the diverse nature of the industry, the hotel will often use many technology platforms to meet all of its distribution needs. Below is a list of some of the technology platforms available for hotels:

Central Reservation Systems. A CRS is often the hub for distribution for hotels. These systems provide hotels with connectivity to the GDS, web booking engines (both tradition and mobile), connectivity to the Pegasus Online Distribution Database (ODD), and possibly connectivity to other distribution channels.

Each chain brand has a proprietary CRS that provides connectivity for its member hotels. Independent hotels and smaller chains contract connectivity through third-party CRS providers. There are dozens of third-party CRS providers to meet the needs of hotels. Below are a few companies that provide these services.

- Sabre Hospitality SynXis CRS
- TravelClick's iHotelier CRS
- Pegasus Connect
- Regatta Solutions
- Trust

Regardless of the provider selected, each CRS allows the hotel to manage inventory and rates within one central location while seamlessly distributing it onward. CRS connectivity, whether via a brand or a third-party CRS, connects the hotel with hundreds of thousands of travel agents and millions of other shoppers via the Internet.

Channel Managers. When OTAs first moved into the marketplace, they were not connected to CRS providers, and therefore could not connect directly to hotels. Each of the OTAs either created their own proprietary user interface or piggybacked on GDS connectivity that allowed hotel staff to manage the rate and inventory of the hotel for distribution.

However, as more sites came online, this became time consuming for the hotel and often created errors where some sites showed rates or inventory that did not match the CRS because they were not synched in a timely manner. Further, reservations acquired through these sites were managed manually. The hotel was required to maintain these reservations offline and manually re-enter an emailed or faxed reservation into the property management system (PMS) and update inventory to their CRS separately.

With the proliferation of OTAs, it became more difficult and time consuming for hotels to manage each of these sites independently. Additionally, CRS providers were sometimes slow to develop or maintain connectivity with them. As a result, channel managers stepped into the fold to allow hotels to manage their inventory and rate for the OTAs.

Channel managers allow hotels to manage alternate points of distribution within one platform. Rather than the hotel having to manage multiple sites across multiple points of entry, they can log into one system, the Channel Manager, and manage all of those sites in one place. There are dozens of third-party channel management providers to meet the needs of hotels. Below are a few companies that provide these services.

- TravelClick's Channel Management
- Rate Tiger
- HotelRunner
- Channel Rush
- Rate Gain

Each of these companies provide a hotel the opportunity to manage hundreds of sites, often including their own CRS, from one point of contact.

Direct Connect. As some of the OTAs grew in size and in terms of the amount of business they contributed to the hotel industry, the OTAs began to work with CRS providers to provide direct connect functionality. This functionality allowed hotels to manage their rates and inventory directly from the CRS without going through a manual interface or a channel manager.

Additionally, this technology allowed the hotel to flow reservations from the OTAs directly into their CRS and potentially their PMSs. It streamlined the way hotels managed those sites with the greatest volumes.

Switch Technology. While CRSs do an excellent job of collecting and maintaining rates, inventory, and content, they are dependent on a second piece of technology to distribute the rates, inventory, and content to third parties like OTAs and GDSs. When an OTA or a GDS has onward distribution to an affiliate network, the switch can convey rates, inventory, and reservations accordingly.

Hotels that are part of large chains, or the smaller groups or independents that use third-party CRSs, may usually connect to these switches for some portion of their distribution. There are several companies that provide this type of connectivity:

- Pegasus
- Hotel Booking Solutions (HBSi)
- Derbysoft

Technology providers abound within the travel space. Each of them plays an integral part of distribution for hotels. The providers are interconnected and dependent on the others to provide hotels with the broadest of distribution opportunities. The technology landscape is complex and with a mix of new and legacy systems, can be costly and difficult to navigate and maintain.

Review Questions

1. *How has the bifurcation of brands between stay brands and booking brands changed the digital landscape for hotels?* Third-party aggregators and search engines

exert a lot of control in the consumer travel shopping path. Hotels pay third parties for traffic and then pay again to compete with each other on the stay experience. The dominance of booking brands has driven up the cost of customer acquisition.

2. *Why is net revenue (or Net RevPAR and Net RevPAR Capture) an important metric to track?* Given that the cost of customer acquisition has risen to 15 to 25 percent of the room revenue paid by consumers, the revenue kept by the hotel after paying acquisition costs (net revenue) is crucial to track and monitor. Like labor costs are managed with a strong focus, acquisition costs have to be similarly measured in order to manage and contain these costs.
3. *What is the optimal channel mix of a hotel and how do you derive it?* Each hotel has an achievable channel mix reflecting room night demand and rates that are indicative of a hotel's aspirations to perform given its advantages or constraints regarding its physical condition, location, room types, meeting space and configuration, market awareness/brand, and competitive position. This mix is unique to the hotel, and management should be realistic about a hotel's prospects in a given market. In order to derive this optimal channel mix, a hotel can look at its historical performance, overall demand by channel in the market, corresponding costs associated with each channel, and benchmark data on competitive net revenue performance by channel.
4. *How can you evaluate how much a hotel should spend on sales and marketing? Can you be efficient in sales and marketing spending and still underperform in terms of net revenue?* Sales and marketing funds are spent only to generate revenue, so it is important to evaluate how well a hotel does this. By looking at how much net revenue (revenue minus direct reservation costs—commissions/transaction fees) is generated for every $1 spent in sales and marketing, a hotel can benchmark its Net Sales and Marketing Efficiency to see how much "bang for the buck" it achieved and compare this to others in the same marketplace. However, a hotel can push this metric up by underspending in sales and marketing and likewise underperforming in net revenue production. This metric has to be evaluated in conjunction with net revenue performance.
5. *What is revenue strategy?* Revenue strategy is the discipline that takes all revenue levers and integrates them into a holistic view of the business to orchestrate all the tactical actions needed to achieve net revenue objectives. It includes digital marketing, direct marketing (email), direct sales, public relations, price optimization, and many more. It takes into account the cost of acquisition and ensures a hotel considers overall trade-offs between revenue generating options.
6. *Why is open pricing a useful way to establish a rate structure and what benefits will ensue vs. BAR-based pricing?* Rather than being constrained by the BAR with discounts off that rate, open pricing allows a hotel to set rates for each individual demand driver unrelated to every other demand driver. Revenue managers can use open pricing to yield all room types across all channels based on the actual demand within each of these individual buckets. The benefit is that customers who are looking for a particular rate in one channel may find

it even if other channels have been closed or are subject to restrictions. The outcomes are that a hotel will derive more revenue by meeting the needs of customer groups who may otherwise have been forced to look elsewhere for a room.

7. *Why is forecasting the most crucial element of the price optimization function?* A good forecast is essential to determining the price the consumer is willing to pay. Anticipating high demand will mean the hotel can charge higher rates; lower demand may mean less competition for rooms and lower rates. Looking at the variables that drive demand can make a better forecast. With today's big data capabilities, examining lost business, website searches, airline arrivals to a destination and weather forecasts can all influence the anticipated demand levels.

8. *How can a revenue strategy approach in a hotel result in improved results?* When a hotel operates with a revenue strategy approach, the overall net revenue objective of a hotel is considered rather than performance in each siloed and individual revenue department. Consideration of trade-offs in acquisition costs is a primary function of the revenue strategist. Revenue strategy does not risk optimizing results in individual channels at the cost of overall optimal results. For instance, a hotel may determine that it should reduce its direct sales spending to increase spending in digital channels or that it needs to spend funds on call center training rather than on public relations. The ultimate outcome is defined by net revenue results.

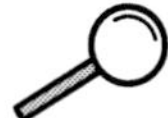

Case Study: The Hotel Stanley

In 2014, the Hotel Stanley spent essentially the same amount in total customer acquisition costs as it did in 2013 and experienced a slight decrease in net revenue. How can the hotel evaluate what is going on? What can it do to improve its net revenue? For this discussion, refer to Exhibits 13–18.

Examine the Net RevPAR Capture to see how much revenue the hotel is able to retain out of the revenue that customers spend. Although acquisition spending overall was contained and third-party spending reduced (all good results), the upshot of reduced room night volume overall with a less than optimal channel mix (an increase in OTA with a decrease in voice and GDS) resulted in a small overall decline in absolute net revenue.

Examine the mix of customer acquisition spending. Direct buying costs (commissions/transaction fees) were reduced and a compensating amount was spent in direct sales and marketing costs. The management team no doubt intended for the increased spending to benefit the direct channel production. Where did the hotel see an upswing? Where did it decline?

The hotel made a decision for 2014 to reduce its FIT wholesale business in order to reduce its high acquisition costs. But the Hotel Stanley was not able to make up the FIT room nights in higher profit channels as the hotel occupancy was flat from 2013 to 2014. While the sales and marketing investment resulted in a nice turnaround in brand.com, more work was needed to point those resources to GDS and voice as well as maintaining the traction in brand.com.

Exhibit 13 RevPAR Capture Rate

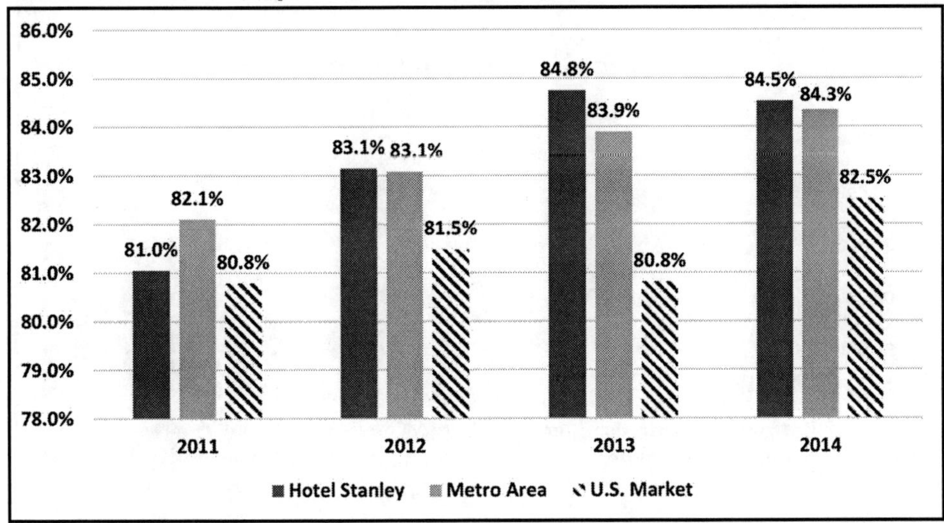

Source: Kalibri Labs, LLC.

Exhibit 14 Net Revenue with S&M and Commission/Trans Fees

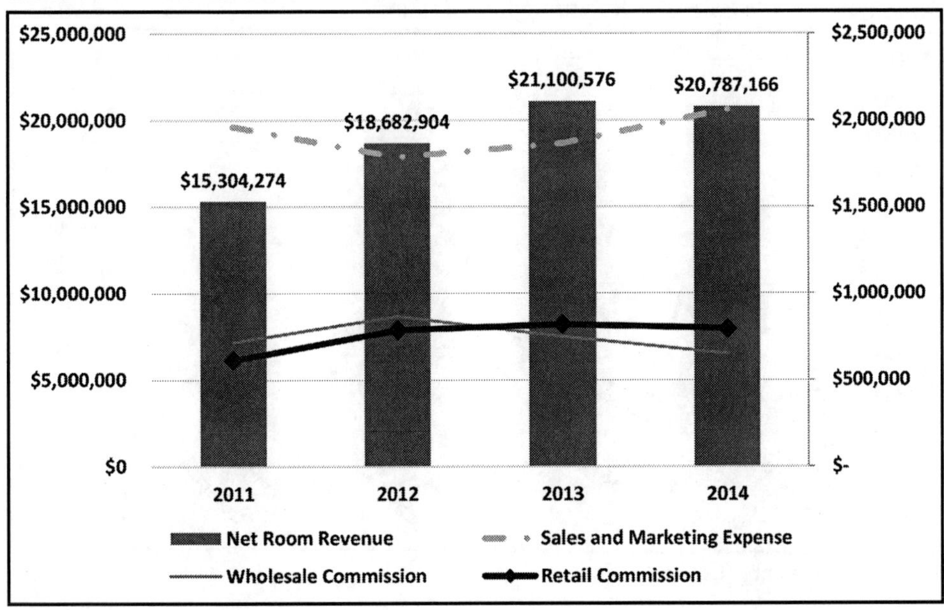

Source: Kalibri Labs, LLC.

The hotel has to look at its demand options and establish an optimal channel mix. One question that could be raised is whether the hotel should have cut back so dramatically on its FIT business and if it should have allowed the OTA channel

Exhibit 15 Customer Acquisition Costs by Center

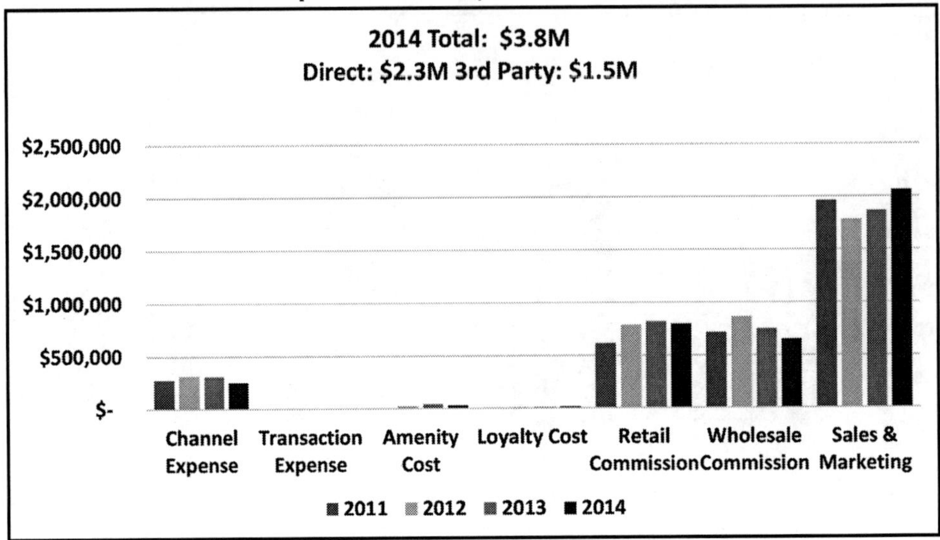

Source: Kalibri Labs, LLC.

Exhibit 16 FIT Wholesaler Room Nights by Month

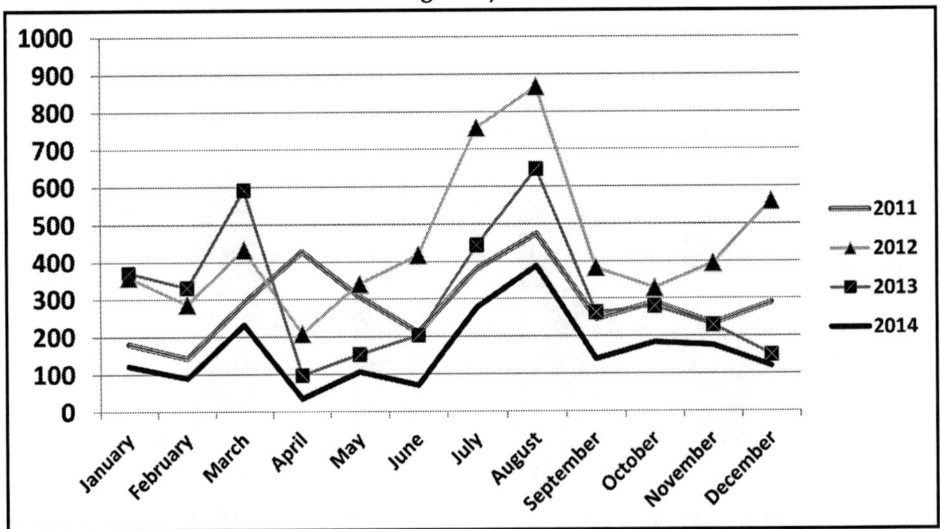

Source: Kalibri Labs, LLC.

to compensate rather than look at GDS and voice. As part of the analysis on this situation, three different net revenue outcomes were evaluated; it appears that some portion of the FIT business may be better than none *in the absence of* growth in the higher contribution channels. This is easy to say in hindsight though. The hotel

Exhibit 17 Channel Mix Demand by Room Nights

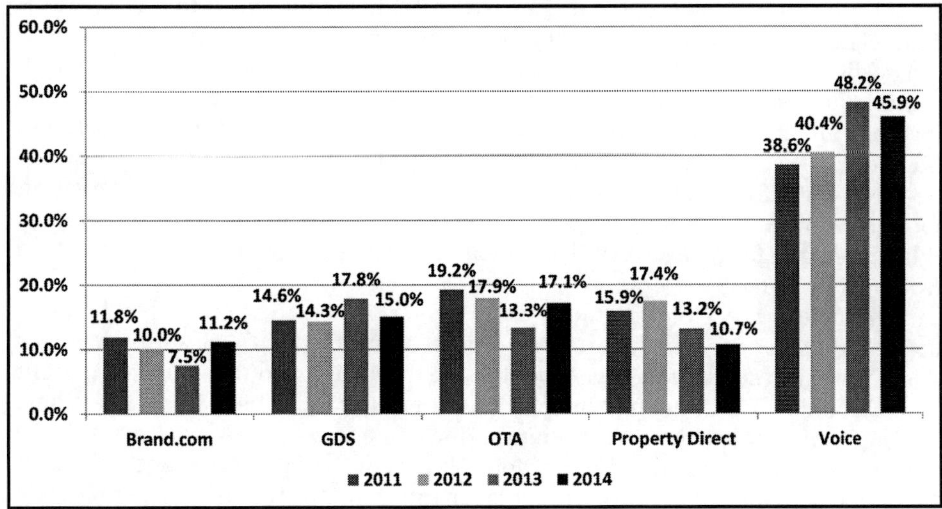

Source: Kalibri Labs, LLC.

Exhibit 18 FIT Wholesale Sensitivity Analysis

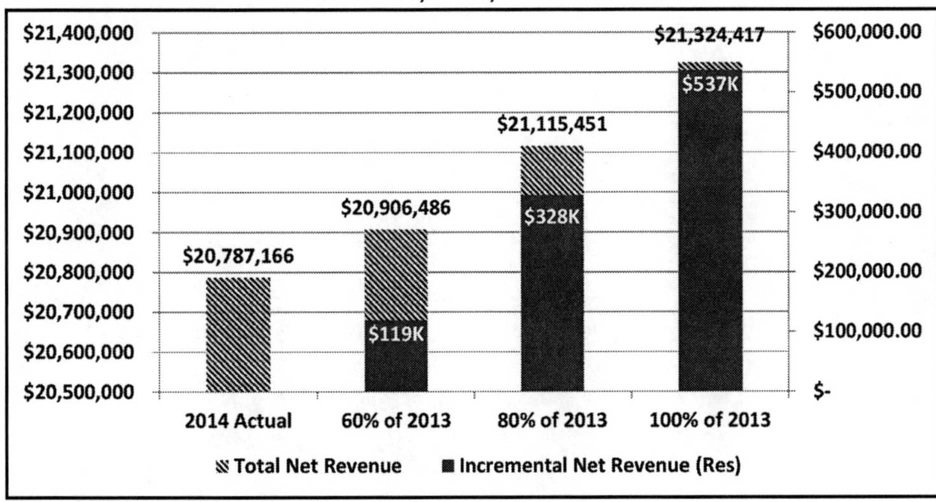

Source: Kalibri Labs, LLC.

would have to get the FIT business on the books well in advance and at the start of the year, management assumed they would get enough in high profit brand.com to make up for the loss in FIT. While brand.com performed reasonably well, they needed to step up efforts in GDS and voice as much as brand.com.

For the following year, they may spend approximately the same in sales and marketing to continue to test ways to grow brand.com, voice, and GDS. They would see a rise in total acquisition costs if they decide to replace a portion of the FIT business, but in spite of this added cost, they would need to find the right channel mix where net revenue still grows. This is the hotel's optimal channel mix. The additional consideration is the relationship between channels. For instance, in many hotels, when OTA business grows, brand.com business declines. There are many channel-agnostic customers who switch between channels. There is less likelihood of FIT business replacing the volume in brand.com. Further, it is necessary for a hotel to examine its net revenue by day of week, lead time (reservation booking window), and length of stay to look for opportunities to find segments of business that fit the needs of the hotel and contribute positively to net revenue growth.

Ultimately, the Hotel Stanley would prefer to cut back on both wholesale and OTA business and make up that volume in brand.com, GDS, and voice. This objective requires adequate investment in the three high profit channels and tight controls on the OTA channel, which is harder to limit than the FIT wholesale one. Raising brand.com without restraining OTA was not enough for the hotel to see benefits in net revenue. In 2015, this hotel should measure and manage all four of the targeted channels in a more granular manner to ensure a higher net revenue contribution.

Part II

Real Estate and the Physical Asset

6

Hotel Development, Construction, and the Real Estate Cycle

By D. Kerry Nickerson and David Johnstone

***D. Kerry Nickerson** joined Miller Global in 2009 as an Executive Vice President and Chief Development Officer with primary responsibility for oversight and management of new development projects and capital expenditures for current real estate assets in the hotel and office markets. He has over thirty-three years of experience leading all phases of development, design, and construction in many industries throughout the United States. In addition to the last seventeen years of hospitality experience, his career also includes major projects in government, industrial, and commercial developments.*

Prior to joining Miller Global, Mr. Nickerson was Vice President, Development for Host Hotels & Resorts from 2004–2009 where he was responsible for managing large and complex repositioning development projects. The hotel real estate portfolio consisted of four- and five-star properties with brands that included Marriott, Ritz-Carlton, Hyatt, Four Seasons, Fairmont, Sheraton, Westin, and Hilton.

Preceding his position at Host Hotels & Resorts, from 1998–2004 Mr. Nickerson was President of Pace Management, LLC, a consulting firm that provided project management services for hospitality, office, and other commercial real estate owners, including all phases of project development. Prior to this, Mr. Nickerson was a Senior Project Manager with a national design/build firm, Facility Group, and a Vice President with a major national architecture and engineering design firm, Rosser International. Mr. Nickerson began his career as a commissioned officer in the U.S. Navy Civil Engineer Corps, managing design and construction projects for the Naval Facilities Engineering Command.

Mr. Nickerson earned a Bachelor of Civil Engineering degree from the Georgia Institute of Technology in 1982, with a focus on Construction Management and Structural Design. He attended Tulane University School of Architecture prior to completing his degree at the Georgia Institute of Technology.

***David Johnstone,** Chief Investment Officer—Hotels for Denver-based McWhinney Real Estate Services, has been involved with hotels and other hospitality real estate for more than thirty-five years. Before joining McWhinney, his responsibilities with Miller Global Properties (1998–2015) in the lodging industry included acquisitions, developments, asset management, and dispositions. Mr. Johnstone began his hospitality real estate career in 1979 in Chicago with Laventhol & Horwath, a hospitality accounting and consulting firm. At his*

departure in 1987, he was Manager of the firm's Denver office. From 1987 to 1989, Mr. Johnstone was an Investment Manager at the Prudential Property Company in Atlanta, Georgia, where he was responsible for an equity portfolio of hotel properties located in the Southeastern United States. From 1989 to 1996, he was a Partner and Executive Vice President with Sage Hospitality Resources, LLP, a Denver-based owner/operator of hotels throughout the United States. In 1996, Mr. Johnstone joined The Ritz-Carlton Hotel Company, a subsidiary of Marriott International, Inc., in Hong Kong as Vice President, Development for the Asia/Pacific region.

Mr. Johnstone graduated from Michigan State University with a B.S.B.A. in Hotel, Restaurant, and Institutional Management in 1979. He received an M.B.A. in Real Estate and Construction Management from the University of Denver in 1986. He is currently a member of the MSU School of Hospitality Business Real Estate Investment Advisory Council and the Fritz Knoebel School of Hospitality Management Executive Advisory Board.

Mr. Johnstone was the founding President of the Hospitality Asset Managers Association and served from 1992–1994.

THE PRIMARY PURPOSE of this chapter is to review the development process for hotels, including a discussion of real estate cycles, the four basic phases of development, and the roles of various participants in the development process. While not an exhaustive presentation, the chapter should provide a solid basis for understanding the fundamental processes involved in the conceptualization, design, and construction of hospitality assets.

Real Estate Cycles

A Brief Historical Perspective

A cycle is defined as a space, or interval, of time between two events with similar characteristics. Economists, scientists, astronomers, and others have been studying cycles and their characteristics for thousands of years, since recurring events were first recorded. As an example, the first lunar and solar calendars are believed to be a series of pits dug in northern Scotland 10,000 years ago and designed to represent months of the year and the lunar phases. It is believed that people used this calendar to track the migration of animal herds and/or the timing of salmon river runs.[1] Today, many kinds of cycles are studied for business and economic reasons. The Foundation for the Study of Cycles (FSC), started by Edward Davey in 1941, is dedicated to the interdisciplinary study of finding and analyzing recurring patterns, including those within the economy, natural and social sciences, and the arts. To date, more than 4,300 natural cycles have been documented with interrelated patterns.[2]

Of primary interest to real estate developers are economic and real estate cycles. The most critical influence on the real estate development cycle is the underlying economic activity. Real estate markets have historically been highly correlated with domestic economic cycles. In recent decades, however, the multi-nationalization of financial institutions and rapidly expanding international trade have led to increasing synchronization and interdependence of international markets. In short, the world's economies are now linked more closely than ever before, and changes in one region often directly affect the others. This interdependence on so many levels can have a direct impact on various kinds of cycles, including real estate development.

Cycle Theory

By definition, a cycle has a beginning and an ending. Most experts and organizations that track real estate cycles agree that "typical" commercial cycles are somewhere around ten years in duration. Individual commercial property-type cycles (office, industrial, apartment, retail, and hotel), primarily due to the length of their lease term and/or their own particular fundamental drivers, can vary greatly within the overall property cycle. Since hotels have the shortest lease term (24-hour) of the real estate classes, they tend to react most quickly to changes in fundamental drivers, both up and down, within the cycle. Thus, understanding the fundamental drivers of a commercial real estate cycle, particularly within the markets where subject assets are located, is critical to successfully managing real estate investment.

Real estate cycles typically have four phases: Transition/Recovery, Expansion/Growth, Peak/Plateau, and Decline/Recession. A sample of the characteristics typical to each phase follows:

- *Transition/Recovery*—Economic fundamentals begin to return; occupancies, ADRs, and asset values bottom out and begin to rise; potential consolidation of investment companies takes place; and debt financing terms begin to improve.
- *Expansion/Growth*—GDP rises, as do occupancies, ADRs and values; debt financing increases in availability; hotel development commences; capitalization rates decline; and construction costs are relatively low.
- *Peak/Plateau*—Supply/demand equilibrium is achieved and eventually exceeded; overly optimistic underwriting occurs; transaction volume is high along with pricing; cap rates are low; and high levels of new construction/development take place.
- *Decline/Recession*—Construction activity is significantly reduced; access to debt financing is limited; occupancies, ADRs and asset values decline; transaction volume is reduced; capitalization rates rise; debt restructuring and/or workouts are widespread; and cash buyers have distinct advantages.

While most people typically refer to the general U.S. real estate cycle, it is important to note that property markets vary widely in terms of product types and economic drivers. While the financial crisis of 2008–2010 hit both domestic and international markets hard, from a lodging standpoint, the Washington, D.C., metropolitan area fared quite well, only to experience a downturn after the rest of the country recovered. Also, certain markets, like Seattle and New York, perhaps due to their technology drivers or their international demand base, rebounded faster than others. Thus, economic drivers can vary greatly from market to market, and by product type within a market. On a micro-market level, no two cycles have the same start and finish time frame, because no two cycles have identical characteristics and economic drivers.

Event Risk

It is always difficult to accurately forecast business cycle timing. Event risk is a factor that can greatly impact both duration and magnitude. Event risk historically was characterized by major political upheaval, such as world wars and/or major economic depressions, occurring at intervals of around 45 years to 65 years. However, since 2000 economic and real estate cycles have been significantly impacted twice by major "black swan" events: the terror events of September 11, 2001, in New York City, and also the unforeseen economic disruption initiated by the U.S. subprime mortgage crisis. Both of these unexpected events caught international markets largely by surprise. Given the world's growing financial interdependence, and the increase in high-profile global terrorist activity, event risk is now thought by many to be the norm for the future rather than the exception. Unfortunately, while some event risk can be insured against, it cannot be fully hedged. This may contribute to the willingness of some investors to accept lower returns in real estate investments or, alternatively, to avoid real estate altogether due to its illiquidity.

Timing Is Everything

The most critical key to successful real estate development is understanding the specific markets and their economic drivers in order to know when to get in and when to get out, thus taking advantage of the cycle. Favorable timing alone has the ability to turn an otherwise marginal investment into a successful deal; conversely, poor timing can doom an investment when every other facet is well-executed. To be sure, entering and exiting the investment cycle in a timely manner with a hotel development doesn't guarantee that your project will be deemed successful. Many other factors will also influence the determination of a hotel development's success, including but not limited to: the choice of a branded versus an independent operation, selection of the property management team, creation of the project's capital structure, strong site selection and investment underwriting, and effective asset management of the property. As other authors in this and previous editions of this book have ably addressed this myriad of factors impacting hotel investment, the remainder of this chapter will focus on the process of hotel development.

The Hotel Real Estate Development Process

Process Overview

Real estate development is the process of determining a real estate need and filling that need by designing, financing, and constructing an asset to fill the requirement. The real estate development process flow chart for a typical development can look like a complex equation or chemical process. There are many branches the process can take and still result in the same successful outcome. It is important to be flexible, have backup plans, and always be in control of all requirements and deliverables that will be required in the process, not just for several weeks, but for several months down the road. Being reactive versus proactive to the risks and pitfalls, which undoubtedly will be encountered, results in a loss of time and leverage relative to cost, schedule, and negotiating contracts. Successful developers need to chart a course well ahead of the process, be proactive, and anticipate outcomes at various stages that may not go their way but do not kill the process.

The basic phases of development, to be discussed in further detail later in the chapter, are pre-development, design and pre-construction, construction, and post construction/project close-out (see Exhibit 1). Since development can move slowly, particularly in the early phases, the most common pitfall early in the process is to think there is a lot of time to accomplish what is required. Failing to constantly monitor the schedule as if an activity that is several months away is tomorrow will most likely result in the inability to overcome adversity in the process, resulting in lost time and money. Timing is critical; if you are pro development because of the positive signs in the cycle, the faster you can execute before the next downturn, the more successful the outcome will be.

Budget Overview. Always establish a project budget from the very inception to evaluate the deal. The preliminary budget may be very limited with only a couple of accounting line items, but it is important to realistically understand the cost to determine if this development potentially lines up with the company's goals and objectives. This will help to eliminate any misunderstandings if a no-go decision is ultimately made and all of a sudden there is a negative reaction to how much has been spent to date. It also creates a cost history for future evaluations. In development there is always a tendency to be optimistic on what construction will cost, so be sure to include an appropriate contingency. Be realistic; think all the pieces through in detail, because it is much harder to go back for additional funds when you are over budget. If you have cost history data, reference it to put together an entire development budget and take a quick internal review of a complete pro forma before spending any funds. Many of the development costs stay within certain ratios as a general rule, but be careful on small projects, as the overhead and soft costs ratio to the overall budget can increase very quickly.

As the development looks more positive the budget can be refined at each stage. In the pre-development stage a development cost contingency of 10 to 15 percent is recommended, depending on the complexity and undefined risks. Never use a general contractor's concept budget estimate in the development budget without at least a 15 percent construction contingency. As the process moves from pre-development through design toward finalizing the construction cost, the contingency may be reduced to the range of 5 to 10 percent. Repositionings or additions to existing assets, depending on complexity, should maintain a heavier 10 percent development contingency.

Schedule Overview. Except in complex developments dealing with many entitlement issues and government approvals, it is fairly easy to put together pre-development, design, and construction schedules with a little research and assistance. As with budgeting, there is a tendency to be optimistic and believe tasks can be accomplished faster than is realistic. This is particularly true with government approvals, so seek advice from local real estate attorneys, design firms, or permit expediters on schedule durations for zoning and permit approvals. Again, be realistic and also include some time contingency. You may want to drive your team on

Exhibit 1 Basic Phases of Development: Typical 200-Key Hotel

Pre-Development	Design & Pre-Construction	Construction	Post Construction/Project Close-Out
6–18 Months	9–12 Months	14–18 Months	12 Months
Land Purchase & Sale Agreement	Consultant Contracts	Construction Monitoring/Coordination	Punch List Items
Site Analysis	Final Hotel Programming	- Construction Permitting	Operations and Maintenance Manuals
Zoning	Final Concept Design	- Quality Control	Substantial Completion and Turn-over
Title Search	Schematic Design	- Schedule Monitoring	Final Lien Waivers
Preliminary Site Plan	Design Development	- Developer/Contractor Meetings	Final Retainage Release
Local Government Meetings	Construction Documents	- Architect/Engineer Construction Reviews	Warranty Tracking
Consultant Selection	Permit Documents	- Contract Change Orders	
Consultant Reports	Branding/Operator Agreements	- Lien Waivers	
- Geotechnical	Market Feasibility	- Government and Brand Inspections	
- Environmental	Final Cost Estimates	- Lien Waivers	
- Utilities	Loan Package & Financing	Finalize FFE, Purchase & Coordinate Delivery	
- Surveys	Projected Investment Returns		
Preliminary Hotel Program	Select Contractor		
Preliminary Feasibility	Insurance and Risk Management		
	Performance/Payment Bonds		
	Finalize Construction Contracts		

a shorter schedule knowing you have some contingency. Be careful in the process; if the schedule is unrealistic then it may become meaningless to the team.

It is easier to establish credibility with other parties when you have a well thought out logistical schedule to present rather than speaking in generalities. While there are many versions of critical-path scheduling software on the market, it only takes a very simple version to create a development schedule.

Development Checklist. A development checklist is a simple tool to keep action items in the forefront of the process from the beginning, and is an efficient way to communicate with your team. The items should be logically organized by phase; state the action item, who is responsible for it, and applicable due dates. Although it seems simple and "Management 101," it takes great discipline to constantly and effectively manage the list. But it will save you time and eliminate mistakes in the long run. Develop an organization of the action items that allows you to deal with different parts of the list for different situations. Again, constantly updating the list sounds very simple but it is surprising how many developers do not use such a process and miss critical items en route. There are many industry checklists available, but keep your checklists to develop a history that you can readily have available for the next project. A sample hotel development checklist can be found at the back of the chapter as an appendix.

Developer's Role. The developer's role involves project leadership, as well as active involvement in the areas of market research, marketing, public relations, design and construction, financing and accounting, and property management. The developer must manage many resources to guide the process, must always have a strategy, and must always be aware of the associated risks in every phase.

Every real estate development involves both the public and private sectors. The developer interfaces with the public sector over (1) politics of the development (is the public supportive or resistant?), (2) zoning and entitlements approval, (3) codes and ordinances affecting the development, (4) transportation planning, and (5) quasi-government entities such as utility companies bringing utility services to the site. The developer is heavily dependent on the successful navigation of a complex governmental system, particularly in urban areas. The government entity may be in favor of the development and the public against it. Many parts of the country want new development, while many others oppose new development.

As development has become increasingly complex and controlled over the past 50 years, the role of development management has changed. Prior to the 1980s, the architect fulfilled the role of designer and project manager for the developer, and many years ago actually fulfilled the various roles of the project manager, designer, and master builder. The architect traditionally managed the general construction contract and represented the developer until the role of an independent project manager started to emerge on the scene in the last 30 years. As the development, design, and construction process became more complex, owners and developers found it advantageous to have a project management consultant represent them to manage all the resources. As the development progresses, the project manager is responsible for keeping the developer updated and recommending scope, schedule, and financial decisions as necessary. In some cases the developer's staff includes the project manager, also referred to as the development manager, and the architect's role becomes solely as a design professional. The project manager is able to give the developer an independent assessment of any issue that involves the design and construction team.

In lieu of "project manager," the term "construction manager" came on the scene to designate someone acting as the developer's project manager and manager of multiple prime construction contracts. This scenario will be discussed further later in the chapter.

Consultants

Role of Design in Hotel Development. In the 1990s, the role of design became increasingly important in our society. Designer products became more affordable and more available on the market to the average person. No longer did you have to be wealthy to have designer-oriented products in all aspects of life. With this change in our society, aesthetic expectations of our physical surroundings gained importance in the selection of hotels for both business and pleasure travel. From large mega casinos in Las Vegas (Bellagio, Mandalay Bay, Venetian, etc.) to boutique (now called lifestyle) hotels from Ian Schrager, Bill Kimpton, and the "W" brand by Starwood, hotel developers started breaking the traditional hotel company brand mold by creating unique interior design and/or interesting architecture. Hotel design trends continued changing rapidly in the early 2000s, with guests becoming more and more discriminating in their choice of lodging. Hotel chains followed Starwood's lead and developed their own boutique/lifestyle brands to compete with more design-centric hotels. Suites, spas, and great guestroom concepts were introduced and became more prevalent. Hotel brands even started partnering with fashion brands. The current decade has seen the design emphasis shift to technology-oriented applications, a more personal check-in and other experience-oriented elements, and sustainable/carbon-neutral designs. Major branded properties are now commonly licensing outside concepts or outsourcing food and beverage outlets to third-party operators to further enhance the experiential nature of their properties.

Excellent design has become increasingly critical to the overall success of a hotel. As a result, the selection of the architect and interior designer has become extremely important. When selecting the design firm, make sure it is a good fit with the proposed type of hotel product. Budget, select service, full service, resort, luxury, and convention hotels are becoming very specialized, and the design team must fit the specific needs of your asset.

The quality of hotel design and construction has improved immensely over time, consistent with the rising sophistication of hotel users. Still, the basic functional elements of a hotel have remained the same. In response to the changing nature of lodging demand, the major hotel companies continue to create, design, and develop new lodging products and brands designed to accommodate the evolving expectations of hotel guests.

Each of today's demographic "generations" has a distinct group of influences, core values, and attributes (see Exhibit 2), and while a person's birthdate may not always be indicative of their individual characteristics, the broad generational commonalities allow group marketing efforts with regard to lodging products.

Exhibit 2 Generational Attributes

	Baby Boomers	Generation X	Millennials (Gen Y)
Birth Years	1946–1964	1965–1980	1981–2000
Current Age	51–69	35–50	15–34
Estimated U.S. Population	80 million	50 million	75 million
% of U.S. Workplace	35%	45%	15%
Attributes			
Value	Success	Time	Individuality
Dealing with Money	Buy now, pay later	Cautious, conservative	Earn to spend
Technology	Acquired	Assimilated	Integral
Education	A birthright	A way to get there	An incredible expense
Personal Focus	Relationship results	Tasks and results	Global and net-worked
Business Focus	Long hours	Productivity	Contribution
Entitlement	Experience	Merit	Contribution
Communications Media	Touch-tone phones, call me anytime	Cell phones, call me anytime at work	Internet, picture phones, E-mail

Various sources, including educational/governmental institutions and businesses, want to understand, for marketing and other purposes, the characteristic differences between the various generations. Each of the generations described below are active participants in the transient commercial, transient leisure, and group travel segments. Understanding the subtle, and not so subtle, differences in generational attitudes is important to designing a successful hotel in a given market. Based on a February 2014 survey of Millennials by The Pew Research Center (www.pewresearch.org), "America is in the throes of a huge demographic shift, and a major factor in this sea change is the Millennial generation, which is forging its own distinct path to adulthood compared with older Americans."

Today's hotel designers need to account for the attributes of the different user profiles. How you design your project today may not be practical ten, fifteen, or twenty years from now. The first of the Baby Boomers are well into retirement age, and by 2020 Millennials are expected to make up half of the U.S. working population. According to the research firm D. K. Shifflet & Associates, by the year 2020,

76 percent of business travel room nights booked will be by Gen X and Millennials. How this knowledge is utilized can and should have major effects on the hotel you plan to develop.

Selection and Roles of Consultants. In a typical pre-development scenario the developer will have pre-development services contracts with the following consultants:

- *Project/development manager*—Manages the overall development as a consultant, if resources do not exist in-house.
- *Architect* —Designs the hotel, produces construction documents, and assists the owner or owner's representative with construction administration. Most architectural firms can also provide land planning, space planning, and landscape design expertise, otherwise one or more specialty consultants will be required.
- *Architect (land planner)*—Designs a master plan for the site in the case of larger developments.
- *Architect (space planning)*—Provides layouts for interior space.
- *Architect (landscape)*—Designs landscape and hardscapes such as exterior spaces, walks, patios, irrigation systems, and trees and other plantings.
- *Structural engineer*—Designs and specifies subgrade structures such as foundations and retaining walls based on recommendations from the geotechnical engineer, and provides design elevated structures.
- *Civil and utilities engineer*—Utilizes the architect's conceptual site design to design the site grading, drives, on grade parking, site hydrology, erosion control, storm drainage, and water quality and detention basins; also provides assistance with land disturbance permits and the site plan approval process.
- *Traffic engineer*—Analyzes the traffic and transportation network to recommend any changes necessary to integrate the development into the transportation system and access the site with the best flow of traffic.
- *Geotechnical engineer*—Identifies soil types on site and makes recommendations for foundation types and the design of the sub-base for drives and parking lots.
- *Legal counsel*—Needed for all of the agreements involved with the development as well as understanding land use laws relative to zoning and entitlements. Legal firms' political connections in the community should also be evaluated, as these connections can be a tremendous asset in securing governmental approval of the development.
- *Environmental engineer*—Provides specialized studies of the site for existing environmentally sensitive issues, hazardous materials, and environmental impacts from the development. The environmental topic has increasingly become a major item in development, as environmental laws and codes become more stringent every year. Development is becoming more difficult, lengthy, and costly every year in environmentally sensitive areas.

- *Registered surveyor*—Provides legal boundary surveys and topographical surveys, as well as legal ALTA surveys.
- *Cost estimator (separate consultant or general contractor)*—Provides cost-estimating and construction-estimating services.

Other consultants to bring into the project as it moves forward from pre-development include the following:

- *Interior designer*—Designs and specifies the interior spaces and interior architecture and finishes as well as furnishings, fixtures, and equipment.
- *Mechanical engineer*—Designs and specifies environmental control systems that provide heating and cooling of the building, and performs energy conservation studies. Mechanical engineering also includes the plumbing design for water and wastewater systems.
- *Electrical engineer*—Designs and specifies the power service from the utility-company connection to the building, interior power distribution, lighting systems (interior and exterior), and fire alarm systems, and performs energy conservation studies.
- *Fire protection engineer*—Designs the connection of the public utility and the building sprinkler system.
- *Sustainability consultants*—The desire for Leadership in Energy & Environmental Design (LEED) certification has become a dominant influence in design. There are two parts to the sustainability consultant services: (1) consulting during the design, including LEED submission; and (2) building commissioning.
- *Other specialty consultants*—Provide engineering and design services relating to parking, signage and other graphics, audiovisual components, technology systems, lighting, food service (F&B), curtain wall, building acoustics, vertical transportation, and water features.

Names of potential design firms may be sourced from publications and prior business contacts. Be sure that the firms have adequate experience with your type of hotel building, since design firms may be very specialized. It is also preferable that the architect and civil engineering firms have business and government contacts in the local community. Only contract for pre-development services, as the development will be further defined during this phase or the decision may be made not to go forward after completing feasibility studies and conceptual design.

As the scope of the project develops and looks positive for moving forward, it may be advantageous to request full proposals and negotiate contracts in preparation for the remaining phases. If you are unable to negotiate an acceptable fee and contract with the current design firm, there is still time to solicit an alternate firm.

Consultant Contracts. There are established forms of contracts for consultants, such as American Institute of Architects (AIA) documents, as well as forms your attorney may draft. Some developers have their own standard contracts. The development manager (DM) should lead all consultant contract negotiations, with assistance from the attorney. The scope of the consultant's services is the responsibility of the DM. The contract sections dealing with ownership of documents, termination, claims, mediation, arbitration, and indemnification and insurance should have significant involvement from the attorney. The risk manager or insurance broker should be involved in all insurance coverage discussions. In lieu of operating with a consultant's proposal, it is highly recommended that the contract be negotiated early in order to obtain the best terms. If time passes there may not be enough time to solicit an alternate firm.

Legal counsel and an insurance professional should be consulted regarding the professional liability policy and coverage limits for the particular design firm involved with the development. Professional liability policies are very complex, and design firms, particularly small ones, are reducing standard coverages. If the developer requires higher limits, then the increased cost is typically being included as an additional cost to the developer.

Project Delivery Methods

Design/Bid/General Contractor. This is the traditional method of project delivery. The developer contracts with the design team and manages the design of the development. The completed design documents are bid to multiple general contractors. The developer typically selects and contracts with the lowest-cost responsible general contractor.

Design/Bid/Multiple Prime Contractors. This approach is the same as above except the developer contracts with more than one prime general contractor for different facets of the project. The developer avoids paying mark-up on the other contractor's work by a general contractor, but must be staffed for the coordination time involved in managing multiple contracts. This time commitment can be significant. Additionally, there is an increased risk for scope of work gaps between contractors, resulting in change orders to the developer.

Negotiated Guaranteed Maximum Price (GMP) General Contractor. This method is similar to the traditional design/bid/general contractor approach except that the developer selects the general contractor any time prior to the design development phase. The developer will request qualifications, fee, general conditions, and an initial GMP from multiple general contractors based on the concept or schematic design. The contractor proposals represent a competitive approach to fees and general conditions, and the developer can make a negotiated selection and also negotiate the initial GMP. The final GMP will be determined when design and construction documents are complete and bid out to multiple subcontractors. Essentially, all parts of the work are competitively bid. It is important to get the contractor on board prior to design development, so cost can be managed to the initial GMP by the contractor during the remainder of the design process.

Design Build (Turnkey). With design build, also known as a turnkey contract, the developer contracts with the general contractor for the design and construction of the project. The developer benefits by only contracting with one party for design and construction, and the contractor has total control of the designers. This method can be utilized with the entire project or just parts of the project, such as mechanical systems, electrical and plumbing systems, or structural systems. Disadvantages of this method are (1) the developer is totally dependent on the general contractor for all phases of the work, and (2) the developer must invest funds and time up front defining the scope of the work and the quality-level of the project to form the basis of the design/build contract, or else many changes in cost will result. The contractor will deliver only the lowest-cost alternatives if not required otherwise. With a design build approach, it is critical to define up front the specific design and quality requirements of ownership.

Construction Management. There are various forms of construction management (CM), both at risk for cost and not at risk for cost. The CM generally fulfills the developer's role of managing multiple construction contracts; however, the difference is that the developer holds all of the contracts, not the CM. The CM is only the manager of the contracts and acts as a project manager for the developer. The basic assumption is that after the CM's fee there should be cost savings because there is no general contractor mark-up of each contractor's cost. There is an increased cost risk by the developer stepping into the shoes of the general contractor, but also there is the reward of potential savings and more control of the multiple contractors.

Various construction contract methods will be discussed later in the chapter in the section covering the construction process.

Phases in Hotel Development

Phase 1—Pre-Development

The goal of the pre-development process is to eliminate as many risks, assumptions, and unknowns as possible in order to determine if the site is feasible for development. This phase will contain just a few—but very important—decisions regarding both what the product will be and how much it will cost. There is a clear correlation to the amount of effort during this phase and the number of risks that can be addressed and eliminated. It is also the phase during which due-diligence seed money will be required to be put at risk to determine if the developer will decide to move forward or pass on the opportunity. For the average hotel development in the United States, these expenses could range from $50,000–$200,000. There needs to be the right balance of adequate money available based on the complexity of the development. For the purposes of this chapter, assume that a hypothetical development will require zoning and entitlement approvals.

The process begins by assembling the team to execute pre-development services and establishing the schedule and budget for the following tasks.

Feasibility—Preliminary. Typically a third-party consultant's feasibility report will be initiated to determine if the market can support hotel development. It may also be required by the lender. Feasibility is discussed in more detail in a subsequent section of the chapter.

Hotel Programming—Preliminary. Programming is the process of taking the feasibility study results and transferring them into actual building spaces and square footage, and describing the functional relationship with other spaces. Each space and size will be identified in a written space program that can be assigned a square-foot cost to determine a construction budget, with input on site and utility costs.

The lack of a clearly defined hotel space program will waste time and money in the design process due to unclear direction. It is very important for the design team to understand the developer's brand product, functional and space requirements, and how the project may need to be customized for the market. The developer should decide what is best for the site and market, and complete an architectural program. This will allow the design team to understand the goals and objectives for the development and also the translation of the developer's vision to building square footage or square meterage. This task of space programming requires significant leadership from the developer, as the decisions are very important and will have significant impacts on the budget. The developer may want to access typical hotel-brand space programs and then customize them for the market in question. It is critical that the developer take charge of the design and not allow the hotel brand to dictate it; if the developer loses control of the process, the project will most likely be over budget.

Site Analysis and Due Diligence. Assuming the market feasibility report supports development of a hotel on the site, to analyze the site's suitability for construction the following tasks must be performed:

- *Geotechnical Report*—Determines the suitability and structural characteristics of on-site soils.
- *Phase 1 Environmental Report*—Determines any sensitive environmental issues and the presence of hazardous materials. The environmental report also determines if any important archaeology is located on the site.
- *Phase 2 Environmental Report*—Determines the quantity and locations of any hazardous materials on the site, if their presence is indicated or confirmed in a Phase 1 Environmental Report.
- *Traffic Report*—Determines how the site will be accessed and what public improvements will be required.
- *Utility Location and Capacity Analysis*—Determines the cost to get utilities to the site boundary. As part of this process, it is advisable to obtain a "will serve" letter from each utility. This is good practice no matter how obvious it may seem to be, and the lender likely will require them. It will also start a dialog on who will pay for what regarding utility extensions.
- *Storm Water Review*—Analyzes how storm water detention and quality control will be handled on the site.
- *Boundary Survey*—Determines the legal boundaries of the site.
- *Topographic Survey*—Determines the topography of the site and any major cost implications due to grading.
- *Zoning Study*—Determines the existing zoning and entitlements for the site—whether they support the projected use, and if re-zoning will be required.

- *Initial Master Planning*—Documents an initial master plan of the site.
- *Preliminary Conceptual Design*—Determines gross building area and parking requirements to determine how the building could potentially be located on the site.
- *Title Search*—Verifies the owner of record and identifies any defects in the title. This will also show recorded deed and land restrictions. It is advisable to initiate a preliminary title search as soon as possible to find out any potential title issues, as they will come into play during the financing.
- *Local Government Agency Meetings*—Assist in determining the level of support for the proposed use. Some of the involved agencies are the local planning department, building department, fire department, transportation department, and utility companies.

Zoning and Entitlements. If the existing zoning and entitlements will not allow a hotel development, then it will need to be determined if there is support from the planning department and community for a land use change. If so, this process could take from 1 to 2 years, depending on the community opposition, if any. If the zoning is determined to be acceptable and only minor variances are required, then it may only take 3 to 6 months to procure necessary approvals.

Phase 2—Design and Pre-Construction

The steps in the planning and design process are feasibility, programming, concept design, schematic design, design development, and construction and permit documents.

Feasibility—Final. The preliminary feasibility report should be finalized during this phase. Further refinements may be necessary to quantify the number of guestrooms and the amount of public space, such as meeting space, food and beverage space, and space for leisure, retail, and other amenities. All of these spaces drive revenue, and requirements need to be defined for the pro forma as much as possible early in the process.

Programming and Concept Design—Final. Programming was previously defined in the discussion of pre-development tasks. Concept design is the process of taking the space program and turning it into actual floor plans and exterior elevations that define the overall architectural aesthetic of the hotel. This will further help to refine the construction budget.

The architect works with the developer and other parties to ascertain the applicable requirements of the development and review the understanding of the program requirements with the developer. The architect prepares conceptual plans and layouts showing the general functional relationships of areas and design concepts; this material will be reviewed and approved by the developer and (if applicable) the hotel brand. Based on a review and analysis of the functional and organizational relationships, the hotel's position in the market, and requirements and objectives, the architect provides a written scope of requirements and conceptual design. The architect assists in review of the construction budget, an FF&E budget (if applicable), and a project schedule.

The food and beverage program and concept design should also be determined and customized for the market at this time. It will have a significant impact on front-of-the-house and back-of-the-house building space, as well as on equipment cost. Typically, for a full-service hotel there will be separate equipment for banquet catering and for the hotel's restaurant/lounge. (Although some equipment may be used jointly.) Close coordination is required with the brand's food and beverage staff and chef (if they are on the team at this point) to determine the program. The developer must be in charge, as food and beverage facilities are expensive, and the budget can easily get out of hand. In some cases, such as with limited-service hotels, the food and beverage requirements are set by the brand and are fairly rigid. However, the developer should not hesitate to challenge the brand if the developer believes the brand's standards do not meet the market's requirements.

Schematic Design. Schematic design further defines the floor plans and architecture of the building, both aesthetically and technically, with written descriptions of construction materials and engineering systems. The architect will evolve the conceptual design into schematic designs, and prepare schematic design documents for the development consistent with the construction budget. Schematic design consists of drawings and other documents illustrating the scale and relationship of the project components, and shall include site plans, preliminary grading and storm drainage plan, colored exterior elevations, colored exterior rendering perspectives, floor plans, structural plans, major systems' descriptions, narrative specifications by each design consultant, conceptual designs of interior spaces, building exterior elevations, and (if applicable) color schemes and furniture selections for spaces covered by the scope. The architect will prepare an overall material palette and typical furniture types to be reviewed.

The architect will also prepare and provide formal schematic design presentations in color board format. The developer may choose to obtain an initial Guaranteed Maximum Price (GMP) from the contractor based on the schematic design documents. If the initial GMP is within the limits of the project cost established by the developer, and the developer approves it, the architect will proceed with completion of design development. Cost and scope will be monitored by the selected general contractor or the developer's cost consultant.

Design Development. Design development starts the process of detailing architectural and engineering systems on the drawings through the use of floor plans, elevations, sections, and details. This is a critical stage to perform a detailed cost-estimating check.

Based on the approved schematic design documents and any adjustments authorized by the developer in the program, schedule, or construction budget, the architect prepares design development documents consisting of drawings, specifications, and other documents to further fix and describe the size and character of the development, and to prepare formal design development presentations. Any proposed deviation from the schematic design shall be specifically identified. A specific list of design development documents will be provided prior to commencing this phase of work. During the design development phase, the architect will consider the availability of materials, construction sequencing, economics, energy conservation, efficiency, safety, and user maintenance. The architect and engineers will review the design development cost estimate and incorporate any reasonable cost-saving alternatives that are presented and accepted.

Construction Documents. Constructions documents are further increased in detail from design development documents and serve as the drawings and specifications that show how the building will be constructed. These documents will be stamped and signed by the design professional and submitted for a construction permit, which will be issued by the applicable government jurisdiction. A typical construction document set includes civil, landscape, structural, architectural, interior design, FF&E, mechanical, plumbing, fire protection, electrical, and low voltage systems.

The architect will prepare construction documents, including drawings, specifications, and other documents setting forth in detail construction requirements that delineate and describe the work in accordance with the design development documents, as well as the developer's criteria for aesthetics, operation, maintenance, and budget. The architect will coordinate documents with services provided by other engineering and design consultants, including consultants and commissioning agents. If the developer has chosen to obtain and has agreed upon an initial GMP with the contractor at the conclusion of schematic design or design development, the architect will complete the construction documents consistent with the GMP so that the developer can secure a final GMP based on the construction documents. The developer, architect, and contractor will agree that the final GMP will not exceed the initial GMP unless the development of the construction documents involves a material change in the current scope of work (or the work as depicted on any subsequent or additional construction documents). If the GMP exceeds the initial GMP, the developer must decide if the construction documents need to be revised through scope reduction or value engineering.

Permit Documents. The architect will incorporate any construction document revisions necessary for the permit submission set.

Phase 3—Construction

Construction Contract Types. There are several construction contract types: lump sum, negotiated (GMP), and cost plus.

Lump sum. A lump sum contract is typically used with the traditional design, bid, and award to a general contractor; however, lump sum contracts also can be used when the developer chooses to manage multiple contractors. The contract is for a lump sum, agreed-upon price and remains fixed for the term of the contract, subject to changes for revisions to the scope of the work. The burden of risk with this contract type is with the contractor; therefore, the contractor will include some cost to cover the risk. Some lump sum contracts include a cost escalation method to mitigate this risk.

Negotiated guaranteed maximum price (GMP). Most GMP contracts are open book and highly recommended. To ensure all costs are accurately documented, developers should ensure that the right is secured by contract to audit the contractor's final construction accounting for the project. If the project final GMP at the end of the design process goes over the initial GMP due to scope increase or market conditions as interpreted by the contractor, the main recourse by the developer is to terminate the contractor. This will cost time and money, and developers are reluctant to choose this option. As the contractor is not liable for nor warrants the initial GMP, the main leverage is the contractor's reputation, the potential for repeat business, and the potential for termination. The final GMP after bidding is frequently higher than the initial GMP due to scope increases during the design process. It is advisable to be wary of an initial GMP that seems too low, and to carry a pricing contingency in the developer's budget.

Fast-track GMP. This contract type allows the developer to set and contract for a GMP early in the project to help the developer obtain financing. It can be combined with fast track delivery to expedite the construction and development process by finishing construction documents for long lead items first, such as site, foundations, structural systems, major building components, and equipment, in the order of construction priority. During the development process, the contractor has the responsibility to constantly monitor and report estimated construction costs to the developer and to continually advise on how to keep within the GMP. Typically, the building is 25 to 35 percent complete before all of the design drawings are complete. This fast track method has an increased potential for cost overrun risks for the developer if the scope of work increases during the design process and the GMP increases. At that point, due to construction ongoing, the developer is committed to the project and its resultant costs.

Traditional schedule GMP. A non-fast-track GMP process, while not achieving the reduced schedule, has less risk, as the developer can agree to none or to small increments of early release work and commitments before the drawings are complete. If none of the work is released early, this will allow the complete, final GMP to be bid to subcontractors and contracted, reducing the unknown cost risk before construction starts. This method still has the benefits of (1) having the contractor on board early in the design process to work with the design team, and (2) open book accounting. It is important to remember that the term "GMP" does not mean that the construction cost will not exceed the initial GMP, because scope of work increases will occur!

Cost plus. This contract has a set fee for the contract regardless of the final construction cost. The developer is billed for the construction cost, plus the fee. In some situations, such as bid award or fast track, the contractor's general conditions and fee may be a percentage of the final construction cost, so that if costs increase, the fees do as well. This method typically is used for a very complex project where it is difficult to determine the complete scope of work at any one time.

Incentives. With any of the contract types just noted, financial incentives for completion under cost, completion on schedule, or early completion can be added to the contract. The incentives must be significant in order to be meaningful.

Selecting the Contractor. Typically three contractors that are known to be qualified for the project are selected to submit proposals. The following criteria should be used in selecting a contractor:

1. Relevant project experience
2. Financial information

3. Proposed management team and organization
4. Cost control procedures
5. Schedule control procedures
6. Quality control procedures
7. Proposed contract changes requested
8. Technical knowledge
9. Recent cost experience on the type of hotel building being developed

After completing the interviews of the contractors, the evaluation of them can be purely subjective, or an objective numerical rating system can be used for assigning a value to each selection criteria for each contractor, or a combination of these methods may be utilized.

Insurance and Risk. The developer should seek legal counsel and professional risk management assistance to establish the risk containment program. Risks can be categorized generally as natural (weather catastrophes or seismic activity), government, utilities, terrorism, and war. Other risks include failure to deliver public services required for the site, design-related errors and omissions, and construction-related risks such as failure to perform and labor disputes.

Liability insurance. Comprehensive general liability insurance protects against legal liability from the public. Workers' compensation insurance protects employers from claims arising from workers' injuries.

Property insurance. Builder's risk insurance protects the insured property from physical damage during the construction period. The types of perils are named in the policy. The coverage reimburses the insureds on actual loss or damage. The contractor or developer can obtain and hold the builder's risk policy. Due to volume, the contractor's policy may cost less, but extreme caution should be exercised to understand the contractor's policy and coverages. It may cost a small additional amount for the developer to obtain the builder's risk insurance, but this can provide the developer with the peace of mind that comes with fully understanding the coverages and selecting the coverage limits.

Other insurance. Consultation should be obtained regarding the advisability of coverage of other perils, such as fire and explosion, water liability, and crime.

Bonds. The developer should obtain performance and payment bonds from the contractor. A performance bond provides for performance of the agreement by the contractor and payment by the surety for the developer's loss up to the penalty of the bond amount. A payment bond provides for payment of all contractors and vendors providing labor and material for the project. In some cases the developer will require a maintenance bond to provide for performance during the warranty period. A release of liens bond ensures that the developer will not suffer loss or damage from a lien claim.

Construction Monitoring and Coordination. Construction monitoring and coordination involves pre-construction services, construction permits, quality control, the construction schedule, developer and contractor meetings, architect and engineering team responsibilities, cost management, contract changes, construction draws and lien waivers, and operations and maintenance manuals.

Pre-construction services. Most contractors are more than willing to provide pre-construction services such as cost estimating and construction scheduling when the scope of the development is established early in the design phase. The typical arrangement is that a fee is established for the services, unless the contractor is awarded the final construction work. The services are generally more detailed if a fee arrangement is established in lieu of no fee. Similar services are also available from a third-party consultant for a fee.

Construction permits. Prior to the start of construction the developer must have building permit approval. The documents for this are submitted months in advance of the start of construction—how many months in advance depends on the jurisdiction. The developer's schedule at pre-development should reflect the zoning, entitlement amendments, and building permit timelines.

Quality control. During the contractor selection process the contractor's quality control process should be outlined and discussed in detail. Those discussions should be clearly outlined in the construction contract. Any quality control issues should be part of the agenda at the developer and contractor meetings. On complex projects, the developer should consider hiring a quality control team for the project. On typical hotel projects, quality control can be accomplished via the materials testing company (which in most cases is the geotechnical engineering firm) with respect to site, structural, and building envelope. Additionally, the architect/engineering team can be utilized for quality control reviews. The developer should insist that the contractor have an internal quality control program.

Construction schedule. A construction schedule should be developed by the contractor, and it should be attached to the construction contract. Construction schedules vary depending on many factors: the weather pattern in a particular geographical region; construction type (materials) and method; size of the hotel; type of hotel; and nature of the facilities and amenities included (meeting space, parking, spa, etc.). All of the components to be constructed impact the construction schedule. In addition to having input on the details of the construction schedule, the developer should provide input on specific milestones required to meet the developer's goals and objectives, as well as milestones that require specific action by the developer, so that there is a clear agreement of responsibility to act. Care should be exercised to review the schedule in detail (or have a consultant do it) and understand it. It is strongly recommended to ensure that what the contractor is proposing is reasonable and not setting the developer up for potential delay responsibility. Developers should also monitor the schedule monthly and require that the contractor use micro schedules such as a 4-week look-ahead on those details that will be accomplished during the look-ahead period.

Developer and contractor meetings. These meetings should be held at a minimum of every two weeks, but weekly is preferred, especially if the project is complex. The developer should attend at least every other week, as too much transpires during these meetings to not be there in person. The architect should be required to attend every meeting. Agenda items should include a schedule report, quality control updates, safety updates, shop drawings, a submittals status report, a request for information status report, and a contract changes status report.

Architect and engineering team responsibilities. To avoid disputes, the developer should clearly identify in the design team contract the frequency of meetings and on-site visits for conformance reviews of work in place. It is highly recommended that a more intensive on-site services agreement be made with the design team. The additional cost should easily be justified by resolving problems quickly and providing an opportunity to catch construction issues before it is too late to avoid impacting the schedule. Significant access to the design team by the contractor will help eliminate a traditional source of frustration in the construction process. The design team can also keep the developer informed on the quality and progress of the construction work.

Cost management. The contractor should provide the developer with an update on costs at least monthly; weekly updates are preferable. Care should be exercised with the contractor at construction commencement to make it clear that absolutely no changes will be paid for unless acknowledged and agreed to by the developer in advance, in accordance with the contract. If a change is not agreed to by the developer, the typical construction contract outlines the process for resolution. It can't be emphasized enough that clear communication on this topic is essential to prevent unknown costs and claims at the end of construction.

Contract changes. All hotel developments have construction contract changes, as it is impossible to include every item and not have errors or omissions. Changes should be dealt with quickly to prevent delays and to avoid compounding construction problems. Change orders may document smaller accretive changes over a time period or may represent one large change. The source of the changes can be from the contractor, developer, or design team, but changes to the contract amount or the intent of the documents must be approved by the developer and the design team whose professional stamp is on the documents.

Construction draws and lien waivers. The general contractor typically will prepare an application for payment draw request monthly. The request will be sent for review and approval by the developer, architect, and consultant representing the lender if a loan is involved. Lien waivers must be attached indicating that the contractor and subcontractor have been paid to date through the previous request. If slow draw request approvals create a timing problem for payment to filter down to sub and vendor levels, lien waivers may only indicate payment through the request prior to the previous month. This really is not an issue with a payment and performance bond in place, but lien waivers should not slip any further behind.

Operations and maintenance manuals. The construction specifications should outline requirements for the contractor to provide operations and maintenance manuals to the developer at the completion of construction for various components of the work. All warranty documents should also be included. Developers should be vigilant in making sure that operations and maintenance manuals are turned over at project completion, or payment should be withheld accordingly.

Phase 4—Post Construction and Project Close Out

The project is complete and ready for developer review when the contractor has corrected all the contractor's quality control and punch list items. At that point, the developer's staff should assist the architect/engineering team in creating the developer's own punch list of items for the contractor to correct. The list will state a required time for correction. The developer's and architect/engineering team's punch list should be substantially complete (95 to 100 percent) before declaring the project substantially complete and useable for its intended use. Additionally, the contractor must have obtained a final or temporary certificate of occupancy.

Substantial completion is a contractual milestone at which point the contractor turns over control of the project to the developer as relates to security, utility costs, and legal control. It also establishes the start date of all warranties. A retention amount for outstanding punch list correction should be established, and the remainder of the contract amount paid to the contractor.

During the warranty period, a warranty call-back procedure should be developed and agreed to by developer and contractor. It is very important for the developer to keep a warranty call-back log in case of multiple problems with one item, in order to establish a potential latent-defect claim if the problem continues after the warranty period. The general construction warranty period is typically one year, but certain equipment and components of construction have warranties that can extend many years.

Development Risk versus Acquisition Risk

Developing a new hotel versus acquiring an existing hotel entails significant additional risk. The time between when a new project is envisioned and when it opens typically takes years, and the level of development complexity compounds the time to project completion. In some jurisdictions, if the site envisioned for development doesn't have entitlements in place, just securing the entitlements can take a year or more. When developing a hotel project, the participants need to feel a sense of urgency, because once construction begins, time turns into money. Being "on time" and "on budget" with the construction component of a hotel development go a long way toward reaching the investment objective.

Examples of Potential Risks During Construction

Examples of potential risks during construction include the following:

- *Increased construction costs*—increased construction costs may be due to increased materials costs, increased labor costs, unforeseen site conditions, or new brand standards.
- *Financing costs*—financing costs may increase due to interest rate increases.
- *Additional supply*—additional supply risks may involve new hotel projects or sister brands of the same hotel company.
- *Political risk*—shifts in political power and philosophy may occur due to national, regional, or local elections.
- *Event risk*—event risks involve unpredictable major events with significant economic and/or political impact.
- *Transaction market*—transaction market risks involve changes in cap rates, discount factors, or the market for buyers.

- *Local demand generators*—the hotel development project may suffer the loss or downsizing of major local demand generators.
- *Technology advances*—the rapid pace of technological advances may render elements of the hotel's design obsolete by the hotel's opening.
- *Jurisdictional policy or tax changes*—jurisdictional policy or tax changes involve unanticipated changes in the business operating environment, such as changes to the property tax mill levy, assessment valuation method, or sales/ occupancy tax calculation methodology.

These are just a few examples of the potential problems that can occur between the time a hotel development is started and when the property opens. Many of these situations can also occur after a hotel is acquired (versus developed); however, the ability to react to them tends to be a greater challenge for hotels that are under construction as opposed to already operating hotels that have been purchased.

Other Development Considerations

Whether developing a new hotel or acquiring an existing one, additional thought should also be given to the following factors:

- *Hold period*—The length of time expected to own the hotel could impact the choice and quality-level of numerous building systems and finishes.
- *Exit strategy*—The profile of the likely buyer could impact many decisions, from project design to potential brand or management encumbrance.
- *Location*—Whether it is expected to improve, stay the same, or get worse over time can impact brand selection as well and other project positioning choices.
- *Site*—Whether the land is freehold or leased, has any unusual site conditions or restrictions (example—height limitations, FAR limitations, zoning restrictions, soil contamination, etc.) will have implications on capital structure, project timeline, and the architectural/design/construction processes.
- *Market*—Barriers to entry and the nature/pattern of market demand will impact branding decisions, project positioning, and design/construction considerations.
- *Branding*—Selection of the appropriate brand (if any) will impact project design and construction, since brand standards must be taken into consideration; FF&E selection and cost will also be affected, as well as soft costs for brand technical service fees.
- *Product type*—Selection of the appropriate product type for the location and the market has broad implications throughout the development process and will also impact the exit strategy.

Conclusion

The hotel development and construction process involves the acquisition of land (or air rights) and the subsequent creation of a tangible hotel building. In some cases it can be the acquisition of an existing building and then the conversion or renovation of that building into a hotel product. The development process involves a multitude of professions including a variety of architects, planners, engineers, lawyers, contractors/sub contractors, construction and project managers, numerous specialty consultants, public officials, hotel specialists (with hotel companies or consulting firms) and others. Each member of the team must incorporate his or her skill set to coordinate the timely delivery of the hotel product. The owner/developer is responsible to synthesize the team through the timely and efficient exchange of information in order to bring the project in "on time and on budget." Starting with the initial feasibility of the project the owner/developer/investor must be sure to find the right site, determine the appropriate product and enter the market/cycle at the right time in order to exit the investment with a successful return.

Endnotes

1. David Keys, "Found After 10,000 Years: The World's First Calendar" (*The Independent*, July 15, 2013; www.independent.co.uk).
2. Foundation for the Study of Cycles, Inc., The World Center for Cycles Research (www.foundationforthestudyofcycles.org).

Chapter Appendix: Sample Hotel Development Checklist

Pre-Development & Due Diligence	
1 Contracts & Proposals	
1	Geotechnical Consultant - preliminary
2	Environmental Consultant proposal & contract
3	Surveyor proposal & contract
4	Civil Engineer Concept Phase proposal & contract
5	Architecture Due Diligence Proposal & Contract
6	Architecture Concept Proposal & Contract
7	Legal - engagement letter
8	Consultant - existing building evaluation proposal & contract
9	Utilities & Location
10	Permit Consultant proposal & contract
11	Market Survey
2 Legal & Financing	
1	Franchise - commitment letter
2	Lender - terms sheet & commitment letter
3	Purchase & Sale Agreement
4	Go Hard On Deposit Date
5	Closing Date
6	Complete title search / report and legal description
7	Independent Consideration
8	Verify and research existing easements
9	Verify any encroachments required
10	Verify future easements required
11	Verify if restrictive covenants
12	Complete Boundary ALTA Survey
13	Future platting changes / parcel consolidation
14	Determine if easements required for utilities or access
15	Evaluate Insurance requirements & cost
16	Liquor license requirements
17	Health / F & B license requirements
18	Mineral rights
19	Water rights
20	Appraisal
21	Tax district & rates
22	Verify if adjacent property federal or state govt boundary
23	Verify if adjacent roadways federal, state or local
3 Schedule	
1	Develop schedule for pre development activities

Pre-Development & Due Diligence

2	Determine feasibility / go hard date
3	Determine closing date
4	Develop construction schedule
5	Design Start & Phase Milestones
6	Base building Completion
7	Additional Tenant buildout Completion
8	Development schedule detail CPM
4 Budget	
1	Development Cost Report - preliminary draft for review
2	Development Cost Report - Final PD Phase
3	Development Preliminary Cost Pro forma & Underwriting
4	Development Cost Proforma - Final PD Phase
5	Develop budget for execution of pre development activities
6	Earnest money deposit amount
7	Determine if construction is Union or Non Union
8	Determine construction area cost index
9	Research for recommended contractors - preconstruction
10	Determine General Building permit fee
11	Determine liquor license process and fee
12	Determine General Impact Fees
13	Determine Development Jurisdcition Improvement Costs
14	Determine Rezoning / Variance fee if applicable
15	Determine Storm impact fee, connection fee & extension cost
16	Determine Water impact fee, connection fee & extension cost
17	Determine Sewer impact fee, connection fee & extension cost
18	Determine Sewer utility equip cost responsibility / rates
19	Determine Transportation Traffic Impact & Curb Cut Fees
20	Determine Gas connection fee & extension cost
21	Determine Gas utility equipment cost responsibilities / rates
22	Determine Electrical connection fee & extension cost
23	Determine Electrical utility equip cost responsibilities / rates
24	Determine Telephone connection fee & extension cost
25	Determine Telephone equipment cost responsibilities
26	Determine real estate taxes
5 Permits & Codes	
1	Maximum building height for low rise - determination
2	Determine applicable Building Codes & complete code analysis
3	Obtain Zoning Regulations & Complete Zoning Analysis
4	Determine Building Dept & obtain development process docs

Pre-Development & Due Diligence	
5	Determine City / County Engineer & obtain dev process docs
6	Determine Fire Marshal & obtain development process docs
7	Determine Planning / Zoning Dir & obtain dev process docs
8	Determine Environmental Agency & obtain dev process docs
9	Determine water & sewer authority & obtain dev process docs
10	Determine gas company & obtain development process docs
11	Determine electric company & obtain dev process docs
12	Determine cable company & obtain development process docs
13	Determine Transportation Agency & obtain dev process docs
14	Determine any FAA permit requirements
15	Determine liquor license permit & process
16	Determine health / F & B permits
17	Bonds required by jurisdiction
18	Wetlands permit
19	Determine permit consultant
20	Other Federal Permits
21	Other State Permits
6 Civil Site & Transportation Evaluation	
1	Civil Engineer review and report
2	Prepare Civil concept site plan
3	Complete Topographic survey
4	Complete Environmental Phase 1 report
5	Complete Environmental Phase 2 Hazmat report if required
6	Complete Wetlands study if applicable
7	Complete seismic fault study if applicable
8	Existing geotechnical report
9	Preliminary geotechnical report
10	Driveway location study
11	ADA accessibility
12	Obtain City / County maps
13	Obtain existing aerial topographic map
14	Obtain sewer and water maps
15	Obtain site plan & flood plain map
16	Obtain existing ALTA boundary survey
17	Obtain electric utility maps
18	Obtain comprehensive land use plan
19	Determine applicable Building Codes
20	Obtain Zoning Regulations
21	Obtain aerial photos
22	Complete ground level site photos
23	Complete existing building photos if applicable

Pre-Development & Due Diligence	
24	Area / description
25	County / City
26	Type of area
27	Acreage
28	Proposed tenants
29	Adjacent roadways
30	Type of soil
31	Type of terrain
32	Significant grade problems
33	Adjoining properties
34	Drainage pattern
35	Roadways / visibility
36	Railroad lines in proximity
37	Are wetlands present
38	If wetlands present - name jurisdictional agency
39	Existing delineation
40	No. acres delineated
41	Estimated depth of topsoil
42	Fill required
43	Cut required
44	Import fill required
45	Excess cut remove from site
46	Rock outcroppings
47	Standing water on site
48	Rubble or dumping on site
49	Large trees on site
50	Vegetation
51	Existing buildings or structures
52	Demolition required
53	Environmental issues / underground tanks
54	Existing poles / hydrants / manholes
55	Existing sidewalks
56	Sidewalks required
57	Cemeteries on site
58	Off site drainage effect property
59	Property in floodplain
60	Pipelines on property
61	Overhead utility lines
62	Wells on site
63	Easements or encroachments
64	Existing geotechnical report
65	Deep foundations requirements
66	Extraordinary soil conditions

Pre-Development & Due Diligence	
67	Earthquake zone
68	Archaelogical / endangered species
69	Jurisdiction
70	Condition of road
71	Required road improvements
72	Future transportation studies & plans effecting property
73	Airports nearby and potential current impacts / future expansions
74	Pavement width
75	R / W width
76	Medians
77	Traffic lights
78	Acceleration / deceleration lanes
79	Street lighting
80	Verify if any proposed improvements by jurisdiction
81	Any problems from site use history
82	Underground tanks or process piping
83	Groundwater
84	Detection for buried drums
85	Confirm any offsite transportation improvements
7 Utilities Checklist	
1	Water - obtain availability letter
2	Water & Fire - location of service
3	Water & Fire - main size
4	Water & Fire - static & residual pressure req / fire pump ?
5	Water & Fire - easements required
6	Water - meter structure required
7	Water & Fire - separate service required
8	Water & fire - vaults required
9	Water & fire backflow preventer required
10	Sewer - obtain availability letter
11	Sewer - size & location / available
12	Sewer - pipe materials
13	Sewer - moratoriums in effect
14	Sewer - line extension necessary
15	Sewer - line extension cost
16	Sewer - connection fee
17	Sewer - treatment plant
18	Storm - obtain availability letter
19	Storm - size & location
20	Storm - retention / detention required
21	Storm - drainage ditches adequate

Pre-Development & Due Diligence

22	Storm - area in flood plain
23	Storm - extension required
24	Storm - extension cost
25	Storm - assessments / impact costs
26	Gas - obtain availability letter
27	Gas - size & location of lines
28	Gas - extension required
29	Gas - extension cost
30	Gas - on site cost to bring to building
31	Gas - service interruptable
32	Gas - easements required
33	Electric - obtain availability letter
34	Electric - overhead or underground
35	Electric - primary service by & estimated load
36	Electric - redundant primary service required
37	Electric - secondary service by
38	Electric - easements required
39	Electric - multiple bldgs / multiple separate services required
40	Electric - transformers by utility
41	Electric - transformer pads by utility
42	Electric - preferred location for service
43	Electric - overhead service cost
44	Electric - underground service cost
45	Electric - emergency power requirements / cost
46	Telephone / Cable / Data - obtain availability letter
47	Telephone / Cable / Data - overhead or underground
48	Telephone / Cable / Data - easements required
49	Telephone / Cable / Data - separate services required
50	Telephone / Cable / Data - preferred location for service
51	Telephone / Cable / Data - building space requirement
52	Confirm private / government data lines in ROW
53	Confirm private / government ROW relocation costs
8	**Zoning Checklist**
1	Permissive use
2	Master zoning plan
3	Rezoning required / public hearing
4	Proposed new zoning
5	Length of time for rezoning / variance
6	Setback modifications required
7	Site plan approval required
8	Sidewalk requirements

Pre-Development & Due Diligence

9	Landscape requirements
10	Screen or fence wall required
11	Signage regulations
12	Traffic study required
13	Neighboring property groups
14	Environmental impact report required
15	Public hearing on EIR - time for
16	Architectural design review time
17	Easements or view corridors
18	Open area requirements
19	Lake or stream buffers
20	Off street spaces required
21	No. of curb cuts permitted
22	Allowable widths at curb cuts
23	Distance required from corner to curb cuts
24	Front / principal street setback
25	Front / principal street parking setback
26	Rear building setback
27	Rear parking setback
28	Side building setback
29	Side parking setback
30	Building coverage limit
31	Landscaping coverage limit
32	Impervious area coverage limit
33	Other limits
34	Maximum height restriction
35	FAA Limitations
36	Maximum stories limitation
37	Rooftop screening
38	Truck dock screening
39	Satellite screening
40	Other required screening
41	Parking ratio required
42	Bay spacing requirement
43	Stall size requirement
44	Compact car requirement
45	Carpool space requirement
46	Signage restrictions
47	Public transportation shelters
9 Code Checklist	
1	Applicable building codes

Pre-Development & Due Diligence	
2	Agency issuing permits
3	Special fireproofing requirements
4	Mezzanine floors
5	Interior partitions
6	Exposed bar joists
7	Special roof loads
8	Draft curtains
9	Stair pressurization
10	Smoke ventilation
11	Exterior skin
12	Other agencies approving plans
13	License required by GC
14	Sprinkler systems required
15	Fire department - full time or volunteer
16	Fire Chief / Fire Marshal
17	Fire risk rating for area
18	Fire district
19	Fire lanes required
20	Painted curb lanes
21	Fire hydrants required on site
22	LEED certification level required by jurisdiction
23	Special geographic weather code requirements
10	**Base Building Program & Systems**
1	Determine number of keys and room mix
2	Prepare Architectural Site Plan
3	Prepare Architectural Building Concept Plan
4	Determine meeting space requirements
5	Determine Food & Beverage requirements
6	Determine SF of each room type
7	Determine pool requirments
8	Determine fitness center requirments
9	Determine LEED certification level
10	Determine building automation system requirements
11	Dtermine green roof requirements
12	Confirm - building area
13	Confirm - typical floor size
14	Confirm - floor to floor height
15	Confirm - atrium connection / main lobby ceiling height
16	Confirm - structural system
17	Confirm - typical bay size
18	Confirm - roof system type

Pre-Development & Due Diligence	
19	Confirm - any special roof loads
20	Confirm - floor system
21	Confirm - exterior wall system
22	Confirm - parking deck or surface
23	Confirm - parking equipment requirements (secured ?)
24	Confirm - elevator requirements
25	Confirm - loading dock & equipment
26	Confirm - trash compactor requirements
27	Confirm - landscaping responsibility
28	Confirm - untility grease interceptor required
29	Confirm - Wet & dry sprinkler systems equip
30	Confirm - Base HVAC system central plant or package units
31	Confirm - special HVAC systems data or UPS rooms
32	Confirm - distributed antenna system
33	Confirm - wireless data system
34	Confirm - emergency power requirements
35	Confirm - special power load requirements
36	Confirm - cable & power tray requirements
37	Confirm - UPS system
38	Confirm - security system
39	Confirm - telephone switch
40	Confirm - emergency generator / inside or outside & screening
41	Confirm - any Food Service buildout
42	Confirm - emergency generator / inside or outside
43	Interior wall finishes - exterior wall / interior walls
44	Ceiling finishes
45	Floor finishes
46	Electrical
47	Data systems / Data processing rooms
48	Telephone systems
49	Security systems
50	Lighting systems
51	Fire protection - special requirements
52	Mechanical systems & connection point
53	Plumbing systems - special equipment requirements
54	Food service
55	FF & E requirements
56	Interior design / space planning - cost / management responsibilty

Contracts	
1 Professional Services	
1	Legal
2	General Contractor - Preconstruction Services
3	Construction Management
5	Landscape Architecture
6	Interior Design
7	Civil
8	Surveying
9	Utilities & Location
10	Geotechnical Report
12	MEP Engineering
13	Fire Systems & Code
14	Structural
15	Acoustical
16	Telecom / Data / AV / Security
17	Parking
18	Laundry
19	Food Service
20	Elevator
21	Window wall
22	Building Envelope
23	Lighting
25	Transportation
26	Permit Expediter
27	LEED Consulting
30	Building Skin
31	FFE Procurement
4	Architecture
11	Environmental Phase 1 & 2
24	Signage / Graphics
29	Construction Testing
28	LEED Commissioning
32	
2 Operational Agreements	
1	Owner Entity
2	Franchise
3	Manager
4	
3 Construction	

Contracts	
1	General Contractor - Site & Building
2	Low Voltage Cable (assigned to GC)
3	Traffic & Roadway Improvements
4	
4 Equipment Vendors	
2	FFE furniture samples required
3	HSIA
4	Audio Visual
5	BOH Computers & Servers
6	PMS System
7	Network
10	MATV & TV Signal
11	Digital Signage
12	Guestroom LCD TV's
13	POS System
14	Music System
15	DAS System
16	OSE
17	FFE Install
20	Warehousing
21	FFE Install
1	Window washing system (in GC)
18	Interior Signage
19	Exterior Signage
22	Parking Equipment
8	Telephones & Switch
9	Security System
23	
5 Utilities & Jurisdictions	
19	Sewer - Determine connection & connection cost
2	Gas - Determine equipment responsibilities & connection cost
4	Electric - Determine equipment responsibilities & connection cost
5	Electric - service by & estimated load
6	Electric - redundant primary service ? Required ?
7	Electric - Secondary service by
8	Electric - Transformers by utility ?
9	Electric - Transformer pads by utility ?
10	Electric - Preferred location for service ?

Contracts	
12	Telephone - Determine equipment responsibilities & conn cost
14	Data / Fiber - Determine equipment responsibilities & conn cost
16	Cable - Determine equipment responsibilities & conn cost
21	Water - Determine equip responsibility & connection cost
22	Centennial - Public Improvement Agreement
1	Gas - Install & Service Agreement
3	Electric - Install & Service Agreement
11	Telephone - Install & Service Agreement
13	Data / Fiber - Install & Service Agreement
15	Cable - Install & Service Agreement
17	Storm Drainage - Agreement
18	Sewer - Agreement
20	Water - Install & Service Agreement
23	Lighting ROW
24	Traffic light
25	

Legal & Finance	
1 Zoning & Entitlements	
1	Traffic Study
2	Parking Study
3	Environmental Impact Report
5	Restrictive Covenants
4	Neighborhood Associations
6	Landscape Architecture
7	Site Plan Approval
8	Streets & Highways
9	Required road improvements
10	
2 Easements	
1	Sanitary
2	Storm Drainage
3	Water
4	Fire
5	Electric
6	Gas
7	Data Communication
8	Cable
9	Telephone
10	Department of transportation
11	Site Signage
12	Access
13	
3 Insurance	
7	Franchise Insurance
1	General Contractor Liability
2	GC P & P Bond
3	Sub P & P Bond
4	Professional Consultants
5	Owner General Liability
6	Owner Builder's Risk
9	Development Bonds
8	Lender Insurance Requirements
10	
4 Legal & Financing	

Legal & Finance

1	Lender term sheet & commitment letter
2	Closing Date
3	

Permits	
1 Permit Process & Approvals	
1	Forestry & Arborist
2	Community Meeting
3	Site Plan - Property Address
4	Streets & Highways
5	Landscape
6	Environmental
7	Address application
8	Fire Marshal
9	Fire Marshal - Water Sign Off
10	Site Plan - 1st Submittal External Packets
11	Site Plan - 1st Submittal Traffic Impact Study
12	Site Plan - 1st Submittal Fees @ Application
13	Site Plan - 1st Submittal Application
14	Site Plan - 1st Submittal Letter of Intent
14	Site Plan - 1st Submittal Taxes
15	Site Plan - 1st Submittal Title Committment
16	Site Plan - 1st Submittal Application
17	Plan Review Fees
18	Waivers & Variances for Roadways & Drainage
19	Site Plan - 2nd Submittal
20	Site Civil - 1st Submittal
21	Site Plan - 3rd Submittal
22	Site Plan - Engineers Cost Estimates
22	Grading Erosion Control Fees
23	Public Improvements - Construction Plan Approval
24	Site Plan - CDs Submittal Fees
25	Public Improvement - Agreement
26	Development Permit
27	Development Collateral LOC
28	Use Tax
29	Site Civil - 2nd Submittal
30	Site Plan - CDs Submittal Fees
30	Site Plan - CDs Submittal
31	Building Permit - Submittal 1
32	Bulding Permit - Submittal 2
33	
2 Permits	
1	Demolition permit
2	Foundation Permit

Permits	
3	FFE Stocking Permit
4	Health Permit - F & B / Pools
5	Liquor License
6	ROW - Streets & Highways Permit
7	FAA Determination & Permit
8	Stormwater Public Improvement Permit
9	Grading Erosion & Sediment Control Permit
10	EPA - Construction Stormwater Permit
11	Development Permit
12	Building Permit
13	Exterior Signage Permit
14	

Design	
1	**Design Schedule Major Milestones**
1	Concept Design
2	Schematic Design
3	Model Room Documents
4	Model Room Review
5	Lobby Design - SD 3 Schemes
6	Site Plan - 1st Submittal
8	Site Plan - 2nd Submittal
7	Design Development
9	Site Plan - 3rd Submittal
10	Permit / GMP Pricing Set
11	Building Permit - 1st Submittal
12	Site Plan - CD's Submittal
13	Site Plan - Final CD's
14	Building Permit - 2nd Submittal
15	Building Permit - Final Construction Documents
2	**Site**
1	Underground stormwater detention
2	Distribute geotech report
3	Repaving of adjacent road required
4	Impervious area coverage limit - Regional Water Authority
5	Site Parking Options
6	Site lighting requirements
7	Soil Bearing design capacity
8	Groundwater design requirements
9	Recommended foundation system
10	Extraordinary soil conditions
11	Import fill required
12	Export soil required
13	Significant grade problems
14	Sidewalk requirements & road coordination
15	Site Signage Location
16	Fire Truck Circulation
17	Utility demand estimates for providers
18	Vaults & Meter Structure
19	Water service 2 sources
20	Generator location & screening
21	Atrium smoke control & fire system requirements
22	Temporary detention with construction sequence

Design	
23	Civil & Electrical site lighting sheets
24	Review lessons learned checklist
3 Building Design Action Items	
1	Fitness Center Requirements
2	Pool Requirements
3	Shower details
4	FFE furniture samples required
5	Retail Requirements
6	Roof equipment screening
7	Exterior Skin Options
8	Acoustic requirements
9	Primary electrical service 2 sources ?
10	F & B Requirements
11	Keycard system - resolve scope
12	Review lessons learned checklist
13	HVAC - system alternatives analysis
14	Generator - verify natural gas or fuel
15	Lighting controls - resolve system
16	Elevators - guestrrom & service quantity
17	Ceiling height
18	Fire Suppression - coord design scope w / pricing
19	Exterior signage - coordinate building face requirements
20	Traffic coating on deck - lower cost alternatives
21	Landscaping - review requirements
22	Renderings
23	Green Roof Structure Design
24	Building Envelope Consultant Design review
25	Window washing system
26	LEED
27	
4 Building Design Direction	
1	Fitness Center Requirements
2	Pool Requirements
3	Shower details
4	FFE furniture samples required
5	Retail Requirements
6	Roof equipment screening
7	F & B Requirements
8	Generator - enclosure height coord with sightlines

Design	
9	Storage Room - add for building supplies & janitorial 12 x 12
10	Central Mail Room - mailboxes
11	Garage Entry - design for security
12	Engineer's Office
13	P1 Parking - at entrance include trench drain
14	Service Drive
15	Colored concrete / Pavers
16	Bike rack locations
17	Car charging stations
18	Smoking area / shelter
19	BAS - tie in
20	Maximum height for low rise classification
21	
4 Brand Reviews	
1	Schematic
2	Design Development
3	Construction Documents
4	Interior Design
5	FFE
6	Construction Site Reviews
7	Progress Reports
5 Equipment Vendors	
1	HSIA
2	Audio Visual
3	BOH Computers & Servers
4	PMS System
5	Network
6	MATV & TV Signal
7	Digital Signage
8	Guestroom LCD TV's
9	POS System
10	Music System
11	DAS System
12	Security System
13	Telephones & Switch
14	Parking equipment
15	
6 FFE & ID	

Design	
1	Concept Design
2	Model Room Documents
3	FFE Brand Review
4	Schematic Design
5	Design Development
6	FFE Artwork
7	FFE Specifications
8	FFE Pricing

Pre-Construction	
1 Construction Schedule	
1	Detailed Construction Schedule
2	Update Development Schedule
3	FFE Schedule
4	
2 Pre-Construction Coordination	
1	Model Room Schedule
2	FFE Procedures
3	FFE Quantities
4	FFE Warehousing
5	Warehouse / Site / Sub FFE delivery coordination
6	Construction GMP update
7	Construction Directives Format
8	Pay Application Procedures
9	Contractor Insurance
10	Materials Testing Coordination
11	3rd Party Inspection Coordination
12	Utilities Locator
13	Lien Waivers - compliance with State's requirements
14	Publicity Events
15	Signage / Graphics
16	Value Engineering
17	Development Budget Updates
18	LEED Coordination Meeting
3 Utilities Construction Install Coordination	
1	Gas
2	Electric
3	Telephone
4	T1 Service / Fiber
5	Data
6	Cable
7	Sewer
8	Storm Drainage
9	Water
10	ROW Lighting
11	Confirm private / government data lines in ROW
12	Confirm private / government ROW relocation costs

Construction

1 General Contractor	
1	Notice to Proceed
2	Construction schedule updates
3	Pending Change Orders status report
4	Change Order status report
5	Submittal Schedule review
6	RFI status report
7	Permit Inspection updates
8	Pay App review schedule / Lender
9	FFE Delivery Coordination
10	FFE Quantities
11	Projected Cash Flow
12	Project Signs & Fencing
2 Owner Subcontractors	
1	HSIA
2	Audio Visual
3	BOH Computers & Servers
4	PMS System
5	Network
6	Telephones & Switch
7	Security System
8	MATV & TV Signal
9	Digital Signage
10	Guestroom LCD TV's
11	POS System
12	Music System
13	DAS System
14	OSE
15	Purchasing Status Reports
3 Utilities	
1	Utility - Gas
2	Utility - Electric
3	Utility - Telephone
4	Utility - T1 Service / Fiber
5	Utility - Data
6	Utility - Cable
7	Utility - Sewer
8	Utility - Storm Drainage

Construction	
9	Utility - Water
10	Utility - ROW Lighting

Construction Closeout	
1 General Contractor	
1	Notice of Substantial Completion from GC
2	Notice of Final Completion from GC
3	Special Inspection Sign Offs
4	Elevator Inspection Certificate
5	Punchlist - attached to Substantial Completion Certification
6	Certificate of Occupancy
7	Area turnover schedule coordinated with Hotel Manager
8	GC As-Builts including submittal drawings - pdf & 1 full size hard copy
9	Systems Training
10	Warranties
11	Manufacturer's Roofing Inspection / Warranty
12	O & M Manuals
13	HVAC Test & Balance Report
14	Building Material Stock Confirmed
15	Building Keys Received
16	G706 - Contractor's Affidavit of Payment of Debts and Claims
17	G706A - Contractor's Affidavit of Release of Liens
18	Consent of Surety to Partial Retainage Contractor Payment
19	G707 - Consent of Surety to Final Contractor Payment
20	Final Unconditional Lien Waivers
21	
2 Owner Closeout	
1	Owner Punchlist
2	FAA Notifications
3	Brand Opening Review
4	Construction Testing Reports - Certification of Compliance
5	3rd Party Inspection - Reports & Certification of Compliance
6	G704 - Certificate of Substantial Completion
7	Punchlist Complete Verification
8	A / E Notice of Final Completion
9	Start Warranty List
10	Roads & Streets Jurisdiction Certification
11	Specifications - PDF & Hard Copy
12	A / E CAD & PDF Record Drawings
13	Civil CAD & PDF Record Drawings
14	Submittals - PDF
15	Closeout MG Subcontractors
16	FFE Punchlist / Missing / Broken Resolved
17	Liquor License Permit

Construction Closeout	
18	Transfer Utilities to Owner
19	Service & Maintenance Agreements
20	As Built ALTA Survey
21	Completion of all easements & revised easements
22	Streets & Utilities Jurisdiction Acceptance
23	Permanent Insurance Policy - Replace Builder's Risk
24	Title Insurance - check
25	Release of Development Bonds / Deposits / Escrows
26	Final Accounting Summary
27	Final Lender Draw
28	Closeout with Lender & Lender's Consultant
29	Complete Office Files

7

Planning and Managing Capital Expenditures

By Richard E. Pastorino and Karen Johnson

***Richard Pastorino** is President of REVPAR International, Inc., a Washington, D.C.-based hospitality advisory and asset management firm that is exclusively dedicated to the hospitality (lodging) industry. The firm was established in 1992, giving it almost twenty-five years of successful service to the needs of the industry at large and its various stakeholders. Among Mr. Pastorino's many contributions to the industry, he co-authored* CapEx 2000: A Study of Capital Expenditures in the Hotel Industry, *which was published by the International Society of Hospitality Consultants (ISHC). For more information on REVPAR International, please visit their website at www.revparintl.com.*

***Karen Johnson,** MAI, CRE, ISHC, is President of Pinnacle Advisory Group West and supervises all of the consulting activities for that office. Ms. Johnson has been active as a hotel asset manager, consultant, and appraiser since 1981. Pinnacle is engaged in a wide range of hospitality consulting services. In 1998, Ms. Johnson led a survey of contract terms co-sponsored by HAMA that was later published in the* Cornell Quarterly. *She was the author of the chapter on negotiating hotel management contracts in the Urban Land Institute's* Hotel Development Handbook. *Prior to opening the West Coast office of Pinnacle in 2011, Ms. Johnson was employed by Warnick + Company as a hotel asset manager and consultant. For more information on Ms. Johnson and Pinnacle Advisory Group, please visit their website at www.pinnacleadvisorygroup.com.*

Overview of CapEx

THE AMOUNT OF CAPITAL EXPENDITURE (CapEx) investment in a hotel—regardless of asset type, location, affiliation, or age—is a critical aspect of the success of a hotel and an ever-increasing cost center that should be thoroughly understood as part of an owner's initial and ongoing financial commitment to a hotel asset.

It is no secret that all buildings require periodic updating, renovation, refurbishment, and/or restoration. However, no other commercial property type requires as much ongoing attention as a hotel. Unlike office or retail space, hotel owners provide a completely "finished" area to guests and their financial success is highly dependent upon its amenities and visual appeal. Unlike apartments, hotel rooms are rented for twenty-four-hour periods, and there is no cost associated with a "move." Also unique to hotel assets is the influence of third parties on the ongoing upkeep and CapEx requirements. Remodeling schedules have been accelerated by the proliferation of hotel branding in our industry over the past twenty-five years and the accompanying contractual requirements to trade out equipment, finishes and signage prior to the end of their useful life. In addition to brands, owners must also comply with new government regulations, such as evolving ADA and/or life safety issues as they are legislated. Ultimately, the cost for all of this upkeep is borne by the hotel owner. By contrast, while in many instances there is a direct return on this capital invested, just as often there is not.

Anticipating and managing CapEx plays a significant role in the ultimate financial success of a hotel asset as an investment vehicle. In this chapter, we will discuss the practical considerations of CapEx evaluations, planning, and management and the framework for doing that.

Evolution of CapEx Theory

The maintenance responsibilities of a hotel owner or lessee are twofold. The first responsibility is for the entire cost of maintaining the physical plant of a hotel, which consists of the building envelope and mechanical systems. The second responsibility is for the hotel's internal improvements and accessories, such as the furniture, fixtures, and equipment (FF&E). In office or retail parlance, this second responsibility is often referred to as "tenant improvements."

In the late 1930s, the American Hotel Association (now the AHLA) recommended that 3 percent of a hotel's gross revenues be set aside or "reserved" for CapEx. It was hoped that this reserve over time would be adequate to cover the periodic replacement or restoration of the building envelope (i.e., roof, brick facades, etc.), landscaping, hardscaping and pools, mechanical systems (i.e., elevators, HVAC systems, etc.), attached fixtures (toilets, sinks and ductwork, etc.), and finishes such as wall coverings, flooring and lighting, and furniture in guest rooms, public areas, offices and employee areas.

However, the three percent rule proved to be insufficient. Any time a hotel changed hands or was sold, the new owner might decide that it needed substantial renovations due to inadequate reinvestment under the prior owner. The frequency with which this occurred gave birth to the Product Improvement Plan or "PIP," an acronym that was used to describe the mandated renovations and refurbishments required by a brand or franchisor. If the new owner opted not to invest the required amount of CapEx to comply with the brand's PIP, then the hotel was converted to an alternative (lesser) brand, where the PIP was not as expensive, or the hotel was taken independent.

In the wake of the savings and loan crisis of the early 1990s, lenders foreclosed on thousands of hotels and became financially responsible for the upkeep of the property and maintaining brand standards. Lenders quickly learned that the amount of CapEx required to maintain the hotel, let alone sustain it over time, was far greater than the three percent annual reserve, while the repairs and maintenance budget was wholly inadequate to cover the shortfall.

In response to all of this, and in an effort to improve consistency and thereby improve brand loyalty, the major brands and franchisors began requiring (through franchise or hotel management agreements) that hotel owners reserve a higher amount of the gross revenue for CapEx as the hotel aged. Most often, these amounts started at three percent when the hotel opened and escalated to five percent of gross revenues by the fourth or fifth year of operations.

In 1995, the ISHC stepped into the fray and undertook a landmark study called *CapEx in the Hotel Industry,* with subsequent editions published in 2000, 2007, and 2015. The 1995 ISHC study documented through empirical research that a minimum of 4 percent of gross revenues should be reserved annually. After some debate among industry participants, the 4 percent recommendation became a minimum underwriting and valuation standard for the industry.

Meanwhile, the brands started specifying in their operating and franchise contracts that the reserves were specific to cosmetic items (soft and hard/case goods), as opposed to the physical plant and building envelope. This stipulation reflected their (correct) belief that 4 percent of gross revenues was still insufficient to cover the entire CapEx needs of a hotel over the long term. Subsequent CapEx studies by the ISHC in 2000 and 2007 concluded (based again on empirical data) that the true cost of CapEx over a hotel's entire life cycle could be as high as 8 to 9 percent of gross revenues on average, depending on the many variables that come into play.

In addition, the composition of CapEx has changed over time, beginning with the ever-increasing importance of technology in the hotel industry. Just think of the cost of periodically increasing the bandwidth necessary to allow for the multiple pieces of IT equipment guests bring with them that require internet access, not to mention streaming music and videos. In addition, the speed of changes in technological requirements make it very difficult to anticipate future costs.

Lastly, it is important to note that CapEx spending is highly dependent upon a hotel's point in its life cycle and the economic cycle during the investment holding period. The charts in Exhibit 1, taken from the 2007 ISHC CapEx study, highlight these points.

As Exhibit 1 illustrates, regardless of product type, the amount of CapEx spending on a hotel asset generally increases as the hotel ages. Moreover, the amount of CapEx needed oscillates, with a dramatic spike around Year 20 when many of the large mechanical systems within the hotel need replacement. Alas, as the charts show, barring a decade of sustained high occupancies and real dollar ADR growth, the amount of CapEx required to sustain a full-service hotel is greater than 4 percent of gross revenues over an extended period of time and can be as much as 7 percent for brand-managed, limited-service hotels.

Even with all of the data collected on this subject to date, the true cost of CapEx for a hotel over its full economic life remains elusive. This is because a significant amount of CapEx funding is still spent as part of a change of ownership and/or is being expensed to the hotel's financial/operating statement as repairs and maintenance. Thus, even the most rigorous surveys have been unable to completely capture the true cost of CapEx for a hotel.

So the question remains, how much of a hotel's gross revenue should be reserved to maintain a hotel asset in a condition that will allow it to remain relevant to its market, generate appropriate levels of profit, and provide for an adequate return to the owner and investor over time? This chapter will explore this and other areas to assist the hotel asset manager in planning and managing CapEx.

Exhibit 1 CapEx Spending and Life Cycle

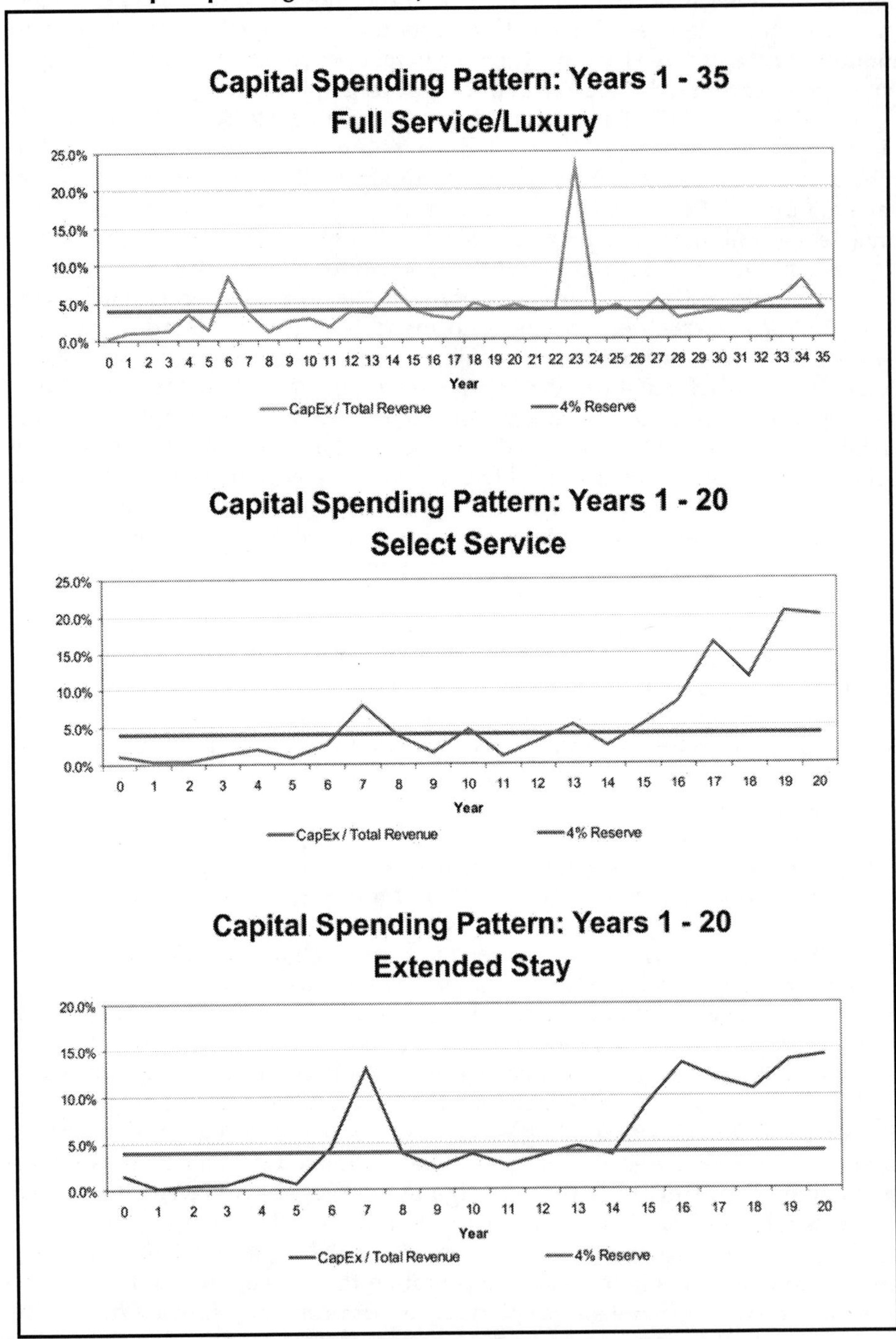

Source: *CapEx 2007: A Study of Capital Expenditures in the Hotel Industry.*

Owner and Asset Manager Roles in the CapEx Process

As the actual building and amenity offering becomes more sophisticated, there has been a corresponding increase in the complexity and cost of maintaining the physical hotel asset, its FF&E, and IT components. In addition, more third parties are requesting or requiring the owner to make further investment in the hotel beyond the initial costs for development. As a result, it has been critical for owners to ensure that a thorough job has been done of overseeing, justifying, monitoring, and validating expenditures. The hotel asset manager has been the logical person to fulfill this role.

As Rick Swig notes, "the ability to predict the timing and cost of major capital expenditures at a hotel or resort requires advanced quantitative tools/databases, analytical abilities, and seemingly at times even some psychic powers. Even now that the data exists, via various CapEx studies, to evaluate the 'typical' capital needs of a property over its life cycle, the 'human factor' always complicates the task and requires constant oversight in order to update progressive assessments."[1]

Thus, the primary role of the owner is to make sure that there is a delineation of investment strategy and that it is properly communicated to the asset manager and operator.

Meanwhile, the role of the asset manager regarding CapEx is to take that investment strategy and develop a "truly comprehensive capital expenditures oversight program" that "include[s] elements of inclusive near-term and long-term planning as well as ongoing physical inspections, evaluations of management performance, and ever-vigilant updating of databases and benchmarking tools. This provides owners with the data that they need to make informed decisions..."[2] To this end, a critical path should be developed by the asset manager for both near-term and long-term capital planning.

It is also the responsibility of an asset manager and owner to review and challenge the requests of third parties who are requiring CapEx be done at a hotel, particularly when the direct ROI to the owner may not be readily apparent. This can oftentimes be an area of friction between the owner and the brand when the CapEx investment is untimely (e.g., required during a recession), does not directly affect the guest experience or reduce liability (life-safety), or serves more to enhance the brand than the asset. In such cases, brands may be amenable to waivers or postponement, but their flexibility is most often a function of the owner-brand relationship (short- and long-term), the industry cycle (as we saw during this last recession when brands relaxed their timing for implementation), the hotel's track record on guest scores for the property, and the brand's strategy for the market over the short- or long-term horizon.

The asset manager, operator, and owner should also be constantly scanning and evaluating potential value enhancement opportunities of an asset where the ROI on a potential CapEx investment yields a true benefit to ownership. A more recent influence has been social media, which is playing an increasing role in CapEx spending now that guests can use a variety of Internet sites to provide their unvarnished opinions on any aspect of a hotel. In turn, owners, asset managers, lenders, and brands access those opinions and use them to formulate a CapEx plan and decision for a property.

Thus, in many respects, an asset manager (and operator) should mimic an owner by asking questions about CapEx decisions such as:

- Are the guests requesting it frequently?
- Is it necessary for the guest?
- Is it strategic?
- What is the ROI?

We will explore the ways to do this later in this chapter.

Repairs & Maintenance Versus CapEx

First, however, we need to distinguish the differences between Repairs and Maintenance and CapEx. Repairs and Maintenance ("R&M") represents the efforts of the engineering department of the hotel to maintain the hotel and to keep all of its component parts in good working order. R&M is expensed to the hotel financial statements. Generally, any material expense (typically above a certain monetary threshold) that extends the life of the building or measurably improves the quality of the property should be capitalized (i.e., a balance sheet transaction) and thus be considered CapEx. Based on these definitions, repairs and maintenance is different, yet related, to CapEx spending, and the two together reflect the true cost of maintaining a hotel asset and keeping it competitive over its economic life.

To put things in perspective, the ISHC CapEx studies from 1995, 2000, and 2007 show that the combined CapEx and R&M expenses for a hotel generally range from about 8 to 14 percent of total revenues, but can vary dramatically from year to year during the life span of a hotel. "Pay me now or pay more later!" This is the mantra of a wise hotel chief engineer, who knows from experience that hotels that adhere to a proper preventive maintenance schedule will have a lower CapEx requirement over time. Ignoring preventive maintenance will inevitably be followed by higher R&M expenses in the form or repairs and parts replacements, culminating in a shorter useful life for the equipment. In addition, new equipment will have to be purchased, increasing the amount and frequency of an owner's CapEx expense.

The difference between an R&M expense and a CapEx expense is not always clear-cut. Computers, for example, can either be expensed or capitalized. In most cases, the hotel operating agreement will attempt to define what constitutes an R&M expense versus a CapEx expense. Less commonly, the management agreement or some other document will do so. If not specifically established in any of these documents, then the owner, asset manager, and operator need to be in agreement on this subject. National tax laws and owner preferences can also influence these classifications.

The annual budgeting process for the hotel is the appropriate forum for these discussions and decisions to take place since all parties are partaking in the process and all major R&M and CapEx items are presented to ownership at this time for approval. If the owner has communicated his/her investment strategy to those involved, then the overall objectives relative to CapEx and R&M should flow from that objective.

As previously mentioned, the hotel operator and the hotel owner may have conflicting motivations about whether to expense or capitalize an item. For example, depending upon the incentive compensation structure of the hotel operating agreement, a hotel operator may prefer to capitalize as much as possible in order to report higher annual profit margins, which in turn may yield higher management fees (primarily as it relates to incentive fees). By contrast, an owner may prefer to expense whenever possible in order to reduce taxable profits. Many hotel management companies establish a standard by which any expenditure for a single item over a fixed amount is capitalized.

In some instances, the hotel may legally have two sets of financial statements—one for the purpose of evaluating the operator's financial performance in generating controllable profit, while the second financial statement is for tax purposes. A recent decision by the IRS indicates that any equipment that is replaced two or more times in a ten-year period should be expensed. The hotel's auditors should be up to date, but readers in the United States may wish to google: "IRS Capitalization v Repair Audit Technique Guide."

The IRS's "Plan of Rehabilitation Doctrine" is a ruling that says that even if an item would normally be expensed if done independently (for example re-painting a guest room), when it is done as part of a larger, comprehensive plan, it should be capitalized. However, a hotel that re-paints every guest room every fifth year in order to maintain its first-class standard, would be permitted to expense even a major expenditure such as that.

If a portion of a renovation is expensed to the R&M line, year-over-year comparisons will be muddied. However, there may be tax advantages to doing so and auditors should be consulted.

One final important consideration is that, technically, the reserve for replacement is not an income statement item. It is an escrow account listed on the balance sheet. However, it is now standard practice to show as an expense deduction on a financial statement or *pro forma* in order to reflect the importance that all hotel asset stakeholders place on the need to have a reserve account for the express purpose of replacing FF&E and/or major building and mechanical components. Otherwise, the ability of the hotel to continue to generate profits will be at risk and could eventually cause the business to fail.

Life Cycles

All property goes through various cycles, most notably economic and physical life cycles, which affect the hotel investment cycle. These cycles can occur concurrently or separately. Due to changes in land utilization (density) and guest tastes and preferences, the economic life cycle of an asset will most likely be shorter than its physical life cycle. Externalities play a role too.

Investment Life Cycle

The typical investment cycle for a hotel is relatively straightforward, as illustrated in Exhibit 2.

Exhibit 2 Typical Investment Cycle for a Hotel

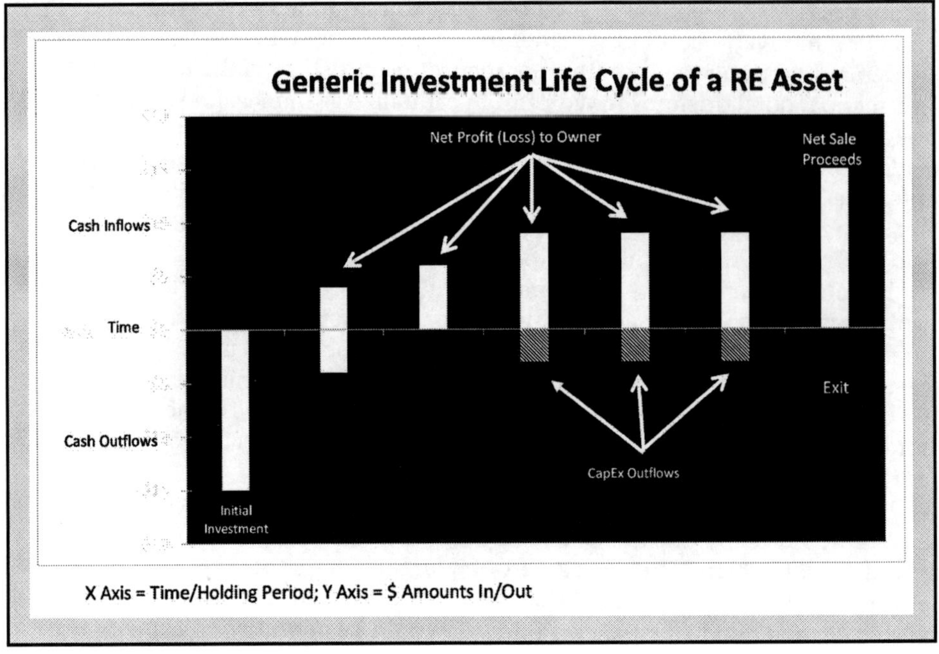

Essentially, Exhibit 2 shows that initial money is invested into an asset at time zero (cash outflow). Over the ensuing holding period, the asset generates a profit that is returned to the investor in the form of a cash inflow until the investor exits the investment, at which point he or she receives the net proceeds of the disposition (sale proceeds). The objective is for the amount of the cash inflows and sales proceeds to be greater than the amount of cash outflows over the designated ownership period. When evaluating the investment life cycle for your hotel asset, the asset manager must be informed as to the likely cash outflows that will occur beyond the initial investment in the form of CapEx requirements.

Long-term holders must recognize that the economic life of a building will be far shorter than the physical life of its steel or concrete. For example, the U-shaped, 2-story exterior corridor Holiday Inn of the 1960s pioneered by Kemmons Wilson is no longer brand-compliant. Even in high-rise, urban properties, the dimensions of a guest bathtub popular in the 1980s are now too small by today's standards. In light of this rapid obsolescence, when estimating the economic life of a hotel investment, many hotel companies assume that the hotel's asset value at the end of forty years is strictly the land value; there is no value attributed to the improvements. The effects of ever-changing consumer tastes are reinforced by ever-changing development patterns within the area. For example, mid-rise buildings are giving way to high-rise buildings, while surface parking is being replaced by new wings and parking garages.

Hotel Asset Life Cycle

According to an article titled "Hotel Asset Management: Managing the Asset Life Cycle" by Colliers International, the typical life cycle of a hotel asset spans four phases. Those phases are depicted in Exhibit 3.

Although this chart depicts the typical life cycle as ten-plus years, Phases 2 and 3 can be extended by a significant number of years if: (1) a proper R&M and CapEx program are in place for the hotel asset, and (2) ownership is spending the appropriate amount of money to extend the economic life of the hotel asset. In other words, a properly maintained asset can avoid Phase 4.

In practice, Phase 4 is the point at which the asset is often sold, either as part of the change in ownership or shortly thereafter. Significant CapEx monies are then reinvested in the property to return the asset to Phase 1, short of any functional obsolescence that a renovation could not cure.

If the holding period is near its end, specialist hotel brokers should be interviewed to determine whether a renovation immediately prior to a planned sale provides a dollar-for-dollar "lift" to the potential sales price. Frequently, the tastes of the buyer and seller differ, meaning that it would have been better to sell the unrenovated product and negotiate a credit for the transfer of the amounts in the CapEx reserve. Hence the key for the asset manager is to understand the owner's objectives and philosophy for the asset in relation to the life cycle. It will then be possible to map out the appropriate near- and long-term strategy to achieve the desired Phase 2 and Phase 3 performance level during the intended holding period of the investment life cycle.

Exhibit 3 Phases of a Typical Life Cycle

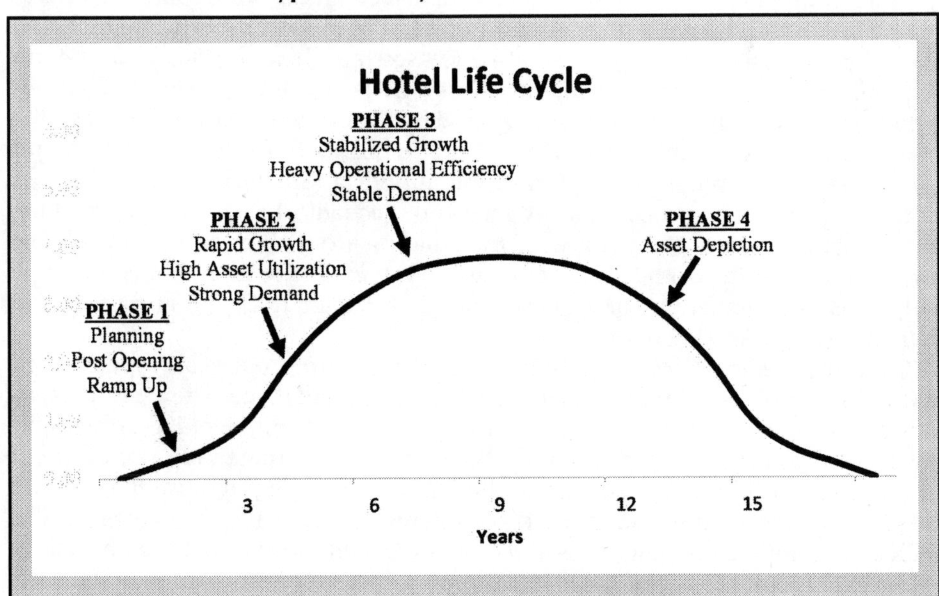

Since different items wear out or become unfashionable at different times, we have presented in Exhibit 4 a summary of the expected life of building components and FF&E, as abstracted from CapEx 2007. Since that time, the authors have made modifications to the table in an attempt to stay current with the ever-changing consumer tastes and preferences—such as showers (versus tubs), grab-and-go food and beverage options in a "market" style format (versus a sit-down restaurant), and higher bandwidth for streaming over the Internet. Thus, the reader should explore current resources available on the Internet or AHLA Educational Institute prior to using the data in Exhibit 4.

CapEx and Strategic Planning

In light of the varying replacement schedules, strategic planning is required to ensure that CapEx spending is focused on the right area of the hotel at the right time and that value is created (or at least not diminished) over the holding period of the investment. Thus, an asset manager must identify and account for the benefits, risks, and other considerations when deciding the monetary resources to allocate for CapEx. In other words, there is no "one size fits all" answer, since there are so many variables that can influence the amount. Those variables will be discussed in the following paragraphs.

Budgeting for CapEx

Budgeting for CapEx is a relatively straightforward process once: (1) the investment objectives of ownership are known, and (2) the research necessary to establish the short- and long-term CapEx needs of the asset has been completed.

While there are many variables that go into establishing a CapEx budget, the time frame that it covers should be established based on the intended holding period of the current owner. Assuming it is a branded property, the first stop should be with the brand representative to ascertain their short- and long-term requirements to maintain the affiliation. This will usually be in the form of a Product Improvement Plan (PIP) that is prepared by the brand (typically for a fee); the owner is then responsible for pricing it out. The PIP will focus mostly on brand standards as they relate to FF&E and the interior and exterior design features of the property. It does not typically focus on mechanical features, except to the extent that the current mechanicals of the building are within consumer use/view and do not meet the brand standards (such as an HVAC system that is two-pipe but needs to be four-pipe, or a guest room that has a PTAC unit and the brand standard is a VTAC unit).

Meanwhile, most owners will have hired a firm to prepare a Property Condition Report (PCR) as part of their acquisition due diligence. The PCR inventories and reviews all the major (and minor) building components and mechanical systems in the hotel and identifies their current and remaining useful life. If appropriate based on the findings of the PCR, lenders may require that monies be set aside or escrowed to replace certain items of concern in the short run. The PCR consultant may review plans and other documents as part of their analysis in order to pinpoint the age of specific equipment, instead of estimating on the basis

Exhibit 4 Expected Lives of Building Components and FF&E

	Guest Rooms	Guest Baths	Corridors	Lobby/ Front Desk	F&B Outlets	Kitchen	Meeting Space	Pool	Fitness Center
Every 4 Years									
Bed Treatment	X								
AV Equipment – Basic							X		
Every 5 Years									
Pool Deck treatments								X	
Pool Furniture								X	
Signage								X	
Every 6-8 Years									
New Wall Vinyl or Paint	X	X	X	X	X	X	X		X
Re-Carpet	X		X	X	X		X		
Paint Doors, Trim, Ceilings	X	X	X	x	X		X		
Refinish millwork	X	X	X	x	X		X		
New Lighting	X	X	X	x	X	x	X		
New Seating	X	X	X	x	X		X		
Artwork & Accessories	X	X	X	X	X		X		
Window Treatments	X		X	X	X		X		
Flat Panel TV	X								
Mattresses/Box Springs	X								
Guestroom Tech	X								
Re-grout Wall/Floor tile		X							
Replace Acoustical Tile Ceilings						X			X
New Mirrors		X					X		
Vanity sink faucets/taps		X							
Refinish Tub		X							
Shower Curtain		X							
Portable Bars							X		
Sound system components									
Rubber Flooring									X
Quarry Tile Flooring						X			
AV Equipment Refurbishment							X		
Sound system components							X		
Guest Laundry Equipment									
Every 8–10 Years									
Internet	X		X	X	X		X	X	X
Point of Sale			X	X	X				
Every 10 Years									
Electronic Guest Rm Door Locks	X								
Replaster pool								X	
Pool Equipment								X	
Wall covering									
Carpet									
Acoustical Tile									
Window Treatments									
Surface Paving									
Every 12–13 Years									
Replace Closet Doors	X								
Replace Guestroom Doors			X						
Replace Drywall	X	X	X		X	X			X
Replace Wood Trim	X		X		X	X			X
Replace Stone/Tile Flooring		X			X	X			X
Replace Wood Flooring	X				X	X			X
Replace Wall Tile		X							
Replace Tub		X							
Re-Tile Shower		X							
Replace Toilet		X							
Replace Vanity/Sink		X							
Replace Case Goods	X		X						X
Replace Stone/Tile Flooring						X			
Replace Storefront type door									
Tables 30", 72" Rounds 14"X72"						X			
Signage			X		X				X
Ice machines			X						
Buffet Equipment						X			
Bar Equipment						X			

(continued)

Exhibit 4 *(continued)*

	Guest Rooms	Guest Baths	Corridors	Lobby/ Front Desk	F&B Outlets	Kitchen	Meeting Space	Pool	Fitness Center
Sound System							X		
Mirrors, floor to ceiling									
Replace toilet stalls									
Office Furniture									
Elevator Cabs			X						
Every 18-20 Years									
Entry Doors							X	X	X
Kitchen Equipment						X			
Life Safety	X		X		X		X	X	X
Telephone Switches	X				X				
Every 20-25 Years									
Roof									
Laundry Equipment									
Every 25 Years									
HVAC guestrooms									
HVAC Public Areas									
Every 25–30 Years									
Elevator Equipment Modernization									
Every 30-35 Years									
Plumbing									
Electrical									
Exterior Cladding/Façade									

of visual review. If the useful life of the equipment is expected to end during the holding period of the current owner, then its replacement or renovation becomes part of the CapEx budget for that future time frame, along with an estimated cost.

Other due diligence items such as a Phase 1 through 3 Environmental Report may alert an owner as to other potential CapEx expenditures that will be required as part of the investment during the holding period. The R&M department may maintain a preventive maintenance system so that much of the foregoing has been documented, along with any prior repairs and potential service issues.

Accordingly, once the above research and data compilation has been gathered, the near- and long-term CapEx budgets can be prepared.

Near-Term CapEx Versus Renovations

Near-term CapEx typically relates to current-year investment requirements put forth by the operator as part of the annual (capital) budget, and are reviewed and approved as part of the annual budgeting process. Having said that, near-term CapEx projects should be developed in the context of the operator's three- to five-year CapEx plan. Otherwise, there may be nothing left for a CapEx project such as an impending renovation or chiller replacement. The current-year items could include owner-requested items, brand-requested items, or items that are nearing or have reached the end of their useful life. The near-term CapEx plan may also include carry-over items from the prior year where they were anticipated but not yet purchased or executed.

The budgeted amounts used for CapEx items scheduled for the three- to five-year plan are typically more "order of magnitude" since they are far enough out that a specific bid or price is not yet required. Rather, the purpose and amounts are provided so that the owner is aware of what is coming down the road and, together with the operator and lender, can prepare accordingly for the funding, along with any potential disruption to hotel operations. An asset manager can develop reasonable "placeholder" numbers by talking to brand representatives, friendly competitors, general contractors, or purchasing agents for the cost of other similar-scale renovations.

A renovation implies a more extensive, comprehensive and expensive effort to improve all or multiple portions of the hotel asset and would typically involve the use of outside consultants and third-party service providers (such as architects, interior designers, purchasing agents, and project managers). The planning process for a renovation is dependent upon its magnitude, but typically commences a minimum of twelve months prior to the actual renovation's start. Even a minor renovation, such as changing out the soft and case goods in the guest rooms, may commence twelve months out with the initial approval of the budget, the hiring of an interior designer, and the ensuing purchasing of FF&E three to six months into the process. Planning for a more extensive renovation will start earlier and should build cushions into the time frame, such that a delay will not push the disruption into a high-occupancy season. It is also important to be mindful of reasons that necessitate an extra-long lead time, such as the need to purchase FF&E manufactured in Asia.

A CapEx budget identifies the operator's suggested priority level of the item, as well as providing for a contingency. Some CapEx budgets, typically at the higher-end hotels, segregate a certain portion of the annual budget as discretionary, which allows the general manager to decide what the funds will be spent on during the year. This has become less prevalent in recent years as owners and asset managers take more control over spending by the operator.

If the hotel is operated by a third party, the owner and asset manager should make sure that the hotel operating agreement identifies a CapEx threshold funding amount, whereby the operator will undertake the project purchasing and project management as part of its base management fee. If it exceeds this threshold amount, then the operator is entitled to charge an agreed-upon fee for providing the service or cause the owner to hire a project manager to execute it. In certain situations, and depending upon the resources of the operator and owner, it may make more sense for one or the other to manage a large renovation. If the operator has an in-house project management team that is fairly active in CapEx for other hotels in their portfolio and, more importantly, has ongoing relationships with the corresponding personnel at the brand level, it may be more efficient on numerous levels to have the operator execute the project. Under these circumstances, the operator may also be able to obtain more competitive pricing, again depending on purchasing volume, knowledge base, and relationships. Alternatively, if the ownership group has a significant platform in the hotel space and has numerous assets, it may be able to execute more efficiently. There may be other considerations as well and these should be explored prior to proceeding with the CapEx project.

Long-Range Planning and the CapEx Planning Model as a Management Tool

Long-range planning of CapEx will extend out ten years, or until the end of that owner's planned holding period. The ten-year term recognizes the need to establish reserves for many major cost items within the hotel that will need to be replaced. Should those reserves not be established, a cash call (i.e., additional paid-in capital) may be required in the future. While specific pricing and costs may not be available today for an item or renovation planned five to seven years out, a target number or "order of magnitude" amount based on available data and information can be used as a placeholder until such time as a more defined scope and price are needed.

There are various secondary source materials that can assist asset managers and owners in determining what will need to be replaced, when it will need to be replaced, and how much it will cost. The ISHC CapEx publications are the most comprehensive source of information on this subject. Each of these ISHC CapEx reports includes an entire section for estimating the future capital requirements of a hotel by property type, by functional area, by line item detail, along with the estimated cost of the individual items. One of the authors of the section has continued to update this forward-looking portion of the study, so this data is readily available to asset managers.

In addition to serving as a planning tool for a property's owner and lenders to adequately underwrite the investment and prepare for future capital expenditure requirements, an effective Long-Term CapEx Planning Model is also used as the framework for assessing the effectiveness of a property's purchasing, maintenance, and preventative maintenance programs. This can be accomplished by adding an element so that in addition to tracking the chronological age of each component of the hotel, an "effective age" can also be assigned to the item.

The introduction of an effective age assessment allows comparison between how the item is actually aging and how a typical "benchmark" item in that category would age. To keep the model current, the property will need to be inspected regularly for the purpose of monitoring the condition of each item and in order to gauge the effectiveness of the property's preventive maintenance programs.

As an added benefit, the effectiveness of the property's on-site maintenance can be better assessed because of the effective age adjustment in the model. For example, if air conditioning units have a theoretical life of twelve years but are able to last fifteen years because of effective maintenance, the value that the property's maintenance staff is adding can be easily quantified and they can be rewarded properly. Conversely, premature aging due to ineffective maintenance would result in an increase in cost to ownership and may be an indicator that the preventive maintenance program is inadequate for that item.

Discretionary Versus Non-Discretionary CapEx

Capital expenditures can be defined as discretionary versus non-discretionary. In some instances, it is easy to determine which silo a proposed CapEx expense item falls into, but this is not always the case.

Non-discretionary CapEx items typically include those dictated by federal or state laws, the most recent one being the mandatory installation of (swimming) pool lifts no later than January 31, 2013, to satisfy a new ADA requirement. Another non-discretionary CapEx expense is any brand or franchise-mandated item that contractually must be completed by a certain date under penalty of default.

Examples of discretionary CapEx items include the development of additional guest rooms, the expansion or addition of a spa, the conversion of a restaurant into meeting space, replacement of the brand-standard 37-inch HD televisions with 42-inch HD televisions to meet the bar set by a competitor, the redesign and repurposing of the hotel's restaurant, and similar projects not mandated by law or contract.

Meanwhile, emergency CapEx items—defined as those that require immediate attention in the wake of some type of equipment failure or life-safety incident—typically take precedence over both types and are most often executed within a very short time period. The parameters of what constitutes an "emergency" CapEx item or issue is normally defined and outlined in the hotel operating agreement.

In most instances, a non-discretionary CapEx item takes priority over a discretionary item. Once again, however, the annual budgeting approval process is the time at which these CapEx discussions occur and priorities are established.

As mentioned previously, brand CapEx items may be more discretionary than mandated. Brands may "request" as opposed to "require" that certain CapEx items be adopted within a hotel. There may also be an alternative that achieves the same objective at significantly less cost. Compliance timeframes may sometimes be extended if an asset manager can demonstrate that the item in question is still serviceable, or meets the local competition. If the physical limitations of the building make compliance impossible from a practical and cost standpoint, that requirement may be waived permanently or until the expiration of the license/sale of the asset. There are firms and individuals available that specialize in negotiating with the brands on these issues.

On the ownership side, there may be discretionary CapEx items that cannot be ignored, even though they are not necessary from a legal or branding perspective. A ballroom roof that is beginning to leak should be replaced before it becomes necessary to relocate a catering function to another hotel, or lose a meeting planners' business due to guests complaining about leaking roofs on their conference table and buffet.

Long-Term Impact to Value Versus No Impact to Value

As we have mentioned, while much of the CapEx investment in a hotel is designed to increase its asset value, there are many CapEx investments made to a hotel that serve only to maintain the asset's functionality or allow it to comply with required standards and regulations. Such expenditures do not have a direct return on investment back to the current owner as investor. Be aware that a future buyer modeling the cost of adding mandated sprinklers, or remediating a mold issue in the guest rooms or public areas, will increase that project's estimated cost to account for the risk. These are underwritten more critically than cosmetic fixes.

A failure to comply with or maintain the asset to "market standards" will also likely detract from the disposition value of the hotel at some time in the future, either through impaired competitiveness, or higher operating costs (both of which impact net operating income). Upon a change of ownership, if the next buyer must play "catch up" due to the current owner's lack of CapEx spending and investment, the additional cost to meet the various compliance standards, or the cost to update the hotel's FF&E package to meet current brand standards, will be factored into the net asset price that the buyer is willing to pay.

ROI Analysis

In an ideal world, every CapEx item would generate a return on investment. The reality is that this does not always happen and, even if it does, it is not necessarily quantifiable for ROI purposes.

On one hand, adding a spa, repurposing a restaurant, or refurbishing guest rooms are all examples of CapEx projects that are intended to generate some level of incremental revenue to the hotel asset that can be quantified such that an ROI can be determined. Conversely, replacing mattresses or a water heater, adding a pool lift to the swimming pool for ADA purposes, or painting the exterior façade of the building may not result in any incremental revenue to the hotel. Thus, the easiest calculations of ROI involve projects that add a new ancillary source of revenue, eliminate a loss, or some combination of both.

Using the conversion of a second, under-utilized restaurant that loses money to additional meeting space is an example that can be analyzed to establish an ROI prior to deciding whether the project is worthwhile or not. For a stabilized year, one would estimate the amount of incremental rooms, food and beverage, and ancillary revenue that could be generated from internal and external groups likely to use the space if converted. From this figure, associated operating expenses, including cost of goods sold, labor, undistributed operating costs, etc., would be deducted to arrive at an incremental profit amount.

After that, one would determine if there are any incremental savings that would result from converting the old restaurant to meeting space. Is there kitchen labor and overhead that can now be saved if the restaurant is eliminated? Is there any salvage value to the restaurant equipment? These savings should be added to the above operating profit. Then, using the ongoing profits and cost avoidance (restaurant operating losses), estimate the recurring annual savings. This annual net profit figure is the absolute dollar value of the return on investment.

Next, one should gather reliable turn-key bids on the construction work. Add to them the one-time costs for terminating employees and contracts, which may be offset by the salvage value of any kitchen equipment. The resultant figure is the total project cost.

One can calculate the return as a percentage; for example, a $100,000 per year increase in profits on a $1,000,000 investment would equate to a 10 percent return and/or a ten-year payback period. Is the renovation likely to last ten years, or will it be necessary to renovate the space again in seven years? This and other such questions should be asked throughout so that the quantitative answer can be factored into the ROI analysis in order to get as accurate an answer as possible so that the owner can make an informed decision.

Another complementary ROI analysis is to undertake a comparable analysis, whereby the asset manager seeks out other hotels and owners that have undertaken similar type projects and interviews them to obtain actual, rather than theoretical results. Based on its applicability to the CapEx project at hand here, this comparable data and information can be used in the preparation of the subject ROI analysis.

The Hotel Asset Manager Role in Annual CapEx Planning

The asset manager's role in the foregoing annual planning process and ROI analysis function for CapEx is multi-faceted, but essentially comes down to that of manager as arbiter.

Initially, the asset manager is responsible for either collecting or delegating the tasks of collecting the pertinent information and data in order to compile an accurate list of all desired CapEx items to be included in the upcoming CapEx budget for the year. Once any owner-related requests or requirements are established, the asset manager should review all other third-party CapEx requirements that need to be executed within the upcoming budget year cycle.

Typically, there should be a formalized document such as a PIP or brand-related CapEx chart that highlights the annual and ongoing CapEx needs of the property. This document should be regularly reviewed by both the asset manager and the operator in order to identify the CapEx needs that must be met in the upcoming year in order to comply with brand standards. Verbal discussions with the brand representative by the asset manager and operator should always accompany this review in order to verify that the need still exists and whether the standards have changed or may be changing in the near future. Any waivers or other time-related issues with the brand requirements should be discussed and documented to ensure compliance and eliminate the threat of a potential default.

Comparable information and data from other branded hotel properties that have already gone through these same CapEx changes can also be shared in order to better understand costs, disruptions to operations, lead times on purchasing items, and return on investment potential. It is beneficial to have the brand representative visit the property to review the physical asset in tandem with the asset manager and operators, with a summary document provided to that effect.

The previously mentioned Property Condition Report should also be consulted. If there is any uncertainty about any aspect of the building envelope, mechanical systems, or other areas of concern, an inspection by an appropriate expert should accompany this annual review process so that any associated CapEx expense to fix or replace the item is established prior to approving all of the upcoming CapEx budget items. Otherwise, this could result in a major expense after the budget is approved and may need to be funded from outside the CapEx budget.

From here, during the annual budget review, the owner, asset manager and operator will prioritize all of the CapEx requests for the upcoming year based on funds available, required CapEx spend, ROI, and desired CapEx spend.

Most CapEx budgets include a contingency amount that allows for a potential unexpected CapEx expense during the course of the year. The amount of this contingency is typically based on a number of factors, with age of hotel and history of unexpected failures or issues playing a major role in the amount reserved for that purpose. In some of the higher-end brand-operated hotels, the management agreement allows for the general manager to have his or her own annual discretionary CapEx budget from which to fund discretionary projects.

If funding is insufficient to cover the CapEx budget, then the asset manager, together with the owner, needs to decide what, if anything, will be pushed to the following year, or alternatively funded from other sources.

Ultimately, the foregoing process allows the asset manager to properly manage the annual and multi-year CapEx process and have sufficient information and data to prioritize needs and approve the annual CapEx budgets.

Obtaining Multiple Bids

It is incumbent upon an asset manager to ensure that the owner is receiving the best overall value for their CapEx funds being spent. To that end, the asset manager should formally require that those responsible for acquiring the CapEx items or services obtain more than one bid. Ideally, three bids should be obtained, but sometimes only two bids are practical. Even if the asset manager is making use of a purchasing agent, the agent should obtain multiple bids for the item.

Depending on the amount of CapEx funds in question, it may also be worthwhile for the asset manager to call other hotel owners or asset managers for references on a prospective project manager, purchasing agent, or vendor. This unfiltered and direct reference may prove invaluable to the asset manager and owner. Kickbacks abound in the construction trades and are devilishly hard to prove. If the cost is significantly lower for one provider over another, make sure the service and workmanship are as advertised.

Be wary, however, of dividing the work/bids into too many smaller projects, as the coordination between contractors can ultimately cost more time and effort than what is saved. In one recent project, the lowest overall cost for a comprehensive mold remediation and re-model project was split between a demolition contractor, a remediation contractor, and a remodeling contractor. The lack of coordination between the parties extended the time frame that the guest rooms were out of inventory and not rentable, which made the apparent savings a false economy.

Monitoring of CapEx and the CapEx Status Report

CapEx spending and execution should be monitored, with the frequency of the monitoring depending on the size, scope and complexity of the CapEx project.

The CapEx status report is a great tool by which to monitor the progress of the current year's CapEx projects and budget. Most operators will include a CapEx status report in their monthly or quarterly owner's financial package so that ownership can be kept current on all CapEx items scheduled to be completed in the current year. This status report should include data on the approved budget, the actual bids/estimates, amounts spent to date, and invoices/obligations outstanding.

Obviously, if the hotel is undergoing a major renovation or will experience major business disruption as a result of a CapEx project, there will likely be significantly more communication with the owners to keep them abreast of conditions and cost, as well as timing to completion. In the case of less intense CapEx items that are scheduled, such as the periodic replacement of PTAC units, the trade out of water heaters or boilers, the repaving of parking lot, the painting of exterior façade of the building, etc., a monthly or quarterly CapEx status report works well.

Conclusion

CapEx management is a strategic process with the goal of maintaining the hotel asset (and its value) over its physical and economic life cycle. Within that process

Exhibit 5 Average CapEx Range by Year

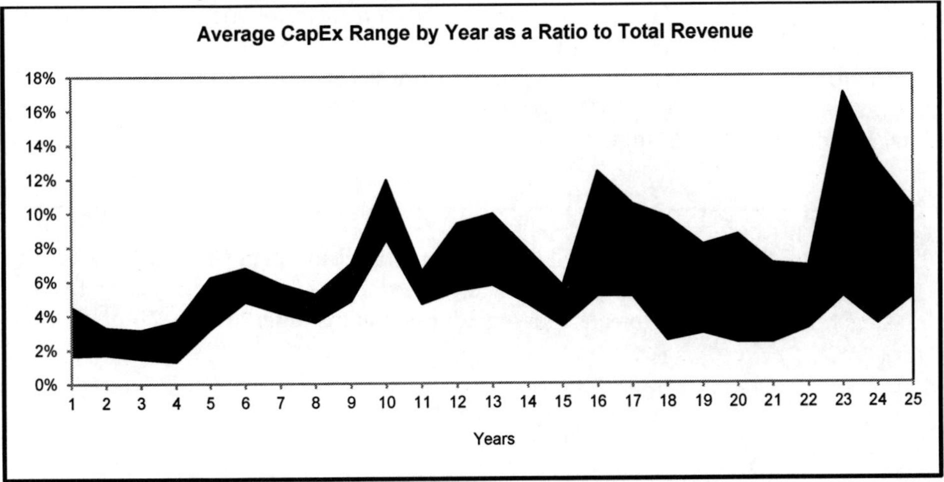

Source: *CapEx 2000: A Study of Capital Expenditures in the U.S. Hotel Industry.*

is the understanding that, although there may be general guidelines, as expressed in this chapter, there are many other issues to consider as part of the short- and long-range planning process for CapEx as part of the investment. As hotel owners, lenders, and operators have learned over many economic cycles, even the best efforts and planning still run afield from unforeseen business cycles or "black swan" events that disrupt the operation and permanently change the course or direction of the investment objectives.

At the same time, because of its potential cost implications and impact to a hotel investment, CapEx planning and managing has become more complex over the years. Despite the industry's best efforts, our industry lags significantly behind many other industries in this particular area when it comes to tracking, forecasting and reporting CapEx. The telecommunications, airline, oil refinery, auto, chemical and energy industries, for example, have a far greater volume of CapEx expenditures on their projects and thus have invested and developed much more sophisticated approaches to planning, budgeting, managing, and monitoring their CapEx needs. The hotel industry thus can learn from these industries as we have in so many other areas of our business, including revenue management and food and beverage operations.

With that in mind, the most important considerations for an asset manager specific to CapEx are: the recognition that planning is needed; that there is no right amount of CapEx investment to be made in a hotel property; that the age, location, product type, brand standards, and historical R&M practices at a hotel will influence the overall cost of CapEx expenditures of an owner; and that CapEx spending in a hotel is highly dependent upon a hotel's point in its life cycle (in other words, the older the hotel, the higher the amount of CapEx investment will be needed to maintain it over the investment holding period). Exhibit 5, taken from the ISHC CapEx 2000 study, underscores this reality best.

Apart from that, be aware that the rapid changes in the tastes and preferences of the consumer are causing more frequent changes to the hotel asset, which tends to drive up the cost of CapEx over a shorter period of time, and cause functional obsolescence to occur more quickly.

In closing, and as stated in the last edition of this book, capital expenditure management remains a metaphor for the hotel business in general: seemingly predictable, yet subject to change.

Endnotes

1. Rick Swig, "Guidelines for Capital Expenditure Decisions," in Greg Denton, Lori E. Raleigh, & A. J. Singh, ed., *Hotel Asset Management: Principles & Practices*, 2nd ed. (Lansing, Mich.: American Hotel & Lodging Educational Institute, 2009), p. 274.
2. *ibid.*

8

Insurance, Risk Management, and Business Continuity

By Angela Giunto and Michael Lettin

***Angela Giunto** is currently a Senior Vice President and Account Executive Practice Leader for Aon plc in Denver, Colorado, where she has been employed over the last 10 years. Aon plc is the leading global provider of risk management, insurance, and reinsurance brokerage services. Ms. Giunto dedicates her time to managing her book of business, serving as an executive client contact for key accounts, and supervising the account executive team. Her book of business is concentrated on real estate and hospitality, where she often advises on and provides solutions for ancillary exposures such as special events and construction. Angela was awarded the 2014 Power Broker by* Risk & Insurance *magazine for Gaming and Hospitality.*

Prior to joining Aon plc, Ms. Giunto was employed by Marsh, Inc. in Philadelphia, Pennsylvania. She graduated from the University of Kansas and the Syracuse University College of Law. She is currently admitted to the Pennsylvania, New York, and Colorado bar associations.

***Michael Lettin** is currently a Vice President and Account Executive for Aon plc in Denver, Colorado, where he has been employed over the last seven years. Mr. Lettin joined Aon immediately after graduating from Colorado State University with a degree in Finance. As an Account Executive, he is responsible for managing his book of business while also brokering complex property and casualty placements for his clients. His book of business consists of Hospitality, Real Estate, Trucking, and Manufacturing, representing over $30 million of premium in the marketplace.*

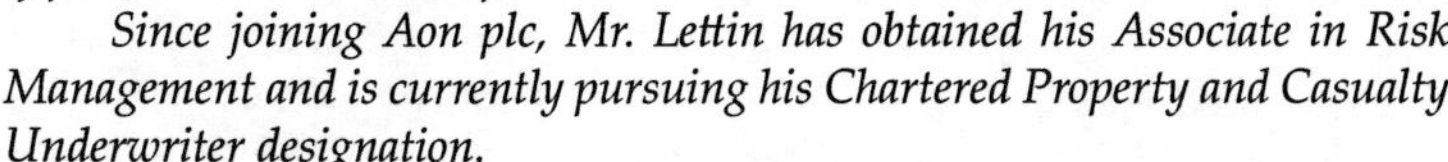

Since joining Aon plc, Mr. Lettin has obtained his Associate in Risk Management and is currently pursuing his Chartered Property and Casualty Underwriter designation.

INSURANCE, BY DEFINITION, is the contractual relationship whereby one party undertakes to protect or indemnify another party for a specified risk in exchange for a payment of premium. This definition of insurance speaks to "risk transfer" in its most basic form. It is important to note that not all risks are insurable, nor are all risks feasibly transferred. A more comprehensive approach to addressing business risks and exposures would be "risk management." Risk management is the practice of identifying and analyzing exposures and taking steps to minimize the overall financial impact of those risks, either to a third party or to an operation's own balance sheet. Hospitality assets and operations lend themselves to a wide array of risks, ranging from basic property losses as a result of a fire, to complex scenarios involving *legionella* and terrorism, and even the rapidly-evolving world of cyber-attacks and other technological vulnerabilities.

A risk analysis should start with a review of hotel operations as they pertain to the four quadrants of risk: operational, hazard, strategic, and financial. This pre-loss exercise aids in determining the various risk factors of an operation as well as deciphering an entity's appetite for risk. Following the analysis, a risk mapping exercise can be utilized to determine how to best deal with a specific risk factor. By mapping risk, you can either decide to retain the risk, finance it, transfer it via insurance, or avoid the risk altogether. An operation's appetite for risk may vary; however, typically operations have more of a tolerance for small but frequent risks, choosing to either retain them or finance them. Alternatively, more severe but less frequent risks more often tend to be transferred or avoided. Unfortunately, despite best efforts, these types of losses still occur. In the case of a severe loss, the use of various mitigation efforts and business continuity and disaster recovery plans are essential to securing the best possible outcome.

The Four Quadrants of Risk

Enterprise risk management provides a framework to review and understand a broad array of risks and their potential impact across an operation. While a formal enterprise risk management process is often initiated by the principals of a company and undertaken through a formal risk review committee represented by representatives from multiple areas of the business, a similar analysis can be conducted by an asset manager. At its core, the analysis applies the four quadrants of risk (see Exhibit 1) to ascertain the risk profile and appetite of an operation. Not every risk has just one quadrant; many fall into several quadrants. It is more important to identify the risk and map it than it is to determine the correct quadrant(s).

Exhibit 1 The Four Quadrants of Risk

FINANCIAL RISK	STRATEGIC RISK
• Interest rate fluctuation • Foreign exchange rate fluctuation • General economy • Dependency on another industry or company	• Industry competition • Regulatory issues, jurisdictional challenges, and political trends • Long-term objectives (i.e., development, condo conversion, resale, etc.)
OPERATIONAL RISK	**HAZARD RISK**
• Day-to-day issues (i.e., human resources, guest safety, etc.) • Pandemics and/or contamination • Ancillary services and activities (i.e., daycare, spa services, etc.) • Cyber risk	• Risk associated with the location: ♦ Fire ♦ Weather-related ♦ Flood/earthquake ♦ Terrorism ♦ Environmental liability

Operational Risk

Operational risks are those associated with a hotel's day-to-day operations and range anywhere from human resources and employee-related issues to guest relations and information technology. Many operational risks can be addressed by the traditional property and casualty insurance offerings (see Exhibit 2).

Most of the traditional types of insurance policies referenced in Exhibit 2 are written on an annual term. The annual policy term is most often renewable but it is important to be actively engaged in the renewal process to ensure that coverage terms, conditions, and pricing remain optimal for your operation. The renewal process is a fairly lengthy process and, depending on the size and scope of a renewal, should often start six months in advance of any policy expiration. At a minimum, the process should closely follow the timetable shown in Exhibit 3.

In the case of asset management, the operation of an asset is frequently contracted out to a third-party management company. Typically, the operator undertakes the procurement of insurance and simply charges back premiums and losses

Exhibit 2 Traditional Insurance Offerings

Property Insurance:
First-party insurance that indemnifies the owner or users of a property for its loss, or the loss of its income-producing ability, when the loss or damage is caused by a covered peril. Common covered perils may include, but are not limited to, fire, earth movement, flood, and named storm.

Casualty Insurance:
General Liability—This policy will pay sums the insured becomes legally obligated to pay as damages resulting from bodily injury or property damage to third parties. The bodily injury or property damage must be caused by an occurrence that takes place in the coverage territory. Coverage is also afforded for personal and advertising injury. Defense costs should be covered in addition to the limits of liability. Coverage is typically written on an occurrence basis, which means the policy will respond only if the injury or damage occurs during the policy period.

Automobile Liability—Involves two basic types of coverage: (1) liability insurance coverage for losses caused by injuries to persons and legal liability imposed on the insured for such injury or for damage to the property of others; and (2) physical damage insurance for losses caused by damage or loss to an insured vehicle.

Workers' Compensation and Employer's Liability—The system by which no-fault statutory benefits prescribed in state law are provided by an employer to an employee (or employee's family) due to a job-related injury (including death) resulting from an accident or occupational disease.

Umbrella/Excess Liability—These policies provide additional amounts of insurance over other insurance policies. Typically, umbrella policies sit over general liability, automobile liability, and employer's liability as well as foreign liability policies, as needed.

Exhibit 3 Recommended Insurance Placement Timetable

120–140 Days Prior to Policy Expiration	The insurance agent or broker should initiate the renewal process by providing a comprehensive list of the exposure data needed and/or relevant applications to the client. A renewal strategy meeting should also take place either prior to the request for information or in tandem with the request.
90–100 Days Prior to Policy Expiration	The client should return all of the requested information, and the insurance agent/broker creates a "submission" consisting of the collected data and includes the desired coverage terms and conditions. The submission is then sent to the insurance carriers (markets) to undergo the underwriting and review process.
30–45 Days Prior to Policy Expiration	The insurance carriers should have completed their underwriting and issued their responses either in the form of a declination or a quotation. The insurance agent/broker continues to negotiate with the various carriers and creates an "insurance proposal" for presentation to the client, with the options received and recommendations for coverage.
25–30 Days Prior to Policy Expiration	The insurance agent/broker should present the final proposal to the client and secure an order to bind the coverage desired for the renewal.
1–25 Days Prior to Policy Expiration	Binders of insurance are issued by the selected carriers, evidencing proof of the renewal terms and conditions. Certificates of insurance and auto ID cards are produced, and premium invoices are generated.
30–60 Days Post-Renewal	Policies should be issued by the carriers; agents/brokers should review them for accuracy and deliver them to the client with a schedule and/or summary of insurance as bound.

through an operating account funded by the owner of the property. When negotiating the management contract, it is important for the asset manager to determine which party is absorbing which risks, so that the risk and insurance program can be designed accordingly. It is also advisable to engage a risk management professional to review the coverage placed on your behalf, to ensure the manager's insurance program has the wherewithal to ensure that your assets are properly covered in the event of a loss, and likewise is compliant with the terms of your management contract. Exhibit 4 provides a practical, non-exhaustive list of questions asset managers should ask when entering into a management contract, to aid them in designing their insurance procurement strategy.

Emerging Issue—Cyber Threats. In the hospitality arena, operational risks can come from many directions and will likely continue to be the area where many emerging risks emanate from. The transient nature of guests, and the desire to

Exhibit 4 Sample Questions for Designing an Asset's Insurance Program

Property:

1. Which party will be responsible for covering the building(s), contents, and business income?
2. Is your business dependent on attraction properties (e.g., amusement park, ski resort)?
3. Is there mobile equipment that must be covered?
4. Are there additional non-traditional assets such as fine arts, valuable landscaping, a golf course, dock, or marina?
5. Are there any particular lender or contractual coverage requirements (e.g., specific limits for flood, earth movement, named storm, or terrorism)?

Human Resources:

1. Who will "own" the employees (i.e., who is the employer—the asset owner, management company, or a separate entity)?
2. Do employees have to re-apply for their jobs upon the sale of the property? If so, what is the action plan?
3. Is there union involvement or regulatory jurisdictional issues to comply with (e.g., Department of Labor filings)? If so, who is responsible for compliance?
4. Who will handle pensions and benefits?
5. Is there a workplace violence program in place?
6. Is the entity that "owns" the employees responsible for placing the employee benefits, crime, fiduciary, and employment practices liability coverages?
7. Will the employees be handling the operation's cash? Will a property manager be collecting dues for a third-party HOA? Employee theft/crime coverage or a fidelity bond may be necessary.
8. How solid is the current staff's safety record? If the current record is not solid, what steps is the management company taking to rectify the performance?

Liability:

1. Who owns the vehicle or lease?
2. What are the driver qualifications? Is there a driver safety program?
3. If there is a liquor license, what entity holds the license?
4. Are there valet operations? If so, the owner of the valet operation should provide garage-keepers liability coverage.
5. Are there childcare or daycare operations? Is it a licensed operation? Is it an owned operation or contracted out? Who will secure abuse and molestation coverage?
6. Are there spa and/or fitness center operations? If so, which party is in charge of the operations and therefore responsible for the insurance?
7. Are there special events or third-party vendors on the premises? If so, is their coverage monitored and evaluated for sufficiency?

(continued)

Exhibit 4 *(continued)*

8. Are there ancillary activities associated with the resort (e.g., beauty salon, scuba, etc.)? If so, are these contracted out to third parties, whereby solid indemnification and insurance provisions are in place?
9. Does your operation receive commissions for concierge referrals at all? If so, you may potentially be legally liable for damage sustained as a result of these recommendations.
10. Are there specific lender requirements for particular limits and/or coverages?

provide guests with more amenities and activities, mean that hotels are vulnerable to new and/or growing exposures. For example, in the summer of 2014, the U.S. Secret Service issued an alert to the hospitality industry related to business center computers being vulnerable to keystroke-logging malware that can effectively provide unauthorized individuals with access to guests' personally identifiable information. Cyber liability is one of the most rapidly growing insurance products. Major retailers such as Target and Home Depot have suffered breaches; no business is safe from attack. The Sony Entertainment Group attack at the end of 2014 may turn out to be the most costly cyber attack to date.

Hazard Risk

Hazard risks are those that may simply arise as a result of your physical location. Hazard risks are typically more severe and less frequent than day-to-day operational risks, which are generally more frequent but less severe. Most commonly, hazard risks derive from natural or weather-related events common to a particular location; for example, earthquakes in California, hurricanes in Florida, and even tornados and floods in the Midwest. These types of events, while rare, can be catastrophic to an operation. An analysis of the environment and location of an operation is imperative, as many insurance costs can be associated with particular locations. Exhibit 5 illustrates some of the variables that contribute to the risk profile of a location.

Exhibit 5 Hazard Risk Continuum

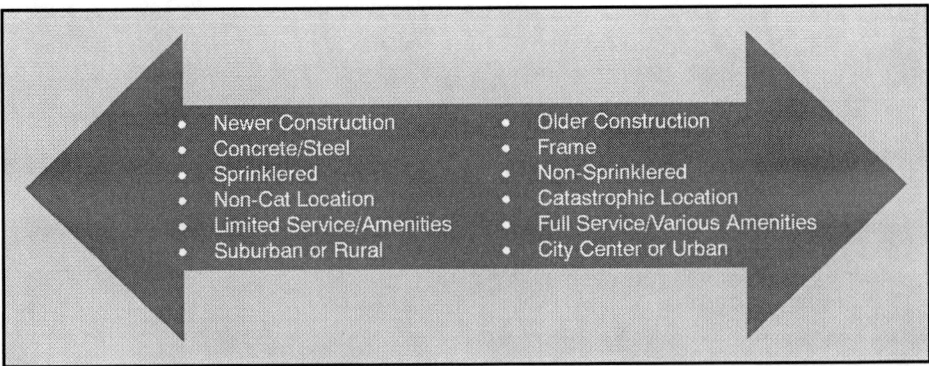

Catastrophic Events. Generally, exposures of magnitude, such as earthquakes or hurricanes, have required amounts of insurance as stipulated either by lending agreements or management arrangements. Typically, the required levels of insurance are derived from a formulaic analysis that determines the probable maximum loss (PML). The PML is the probable amount of loss that may result from events ranging in magnitudes of 100-year, 250-year, or 500-year. For example, a resort in California may have a probable maximum loss of $10 million from an earthquake event that would occur once every 100 years. The same resort may have a PML of $25 million from an earthquake event that may occur once every 250 years, and a $40 million PML for a once-in-every-500-years type of event. Property engineering reports, surveys, and detailed construction and protection information are utilized in the hazard modeling of a risk and formulation of the PML. The PML is often used as a baseline in negotiations with the lender regarding limits of coverage that may be required to be purchased. Depending on a hotel's exact location and type of construction, it is reasonable to insure for a 250-year event. While there are more conservative lending institutions that will push for higher limits, it is important to weigh their desires with what is reasonably, commercially available in the insurance marketplace. For example, after Superstorm Sandy the flood marketplace for insurance became much stricter: the definition of "flood" was narrowed, deductibles were increased, premiums were increased, and areas were designated where insurance carriers simply could no longer offer the coverage. It is often advisable to engage the agent/broker during negotiations with the lender so that you do not suffer the unintended consequences of being unable to afford compliance with your loan.

Terrorism and Political Risk. In addition to the natural climate, the local political climate will also have an impact on an operation. Foreign political risks are nothing new to the global hospitality arena. The risks of doing business in another country are varied, not to mention the added risk of housing people within your business in a foreign country. From an insurance perspective, every country is different, and it is important to know each country's regulatory environment to ensure compliance with local laws, as well as fully understand the potential penalties for non-compliance. A full insurance analysis of each country's laws on compulsory, admitted, or non-admitted insurance is necessary. Purchasing insurance for operations abroad should be informed and deliberate in order to comply with local regulations.

Emerging issue—terrorism. Domestically, the United States has been victim to terrorist acts, most notably the terrorist attacks of September 11, 2001. In response to the 9/11 attacks, the United States Congress enacted the Terrorism Risk Insurance Act (TRIA). First signed into law in 2002, the Act created a federal "backstop" or effectively reinsurance for insurance claims arising from "certified acts of terrorism." At the Act's expiration, a "certified act of terrorism" was generally one to be deemed as such by the Secretary of Treasury, Secretary of State, and the Attorney General, and must cause damage in excess of $100 million within the United States. The Act was renewed in 2005, and again in 2007 when it was re-titled the Terrorism Risk Insurance Program Reauthorization Act (TRIPRA), with slight modifications and an expiration date of December 31, 2014. On December 16, 2014, after the U.S. House of Representatives passed a 6 year extension, the

Senate adjourned for the year without passing the extension. This failure to renew the federal program resulted in a flood of insureds scrambling for terrorism coverage to remain in compliance with loans as well as to fill the gap in coverage for their potentially high-target assets. (Major metropolitan areas in the United States are considered higher risk, with restricted zip codes for many carriers across the country where they are limited as to the amount of coverage they either can afford to or are willing to provide.) The impact of the failure to extend the Act was notable. On January 12, 2015, Congress passed the Terrorism Risk Insurance Program Reauthorization Act of 2015, effectively extending the Act until December 31, 2020. Throughout the term of the 2015 Act, definitions on the size and scope of loss-trigger and subsequent backstop protection become increasingly more narrow. Assets that are considered to be in high-target locations in terms of possible terrorism events should not rely solely on TRIPRA coverage but instead seek options for stand-alone terrorism coverage.

Other Hazard Concerns. In addition to catastrophic or political risks, there are basic location and environmental hazard risks that are worth noting. Your resort location may be near another destination or attraction property such as an amusement park or national landmark. In this event, a loss to the attraction property may have a significant impact on your hotel or resort's income stream, even if your asset has not suffered any physical damage itself. A typical property policy only responds if there is direct physical damage to your property as a result of a covered peril; it may not respond if there is physical damage to another operation's property. Likewise, if you have a remote location where there is only one means of ingress/egress to your location and that road is blocked by some natural means like a mud-slide or avalanche, you may want to negotiate a way for your property policy to respond in the event of lost income. While these examples are not standard coverages, there are potentially ways to negotiate these coverages for a price, with good data gained from your risk assessment and evaluation practices.

Emerging issue—environmental. Another continually evolving area of hazard risk is that of environmental risk. Most property and general liability policies exclude mold, fungi, bacteria, and contamination. While historically the hospitality industry may not have thought much about exposure to environmental risks, the transient nature of resort guests, along with varied climate ranges and expanding operations, can open up a resort to a myriad of risks not previously addressed. Guests from all over the word descend upon a resort for a brief period of time, bringing with them any number of germs or infestations that may then be transmitted to other guests. Infestations, pandemics, and infectious diseases remain a hot button issue after continued reported cases of bedbugs, noroviruses, *legionella* outbreaks, and, most notably in 2014, the Ebola crisis. Aside from the obvious risks to guest and employee health, these types of outbreaks can also result in lost income and substantial remediation costs. Environmental or pollution legal-liability policies exist to address any number of environmental risk concerns, ranging from pre-existing conditions to mold to pesticide and fuel storage. Even the more traditional hotel operations of chemical storage for pools or golf courses can also benefit from the broadened coverage offered by an environmental policy in the event of an inadvertent leak or distribution of chemicals.

Strategic Risk

Strategic risks can range from regulatory and jurisdictional concerns to political risk to those geared toward brand reputation and competition. Brand reputation is particularly important for an asset manager contracting with a brand flag for its property. The franchise brand may suffer a loss from an operation that has nothing to do with your asset, but, depending on the nature of the issue, your operation may suffer lost business as a result. This type of lost income is a business risk that deserves attention, as there is not a traditional insurance product to offer reimbursement for this type of loss of income. Strategic concerns of an operation often involve mergers and acquisitions activity, renovations of current assets, or development of new assets. Mergers, acquisitions, and/or divestitures come with a set of transactional risks for which there are insurance products that may be able to respond, such as representations and warranties, tax indemnity, fraudulent conveyance, and environmental liabilities.

Strategic risk also includes competition. In an effort to make an asset more attractive relative to its competition, significant renovations and even ground-up construction of assets may be employed. Construction risk involves a substantial amount of exposure, especially when habitational in nature. At a minimum, construction projects require an element of property coverage called "builder's risk" as well as general liability and workers' compensation coverage, which can be provided either on an individual basis by each contractor or in a "wrap-up" format.

Builder's Risk. An asset owner/developer's first insurance concern likely involves insurance coverage for the actual building while it is being constructed or renovated. "Course of construction" or builder's risk coverage is most advantageous in scope when placed by the actual owner/developer versus the contractor providing the coverage on the owner's behalf. A builder's risk policy should have a policy limit equal to that of the estimated completed value of the project, plus coverage for "soft costs," which is the equivalent to business income coverage within a standard property policy. Soft costs coverage will provide coverage for loss of income and/or specific additional expenses incurred from construction delays resultant from a covered peril. These policies can be placed on a stand-alone basis for each asset or, if there is a construction pipeline of multiple projects within a three- to five-year period, it may behoove the owner to place a "rolling" program. A "rolling" program may afford more attractive pricing and terms for an entire project pipeline, as there may be more insurance carriers interested in participating with more values and a greater spread of risk. Terms can be negotiated for the entire pipeline up front, and the assets simply "roll" onto the program when each project starts. While asset owners should seek to place their own builder's risk policy to ensure their asset is covered adequately, there are pros and cons regarding the owner- or contractor-placed coverage on the liability coverage versus insurance placed separately by the general contractors and subcontractors on a project.

Wrap-Up Programs. Historically, the approach to insurance on a construction project would be to have the general contractor and all subcontractors secure their own insurance coverage for a project. More recently, "wrap-up" insurance programs have been fashioned to "wrap" all contractors into one master insurance program for general liability, umbrella/excess liability, and sometimes workers' compensation. Each contractor simply enrolls in the insurance program upon entry to the project, and the program provides consistent and seamless coverage for all enrolled contractors across the term of a project. The two main types of wrap-up programs are referred to as owner-controlled or contractor-controlled insurance programs (OCIPs or CCIPs). The use of these programs are common now, as they can lead to some cost savings, enhanced and consistent coverage terms, and elimination of disputes between multiple contractor policies in the event of a loss. These programs can also be written on a "rolling" basis, which is particularly useful if you have a series of smaller projects. Oftentimes a "wrap" style project is not financially viable with less than $100 million of construction values. However, a series or pipeline of smaller projects can be marketed to the insurance carriers at the same time to entice the marketplace to create a master "rolling" wrap-up program. See Exhibit 6 for a comparison of the respective pros and cons of OCIPs and CCIPs.

Financial Risk

Many of the risks previously identified may ultimately have a financial impact, such as losses to business income that may not be fully recoverable, deductible or retention obligations, and even those risks that are under-insured or uninsurable. However, in its truest sense, a financial risk is one that directly impacts the company's balance sheet. Financial risks include fluctuating interest and foreign exchange rates as well as the general state of the economy, inflation, and consumer spending. Financial risk is the most elusive type of risk for a service-based industry. Where a products-based industry has set costs for tangible products, the hospitality industry is often subject to the state of the global economy, the travel industry, the weather, the success of a nearby attraction property, and various seasonality factors, many of which are not insurable. While not insurance tools, exchange rate risk can be fairly easily hedged in the futures and options markets, some derivative products may be tailored to address seasonal and/or weather concerns, and even commodity procurement in remote locales can be employed to alleviate some financial risks.

Despite best efforts to avoid and/or mitigate loss, losses do happen, and, when they do, it is important to have a business continuity or disaster recovery plan in place to minimize the loss and subsequent financial impact.

Risk Mapping

The "risk map" in Exhibit 7 can help asset managers gauge the risk of an asset or operation under review; it's a tool to help them determine how to handle the various risk exposures either through risk retention, risk finance, risk transfer, or pure risk avoidance. This risk-mapping technique should be done initially during the property acquisition and revisited annually during the renewal-strategy phase to aid with the insurance program design for the next year. While this technique is helpful, it should be remembered that classifying various risks into one of the four risk quadrants is merely one of the first steps in the insurance and risk

Exhibit 6 OCIP versus CCIP

	Owner-Controlled Insurance Program (OCIP)	Contractor-Controlled Insurance Program (CCIP)
Definition	Owner of the project is in charge of the placement and structure of the program. Contractors either submit their bids without a line-item for insurance, or insurance costs are included in the initial bid and the costs are then deducted when their work on the project is complete to track potential cost savings.	The general contractor is charged with organizing and administering the insurance program for all of the subcontractors that awarded work on a project and eligible for participation.
Pros	• Greater control • Clearer understanding of coverage purchased • Dedicated limits of insurance • Potential cost savings • Leverage of volume purchasing	• Certainty of costs at time of bid • Less owner resources needed to manage the program
Cons	• Resources to procure and monitor program • Owner is the first named insured ultimately responsible for premium or retentions/deductibles • Uncertainty in final costs due to loss variables	• Lack of control • May actually cost the owner more than the traditional method • Contractor receives the benefit of potential cost savings

management process. The asset manager still must determine how to best manage the various exposures, always keeping in mind the asset owner's appetite for risk.

To see how the risk-mapping technique works, let's focus on an exposure of typical concern to an operation, such as the day-to-day "slips and falls" of guests on the premises. Since these situations may occur somewhat frequently but are typically not very severe and result in minimal compensation, this exposure would be plotted in the lower left "Retain" square. These low-level losses would likely be retained on the books of the operation, through either a deductible or self-insured retention. In contrast, the more severe and less frequent exposure of a damaging hurricane would be plotted in the upper left "Transfer" quadrant, whereby the high risk is transferred to an insurance company after the operation retains a portion of the loss via a deductible or self-insured retention. The risks a resort may choose to avoid may be ancillary activities or facilities such as scuba diving, jet-ski operations, or even a day-care operation. These risks can be avoided by contract-

Exhibit 7 Risk Map

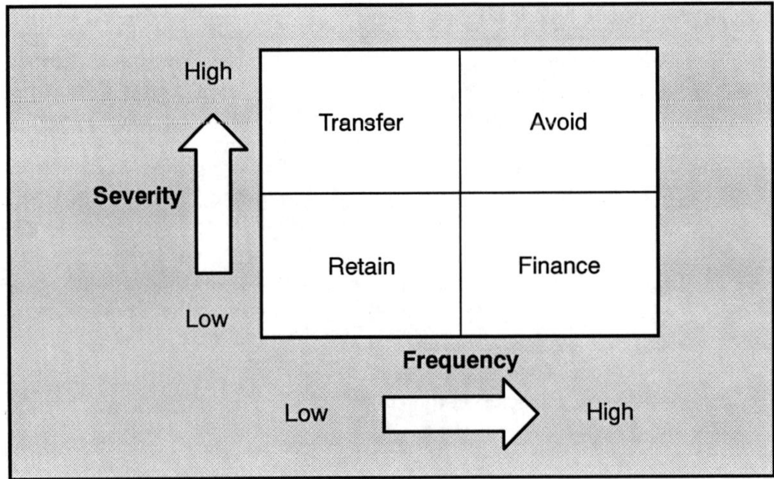

ing with a third party and securing indemnification and proof of insurance from another party. Finally, large, sophisticated risk management programs may choose to finance losses instead of transferring all exposures to insurance.

Business Continuity and Disaster Recovery Planning

Despite the most careful due diligence planning, it is inevitable that emergencies, crises, and disasters will occur. In order to be prepared when a catastrophic event occurs, hotel businesses must have certain procedures in place to ensure the safety of their employees and guests as well as their continued operations. Preparation and planning is critical to any hospitality risk, whether insurable or not. In this section we will discuss the development of a broader Business Continuity Plan (BCP), of which a Disaster Recovery Plan (DRP) is an element, and the key factors that should be considered when creating a BCP.

A BCP is simply an enterprise-wide plan to continue to do business during a disaster. A BCP consists of many elements, but broadly speaking includes three main phases:

1. An emergency/crisis identification and response phase
2. A crisis management and communications phase
3. A disaster recovery and operational restoration phase

A BCP should address the different types of losses that are likely to occur across an operation and then provide a specific set of guidelines to follow for each type of loss. The main objective of the plan is to continue operations safely and ensure a structured and speedy recovery by addressing the following:

- Identification of an event
- Employee and guest safety and security

- Coordination and communication protocols (internal and external)
- Damage assessment and stability
- Brand reputation preservation
- Maintenance of operations

The first step is to form an internal BCP committee and assign each member a specific position. Each operating department should be represented on the committee, and cross-training is essential. The goal is to try and not be dependent on certain individuals and balance the tasks amongst the team members. The committee should meet regularly to discuss ongoing issues and the different ways to address them. The committee will be responsible for continually testing the BCP to ensure its viability.

Once a committee is formed, it will need to identify and review all risks associated with the operation and perform a business impact analysis. Since BCP's are meant to address catastrophic events, the plan should focus mainly on external risks along with the specific operational risks. The committee will need to assign specific tasks by department and individual for each type of loss. Each department should have an emergency contact list available and everyone should know what steps they need to take once an incident occurs. There should be redundancy built into the plan for ownership of tasks and a clear hierarchy of committee members to trigger the plan.

The business impact analysis will identify critical processes and organizational impacts for the identified risks. Exhibit 8 provides a list of areas the committee should focus on when analyzing how a business will be impacted by a loss.

In hospitality organizations, people are providing services to other people, so the ability for employees and guests to continue to be safe and protected is paramount. Below is a brief list of critical business functions related specifically to hotels and resorts:

- *Power.* It is imperative for hotels to have power to ensure guest safety. Backup generators are essential for all operations. HVAC and temperature control may be critical to maintain in certain climates to minimize property damage.
- *Technology systems.* This includes the ability to communicate with guests, provide room access, and functioning reservation systems.
- *Food and water.* If guests cannot leave the premises due to an ingress/egress issue, it is imperative to make sure there are adequate essentials on site to keep people in good health.
- *Structural integrity and sustainability.* In the event of a loss, how much of the building is damaged and how long can guests be kept safe?
- *Transportation to and from the resort.* If there is an evacuation, how will you transport guests and where will they go?

The BCP committee must assess each of these functions in terms of what the impact would be if the hotel had to function without that function for a period of time. The committee also needs to determine the maximum amount of downtime the operation can withstand and determine contingency plans.

Exhibit 8 Business Impact Areas of Focus

Business Impact Analysis—Areas of Focus	
• Guest and employee safety • Critical services—power, HVAC, laundry, security, food and beverage • Communication protocols • External risks—evacuation planning • Key suppliers or vendors for goods or services • Attraction properties	• Competition disruption • Recovery complexity • Relative replacement for equipment/information • Desired recovery time • Reliance on IT • Single/sole sourcing • Key staff • Ingress/egress • Outside partners for food, water, and shelter

Once the committee has identified and analyzed the risks associated with the operation, it can start planning how to respond to each type of loss. There are certain priorities that need to be taken into account when planning:

Once all of the factors have been identified and discussed, the committee can start the formulation of the BCP. The plan should consist of at least three phases:

Priorities When Planning	
Ensure Safety	• Employees and guests • Hazard awareness • Evacuation planning • Shelters in place • Local authorities contacts (fire, police, hospitals)
Communication	• Alert notification system • Security • Fire system monitoring • Backup phones/internet
Identify Alternatives	• Generators • Data backup systems • Third-party locations to house guests • Other vendors/suppliers • Transportation for guests and employees • Restaurants
Resources	• Fire department • Police • Hospitals • Utilities • Local water supply • Restoration companies

Priorities When Planning	
Ensure Safety	• Employees and guests • Hazard awareness • Evacuation planning • Shelters in place • Local authorities contacts (fire, police, hospitals)
Communication	• Alert notification system • Security • Fire system monitoring • Backup phones/internet
Identify Alternatives	• Generators • Data backup systems • Third-party locations to house guests • Other vendors/suppliers • Transportation for guests and employees • Restaurants
Resources	• Fire department • Police • Hospitals • Utilities • Local water supply • Restoration companies

1. *Emergency identification and response.* This initial response would occur during the first hour to two after the incident has occurred. The primary goals are to evacuate the location, stabilize the facility, and conduct an initial assessment of the damage. Ensuring guest and personnel safety is essential while coordinating with authorities and stabilizing the situation. Internal communications should be frequent and coordination with emergency services should be emphasized.

2. *Crisis management.* After stabilization, the actual management of the incident and operation are required. Coordination of remediation activities, internal/external communications, and making informed decisions all fall under the crisis management phase of the plan. The crisis management phase typically occurs after all emergency responses have taken place, generally up to three days post-incident.

3. *Operational restoration and recovery.* Roughly 3 to 4 days post-incident and until the operation is back up to pre-loss activity, the focus becomes fully restoring operations (starting with critical processes), making sure that essential staff members are back in place, restoring technology equipment, and dealing with

infrastructure issues. Third-party disaster recovery and property restoration firms are often engaged to help, and can be vital to this process. It is important to note that effective and prudent contingency planning dictates that hotels should identify third-party resources *before* an incident occurs (this is particularly important in cases of market-wide catastrophic events such as earthquakes and terrorism attacks).

The proper implementation of the BCP and continual staff training regarding the BCP are essential for the plan to be successful. Current and emerging risks should be monitored regularly and the plan adjusted accordingly. It is also helpful to engage outside firms to aid in plan formulation and/or audit. To test its ongoing viability, it is recommended that the plan be tested annually using various scenarios. It is nearly impossible to have a perfect response to a catastrophic event, but knowing your operation's risks and having assessed vulnerabilities will provide a solid foundation for successfully managing a disastrous situation.

Conclusion

Ongoing risk identification and risk assessment before a loss occurs not only aids in crafting your risk management and insurance purchasing strategy, it also provides a solid framework for business-continuity planning in the event of a disaster. It is vital to have enterprise-wide participation in the evaluation of risks to determine your operation's appetite for risk and its wherewithal to withstand a catastrophic loss. The hospitality industry is subject to an amplified duty of care during a catastrophe, as the priority of either evacuating or housing guests safely is paramount and not without its own risks. A comprehensive and tested business-continuity plan will increase an operation's likelihood for a successful recovery following a disaster. Partnerships with agents/brokers, insurance carriers, emergency responders, contractors, and property restoration firms are also advisable to support efforts in returning to pre-loss operations. Risk and safety will remain a large expense line item in the hospitality industry, but the proper attention given to risk management and insurance can enhance an asset fiscally, operationally, and strategically.

Mini-Case Scenarios Highlighting Risk and Insurance Issues

I. An asset owner seeks to acquire a new portfolio of resorts in order to further diversify the owner's holdings. Use the hazard risk continuum to determine which portfolio would come with greater hazard risks. Focus on the qualities of age, construction type, protections, amenities, and locations.

   a. Portfolio 1: Ski resort lodges and hotels throughout the U.S. and Canada; older, frame construction with limited or dated protection systems.

   b. Portfolio 2: Portfolio of U.S. urban, coastal, high-rise hotel properties with newer construction dates and protections.

Answer: Depending on the asset owner's current portfolio mix, the most important tenant from an insurance cost perspective is to enhance diversification. So if the asset owner's current portfolio is comprised mostly of urban coastal locations, then the spread of risk to non-CAT areas such as Colorado would relieve the need for added CAT capacity. While ski lodges are often older, wood-frame construction, they are not in urban centers and often are not faced with the traditional critical CAT type of exposures such as named windstorm, flood, and earthquake. That being said, wood frame construction in remote locations with limited fire protection systems are also at high risk for fire and access to a water source. An unbalanced load either way in an insurance program will affect the premiums. Likewise, foreign operations also bring with them local compulsory and regulatory insurance concerns.

II. A hospitality REIT is looking to acquire a ski resort, including all of the lodging and base operations as well as the ski mountain operations. From an insurance perspective, list all of the possible types of relevant insurance.

Answer: Relevant insurance includes property, equipment breakdown (ski lifts), general liability for the guest activities, liquor liability, automobile and mobile equipment, umbrella/excess liability, workers' compensation/employer's liability, environmental, crime, fiduciary, director's and officer's, employment practices, cyber attack, terrorism.

III. An asset manager acquires a large resort that is near a major amusement park. The resort offers a wide range of amenities and services, from child care services to servicing large private events. The asset manager is very risk-adverse and has asked for a review of the various exposures and a determination of what can be covered by insurance.

Answer:
Traditionally Insurable:

1. Property, equipment breakdown, business income, attraction property issues with amusement park
2. Terrorism
3. General liability for guests, special events, liquor
4. Spa and salon services
5. Child care services and activities
6. Food and beverage (including liquor)
7. Pools, slides, diving boards, hot tubs, saunas, fitness facility
8. Automobiles, valet and livery services, and mobile equipment (including golf carts potentially)
9. Workers' compensation and employer's liability
10. Employee benefits and fiduciary liability
11. Crime

12. Director's and officer's liability
13. Employment practices liability
14. Cyber liability
15. Professional services related either to property management and/or spa services
16. Environmental

Limited to No Insurability:

1. Weather
2. Seasonality
3. Closure of attraction property not resulting from covered peril
4. Poor economic climate—i.e., reduction of discretionary spending
5. Pandemics—resulting decline in travel

9

Sustainable Hospitality

By Jeanne Varney and Jennifer Moon

Jeanne Varney, *LEED Green Associate, GGP, CHA, is a Lecture Faculty member in the Property Planning, Design and Management Department at the Cornell University School of Hotel Administration. She is responsible for the curriculum in Hospitality Facilities Management and sustainable hospitality electives. In Hospitality Facilities Management, she combines the technical facilities curriculum with a practical management perspective. In sustainability electives, she leads students through the principles, methodology, and tactical application of green hotel development and operational practices.*

Outside of Cornell, Jeanne is a Principal with Olive Hospitality Consulting where she provides practical sustainability solutions to businesses looking to improve the triple bottom line. She has more than twenty years of real estate, operational, and sustainable hospitality experience. Before establishing Olive Hospitality Consulting, Jeanne was Vice President of Asset Management at Host Hotels and Resorts, administering the full range of hotel real estate ownership responsibilities. Jeanne has held positions with Marriott International Corporate Headquarters, Horwath Landauer Hospitality Consulting, The Ritz-Carlton Hotel Company, and Four Seasons Hotels and Resorts.

In addition to her professional duties, Jeanne is an International Past President for NEWH, Inc. and is a founding member of the NEWH Sustainability Committee. She is also a member of the U.S. Green Building Council and the Cornell Hotel Society. Jeanne holds a Master of Business Administration from The George Washington University and a Bachelor of Science in Hotel Administration from Cornell University.

Jennifer Moon *is a consultant with Greenview, a sustainability consultancy specializing in the hospitality, meetings and events, and travel and tourism industries at the organizational level. Greenview was founded in 2008 to play a pivotal role in advancing sustainability through increasing the prevalence of metrics, measurement, and reporting. Jennifer has experience working in corporate ESG advisory and reporting, sustainable event services, destination reporting, and industry research. She has earned a Bachelor of Science degree from the Cornell University School of Hotel Administration and a Master of Science degree from Columbia University in Sustainability Management.*

THERE WAS A TIME when some hospitality industry executives debated whether sustainability, as it applied to their operations and assets, was a trendy topic that was likely to pass. It has now become clear that the issues surrounding sustainability in the hospitality industry will continue to grow in importance to all stakeholders.

It may be a daunting task to understand all of the pros and cons of various "green" choices. Even when a property is trying to make the best choices on sustainable practices, there may still be negative repercussions. For example, is it really sustainable if a hotel chooses to have organic food ingredients on their restaurant menu and advertises it as a green initiative? Maybe yes, maybe no. If the hotel is located in New York City and it has to fly its organic tomatoes in from Mexico, is that considered environmentally responsible? As Exhibit 1 demonstrates, just a simple decision related to placing an organic tomato on the menu has many considerations.

This chapter will focus on higher level issues illustrated with various examples. There will be repeated references to the benefits and negative results of decisions related to sustainability in hospitality operations and asset management. The chapter begins with a brief history of the sustainability movement, then moves through various aspects of hotel engineering and operations, certifications, renovations and regulatory influences, available resources, and sustainability reporting that features important aspects of environmental social governance and its value in asset management.

Before proceeding, we should look briefly at a few terms and definitions that will help set the stage.

- *Sustainability:* A method of harvesting or using resources so that the resource is not depleted or permanently damaged.[1]
- *Triple Bottom Line (TBL):* This is an "accounting" framework that measures the impacts of the three P's: people, planet, and profit. It is often referred to as the "bar stool" analogy because there needs to be a proper balance of all three legs

Exhibit 1 Organic Tomatoes from Mexico

Organic Tomatoes from Mexico to be Used in New York	
PROS	**CONS**
Organic means no synthetic chemicals, fertilizers, or pesticides/herbicides are used in the growing process. This avoids harmful contamination of the ground soil and water table.	Assuming our organic tomato has to travel an estimated 2,500 miles from Mexico to New York, the estimated carbon footprint from its travel is approximately 2.2 tons of carbon dioxide.
No synthetic chemicals is also good for the consumer because they will be eating a "clean" tomato. It is considered a healthier option for the individual.	Costs. The crop yields for organic produce are often lower and growth time longer, thus the unit costs are higher.
Some argue that organic farming methods that involve crop rotation, more nutrient-rich soil, and slightly longer growth times lead to more nutrient-rich food.	

for the stool to function—that is, for the business to function properly. If one or two P's are sacrificed, the business cannot in the long run be sustainable (economically, environmentally, or ethically).

- *Corporate Social Responsibility (CSR)*: A management method by which a company integrates interactions with stakeholders related to the concerns of economic, environmental and ethical functions within the business operation.
- *Environmentally Responsible:* This attribute refers to goods, services, or policies that cause little or no harm to the environment.
- *Sustainable Stakeholders:* Customers, guests, associates, owners, managers, brands, investors, vendors.

Brief History of the Sustainability Movement in Hospitality

The global movement of sustainability in hospitality operations and activities has evolved over the last fifty-plus years. Due to resource and landfill constraints, conservation activities were implemented in Europe and parts of Asia well before many Western Hemisphere businesses adopted them. Most historians specifically cite environmental disasters in the 1960s and the energy crisis of the 1970s as the main catalysts for formalizing sustainability activities in hotels.

The United Nations–funded Brundtland Commission released the report *Our Common Future* (commonly known as the Brundtland Report) in 1987, which became the basis of many other sustainability organizational standards, principles, and guidelines. This report established the definition of sustainable development as:

> "... development that meets the needs of the present without compromising the ability of future generations to meet their own needs."[2]

The Brundtland Report strongly influenced the formation of Agenda 21, which was created after the Earth Summit of Rio de Janeiro in 1992. In 1995 the World Travel & Tourism Council (WTTC), the United Nations World Tourism Organization (UNWTO), and the Earth Council collaborated to launch *Agenda 21 for the Travel & Tourism Industry: Towards Environmentally Sustainable Development* (Agenda 21 TTI). Agenda 21, in which "21" indicates the twenty-first century, outlines ten priorities/action areas for governments and organizations to follow to implement sustainable development for the travel and tourism industry (see Exhibit 2). These ten areas and the supporting implementation information were the building blocks of many hospitality industry corporate sustainability strategies. In fact, Accor named its sustainable development program—Planet 21—with this in mind.

As public awareness of environmental and social issues related to hospitality organizations grew, so did governmental regulations. The good news is that resources, technologies and products also grew in availability. Today, we see demand and in some cases requirements for green-building design, technologies, products, employee engagement, and CSR reporting.

Exhibit 2 Agenda 21

Priority Area 1	Waste Minimization
Priority Area 2	Energy Conservation and Management
Priority Area 3	Management of Fresh Water Resources
Priority Area 4	Wastewater Management
Priority Area 5	Hazardous Substances
Priority Area 6	Transportation
Priority Area 7	Land-Use Planning and Management
Priority Area 8	Involving Customers, Employees, and Community in Environmental Issues
Priority Area 9	Design for Sustainability
Priority Area 10	Partnerships for Sustainable Development

Source: *Agenda 21 for the Travel & Tourism Industry: Towards Environmentally Sustainable Development* (London: WTTC, WTO, The Earth Council, 1995).

Once Agenda 21 TTI was released, hospitality companies began to strategically identify a variety of priorities. Many early practices had economic advantages such as energy savings, which made the adoptions both economically and environmentally beneficial. As internal expertise grew and the C-suite prioritized activities, many companies developed full sustainability programs by the turn of the century. Some companies continued to sit on the sidelines, but as stakeholder education grew, so did the pressure on these companies to provide some sort of organized sustainability programming. It is now the exception to find a company with no CSR program in place. Regardless of when a company began its initiatives, it must continuously evolve to remain competitive. It is the responsibility of asset management and ownership groups to pressure management companies to continue this evolution to drive progress in the industry. Likewise, asset management and ownership groups must assume their fair share of the logistical and financial responsibility to support these efforts.

Getting Started

As with any hotel initiative, asset hold strategy will play a large role in the degree to which ownership invests in sustainable programming. The shorter the hold period, the more constrained the activity. However, even if a property is for sale, there are activities that may take place that will contribute to a sustainable hotel (and likely cost savings). This section will discuss a variety of strategies that may be used at varying times during the hold-cycle of the asset.

In order to optimize the success of sustainability initiatives, several key strategies need to be in place. The first important element is to have support from the top—both the asset manager and the general manager (GM) need to strongly support the program and to convey that message to all stakeholders. Once everyone understands the importance of the initiatives, organized planning should take place.

A best practice that is used in many hotels is the establishment of *green teams*. Green teams should comprise volunteer associates from all departments, with a variety of hourly and management positions, and should include the GM and director of engineering (DOE). It is important to include the DOE because this employee is responsible for energy and waste, which are two of the largest target areas. It is also important to include the GM because it demonstrates that leadership in the hotel supports the initiatives, starting with the most senior manager at the property.

Next, to increase the likelihood of successful implementation, the team should meet to develop a strategic "green" plan that outlines activities, goals, communications, and education for the property. This should be done annually, with adjustments as appropriate throughout the year. When a diverse mix of hotel employees develop the plan, several benefits occur. First, the associates are the author of the plan, and therefore there is a higher degree of ownership driving the success of the plan. In addition, most very good ideas come from associates. Representatives from all departments will be able to bring together ideas from all over the property, consolidate the good ideas, and disseminate them back to the different areas.

An excellent first resource to assist green teams to get started is the Going Green guide from International Tourism Partnership. A link to the guide is in Chapter Appendix 2. The guide is published in eight languages and outlines how hotels should approach managing sustainability programming in their properties.

Engineering

There is usually little question that the area of engineering has the greatest potential for environmental and economic impact, positive or negative. Asset managers should focus on this department as a priority. Many ownership groups look to the area of energy savings first for their sustainability initiatives, and rightfully so. According to the 2014 PKF *Trends*, utility expenses account for 3.2–4.6 percent of sales. Keep in mind that saving energy is work that is never really done. Energy consumption is a constant process in hotel buildings. Operational practices play a significant role in energy efficiency, and there are constantly new technologies coming to market related to new equipment and energy-smart software.

Engineering Operational Practices. Just as every physical building is different, so is the formula for effective energy management practices. It is crucial that the asset manager partner closely with the DOE to establish the best program possible for their asset. The first step is to ensure accurate baseline measurements of all utilities (water, electric, gas, steam, other) and waste. This will be the starting point for setting goals and strategizing methods of improvements.

Once energy consumption and waste generation volumes are understood, the property should ensure that all green operational strategies are being employed. This involves education and training of various departmental associates. A consolidated list of operational practices is included in Chapter Appendix 1.

An assessment of the age and efficiency of building system equipment should also be documented. A sample checklist is referenced in Exhibit 3. This data may

Exhibit 3 Building System Equipment Inventory

Equipment	Manufacturer	Age	Location	Efficiency High/Med/Low	Notes and Ideas for Improvement
Chiller					
Boiler					
AHUs/FCUs					
Cooling Tower					
Thermostats					
PTACs					
Windows					
Elevators					
Other					

be readily available in the property's building management system. Once there is an understanding of what is in place, ideas may be generated for improvements. Improvements for equipment efficiency may be anything from recalibration, to recommissioning, to recapturing energy, to full replacement.

From here, the engineering team should engage in internal and if possible external benchmarking to determine how well they are performing in designated key performance indicators (KPIs). Typically, sustainability KPIs involve all energy consumption sources, waste, recycling weights (including composting), and carbon footprint measures if possible. Typically, these are all considered variable costs, so a common denominator is per occupied room (POR). The purpose of benchmarking is to identify best practices, determine reasonableness, and set goals. Regularly repeat the process.

Building Systems. To calculate basic savings in energy, water, and waste, the Environmental Protection Agency (EPA) has many excellent tools available at www.epa.gov that are referenced in this chapter.

A good building management system. It is estimated that on average 30 percent of a commercial building's energy use is wasted.[3] More than half of the energy used is for HVAC and lighting. Hotels have proven to be more energy intensive because of their 24/7 operating model. Therefore, the more efficiently these energy functions are managed, the more energy and costs the hotel will save. Computerized building management systems (BMS) are available that allow hotels to program the functioning of HVAC (timing, temperature, humidity, variable frequency drives, economizer cooling, etc.) and lighting (timing and light levels) in various spaces in hotels (public spaces, guestrooms and/or back of house). These programmable systems are reliable and may be remotely and easily managed. Many of the major brands have a customized BMS that hotels may or must use. But regardless of the manufacturer of the system, a well-integrated, relatively modern BMS will produce a strong ROI as long as it is actively managed and occasionally serviced.

Water. Water aerators are the most popular and easiest tool to use to conserve water. They are inexpensive and take only minutes to install. Many products today come with low-flow aerators already installed. It is up to the designer or engineer to specify the gallons-per-minute (gpm) for the fixture. Exhibit 4 compares traditional fixtures with low-flow fixtures. The EPA has established a program called WaterSense with customized recommendations for hotels. The link for the site is at: http://www.epa.gov/WaterSense/commercial/challenge_pledge.html. This site contains a *very detailed* water use tool that properties may use to calculate consumption and savings. Supporting guides, recommendations, and webinars also are available.

On a sustainability and financial note, do not forget to sub-meter water use, particularly areas that do not feed back into the sewer system. Remember that most commercial water bills charge for the water use and the wastewater sent back out. If the hotel can prove that it is not sending wastewater back out, the municipal water company will deduct this from the wastewater portion of the bill. These areas are typically pools/hot tubs, irrigation, and secondary water systems.

Chapter Appendix 1 contains a listing of engineering equipment that is often used to conserve energy, water, and waste.

Operations

Ownership groups can invest in the latest and greatest sustainable technologies, but if they are not managed well, the investment is wasted. Just as a skilled DOE must execute on the energy side, other departmental leaders must take ownership of green initiatives.

Rooms Division. Green activities often benefit both the guest and the hotel's associates. The rooms division plays a large role in executing sustainability initiatives that enhance the experience of both.

Exhibit 4 Low-Flow Filters

Fixture	Traditional	Low-Flow	Water Savings	Average Usage
Lavatory (guestroom)	2.2 gpm	1.5 gpm	0.7 gpm	8.1 minutes/day POR
Shower Head	2.5 gpm	2 gpm	0.5 gpm	8.2 minutes/day POR
Toilet (gal/flush) (guestroom)	3.5 gpf	1.3 gpf	2.2 gpf	5.05 flushes/day POR
Urinal	1 gpm	0.5 gpm	0.5 gpf	1 flush/day/male visitor and 0.5 flush/day/male employee
Kitchen Steamer	40 gal/hour (boiler based)	3 gal/hour (connectionless)	37 gal/hour	Varies

Source: epa.gov.

When evaluating the value and feasibility of initiatives, the simple pro-vs.-con approach often works well. For example, an evaluation of using green cleaning chemicals might look like this:

- Pros: pose a much lower risk to associate and guest through lower toxicity, volatile organic compounds (VOCs), accidental physical injury, fewer respiratory and skin allergens, higher housekeeping associate satisfaction
- Cons: time and training costs required for proper effective use
- Costs: may be higher for chemicals (note, costs have become more in line with traditional chemicals), training time

Similarly, a linen reuse program might be evaluated as follows:

- Pros: keeps laundry chemicals from entering the sewer system, saves hot water (energy), guest feels empowered by environmentally responsible decision, extends life of linens, saves labor, laundry cleaning chemicals
- Cons: perceived by many as "greenwashing" (meaning the party is making the claim of being green when the act is either not green or the intent is not for environmental benefit) because of greater financial benefit than environmental benefit, execution is inconsistent, which creates guest dissatisfaction, and training costs
- Costs: saves costs in chemicals, energy for hot water, labor time for changing linens, purchase fewer linens over lifetime of asset due to extended life

Guestroom amenity waste. There are several solutions to the massive amount of product and plastic waste that is generated from the small bottles of amenities that are tossed into landfills each year. Bulk amenity dispensers are the easiest solution to the issue. Many manufacturers have tamper-proof and attractive presentations that offer different configurations (attach to the wall, set on bath shelves). However, some guests do not feel comfortable using these products. A way to deal with this issue is to place a note next to the hand soap amenity dispenser that tells guests that if they would like to have the small bottles brought to the room, housekeeping would be happy to deliver a set.

Another option is to use a program such as Clean the World, which offers comprehensive reuse and recycling of the soaps and packaging. Every hour, people around the globe die because of diseases that could be alleviated if they had soap for sanitation. In the Clean the World program, hotels collect the partially used amenities and soaps, then package and send them to a processing center. The staff at Clean the World sanitizes the soaps, repackages them, and sends them to areas around the world in need of sanitation products. They then recycle the packaging to the greatest extent possible. Hersha Hospitality states that it will provide Clean the World with more than one million bars of used soap annually—enough to provide soap for more than 9,000 children for an entire year. That is a very positive environmental, social, and economic impact.

More ideas are included in Chapter Appendix 1.

Food and Beverage Division. Just like there are endless facets to the F&B area, there are endless opportunities to integrate sustainability into this division. Many find it easier to break this area down by food (with the responsibility with the executive chef), beverage (with the responsibility with the beverage manager), and materials and practices (with responsibility with the F&B director). Looking at pros and cons is again a valuable way to prioritize and decide which initiatives to proceed with and when. An evaluation of using local foods might look like this:

- Pros: freshness, supporting local economy, lower carbon emissions due to transport, makes good material for menu stories
- Cons: reliability of supply (use more than one vendor for higher volume items), limited by what is available regionally, need to take the time to educate staff on food product origin, may take time to research
- Costs: could go either way

Buying in bulk might be evaluated as follows:

- Pros: saves packaging materials, lower shipping weight (thus lower carbon footprint), less pilferage
- Cons: sanitation concerns over open food containers, labor for preparation (individual ramekins, refilling condiment dishes, etc.)
- Costs: increased costs for labor for preparation, significant cost savings for materials

Minimizing food waste. Food waste is a significant issue globally. According to a report by the United Nations Environment Programme and the World Resources Institute, about one-third of all food produced worldwide, worth around US$1 trillion, gets lost or wasted in food production and consumption systems.[4] Exhibit 5, the Food Recovery Hierarchy, describes the many strategies that may be employed to reduce food waste. Once source reduction is employed, the remaining strategies deal with excess food.

Currently, only about 3 percent of food waste is recycled.[5] Composting is a practice that many hotels avoid because it requires an investment of time to organize the physical logistics of the system and consistent employee training is necessary to successfully execute the program. However, mandatory programs are gaining steam and are already in effect in some jurisdictions. (Note that many sustainability initiatives that are currently good business practices will be mandatory in the future.)

There is actually a significant financial and environmental payoff for a property's composting efforts. Some composting systems bring special machinery to the hotel site where the stewarding team places the organic matter in the machine for decomposition. Other systems are as simple as just sorting your waste. Organic waste goes into one bin, recycling into another bin, and landfill into a third bin. In almost all cases, the haul rate for landfill trash is the highest per ton/bin. Thus, anything that a property team can divert from this container will save money and help the environment by either reconstituting or recycling the matter.

Benefits of green meetings. Because some of the food and products associated with green meetings cost more, green meetings began to earn a reputation for costing more. This does not need to be the case. Like many sustainability initia-

Exhibit 5 Food Recovery Hierarchy

Source: http://www.epa.gov/epawaste/conserve/foodwaste/images/fd_recovery_hierarchy_lg.jpg.

tives, green meetings come in a variety of formats. Some are modest in effort and some are robust. Likewise, some cost hotels more money and some save hotels money.

There are some capital expenditure investments that have favorable ROIs that asset managers should consider to aid green meetings. Linenless meeting tables are one of those investments and they come in many forms. The analysis in Exhibit 6 was provided by Remington Hotels. Their sustainable banquets set-up involves a refresh station at the entrance of rooms with water dispensers (no bottled water), stationery and pens (instead of paper and pens at each station), and a candy dish. The meeting tables are Southern Aluminum tables that do not require linens. This set-up shows how a hotel can purchase an environmentally friendly product, use an efficient meeting supply station set-up, save labor and supplies, and improve customer satisfaction.

For more tactical ideas, see the operational practice ideas in Chapter Appendix 1.

Exhibit 6 Remington Hotels Sustainable Banquets and Southern Aluminum Tables

OPERATIONS—Execution Benefits	SALES—From Sales Manager's Perspective
Houseman $ labor savings—decreased time to set rooms as rooms are kept set, decreased time to water rooms in morning—can be executed by anyone as refresh station is used vs. traditional method of putting water/glasses/set up at each place setting	Ability to sell sustainable nature of tables to companies that ask about sustainable practices in RFP process—both the linen-less table program with Remington and the sustainable practices of Southern Aluminum are notable
Savings of Water $—not washing table cloths and decreased washing of skirts (spandex washed less frequently)	"Room is always ready" program allows potential customers to see what the room will look like
Savings $ on decreased use of pads, pens, candy—while still offered, with the use of refresh station at the back of the room, the usage of these items is drastically decreased	Meeting set ups look clean/contemporary
Further savings of labor $ Houseman—easier to refresh rooms during breaks, can be done by fewer people or even by coffee break/waiter staff	Different than other hotels—"you said the goal of your meeting was to be cutting edge, different"—that's why your meeting needs to be with us
"Pop up" meetings handled more easily—since rooms are always ready, makes it simple to add a meeting at any time	Shorter turn times between events—maximizes use of space and ability to book events closer in time
Decreased frustration and time for staff to find linen not stained or with holes, skirts not wrinkled—spandex stays on the tables even when stored	Meetings—linenless tables—perfect for use of laptops—no water risk of spill—and solid writing surface appeals for note taking
Increased ease in satisfying last minute client needs—changes, or additions of registration table, materials table—easy to pop up a table and be ready for guest use	The metal colors of the tables create a "blank slate" for style creation for social clients—the room can take on any color or style from classic to contemporary
"Turns" easier and faster	

Source: Amy McDaniel, SVP Operations, Remington Hotels.

Certifications

There is great debate among the professionals who work in the field of sustainability as to the validity and reliability of green certifications. This chapter will not attempt to sway the reader one way or the other. However, it is important that the asset manager have a basic understanding of the potential benefits and downsides of such programs.

There are two main green building certification systems: Leadership in Energy and Environmental Design (LEED) and Green Globes. Both have similar credit categories that basically focus on the building site, energy, water, waste, materials, and indoor environment. Both use a point system.

LEED

LEED is the most widely recognized green building certification program in the world. This program was developed by the United States Green Building Council (USGBC), a non-profit organization founded in 1993. The first version of LEED was released in 1998; the most recent version 4 (v4) was released in 2014. Up until v4, there was not any specific guidance for hotels. However, after many years of collaboration with multiple stakeholders from the hospitality industry, USGBC has finally developed three different rating systems specifically for hotels: LEED Hospitality—New Construction; LEED Hospitality—Existing Buildings; and LEED Hospitality—Commercial Buildings.

Both Marriott International and Starwood Hotels and Resorts have partnered with USGBC to develop the LEED Volume (New Construction) program where hotel building prototypes are designed and LEED credits are "pre-approved." This assists developers in fast-tracking the certification process and increases the assurance that the building will successfully obtain LEED certification. InterContinental Hotels & Resorts has the LEED Volume program for hotels to certify with the LEED Existing Building Operations and Maintenance (EBOM) program.

LEED holds the largest market share for green building certifications in the hotel industry. The basic summary of the point system is outlined in Exhibit 7. Exhibit 8 presents some of the pros and cons to the LEED certification system.

Exhibit 7 LEED Certification Levels and Credit Categories

Certification Levels		Credit Categories and Maximum Points	
Certified	40–49 points	Integrative Process	1 point
		Location and Transportation	16 points
Silver	50–59 points	Sustainable Sites	10 points
		Water Efficiency	11 points
Gold	60–79 points	Energy and Atmosphere	33 points
		Materials and Resources	13 points
Platinum	80+ points	Indoor Environmental Quality	16 points
		Innovation and Design	6 points
		Regional Priority Credits	4 points
		Total:	110 points

Source: www.usgbc.org, LEED v4 for BD+C: New Construction and Major Renovation.

Exhibit 8 Pros and Cons of the LEED Certification System

PROS	CONS
• Global recognition • Rigorous standards • Global distribution with criteria in multiple languages • Strong pool of professionals trained to consult on LEED projects • Lower levels of certification carry very low cost premiums for projects	• No requirement for ongoing green operations (exception EBOM), which means a building that was built very green may be run very inefficiently • Time-consuming certification process • No standards related to community • Higher levels of certification can carry high cost premiums for projects

Numerous studies of commercial buildings link higher rental and occupancy rates to LEED certification. Unfortunately, there is limited research data available related to hotels. However, a recent study looked at ninety-three LEED-certified hotels and, using STR data, compared their overall performance to competitors (see Exhibit 9). Notably, the LEED-certified hotels achieved comparable occupancies within one year of their competitors. The largest gains made by LEED-certified hotels were in average daily rate (ADR), yielding ADRs in excess of $10 in year one and $20 in year two over the non-LEED-certified competitor hotels.[6]

USGBC also offers professional accreditations and educational opportunities that are beneficial for asset managers. There are two levels of accreditations: LEED Green Associate and LEED Accredited Professional (LEED AP). The LEED Green Associate is an accreditation that every asset manager could obtain with a moderate amount of study and its benefit goes beyond the knowledge gained of the LEED system. Studying for this exam would provide a strong foundation of knowledge in green building principles. A link to the handbook is provided in the Resources table in Chapter Appendix 2.

The LEED AP is a much more difficult designation to achieve. Typically interior designers, architects and engineers will sit for this exam. It requires an in-depth technical knowledge of all of the credits, such as ASHRAE standards, lighting densities, water efficiency measures, and so on. The exam is far more rigorous in difficulty and continuing education unit requirements are double that of the LEED Green Associate (thirty hours every two years versus fifteen hours every two years).

Green Globes

The Green Globes environmental assessment and rating system was first incubated from the United Kingdom's Building Research Establishment's Environmental Assessment Method (BREEAM) and transformed through several other measurement systems until its formal launch in Canada in 2000. In 2004, the Green

Exhibit 9 LEED Certified vs. Non-LEED Certified Hotel Performance

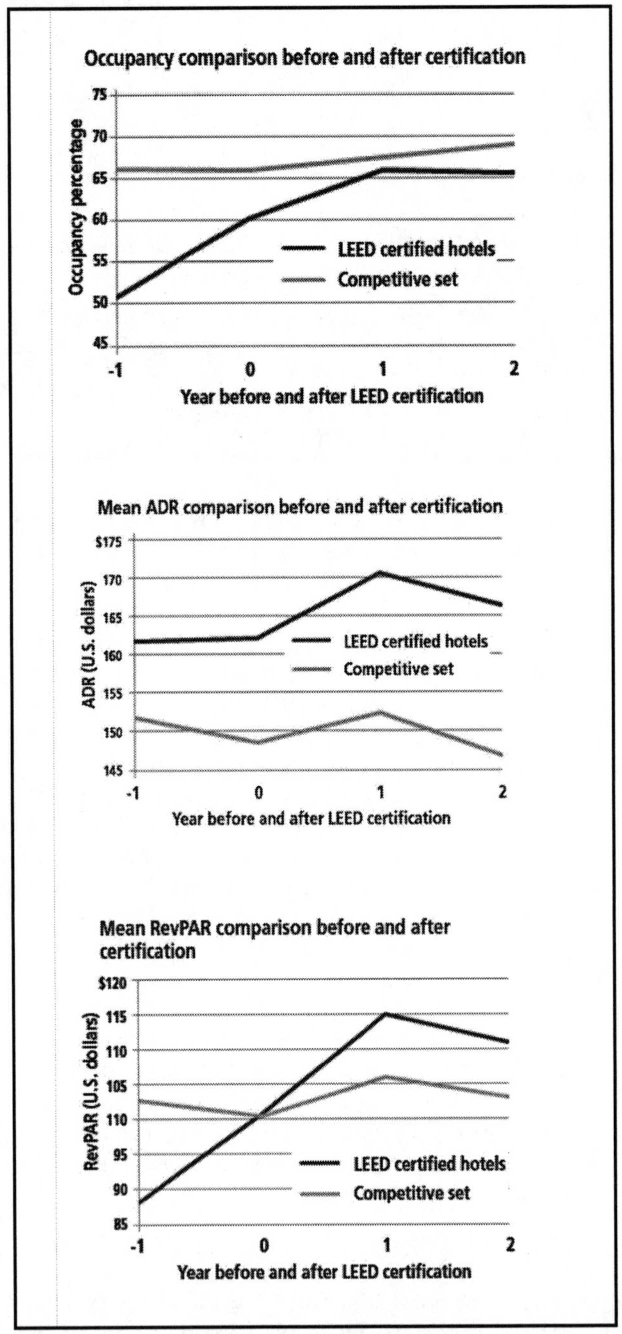

Source: "The Impact of LEED Certification on Hotel Performance," *The Center for Hospitality Research,* 14(15), July 2014.

Building Initiative acquired the rights to distribute Green Globes in the United States.[7]

For hotels, certifications available are Green Globes for New Construction, Green Globes for Continual Improvement of Existing Buildings, and Green Globes for Sustainable Interiors. There is no certification system customized for hospitality at this time. The basic summary of the point system is outlined in Exhibit 10. Exhibit 11 presents some of the pros and cons of the Green Globes certification system.

The GBI also offers personal certification and educational opportunities, including many interesting webinars and articles on the Green Globes system and other green building information. The professional certifications require experience in the sustainability field or technical training before one may sit for any of

Exhibit 10 Green Globes Rating System and Environmental Assessment Areas

Rating System	Environmental Assessment Areas and Maximum Points	
85% - 100%	Project Management	50 points
	Site	115 points
70% - 84%	Energy	390 points
	Water	110 points
55% - 69%	Materials & Resources	125 points
	Emissions	50 points
35% - 54%	Indoor Environmental	160 points
	Total:	1,000 points

Source: The Green Building Initiative: Green Globes New Construction Module.

Exhibit 11 Pros and Cons of the Green Globes Certification System

PROS	CONS
• Very strong North American and UK presence	• Must pay for on-site third-party assessor
• Rigorous standards	• No standards related to community
• Shorter certification processing time	• Not as well known as LEED
• Trustworthy: third-party assessor verifies all conditions	

the exams. There are two levels of personal certifications, Green Globes Professional and Green Globes Assessor. For more information, a link to the website is provided in the resources table in Chapter Appendix 2.

Other Notable Certifications

For hotels in the Boston, New York, Chicago, Washington, D.C., San Diego, and Los Angeles areas, the Certified Green Restaurant certification is growing in popularity with hotel restaurants, particularly those that focus on wellness and healthy food choices. There are more than 400 certified restaurants that can be easily found on their website.

Green Key Global Certification and the TripAdvisor GreenLeaders Award are also notable programs that the American Hotel & Lodging Association's Green Task Force recommends. Green Key Global is a graduated rating system that rates performance in the areas of energy conservation, water conservation, solid waste management, hazardous waste management, indoor air quality, community outreach, building infrastructure, land use, and environmental management. Hotels may earn from one to five keys. The system is designed for properties to continuously improve their performance and eventually earn more keys. There are more than 2,000 certified U.S. properties.

The TripAdvisor GreenLeaders Award is a voluntary program that TripAdvisor members may participate in by filling out a questionnaire about their environmental practices and impacts. Guest comments and audits verify practices. Hotels may achieve one of four statuses: Bronze, Silver, Gold, and Platinum. There are more than 2,100 TripAdvisor GreenLeaders Award properties.

Renovations

Design and construction experts agree that the most successful approach to incorporating sustainability into a renovation project is through the "integrated design" approach. This is a holistic approach with the project team collaborating from the beginning of the project on the goals, including sustainability. It includes what practices and products will be used and, if there is a certification, what level of certification the project will target. Like any aspect of a renovation project, it can be difficult to incorporate changes in the later stages, so detailed upfront planning is important.

Green design, products, and technologies are a specialized field. Not all service providers have enough knowledge to work on sustainable projects. Hiring qualified professional services team members with training and experience in green renovation and construction projects will increase the level of sustainability that the project can achieve.

Renovations present an excellent opportunity to incorporate sustainable materials into a hotel. Manufacturers of almost any type of furniture, fixture and equipment (FF&E) have sustainable options. Many options are cost neutral with comparable or even superior quality. Asset managers need to direct the CapEx project teams to request sustainable products. Otherwise, many designers and purchasing agents will proceed using traditional, possibly even wasteful materials. What exactly is a sustainable product? In general, sustainable product attributes are as follows:

- Biodegradable
- Energy efficient
- Recyclable
- Recycled content
- Water efficient
- Avoid virgin materials whenever possible
- Minimize/eliminate toxins (VOCs)
- Consider life-cycle costs
- Minimize packaging
- Use "Smart Way" shipping
- Upcycle
- Understand chain of custody
- Local purchase
- Natural product/organic
- Rapidly renewable (under ten years)
- Fair labor practices/no child labor
- Safe working conditions
- Highly durable

Earlier, several different certification systems were discussed that could be coordinated with renovation projects, particularly if a property was certifying an existing building where materials play a larger role. However, even if the hotel is not seeking a certification, it may still tell an excellent story and receive significant press like the Courtyard by Marriott Denver Downtown. Sera Architects, a well-known firm out of Portland, Oregon, that specializes in sustainable design, provided the case in the sidebar.

Hotel Carbon Measurement Initiative

Launched in 2012, the Hotel Carbon Measurement Initiative (HCMI) is a methodology that was created by a large and diverse working group of hospitality industry companies, consultants, and NGOs. International Tourism Partnership, the World Travel & Tourism Council, and KPMG in the U.K. were the primary authors. The methodology was developed to calculate the carbon footprint of hotel stays and meetings. It is not intended to be a comprehensive greenhouse gas measurement tool for buildings. The design and the metrics in the model attempt to balance the need for ease of implementation with the need for accuracy.

HCMI provides a template that is designed for global use with a standard set of measurements for all hotels to use. This tool allows hotels and hotel clients around the world to take a uniform approach to carbon footprint calculations. The methodology provides users with the ability to measure a carbon footprint on

Courtyard by Marriott Denver Downtown Case Study

Unlike the majority of hotel rooms on the market, the rooms at the Courtyard by Marriott Denver Downtown have sustainable measures that go beyond the basics. Many hotels have adopted environmentally sensitive operational features (reducing multi-stay laundry and linen needs, using fluorescent lighting, to name a few) that an increasingly savvy public has come to expect. However, the renovations at the Courtyard Denver Downtown have pushed further into the design and purchasing world, beginning to change how and why hospitality case goods are specified.

This more environmentally aware approach to the Property Improvement Plan (PIP) begins as soon as the guest gets off the elevator. The corridor carpeting is Green Label Plus, the walls have been repainted with low VOC paint, and existing light fixtures were reused in the new design.

As the guests arrive at their room for the night, they are unaware of the variety of sustainable measures that lie beneath the fresh design. The finishes on the wall—low VOC paint for the majority of wall and ceiling surfaces and a 100 percent spun polyester PVC-free wall covering at accent walls—are healthier than the standard vinyl that coats most hotel rooms.

Material toxicity and the chemical makeup of the built environment is an area that is just beginning to be fully explored in order to make healthier environments. Choices that result in cleaner, healthier surroundings, and avoiding chemicals of concern like PVC that emit a variety of harmful chemicals are becoming increasingly important in providing sustainable solutions. A majority of the guestroom furniture was manufactured to low E0 finish levels of urea-formaldehyde (< 0.05 parts per million) and used FSC-certified wood stock and veneers. The faux leathers used on the headboard, task chair, and ottoman are all PVC-free polyurethane. Even the shower curtain, with its snap-on 100 percent nylon (and non-vinyl) liner, keeps guest health in mind.

Recycled content is another feature of many of the guestroom's furniture and fabrics. The custom duvet cover has 100 percent post-consumer recycled content polyester. The bed skirt and red accent pillows on the bed are also made of 100 percent recycled content fabric, while the majority of fibers used in the striped accent pillow are natural wool and cotton. Guests staying in one of the presidential suites with a skyline view patio sit on bold, brightly colored furniture that is made completely out of recycled soda bottles.

Energy use is always a factor in the sustainable story of any hotel. All lighting in the room is fluorescent and the in-room refrigerator provided to the guest is plugged in only when needed.

Even the art in the rooms has a sustainable story through its ties with the community. All of the various art pieces were done by local artists, each artist offering a unique portrayal of Denver and Colorado. One piece in each room was also produced by students at the local art school, grounding the guest in a truly community-oriented experience and tying in with a meeting room level rotating art gallery space.

In the hospitality sector, price point is everything. In this project, 70 percent of the products specified had a green component with only a 4 percent overall cost premium when compared to more standard goods. The breakdown of what product types had a premium is enlightening (see below) in that it highlights where sustainable thinking has been long entrenched and where there are greater opportunities for change.

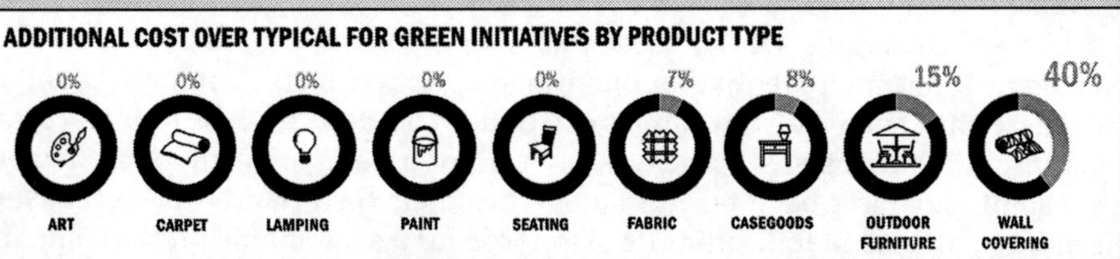

Steps in the greening of hospitality FF&E can involve a variety of initiatives. These include lowering urea-formaldehyde to below California's CARB standards, working with wall covering manufacturers to lower the cost differential on PVC-free wall covering, specifying hospitality carpet with recycled content, working with vendors in the project's bio-region, end-of-life operational manuals for a hotel's FF&E, and designing case goods to last longer than one PIP cycle.

With the PIP process and the constant change-out of hospitality goods and materials generating so much waste and embodying a tremendous amount of energy (much of it still being manufactured outside of this country), clearly changes need to be made. We can't responsibly burn through resources as we have in the past—decision-making processes need to change. Designers (and managers and owners) need to factor their environmental impact into the design process and way of doing business, ultimately improving environmental performance with each project.

Note: This hotel is also a TripAdvisor GreenLeaders Silver Award Winner.

Source: Sera Architects, Portland, Oregon (www.serapdx.com).

a POR-per-day basis and per-area-of-meeting-space on an hourly basis. Back-of-house spaces (in the template referred to as "private spaces") are not incorporated into these measurements. The tool includes recommendations for carbon emission measurements of Scope 1 and 2; Scope 3 emissions are excluded. The tool calls for a twelve-month data set for a reporting period.

Globally, more than 21,000 hotels are using this tool for themselves and their clients.[8] The tool is free and available to any hotel in the world. A link to detailed information on the methodology of the tool and the template is provided in the Chapter Appendix 2 Resources, under the General category.

Regulatory and Other Influences

Governmental regulations related to the environment are increasing. Energy consumption reporting requirements are in place in several major cities and this trend is increasing. Carbon emission reporting is largely voluntary, but this trend is tightening with more states beginning to require this. This type of reporting may not have any significant implications yet, but it is worthy of note that this information is public. There is also speculation that this first step will lead to the requirement that building owners will next need to report *and* then reduce consumption. Carbon cap and trade discussions were prominent in the United States in the mid-2000s, but there does not appear to be anything of this nature on the immediate legislative horizon.

For asset managers working for public companies, the issue surrounding reporting now has the potential for quantifiable influence on a company's trading price. There have been many examples of a public company's environmental disaster significantly hurting share prices, some temporary and some more permanent. Sustainability analysts have taken matters into their own hands and established their own set of criteria for minimum standards for a sustainable public company. These agencies rate companies and publish the results. Others have set up stock indexes for individual and institutional investors. For example, the Dow Jones Sustainability Indices have been in existence for over fifteen years and many of the major hospitality brands, ownership groups, and REITs are traded in these funds.

There are varying methodologies for rating a company. Some speak to corporate representatives. Some use questionnaires. Some use only a company's annual report to determine the range of CSR activities. This more narrow approach was purposefully taken by rating companies to drive more transparency on the part of public companies. Because of this, more companies began to author CSR reports (sometimes referred to as corporate governance or environmental social governance reporting).

Governmental agencies, such as municipal building code departments, permitting departments, and even the General Services Administration (GSA), are using green certification systems such as LEED and Green Globes as models for their standards. In the District of Columbia, the Green Building Act (2006) requires that any non-residential building built after January 1, 2012, that is more than 50,000 square feet must be LEED-certified.[9] The GSA identified both LEED and Green Globes as being "deem(ed) to be most likely to encourage a comprehensive and environmentally sound approach to certification of green buildings." It is stated that either system could be used by federal agencies for green building design and construction certification.[10]

Overview of Environmental, Social Governance (ESG) Corporate Reporting

According to "Hospitality 2015, Game changers or spectators?" (an industry outlook study conducted by Deloitte), "Sustainability will become a defining issue for the industry in 2015 and beyond. Rising populations and increasingly scarce resources will provide a challenging business environment in which sustainability will need to be embedded within all facets of the industry, rather than regarded as a standalone issue." Already there has been a concerted effort within the hospitality industry to address sustainability issues. Many of the largest hotel groups have established their understanding and outlook around key issues and some have even vocalized their commitments to minimize impacts (see Exhibit 12 for summary of key sustainability commitments by hotel companies).

Exhibit 12 Key Hotel Company Sustainability Commitments

	Publicly announced sustainability targets?	Target summary
Hilton	Yes	Five year reduction targets (energy, waste, water, and CO_2 emissions) from direct operations.
IHG	Yes	Three-year energy reduction targets per available room night and plans to launch 'Green Engage' programme in 100% of owned and managed facilities.
Marriott	Yes	Ten-year energy and water consumption reduction targets per available room Established green building targets and implementing green-sourcing programmes.
Starwood	No	No formally announced targets – however, the company has launched the Element brand which incorporates the LEED construction standards.
Wyndham	No (In-Progress)	Defined sustainability strategy and identified core focus areas. In-process of establishing sustainability targets.

Source: Based on information on company websites and Deloitte interviews

Source: Deloitte, "Hospitality 2015, Game changers or spectators?"

What Is ESG Reporting?

The ESG corporate reporting movement represents how businesses are communicating with key external audiences (corporate customers, investors, employees, and stakeholders) on material sustainability issues (see Exhibit 13 for examples of material issues for hotel REITs).[11] As a result, ESG reporting has become a tool for transparency and a continuous exercise in understanding key impacts and future vulnerabilities for companies that choose to participate. This movement of reporting has taken shape over several decades, but has gained the most momentum in the most recent decade and continues to grow quickly due to both external business and regulatory pressures.[12]

ESG Data Helps Determine Intangible Value. ESG reporting holds vital information that helps assess company performance more accurately, especially when it comes to intangible value.[13] Nearly 80 percent of S&P 500 companies' value is represented by intangible assets, a drastic shift from 20 percent in 1975.[14] As a result, investors will need to utilize ESG data to better assess future company performance and value.[15] Unfortunately there is still a large gap in the integration of ESG data and "mainstream investing," where the financial industry has yet to embrace

Exhibit 13 Possible Material ESG Topics for REITs

- Energy and water usage (across portfolio)
- Waste
- GHG emissions
- Reduction initiatives for energy, water, waste
- Labor practices
- Charitable giving
- Volunteer hours

the fundamental shift in how businesses should understand sustainability issues as integral to "investment performance."[16] This gap is largely due to the lack of quality ESG data that is easily quantifiable. But, as more methodical approaches and frameworks continue to define and improve ESG reporting, the data will reflect such efforts. And that is the crux of how ESG reporting will help companies not only address key sustainability issues, but foster the necessary transparency and competition for industry-wide solutions (see Exhibit 14 for how ESG data integration drives market transformation).

ESG and Asset Management

Further narrowing down the ESG context as it pertains to asset management is quite simple—the hospitality industry is an "asset heavy sector with a large environmental footprint."[17] The green building trend has gained significant traction globally, with third-party green building certification systems such as LEED gaining popularity across all asset classes.[18] The hotel industry is no stranger to this growing trend and is keen to incorporate green building best practices in all aspects of the hotel development process. In addition to building greener hotels, the industry is also aware that the asset itself needs to operate more efficiently as resources become scarcer. A more holistic view to take is that the hospitality industry has an environmental footprint that extends alongside the life cycle of an asset, from the initial resources used to develop the physical asset to the resources (energy, water) consumed and waste generated as a result of operating the asset. It is important to note this life cycle viewpoint because there is often a disconnect between building/acquiring new assets and operating/maintaining the performance of existing assets. The latter is a fundamental part of what makes a good

Exhibit 14 Creating a Virtuous Cycle: From Standards to Innovation

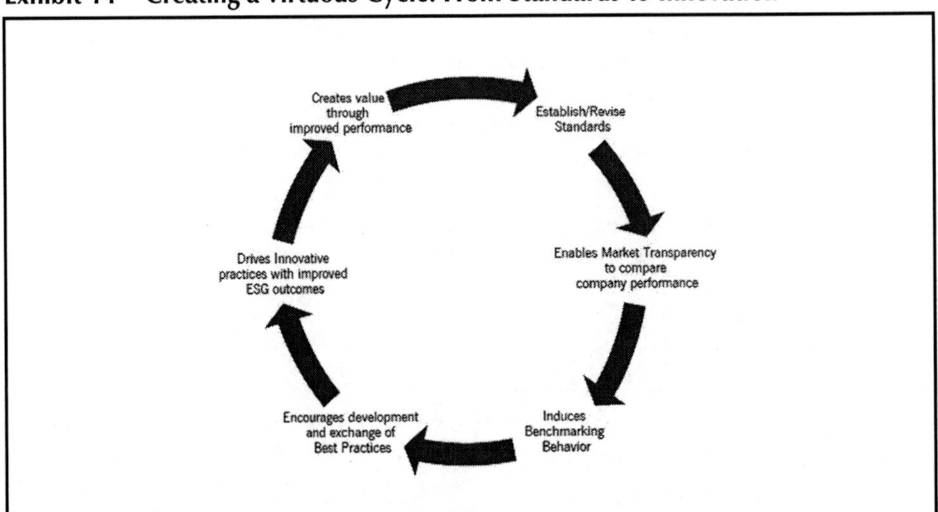

Source: Park and Ravenel, "Integrating Sustainability into Capital Markets: Bloomberg LP and ESG's Quantitative Legitimacy," *Journal of Applied Corporate Finance*, 25(3), 2013, 63–67.

asset manager. Asset managers will be expected to navigate the pressures of sustainability that will affect the real estate industry.

Addressing Sustainability within Asset Management

It is easy for a savvy asset manager to view sustainability from the lens of building operational efficiencies and invest time and money into green initiatives with quicker paybacks and ROIs. This approach has been the industry norm for addressing sustainability for some time, which makes business sense. An industry-wide EPA study indicates average energy costs for each available room equal $2,196 per year in the U.S., representing roughly 6 percent of a hotel's operating cost.[19] Another way to understand energy costs is to look at energy consumption strategically and set sustainability goals that translate into financial benefits. For example, the same EPA study indicated that reducing energy consumption by 10 percent is equivalent to increasing the ADR by $0.62 and $1.35 in limited-service and full-service hotels, respectively.[20] But beyond the obvious financial benefits to addressing key sustainability impacts, asset managers should also understand the broader context in which sustainability is driving change in real estate.

Circling Back to the Value of ESG Reporting

The uptake of sustainability for the hospitality sector will only continue to grow stronger as external pressures mandate and regulate the conversation. The real estate industry is also included in that conversation, with expectations for ESG transparency on the rise for the industry. It would be incredibly shortsighted for asset managers to miss the proverbial boat on understanding the importance of addressing sustainability as a strategic business issue and adapting to changing market demand.[21]

In October 2014, the Green Building Certification Institute (GBCI), acting certification body for LEED, acquired the Global Real Estate Sustainability Benchmark (GRESB), an emerging sustainability performance assessment for the real estate industry at the enterprise and portfolio level.[22] GRESB defines itself as follows:

> GRESB is an industry-driven organization committed to assessing the sustainability performance of real estate portfolios (public, private and direct) around the globe. The dynamic benchmark is used by institutional investors to engage with their investments with the aim to improve the sustainability performance of their investment portfolio, and the global property sector at large.[23]

GRESB has rapidly gained momentum within the real estate industry since 2009. GRESB's 2014 report represents data from 637 listed property companies and private equity real estate funds, collectively worth US$2.1 trillion in assets under management (AUM).[24] As the demand for transparent ESG data increases, GRESB's presence will continue to dominate the global real estate sector further driving competition among real estate companies to disclose and improve performance of ESG issues.

Overview of ESG Reporting Marketplace

It is important to note that GRESB is just one of several ESG reporting frameworks that exist in the marketplace currently. While GRESB is a framework specific to real estate, there are other popular frameworks for ESG reporting to consider. These include Global Reporting Initiative (GRI), CDP (formerly known as Carbon Disclosure Project), Climate Disclosure Standards Board (CDSB), Sustainability Accounting Standards Board (SASB), and International Integrated Reporting Committee (IIRC) to name a few.[25] There is a proliferation of ESG frameworks that have entered the marketplace over the last few decades. Some frameworks address broader ESG issues, while others work to address sector-specific issues. To better understand this dynamic, it is important to understand the layers of the ESG reporting marketplace:[26]

- *Commitment Formers*—Leading commitments include the U.N. Principles of Responsible Investment and the U.N. Global Compact, which drive market demand for ESG reporting.
- *Framework Providers*—GRI, CDP, CDSB, SASB, IIRC, and GRESB represent ESG frameworks, guidelines, and standards that companies use to disclose material ESG information publicly.
- *Rankings, Ratings and Indexes*—The Dow Jones Sustainability Indices, FTSE4Good Indexes, Newsweek Green Rankings, CDP Leadership Index, and others use ESG data from reporting companies to further promote transparency and competition.

Companies can pursue disclosure and recognition in any number of these ESG marketplace products and often do strive for many if not all channels. Think of the ESG marketplace as a company's best bet to gain competitive advantage against its competition. However, there is a caveat: the way to truly distinguish themselves from the competition depends on how well and how much ESG data is disclosed. This is the whole point of ESG reporting, which creates transparency within the industry that in turn leads to competition and catalyzes market innovations for scalable solutions to sustainability.

Will ESG Reporting Be Enough?

For the most part there seems to be a clearly marked path for successful market transformation when it comes to addressing ESG issues, but the key questions remain: Will it happen soon enough? And when it does occur, will it be enough?

Extreme weather-related events continue to occur and are anticipated to not only become more frequent but also stronger in future years.[27] A warming planet is raising sea levels and rising population growth will continue to strain resources.[28] The culmination of these global issues represents what sustainability is supposed to address at all levels of the public and private sector—a concerted global effort in which ESG reporting is at the epicenter. Time is an important factor to consider when setting sustainability goals for reporting. When it comes to sustainability, keep in mind the bigger picture, why this matters, and that while setting goals is important, setting *timely* goals will be the most crucial driver of change. In understanding ESG issues, it will become markedly clear that fundamental shifts in "business as usual" also have to occur. It is imperative to understand sustainability as a "core pursuit of business."[29] The better companies can address and align their strategies for growth and mitigating future risk, the better they can address ESG issues.

Conclusion

The field of sustainability is fast changing and will be for the foreseeable future. It is the asset manager's responsibility to maximize the value of the asset. Using the triple bottom line approach of balancing the interests of people/planet/profit, asset managers should actually enhance profitability and increase guest and associate satisfaction, while minimizing any harm to the environment. It takes thoughtfulness, questioning, planning, innovation, and some willingness to occasionally invest in technologies that make a material difference to the environment.

Asset managers are often referred to as "stewards" of their assets. We are all stewards of the earth and have the ability to be a positive influence on its health and prosperity for the future. Although many of the global environmental issues may seem very large, if the hospitality industry strongly engages to do its collective part, great positive change will take place. Asset managers have an enormous opportunity to be the leaders of this positive change. Engage.

Endnotes

1. www.Merriam-Webster.com
2. Brundtland Commission, *Our Common Future* (Oxford: Oxford University Press, 1987, 43).
3. www.siemens.com/sitecontrols, Quantifying the Benefits of an Energy Management System
4. http://www.wri.org/sites/default/files/reducing_food_loss_and_waste.pdf
5. www.nofoodwaste.com
6. "The Impact of LEED Certification on Hotel Performance," *The Center for Hospitality Research*, vol. 14, no. 15, July 2014.
7. www.thegbi.org
8. http://www.tourismpartnership.org/what-we-do/products-programmes/hotel-carbon-measurement-initiative
9. http://www.usgbc.org/articles/taking-sustainability-seriously-washington-dc
10. http://www.gsa.gov/portal/content/131983
11. WTTC, Travel & Tourism ESG Reporting Trends & Guidance, 2014.
12. Ibid.
13. BSR, Trends in ESG Integration in Investments: Summary of the Latest Research and Recommendations to Attract Long-Term Investors, 2012.

14. International Integrated Reporting Council, Towards Integrated Reporting: Communicating Value in the 21st Century, 2011.

15. Park and Ravenel, "Integrating Sustainability Into Capital Markets: Bloomberg LP And ESG's Quantitative Legitimacy," *Journal of Applied Corporate Finance*, 25(3), 2013, 63–67.

16. Ibid.

17. Deloitte, Hospitality 2015: Game Changers or Spectators? 2014.

18. Marc Heisterkamp, LEED and the Growth of Green Building in Lodging, Hotel Sustainable Development: Principles & Best Practices, 2012

19. ENERGY STAR, Hotels: An Overview of Energy Use and Energy Efficiency Opportunities, http://www.energystar.gov/sites/default/files/buildings/tools/SPP%20Sales%20Flyer%20for%20Hospitality%20and%20Hotels.pdf (Accessed December 2014).

20. Ibid.

21. Deloitte.

22. USGBC, GBCI Joins Forces with GRESB, http://www.usgbc.org/articles/gbci-joins-forces-gresb (Accessed October 2014).

23. GRESB, About GRESB, 2014.

24. GRESB, 2014 GRESB Report, 2014.

25. WTTC, Travel & Tourism ESG Reporting Trends & Guidance, 2014.

26. Ibid.

27. Andrew Winston, *The Big Pivot* (Boston: Harvard Business Review Press, 2014).

28. Ibid.

29. Ibid.

Chapter Appendix 1

Operational Practice Ideas

The following list is by no means intended to be complete, but it provides a fair sampling of the products, practices, and policies that a hotel could choose to employ in any given area.

DEPARTMENT			
ENGINEERING	• Building management System • Digital thermostats • Changing filters • Calibrating machinery • Efficient lamp choice • Xeriscaping • Aerators for all faucets and shower heads • Timers and motion sensors for all public and employee restroom faucets • Waterless urinals	• Total hotel recycling program • Proper handling and disposal of toxins • Environmentally friendly refrigerants • Sub-metering • Heat-plate exchangers • Life-cycle costing for equipment that uses energy • Monitor indoor air quality	• Variable speed drives • Heat-pumps • Economizer cooling (outside cold air mix into HVAC in winter for AC) • Tint/glaze windows • Overall excellent preventive maintenance program
HOUSEKEEPING	• Closing guestroom drapes (minimizes sunlight heat load) • Setting thermostat to baseline temperature • Turning off ALL lights when room not in use or leaving space	• Strong execution of linen reuse program • Amenity recycling program • Green cleaning chemicals • HEPA filter vacuums	• Lighting timers BOH • Motion sensors BOH • Laundry—Ozone System • Sustainable laundry detergent
FOOD AND BEVERAGE	• Linenless tables • Buying in bulk (avoid individual F&B containers with high waste factor) • Composting (on or off-site) • Recycle cooking oil • Minimal use of bottled water (use a system similar to Natura that a hotel can bottle itself)	• Sustainably sourced seafood • Use local ingredients • Use organic ingredients • Beeswax or soy candles (not paraffin) • China, glass & silver (minimize paper & plastic—Never use Styrofoam) • High efficiency steamers	• Minimize cut flowers • Use centerpieces with whole fruits, stones, marbles, grasses, etc. • Thaw frozen items in the refrigerator (not under running water when health code permits)

DEPARTMENT			
RENOVATIONS	• Hire service providers educated and experienced in sustainable renovations • Use integrated design strategies to ensure sustainability products, design and practices are used in project • Use sustainable purchasing protocols • Purchase regionally or within country whenever possible • Request chain of custody information when available	• Use products with recycled content • Upcycle products • Recycle old FF&E • Donate old FF&E • Reuse old FF&E • Require construction contractor to recycle waste • Use natural products when available and make sure that they meet durability standards • Use rapidly renewable materials	• Require low or no VOCs in finishes, paints, sealants, glues, etc. • Use nylon 6 carpet (infinitely recyclable nylon fiber) • Consider carpet squares where appropriate to minimize waste when needing replacements
ADMINISTRATIVE & SALES OFFICES	• Purchase paper with recycled content • E-sales proposals • E-hotel brochures • Set all printers to default 2-sided printing	• Educate staff on all sustainability practices • No bottled water • Offer to print materials for clients on site to avoid carbon footprint of shipping	• Lighting motion sensors • Turn off ALL lights when not in use or leaving space • Offer community engagement activity for client
HUMAN RESOURCES	• Organized community service programming (combination of charity, volunteering and education) • Integrate community service throughout the year	• Fair wages • Ongoing training • Provide framework for sustainability education in hotel • Include sustainability in Town Hall, Newsletter or other communications	• Emphasize local service providers for hotel • Subsidize public transportation for employees • Incentivize carpooling
MISCELLANEOUS	• Support a Green Team • Purchase green power • Use Energy Star equipment • In all areas, use the most efficient bulbs possible and where appropriate use dimmers, timers, or motion sensors	• Smoke-free environment • Minimize use of toxins throughout hotel and substitute with more environmentally friendly chemicals • Purchase all paper products w/recycled content (napkins/plates/etc.)	• Install alternative energy source if feasible (solar, co-generation, geothermal) • Green roof • High solar reflectivity outdoor surfaces • Pursue green certification if feasible/appropriate

Chapter Appendix 2

Selected Resources and References

Presented below is a listing of various resources by area that provide greater detail for accomplishing various sustainability initiatives. The field of sustainability is continuously evolving, so new resources will continue to become available. Subscribing to newsletter sources such as *Green Lodging News* is highly recommended. These sustainability field professionals will do the research for you and provide much of the latest and greatest in innovations in the field of green hospitality.

Another excellent resource is the AH&LA website and webinars. Although it is a U.S.-based association, its work in the area of sustainability may be adopted globally and many resources are available for free on its website. If you are a member of AH&LA, there are extensive resources available in the Green Resource Center.

General

Hotel Carbon Footprint Initiative Tool information: http://www.tourismpartnership.org/what-we-do/products-programmes/hotel-carbon-measurement-initiative

AH&LA Green Resource Center link: http://www.ahla.com/green.aspx

AH&LA Green Guidelines link: http://www.ahla.com/uploadedFiles/AHLA/Members_Only/_Common/Minimum%20Green%20Guidelines.pdf

Hotel Sustainable Development: Principles and Best Practices, A. J. Singh and Hervé Houdré, Eds. (Lansing, Mich: American Hotel & Lodging Educational Institute, 2012).

International Tourism Partnership Going Green guide: http://www.tourismpartnership.org/what-we-do/products-programmes/going-green

DSIRE US National Website Resource for Rebates, Tax Incentives, etc. link: www.dsire.org

International Tourism Partnership: http://www.tourismpartnership.org/

Engineering

EPA energy efficiency calculators link: http://www.energystar.gov/buildings/facility-owners-and-managers/existing-buildings/find-financing/calculate-returns-energy-efficiency

WaterSense at Work: Best Management Practices for Commercial and Institutional Facilities, Environmental Protection Agency http://www.epa.gov/WaterSense/docs/ws-at-work_bmpcommercialandinstitutional_508.pdf

Hospitality Facilities Management and Design, Fourth Ed., David M. Stipanuk (Lansing, Mich: American Hotel & Lodging Educational Institute, 2014).

Engineering staff energy management training from Schneider Electric link: http://www2.schneider-electric.com/sites/corporate/en/products-services/training/energy-university/energy-university.page

Building Owners & Facilities Executives Magazine: http://www.facilitiesnet.com/bom/#

BOMA Sustainability information: http://www.boma.org/sustainability/Pages/default.aspx

F&B

IFMA Foundation Sustainability "How To Guide" Series: *Sustainability in the Foodservice Environment*: www.aramark.com/.../WhitePapers/IFMA-Sustainability.aspx

National Restaurant Association sustainability resources: http://www.restaurant.org/Industry-Impact/Conservation

Green Meetings Industry Council link: http://www.gmicglobal.org/

EPA Green Meetings guidelines & resources link: http://www.epa.gov/oppt/greenmeetings/

Monterey Bay Aquarium Seafood Watch: http://www.seafoodwatch.org/

Marine Stewardship Council: http://www.msc.org/

Commercial Guide to Food Composting: http://www.epa.gov/foodrecovery/fd-tools_rescrs.htm

Natura Water System link: http://www.naturawater.com/index.php

Rooms

Clean the World link: http://www.cleantheworld.org/

Ecogreen Hotel Housekeeping link: https://ecogreenhotel.com/housekeeping.php

Green Hotelier, Ozone Systems for Laundry: http://www.greenhotelier.org/our-themes/energy/green-solutions-for-hotels-ozone-laundry/

"Sustainable Products: The Skinny on Laundry Detergent," Arthur Weissman, Hotel Business Review: http://hotelexecutive.com/business_review/1634/sustainable-products-the-skinny-on-laundry-detergent

Certification, Design

"The Impact of LEED Certification on Hotel Performance" link: https://www.hotelschool.cornell.edu/research/chr/pubs/reports/abstract-18084.html

United States Green Building Council (USGBC): www.usgbc.org

Green Globes Certification: www.thegbi.org

Green Restaurant Association Certification: www.dinegreen.com/

Green Key Global: www.greenkeyglobal.com

TripAdvisor GreenLeader Award: http://www.tripadvisor.com/GreenLeaders

Newsletters, etc.

Green Lodging News weekly online newsletter: www.greenlodgingnews.com

Smartbrief on Sustainability: https://www.smartbrief.com/signupSystem/subscribe.action?pageSequence=1&briefName=sustainability

Today's Facility Manager: http://todaysfacilitymanager.com/

Green Hotelier: http://www.greenhotelier.org/

Professional

LEED Green Associate Handbook Download link:
http://www.usgbc.org/resources/leed-v4-green-associate-candidate-handbook

Green Globes Professional Certifications link:
http://www.thegbi.org/professional-certification/

10

Managing Technology

By Jon Inge

Jon Inge is an independent consultant in hotel technology with over thirty-five years of experience in hotel systems, gained through working with both vendor and hotel companies and, for the last seventeen years, through his own consulting practice. His clients range from eight-room boutiques to international chains; he writes a bi-weekly e-newsletter on hospitality technology, and his articles appear frequently in the trade press. A founding member of the HTNG (Hotel Technology Next Generation) initiative for greater system inter-operability, he has served on Hospitality Financial and Technology Professionals' HITEC Advisory Committee and the American Hotel & Lodging Association's Technology Committee, and is a member of the International Society of Hospitality Consultants. In June 2006, he was inducted into the HFTP International Hospitality Technology Hall of Fame.

TECHNOLOGY IS ONE OF THE LESS VISIBLE topics among asset managers' priorities, but it is one of the most critical areas on which to keep current. Failure to keep it in good order may not be as immediately obvious to the guests as furniture, fixtures, and equipment—except perhaps for Wi-Fi service!—but nevertheless it affects the ability of every area of the operation to run effectively, especially marketing.

It's not possible to run any but the smallest and simplest properties today without computerized management systems. Because they contain every piece of information about the operation and its guests, for effective and efficient management these systems must be kept current and well-protected and the staff well-trained in their use. Further, technology has become a critical interface point with the guests. Any failure to meet their ever-evolving expected levels of service will be instantly reported widely over the social networks, affecting the property's reputation—and its value.

In addition to the impact of technology on operations, the guests' personally identifiable information that passes through the management systems (including the credit card information covered under payment card industry [PCI] regulations[1]) is in itself a digital asset that must be protected, with failure to do so bringing significant legal and financial risks. The degree of data protection and restriction on its movement across national and international borders varies considerably from one country to another, which has added a new level of legal complications to its management.

The rapid pace of technological change has raised expectations among both guests and management. The increasing focus on data-driven decisions means that no property can afford to slip behind its peers in the collection, consolidation, and analysis of accurate information for more effective management and marketing. This isn't easy to plan for, partly because it's not always obvious when and where technology investments will need to be made for maximum effect. But it's guaranteed that some area of technology will need to be upgraded every year, so capital funds must be allocated for this general purpose.

What do hospitality investors want from their hotels' technology systems? Typically, their primary need is accurate, comprehensive data that tells them how well each property is performing and allows them to conduct highly effective targeted marketing campaigns to bring in new business. However, the systems also need to provide enough day-to-day functionality, flexibility, and power to help management keep producing those great results, along with a reasonable (i.e., low) cost of installation and support.

The challenges to providing this are many. There are very few fully comprehensive enterprise resource planning (ERP) systems available for hospitality, so virtually all hotels need to use multiple systems from multiple vendors to manage their operations, each specializing in a different area. Consolidating their data for effective reporting can be difficult, error-prone, and subject to inconsistencies of meaning from one system to another.

Implementation and support are also challenging. It used to be the norm that each system at a property needed its own server, although virtualization is now reducing the amount of physical hardware. An equally daunting issue is that few individual properties can afford the level of technical expertise required for proper support of these multiple platforms, a situation that is becoming even more critical given the increasing importance of data security.

All of these factors contribute to the growing interest in remotely hosted systems, whether cloud-based or located at a hotel chain's own facilities. Although this approach has its own challenges, the reduced CapEx at the property level, improved data consistency, and greater security all are very attractive. Counterbalancing this, remotely hosted systems are obviously completely reliant on the stability and performance of the connecting networks, and operating expenses may go up to cover the more capable network and remote-system hosting fees. Combined with the huge growth in travelers' use of mobile technology and reliance on the Internet for entertainment, every hotel faces constantly increasing demands for investment in Internet bandwidth and Wi-Fi signal coverage.

Despite its challenges, technology is critical to every property's operational success. Management and marketing both need complete, accurate information on guests and operations, together with the ability to analyze it flexibly to target ever more granular market segments and to track their response in real time. Management efficiency can be boosted significantly through the use of appropriate, well-integrated systems, and guests simply won't stay at a hotel that can't provide them with widespread, reliable and fast Internet access.

Proper investment in technology throughout a property has never been more essential.

Hotel Technology Trends and Issues

Hospitality management shows no signs of becoming simpler. Resorts continue to add new facets such as condominium units, membership clubs, fractional ownership, spas, golf, tennis, and all kinds of other activities. Business-oriented properties need ever more comprehensive information on their individual and corporate group customers to provide repeat-guest recognition and to support effective marketing. In common with other areas of general public life, hotel guests are encouraged to expect more personally tailored levels of service, and distribution channel management has become almost impossibly complex as marketing is forced to target increasingly specialized segments. Competition is fierce and requires continued close attention to cost management and operating efficiencies if investors are to see an acceptable return on their funds.

To manage these influences, hotel systems have continued to grow in power and flexibility. However, no one application does everything and the number of different systems required by a typical property is still a major operational and support problem. Exhibit 1 provides a list of the more common system types. The demand for data consolidation and analysis has skyrocketed as managers and owners need a wider-ranging view of their guests and operations, and need it in greater detail. Effective interfaces and data integration are therefore essential to consolidating information into a meaningful, usable whole.

Many vendors are expanding their software to cover more operational areas and reduce the number of interfaces, and indeed the first full ERP systems for hospitality (from Cenium and Indra) have made their debut in the United States. Individual best-of-breed applications still maintain a functional advantage in some situations, however, and it's seldom feasible to replace every system in a property with an ERP, especially if some best-of-breed software was only recently implemented and has not been amortized. Interface power and flexibility are still essential factors, therefore, and while these continue to grow through the efforts of HTNG and others, much remains to be done.[2] Selection of the right mix of systems with the fewest compromises for a property's particular operational needs thus remains a complex but essential undertaking.

Current Issues

Two new issues having a significant impact on investments are cloud computing and consumer-driven mobile technology. The former has the potential to simplify the CapEx investment at the property level, improve systems reliability, and greatly enhance the speed and accuracy of multi-property reporting and analysis. There are trade-offs, though, including increased operating expenses, the need for upgrades to the infrastructure, and in the areas of data access and interfaces.

Adaption to mobile technology is being forced on the hospitality industry by the sheer numbers of guests relying on it as their main source of communications, for both business and entertainment. The growth in usage of smartphones and tablets has been phenomenal, leaving hotels with little choice but to expand their marketing, management, and infrastructure approaches to cater to it if they are not to lose business. Fortunately, upgrading the infrastructure to cater to

Exhibit 1 Typical Hotel System Set

The following is a list of software applications that are typically found in hotels and resorts. While several vendors now make comprehensive systems that cover multiple areas (typically GMS, S&C, activities management and, sometimes, POS), it is very common for each system to be purchased from a different vendor and to rely on some form of interface with the others for effective data management.

BI	Business intelligence, the consolidation of operating data and its flexible analysis for decision support.
BOS	Back office system, an older acronym for the financial accounting system. Since most GMSs include accounts receivable, BOSs usually cover primarily general ledger and accounts payable. Most can be extended to include asset management, payroll, and several other areas.
CRM	Customer relationship management, the consolidation of guest profile, stay information, and preferences. It is used for the recognition and reward of repeat guests, for generating targeted marketing campaigns, and in general for personalizing every interaction with a guest.
CRS	Central reservations system, an application that allows call center agents to search availability for multiple properties at once and to take reservations. Bookings are then transmitted to a GMS to allow the hotel to prepare for the arrival of the guest(s).
EMS	Energy management system, a combination of intelligent guestroom thermostats, door-opening sensors, occupancy sensors, and an interface to the GMS, such that default room temperatures are set back when the room is unoccupied or unrented.
F&B	Food and beverage systems, including restaurant/bar POS, dining reservations, and banquet operations.
GMS	Guest management system, the core technology for every hotel. Handles guest reservations, check-in, folio charge posting, housekeeping, check-out, and (usually) accounts receivable. Interfaces to multiple sub-systems at the property to collect charge data from F&B outlets, spa/golf/tennis and other activity centers, telephone/Internet/movie charges, credit card authorizations/charging, door lock key generation, etc.
I/P	Inventory/purchasing systems that cover the ordering, receiving, requisition, and issue of both F&B and general items for a hotel. Not to be confused with Internet Protocol (IP), and thus often called *procurement systems* instead.
Locks	Electronic guestroom door locks, usually using magnetic stripe cards but increasingly moving to contactless RFID cards and cell phone signals.
Payroll	Usually contracted to an outside service supplier.
PBX	Private branch exchange, an antiquated but convenient acronym for a property-based telephone system. Typically includes a call accounting system to calculate call charges and post them automatically to guests' folios, and a voice mail system for taking guest messages.

Exhibit 1 *(continued)*

PMS	Property management system. Obsolete and inaccurate term for guest management system, first used when hotel operations focused on rooms availability rather than guest profile data.
POS	Point of sale, for both food/beverage outlets and retail, covers ordering and cash register functions.
PPV	Pay-per-view movies.
RMS	Revenue management system.
S&C	Sales and catering system, which manages bookings for groups and for function/banquet spaces.
T&A	Time and attendance, captures time stamps for hourly paid staff and transmits the data to payroll systems.

guests' needs also allows management to improve efficiency by using its own mobile tools.

Other major trends in hospitality technology include:

- more powerful revenue management, allowing for better-informed and finer-grained control of rates and availability to take advantage of even minor variations in markets and their ancillary revenue streams
- improved customer relationship management (CRM) functionality, allowing for greater knowledge of guest trends and preferences and, consequently, more effective targeted marketing
- greater use of business intelligence (BI) tools for more informed and responsive management of operational factors

Note that all three of these areas depend significantly on the analysis of large databases of similar guest and operational information. As management and marketing decisions are increasingly data-driven, any complex hotel and all chains should give serious consideration to the creation of a single data warehouse with powerful and flexible analysis tools (i.e., to big data consolidation and big data analytics). Such systems and vendor consolidation reduce the number of different systems required and simplify their support. Tighter integration of guestroom technology infrastructure supports guests' needs and improve management efficiency. Each of these issues is discussed below.

Return on Investment

While every technology implementation must be done with a clear definition of what it is expected to achieve, it is very often impossible to define the return on investment (ROI) in financial terms. Some systems do have quantifiable outcomes—implementing a purchasing system will typically lead to around a 5 percent reduction in inventory costs, for example, and revenue management systems typically provide a 3–6 percent revenue uplift. However, the more guest-facing and marketing-oriented systems cannot be evaluated in this way.

For instance, investing in higher Internet bandwidth and more uniform Wi-Fi coverage throughout the hotel will not generate any additional business. It is nevertheless essential, because *not* doing so will lead directly to the *erosion* of business; it's necessary to continue to offer competitive levels of guest service just to stay in the game. There might be a goal of reducing the number of Wi-Fi complaints on guest satisfaction surveys by x percent, but it's virtually impossible to translate that into additional bookings.

Similarly, new management and marketing tools can lead to greater efficiencies and increased business, but only if operating procedures are changed to take advantage of them and if marketing analyses and campaigns are carried out appropriately. The tools are necessary investments to improve the operation, but don't produce an ROI without being used properly.

Every technology investment, therefore, must include a written statement of the desired outcome and benefit to the operation (quantified if possible but not essential) from the head of the operations department most affected, and be sponsored and signed off by a senior operations executive. Without this commitment to change the organization to take full advantage of the new tools, the full potential of the investment will not be realized.

Cloud Computing

Much hyped in the news at the time of writing, cloud computing genuinely does have the potential to change the way hospitality technology is delivered to hotels and how it is paid for.

As discussed above, the number of systems required by the average property continues to cause challenges in data integration and support. Few properties can afford the resources to support them in-house, so outsourcing support to a centralized, well-trained staff—whether at a chain's HQ or at a vendor's data center—is much more cost-effective. Similarly, credit-card and personal-data security concerns, both for PCI compliance and for general data security, complicate things at the property level by requiring strict partitions between different parts of the systems and networks and in the encryption of sensitive data. Off-loading these concerns to remotely hosted systems "in the cloud" makes PCI compliance at the hotel level much simpler and is receiving significant attention.

Note that there's a technical difference between "the cloud" as a generalized term for "that place remote from the hotel where the computer systems' servers physically live" and "cloud computing," which refers to a specific technical architecture. Remote-hosting in "the cloud" has been popularized as "Software as a Service" (SaaS) or, earlier, as an Application Service Provider (ASP) approach. While these remotely hosted approaches do offer many of the same benefits (improved security, support, data consistency, and analysis), true cloud computing offers much more flexibility and consistency in performance (being able to respond automatically to peaks in traffic demand), as well as the additional benefit of being priced according to monthly usage.

This flexibility arises from their architecture. True cloud systems run on massive banks of servers in major data centers, with control systems that automatically and dynamically allocate the combined computing, memory, and storage resources between whichever applications need them most. This not only maintains performance standards, it allows for new properties to be added remarkably quickly through a simple copy-and-edit process, a significant advantage to expanding hotel chains. By comparison, adding resources to a non-cloud system requires the acquisition of new server hardware, followed by its configuration, testing, software loading and incorporation into the rack, a decidedly non-dynamic process.

Cloud systems are also priced according to monthly usage—the amount of computing power, memory, storage, and/or data transmitted—which means they can be implemented with significantly less CapEx.

Advantages

Greater Reliability and Availability. Very few individual properties can afford to run their critical applications in the kind of access-secured, fully protected environment available from professional hosting companies, with the software running on duplicated, redundant servers with duplicated power supplies, backups, 24/7 monitoring, and full protection against viruses and spam, all designed to keep the systems available and performing efficiently all the time. Sharing the costs of such an environment between many hotels, or even hotel chains, however, makes it affordable and practical to each.

A frequent concern expressed over centralized systems is their vulnerability if the communications link goes down, though this disregards the fact that, for many properties, keeping on-premises hardware and software running can be at least as challenging. Some remotely hosted systems provide for the caching of critical data (such as in-house guest list and folio balances, next day arrivals, etc.) on a PC at the property, but in many areas communication reliability is so high that brief outages are not a problem. If cellular signals are strong at the property, it is even possible, if tedious, to run a browser-based guest management system over a smartphone connection in an emergency.

Larger or more complex hotels can ensure against a single-point communications failure by having multiple communications lines from different vendors. This is highly desirable in any event as a means of supplying sufficient bandwidth for guest and staff Internet usage, too, allowing traffic demands to be balanced across the most suitable connections.

Performance. A key aspect of cloud systems is that they can be configured to be self-managing in response to traffic demands, automatically adding more computing power, memory, and disk storage as needed, then reducing it when demand drops off. Peak-hour slowdowns in system response times are avoided, while short-term loads from new marketing campaigns (for example) can be handled without problems.

Remotely hosted but non-cloud configurations do not have this flexibility; additional resources have to be configured and tested before being brought on-line, and are equally hard to de-commission.

Vendor Support. Cloud computing data centers automatically reconfigure themselves around hardware failures to maintain service without interruption, and technical support at a central site is more available and of higher quality than at an individual hotel. Software upgrades and patches can be installed consistently by the vendor technicians at one location, and do not have to be done by multiple IT coordinators at the individual properties whenever they find time (and thus potentially not in complete accordance with the instructions). And if there are problems with a new release, a central system can be quickly rolled back to the previous release without drama.

The vendor has more incentive to perform high-quality testing before implementing any patch or upgrade, too, since any such change will immediately affect many more properties. Smaller properties should see a higher level of support responsiveness, since any problem they experience will likely also affect the biggest multi-property users, who will exert considerably more influence on the speed of identifying and resolving the issue.

Security. Firewalls, anti-virus, anti-spam, user authentication, intrusion detection, and remote access management for the sales managers are all better managed centrally on a skilled, professional level rather than left to overworked management and staff at the property. Further, PCI compliance is simplified if all credit card transactions are handled off-property in an isolated part of the configuration.

Fewer CapEx Battles. Remotely hosted systems are often priced on a monthly or transaction-based fee basis; cloud systems are more commonly priced according to usage (e.g., the amount of processing power or memory used or the amount of data processed or transmitted per month). New systems can thus be implemented with minimal CapEx, reducing the typical competition for capital funds from lobby or guestroom renovation projects, for example.

Hotels still need to budget for regular workstation upgrades or replacement, but this can be covered in a lease program. Further, since centralized systems require only a browser or thin-client application instead of a full PC software suite, the workstations can be simpler and less expensive.

There is, of course, a corresponding rise in operating expenses, an issue that must be resolved within management agreements.

Ease of Introduction. A prime benefit for many hotel chains is the ability to introduce a new system to the organization quickly, a huge benefit when a property is re-flagged and needs to be brought into the chain as quickly as possible. As long as the hotel already has a standard PC/browser environment, just typing the new URL into the users' browsers establishes the connection to the new system. Of course, there is still much operational work to be done in setting up the standard data parameters used by the new management company and in training the staff on the new system, but the technical issues become almost insignificant.

Multi-Property Benefits

Data Consolidation and Reporting. All of the above benefits accrue to a single hotel just as much as to a multi-property organization, but the latter also enjoy other advantages, whether they decide to host a system for their properties themselves or rely on the vendor. Key among these are the twin benefits of (a) having standardized data across all properties for consistency and accuracy, and (b) far simpler consolidation of that data for accurate, timely comparative reporting, data analysis, and building complete guest profiles. Sharing operational data so all hotels in a group can see which sites are overperforming or underperforming in certain areas also brings peer pressure into play, a powerful driver of improved efficiencies and profitability.

Fewer Interfaces. A multi-property chain using a centralized guest management system (GMS) can implement one interface each to its central reservation system (CRS), to its centralized revenue management system (RMS) or sales and catering system, to the Internet for Web bookings, and possibly even to a centralized VoIP (voice over Internet protocol) telephone and call accounting system, instead of having to implement and manage one version of each interface at every property. Some interface links still need to remain on-site to local implementations of POS, PBX, pay-per-view movies and so on, but the improvements in reliability and supportability by concentrating as many as possible in a central location are obvious and enticing.

New-Hotel Integration. When a new property joins a group that already has a defined standard system configuration, it is significantly more efficient and faster to produce a copy of that and customize it for local variations than to build a new one from scratch. And because it's hosted, it's already installed on the servers, one less major task to perform.

Allows Spread of Systems to Smaller Properties. Centralization can make it feasible to implement higher-quality systems in smaller properties where they were previously cost-prohibitive. If the service is delivered over a network from a remote central site, the only cost is that of servicing the additional rooms, and that cost is purely incremental; there's no new base price to cover. Pay-per-view movie systems, VoIP telephone systems, call accounting, and voice messaging all offer examples of potentially significant cost savings from remote-hosting.

Drawbacks

Licensing. While most hospitality systems' license fees are based on an operational parameter (such as the number of guestrooms, meeting spaces, concurrent users, etc.), the vendors of some supporting applications (Oracle, for example) charge by the number of servers running their software. Because this is very difficult to define in the dynamic world of a cloud's data center, these vendors do not support virtual-server usage in any form, whether at a local implementation or in a cloud. Unfortunately, this category includes Micros, the industry's largest vendor, whose applications are all based on Oracle (and which was acquired by Oracle in June 2014).

This is likely to change, but until it does these vendors will continue to require physically identifiable servers for their applications, preventing properties and chains from realizing the hardware and security benefits of virtual servers.

Interfaces. As mentioned above, cloud systems have fewer interfaces to configure than premises-based ones. However, not all of the systems needed for a hotel are yet available in cloud format, and those that are may not have all the functionality a particular operation needs. Most implementations will therefore still need some interfaces. A chain with a cloud-based GMS and CRS may still need to link to vendor-hosted RMS or sales and catering (S&C) systems, for example. This complicates interface support, because, in addition to the vendors debating which of them is at fault in the event of an interruption, the hosting companies and their communications vendors will also need to be involved, making it harder to pinpoint the true root cause.

This is a key point to be addressed in hosting contracts, because third-party cloud hosting companies typically support a great variety of systems for companies in multiple industries, and may not have much focus on the specific needs of a multi-vendor, 24/7 vertical such as hospitality. Nevertheless, interface technology is improving steadily in power, flexibility, and maintainability, and careful, accurate monitoring of traffic and data flow will help resolve most issues.

Service Level Agreements

Service level agreements (SLAs) are essential to ensuring the effective delivery of services, but they need to be approached with a sense of reality from both sides. Vendors need to understand how critical their service is to the hoteliers and the true impact of downtime in a 24/7 environment. Hoteliers need to understand that achieving those last few percentage points toward 100 percent uptime can get very expensive. An uptime of 99.5 percent uptime might sound good, but it means that service is likely to be unavailable for 0.5 percent of a year, which is nearly two days. Fortunately it's relatively affordable to get to 99.95 percent uptime and most services offer this, though not perhaps in all parts of the globe. Each hotelier has to strike a balance between cost and the impact of occasional interruptions.

Clearly, there must be financial penalties if the vendor fails to meet the guaranteed uptime. These too must be kept in proportion, but they do have to be significant enough to get the vendor's attention. Waiving support fees for periods of downtime is the absolute minimum, but that usually amounts to far less than the economic impact on the property. While you can't impose consequential damages on the vendor (even if downtime causes you to lose a major piece of business), some form of meaningful but realistic penalty is only fair.

Vendor-Hosting Versus Self-Hosting

Data centers are expensive, and only the largest chains and vendors can afford to build and maintain their own. Most vendors who provide remotely hosted software do so through contracts with third parties, either a public cloud such as those from Microsoft, Google, and Amazon or a secure co-location facility from one of many suppliers. "Co-location" refers to the fact that these data centers host multiple applications for many different companies, sharing the same hardware but with software and data kept protected from each other.

This highlights the benefits and drawbacks of third-party hosting in general, namely that while the costs and responsibility for uptime and security are shared across many clients, the third-party company is unlikely to know—or care—as much about the 24/7 nature of a hotel's operation. While SLAs define the required uptime and response time, as well as the penalties for failing to meet them, third-party hosting typically requires hotels to manage three SLAs: one each with the software vendor, the hosting company, and the communications network provider.

Some hoteliers are uncomfortable in general with having their critical data hosted elsewhere and prefer to set up their own "private" clouds, though this obviously transfers responsibility for maintaining the data center to the hotelier. A compromise configuration uses a third-party center to house the hotel servers, with the software vendor or hotel company taking responsibility for maintenance of the application software.

It's a trade-off based on the degree of comfort with the vendor's ability to provide the service reliably and the desired degree of control over the whole process and data. Some hotel chains centralize many systems but still install GMS servers at the properties, often in secure rooms and monitored remotely by central support technicians. This complicates both support and the roll-out of software updates, but it does remove concerns about data inaccessibility at the properties in case of communications failure. It all comes down to comfort level and individual circumstances.

Communications—Internet Versus Dedicated Lines

With the rapid expansion of broadband coverage, encryption, and the adoption of virtual private networks (VPNs), many centralized hotel systems work very well over the Internet. As demand for guest Internet access has risen, many properties have established multiple reliable broadband connections from different trusted Internet service providers (ISPs). This bandwidth can easily accommodate the comparatively minimal requirements of the management systems.

In areas where Internet coverage is less predictable, it may be possible to contract for a private dedicated network, though there is a cost for this predictability. In other regions where even routine Internet access is prohibitively expensive, it may be more feasible to run the systems in stand-alone mode at the property and synchronize them on a periodic basis throughout the day, rather than providing full-time access.

Cloud Versus Web-Native Versus Web-Enabled

Vendors are likely to describe their centralized systems as cloud-based, web-native, or web-enabled. Web-enabled systems, usually the older, more established ones, provide remote access over the Internet or other Internet protocol (IP)–based network by using Citrix or Microsoft's Terminal Services on the workstations, or a web browser. These utilities off-load the actual software application processing work from the workstation to the central server and just use the workstation as a display device to show the changed screens. However, they don't change the way the underlying application works, and they require extra bandwidth to handle the greater traffic. Citrix/MTS can also be expensive.

In contrast, web-native systems are usually newer, have been written directly for this environment using more modern languages and approaches, and are inherently designed for use by browser-equipped PCs via any IP-based network. The browser is used to reach the central site, but the application then usually loads a small client application on the workstation to handle screen displays and whatever minor local processing might be required.

Since they tend to be more recently developed, web-native systems may not always have the rich functionality or established reliability of web-enabled ones. However, they're likely to be much better positioned for future development, especially for integrating with other systems. Either approach means that simpler and less powerful "thin-client" workstations can be used at the property level than are required for traditional client-server software architecture, a major advantage for the centralized approach.

Given the imprecise way the term is often used, it's important to clarify what a vendor means when they claim a system is "cloud-based." Make sure to specifically ask whether it is actually running in a cloud environment or just running off-premises on remotely hosted servers in a traditional client-server architecture. A true cloud system will provide more performance flexibility and stronger support, which should be reflected in the vendor offering both lower costs and better SLA terms.

Commitment

One objection raised to the concept of buying cloud or SaaS systems is that the payments never end; you sign up for a minimum commitment (usually three years) but continue to pay as long as you use the software. But this is also true with the more traditional practice of licensing a system outright; even if the hardware is leased, the acquisition payments do stop eventually, but support costs always continue.

In summary:

- Limited-service chains should be running on remotely hosted systems; the advantages are too numerous to ignore. If they're looking to move toward that goal, a true cloud system will pay long-term dividends.
- More complex operations should evaluate their functional needs, including interfaces, and compare products from several vendors. If functionality is comparable between two systems, and if the communications links are reliable and affordable, choosing the cloud system will have greater upside in the long run.
- If the functionality needed isn't available in a cloud system, or if communications are unreliable or prohibitively expensive, there are several good systems available for use on-premises. However, their support will need to be considered seriously.

There will always be hidden operational costs to a hotel of running on older, under-supported, poorly integrated systems on hardware that's not kept up-to-date and running efficiently, whether these are accounted for or not. Paying a monthly fee for reliable, well-managed, perpetually up-to-date systems allows the hotel management to concentrate on using those tools to run the operation more effectively and imaginatively. The payback in terms of time and focus is well worth the investment.

Mobile Technology

It's impossible to miss the impact that mobile technology, especially smartphones and tablets, has had on life in general, leaving the hospitality industry with no choice but to invest in it so as to meet guest demands. Wi-Fi Internet access has become a deal-breaker for many, many guests; lack of it will immediately disqualify a hotel from consideration, and a poor experience will discourage guests from ever returning. Fortunately, this investment also provides an excellent infrastructure for management-oriented mobile tools, which can bring significant benefits in efficiency.

The four major areas of impact have been in:

- the development of guest-facing software applications (for booking rooms, dining, or other activities, requesting guest services, etc.), both for guests to download onto their devices and for hotels to load onto guestroom tablets.
- enhancing marketing software to identify specific sub-sections of the guest mix and send special offers to them on new channels, such as via Twitter, Facebook, Instagram, and others.
- improved management tools and greatly improved Wi-Fi service, in both bandwidth and signal coverage.
- increased demand for cell phone signal coverage throughout the property.

Guest-Facing Applications

Strong trends in traveler booking behavior mandate that hotels need a mobile-compatible booking and information application, either a page on its website compatible with (and optimized for) a phone's web browser or a property- or chain-specific app downloadable to the guest's phone or tablet. This is because booking lead times have shortened as guests become more spontaneous in their travels and have become used to the convenience of location-aware searches on their phones, sometimes even booking a room while standing outside the property.

Investment in these tools is thus essential to capturing this market segment, but they also have great benefits in strengthening guest loyalty through the opportunity to provide useful and appreciated functions. In addition to booking rooms, these include guests being able to book other activities such as spa, golf, or dining, access their group's meeting agenda and a map of the function rooms, order room service, place housekeeping requests, order car valet service, check and update their frequent-guest profile with the chain, and so on. Typically, they will also escalate a guest request if it has not been satisfied within pre-set service targets, helping to ensure a prompt response while also compiling management statistics that can be used to improve service in general.

Versions of these applications are increasingly being used on tablets that hotels place in their guestrooms. In addition to providing excellent service to guests who don't wish to be disturbed by too much staff interaction, the apps also generate increased guestroom revenue. One reason for this is that the convenient design of the apps makes it very appealing to book other activities. In addition, the apps can make well-targeted upselling offers, such as suggested wine pairings for room service orders or personalized spa/golf packages.

Another advantage of guests' near ubiquitous possession of cell phones is that it's easier for hotels to send them text messages. One benefit is the capability to broadcast emergency messages if needed (often a consideration for ocean resorts in tsunami-prone areas). In addition, guests whose flight schedules bring them to the property early in the day can receive a text message when their rooms are ready, a greatly appreciated service.

Enhanced Marketing Functionality

Customer relationship management aspects are discussed below, but mobile technology in general adds more channels through which guests can communicate with a property, whether for bookings, checking-in via location-based services such as Facebook, Twitter, Instagram, and so on. This usage must be identified and tracked. Marketing software must be updated to be able to send special offers to appropriate guest segments on all of these channels.

Management Tools

Taking advantage of the guest-driven expansion of Wi-Fi coverage throughout a property, many management tools have become available for smartphones and tablets. Some are quite specific, such as housekeeping management tools that allow the reporting of room status changes directly from a smartphone (or iPod Touch) and also identify the next room to be cleaned. This dynamic response allows a room to be moved up in priority for a guest who has already arrived on property and is waiting, or to tell the attendant that a guest has just checked out of a nearby room that can now be accessed for cleaning. The dual benefits are greater guest satisfaction and improved staff efficiency.

Similar systems are available for engineering work order management, allowing engineers to be notified of urgent tasks while they're away from their workshop location and giving them access to key information (e.g., TV set model, light bulb type and wattage, etc.) or even a photo of the problem so that they arrive prepared. Guest service and staff efficiency are thus again both improved.

Other tools are more general, providing managers with access to guest and conference/meeting data and to daily operating statistics and sending them alerts that tell them, for example, that VIP guests have just arrived. The advent of the tablet has provided a far more usable device than the frequently cramped screen of a smartphone, making it feasible to run guest management, revenue management, and, increasingly, point-of-sale (POS) systems on a mobile unit. This in turn allows front desk staff to check in guests when away from the front desk or to update revenue management controls from anywhere on property—or even from home.

Signal Coverage

Signal coverage is especially challenging. Hotels have already been improving both Internet bandwidth and coverage in response to guests' strong demand for Internet access and their preference for wireless over wired connections. The difficulty is that the cost of providing sufficient Wi-Fi bandwidth continues to grow, while guests still expect that it will be offered for free. Consequently, many hotels are introducing tiered-service offerings, with basic service at no charge but higher levels, suitable for streaming video, available for a fee. Either way, increasing Wi-Fi coverage is an essential, regular investment and is discussed in more detail later in this chapter.

On the other hand, cell phone coverage, which uses different network protocols, has not kept pace and is in turn becoming a rising source of guest dissatisfaction as smartphone usage becomes more widespread. It's true that many smartphones can use Wi-Fi for communications, but this usually requires the guest to specifically allow connection to the hotel's network to do so, a noticeable disincentive.

Providing strong, consistent cell phone coverage throughout a property can be quite expensive. In rare cases, the telephone carriers can be persuaded to subsidize the installation of a distributed antenna system (DAS), but these are costly and the carriers are often reluctant to add more traffic to their already overloaded local access points. Hybrid approaches whereby cell phone signals can be carried over the Wi-Fi or wired Internet network and broadcast from transmitters plugged into access points are becoming more available. These may be more feasible for retrofit to existing properties.

Currently, the necessary investment is being made more often by high-end properties. The importance of this issue is sure to grow in the years ahead, as demand for coverage will only increase. Bandwidth needs may be partially met by faster 4G networks as the carriers implement them, but those signals will still be unable to penetrate most hotel structures (especially those with reflective treatments on their windows) and will still need to be re-broadcast inside the building.

Revenue Management

With the trend toward more personalized travel experiences showing no signs of slowing down, hotel guest mixes have become more and more granular, divided into increasingly smaller market segments that have their own preferences and booking patterns. Maximizing revenue therefore means having:

- systems capable of analyzing all booking and stay data to identify these micro-segments, including the ancillary revenue streams each segment brings in over and above the room rate.
- accurate, up-to-the-minute information on what your competition is offering.
- the ability to post appropriately configured packages to multiple sites simultaneously and at the right time to catch the attention of specific market segments.

Each of these functions used to be the prerogative of discrete systems, but the complexity of the situation requires that more of them are being integrated into more usable packages. Furthermore, the speed at which market demand changes has shifted the emphasis of the systems. Instead of focusing on comparisons between the current booking pace and historical trends, it's now at least as important to offer dynamic real-time monitoring of the market's reaction to a hotel's offerings.

Revenue management itself has always been an integral part of hotel operations—after all, even a strategy as simple as posting different rates for weekdays and weekends is a form of revenue management. Early automated systems added new possibilities, such as comparing the current booking pace for different market segments against their historical patterns, then recommending rate and/or length-of-stay adjustments that would encourage guests to book when it was most beneficial both to them and to the property's goals. However, it seemed that the best results were realized only by larger hotels that had guests in several distinct market segments, each with clearly identifiable stay patterns and price sensitivities that could be easily manipulated.

The situation has become more complex in recent years. Price comparison shopping has become remarkably easy, and market segments have become harder to distinguish as travelers use different booking channels for different trips, depending on their needs. More impulsive buying habits give hotels less time to react to trends, while the growing influence of peer reviews adds another new factor. Three major travel disruptions in the past decade have reduced the usefulness of historic data as a comparison. Although seasonal and day-of-week patterns are still important as the underlying groundwork for forecasting, the variations in booking patterns for individual segments have become much harder to distinguish.

Older systems and weekly/monthly data reviews mask a great number of subtle variations. These may balance themselves out over the longer period, but close analysis of the wealth of booking and stay detail that systems now capture can identify many micro-market segments. Each will have its own patterns and preferences as to booking channel, lead times, and combinations of rates and activities that it finds appealing. Micro-managing them is essential if money is not to be left on the table.

Collecting more information about group visits is also valuable. Tallying the delegates' expenditure in all areas throughout their stay, beyond just the room rate and banqueting functions, will give revenue per occupied group room figures that help identify the most profitable groups for future bookings.

The result is a need for data awareness and management at a level far too complex to handle manually. The current range of revenue management systems allows this detail to be identified in more depth by pulling it from a wider range of sources and distribution channels, while also providing the means to manage it effectively in real time. Investing in one will thus pay dividends for most properties. Even those with only a single room type sold at a single rate can maximize profitability by using revenue management to adjust that rate very precisely.

The ease of comparative pricing and the difficulty of distinguishing between competing brands in the same quality segment have meant that shopping is often done first on the basis of price. This makes it essential for hotels that aren't competing on price alone to distinguish themselves, not necessarily in the marketplace at large but certainly in the minds of the guests in their principal and most profitable market segments. Every hotel thus must know its own value proposition (market leader, follower but good value, technology specialist, great resort location, etc.) and state it clearly and often, on-line and off-line. Only then can it target different market segments individually within that overall philosophy, offering specific rates and packages to each that are clearly worth their higher prices.

Search engine optimization is essential for making sure the property is easily found in searches by the right type of guests, but it must be carefully targeted for appropriate search keywords. Trying to be at the top of every page of search results is ineffective and just dilutes the message. It's also critical to keep on top of changes in Google's search algorithms to maintain visibility, and well worth the investment in specialized knowledge and abilities.

All of these factors have led to a more marketing-oriented approach to revenue management, with an emphasis on real-time monitoring and adjustment. Revenue managers now operate much more as part of a team that includes all major operating departments. They can especially work closely with marketing to identify suitable segments to approach with specific offers, and which ones aren't worth the effort.

Rate Search and Channel Management Tools

The number of specialized travel websites has grown exponentially. These range from the very specific (e.g., hiking treks in the Himalayas) to the very general (e.g., cruises), from hotel chains' own-brand sites (e.g., Marriott.com) to all-purpose travel search engines (e.g., Expedia.com). As the number of different target market segments increases, each with its own preferences for where to look for travel information, distribution channel management has become one of most complex and difficult tasks that hotel management faces, as well as one of the most important.

Knowing what a property's peer group of hotels is offering is equally important, and so an abundance of rate search services has become available to hoteliers, typically feeding the data directly into a revenue management system to provide on-screen assistance. Two ongoing issues are (1) being sure that an accurate apples-to-apples rate comparison is being made, and (2) making sure that the most important distribution channels for the hotel are all being tracked, because they may be different for different hotels in the peer group.

Given the number of different websites and booking channels used by different market segments and the fact that many of them must still be accessed through their own extranets, updating them has become almost impossible to do manually. This is especially so where sales contracts demand rate parity (i.e., making sure that offers are always available at the same price on every site). Several vendors have developed excellent channel management tools that allow for the distribution of rate and room availability updates from a single screen out to multiple websites. These are essential tools.

Another aspect of information gathering that's become more important is reputation management, the consolidation of all mentions of a property online, especially on consumer sites where travelers post comments about their stay experiences. To even out the impact of individual reports, many such sites (e.g., TripAdvisor, Expedia) assign a one- to five-star rating to each property listed based on an analysis of the overall tone of the reports. Travelers can then search by rating as well as by price and location.

Many third-party tools such as Revinate, ReviewPro, and TrustYou offer widespread reputation data collection and analysis. This means that in addition to helping hoteliers respond promptly to guest comments, they can provide valuable input when setting rates. For example, if a hotel consistently gathers five-star reviews, it ought to be able to raise its rates without decreasing occupancy much, if at all. Conversely, if it frequently gathers three-star comments, it may not be targeting the right market segments because the value proposition it represents to guests is likely different from the one it thinks it offers.

Websites

In the never-ending battle to capture travelers' attention, hotel, chain and third-party websites are becoming more elaborate in functionality and (fortunately) better-designed. In addition to improved quality of descriptions, the text is accompanied by steadily better photography including videos and 360-degree panoramic tours. To maintain consistency of the property or chain brand presentation, especially given the different formatting demands of mobile devices, this "rich data" is often sourced from a central graphical image library maintained by the hotel or chain. This library, which typically also includes general descriptive information about a hotel and its function space, is also often interfaced to automated RFP-response systems to allow a faster turnaround of inquiries for contract bids.

On-line booking engines are becoming more streamlined and more user-friendly, which makes it easier for travelers to retrieve and modify their bookings directly. Many provide the ability for frequent-guest program members to access their accounts and update their profiles on-line, as well as to reserve additional on-property services (spa, golf, dining, etc.).

Customer Relationship Management

Competition for guests is fiercer than ever. As hotel brands increasingly overlap and become harder to separate meaningfully, differentiation through service is critical to encouraging repeat business. All properties must place a strong emphasis on CRM to make each guest feel valued, appreciated, and understood.

This requires the gathering and careful, flexible analysis of as much information as possible about the guests, their booking/stay preferences, and their spending habits. This in turn allows for the creation of finely targeted marketing promotions so that guests in the most profitable market micro-segments can be encouraged to return (and recognized when they do). It also facilitates more productive prospecting for new guests with similar profiles.

Consolidating all the appropriate information from the multiple systems involved throughout a guest's booking process and visit, both for a single property and across all properties in a chain, has become easier with the development of more flexible and powerful interfaces. However, getting that data back into the hands of the staff interacting with the guests is still challenging. Fully integrated system suites have the significant advantage of allowing front-line staff to access this data in the same system they use to interact with the guests, instead of having to look it up in a separate application. Few things improve staff confidence and service levels more than knowing they have immediate access to all pertinent information about the guest—and that it's accurate.

Keeping it accurate is a constant challenge, but is absolutely essential; nothing will undermine a hotel's reputation faster than trying to meet a guest's personal preferences based on faulty or obsolete information. Many systems provide de-duplication assistance to identify and merge multiple profiles for a single guest, but it is also valuable to run the database through an outside data cleansing company periodically to pick up changes of address and other public information. As much as anything, though, accurate data depends on a management culture that rewards the staff for entering it accurately and consistently in the first place.

Marketing campaign tools have grown more sophisticated as well as more precise. It's now common for management systems not only to send an e-mail confirmation for a booking, but also follow-up e-mails to encourage pre-arrival booking (through active links in the message) of other activities such as spa, golf, or dining that may be hard to reserve at convenient times after arrival. This frequently increases the guest's total spend for the visit and creates a stronger buy-in to the stay, thereby discouraging last-minute cancellations and improving the hotel's bottom line from both directions.

Another improvement comes from the growing use of electronic guest satisfaction surveys and their integration into the management systems. Sending post-departure "thank-you" e-mails with links to electronic surveys generates a usefully higher response rate, while automatically integrating the responses back into the guests' stay records provides much valuable information. This includes being more aware of any problems a guest had so that they can be pre-checked before his or her next arrival, as well as being able to tie any comments about good or bad service back to the specific staff who interacted with that guest.

Business Intelligence

The demand for accurate, comprehensive operational data and intelligent analysis tools has never been stronger. Revenue may be on an upswing, but profits have not grown at the same rate. Consequently, the intelligent management of expenses and costs is just as critical as making the right operational and marketing decisions. Given this reality, the need continues to grow for the central consolidation and analysis of data, both operational and guest profile; in other words, for performance management and business intelligence (BI) tools. In fact, a single comprehensive database can form the basis for all three major data-driven disciplines in the hotel: revenue management, customer relationship management, and business intelligence.

What makes BI more challenging is the increased complexity of the business, the pressure on margins from ever-rising customer-service expectations, and the unpredictability of travel volumes due to wars, government actions, and terrorist threats and actions. Owners, investors, and operators all need real-time access to the critical measures driving the business so that they can provide timely, useful information to decision makers, identify problems while they are still small, and assess trends as quickly as possible as they develop.

The two biggest developments recently have been time compression and reporting flexibility. We've moved from monthly STR reports that arrived three or four weeks after the close of the month to weekly reports and, most recently, to daily data reporting. Many multi-property data consolidation tasks now include web-based daily entry and reporting, with flash data distributed early in the morning and audited data available before the end of the day.

At the same time, with the multi-owner complexity of many (if not most) properties, the number of people needing their own sub-set of data continues to expand. A multi-hotel operation will typically need to provide reporting and analysis tools for management staff at property, regional, headquarters, and brand management levels, for functional area management on-site, and for development, owners, asset managers, investor relations, and so on. Modern systems can provide all these clients with the data they need, in their own format, quickly and at secure websites. This allows each of them to access their reports and drill down to the underlying detail from wherever they happen to be, even from smartphones and tablets.

The better BI systems now have more data collection options, being able to attach to any open data sources (SAP, Peoplesoft, SAS, Oracle, DB2, SQL, MS Access, STR, TravelClick, financial indices, currency exchange rates, etc.), as well as to relevant hospitality systems (such as the GMS, POS, sales and catering, spa/golf/other activities management, CRM, accounting, payroll, satisfaction surveys, and so on). They have flexible drag-and-drop ad-hoc query builders and also allow companies to pre-configure their own OLAP (OnLine Analytical Processing) "cubes" of sorted data to give line managers access to fast, flexible analysis with full drill-down capability. Dashboard views are easily constructed to give near-real-time indicators of key performance indicators and can guide users through the entire budgeting/forecasting process by property, region, etc.

After the extraction of data from all these disparate sources has been completed, its normalization and consolidation must also be performed before BI tools can help provide intelligent decision guidance. Most hotel systems have at least rudimentary (and often quite sophisticated) data extraction and export tools, but several now also have their own built-in BI analysis tools or optional third-party modules providing similar functions. The growth of more comprehensive systems that reduce the need for data translation between different vendors' products, and the significant benefits of cross-industry data definition standards being established by groups such as OpenTravel[3] and HTNG, have all made data consolidation more effective.

However, the operational challenges of collecting clean and complete data at the point of entry show no signs of diminishing and will always remain the primary obstacle to accurate analysis. Those tasked with entering the data are seldom those gaining the most benefit from it. Accordingly, it must become part of the culture to keep them motivated to strive to compile the most complete and accurate information by making sure that they are aware of the benefits that this meticulousness brings to the whole operation. This drive for data consistency is a key reason so many hotel chains require their properties to use standard systems for all critical areas of operations. It is also a strong incentive for them to consider using centrally hosted systems instead of each property having its own, as this guarantees that all sites are at least using the same software release configured in the same way.

Guest Management Systems

Guest management systems (GMSs), frequently and inaccurately known as property management systems (PMSs)—they don't manage the property, they manage the guests' experiences while they are at the property—are still the core for guest data management. They continue to expand in depth of functionality in guest profile, stay, and preference tracking, in group block bookings and charge routing flexibility, in housekeeping schedule flexibility, and through a myriad of other, smaller improvements.

Many have also expanded in breadth as well as depth of coverage, allowing them to include modules that were long the preserve of specialized systems. What used to be a mostly guestroom-oriented system will now quite often also include POS functionality, sales and catering, spa management, condominium owner accounting, and club membership management modules. As GMSs grow into these other areas, hoteliers need fewer systems to provide the same breadth of guest data. That data will also be of higher accuracy since it hasn't needed to be translated from one system to another.

Unfortunately, no one system currently provides everything a hotelier needs (although the ERPs from Cenium and Indra come close). Indeed, despite the advantages of integrated systems, if an existing application is performing well and provides essential functionality, it may not be appropriate or desirable to replace it with the equivalent module from a more comprehensive system. Interfaces therefore are and will remain a fact of life for every property.

Reflecting the marketing trend toward dynamic packaging, vendors now provide much more flexibility in the package plan capabilities of their systems. This manifests itself in both external and internal choices. Many GMSs allow agents to build packages on-the-fly, offering guests more choices in building their own combination of services, such as spa, golf, tennis, horseback riding, dining reservations, room upgrades, higher-quality Wi-Fi service, and so on. This has come about both through the increased scope of GMSs (since many of these package components are now an integral part of the system's database) and through better interfaces to third-party activities management systems.

A Trend Toward Usability

One recent but very welcome trend is that several vendors are redesigning their systems to make them more usable, reliable, and supportable. As the applications have grown over the years, they've become more and more complex architecturally, to the point that enhancements have become difficult to make quickly and without breaking any existing functions. At the same time, adding ever more functionality into the software, while beneficial, has complicated the user interface and made it harder to learn and to use.

To get around this challenge, a number of vendors are building new systems using more modern tools for faster development and more automated regression testing. They are also taking a more user-oriented approach to the screen designs, providing as much detail and functionality as each user's role requires, but no more. Some incorporate workflow indicators to help new users understand where they are in a process and what options might be useful next. All have more visual, graphic layouts that are likely to be more intuitively understandable.

The result should be more systems that help staff members instead of confusing them, thereby reducing training costs and increasing effectiveness. These systems should also be capable of being enhanced more quickly in response to market demands. Users of older systems will increasingly find themselves handicapped as this new breed comes to market.

Service-Oriented Architecture

Most vendors are basing their new systems development on service-oriented architecture (SOA). Another term that's become almost as hyped as "cloud computing," SOA is based on the concept of a "bus," an electronic pipeline into which multiple different systems or system modules are connected to exchange data and to combine appropriate parts of each other's functionality.

For example, if a reservations system, guest management system, and POS system are all connected via an SOA bus, they don't each need to continue using their own credit card charge-processing functions. It makes more sense to decide which one has the best approach and use that particular system's module to service the charge-processing needs of all three. This SOA approach, which has been widely accepted in other industries, leads to more efficient systems, easier integration, and more accurate data, since it's all managed by a single module. Keeping that payment processing module identifiably separate also simplifies PCI compliance.

This has two consequences for hospitality systems. One is that it encourages vendors to form closer partnerships, sharing the best parts of each other's systems for a more effective whole and thus a more appealing offering to hotels. They are also more inclined to support each other's systems, simplifying support for the properties.

The other is that it is attracting Tier 1 companies such as Microsoft, Accenture, Oracle, and others to consider entering the hospitality vertical. They already have considerable expertise in SOA architecture in other industries, as well as their own worldwide high-bandwidth communications networks. This gives them an advantage in assembling systems into a comprehensive offering and in making it available over a cloud-based network.

It's too early to say whether their interest will lead to serious involvement, although Oracle's recent purchase of Micros Systems, the largest vendor in the market space, is certainly encouraging. The appearance of more global providers able to supply and support hospitality systems to hotel chains on a worldwide usage-fee basis has the potential to change the way software is provided to the industry.

Kiosks

Self-service kiosks have become a mainstream option for most property types. They won't replace the need for front desk staff, but can provide a useful supplement at peak check-in/check-out times and for any guest who prefers a swift, automated process. Most current designs are deliberately limited to retrieving reservations, checking in the guest, producing a guestroom key, and handling check-out and folio print.

The opportunity and technology exist to add several more options to these functions, such as:

- a hotel room layout plan to help guests select a room with specific attributes or location
- group delegate check-in messages and printable agendas
- upselling the guest to a higher rate room or package
- printing airline boarding passes at check-out
- full Internet access so that guests can research local restaurants and attractions, printing out directions and maps as needed

However, care needs to be taken not to overly complicate the user interface and delay both the guest using the kiosk and those in the queue forming behind him or her. Concierge-like activities are best handled on a dedicated kiosk further removed from the front desk, more often these days using tablets instead of kiosks.

Kiosks are never going to be the answer for every guest, and labor savings will be limited as front-desk staff still needs to be available to answer queries. However, they have a very definite place in the lobby of extended stay and limited-service properties where the front desk may be unattended at night, and there's a considerable segment of guests who'll be very happy to use them in most other types of operations.

Guestroom Technology

Certainly one of the most visible trends continues to be in upgraded guestroom technology, both in terms of the guest experience and in the investment needed to meet it. As consumers' entertainment has switched more to the Internet, and as it has become much more common for guests to carry multiple entertainment devices with them—smartphones, tablets, portable game controllers, etc.—hotels simply have no alternative but to provide consistent, reliable Internet access in all guestrooms. Flat-panel displays have also become the norm, preferably with the ability for guests to use them as displays for their own equipment.

Internet Access

The dominant trend is unquestionably toward wireless (Wi-Fi) access for its sheer convenience. Some major corporations (and the United States government) still require their personnel to use wired connections for their greater security, but that requirement is likely to become less common as Wi-Fi security improves. There are two major challenges to providing effective Wi-Fi service, however: achieving consistent coverage throughout the property and supplying sufficient bandwidth to meet guests' demands.

Wireless coverage is certainly simpler than wired to implement on a retrofit basis, but it does still require cable to be run to each access point (wireless transceiver). Each property must be surveyed to determine the number and placement of access points to ensure coverage in all areas, which will depend on the building's layout and construction. Mesh networks—where each access point acts as a wireless link to the next and so reduces the need for physical cabling—sound attractive but are best used only as a way to extend coverage to remote locations. If used throughout a hotel, the units closest to the communications base can quickly be swamped by having to handle the traffic from all of the remote points as well as their own.

Bandwidth. Bandwidth management is perhaps the most challenging aspect. What used to be satisfactory for many guests to check e-mail at the same time—often a 1.5MB T-1 line—has become hopelessly inadequate now that so many download streaming video during their stay. The sources are many—YouTube videos, Netflix movies, Hulu TV episodes, Skype video chats, etc.—but the cumulative effect is the same: a far greater demand for overall bandwidth coming into the property (100MB is now common) and the need to prevent high-demand guests from locking out access for others.

Providing more incoming bandwidth is relatively easy, both through buying more from the principal communications provider and through implementing connections from multiple providers—T-3 and DSL phone lines, cable service, even streaming wireless. These provide security against total loss of access through failure of a single source, and competition between the vendors prevents monopoly pricing. Further, installing load balancing equipment at the property can automatically spread peak demands across multiple channels, making more efficient use of each.

Load balancers also address the management of individual guests' usage, making sure each has an appropriate level of service by detecting which rooms have the highest demand and throttling back their bandwidth if it threatens to dominate the network. They can also switch bandwidth availability between guestroom usage in the evenings to public area and meeting/conference room usage during the day, so as to suit their differing peak demand periods.

Tiered Pricing. While the majority of hotels still provide free Internet access, demand continues to soar and the cost of doing so is becoming increasingly difficult to bear. The great majority of guests expect that free access will always be available, but more of them are beginning to accept that it is a limited resource and will slow down as more people take advantage of it.

Tiered pricing is thus becoming more acceptable: free if a guest just wants to check e-mail, but charged for if they want to watch streamed movies. Load-balancing equipment can provide tiered pricing, but more flexibility still needs to be built into it. Charging a guest at the high-bandwidth rate for an entire stay because that guest chose watch a movie on one evening may be profitable but is seen as unfriendly and poor service. It's preferable for each room to have free access as a baseline, but with a pop-up warning and the opportunity to pay if a high-bandwidth source is selected. Network controls should soon be able to provide this.

Some hotels have also attempted to control the number of devices that a guest can connect, since each adds to the load. This has added some technical complexity—each device must also be able to connect to access points both in the guestroom and in the public areas—and is also a guest-relationship challenge. With more guests carrying their own small "Mi-Fi" devices, where one laptop or phone can connect to the hotel service and re-broadcast to all other devices brought by the guest, this restriction is becoming very difficult to enforce. While some networks allow the hotel to detect such unauthorized "hot spots" and shut them down, doing so can quickly turn into a major public relations nightmare.

Eventually, I believe, Wi-Fi coverage will be universal enough, fast enough, and affordable enough to be effectively free, and then the issue will go away. But we're not there yet, so constant investment in Wi-Fi will be necessary for some years to come.

One inevitable consequence of the widespread choices available through the Internet has been the decline in guest usage of hotel-based pay-per-view movies. These are rapidly falling out of favor as offering too limited a selection and are no longer a requirement for many properties. More commonly, vendors offer bundled guestroom services that include Internet access, IPTV programming with its great variety of channels and ability to be customized to individual guests' preferences, and, sometimes, IP telephone service. If they do offer a selection of movies, their only advantage is in acquiring distribution rights to the hotel market for new-release movies before they're available via other channels.

Flat Panel Integration

Flat-panel displays are increasingly being integrated into more areas of the guest's stay than just showing movies and television channels. With an appropriate wireless keyboard, they are often suitable for general Internet access, and their connection to the hotel's internal network facilitates the guest being charged for this. They can also display the guest concierge service applications mentioned above for ordering room service, laundry pick-up, dining reservations, etc., as well as showing controls for the room's thermostat, lighting, drapes, and so on. Future uses being explored include a video display of the corridor outside the room, which would serve as a "video intercom" to replace the door peephole.

All of these functions can also be managed through other device screens in the guestroom. These can include a stand-alone wireless tablet, a dedicated concierge-style workstation, or even an IP telephone. There is much debate over how many screens a guestroom needs, given that the guest will very often also have a smartphone that can use the same service applications. The best answer will depend largely on the preferences of the predominant guest market segment at the property. For example, at a family-oriented property where the children may monopolize the television as a game display, it's convenient for the parents to have an alternative means of checking dinner reservations or booking the next day's activities. In any case, a large flat-panel television/Internet display and fast, reliable Internet access are essential in virtually every guestroom.

VoIP Telephones

VoIP technology has definitely proven itself and is now the basic telephone platform for all new and retrofit installations, especially as installation and support can be handled by existing network and PC maintenance staff instead of telephony specialists. However, IP telephones themselves are still relatively uncommon in guestrooms because VoIP's advantages in general commercial use (ease of programming, transportability to different locations, etc.) simply don't apply to guestroom usage. Thus, a property's existing analog instruments continue to work well with most VoIP systems.

Furthermore, IP phones are often equipped with large-screen displays and extra functions that increase their cost without significant benefit in a guestroom. If there's no need for a display, conventional-appearance IP phones cost much the same as traditional analog phones and will become the default for new-build properties.

IP telephony itself is becoming more common as an outsourced, remotely hosted service, with the operators and system itself off-property. This is often a viable option if a hotel's traditional telephone switch needs to be replaced.

Energy Management

As energy costs continue to increase, guestroom energy management pays noticeable dividends. This typically comprises an intelligent thermostat communicating with the guestroom door, an occupancy sensor, and the guest management system. When the door is opened, the sensor checks for movement or infrared emissions from a person; if none, indicating that the room is now empty, the thermostat is set back a few degrees. It automatically kicks back up when someone enters the room. The more sophisticated ones have two levels of set-back: one for when the room is rented to a guest, changing to a more significant one when the guest checks out.

A new technique being tried with good results involves monitoring the carbon dioxide levels in the room. The temperature and air flow are then adjusted as needed to maximize both guest comfort and energy efficiency.

Implementation has become simpler over the years as wireless links (especially Zigbee-based) have replaced wired or infrared transmissions between the various components. Recent developments have also produced very efficient self-powered devices, such as door sensors that generate small amounts of energy from the door movement itself and ceiling-mounted occupancy sensors powered by photo cells sensitive enough to run on the light of a television display. These reduce the implementation cost and maintenance of the controls significantly.

Door Locks

Magnetic-stripe keycards dominate the industry as a secure, relatively inexpensive approach, but are beginning to be replaced by radio frequency identification (RFID) cards. These have the dual advantages of being easier to use because they only have to be brought into close proximity to the door lock's sensor to unlock it, while also increasing lock reliability, since these are sealed and not subject to contamination from, for example, a guest's sunscreen-and-sand-covered mag-stripe card.

Traditionally keycards have been used in stand-alone mode, which means that each card carries not only the code applicable to that door for the duration of the guest's stay but also the next code that will be assigned to that room for the next guest. The advent of more widespread and affordable wireless links makes it increasingly practical to have the door locks communicate with a central control unit. This has the dual benefit of alerting the security office if door entry is attempted with an incorrect key, while also allowing a guest's code to be transferred to a different room to enable a room move without the need to return to the front desk for a new key.

RFID door locks are also compatible with mobile telephones equipped with near-field communications (NFC), a useful hedge against the future. NFC is another short-range proximity communications approach, used more in Europe and Asia than in the United States to date, that allows phones to be used, for example, to pay for goods at vending machines and in stores. In hotel use, a pre-arrival message would be sent to the guest's phone, which would then transmit the door code to the lock when placed close to it. Although requiring the extra step of pre-loading an application (which may be different for different hotel chains) onto the phone, this approach allows guests to go straight to their rooms upon arrival without needing to stop at the front desk for a key.

A similar front-desk-bypass approach applicable to every type of mobile phone is being tried by OpenWays. Instead of an NFC-coded transmission, the message sent to the phone is a coded series of audio tones replayed over the phone's normal earpiece speaker to a receiver in the door lock. While potentially interesting, this approach requires hotels to equip all door locks with acoustic couplers and to ensure that consistent, reliable cell phone coverage is available outside every guestroom door so that the coded signal can be received by the phone on demand. Several hotels are testing this currently, but it's too early to tell whether it will gain widespread popularity. Much will depend on whether demand for cell phone coverage inside hotel buildings grows to the point where most hotels will provide it.

Despite these last caveats, the trend is definitely toward some form of phone-based door lock. Hilton has committed to introducing this capability chain-wide and Starwood is experimenting with it at some brands. Bluetooth Low Energy (BLE) is the preferred technology for these early installations, but this is a rapidly evolving area and things may well change as implementations are refined. In particular, there are some reservations about the security of BLE transmissions, as well as liability concerns about using a device not owned by the hotel to provide access to guestrooms. Even then, the door locks will also need to handle either mag-stripe or RFID cards for guests who prefer not to use their phones or who don't have one.

Audiovisual Meeting Technologies

With a general move away from annual large national presentation-style meetings to more frequent, smaller, regional collaborative-style meetings, there's been a corresponding trend toward maximizing their effectiveness through technology. Video conferencing technology has become more widespread and affordable, but still does not seem to be decreasing the number of meetings being held, as was feared a few years ago. Instead, video-conferencing and other advanced hotel-based systems are being added to on-site meetings to get the maximum value out of them. Examples include:

- *Virtuality/Simulations*: Multiple small workgroups are led through a series of experiences to enhance their decision-making skills in competition with each other, with their decisions and results compiled and later analyzed centrally for everyone's benefit.
- *Video Teleconferencing*: Provides two-way audio and video, mostly for smaller groups of twelve or fewer.
- *Webcasting*: Uses the hotel's high-speed Internet access to broadcast events on the Internet, either real-time or later, such that remote participants can browse into the event, watch and listen to the presenter, and view the presentation materials.
- *Webconferencing*: Allows participants to interact with the presented materials (document sharing), and if necessary the application itself (application sharing).
- *Digital Events*: This is the generic term covering meetings that include any or all of the above, plus audio and video conferencing, web newsletter input from Listserv distributors, feeds from blogs, RSS news updates, etc. Digital audio/visual input/output is fast becoming an essential and integral part of business life, and providing a flexible, powerful infrastructure to meet clients' needs is the way to attract their business.

Technologically, the move from analog to digital A/V equipment has only become stronger as prices for the latter have fallen. Digital signal processing greatly simplifies systems through combining the functions of several previously separate components into one unit. Additionally, it provides far more flexibility and control over the signal processing, requires less rack space and air-conditioning, and takes less labor to install. The systems themselves are becoming more intelligent and communicative with one another, which allows for more interconnectivity and integration with telecommunications services, including the Internet.

However, in contrast to hotel management systems, this has led to increased competition among manufacturers who were once collaborators, and a counter-intuitive trend away from standards-based communications protocols. While the industry has reluctantly accepted standards for communications, manufacturers are competing to maximize the performance of their equipment at the cost of standards compatibility. This can cause problems if A/V equipment is hooked up to the same network as other hotel systems and can make it very difficult to make substitutions of equipment on the fly.

This in turn is causing challenges in the specifying and contracting world, where each party has its own "right" way of designing the systems. Installation and support will be easier if a complete system is acquired from a single vendor, but this usually restricts the ability of the hotel to make any changes or enhancements without going back to the vendor.

Electronic signage is fast expanding in the hospitality arena as well. Visual information systems (VIS) or electronic reader boards located in public assembly areas serve several functions, primarily to provide information on the location and times of the meetings and activities, but also for the hotel to promote such amenities as golf, spas, gift shops, and the food and beverage outlets.

Public area displays are typically flat panels, often with door-side alphanumeric or LCD displays adjacent to each meeting room entry. These messaging systems can also be integrated with the PMS and S&C systems to distribute meeting information to the appropriate guestrooms. Future developments being explored include picking up signals from a guest's RFID room card or NFC smartphone, then customizing the display to show only those events relevant to his or her conference.

As for the infrastructure in the meeting rooms—the power, telecom and Internet services, cabling, and connectivity—standard practice is to install multiple bundles of Category 5e cabling tie lines to all function spaces, with fiber to the larger rooms. All lines are brought back to patch panels in the A/V room so any connector can be assigned any service in any room at any time.

It is also important to provide wired high-speed Internet services, in addition to the ubiquitous Wi-Fi. All presentation or meeting functions that are Internet-based must be wired; wireless is still a security concern, and many corporate clients and government agencies do not permit it in their meetings.

This cabling infrastructure must be able to provide telephone services as well. Corporate LANs can be securely accessed via dial-up switched services. The current best practice for video teleconferences is often still via switched-services such as ISDN and T1 lines.

It's critical to start with the right foundation of good architecture, interior design, and infrastructure; even the best technology can't fix a meeting space that is noisy, dim, or poorly designed. For all the possibilities for digital audiovisual systems, quality meetings start with a high-quality sound system (for voice) based on an array of ceiling speakers. All meetings need voice reinforcement, and there is no better way to provide high intelligibility in the typical flexible function space than this approach.

Other Areas

Virtually every area of a hotel requires some form of technology for most efficient operations. In addition to the above areas, the most obvious need is for a good accounting system. This does not necessarily have to be one developed specifically for the hospitality vertical. Many properties use standard accounting packages that include QuickBooks, SAP, Sage 100, and Microsoft's Dynamics Great Plains or NAV. Most GMSs include an accounts receivable module, too, so that accounting packages really only need general ledger and accounts payable functionality, and all can export a daily journal file of the day's activities for accounting to audit and import into the general ledger.

Purchasing departments can also be helped by automation. Those benefits include streamlining the requisitioning of goods and supplies from the storeroom to the kitchen(s) and outlets and providing strong controls over both the purchasing process and inventory management. Most will track multiple bids from vendors for key items and will automatically generate draft item reorders when on-hand inventory drops below a preset level.

All retail and F&B outlets need some form of POS system and cash register with at a minimum the ability to post a charge to a guest's room or a member's account. Better systems have GMS interfaces that allow front desk staff to access the line item details of any particular POS check, which is especially valuable in helping to resolve guests' challenges to charges on their folios. Retail systems need to be able to handle color/size matrices for clothing items and generate bar code labels upon the receipt of goods. F&B systems need great flexibility in menu item ordering and modification, as well as in combining and splitting orders and checks. POS systems of both types often need to be able to handle quite complex gratuities and service charge splits between various staff members.

Spa, golf, tennis, and other activity management systems need very complex and flexible booking functionality, so as to be able to handle the availability of suitably qualified staff, the facility being used, and the possibility of multiple guests being booked to the same activity at the same time. They typically include retail POS modules, which need to be integrated into the overall purchasing operation.

Sales and catering systems, which manage group bookings and banqueting events, need to include full sales management operations from initial contact through follow-ups, proposal generation, and contracts. They must allow for the booking at fifteen-minute intervals of multiple rooms combinable into multiple different configurations. They must also be able to generate banquet event orders that cover all details of the event set-up, F&B menus, audiovisual requirements, floor and table decorations, and so on.

Engineering systems cover scheduled preventive maintenance tasks for all service items on property, as well as ad hoc work orders generated for such guestroom problems as faulty lamps, leaking toilets, etc. They often also have their own inventory/purchasing functionality to maintain dedicated engineering storerooms.

Time and attendance systems record staff working hours, often using biometric techniques such as hand-shape profiling to ensure accuracy. The recorded hours are audited and sent to a payroll system or service, ideally linked to an HR system for proper tracking of benefits. Workforce management and scheduling systems are becoming one of the fastest-payback applications, allowing the precise customization of staffing levels to forecast traffic.

Putting It All Together

As beneficial as each of these systems is to each area, they really come into their own and improve the overall efficiency of the operation only when they are integrated together. For example:

- POS systems link to purchasing, automatically decrementing on-hand inventory by the amount of each sale and uploading the latest prices based on the cost of goods received.
- Purchasing systems integrate with accounts payable modules to synchronize vendor profiles and allow for electronic payment of invoices.
- S&C systems link to GMSs to coordinate the sale of guestrooms along with the function space and to consolidate individual delegate spending with billing for the group's function. They can also link to the purchasing system for proper costing of banquet menus.
- Guest-request systems can link to engineering applications, such that a guest's on-line request to fix a leaky toilet automatically generates an engineering work order and transmits it to the appropriate person, escalating it to a manager if it is not corrected within a pre-set time. A link to a GMS alerts the front desk staff that the guest has had a problem so that they can make sure it was corrected appropriately before the guest checks out. It can also place a marker on the guest profile that will automatically generate a work order a few days before the guest's next visit to make sure the same problem doesn't happen again. And if the problem is billable to the owner of a condominium unit, it can be charged to the owner's account automatically when the work order is closed.
- Labor forecasting and management systems tie in to GMS and S&C systems to predict demand, as well as to HR and time and attendance systems to schedule staff of the appropriate skill sets in the most efficient manner.
- And so on.

As should be clear by now, technology is essential to the effective operation of every department in a hotel, but no department operates alone. Implementing a stand-alone system for a single department may improve that department's operations, but it will shift any processing bottlenecks to other areas, which will operate less efficiently as a result. The essential approach is to look at the entire property as a single whole, identify challenges and opportunities, and then develop an overall technology plan to optimize the competitiveness and profitability of the entire operation.

This doesn't mean that everything must be done at once. However, it is critical to have a road map to track which areas will be upgraded at what times and what temporary interfaces will be needed until the end of the project. It may—and probably will—also mean that some departments may not get the absolute "best" system they want for their specific needs, but that sacrifice is worthwhile if it benefits the overall property. To optimize the whole, it is usually necessary to sub-optimize at least some of the parts. But optimize the whole you must, or lose ground to your competitors.

General Considerations for Asset Managers

As with all other areas of hotel operations, managing the funds available for technology is a constant balancing act. Different owners have different approaches. Some really understand the benefits well-integrated technology can bring to the operation and its efficiency and are willing to invest in it accordingly. Others see it as a lower priority to be updated only when absolutely necessary.

If the property operates under a brand's flag, of course, the brand's technology standards and initiatives play a very significant role and must be included in the budget. All such projects must be scrutinized for their impact on costs and operations, as well as for their effect on other systems and technology on-premises; as mentioned above, few systems operate in isolation any more. This situation has improved over the last few years, however. It was once common for new initiatives to be dropped on the hotels with little notice and certainly before the previous one could be amortized, but most brands are now much better at providing advance notice and cost estimates for their initiatives. There is also much more awareness of the legal issues surrounding technology, which has led to more willingness to pay for software user licenses and not use unlicensed copies.

Where possible, regular involvement with a brand's technology standards committee will pay significant dividends. For example, an asset manager may be able to have some influence on the direction and timing of such initiatives, while also providing more context and advice to the owners. In cases of hardship, it may be necessary to ask the brand for delayed implementation; when doing so, the more contacts that have been cultivated, the more influence can be brought to bear. In the end, however, the management contract will prevail, of course.

Keeping in touch with key vendors and their development programs is also valuable, not only in providing advance warning of likely developments but also in building a wider awareness of industry trends and system interactions. Hotel asset managers don't always get good advice from their vendors, who not unnaturally tend to take a very parochial view of what constitutes a priority for the property and frequently minimize their impact on related systems. Franchise brands are often equally optimistic in making revenue projections based on out-of-date or unrealistic assumptions, so they frequently provide budget estimates too late in the year to be included in a property's standard budget timetable.

Developing a wider general knowledge through contacts with multiple vendors, reading industry publications, and attending trade shows helps build a position of greater knowledge and negotiating strength. It also facilitates the preparation of a budget that allows for the inclusion of technology upgrades that are highly likely to be needed in the next year, even if they haven't been specifically identified by the brand.

A major challenge comes from the very rapid developments in consumer technology and consequently in guest expectations. The explosive growth in demand for Wi-Fi connectivity and adequate bandwidth continues to catch many hotels by surprise, just as the demand for flat-panel television displays did a few years back. It's not always possible to budget for regular technology upgrades because it's not always clear where the money will need to be spent, but it is certain that investments will need to be made in some area of technology every year.

The best that can be done is to budget for the most likely areas, make sure the overall budget includes a contingency fund, schedule formal mid-year budget reviews to see what's changed in the last six months from both the business and technology standpoints, and be prepared to be flexible in switching funds between budgets as needed.

Other Sources of Hotel Technology Information

Information can be gathered from a variety of resources. Some trade magazines focus exclusively on technology, such as *Hospitality Upgrade* and *Hospitality Technology*. The more general publications such as *Hotel & Motel Management, Hotels, Lodging, Lodging Hospitality,* etc., all have sections that cover technology developments and issues, and a number of electronic newsletters provide valuable regular updates—*Hotel-Online, HospitalityNet, HotelInteractive,* and others. The AH&LA's Technology Advisory Committee publishes a series of primer booklets as introductory guidelines on hotel technology, which give a good grounding in the fundamentals.

The most comprehensive and useful annual trade show is HITEC, sponsored each June by HFTP and focusing exclusively on all aspects of hospitality technology. Other valuable events include HTNG's annual conference, which covers developments in system integration and has developed a reputation for thought-leadership education sessions, and the Hospitality Technology Forum, sponsored each March/April in Las Vegas by *Hospitality Technology* magazine. The IHM&RS exhibition, held each November in New York, also incorporates a technology section within its "total hotel" coverage of equipment, services and supplies.

Consultants can also provide valuable independent advice, along with help in technology selection and implementation. If using their services, be sure to select carefully, checking references and distinguishing between generalists and specialists to ensure the most appropriate match of approach and experience for your needs.

Case Study

A 400-room city center property with significant convention business had been struggling with older guest Internet access for some years, but had considered the relatively low level of complaints to be tolerable. However, the combination of a large group being in-house shortly after Apple released new versions of both the iPad and the iPhone led to a steep rise in adverse comments.

The unusually high peak demand for access, coupled with the newer devices' greater capabilities and weaker antennae, caused many access points to overload and dead spots to occur in coverage that had previously been adequate, if marginal. This led to many more guest complaints that the bandwidth was too slow or that they couldn't connect at all. A wider survey of social network comments across multiple sites confirmed that even more guests had been venting in public than had complained to the management; it also brought to light that the user interface to connect to the Internet was clunky and hard to use.

When a couple of group bookings were cancelled with direct reference to the problem, and with transient traffic also being affected, the ownership was faced with no choice but to implement a mid-year upgrade. Two vendors were brought in and carried out their own surveys and assessments, but came up with noticeably different recommendations. Consequently, an independent third-party communications firm was hired to conduct its own survey. It recommended a phased approach that replaced the existing access points with newer models that were more amenable to future upgrading. They also allowed for mesh network extensions to broaden coverage more easily as needed in the future. The final proposal also included a reworking of the guest sign-in process for Internet access to make it more intuitive and faster.

None of this came cheaply, of course, but the direct impact on business made it essential. Some funds were allocated from the contingency account, but the majority had to be found by postponing other projects slated for that year. After much debate between the various operating departments affected, some guestroom renovation was cut back in scope and lobby refurbishment postponed for one more year.

Endnotes

1. PCI is shorthand for the regulations covering the security of data involved in handling credit card charges. Note that a computer system cannot be PCI-certified, only an operation can. To be PCI-certified, an organization must comply with requirements concerning the physical security of the data network, the handling of sensitive data documents, etc. Nevertheless, systems can (and should) be certified and the use of such systems is necessary for PCI compliance. Payment Alliance Data Security Standards are a set of requirements issued by the payment card companies to systems vendors covering such things as credit card number encryption, password management, user access security controls, etc. Use of PA/DSS systems is necessary for PCI compliance.

2. Hotel Technology Next Generation is a hotel-sponsored initiative to encourage and support vendors in developing powerful, flexible XML-based interfaces and integrated sets of systems that hotels will buy. XML (extended mark-up language) is used to create self-describing messages ("here's a guest name, here are its properties and how it can be used," "here's a room number," etc.) that allow for very flexible interface messages.

3. OpenTravel is a travel industry group defining standard guest/traveler profiles and data exchange messages between the airline, car rental, and hotel industries. Formerly called OTA for OpenTravel Alliance, it changed its name to OpenTravel to avoid confusion with online travel agencies (OTAs).

Part III

Contracts and the Legal Aspects of Asset Management

11

Hotel Management Agreement Structures

By Jan A. deRoos

***Jan A. deRoos** is the HVS International Professor of Hotel Finance and Real Estate at Cornell University's School of Hotel Administration. He has been on the faculty of the hotel school since 1988 and has devoted his career to hospitality real estate, with a focus on the valuation, financing, development, and operation of lodging, timeshare, and restaurant assets. He holds B.S., M.S., and Ph.D. degrees from Cornell University, all with majors in Hotel Administration. His areas of teaching expertise span the entire range of hospitality real estate topics: property valuation, hospitality asset management, investment analysis and capital structure, hotel/resort planning and design, hotel/resort development and construction, and timeshare/vacation ownership.*

An expert and frequent speaker on these topics, Mr. deRoos continues to contribute to lodging industry conferences around the world and provides litigation support services to hospitality clients. Mr. deRoos's current research is focused on three themes: the design and implementation of hotel management contracts and hotel leases, investment returns to lodging properties, and supply/demand dynamics of lodging markets. He has developed two software tools to support the feasibility analysis of hospitality property: Hospitality Valuation Software, which was co-developed with Mr. Stephen Rushmore of HVS International, and a second proprietary tool called Timeshare Valuation Models.

Prior to his teaching career at Cornell, Mr. deRoos worked extensively in the hospitality industry. His industry experience includes work for the Sheraton Corporation in New York City as an engineering professional. He also worked for Remington Hotel Corporation as Director of Engineering, responsible for the engineering operations and renovation planning of the firm's owned and managed hotel portfolio, and as Senior Project Manager, responsible for the construction of new properties and the renovation of existing hotels. During this period, Mr. deRoos was responsible for the construction of Marriott Hotels, Hilton Hotels, and Hampton Inns.

"AT NO POINT IN RECENT HISTORY have so many forms of management agreements been in use or so many different balances been struck between owners and management companies in their operating relationships."[1] The corresponding chapter in the second edition of this book started with this quotation, which still rings true. In fact, the playing field for hotel management agreements (HMAs) has become more complex since that chapter was written. The continued growth of the hotel industry around the world has solidified the use of the HMA as a means for owners of hotels to obtain the services of professional managers and well-recognized brands. In this chapter, we provide an assessment of the major trends influencing new agreements and their impact on existing agreements, give a perspective on how HMA practice differs (or does not) in North America, Europe, and the Asia Pacific regions, focus on how specific clauses in HMAs are used to meet owner and manager objectives, and end with a primer for owners desiring a process for negotiating the HMA. This chapter has benefited greatly from the recent "HVS Hotel Management Contract Survey"[2] and numerous conversations and e-mail exchanges with owners, managers, and lawyers. I am indebted to them all for their time and expertise.

Major Trends Shaping Hotel Management Agreements

Hotel management agreements were born out of a desire for owners of hotels to obtain the services of professional managers and an affiliation with a brand that has meaning with customers. The continued embrace of the HMA by both owners and managers is a testament to the strength of these agreements as a business relationship and their ability to create value for both sides. The playing field is not static, however, and there are several factors that are major influences on the way HMAs are negotiated and used. We will look at four.

Post-Recession Post-Mortem

The recent Great Recession has provided a test of HMAs, as no downturn in recent memory has created the widespread financial distress witnessed within the industry. With this distress came the inevitable strains on the relationships between owners and managers as well as the legal foundations on which these agreements are built. One of the most striking lessons of the Great Recession is that owners are not hesitant to terminate agreements when they feel it is in their best interests, even if the agreement does not provide that right. Here is a list of recent examples of hotels with pending or completed HMA terminations:

- The Paris Hilton Hotel is now L'Hotel du Collectionneur Arc de Triomphe as of August 2012. A French commercial court found in favor of owner SIHPM in ending the HMA.
- The Eden Roc Renaissance Miami Beach is now the Eden Roc Hotel, Miami Beach, as of July 2013. Litigation to terminate the HMA resulted in a change of management. Renaissance has pending litigation for damages resulting from the termination.
- The Shelbourne Dublin, A Renaissance Hotel: Litigation to terminate the HMA was initiated in 2008 and resolved in 2010.
- The Edition Waikiki is now the Modern Honolulu, as of September 2011.
- The Four Seasons Aviara is now the Park Hyatt Aviara. Four Seasons management was removed from the hotel in 2009, and the matter was settled via arbitration in 2011.
- The Fairmont Turnberry is the Turnberry Isle, an Autograph Collection Hotel, as of August 2011.

- The Hyatt Regency in Dearborn, Michigan, is the subject of an HMA termination. On January 22, 2014, owner Royal Realties served a thirty-day notice to terminate the management agreement of Atmosphere Hospitality. The matter is currently under litigation.
- The Setai Miami Beach is under new management as of March 31, 2012. An international arbitration panel found in favor of the former manager and awarded damages on July 13, 2014.

It is important to note that these terminations were not free of cost to the owners, as in several cases courts or arbitration panels awarded significant sums to the former managers.[3] However, in spite of the threat of significant damage awards, owners have been uniformly successful in removing managers via their unilateral termination of the HMA. With managers having been unsuccessful in maintaining their control over hotels, the fight has shifted to the damages suffered by the manager.

The Eden Roc hotel mentioned above has solidified the view that the relationship and duties of the manager and owner continue to be defined by the courts, not the agreements themselves. Citing a decision in the *Marriott International v. Eden Roc* case in their recent handbook, lawyers Jim Butler and Bob Braun argue that "... virtually all hotel management agreements are now terminable at will by owners. And this result will prevail even against ... management agreements that seek to avoid an 'agency' characterization of the owner-operator agreement."[4] This does not mean that owners can unilaterally terminate HMAs without consequence; while this decision may provide owners with the *power* to terminate the HMA, the *right* to terminate remains in force and owners are potentially liable for significant damages if it is found that a terminated manager did not breach the agreement. This important decision will undoubtedly reverberate for several years, but the bottom line is that the courts have shown a willingness to make decisions that contravene specific language in agreements if that language contradicts long-established legal principles of agency and the resulting fiduciary duties that accompany agency. In turn, owners have become increasingly aware of their options regarding their relationships with their managers.

Shorter Agreements Are the Norm

Hotel management agreements appear to becoming shorter, at least for the initial term of the agreement. This trend is most striking in the United States, as we will see in the next section of this chapter. Reasons for the shorter terms include:

- Increased competition among managers for a limited number of new hotels in relatively slow-growing markets.
- A shift away from branded managers to franchised hotels being managed by independent managers.
- An increase in the number of non-branded hotels managed by independent managers.
- A desire by owners to have the option to cancel the HMA at the end of each term, generally subject to a performance termination clause.

- A desire by branded managers to have the option to cancel the HMA at the end of each term, especially in rapidly growing markets. This gives the manager the option to associate their brand with a bigger or better hotel.

We see these factors continuing to be in force in the near future. This trend does not mean that the total term of the agreement, including renewals, is getting shorter. In fact, there is some evidence that the length of agreements, especially agreements with branded managers, is getting longer. However, both sides of the agreement have reasons to break agreements into shorter terms and to negotiate very specific language for termination and continuation rights at the end of each term.

For independent (non-branded) managers, the shorter terms are clearly the product of two factors. First, a relatively large number of very short-term agreements arose from bankruptcies, foreclosures, and other changes of ownership as a result of the recent recession. New owners, especially banks, are reluctant to sign long-term agreements that might inhibit the sale of a property. With the branded managers insisting on relatively long-term agreements, these so-called "distressed" situations have become the domain of the independent managers. Second, independent managers are in a much weaker negotiating position than are branded managers, and the owner's option to have the right to terminate (in addition to the power to terminate) at the end of the agreement term is a compelling option. One mitigating factor is the use of "key money" by independent managers, which is clearly tied to longer terms, sometimes significantly so.

Increased Conversation About Key Money

Paraphrasing a comment by the senior counsel of a major hotel brand gives the key money discussion some context. "Our policy is that we do not use key money," he stated, "but when we do, it looks like this." Key money is best understood as an up-front rebate of management fees in exchange for language that makes HMAs more favorable to managers. Owners often characterize key money as a way to "align the interests" of the owner and manager by asking the manager to "invest" in the hotel. Nothing could be further from the truth. Key money agreements almost universally provide no return for the manager; they simply are a way of providing working capital to the owner. In addition, most key money agreements provide for a return of the unamortized key money if the agreement is terminated before the end of the initial term, regardless of the circumstances. Key money is found in a minority of agreements but the idea is intriguing to owners who see a potential source of capital that can offset their equity investment.

When considering key money, owners should keep the following points in mind:

- Key money is almost universally structured so that it is not an equity investment in the hotel or venture. The reason is that owners are reluctant to place the manager in the position of being both the manager and the owner's partner. If the manager is also the owner's partner, it changes the relationship in meaningful ways, especially with regard to the ability to terminate the HMA.

- Key money is "sliver capital"; it is rarely more than 5 percent of the total capital in a given hotel investment and is often a fraction of that. Remember, managers are rebating their fees in order to obtain the HMA and to obtain a more favorable HMA; they are not likely to rebate a significant portion of their fees.
- Key money is not free money; it comes with conditions.
    - Many managers insist that the agreement is non-terminable for any reason during the initial term if key money is provided. Failing that, almost all key money agreements provide for a return of the key money (or its unamortized portion) should the agreement be terminated for any reason during the initial term.
    - Many managers insist on longer terms if key money is provided.
    - Many managers insist on market or above market fees if key money is provided, especially if the owner appears to be capital constrained.
    - Key money rarely (meaning almost never) is provided until the hotel is open and the manager is actively operating the hotel (i.e., it is the last money in).

While key money can be a seductive concept, owners are well advised to carefully consider its use and how it can transform the relationship between the parties.

Franchising as an Alternative to the HMA with a Branded Manager

Although it is hard to imagine that HMAs with branded managers will be replaced by a franchising/independent manager model, it is clear that the use of the franchise to obtain brand services coupled with the services of an independent manager is on the rise. One of the clearest indicators of this trend is in co-located facilities in which more than one hotel occupies a single site with more than one brand represented in large convention-oriented hotels. In Chicago, White Lodging operates a property with a total of 664 keys, including an Aloft, a Fairfield Inn & Suites, and a Hyatt Place, all operated under franchise. This same firm operates the 1005-room JW Marriott Indianapolis and the 1012-room JW Marriott Austin; hotels of this scale and complexity historically had been operated by a branded manager, but this is changing rapidly, with many independent managers operating hotels with room counts in excess of 750 rooms. In such cases, the brands provide their brand services under a franchise agreement and obtain a royalty fee in lieu of a management fee. Owners prefer the franchising/independent manager model as they claim to be able to negotiate a better agreement with an independent manager than with a branded manager.

One area resisting this trend is luxury hotels; the hotel brands almost universally offer their luxury tier brands only via a company-managed model. This is undoubtedly due to the ability of the brand to have a higher level of control over the brand offering and its consistency around the world. It is hard to make the case that a hotel company obtains a higher fee from management than from franchising with most brands charging a royalty fee roughly equivalent to the total management fee for the same property.

Global Hotel Management Practice

In this section, we will discuss the "Global HMA Term Sheet"; the major clauses of HMAs will be discussed from a global perspective with commentary about how they differ in the United States from Europe and the Asia-Pacific region. The work relies heavily on the recent "HVS Hotel Management Contract Survey" previously mentioned and cited (the HVS Survey); interested readers should obtain the full report from HVS. Let us start with the understanding that there is no truly global HMA term sheet; legal systems, labor laws, and property rights differ widely around the world and a hotel management agreement must be drafted within the structure of the laws of the country where the hotel is located and the jurisdiction chosen by both parties for the settlement of any disputes. However, as we will see, there is a convergence within the industry on the major clauses and their operation. This section continues by listing the major negotiating points of an HMA, providing a brief overview, and then discussing global practice. To avoid having to constantly reference the HVS Survey, note that all figures stated in this section come from the HVS Survey unless stated otherwise. In addition, we will use the acronym APAC when referring to the Asia-Pacific region.

The fundamental story is that management agreements in the United States are better for owners than they are elsewhere. This is due to the long history of HMA use in the United States and a full understanding of their operation by owners, the legal community, and asset managers. European practice has transitioned from a very fragmented owner-operator model to a financial owner model over the past twenty years, while the growth of the lodging industry in Asia has brought a number of new hotel owners into the business, many of whom, while familiar with the real estate business, are not skilled in their understanding of HMAs. These factors have given managers an advantage in negotiations that is clear in the data.

Manager's Financial Contribution

As mentioned earlier in this chapter, the manager's decision to provide key money to the owner has generated substantial interest but is found in a minority of agreements. Ten percent of global agreements have key money: 15 percent in the United States, 9 percent in Europe, and 5 percent in APAC. Interestingly, nearly half the agreements with key money in the HVS Survey were signed before 2005, indicating that key money is not a new phenomenon. Key money agreements generally have a so-called "claw-back" provision that would make the key money refundable (either in whole or a share corresponding to the remaining term) if the agreement is terminated for any reason before the end of the initial contract term. Owners should be aware that key money puts managers in a much better position to negotiate a longer term with unilateral termination rights in favor of the owner, a better performance termination clause, and a better management fee structure.

No discussion of key money would be complete without a passing mention of two alternatives to key money when owners seek a manager's financial contribution. The first is a mezzanine loan from the manager to the owner; the second is a cash flow guarantee from the manager. When the owner seeks a significant amount of capital from the manager, there are two fundamental alternatives: debt and equity. Equity is rarely used due to the position of the manager as partner. As for debt, senior (mortgage) debt is rarely used due to the size of the request—senior debt is often 50 to 70 percent of the capital structure. The manager's position is that an investment of that scale is an alternative to owning the hotel; in most cases, the manager would simply prefer to own the hotel and have control over its destiny than be put in the position of lender and manager. Thus, the alternative of a mezzanine is considered by some managers. Mezzanine loans are generally 10 to 25 percent of the capital structure, require a rate of return higher than debt capital but lower than equity capital, and are generally secured by the right to foreclose on the owner's equity interest in the hotel in the event of a default.

Cash flow guarantees are an attractive alternative to key money for managers. Conceptually, a cash flow guarantee can be thought of as contingent key money; that is, the funds are provided only if the hotel does not meet certain levels of operating performance. In addition, cash flow guarantees are often subject to significantly stronger claw-back provisions when the hotel's performance improves. The general outline of a cash flow guarantee takes the following form: there is a maximum guarantee amount over a defined period of years, typically the early years of the agreement; there is a cap on the annual guarantee amount; the cash flow to be guaranteed is carefully defined and is subject to *force majeure*; there is a provision for the return of funds provided under the guarantee, generally without interest, but before an owner's return. One reason for the owner and the manager to agree to a cash flow guarantee is to secure more favorable terms from senior lenders. The cash flow guarantee is seen as a form of credit enhancement for the lender and gives them an alternative source of funding should the property fail to produce its projected cash flow.

It is highly unlikely for owners to obtain more than one of the three types of contribution outlined above; owners must choose between them. The mere fact that an owner is asking for a contribution changes the dynamic in favor of the manager as it is generally a sign of weakness by the owner or the owner's hotel. This changed dynamic affects the negotiation of the remainder of the agreement. It is difficult to say which of the three changes the dynamic the most, as practice varies across the globe. In general, however, the manager is willing to provide the largest contribution via a mezzanine loan, the second largest with a cash flow guarantee, and the smallest contribution via key money.

Initial Term of the Agreement, Renewals, and Territorial Protection

The length of the agreement's initial term, the number of renewals, the length of each renewal, and who holds renewal options are major concerns to the owner and the manager. Long terms provide stability for both parties but decrease the owner's flexibility and can be a significant disadvantage to an owner who desires the right to unilaterally terminate the agreement, since the remaining term and renewal periods serve as a basis for a negotiated termination fee or a damage claim if the owner does not have the contractual right to terminate. A shorter term increases the flexibility of each party but is considered to be a major drawback for the manager, who wants to manage the property over an extended period of time in order to realize a return for the significant up-front costs and effort involved, and to maximize the value of the HMA. The project lender is often the party that determines the initial term to ensure that the HMA initial term is at least as long as the senior debt term.

The HVS Survey finds that the most common initial term across the three regions is twenty years. The overall initial term averages 18.3 years: 15.6 years in the United States, 21.1 years in Europe, and 18.3 years in APAC. Agreements in the United States signed before 2005 have terms that average five years longer than those signed after 2005, while pre-2005 HMAs in Europe average four years shorter than post-2005 HMAs. There is less than a year difference between pre- and post-2005 agreements in APAC. Interestingly, while the initial term is significantly shorter for hotels with fewer stars in the United States and APAC, it is virtually the same for all chain scales in Europe. For example, budget hotels in the United States have an average initial term of 9.9 years, while luxury hotels average 22.1 years; the corresponding figures for Europe are 20.0 years and 22.6 years.

Global practice on renewals is not uniform. Globally, 22 percent of agreements have no renewals or are silent on the matter, 56 percent have one or two renewals, and 22 percent have three or more renewals. The average length of renewals is 8.1 years. Agreements in the United States have more renewals for a shorter period: 20 percent have no renewals, 42 percent have one or two, and 38 percent have three or more, with the average renewal length being 6.6 years. HMA renewal numbers in Europe mirror the global numbers with the average length being ten years. HMA renewals in APAC tend to be fewer in number: 24 percent with none, 71 percent with one or two and 5 percent with three or more. The average length of APAC renewals is 8.2 years.

The HVS Survey provides interesting insight into the nature of the renewal option. For those agreements providing data, 50 percent renew automatically or upon mutual consent, 32 percent renew at the manager's option, with the remainder having another mechanism. Note, however, that 28 percent of the sample had no data on the nature of the renewal. Another point to note is that there is little to suggest that agreements renew solely at the owner's option; owners seeking to terminate the agreement find a mechanism in the performance termination clause.

Another notable aspect of the agreement is the manager's willingness to provide territorial protection to the owner. The global sample indicates that this is found in 46 percent of all agreements. Here global practice varies widely. Territorial protection is found in only 30 percent of agreements in the United States, 61 percent of HMAs in Europe, and 49 percent of HMAs in APAC. Hotels in higher chain scales tend to have this protection with greater frequency, for a larger radius, and for a longer period of time.

Management Fees

The HMA provides for a number of fees that fall into three general categories. We will discuss each in turn:

- *Pre-Opening Fees*: This set include a commitment fee (a rare occurrence), fees for technical services to advise the owner during the development phase, and fees for pre-opening services to prepare the hotel for operation.

- *Ongoing Management Fees*: These are fees paid to the manager for performing the duties enumerated in the HMA. This set generally includes a base fee based on gross hotel revenues and an incentive fee based on hotel profitability.
- *System Reimbursable Charges*: This set includes charges for guest reservations, system-wide advertising and marketing, loyalty programs, international, national, and regional sales offices, centralized reservation and distribution systems, centralized accounting and management information systems, centralized procurement services, and centralized educational and training programs.

Pre-Opening Fees. The commitment fee is found in less than 10 percent of agreements, generally for economy and midscale hotels. This fee is in the range of US$125 to US$250 per key. This type of fee is generally associated with a franchise license, not an HMA. The technical services fee is associated with the development of new hotels or the conversion of a hotel from one brand to another. Managers generally bundle this fee with pre-opening fees, which compensate the manager for preparing a new hotel for operation and include funds for training, marketing, provisioning, and setting up management systems at the hotel. Agreements for technical services and pre-opening are distinct from the HMA and are negotiated separately. For the lower chain scales, these fees range from US$25,000 to US$200,000, while for the higher chain scales these fees range from US$50,000 to US$500,000. The high end of the range is associated with luxury hotels, which by definition have a significantly more customized physical and service product. In some cases, fees are charged by the manager for major renovations at the hotel during the term of the HMA. These fees are generally in the range of 3 to 8 percent of the total cost of the work; the low end of the range is used for large, construction intensive work, while the high end of the range is used for work that is primarily removal and replacement of interior furnishings and equipment. These fees are consistent across the globe.

Ongoing Management Fees. As stated above, the management fee is (almost) universally broken into a base fee and an incentive fee. Outside the United States, some managers break the base fee into an operating fee and a royalty/licensing fee, as licensing fees are taxed at a lower rate than operating fees; however, the total base fee remains within the figures cited here. In addition, for distressed situations in which hotels have little revenue or hope of profit, the manager may be paid a flat fee on a monthly basis to manage the hotel. For new hotels, the basic fee may be discounted in the early years of the agreement.

The HVS Survey shows the average base fee to be 2.65 percent of hotel revenues. This is consistent with other surveys, which have shown fees declining over the past twenty years. Base fees are highest in the United States at 3.58 percent of revenues, but this may be an artifact of the sample, which includes a number of extended-stay properties. When these are removed from the numbers, the base fee is 3.35 percent of revenues. In Europe, the base fee averages 2.09 percent, although this figure may be low because many of the agreements surveyed did not have information on the licensing fee. APAC base fees average 2.25 percent of total revenues, again lower than the global average. The reason is that many older Asian hotels have a "no base fee" agreement but a much higher-than-average incentive fee. It appears that this is changing rapidly, however, as APAC agreements signed after 2005 have a base fee of 2.37 percent versus 0.97 percent for pre-2005 agreements. Globally, there is little difference in the fee based on the size of the hotel. Lastly, there is strong evidence to suggest that managers are accepting lower base fees in exchange for higher incentive fees.

Incentive fee design is both art and science. The idea is to compensate the manager for driving hotel profitability by providing a larger share of profits as they grow. The industry has recently witnessed a shift in how incentive fees are earned and paid, shifting the definition deeper into the cash flow statement. In a nutshell, incentive fees were historically paid as a percentage of Gross Operating Profit or GOP.[5] In a major shift over the past two decades, incentives fees have been increasingly earned and paid after an owner's priority return. The owner's priority is an annual amount deducted from GOP to determine the incentive fee base. In the HVS Survey, 38 percent of agreements have an owner's priority. This percentage varies widely on a global basis, however: 58 percent of agreements in the United States, 45 percent of European agreements, and only 11 percent of APAC agreements have this arrangement. Thus, this is fundamentally a non-Asian phenomenon. The operation of this incentive fee structure is described in detail later in this chapter. Global incentive fee design is summarized as follows; the figures are given for, respectively, the global sample, the United States, Europe, and APAC.

- No incentive fee or no information provided—17 percent, 25 percent, 20 percent, 6 percent
- Incentive fee is a constant percent of GOP—28 percent, 10 percent, 30 percent, 45 percent
- Incentive fee is linked to GOP or Cash Flow performance—39 percent, 56 percent, 25 percent, 33 percent
- Other incentive fee designs—16 percent, 8 percent, 25 percent, 16 percent

For those agreements featuring linked incentive fees, the general trend is to link the fee to GOP expressed as a percent of total revenues (the GOP margin).[6] The HVS Survey indicates that this fee averages 5.4 percent of GOP if the margin is less than 30 percent and averages 8.72 percent if the GOP margin is above 50 percent, with the percentage rising as the margin improves. Anecdotally, they report that certain owners have been successful in negotiating an incentive fee of zero if the GOP margin fails to reach a certain level.

System Reimbursable Charges. In discharging their duties under the HMA, managers use centrally provided services developed and provided by the manager for the benefit of the entire chain or management company. The major categories were enumerated at the opening of this section. Owners new to the business are often surprised at the extent and the cost of these services. Below we summarize the major categories and their cost structure:

- Reservation Fees—these fees take several forms:
    - Fixed fee per room per month, in the range of US$25 to US$50.

  - Percentage of total revenue, in the range of 0.75 to 1.5 percent.
  - Percentage of rooms revenue, in the range of 1.0 to 1.5 percent.
  - Fixed fee per reservation, in the range of US$2.50 to US$10.00.
  - Some agreements provide for a reservation fee that is a combination of the above.

- Marketing Fees are generally charged as a fixed percentage of total revenue or a fixed percentage of rooms revenue. When based on total revenue, the fee is usually in the range of 1.0 to 2.5 percent with a few outside this range. When based on rooms revenue, the fee is usually in the range of 1.5 to 4.0 percent, again with a few outside this range.
  - This fee is found is 40 percent of agreements in the United States, 60 percent of European agreements, and 70 percent of APAC agreements.
- Training fees are found in a minority of agreements and are charged as an annual per employee fee or fee per available room. The range is US$150 to US$750 per employee per year, depending on seniority, or US$17 to US$48 per available room.[7]
- Loyalty program fees are identical for the same brand across the globe. They range from 2.75 to 6.0 percent of a loyalty member's total folio during the stay.
- Other fees that are found in the minority of agreements:
  - Technology and system support fees range from US$480 to US$920 per month.
  - Centralized accounting fees are in the range of US$1000 to US$3000 per month.
  - Purchasing fees for operating supplies are in the range of 5 to 10 percent of the total amounts purchased.

Performance Test and Termination for Non-Performance

A performance test is found in 64 percent of all HMAs in the HVS Survey, with virtually no variance across continents. We provide detail about the operation of this test later in the chapter. The operation of this test is based on several characteristics:

- The year the test commences is generally not the first year of the agreement, giving the manager time to stabilize the property.
  - Globally, only 22 percent of tests commence in the first year, 25 percent commence in year two or three, and 54 percent commence in the fourth year or beyond.
  - In the United States, 31 percent of tests commence in the first year, 31 percent commence in year two or three, and 38 percent commence in the fourth year or beyond.

  - In Europe, 16 percent of tests commence in the first year, 18 percent commence in year two or three, and 64 percent commence in the fourth year or beyond.
  - In APAC, 14 percent of tests commence in the first year, 27 percent commence in year three, and 59 percent commence in the fourth year or beyond. Interestingly, none of the APAC agreements have a test that begins in year two.
- The tests are generally based on a failure to meet budget, the failure to maintain RevPAR penetration, or some combination of the two.
  - Globally, 41 percent of agreements have a test that is either failure to meet budget, failure to maintain RevPAR penetration, or failure to meet either budget or RevPAR penetration (a particularly onerous test for managers). Requiring the manager to fail both the budget and RevPAR tests is found in 36 percent of agreements, while 23 percent have some other test.
  - In the United States, 28 percent of agreements have a test that is either failure to meet budget, failure to maintain RevPAR penetration, or failure to meet either budget or RevPAR penetration. Requiring the manager to fail both the budget and RevPAR tests is found in 43 percent of agreements, while 20 percent have some other test.
  - In Europe, 24 percent of agreements have a test that is either failure to meet budget, failure to maintain RevPAR penetration, or failure to meet either budget or RevPAR penetration. Requiring the manager to fail both the budget and RevPAR tests is found in 46 percent of agreements, while 30 percent have some other test.
  - In APAC, 74 percent of agreements have a test that is either failure to meet budget, failure to maintain RevPAR penetration, or failure to meet either budget or RevPAR penetration. Requiring the manager to fail both the budget and RevPAR tests is found in 18 percent of agreements, while 8 percent have some other test.
    - Thus it appears that the tests are most onerous for managers in APAC. Note that the failure to meet either test is found in only a minority of agreements, 6 percent globally; this percentage does not vary meaningfully across the globe.
- The time frame for the test is also a negotiable item. The vast majority of agreements (69 percent) require the manager to fail the test for two consecutive years in order to be found "non-performing." Only 10 percent of agreements allow for failure in any given year, an additional 11 percent define the test period as a three-year span, and the final 10 percent have some other arrangement.
- Next, there is the threshold for non-performance, that is, how is failure defined?

    - Budget tests are universally based on achieving some percentage of the budgeted gross operating profit or GOP. In 32 percent of cases, the global sample defines failure as achieving 85 percent of the budgeted figure or higher, with the remainder setting a lower threshold for failure. An 85 percent threshold or greater is found in 70 percent of agreements in the United States, 41 percent of European agreements, and only 8 percent of APAC agreements.
    - RevPAR tests are based on RevPAR penetration relative to the competitive set of hotels. Again, failure is defined as achieving less than an agreed-upon percentage of RevPAR penetration. The global sample shows that 58 percent of agreements define failure as not meeting at least 85 percent RevPAR penetration or better. These figures by region are 78 percent in the United States, 46 percent in Europe, and 33 percent in APAC.
        - It appears that the United States has the most stringent thresholds for non-performance.
- Lastly, there is the matter of whether the manager is allowed to "cure" the failure by making a monetary payment to the owner. Globally, 15 percent of agreements do not allow the manager to cure the failure. One cure is allowed in 12 percent of agreements, 21 percent of agreements allow two cures, 50 percent of agreements allow three or more cures, and 2 percent are silent on the matter of cures. The HVS Survey finds that global practice is very similar across continents.
    - Interestingly, 62 percent of agreements with no cure were signed after 2005 and the majority of these are found in Europe.
    - The parties will also negotiate several other matters related to cures:
        - The first is whether the cure is mandatory or optional for the manager to remain in the agreement. If mandatory, the performance test takes on the operation of a cash flow guarantee.
        - The second is the amount of the cure, generally negotiated as the amount necessary to bring GOP equal to the failure threshold.
        - The third is whether the cure is a cash payment or a reduction in management fees and whether any cures have a "claw-back" from future cash flows.
        - The fourth is whether the cure applies to only a single year or multiple year for tests that have a multi-year test period.
        - The fifth is how disputes are treated. Generally, they are to be resolved by arbitration (or expert) and are not allowed to be litigated.

In summary, performance tests are complicated matters that tend to favor managers. Let's end with a paraphrased remark by an asset manager in a recent guest lecture that summarized their value: "I am not aware of any manager who has been terminated as a result of a performance clause; on the other hand, having the clause is a very useful club at the negotiating table."

Termination by Owner and Manager

Universally, HMAs give both parties the right to terminate the agreement for several reasons. These provisions allow either the owner or the manager to terminate the agreement if:

- The other party fails to keep, observe, or perform any material covenant, agreement, or provision, and the default continues for a period of thirty days after that party is given notice to cure the default.
- The other party files a petition for bankruptcy or reorganization or assigns the property on behalf of creditors.
- The other party causes the property's licenses to be revoked or suspended.

Most agreements also permit the manager to terminate if:

- The owner fails to maintain an agreed-upon minimal balance in the property's operating bank account.
- The property is significantly damaged or destroyed by fire or other casualty.
- The property is condemned in whole or in part.

Three provisions allowing the owner to terminate the agreement require negotiation. These are:

- The owner's desire to terminate the agreement due to the manager's "non-performance" as detailed in the previous section.
- The owner's desire to terminate the agreement in the event of the property's sale.
- The owner's desire for the option to terminate the agreement without cause. This is the most contentious termination right.

The HVS Survey notes, "An increasing number of owners … want out should the manager fail to meet their expectations in terms of performance and compatibility."[8] Owners continue to seek these provisions and managers continue to resist. Here we detail the current state of the market.

The survey shows that 29 percent of global agreements have a provision that allows the owner to sell the hotel with appropriate compensation to the manager and without the manager's involvement or consent. The remaining 71 percent not only prohibit such termination, but require any purchaser to explicitly agree to the terms of the agreement and require that the manager approve the purchaser or that the purchaser meet a specific set of requirements. Some agreements give the manager the right to purchase the hotel before allowing the owner to bring the hotel to the market, with a few agreements even stipulating a minimum purchase price for the property. The 29 percent global figure for agreements that provide for termination upon sale breaks down as follows: 45 percent in the United States, 24 percent in Europe, and only 17 percent in APAC.

Termination without cause is a rare occurrence, found in only 16 percent of global agreements (20 percent in the United States; 14 percent in both Europe and APAC). Once again, appropriate compensation is part of this termination right; owners are expected to pay an amount equal to two to four times the most recent annual management fee (base plus incentive) for the right to terminate. It is often the case that the amount of the termination fee is reduced in the later years of an agreement.

Financial Matters

Hotel managers are expected to produce an annual operating budget and an annual capital expenditures (CapEx) budget as part of their duties. While these budgets are prepared by the manager, both parties recognize that the budgeting process is a collaboration between the owner and manager. In general, while the budgets are prepared and sent to owner for review or approval 90 to 120 days prior to the start of the next fiscal year, the collaborative process generally starts 180 days in advance of the start with the owner and manager agreeing on the general outlines of the revenue plan and any major changes to the property and its operation. The agreement calls for specific actions on both parties, which we now detail.

The CapEx budget, also known as the FF&E budget, is established as a fund to renew and refurbish the hotel to maintain its operating position in the market and to comply with brand standards. Owners are required to fund this budget out of the revenues from the hotel or via a separate cash contribution equivalent to a stipulated percentage of revenues. Managers insist on adequate funding to ensure that the property is properly maintained. Not having an established fund has traditional devolved into a particularly nasty fight over both the level of funding and the nature of the investments. Sophisticated parties recognize that hotels require an ongoing reinvestment of equivalent to approximately 5 percent of total revenues to remain competitive. The manager is allowed to spend funds from the CapEx reserve in accordance with the approved plan. Over the long term, the amount of CapEx funding is 4.15 percent of total revenues for the global sample (4.30 percent for the United States, 4.37 percent for Europe, and 3.78 percent for APAC). These amounts are generally reduced in the first five years of a new hotel's operation.

As for the operating budget and operating accounts, the manager expects to have full control over these funds, subject to limits on spending set by the owner in accordance with the annual operating plan. The HVS Survey shows that the manager has exclusive control in 86 percent of U.S. and European agreements and only 61 percent of APAC agreements. That meaningful difference for APAC is attributable to cultural norms in which owners desire control over financial matters. In terms of the budget, once the manager and owner agree on the annual operating plan, the manager has the right to spend funds in accordance with the plan, with few restrictions. These restrictions include:

- A requirement for the owner's approval if actual expenditures exceed the budgeted amount, generally with a threshold of 10 percent or more.
- Restrictions on entering into contracts with third parties, which require the owner's approval.
- Restrictions on entering into leases, either as landlord or tenant, or equipment leases without the owner's approval.
- Restrictions on the emergency expenditure of funds, which require the owner's approval.

Personnel Matters and Owner's Approval of Personnel Hires

Several personnel-related provisions in the manager's standard agreement are of concern to the owner. These provisions are as follows:

- All employees shall be on the owner's payroll, and the manager shall not be liable to such employees for their wages or compensation.
- The manager will hire, promote, discharge, and supervise the work of the executive staff of the property and the owner shall not interfere or give orders or instructions to personnel employed at the property.
- The manager may change or replace the general manager of the property at any time, at the sole discretion of the manager.
- The general manager shall be an employee of the manager, and owner shall reimburse the manager monthly for the manager's salary and fringe benefits.
- The owner agrees that if the general manager of the property leaves the employ of the manager for any reason, the owner shall not hire the general manager in any capacity for at least one year following such termination.

Neither the owner nor the manager wishes to carry the employees of the property on their respective payroll. Each is reluctant to assume the continuing business obligations for keeping payroll and pension records and for negotiating and adhering to labor agreements. Also, neither wants to be liable for potential tort actions or discrimination claims. In most cases, property employees are on the owner's payroll. However, they are employed by the manager in the following cases:

- When the ownership entity is an insurance company or a real-estate investment trust that is prohibited by law from managing and operating properties.
- When the ownership entity is a government, and it is in the best interest of both parties not to have civil-service rules governing hotel employees.

The owner's most important personnel-related concern is to influence or control the selection and the dismissal of the property's general manager and executive-staff members, since the owner is prohibited from interfering with or giving instructions to personnel employed at the property. In recent years, negotiated agreements more frequently contain provisions that permit some ownership influence in management selection. The HVS Survey indicates that 68 percent of global agreements provide for the owner's approval or consultation with the manager in the selection of the general manager, a percentage that is very similar across continents. The data for other positions is quite different; for example, about 60 percent of European and APAC agreements provide for the owner's approval or consultation for the financial controller, while only 18 percent of agreements in the United States have this provision. For all other executive positions, the percentage of agreements providing for approval or consultation is below 15 percent.

Dispute Settlement

Dispute settlement mechanisms are an important component of the legal framework. Absent any language to the contrary, the parties have full access to the courts at any time in matters under dispute. In the vast majority of cases, managers insist on language that creates formal dispute settlement mechanisms, which have the effect of preserving the status quo while the dispute is under consideration or uncertain in outcome. While practice varies considerably around the world, arbitration and the use of experts are the dominant methods.[9] As an example of current practice in the United States, agreements are found all along a continuum. At one end of the continuum are agreements that use arbitration for some, but not all contract disputes—these include disputes over the budget, budget definitions, performance termination, and capital expenditures. At the other end of the continuum are agreements in which the use of experts and/or arbitration is the sole remedy of the parties in all disputes.

What the Agreement Says—What the Agreement Means

Certain management agreement clauses and terms have transformed over time to be used in a very different manner from what was envisioned when the clause was first introduced.[10] What is interesting about these agreement matters is that they were historically negotiated with one intention in mind, but they have become the subject of negotiation over an entirely different matter in contemporary agreements. Let's take a look at a few.

Performance Termination Clause = Cash Flow Guarantee

What the Agreement Says—The performance termination clause was traditionally seen by owners as a safety valve, a way to contractually stipulate the automatic termination of the manager if the manager is not operating the hotel properly. These clauses generally work by specifying a "two-pronged test"; there is both a benchmark cash flow and benchmark operating performance metric that are tracked on an annual basis. Repeated failure to meet both benchmarks is an event of manager default under the agreement and places the manager in jeopardy of being terminated by the owner, subject to a *force majeure* provision.

A typical clause for an average hotel would have a cash flow failure benchmark (generally 90 percent of annual budgeted cash flow), an operating performance metric benchmark (generally 90 percent of the historical RevPAR penetration), and a multi-year time horizon (generally the manager must fail both benchmarks for either two consecutive years or two of three consecutive years). The two-pronged test protects the manager from being terminated for the wrong reasons. For example, if cash flow drops due to bad economic conditions and the hotel maintains its RevPAR penetration, the owner should not have the right to terminate, as the manager has demonstrated that the hotel's market share of revenues has been maintained.

What the Agreement Means—Over time, the terms of performance termination clauses have been expanded to give the manager the right to cure defaults via monetary compensation. The typical case provides cures even if the property is found to have failed the two-pronged test repeatedly; the manager has the unilateral right to "cure" the cash flow shortfall, with the number of allowable cures a negotiating item. If the manager exercises its right to cure the cash flow shortfall, they are also curing the default, thus removing the right of the owner to terminate the agreement. Managers negotiate vigorously over the terms of the performance termination provision, especially the right to have multiple cures. Multiple cures give the manager the ability to preserve their status as manager, protecting the flow of fees, market presence, and market share. With the ability to cure multiple times, owners have come to understand that it may be difficult, if not impossible, to terminate a non-performing manager and increasingly see the performance termination clause as a cash flow guarantee equivalent to (say) 90 percent of budgeted cash flow for the year. This increases the importance of obtaining benchmarks that are accurate, meaningful targets for the property and of getting the rights and responsibilities correct during the negotiating process.

Right of Unencumbered Sale = Value Creation for Owner

What the Agreement Says—Owners are naturally eager to obtain unilateral termination rights in the agreement; the option to terminate is very valuable. Managers are just as naturally inclined to restrict any right of unilateral termination by the owner. In the negotiation process, there are three owner termination rights that must be negotiated separated: termination without cause, termination upon sale, and termination upon foreclosure. Here our focus is on the right to terminate upon sale. Termination upon foreclosure is (almost) always part of the non-disturbance agreement between the owner, manager, and lender and is not covered here. Termination without cause is covered below.

What the Agreement Means—There is strong theoretical and anecdotal evidence that the ability to sell a hotel unencumbered with a management agreement will result in a higher selling price. One of the primary reasons for the higher selling price is that optimal offer prices are a function of the number of expected bidders. Using a set of reasonable assumptions, it can be shown that the optimal offer is for individual bidders to offer $(n - 1)/n$ of their reservation price. Thus with only one other bidder, the optimal offer is half (50 percent) of the reservation price; if ten total bidders were expected, however, one would bid 90 percent of the reservation price. Note how the offer price changes even though the object being bid upon (the hotel) stays the same. Anecdotally, the argument in favor of an unencumbered sale is that certain investors will not bid on assets managed by certain managers. For example, as a class, most owner-operators prefer to purchase hotels that can be franchised from a brand, not managed by the brand—thus these buyers would not bid on a brand-managed property. The bottom line for owners is that an unencumbered sale may mean more bidders, which translates into a higher potential selling price.

Termination Without Cause = My Way or the Highway

What the Agreement Says—Owners in strong negotiating positions are able to obtain the unilateral right to terminate the HMA in some cases; such a right to terminate is universally coupled with an obligation to pay a termination fee to the manager tied to a multiple of the annual management fees. The most commonly stated reason for this right is that owners would like the ability to sell their hotel unencumbered with a management agreement, and the unilateral right of termination provides an uncomplicated mechanism to achieve this end. As stated previously, the ability to sell the hotel unencumbered by an HMA opens the field of potential bidders on any given hotel, and auction theory strongly suggests that this will result in an increase in the ultimate sale price. Accordingly, owners have an incentive to negotiate this clause, so long as the value premium exceeds the cost of the termination fee. There is thus no doubt that the "unencumbered sale" story is reasonable. However, there is an additional factor to be considered.

What the Agreement Means—Owners, and especially owners' asset managers, are delighted with having the right to terminate because it tilts the asset management dynamic decidedly in favor of owners. The ability to terminate is a very potent tool in an asset manager's toolkit if used in a strategic and credible manner. If used with repeated, empty threats, the value of this right is significantly diminished. Paraphrasing the CEO of a major hotel real estate investment trust, "... the owner's unilateral right to terminate the HMA [subject to payment of a termination fee] is the most important clause in the HMA during the term of the agreement." If the (lack of the) right to terminate is a "deal killer" for the owner and the manager desires to continue with contract negotiations, the manager is well advised to be thoughtful in negotiating those items that will affect the owner-manager relationship during the contract term. For example, does the owner have the right to "review" the annual operating and CapEx budgets, or does the owner have the right to "approve" these budgets? Approval rights are much stronger and can prove more problematic for managers than review rights, especially if the agreement has a performance termination clause.

Right of First Offer = Sale-Manageback Option for Manager

What the Agreement Says—As part of the negotiation over the owner's ability to terminate the HMA upon sale, many managers ask for the right of first offer. This obligates the owner to offer the property to the manager before offering the property to the market. The right of first offer is often written as follows: the owner gives notice of the desired sale and invites an offer from the manager; the owner and manager agree to negotiate in good faith over the offer (usually no more than ninety days), but the owner is under no obligation to accept the offer. The owner is then free to bring the property to market, with no obligation to accept any offer from the manager, unless the manager's offer exceeds any received from the open market. This exception prevents the manager from being unfairly excluded. Owners agree to a right of first offer to secure the right to terminate the hotel upon sale; should the owner and manager fail to agree during the right of first offer period, the owner obtains the right to sell the hotel unencumbered by the HMA. Another reason for owners to use the right of first offer is as an alternative to the more onerous right of first refusal.

What the Agreement Means—For managers, the right of first offer is a valuable option. The manager obtains the option to purchase the property at the market price and become the owner. This option is exercised for properties considered strategically important to the manager. While the purchase has an impact on the manager's balance sheet, many managers will purchase the property and then immediately resell it, subject to an agreement, with terms that are favorable to manager. With the right of first offer/sale-manageback strategy, managers obtain the right to continue to operate properties but must use their balance sheet in the short term in order to retain control of the hotel.

Territorial Protection = Protect Owner's Market Share

What the Agreement Says—This clause goes by many names: a non-compete clause, a restricted territory clause, a territorial protection clause, an area of protection. Whatever the name, the intent of this clause is to constrain the manager's ability to operate properties that directly or indirectly compete with the owner's hotel. While owners desire to constrain managers' ability to operate competing facilities, managers want maximum flexibility to grow their brands and to protect market share.

Interestingly, this is one clause that sees a huge range of outcomes in practice. Clauses that favor the manager contain language that allow the manager to operate any facility at any location except as explicitly specified; the owner may obtain a restriction limited to a small geographic region, limited to specific brands, and limited in time. Clauses that protect the owner contain language that the manager may not operate any facility within the metropolitan area so long as the current agreement is in effect. These approaches are clearly at odds with each other and they come into very sharp focus when the owner negotiates with a branded manager; they play a less important role when an owner negotiates with an independent manager.

What the Agreement Means—Both parties understand the concept of market share. This clause defines the parties' intentions to nurture and protect market share for any given hotel. Owners are understandably reluctant to allow any dilution of market share that comes from the addition of competing facilities; if they can prevent the manager from doing so, owners are better off. Managers are understandably reluctant to allow their competitors access to a market by signing agreements that constrain their own ability to compete. By saying yes to significant territorial, brand, or time constraints in any given market, managers are removing the option to grow. They must be convinced that the benefits of saying yes to Owner A outweigh these other considerations. Further, the most "owner-friendly" clauses allow the owner the unilateral right to allow competing facilities, which gives the owner a seat at the table when the manager has opportunities for growth, a seat that may not be welcome. As a result, negotiations over this clause are difficult due to the win-lose nature of the bargaining; owners are focused on protecting market share for a given property, while managers are focused on growing market share for their management company and for their brands.

Input on Hotel Personnel Selection = Owner Control Over a Major Relationship

What the Agreement Says—The agreement specifies the degree to which the owner may be involved with personnel decisions at the property level. In the United

States, owners desire that all employees be employed by the manager with the owner reserving the right to have influence over decisions involving "key personnel." In owner-oriented clauses, this influence takes the form of the right to approve hiring decisions and the right to require replacement of personnel if the owner is dissatisfied with a hiring decision, after consultation to resolve the dissatisfaction. Key personnel usually include the roles generally known as hotel general manager, hotel assistant general manager, hotel controller, and director of sales and marketing. The manager is understandably reluctant to allow such direct involvement in these decisions, especially when staff members are in the employ of the manager. Manager-oriented clauses are written so that all personnel are employed by the manager, with the manager having absolute discretion over all personnel matters and treating all employment records and employee information as confidential and proprietary.

What the Agreement Means—Resolution of this matter helps to define the relationship between the owner and the manager. Managers desire a relationship in which the owner does business with the manager's central (or regional) offices, who in turn direct property-level staff. Managers desire contract language that has the effect of distancing the property-level personnel from the owner and placing corporate staff in the role of the owner's liaison. This language frustrates many owners, as it serves to reduce their control over the day-to-day operation of the property. This relationship is shown in Exhibit 1. Owners, especially owners who embrace an asset management paradigm, prefer the relationship shown in Exhibit 2. In this exhibit, note that the manager's central office is pushed away and the general manager is pulled closer to the owner. To make this relationship even stronger, owners employ language that allows some influence over the selection

Exhibit 1 Manager's Desired Relationship with the Owner

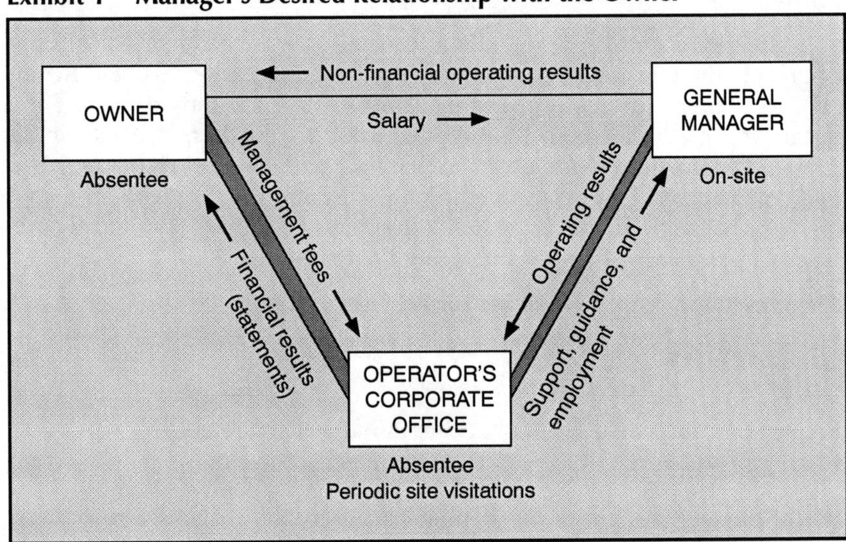

Adapted from Eyster and deRoos, *The Negotiation and Administration of Hotel Management Contracts* (Ithaca, NY: Pearson Custom Publishing, 2009)

Exhibit 2 Owner's Desired Relationship with the Manager

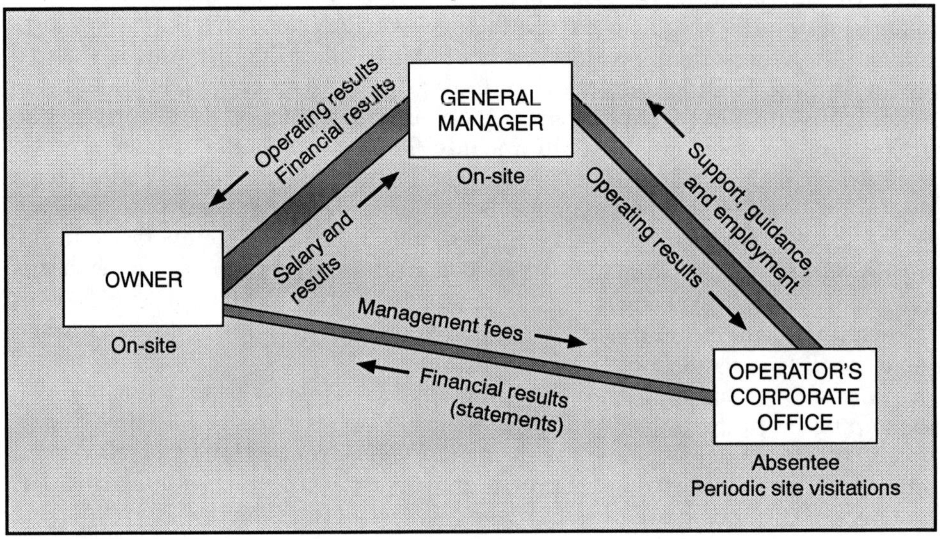

GENERAL MANAGER
On-site
OWNER
On-site
OPERATOR'S CORPORATE OFFICE
Absentee
Periodic site visitations
Operating results
Financial results
Salary and results
Operating results
Support, guidance, and employment
Management fees
Financial results (statements)

Adapted from Eyster and deRoos, *The Negotiation and Administration of Hotel Management Contracts* (Ithaca, NY: Pearson Custom Publishing, 2009)

of key personnel (personified as the general manager in Exhibit 2). The greater the influence over the personnel selection decision, the greater the degree of control over the relationship at the hotel itself.

Formal Dispute Resolution = Manager Control over Process and Outcomes

What the Agreement Says—Formal dispute resolution mechanisms are found in many agreements. The most manager-oriented language subjects the entire agreement to dispute resolution via a binding arbitration proceeding or a combination of non-binding mediation and binding arbitration.[11] Further, these same agreements would typically include a clause waiving both parties' rights to a trial by jury and consequential and punitive damages. In other agreements, the contract specifies which clauses in the agreement are subject to mandatory binding arbitration. These are typically disputes involving the following:

- Changes to the "competitive set" or benchmarking data
- The annual budget and business plan
- Calculation of the management fee
- Preparation and correctness of audited financial statements
- Fees related to loyalty programs or similar programs

While owners recognize the benefits of alternative dispute resolution, an owner-oriented agreement would have language that has no reference to mediation or arbitration, leaving litigation as an option. The agreement would have no reference to any waiver of trial rights or waiver of the right to receive damages related to the agreement. However, even the most restrictive agreements allow for certain disputes to be resolved by third parties; for example, one agreement places the resolution of disputes involving working capital funding, matters involving statements and reports, and the computation of the management fee in the hands of the owner's independent certified public accounting firm.

What the Agreement Means—Negotiation over dispute resolution procedures is about control of the process and the ability of the parties to preserve the "nuclear" option of a jury trial. Alternative dispute resolution mechanisms are designed to help parties find common ground and to defuse disagreements. Traditional dispute resolution mechanisms push parties to take "polar opposite" positions and often devolve into bitter and acrimonious clashes. However, placing decisions in the hands of experts removes the owner's ability to use litigation as a strategic lever in disputes in order to obtain an outcome that is not possible when seeking common ground. In their negotiation of this clause, both owners and managers signal their future intentions with respect to dispute resolution. While many owners are amenable to alternative dispute resolution mechanisms in certain situations, making these decisions binding is another matter entirely.

Incentive Fee Subordinate to Owner's Priority = Shift Risk from Owner to Manager

What the Agreement Says—In the vast majority of HMAs, the manager earns a management fee composed of two parts: a so-called base fee that is a function of the hotel's total revenues and a so-called incentive fee that is a function of the hotel's "profits" broadly defined. The fee structure is designed to reward managers for driving revenues to the property (base fee) and for operating the property in an economically efficient manner (incentive fee). Owners often claim that good incentive fee design aligns the interests of the owner and manager, as they are both working toward the same end—the cash flow from the property.

Traditionally, the incentive fee was based on a given hotel's income before fixed charges, known within the industry as gross operating profit or GOP. See Exhibit 3 for an illustration. This measure of operating profit is interesting, as it defines the manager's span of control at the property; that is, the manager is responsible for driving revenues, controlling departmental expenses, and controlling the undistributed operating expenses. Traditionally, the manager was seen as having no control over any expenses "below" income before fixed charges, and certainly no control over any payments to capital providers such as lenders and equity partners.

During the last two decades, however, there has been a decided shift toward an incentive fee that is subordinated to some measure of a return on the owner's total investment in the hotel. What has emerged is a fairly uniform solution involving the payment of an incentive fee using the notion of an "owner's priority return."[12] In lieu of obtaining an industry standard of (say) 8 percent of income before fixed charges, the manager would agree to an incentive fee of (say) 32 percent of the cash flow after owner's priority. Using the figures in Exhibit 3, either

Exhibit 3 Abbreviated Pro Forma Statement of Revenues and Expenses

Room Revenues	$26,700		(250 keys, 4+ stars, $293 RevPAR)
Other Revenues	$11,300		
Gross Revenues		$38,000	
Departmental Expenses	$15,000		
Undistributed Operating Expenses	$ 7,000		
Income Before Fixed Charges (GOP)		$16,000	
Base Management Fees	$ 1,140		(3% of Gross Revenues)
Property Taxes	$ 890		
Property Insurance	$ 450		
CapEx Reserve	$ 1,520		(4% of Gross Revenues)
Cash Flow from Operations		$12,000	(After Base Management Fee)
Owner's Priority		$ 8,000	(8% of the $100M Asset Value)
Cash Flow After Owner's Priority		$ 4,000	

incentive fee structure would result in a $1.28M payment to the manager (8 percent of $16,000 = 32 percent of $4,000 = $1,280).

What the Agreement Means—While the two payments are identical in the example, they are by no means the same. An incentive fee subordinate to an owner's priority return is a much riskier fee for the manager. Any reduction in the GOP from $16,000 reduces the incentive fee by 32 percent and a reduction in GOP from $16,000 to $12,000 completely eliminates any incentive fee, even though the owner would obtain the defined owner's priority return of $8,000, presumably enough to pay senior debt service on the hotel and a minimal return to equity.

The reduced GOP scenario outlined above would generally occur during a market downturn, during which both revenues and GOP would be reduced. This has the effect of punishing the manager when times are bad, even if it is turning in an outstanding performance. In practice, managers demand a larger incentive fee when it is subordinate to an owner's priority return in order to compensate them for the additional risk they are taking. There is a bright side to the subordinated incentive fee, however; a market upturn combined with superior management skills could result in incentive fees that have significant upside relative to a GOP-based incentive fee. Properly designed, the use of a subordinated incentive fee can be a powerful motivator, but managers need to be convinced that there is a real probability of upside relative to a GOP-based fee if they are expected to embrace the idea.

Management Agreement Negotiation Process

Exhibit 4 sets forth a stylized process for owners and managers to negotiate a management agreement. Although the exhibit shows only one owner and one manager, the owner may well duplicate the same process with several managers until a negotiated agreement is signed. Developing a project's concept (step 1) and initiating contact with prospective managers (step 2) are important preliminary

Exhibit 4 The Process of Negotiating a Management Agreement

1. *Owner proposes project:*
    - Evaluation of project's suitability to firm's objectives
    - Market study and other due diligence performed
    - Preliminary discussions with prospective lenders
    - Research prospective brands/managers for suitability to project
    - Develop Request for Proposal (RFP)
2. *Owner* contacts prospective managers:
    - Issue RFP and make presentation to managers
    - Managers' expression of varying levels of interest in project
    - Select manager based on responses and suitability for project
3. *Owner and Manager* engage in first round of discussions:

Owner:	Manager:
• Assesses own position and basic concerns • Assesses manager • Develops operating projections	• Assesses own position and basic concerns • Assesses owner • Develops operating projections
• Owner and Manager discuss and develop agreed-upon projections. • If no agreement, go back to step 2.	

4. *Owner and Manager* engage in first round of agreement negotiations:

Owner:	Manager:
• Presents going-in key terms to manager for consideration • Identifies "deal-killers" • Pursues back-up options, if needed	• Presents going-in key terms to owner for consideration • Identifies "deal-killers" • Pursues back-up options, if needed
• Owner and Manager agree on key terms and develop a letter of intent. • If no agreement, go back to step 2.	

5. *Owner and Manager* engage in second round of agreement negotiations:
    - Convert letter of intent into a legal document.
    - Negotiate legal document in detail.
    - Sign negotiated legal document when both parties are satisfied.

steps. The evaluations conducted concurrently by each party and the development of realistic operating and financial return projections for the project (step 3), the development of negotiating strategies and a letter of intent by the parties (step 4), and the negotiation of the legal contract document by both parties (step 5) are the most important steps in the process, as considerable time and resources are devoted to these steps once the parties decide to negotiate with each other.

The successful negotiation of an agreement depends as much on the owner's and the manager's preparation as it does on the decisions reached when the parties face each other across the bargaining table. After the initial contact between an owner and manager, each party should evaluate their position, define the goals they wish to achieve through the hotel project, and identify the specific concerns raised by the prospect of working with the other party. It is essential that these considerations be evaluated exhaustively in writing so that the resulting document can be used as the basis for assessing the other party and, later, for developing "going-in" and "fallback" positions to be used during the contract negotiations. The categories of considerations reviewed by each party to the agreement are discussed below.

Owner Self-Assessment

The owner should identify the following critical factors:

- The financial objectives of the investment
- The relative bargaining power brought to the negotiations
- The concerns raised by the agreement forms provided by each management company at the initial meeting with the owner

The owner's definition of the project's financial objectives should be expressed both in terms of specific quantitative measures—cash flow from operations, appreciation of the real estate, earnings per share, tax benefits, diversification, and hedging benefits—and the owner's view of the project as a short-, intermediate-, or long-term investment. Non-quantitative objectives—control, image enhancement, support for related products or services, employment of family members—should also receive explicit evaluation as part of the process.

The owner's review of the standard agreement provided by each prospective manager leads inevitably to the identification of provisions that cause concern. It is imperative that the owner identify these concerns and incorporate all questions about them in any formal request for information from the manager.

Manager Self-Assessment

Managers should analyze their position, defining:

- How the proposed project fits into strategic objectives.
- Corporate resources required for the project.
- Their relative bargaining power.
- Any concerns or strategic considerations regarding the owner.

In defining the strategic objectives of the project, the manager should identify the anticipated impact of the project on the firm's financial performance, as well as the likely effects participation in the project will have on the operating firm's reputation, brand positioning, and market position. In addition, the manager should analyze how the proposed hotel will be integrated into the portfolio, estimating the commitment of management time and energy required by the proposed venture. Finally, if an equity, loan, or key money contribution to the project is indicated, the manager should specify the financial objectives expected from this investment.

Developing Financial Projections and a Letter of Intent

Steps 3 and 4 are the heart of the owner's negotiations. This is not to trivialize the importance of step 5, but in the absence of acceptable outcomes in steps 3 and 4, the writing of the legal document in step 5 is moot. Experienced owners know that significant sums can be wasted rewriting the legal document if step 3 and 4 are not taken seriously. Let's take a look at each step in turn.

Step 3 ends with both parties developing agreed-upon operating projections. The process forces the owner to be very forthcoming about his or her vision for the project and for the manager to be very forthcoming about the anticipated operating results for the property. It is in this critical step that clarity is obtained. The physical program is refined to a great level detail. In order for the manager to prepare defensible operating projections, details such as the rooms mix, service standards, target markets, seasonality, F&B program, amenities, and staffing must be specified. It is also in this process that the owner and manager set the tone for their long-term relationship. The essence of this step is that until the owner and manager come to agreement on the hotel's potential, there is little reason to discuss any particulars related to the management agreement.

Step 4 begins with the parties combining their expectations, bargaining power, and mutual understanding of the financial projections and preparing to start the contract negotiations. Each project is unique, making the possibility that a manager or an owner will agree to a predetermined agreement package is highly unlikely. The work done by the two parties in preparing financial projections will lead to some common ground for negotiating management fees commensurate with the project's ability to generate returns to both parties. The form that these fees take will be determined by the relative bargaining power of the owner and the manager and by each party's willingness to participate in give-and-take bargaining on the other key provisions of the agreement.

In negotiating these major provisions, many outcomes are possible, but only a few will be mutually acceptable. Each party views some provisions as more important than others. As a result, it is important that before formal negotiations begin, each side separately evaluates the relative importance of every provision of concern and develops preferred "going-in" positions—as well as acceptable fall-back positions on those provisions where compromise is possible, given reciprocal concessions from the other party.

Defining one's position on these provisions is the culmination of assessing the opposite party's relative bargaining strength and ability to perform the required contractual obligations. Step 4 ends with the parties signing a letter of intent that contains a brief description of the major clauses in the agreement. A well-drafted letter of intent uses language that is clear in its meaning; both parties wish to use the letter of intent to provide clear direction to the legal teams who will draft the legal document. The legal teams then take over the process (Step 5) and produce the legal document. The legal teams generally have very little latitude to renegotiate the provisions of the letter of intent. Their job is to turn the letter of intent into a legal document.

Closing Summary

The global hotel industry has embraced management agreements as the dominant means to separate control and ownership of hotels. Both owners and managers gain by employing management agreements. Managers can focus on their key competencies—bringing their management expertise and brand services to properties owned by others; owners secure the services of third-party professionals in ways that can enhance the rewards of ownership. It is vital that owners and managers craft their agreements in a way that allows each side to derive benefits; if this is not the case, both sides are left with options that are potentially damaging.

Endnotes

1. From K. C. McDaniel, "Current Issues in the Negotiation of Hotel Management Agreements" in M. T. Carroll, ed., *Modern Real Estate Transactions* (Philadelphia, PA: American Law Institute/American Bar Association, 2005), pp. 597–646.
2. The full citation is M. Thadani and J. S. Mobar, "USA | Europe | APAC—HVS Hotel Management Contract Survey," HVS, August 2014. I would like to thank Manav Thadani for his permission to summarize and use the data from the report in this chapter.
3. See J. A. deRoos and S. D. Berman, "Calculating Damage Awards in Hotel Management Agreements," [electronic article] *Cornell Hospitality Report*, 14(16), 6–16, for more detail. Damage awards have exceeded $10 million in several cases.
4. J. Butler and B. Braun, *The HMA and Franchise Agreement Handbook*, 2nd edition, Global Hospitality Group of JMBM, April 2014, page 97. We urge interested parties to obtain the handbook, which is freely available for download.
5. GOP is loosely defined as gross revenues less all operating expenses of the hotel but before paying property taxes, insurance, rents, and any returns to capital.
6. We use the term GOP margin as an imprecise term here. Various agreements have various definitions of the GOP margin, often deducting the base fee from GOP or a fixed return to the owner. These definitions of operating profit are known as AGOP or "adjusted GOP."
7. Note that the marketing and training fees charged as system reimbursable expenses are in addition to property level allocations for these activities.
8. HVS Survey, *op. cit.*, p. 25.
9. K. Wales and L. Ferroni, *Hotel Management Contracts* (New York: Jones Lang LaSalle Hotels, 2008) present tables showing that arbitration or the use of experts is found in 81 percent of North American contracts, 72 percent of contracts in EMEA, and 72 percent of contracts in Asia-Pacific. Globally, the use of arbitration is growing rapidly, it is found in 75 percent of North American contracts, 33 percent of contracts in EMEA, and

42 percent of contracts in Asia-Pacific. The use of experts is the dominant mechanism in EMEA, but is becoming less dominant.

10. This section is adapted from J. A. deRoos, "Current Management Contract Terms," chapter 13 in L. E. Raleigh and R. J. Roginsky, eds., *Hotel Investments: Issues & Perspectives*, 5th ed. (Lansing, MI: American Hotel & Lodging Educational Institute, 2012). It has been edited and updated for this publication.
11. In some agreements, the language specifies the use of "experts" to resolve the dispute, with the sides selecting an expert (or experts) whose decision is final.
12. Early attempts subordinated the incentive fee to hotel debt service, which proved difficult to administer when the owner recapitalized or refinanced the hotel.

12

Hotel Franchise and Brand Licensing Agreements

By Robert Braun and Melissa Silvers

Robert Braun *is a partner in Jeffer Mangels Butler & Mitchell LLP and a senior member of the firm's Global Hospitality Group. He represents clients in the negotiation of hotel and spa management and franchise agreements; the acquisition and divestiture of hotels, resorts, restaurants, and other hospitality properties; hotel and hospitality workouts and turnarounds; and ongoing operating issues of hotels, spas, resorts, and restaurants. Mr. Braun is also a frequent lecturer as an expert in technology and hospitality issues.*

Melissa Silvers *is a Principal of SCS Advisors, Inc., a multi-discipline hotel investment firm specializing in asset management, operations oversight, transactions, development, and property management services to lodging investors. Ms. Silvers, who has more than twenty years of experience in the hospitality industry, joined SCS in July 2001. She currently serves as the Education Chair on the board of the Hospitality Asset Managers Association and has earned her Certified Hotel Asset Manager designation from the American Hotel & Lodging Educational Institute.*

DURING THE PAST SEVERAL DECADES, it has become increasingly popular—and often a business necessity—to operate a hotel as part of a brand. Hotel guests look for familiar names to ensure a consistent experience, gain access to anticipated amenities, participate in loyalty programs, and for other reasons. Hotel brands, as discussed below, have increasingly turned to franchising as a way of expanding. Franchising allows hotel companies to expand their market penetration at a lower cost, and to focus on their ability to develop and redefine the guest experience. At the same time, franchised properties create opportunities for owners, developers, and managers to expand their impact on the industry. Because so many hotels in the United States (and, increasingly, outside the United States) are operated under franchise agreements, hotel professionals need to understand the basics of franchises and how they impact the operation and profitability of hotel properties.

What Is a Franchise?

Hotel guests are often surprised to find out that the name of a hotel doesn't identify its owner. In fact, only a small percentage of branded hotels in the United States are actually owned by brands; brands, for the past twenty years or more, have pursued an "asset light" strategy, reducing the number of hotels they own and focusing instead on selling licensing rights to others who wish to use their brand names.

The key to this strategy, and a vital element of the structure of hotel ownership, branding, and management in the United States, is the use of franchises to build a hotel brand. The franchise structure is particularly valuable to the hotel industry. Hotels require significant initial and continuing capital investments; few, if any, hotel brands or operators are willing to make those investments. Franchisees, on the other hand, see branded hotels, with turnkey market access, reputations, and operating models, as attractive investments.

So, what exactly is a franchise? Simply stated, a franchise is a business relationship. It has much in common with other business relationships, most notably a license, but has come to embody a unique arrangement between two legally independent parties, an arrangement that has three distinct elements:

- One entity (the franchisor) grants another person or entity (the franchisee) the right to market a product or service using the trademark, trade name, or other intangible personal property of another business.
- The franchisee is given the right to market a product or service using the operating methods of the franchisor, and the franchisor has an obligation to provide rights and support to the franchisee.
- The franchisee must pay the franchisor royalty fees for these rights.

Franchises cover a wide array of businesses, including not just the most obvious candidates (hotels, restaurants, and cleaning services, to name just a few) but also businesses that would not immediately be thought of as a franchise, such as certain kiosks or outlets within existing stores.

Franchisees and potential franchisees should be aware that the definition of a franchise is not based on whether the franchise is *called* a franchise. A franchise is defined by the relationship and whether the business terms encompass those factors which cause it to be a franchise—whether or not it is called one, and whether or not the parties intended to enter into a franchise relationship. Many franchise agreements are called *license agreements*; however, just as a rose is a rose, a franchise is a franchise.

What Are the Benefits and Obligations of a Franchise?

In return for paying franchise fees and agreeing to extensive and often restrictive agreements, franchisees gain privileges, including the rights to sell a proven and recognized product or service, use the franchisor's business practices, and receive initial training and ongoing support. Franchisees also have responsibilities, which typically include:

- Requirements to meet a variety of quality controls for products and services sold.
- Restrictions on what they can sell or how they can operate using the company's name.
- Specifications for their business location and site appearance.
- Prohibitions on the operation of any similar businesses during or after the term of the franchise agreement.

Franchisees usually have an advantage over their non-franchisee competitors, since they have the rights to use the key properties developed by the franchisor, such as:

- Brand names, trademarks, copyrights, trade secrets, and patents
- Uniform logos, storefronts, and interiors

Regulation of Franchises

There are two important factors for both franchisors and franchisees to understand. First, both the granting and operation of franchises can be regulated by the federal government through the Federal Trade Commission and by some (but not all) of the states. Second, it does not matter if the parties intend to enter into a franchise or elect not to do so; if a business arrangement falls within the legal description of a franchise, it will be regulated as a franchise, and the franchisor will be obligated to comply with registration and other laws and regulations pertaining to franchises.

There are three general categories of laws regulating franchises:

- *Disclosure laws.* Disclosure laws regulate things like pre-sale disclosures, franchise sales practices, and a mandatory cooling-off period before a franchise sale becomes final.
- *Registration laws.* Registration laws require things like registration of the franchise with a state regulator, registration of salespersons authorized to market franchises, and registration of franchise advertising.
- *Relationship laws.* Relationship laws govern certain aspects of the relationship between franchisor and franchisee, such as when a franchisor can terminate a franchise; whether a franchisee is required to have notice of, and an opportunity to cure, defaults before termination; the grounds under which a franchisor may choose not to renew a franchise; and equal treatment of all franchisees.

The regulation of franchises is seen by the states and the federal government as a matter of consumer protection. The laws themselves developed out of the observation that unscrupulous parties were offering franchises without meaningful disclosure of the rights of the franchisee, the history of success (or failure) of the franchisor, the costs of the franchise, and so on. As a result, beginning with California, a number of states and the federal government adopted laws that require extensive disclosure of the franchisor's background and experience and the costs of acquiring, establishing, and maintaining a franchise. A number of states also adopted franchise relationship laws that regulate some key aspects of the franchise relationship, such as when a franchisor may terminate a franchisee.

Dual Regulation by State and Federal Law

State Law. Twenty-four states regulate the sale and operation of franchises (see Exhibit 1 for a listing of states with and without franchise laws). There are a number of variances between the laws, but they can be broken down into a few common themes.

Twelve states (California, Illinois, Indiana, Iowa, Maryland, Michigan, North Dakota, Oregon, Rhode Island, Virginia, Washington, and Wisconsin) identify three elements that define a franchise:

- *A marketing plan.* The franchisor grants to the franchisee the right to engage in the business of offering, selling, or distributing goods or services under a marketing plan or system that is substantially prescribed by the franchisor.

Exhibit 1 State Franchise Laws

States with Franchise Laws	
Arkansas	Mississippi
California	Missouri
Connecticut	Nebraska
Delaware	New Jersey
Florida	New York
Hawaii	North Dakota
Illinois	Oregon
Indiana	Rhode Island
Iowa	South Dakota
Maryland	Virginia
Michigan	Washington
Minnesota	Wisconsin
States without Franchise Laws	
Alabama	New Hampshire
Alaska	New Mexico
Arizona	North Carolina
Colorado	Ohio
Georgia	Oklahoma
Idaho	Pennsylvania
Kansas	South Carolina
Kentucky	Tennessee
Louisiana	Texas
Maine	Utah
Massachusetts	Vermont
Montana	West Virginia
Nevada	Wyoming

- *Association with trademark.* The franchisee's business is (and must be) associated with the franchisor's trademark, trade name, service mark, etc.
- *Fee.* The franchisee is required to pay a fee (which can be direct or indirect) for the right to engage in the franchised business.

In five other states (Hawaii, Minnesota, Mississippi, Nebraska, and South Dakota), the three elements of the legal definition of a franchise are:

- *Trademark license.* The franchisor grants the franchisee the right to engage in the business of offering, selling, or distributing goods or services using the franchisor's trademark, trade name, service mark, etc. (but without the need for a marketing plan).
- *Community of interest.* The franchisor and franchisee have a "community of interest" in the marketing of goods or services.
- *Required fee.* The franchisee is required to pay a fee, directly or indirectly.

Four states—Connecticut, Missouri, New York, and New Jersey—incorporate some, but not all, of these elements in the definition of a franchise. Finally, Arkansas, Delaware, and Florida have unique definitions.

It should be noted that some states have specialty franchise laws relating to specific industries (for example, the automobile dealer industry or the fuel distribution industry), and some states have franchise laws related to specific industries in addition to their general franchise laws. No state currently has a specific law relating to hotel franchises.

A state's franchise laws will generally apply only if the offer or sale of the franchise is made in the state, the franchised business will be located in the state, or the franchisee is a resident of the state. However, with many franchises (including many, if not most, hotel franchises) the fact that twenty-four different states have variations of the essential elements of a franchise creates challenges for franchisors. In addition, the multiplicity of state laws can create additional confusion, since the laws are subject to change (and often do).

Federal Law. In 1979, the U.S. Federal Trade Commission (FTC) adopted the "FTC Franchise Rule" as part of its authority to regulate trade practices. The FTC Rule incorporates three elements of a franchise:

- *Trademark.* The franchisee is given the right to distribute goods and services that bear the franchisor's trademark, service mark, trade name, logo, or other commercial symbol.
- *Significant control or assistance.* The franchisor has significant control of, or provides significance to, the franchisee's method of operation. Significant control or assistance includes:
  - Site approval
  - Standards or requirements for site design or appearance
  - Required hours of operation
  - Production techniques

  - Accounting practices
  - A requirement to participate in promotional campaigns
  - Mandatory training programs
  - An operations manual

- *Required payment*. The FTC Franchise Rule provides that a franchise exists if the franchisee is required to pay the franchisor (or an affiliate of the franchisor) at least $500 either before or within six months after opening for business. A required payment can include any payments the franchisee makes to the franchisor for the right to be a franchisee, and can include franchise fees, royalties, training fees, payments for services, and payments from the sale of products. However, purchases of reasonable amounts of goods at bona fide wholesale prices will not be considered a required payment.

If all three elements are present, then the relationship will be a "franchise" for purposes of the FTC Franchise Rule.

Franchise Violations

The most common types of violations of franchise laws include the following:

- Offering or selling a franchise without registration
- Failing to provide a Franchise Disclosure Document (FDD) when required
- Failing to provide the franchisee with all disclosures required in the FDD
- Making misrepresentations to franchisee prospects
- Improperly terminating or not renewing a franchise

States impose a variety of penalties for violating franchise laws, which can include fines, bans on engaging in franchising, freezing of assets, money damages, and—in some extreme cases—jail sentences. These penalties can be applied to the franchisor, and to its officers, directors, and managers who formulate, direct, or control the franchisor's activities. Since state franchise laws are consumer protection laws, their violation is typically treated as either a fraudulent and deceptive trade practice, a misdemeanor, or a felony. In some states, a franchisee which has been harmed by the franchisor's conduct can be awarded money damages (including punitive damages and attorneys' fees), or can terminate the franchise agreement and receive reimbursement of all fees paid to the franchisor.

Disclosure Laws

The FTC amended Franchise Disclosure Rule, which took effect in 2008, requires franchisors in the United States to provide each prospective franchisee with a Franchise Disclosure Document (FDD), formerly known as a Uniform Franchise Offering Circular (UFOC), at a certain point early in the process of offering and selling a franchise.

There are a number of changes imposed under the FDD that differ from the UFOC. Among the more substantive changes are the following:

- *FDD electronic delivery allowances*. In addition to being able to deliver the franchise disclosure document in hard copy or CD-ROM, franchisors can e-mail it to potential franchisees or offer a download from a website. The cover page of the FDD also now includes the franchise company's website and e-mail address, if the company has these. The new rule also allows a prospective franchise buyer to "sign" an FDD receipt electronically. At the same time, disclosures must not include electronic features such as pop-up windows, audio, video, and links to external documents, and the recipient of the FDD must be able to store it on a local computer and print it.
- *First meeting between franchisor and franchisee*. Previously, a franchisor was required to provide a potential franchisee with the UFOC at their first meeting. Now franchisors are not required to provide a potential franchisee the FDD at their first meeting, but it needs to be provided at least 14 calendar days before the franchisee signs a contract. However, the franchisee may reasonably request the document earlier in the process.
- *Franchise closings*. According to the UFOC, final documents were required to be provided five business days before closing. However, under the FDD, the franchisor must provide the final agreement seven calendar days before execution only if the franchisor makes unilateral and material changes to the franchise agreement or other agreement attached to the FDD. Switching to calendar days from business days was designed to avoid some of the prior confusion.
- *Increased franchisor transparency*. The FDD includes more detailed information about direct and indirect parent companies, including disclosure of any lawsuits or bankruptcies:
    - The franchisor is required to reveal whether any officer of the franchise has any interest in any approved suppliers.
    - The franchisor must also include in the FDD information about whether the franchisor or any affiliates make use of any other types of distribution channels (such as the Internet, telemarketing, or catalog sales).
    - The franchisor must notify potential franchisees of any restrictions prohibiting previous or current franchisees from discussing their experiences with prospects.
    - The FDD must also include any confidentiality clauses (sometimes referred to as "gag clauses") in agreements with the franchisor in the past three years.
    - Franchisors are also required to disclose how many franchises over the past three years were sold, terminated, or transferred.
    - If a franchisor is selling a previously franchised channel, the franchisor must provide a supplemental disclosure with the name and contact information of any previous owners from the prior five years. The franchisor must also include the reason for the changes in ownership.

Laws in more than a dozen U.S. states also require franchisors to provide a similar disclosure document. The FDD format is acceptable, with some amendments, in all of the states requiring registration, and most franchisors use its format instead of creating a unique disclosure document for each state requiring disclosure. Because many states have specific disclosure requirements not covered in the FDD, the FDD format must be amended, typically by the use of exhibits, to include the special information which is required by each state.

Relationship Laws

The FTC does not govern franchise relationships, although legislation to do so has been proposed in the U.S. Congress several times. There are nineteen states that regulate some aspect of the franchise relationship: Arkansas, California, Connecticut, Delaware, Hawaii, Illinois, Indiana, Iowa, New Jersey, Michigan, Minnesota, Mississippi, Missouri, Nebraska, North Dakota, South Dakota, Virginia, Washington, and Wisconsin.

Restrictions on Termination. In all of the nineteen states that have relationship laws other than North Dakota, it is illegal for a franchisor to terminate a franchise agreement without good cause. "Good cause" can include:

- Insolvency or bankruptcy.
- Voluntarily abandonment of operations.
- Conviction of a crime relating to the franchise operations.
- Failure of the franchisee to comply with its material obligations under the franchise agreement.

These laws typically require the franchisor to give the franchisee written notice of the proposed termination a certain number of days before the termination, ranging from 30 to 120 days. Franchisees can usually cure the default, other than for certain non-curable defaults, such as voluntary abandonment, bankruptcy, and criminal conviction.

Restrictions on Non-Renewal. State laws do not require franchise agreements to include a renewal right after the end of the initial term; however, if a franchise agreement does have a renewal provision, franchise relationship laws in twelve states can restrict the franchisor's ability to elect not to renew the franchise. This means that a franchisor must renew the franchise unless there is good cause not to do so, and the franchisee has been given the required advance written notice and opportunity to cure. These states include: Arkansas, Connecticut, Delaware, Hawaii, Iowa, Indiana, Minnesota, Mississippi, Missouri, Nebraska, New Jersey, and Wisconsin. As a practical matter, very few, if any, major hotel brands grant renewal rights in their franchise agreements.

California, Illinois, Michigan, and Washington require the franchisor to give the franchisee advance written notice of non-renewal (typically at least six months), and impose certain restrictions or requirements on the franchisor in some circumstances, such as repurchase of the franchisee's assets, or waiver of any non-competition restrictions.

Repurchase Obligations. Arkansas, California, Connecticut, Hawaii, Illinois, Iowa, Michigan, North Dakota, Washington, and Wisconsin require the franchisor to repurchase some or all of the franchisee's furnishings, equipment, inventory, supplies, and other assets following the end of the franchise relationship. The specific repurchase requirements vary from state to state.

Transfer Restrictions. Hotel franchisees typically seek the ability to transfer a franchise so as to monetize their investment, something that is particularly important in long-term agreements. Arkansas, California, Hawaii, Indiana, Iowa, Michigan, Minnesota, Nebraska, New Jersey, and Washington make it illegal for a franchisor to refuse to allow a transfer of the franchise without good cause, and franchise agreements establish specific standards to meet those requirements. Many of these states permit a franchisor to have a right of first refusal to purchase the franchise prior to a transfer.

Other Restrictions. There are various other restrictions or requirements imposed on franchise relationships by state law. Some of these include:

- *Encroachment.* Franchisors are restricted from opening a new unit in the vicinity of a franchise's existing unit in Hawaii, Indiana, Iowa, Minnesota, and Washington.
- *Free association.* A franchisor may not prohibit free association among franchisees or prohibit them from participating in a trade association in Arkansas, California, Hawaii, Illinois, Iowa, Michigan, Minnesota, Nebraska, New Jersey, Rhode Island, and Washington.
- *Good faith/reasonableness.* A franchisor must deal with its franchisees in a commercially reasonable manner and/or in good faith in Arkansas, Hawaii, Iowa, Minnesota, Nebraska, New Jersey, and Washington.
- *Management.* A franchisor may not require or prohibit any change in the management of the franchisee without good cause in Arkansas, Minnesota, Nebraska, and New Jersey.
- *Marketing fees.* Arkansas prohibits franchisors from collecting marketing fees from franchisees and not spending them for marketing purposes.
- *Non-compete agreements.* Indiana and Louisiana limit non-compete provisions in franchise agreements.
- *Non-discrimination.* A franchisor may not discriminate among similarly situated franchisees in Hawaii, Illinois, Indiana, Minnesota, and Washington.
- *Non-waiver.* Every state makes it illegal or unenforceable to require a franchisee to waive any of the protections provided to it under state law.
- *Required purchases.* Hawaii, Indiana, Iowa, and Washington limit a franchisor's ability to require franchisees to purchase supplies, inventory, goods, and services from the franchisor or designated sources.

Franchise Disclosures—the Franchise Disclosure Document (FDD)

The FDD contains important information regarding the franchise, the cost of acquiring and operating the franchise, and the contractual relationships between the franchisor and the franchisee. The FDD discloses extensive information about the franchisor and the franchise organization, which is intended to give potential franchisees enough information to make educated decisions about their investments. The disclosure document gives important information about the franchise company's financial status, including audited financial statements. A franchisee can find explanatory information about the franchisor's financial status in notes to the financial statements. Investing in a financially unstable franchisor is a significant risk; the franchisor may go out of business or into bankruptcy after a franchisee has invested its money, leaving the franchisee without the benefits it sought by investing in a franchise. The FDD may disclose whether the franchisor has steady growth plans; whether the franchisor makes most of its income from the sale of franchises (which may be a signal that the franchisor does not provide meaningful support to franchisees) or from continuing royalties; or devotes sufficient funds to support its franchise system.

The FDD is divided into a cover page, table of contents, and twenty-three categories called "Items." Twenty-one of the items contain information primarily pertaining to the franchisor, only two of which contain information directly relating to the performance of the franchise that is being offered for sale. One of these items, Item 19, "Earnings Claims," is an optional disclosure under the FTC Rule and State FDDs. Consequently, the franchisor is not obligated to disclose the performance of the franchise in terms of unit "earnings."

Item 20 provides a current accounting of the number of units that comprise the franchise system and reports the terminations and sale-transfers which have been applied to report the total number of units that comprise the system. Item 20 also provides the names and contact information of franchisees (both current franchisees and ex-franchisees) who may be contacted for information during the due diligence process conducted by prospective franchise buyers. A franchisee should note that this information may have less value than they anticipate, because these references have no legal duty to disclose the performance statistics of their independent businesses to new buyers of franchises. Also, the information in Item 20 does not disclose that the transfer or sales can be transfers and sales that resulted in gains or losses for the franchisees who have transferred or sold their units.

Brief Descriptions of the Individual Items in the FDD

1. The Franchisor and Any Parents, Predecessors, and Affiliates. This section tells how long the franchisor has been in business; discloses likely competition; and identifies any special laws that pertain to the industry, like any license or permit requirements. This is intended to help prospective franchisees understand the costs and risks they are likely to take on if they purchase and operate the franchise.

2. Identity and Business Experience of Key Persons. This section identifies the executives of the franchise system and describes their experience.

3. Litigation History. This section discusses prior litigation—whether the franchisor or any of its executive officers have been convicted of felonies involving fraud; convicted of violations of franchise law, or unfair or deceptive practices law; or are subject to any state or federal injunctions involving similar misconduct. It also discloses whether the franchisor or any of its executives have been held liable for—or settled civil actions involving—the franchise relationship. A number of claims against the franchisor may indicate that it has not performed according to its agreements, or, at the very least, that franchisees have been dissatisfied with its performance. This section also should say whether the franchisor has sued any of its franchisees during the last year, a disclosure that may indicate common types of problems in the franchise system. For example, a franchisor may sue franchisees for failing to pay royalties, which could indicate that franchisees are unsuccessful and therefore are unable or unwilling to make their royalty payments.

4. Bankruptcy. This section discloses whether the franchisor or any of its executives have been involved in a recent bankruptcy, information that can help potential franchisees assess the franchisor's financial stability and whether the company is capable of delivering the support services it promises.

5. Initial Franchise Fee. This section describes the costs involved in starting and operating a franchise, including deposits or franchise fees that may be non-refundable, and costs for initial inventory, signs, equipment, leases, or rentals. It also explains ongoing costs, like royalties and advertising fees. This item, and item 6 which follows, are among the most important provisions for a franchisee to review, especially with respect to hotel franchises, since hotel brands include a wide variety of fees, costs, and reimbursements. In order to evaluate the benefits of the hotel brand in question, a franchisee must have a full understanding of these costs.

6. Other Fees and Expenses. This section explains the franchisor's training and assistance program, and provides information on advertising costs. Franchisees often are required to contribute a percentage of their income to an advertising fund; it is almost universal in the hospitality industry.

It is not uncommon for a hotel franchise to list 25 different potential expenses. These may include costs as disparate as fund contributions, loyalty program fees, comfort letter fees, annual convention costs, liquidated damages, audit expenses, and other fees. Reviewing these fees, with the attached notes and explanations, will give a franchisee a much better idea of the true cost of a franchise.

7. Franchisee's Estimated Initial Investment. These costs range from application fees to permit costs, construction expenses, signage, inventory, and the like. These are not limited to amounts paid to the franchisor; they include sums paid to others, but which are necessary to start the franchise or are required by the franchisor.

8. Restrictions on Sources of Products and Services. This section tells whether the franchisor limits the suppliers from whom a franchisee may purchase goods. This is a significant issue for hotel franchises, since hotel brands often specify the sources for a variety of goods—bedding, case goods, stationery, consumables, etc.—which can constitute a significant cost of the operation of the franchise. It may also identify resources available to the franchisee, such as purchasing agents, and whether those are mandatory or optional.

9. Obligations of the Franchisee. This item provides a description of the franchisee's contractual obligations, with cross-references to the franchise agreement and the rest of the FDD.

10. Financing Arrangements. If the franchisor offers a lending program, or has arrangements with lenders who have agreed to help finance its franchisees, the existence and terms of those relationships are described in this item. The item also discloses any financial relationship the outside lender has with the franchisor.

11. Obligations of the Franchisor. This item outlines the content and scope of the franchisor's support services. Hotel franchisors typically include site approval, comments on and approval of designs (ranging from concept designs to final plans and specifications), marketing plans, training of key personnel, access to the franchisor's operating or system manual, and other resources. The item also discloses continuing support obligations of the franchisor, such as quality assurance and guest loyalty programs, and central reservations systems. Many of the franchisor's obligations are qualified; because franchisors expect to revise their services during the term of the franchise agreement (which is typically long), franchisors retain the ability to change their obligations.

12. Territory. A key concern for a hotel owner is that it not be forced to compete directly against other hotels operating under the same brand in its market area. This item describes the terms under which the franchisor will grant exclusivity, which is typically for a limited geographic area in the near vicinity of the hotel, and for a limited period of time.

13. Trademarks. This item lists the trademark registrations the franchisor has obtained or applied for. It also indicates whether there are marks that are not owned or used by the franchisor, and describes the rules and limitations imposed on the franchisee for the use of the marks. This may include the right of the franchisor to discontinue the use of any or all of its trademarks and other distinguishing marks.

14. Patents, Copyrights, and Proprietary Information. Covers franchisor items such as copyrighted advertising copy and designs, training films, workbooks, operating manuals, and so on.

15. Obligation of the Franchisee to Participate in the Actual Operation of the Franchise Business. Some franchisors require franchisees to run the business themselves; others allow them to be passive owners and hire someone else to manage day-to-day operations. Hotel franchises typically allow the franchisee to engage a professional, third-party manager for the operation of the hotel. Hotel franchisors often include provisions regarding the financial obligations of the franchisee, which may include obtaining guaranties of payment and performance, and maintenance of net worth requirements.

16. Restrictions on Goods and Services Offered by the Franchisee. Hotel franchisors seek to restrict the ability of franchisees to sell goods and services that are inconsistent with the operation of the hotel or the brand.

17. Renewal, Termination, Repurchase, Modification, and/or Transfer of the Franchise Agreement, and Dispute Resolution. This section spells out the conditions under which the franchisor may end a franchisee's franchise, and a franchisee's obligations to the franchisor after termination. It also defines the conditions under which a franchisee can renew, sell, or assign the franchise to others.

18. Public Figures. If a franchise uses a public figure to promote its business, that usage is disclosed under this item.

19. Financial Performance Representations. Franchisors are not required to disclose information about potential income or sales, but if they do, the law requires that they have a reasonable basis for their claims and that they provide substantiation for their claims. Although this is one of the most important pieces of the FDD, only 30 to 40 percent of franchisors provide information on how much their current franchisees are earning; the others must state that they choose not to make such a claim. There are a number of factors that make these financial representations less valuable than one might assume:

- *Gag orders.* Franchisors practicing franchise fraud may have a high number of former franchisees under a gag order, preventing a potential new franchisee from obtaining a clear picture of financial performance.
- *Sample size.* The disclosure document should tell the sample size and the number and percentage of franchisees who reported earnings at the level claimed. Sometimes the sample size is too small for the numbers to be meaningful.
- *Average income.* Average figures tell very little about how individual franchisees perform. An average figure may make the overall franchise system look more successful than it is because just a few very successful franchisees can inflate the average.
- *Gross sales.* These figures don't really tell about the franchisees' actual costs or profits. An outlet with a high gross sales revenue on paper may be losing money because of high overhead, rent, and other expenses.
- *Net profits.* Franchisors often do not have data on the net profits of their franchisees.
- *Geographic relevance.* Earnings may vary with geography. The disclosure document should note geographic or other differences among the group of franchisees whose earnings are reported and a franchisee's likely location.
- *Franchisees' backgrounds.* Franchisees have different skill sets and educational backgrounds. The success of some franchisees doesn't guarantee success for all.
- *Reliance on earnings claims.* Franchisors may ask a franchisee to sign a statement—sometimes presented as a written interview or questionnaire—that asks whether a franchisee received any earnings or financial performance representations during the course of buying a franchise.

20. List of Franchise Outlets. This section has important information about current and former franchisees. Many franchisees in an area may mean more competition for customers. The number of terminated, cancelled, or non-renewed franchises may indicate problems. The sale-transfer columns can obscure churning of units through fire sales to third parties by failed or failing franchisees. Some companies may repurchase failed outlets and list them as company-owned outlets. Some of the former franchisees may have signed confidentiality agreements that prevent them from speaking. Franchisors practicing franchise fraud may have a high number of former franchisees under a gag order. If a franchisee buys an existing outlet that was reacquired by the franchisor, the franchisor must tell the franchisee who owned and operated the outlet for the last five years. Several owners in a short time may indicate that the location isn't profitable or that the franchisor hasn't supported that outlet as promised.

21. Financial Statements. The audited financial statements in this section can give important information about the company's financial status.

22. Contracts. These items include the contracts that the franchisee will be required to sign.

23. Acknowledgment of Receipt. The FDD is used not only as a disclosure document but as a means of protecting the franchisor from claims by franchisees. The franchisor is required to obtain a receipt showing that the franchisee received a copy of the FDD.

The Franchise Application

Once a hotel owner has selected an appropriate franchise affiliation, a franchise application needs to be completed and submitted to the franchisor. A franchise application typically requires basic information such as a disclosure document receipt signed and dated by the applicant, an application letter, a letter of intent, a certification of formation, a complete ownership structure form for the ownership entity and any underlying ownership entities, a complete ownership structure form for the fee title holder, a market or feasibility study, and the payment of a franchise application fee.

The letter of intent or LOI is a document that outlines an agreement between two or more parties before the agreement is finalized. LOIs are typically not binding on the parties in their entirety, but many LOIs contain provisions that are binding, such as exclusive dealing provisions or confidentiality requirements. An LOI may be negotiated before execution. The most common purposes of an LOI, sometimes referred to as a "term sheet," are:

- To clarify the key points of a complex transaction for the convenience of the parties.
- To declare officially that the parties are currently negotiating.
- To provide safeguards in case a deal collapses during negotiations.
- To verify certain issues regarding payments that may be made prior to entering into the franchise agreement (for example, most hotel franchisors require

a significant deposit, only a portion of which may be refundable if the franchise agreement is never executed).

Once the franchise application is submitted, the franchisor must provide the previously discussed FDD for review by the potential franchisee. The franchisor will review the applicant's financials and credit. If the application is approved, the franchisor may request additional information and ask for the franchise agreement to be signed within a specific amount of time.

Franchise Agreement Terms

While the franchisor is waiting for the franchise application to be approved, the franchise agreement can be negotiated. During the negotiation process, many areas are standardized, but several terms may be subject to negotiation.

Items Subject to Negotiation

Franchise agreement terms that are subject to negotiation include brand standards; royalty fees; advertising or marketing fees; the reservation fee; the frequent traveler program fee; other miscellaneous fees; protected/non-compete areas; management; property improvement plans; reserves; liquidated damages; purchasing programs; termination rights; financing; and transfer, assignment, and sale.

Brand Standards. The franchise agreement will refer to the brand standards and the obligation of the hotel owner to maintain the brand standards during the franchise agreement term. Brand standards are tools used to support the brand strategy. The brand strategy involves the positioning of the brand, the target guest, the uniqueness of the brand, and the brand principles. The operating budget must include items that the franchisor deems appropriate to maintain the brand standards. It also usually means that even in those circumstances where the hotel owner has the right to approve the operating budget, the owner cannot object to any elements of the operating budget that represent expenditures to maintain the brand standards. Brand standards change over time and the franchise agreement is typically specific that the brand standards must be followed to stay within the franchise. Brand standards are not typically negotiable but a hotel owner can get an exception to a brand standard, depending on the circumstances.

Royalty Fees. Royalty fees represent compensation for the use of the brand's trade name, service marks and associated logos, goodwill, and other franchise services. Almost all franchisors collect royalty fees based on a percentage of revenue (rooms revenue and/or food and beverage revenue). The royalty fee percentage can vary depending on the value of the brand.

Advertising or Marketing Fees. Brand advertising and marketing consist of national or regional advertising in various types of media, the development and distribution of a brand directory, and marketing geared toward specific groups and segments. In many instances, the advertising or marketing contribution fee goes into a fund that is administered by the franchisor on behalf of all members of the brand. There are many fee structures that can be negotiated, including fixed fees per property or fees based on a percentage of room revenues.

Reservation Fee. If the franchise brand has a reservation system, the reservation fee includes the cost of operating the central office, telephones, computers, reservation personnel, and all distribution-related fees, including fees payable to third parties such as travel agents and distributors. Reservation fees can be calculated on a fixed percentage of room revenue, cost per reservation, or a combination of fixed plus cost. Many brands have various reservation fees that vary depending on the source of the booking.

Frequent Traveler Program Fee. Many franchisors have incentive programs that reward guests for frequent stays and brand loyalty. The frequent traveler program fee is typically based on a percentage of total or rooms-only revenue generated by a program member staying at a hotel, or a fixed dollar amount for each room occupied by a program member. Many brands also charge hotels a one-time participation fee when the guest stays at the hotel for the first time.

Other Miscellaneous Fees. Other fees may be required to be paid to the franchisor or third-parties for additional systems, training, conferences, and support.

Protected/Non-Compete Areas. Franchise agreement negotiations typically include "radius restrictions" or geographic areas of protection (AOPs)/non-compete areas, that limit the tenant, manager, or licensor from opening, operating, permitting, or otherwise engaging in their business in another location within a certain radius or area. A radius restriction can be for a set number of years or for the life of the franchise agreement. The radius restriction effective date can be when the franchise agreement is executed or when the franchise operation is opened.

Management. Franchise agreements allow hotel owners the flexibility to contract with an independent hotel manager to operate the hotel based on a separate management agreement. The selected management company should be owner-loyal and should report directly to ownership.

Property Improvement Plans (PIPs). A property improvement plan or PIP generally is required by a franchisor to ensure the hotel is compliant with brand standards. A PIP typically represents a substantial capital investment by the hotel owner that a brand will require when there is a change in ownership or a change in brand.

Reserves. Franchise agreements typically require a furniture, fixture, and equipment (FF&E) reserve, but some may also have an insurance reserve and/or a real estate tax reserve. These reserves are kept to pay for capital needs, insurance invoices, and real estate tax bills when due for payment. These funds are not distributed to ownership but also cannot be used for anything else but the need specified in the franchise agreement. An FF&E reserve is typically 4 percent for full-service hotels, but can vary in range, depending on the hotel's age and need.

Liquidated Damages. Liquidated damages in a franchise agreement give the franchisor the ability to collect damages on a specific breach of the franchise agreement, such as the early termination of the agreement. There are ways to reduce the amount of the damages.

Purchasing Programs. Purchasing programs are typically voluntary for a fee. Participation in the program gives the hotel the right to purchase the products and services offered through the program at the program-negotiated prices. Most of the purchasing programs have a platform that electronically connects hotel buyers with suppliers in a secure marketplace. There are many hotel purchasing programs available that integrate eProcurement, AP automation, inventory control, recipe management, and capital budget management modules. The fee charged by the franchisor is typically a percentage of total purchases under the program.

Termination Rights. Termination rights are the rights to terminate a franchise agreement early. Early terminations are not common, except in connection with a default or performance test failure. The termination right is typically negotiated on behalf of the hotel owner when the franchisor is negotiating the length of the franchise agreement. The most common termination right is upon sale. This allows ownership to terminate the franchise agreement before the end of the term in connection with a sale of the hotel, in exchange for payment of a termination fee. There are various kinds of terminations (with cause or without cause) in a franchise agreement, and many of them can be cured in a set amount of time.

Financing. Financing is not typically part of a franchise agreement, and most brands do not get involved with financing a hotel. "Financing" refers to the sources of funding for a hotel. Franchisors will sometimes finance the initial franchise license fee with a promissory note.

Transfer, Assignment, and Sale. "Transfer, assignment, and sale" includes the conveyance of any interest the hotel owner has in the franchise agreement or hotel to another entity. These three actions are typically subject to approval by the franchisor with or without conditions and with or without fees due to the franchise. In some cases, the franchise will have the right of first refusal to acquire the hotel.

Considerations in Negotiating Franchise Agreements

Relationship of the Parties

Franchisors are extremely reluctant to change the terms of their form agreements. While some provisions described below may be subject to negotiation, franchisors will typically not negotiate more than a handful of terms. There are good business reasons for this reluctance: the essence of a franchise is the consistency of the service or product throughout the franchise system, and any changes can dilute that consistency. Moreover, franchisors often have hundreds of franchise agreements; when there are significant differences among a large number of franchise agreements, the franchisor faces practical challenges in enforcing its agreements effectively or efficiently.

The extent to which a franchise agreement may be negotiated is also a matter of leverage. If a franchisor particularly desires representation in a particular location, whether to fill in its delivery system or prevent a competitor from becoming established in the location, the franchisor may be more flexible in its negotiations. Franchisors are also more willing to make concessions to franchisees who have long relationships with them covering multiple properties.

Negotiable Provisions

Notwithstanding the observations made above, hotel brands are willing to negotiate a number of important terms in hotel franchise agreements, including the following.

Term. The contract duration can vary from agreement to agreement, although brands tend to have a strong preference for long, no-cut agreements. Franchisees may sometimes negotiate either a shorter term, the right to terminate at specified intervals, or the ability to terminate with payment of a fee. In some special instances, typically where the brand is highly motivated to achieve market representation, a franchisor might be willing to provide a free termination option.

Protected Territory. Most franchisors will agree to a limited period of time in which it will not open up a competing hotel within the immediate vicinity of the franchised property. The protected territory, or AOP, is typically limited to the first few years of the agreement, applicable for a limited radius around the hotel, and excludes any other flags operated by the brand (even if they actually compete with the subject property). It is sometimes possible to extend the term of the protection through the full term of the franchise agreement, and tailor the protected area to a meaningful market area.

Royalty Fees. Royalty fees are often negotiated to a ramp-up during the initial years of the franchise; it may be possible to have them eliminated entirely for some period of time. A franchisee should note that franchisors will sometimes defer, but not actually reduce, the royalty fee, so that the full fee can be recaptured if the franchisee defaults in its obligations under the agreement.

Transfer Provisions. Franchisees should always consider the restrictions on transfer in light of their own legal structure, and request changes to reflect likely transfers. For example, private equity groups, which often change ownership (but not control) of assets, may request a more liberal transfer provision.

Liquidated Damages. Franchisors assess liquidated damages for the early termination of a franchise agreement based on the franchisee's default. These fees have escalated to as much as five to seven years of fees (including royalties, marketing fees, and other fees). While franchisors are extremely reluctant to make any change in this structure, it may be possible to "nibble at the edges" to make liquidated damages less onerous.

Personal Guaranties. Franchisors regularly require franchisees to provide personal guaranties of performance and payment, reflecting the fact that, particularly for institutional owners, the actual owner of the property is likely to be a single asset entity. Franchisees should push back against providing a guaranty; if ultimately required to do so, franchisees should attempt to negotiate limitations on the guaranty (monetary or duration) and the provision of a corporate, rather than a personal, guaranty. Franchisors are sometimes willing to consider other means of ensuring that the franchisee maintains the financial capacity to meet its monetary obligations (such as net worth covenants) in lieu of requiring guaranties.

Key Money. Franchisees can sometimes negotiate cash payments of "key money" from brands to help defray the cost of developing or converting a project. While additional cash is always welcome, franchisees should be aware that it can be the most expensive funds available. While key money typically does not bear interest, brands will, with very few exceptions, only provide the funds upon the actual opening of the property, making the attainment of the key money less valuable, and when key money is asked for franchisors will be even more reluctant than otherwise to concede on other franchise agreement points that are under negotiation. In addition, franchisors will nearly always require repayment of all or an amortized portion of key money if the franchise is terminated prior to the end of the contractual term.

Casualty and Condemnation. Franchisors will often revise the provisions of a franchise agreement relating to the impact of the damage or destruction of the hotel property, or condemnation of the hotel property, to meet the requirements of lenders. This is important to avoid a disconnect between the obligations of the franchisee to lenders and to the franchisor. Particular attention should be given to provisions that would give the franchisor an interest in insurance or condemnation proceeds.

Recordation of the Franchise Agreement. Franchisors often require that a memorandum or other notice of the existence of the franchise agreement be recorded in the real estate records of the jurisdiction in which the hotel is located. Franchisees should note that this could prove problematic in financing or selling the hotel.

Management Company Acknowledgements. Franchisors typically require management companies to enter into agreements that require the management company to conform to the terms of the franchise agreement. This can prove problematic if the franchisee and franchisor have a dispute, since the franchisor can effectively ignore the franchisee and impose obligations directly upon the manager operating the property.

Comfort Letters. The franchise agreement should include an affirmative obligation of the franchisor to provide a comfort letter to a lender to facilitate the financing of the hotel.

Terminating the Franchise

Hotel franchise agreements generally are difficult to terminate. Hotel franchise agreements are typically long-term—twenty to thirty years is not uncommon—and rarely provide for early termination. Hotel brands do this for several reasons. Brands take the position that they have invested significant time and effort in establishing a presence in a particular location, and that investment will be lost unless the brand is able to retain a property. This issue becomes more important to the brand, since it may not have any other opportunities to establish a presence in that market, or will have a delay in doing so while a location is identified and developed. Moreover, since brands are valued, at least in part, by their portfolio of long-term franchise or management agreements, termination of a management agreement will have an impact on the value of the hotel company as a whole. For this reason, hotel franchisors establish barriers against early termination.

Termination for Cause

While most franchise agreements provide for termination by the franchisor if the franchisee breaches its obligations, and by the franchisee if the franchisor breaches its obligations and fails to cure within a reasonable period of time, the fact is that this is often a one-way provision. Franchisors have very few explicit obligations; the franchise agreement is slanted in favor of the franchisor and does not require the franchisor to provide any explicit services. The franchisee, on the other hand, is required to meet all of the franchisor's standards, and failure of the brand to drive occupancy, rate, or profitability is not grounds for termination. Moreover, the state relationship laws noted earlier are focused on addressing the possibility that a franchisor will terminate the franchise agreement without adequate cause; they rarely address the possibility that a franchisee may find it necessary to terminate the franchise agreement, which is often a concern in hotel franchise agreements. Hotel franchisees should note that it is exceedingly rare for a franchise agreement to include a performance termination clause. Franchisors almost never provide assurances regarding the performance of the franchise, and thus will not be subject to termination simply because the property does not perform as anticipated (even if that failure can be traced to the brand) unless failure is due to an uncured breach.

Termination without Cause

Few hotel franchise agreements provide for termination without cause by either party (and franchise relationship laws generally restrict that right on the part of the franchisor). Franchisors may be willing to negotiate early termination provisions, including the right of the franchisee (and often the franchisor) to terminate the franchise agreement at specific intervals. When the agreement does include such a provision, the franchisee is often obligated to pay liquidated damages.

Liquidated Damages

Most hotel franchise agreements provide that the franchisor may seek liquidated damages, often reaching five to seven years of fees, if the franchisor terminates the franchise agreement for cause. Notably, the calculation of fees may include not only the base franchise or license fee, but also marketing fees, loyalty program fees, and any other payments by the franchisee to the franchisor. This provides an obvious, and strong, incentive for a franchisee to fulfill its obligations. At the same time, even when an agreement does not provide an affirmative right to the franchisee to terminate without cause, the existence of liquidated damages may provide a cap on damages should a franchisee terminate the franchise agreement without cause.

Franchise Issues in Hotel Sales

When a hotel sells to a new owner, almost all franchise agreements terminate. A new buyer would have to enter into a new franchise agreement if the new buyer wants to keep the current brand. If the sale occurs before the end of the term of the franchise agreement, the current owner may have an obligation to pay a termination fee. Many times the franchise will waive applicable termination fees if the new owner signs a new franchise agreement.

Upon a hotel sale, a franchisor likely will require a PIP or upgrades to the condition of the hotel before approving the new owner's franchise agreement. The PIP's scope generally is negotiable, and will depend in part on what capital investments the current hotel owner has made in recent years.

Before a hotel purchase and sale agreement is documented, the buyer should submit the franchise application and determine how long it will take to get approval for the new franchise. The required time to get approval should be included in the closing timeline of the purchase and sale agreement. If the buyer is already a franchisee of the brand, the approval process may only take a few weeks. If the buyer is not an existing franchisee, the approval process can take up to several months.

International Franchising

The United States is not alone in regulating franchises. More than 160 countries have franchised businesses, and many countries regulate the sale and operation of franchises. Many franchisors in the United States offer franchises outside the United States, and many franchises operate entirely outside the United States.

While the United States is generally considered to have the most extensive and developed franchise laws, many countries do have pre-sale regulations. At least twenty-four countries specifically regulate franchising. Australia, Brazil, Canada, China, France, Indonesia, Japan, Malaysia, Mexico, Romania, South Korea, and Spain have laws regarding pre-sale disclosure and require franchisors to provide prospective franchisees a disclosure document prior to sale. Some countries also require that the disclosure document be filed with a specific government agency. In addition to pre-sale disclosure regulation, international franchising is affected by a wide range of laws, including those which relate to trademark, antitrust, contract, tax, and technology transfer issues; currency control; foreign investment; import and export restrictions; and dispute resolution. A prospective franchisee should seek assistance in such laws, which include U.S. federal and state statutes and regulations, laws of the foreign nations where the franchise will be located, and even any bilateral or multilateral treaties which may apply.

Many U.S. franchisors are expanding internationally; Canada is the most popular country for U.S. franchise expansion, but Asia, Europe, South America, Central America, and Mexico are also experiencing great international franchising growth. The most common form of international franchise relationship is the master franchise, sometimes referred to as sub-franchisor. The master franchisee is granted a franchise for all or part of a particular country, and is granted the right to develop the entire territory or sub-franchise the units to third parties (sub-franchisees). Master franchisees are attractive to franchisors because they have the knowledge of local markets and the business/political connections to make the franchises there successful. The master franchisee is trained by the franchisor, and in consideration for a portion of the royalties, the master franchisee recruits, trains, and supports sub-franchisees to operate individual units of the franchise in the territory. In effect, the master franchisee is now the franchisor for that particular country, and normally there is no privity of contract between the sub-franchisee and the international franchisor located in the United States, or other countries.

Another form of international franchisor-franchisee relationships is the "Area Development Franchise." With an area development franchise, the franchisor grants the area developer the right to develop an entire country or part of it. Unlike those holding a master franchise, the area developer focuses on running the business, rather than selling franchises.

Finally, some international franchise relationships take the form of more traditional single-unit franchises. A single-unit franchisee is granted the right to open one franchise. While many franchisors steer away from this type of arrangement because of the costs of servicing one unit outside the country, hotel franchisors often establish significant operations outside the United States and will engage in single-unit franchising.

Conclusion

Franchising provides a myriad of opportunities for hotel owners and brands alike. By understanding the laws and regulations underlying hotel franchises, the ways in which owners and managers can work with hotel brands, and the impact of the franchise relationship on the business of the hotel, all parties can create a mutually beneficial and highly profitable relationship.

Review Questions

1. *What are the benefits of a franchise?* The benefits of a franchise are the right to sell a recognized brand, the use of franchisor's business practices and to receive initial training and ongoing support.
2. *The FTC Franchise Rule incorporates what three elements of a franchise?* The FTC Rule incorporates (1) trademark, (2) significant control or assistance, and (3) required payment.
3. *What are some of the most common types of violations of franchise law?* The most common types of violations of franchise law are selling a franchise without registration, failing to provide an FDD, failing to provide the franchisee with all disclosures required in the FDD, making misrepresentations to franchisee prospects, and improperly terminating or not renewing a franchise.
4. *What is the name of the document that franchisors in the U.S. are required to provide each prospective franchisee?* The Franchise Disclosure Document.
5. *What information is contained in the Franchise Disclosure Document?* (1) The franchisor and any parents, predecessors, and affiliates, (2) identity and business

experience of key persons, (3) litigation history, (4) bankruptcy, (5) initial franchise fee, (6) other fees and expenses, (7) franchisee's estimated initial investment, (8) restrictions on sources of products and services, (9) obligations of the franchisee, (10) financing arrangements, (11) obligations of the franchisor, (12) territory, (13) trademarks, (14) patents, copyrights, and proprietary information, (15) obligation of the franchisee to participate in the actual operation of the franchise business, (16) restrictions on goods and services offered by the franchisee, (17) renewal, termination, repurchase, modification, and/or transfer of the franchise agreement and dispute resolution, (18) public figures, and (19) financial performance representations.

6. *What basic information is required on a franchise application?* (1) Disclosure document receipt signed and dated, (2) an application letter, (3) a letter of intent, (4) certification of formation, (5) complete ownership structure form for the ownership entity and any underlying ownership entities, (6) complete ownership structure form for the fee title holder, (7) market feasibility study, and (8) payments of a franchise application fee.
7. *What does LOI stand for and it is binding?* LOI stands for Letter of Intent and it is not binding.
8. *What key terms should a franchise applicant look for in a franchise agreement?* Brand standards, royalty fees, marketing fees, reservation fees, frequent traveler program fees, non-compete areas, management, PIP, reserves, liquidated damages, purchasing programs, termination rights, financing and transfer, assignment and sale.
9. *What is a PIP?* A PIP is a Property Improvement Plan.
10. *What few items should a franchise applicant expect the hotel brands to negotiate in a hotel franchise agreement?* The term, protected territory, royalty fees, transfer provisions, liquidated damages, personal guaranties, key money, casualty and condemnation, recordation of the franchise agreement, management company acknowledgement, and comfort letters.

13

Leases, Licenses, and Related Agreements for Hotels

By Nelson F. Migdal and Derrick Yee

***Nelson F. Migdal** is a Principal Shareholder at Greenberg Traurig and the Co-Chair of the Global Hospitality Group. He has been practicing law in the hospitality area for more than thirty years, and has extensive experience in hotel and gaming transactions, including negotiating hotel management, franchise, licensing, and branding agreements. Mr. Migdal is an officer of the Academy of Hospitality Industry Attorneys, a member of the International Society of Hospitality Consultants, a member of ULI's Hotel Development Council, and Adjunct Associate Professor of Law at the American University College of Law.*

***Derrick Yee** is an Assistant Vice President at Watermark Capital Partners, responsible for asset management activities. Before joining Watermark, he was responsible for hotel asset management at Istithmar World/Dubai World, managing their multi-billion-dollar North American portfolio of luxury and resort assets. Prior to that, Mr. Yee was an asset manager for the Chartres Lodging group, where he was responsible for a portfolio of large convention hotel and upper-upscale hotels throughout the United States. While at Chartres, he oversaw several significant turnarounds, renovations, and repositionings. Mr. Yee is a graduate of Georgetown University, where he received a B.S.F.S. focused in International Relations. He also has an MBA from the Johnson School at Cornell University as well as a Masters in Management of Hospitality from the School of Hotel Administration at Cornell University, where he concentrated in Hotel Asset Management and Hotel Real Estate Finance. Mr. Yee is also a Certified Hotel Administrator and a member of the Hotel Asset Management Association.*

HOTELS ALL ACROSS THE PRICE AND QUALITY SPECTRUM, from economy to ultra-luxury, operate with a variety of leases, licenses, and other agreements with third-parties. Some of these agreements generate revenue for the hotel and represent an element of total operating revenue, while the expense to the hotel is captured as a departmental expense or undistributed operating expense. In this chapter we will explore these third-party relationships and their importance to the asset management process.

Leases, Licenses, and Related Agreements—Why Implement Them?

Leases, license agreements, and other related agreements, such as revenue share agreements, are useful asset management tools. In some cases, these agreements are clearly revenue focused, either introducing new revenue streams into the property or optimizing existing revenue streams. Examples of these revenue-focused agreements include:

- Self parking (at most urban hotels)
- Retail leased space on busy street frontages
- Hotel lobby kiosks
- ATMs
- Vending machines
- Exterior signs
- License agreements to use brands/concepts
- License agreements to use music protected by a copyright

Sometimes, asset managers can leverage these tools to mitigate expenses or reduce the operating risk of certain aspects of the property. Examples include:

- Gift shops
- Audiovisual departments
- Concierge services
- Valet parking

Not all agreements will either be specifically income-generating or expense-savings-focused agreements. In fact, many agreements will have both benefits. However, for ease of classification and discussion, we have broken them down into these two broad categories.

Beyond these two categories, there is also one special type of lease that asset managers may encounter: a ground lease. In some markets, where purchasing a property "fee simple" is difficult or not possible (such as New York City or Hawaii), ground leases will be a common occurrence. In a ground lease scenario, the lessee will make rent payments to the owner of the land for the right to develop or operate the improvements. In other cases, this structure can be used to separate the operations from the land, enabling an owner to divide revenue streams. Given the nuance of this specific type of agreement, we will address this separately later in the chapter.

Income-Generating Agreements

Nearly every aspect of the hotel can be a source of revenue for the owner. Leveraging leases, licenses, and other agreements, asset managers can create tremendous additional value for a hotel, maximizing the revenue generated per square foot.

With all revenue-related agreements, there are several general items that must be considered:

- Financial objective
- Term of agreement
- Obligations of each counterparty
- Promised rights/services
- Termination rights
- Fees
- Performance standards
- Brand approvals

Depending on whether you enter a license agreement, a lease, or another type of related agreement, there are several additional specific items that must be considered, which we will discuss in further detail in the following sections.

Leases

Asset managers are most likely to encounter leases when looking for new revenue streams for a hotel. Leases can take the form of space leased to third-party retail tenants, leases for billboards, or even leases of exterior spaces for antennas/radio transmitting equipment. While leases can be excellent tools, there are several key concerns that must be considered:

- *The leased space must be clearly defined, both as to location and size.* In addition, should there be the need for easements/access agreements, those should be clearly understood and documented.
- *The impact on other outlets/operating departments and operating procedures must be defined.* Agreements should clarify if there will be any sharing of services (garbage, receiving, shipping), and the cost, and potential expense reimbursement from the tenant, should be documented.
- *Tenant information must be provided.* In some cases, depending on affiliations and lender requirements, tenant qualifications will be critical to a successful lease.
- *If there is a guarantor of the tenant's obligations, the guarantor's information should be included.* Agreements should also specify any conditions where guarantor's obligations decrease or "burn off," such as the tenant's achievement of contractual sales volume hurdles, or the approved assignment or transfer of the guarantor's interests.
- *The date of the lease and term (including renewals, and which party has the right to renew) must be stated.* Agreements contemplating construction in the space should be clear as to the date of rent commencement.
- *The amount of the security deposit must be stated, and whether it is in the form of cash or a letter of credit.* As with guarantor's obligations, any potential reduction in the security deposit or letter of credit should be clearly documented.

- *The permitted use of the space must be clearly defined.* It is critical to clearly define the use of the space and its mandatory operating hours (ensuring it is complementary to guest activities and hotel operations).
- *The rent must be stated, including whether there will be additional rent and/or sales reporting requirements.* This area can be very flexible, and there are many rent structures available (see Exhibit 1).
- *Any tenant allowance being provided by the landlord should be stated.* In competitive markets, it will be likely that a tenant allowance would be demanded by the tenant. This will be critical to consider when developing ROI analyses.
- *Maintenance and repair obligations should be outlined.* Agreements should clarify who will maintain specific areas. Additionally, rights and obligations should be spelled out to ensure the performance of specific repairs, should other parts of the property be impacted.
- *Events of default and remedies should be outlined.* Although local statutes can impact the available options, the rights of all parties should be defined to help avoid future disputes.

In many markets, it may be helpful to engage a third-party broker to assist in the leasing of spaces. When working with a broker, asset managers should remember to specifically outline the financial as well as conceptual objectives of the project and the space available for lease. Leased space can have a significant impact on the overall feel and marketability of the property, and a strong brokerage partner can help you identify appropriate prospective tenants, determine market rents, and secure competitive offers. Additionally, qualified brokers should be able to provide rental comparisons that are useful when analyzing offers and the need for additional investments to secure prospective tenants.

A subset of general leases that may be encountered by asset managers will be billboard or signage leases. In areas of high visibility, leasing parts of the building or areas that can act as marketing platforms can be a very lucrative way to generate additional revenues. These types of leases do have some additional nuances that must be considered, however:

- Will the operator be involved in sourcing advertisers?
- Who will review and decide on the suitability of potential advertisers?
- What is the frequency of changes in advertising content?
- Will the process of changing advertising content affect property operations?

Finally, another commonly encountered lease type is the antenna lease. Rooftop "farming" is a concept available to any hotel in any market. In many markets where the hotel may be one of the tallest structures in the area, this can be a lucrative way to turn the area into revenue-generating space. As the demand for wireless services increases, antenna or radio leases are not only a great way to add revenue, but additionally improve critical service to the property to increase guest satisfaction. However, these agreements require special care and attention for a variety of reasons. Some of these key concerns include the following:

Exhibit 1 Common Lease and License Agreement Terminology

Additional Rent—Broadly defined, all rental payment due from tenant to landlord other than base rent. The most common types of additional rent generally found in commercial leases are variable rent and operating expense recoveries.

Base Rent—Minimum contractual rent under a lease.

Base Year—A type of expense stop sometimes included in a modified gross lease; the base year refers to a benchmark year for expenses, beyond which any increases are to be passed through to the tenant.

Breakpoint—A monetary level, typically a specified level of gross sales, where percentage rent begins to apply. A "natural breakpoint" occurs at the calculated level where the gross sales multiplied by the applicable variable rent percentage equals the base rent (Natural Breakpoint = Annual Base Rent ÷ Variable Rent %).

Commencement Date—Contractual date typically tied to when the lessee will make rent payments to the landlord. This can be either the date the lease is signed, or the opening date.

Common Area Maintenance (CAM)—A catch-all term referring to operating expenses for maintaining "common areas" that is subsequently passed through to the tenant, typically on a pro-rata basis.

Expense Stop—A monetary limit in a modified gross lease, above which the tenant in a commercial lease agrees to pay operating expenses over the lifetime of the lease. Different classes of expenses may have distinct expense stops, and frequently the base-year level of expenses is established as the level of expense stop.

Gross Lease—A classification of commercial lease denoting that the landlord will bear some portion of the cost of building operating expenses rather than passing them through to the tenant as additional rent. With full-service gross leases, all operating expenses are typically included in the base rent, while with modified gross leases, the tenant pays some portion of the operating expenses (may be all certain expense classes or some level of expenses above a contractual expense stop).

Hold-Over Tenant—A tenant whose lease has expired but continues to occupy the premises without the landlord's consent.

Opening Date—Typically defined as the date when an outlet commences operations, rather than when it takes over a space.

Operating Year—For leases that start during a calendar year, the rent schedule may be tied to a specific operating year. However, sometimes the operating year will shift to the calendar year after the first, stub year.

Percentage Rent—A common type of variable rent, generally calculated as a percentage of tenant's gross sales, and often taking effect (or changing calculations) above contractual breakpoints.

(continued)

Exhibit 1 *(continued)*

Subordination, Non-Disturbance, and Attornment Agreement (SNDA)—An agreement which defines how and when the rights of the tenant will be subordinate to rights of lenders and ground lessors, or when its rights will be senior to rights of lenders and ground lessors. In general, it ensures that tenants will have access to their premises, even if the landlord defaults and the lender attempts to foreclose on a property. It also assures the lender than the tenant will agree, should it wish to remain a tenant, to certain lender rights following a foreclosure or purchase.

Triple Net Lease—Also referred to as "net-net-net," a triple net lease is a lease requiring that the tenant is responsible for all operating expenses of the space being leased, including specifically the real estate taxes, insurance, and common area maintenance. The method for determining the amounts (whether by allocation or another method) can be negotiated.

Variable Rent—Rent that is variable, tied to revenues or possibly escalated by a factor such as CPI.

- *Roof integrity.* Roof warranties could be rendered void if the telecommunications equipment requires penetrations into the roof in order to be installed.
- *Service and maintenance.* In order to provide continual service, many groups may request 24/7 access to the roof in order to maintain the equipment and address service issues. However, given the security concerns that have arisen in the post-9/11 era, continuous access may be impractical or unrealistic.
- *Interference.* Any new installations must not interfere with existing antennas or other wireless communication devices that service the hotel or its primary functions. Language in any agreement should protect the hotel and ensure that any interference is resolved at the cost of the lessee.

The goal of a successful lease will be to add incremental value. In cases where the venue/outlet could be self-operated, there are several other factors to consider:

- Does the lease make the outlet more profitable than the current operating scenario?
- What additional investments must be made to successfully lease the space?
- What sort of restrictions/complications could the lease have on future redevelopment/transfer/sale?
- Will managing the tenant place additional unnecessary burdens on either the asset manager or the hotel manager?
- Does this lease eliminate operating risks associated with self-operation?
- Does leasing the space negatively impact other key operating departments (e.g., banquets and catering, engineering, etc.)?

While leasing can be a terrific way to eliminate some operating risk and allow the hotel to focus on the most important part of its operations, leasing is not always the optimal solution. In some cases, having flexibility may be more valuable to the investment objective. All these ancillary impacts must be reviewed to make the property investment decision.

It is worth noting that many states have different laws governing leases and lease termination. When negotiating leases, it is wise to understand your rights as a landlord in each jurisdiction in order to fully understand the risk involved should a tenant fail to live up to its obligation, and should you want to evict a tenant or exercise additional initiatives as the property owner.

License Agreements

License agreements can be useful for asset managers who want to leverage a brand to increase the visibility of an outlet at a property, but retain in-house management and operational control. A common license agreement will be a coffee shop/restaurant franchise agreement, where the property uses the name of an organization (e.g., Starbucks, Peets, Caribou, Shula's, ESPN), but continues to operate the outlet internally. Another type of license agreement commonly encountered is an antenna license. Many of the concerns in license agreements will mirror those previously mentioned when considering lease agreements; however, there are some additional considerations to keep in mind for license agreements:

- *Definition of trademarks and branding materials.* It is critical to understand how the hotel can use the licensor's trademarks and branding items in advertising and collateral.
- *Licensor restrictions and operating standards.* The hotel must understand its obligations to the licensor and consider whether it can comply with all of the licensor's operating standards, and if those standards make financial sense for the hotel.
- *Licensor access for inspections/training.* Depending on the licensor, access for inspection or training may be required. Understanding the access requirements and the frequency of inspections is critical to understanding the ongoing operational impact of entering such an agreement.
- *Sourcing.* Some license agreements will be strict on where products may be sourced. This can have a significant impact on the financial feasibility of any licensed outlet or product. For example, some coffee-focused licensors may be fanatical about the sourcing of the beverage products, but may give leeway on the sourcing of the food components in the outlet, enabling the licensee to leverage purchasing power of other departments to improve the effectiveness of the overall operation.

Sometimes, use of either a lease or a license is available for similar types of relationships, but they are not the same and do not provide the same benefits to the recipient of the rights. Leases are hybrid documents that can grant the tenant both contract interests and real estate interests. Property owners often seek to avoid use of a lease, because the concept of the grant of an interest in real estate can allow the tenant to also claim the benefits, rights, and protections of tenants granted under the laws of the state in which the hotel is located. A license, on the other hand, represents the granting of permission that would not exist without that grant, and is therefore governed solely by the language of the grant itself. For example, a rooftop antenna arrangement could be achieved through a lease or a license. If a lease is used, the tenant can assert all the rights afforded to tenants in that jurisdiction, which can make it a longer and more costly process to remove the tenant. Use of a license in the same context grants the licensee permission to have the antenna on the roof based solely upon the terms and conditions stated in the license itself. Upon the termination of the license, the licensee has only the contract rights under the license and no statutory tenant's rights.

Leases and licenses are both terrific tools to increase revenue generation at the property. However, these items should not take away from the primary focus of running and operating the hotel. Any potential negative impact that these agreements could have on the property's operations and guest satisfaction must be considered when evaluating whether to proceed with a new lease or license agreement. In addition, should ownership be considering a capital event, such as a sale, it is of utmost importance that all agreements be transferrable or terminable with minimal hurdles and difficulties.

Other Operating Agreements

For many hotel owners, entering into operating agreements with third parties to take over specific functions of the hotel can be a way to minimize operating risk and reduce expenses. These models are very common for food and beverage outlets, as well as other operated departments such as valet services, audiovisual services, and spa departments. As these agreements bring outside parties to operating departments within the building, these agreements must be carefully assessed. Some key considerations include the following:

- *Operating partner history.* As the partner will be operating within your hotel, the quality of the partner's operations will impact the overall image of the property. Vetting the operating partner's capabilities is critical to the success of any of these types of arrangements.
- *Term of the agreement.* The ideal term will be dependent on the investment objectives. While operators generally will look for longer-term contracts, there may be significant flexibility depending on the situation.
- *Fees and the structure of fees.* Most agreements will include a flat percentage fee. However, participation or performance fees can be highly negotiable. Establishing the correct fee scenario can align interests and improve cooperation among all parties.
- *Operating covenants, such as hours of operation.* Understanding these covenants is critical to smooth operations. In some cases, a third-party operator will want to restrict hours or limit services, which can negatively reflect on the hotel and impact guest satisfaction. When evaluating these agreements, make sure the hours of operation are standardized and reflect the needs of the hotel's guests.
- *Room service and catering obligations.* The topic of in-room dining can be particularly sensitive in union environments. If an outlet is operated by a non-union entity, delivering to guestrooms may be impossible or difficult to implement

based on the existing work rules and agreements. Additionally, operators may not want to work with union labor if they are non-union, for fear of encouraging organizational activity within their own companies.

- *Interaction with sales team/sales discounts.* Potential sales comps or discounts, which are common in group sales contracts, need to be documented up front.
- *Licenses and permits.* Rights and responsibilities for obtaining and maintaining all necessary licenses and permits should be clarified in the agreements.
- *Repairs, alterations, and maintenance.* The rights and obligations of all parties in these areas should be documented.
- *Shared services/shared access.* Any shared services or shared access should be addressed in the agreements.
- *Security.* Security can be a particular concern for night-life and beverage-centric venues. Should the outlet be popular, driving a significant volume of non-hotel guests into the property, it will be necessary to establish security protocols to protect guestroom access, as well as protect the overall safety of guests from those individuals who may become overly intoxicated or rowdy.
- *Food safety and sanitation.* While typically the responsibility of the operator, that responsibility should be clarified.
- *Containment of noise and fumes.* Noise and fumes, either from food preparation or smells from salon services, can negatively impact guest experiences if not contained. This is of particular concern if impacted spaces are in close proximity to guestrooms or meeting space.
- *Legal compliance.* The rights and obligations of all parties should be documented.
- *Insurance.* The insurance requirements of all parties should be spelled out.
- *Defaults.* As previously noted, in terms of defaults, the rights of all parties should be defined to help avoid future disputes.
- *Casualty and condemnation.* The rights and obligations of all parties should be documented.

Entering an operating agreement is similar to entering a partnership, as the operations of each party will be critical to the overall success of the hotel. As the relationship between the hotel operations team and the third-party operator will be tightly intertwined, having all parties at the negotiation table early will ease the implementation of any negotiated agreement. When executed appropriately, these agreements will make the third-party operator a true part of the overall hotel operation, resulting in improved performance and guest satisfaction.

Ground Leases

Ground leases typically exist in markets where land is in high demand or difficult to secure. In these cases, the lessee will generally be the owner of the property improvements (the physical building) while leasing the land from a landlord. Typically, these agreements are for a long duration (50–99 years), making it palatable for the lessee to improve the land. Ground leases can reduce the overall initial costs of developing a hotel (eliminating the need to purchase the land upfront and effectively serving as partial financing). However, ground leases do have certain drawbacks and can have implications on exit valuations.

When dealing with ground leases, there are several items that you must keep in mind:

- *Term.* As just mentioned, typically new ground leases will be for a term of 50–99 years. If purchasing a property that has a limited term left on the lease, it will be critical for the asset manager to understand the renewal terms of the ground lease (if any) and what notices may exist in order to execute on a renewal. It is worth noting that many investors will avoid short-term ground leases, and many lenders may be unable or unwilling to underwrite mortgages involving them.
- *Rent reset.* Many ground leases will incorporate an escalation clause, which may be based upon pre-negotiated "steps," an annual percentage increase, or some other methodology, which will grow the annual rent every year. However, some ground leases will fix the rent over a specific period and then have a rent reset date, which will reset the rent to a new level at the agreed-upon date. Understanding the mechanism of the reset will be critical to understanding the financial obligations of the hotel and overall profitability of the investment.
- *Percentage rent.* Some ground leases will incorporate a percentage rent provision, enabling the landlord to benefit from any potential upside from the land improvements.
- *Casualty and condemnation.* With the ownership of the land being separated from the ownership of the improvements, there are often unique provisions in ground leases with respect to allocation of any casualty and condemnation proceeds.
- *Subordination.* The hotel management agreement generally will be subordinate to the landlord's interests under the ground lease, absent specific non-disturbance provisions for the benefit of the hotel manager.
- *Ground lessor consent requirements.* While the lessee typically owns the improvements, many ground leases contain provisions requiring lessor consent for major additions or changes in use.
- *Lease expiration and reversion provisions.* Responsibilities of the lessee and what happens to the improvements upon ground lease expiration may have significant financial implications on the value of the leasehold interests. Many ground leases provide that ownership of the improvements revert to the lessor upon expiration, and contain specific provisions about the required condition of the improvements upon reversion.

Negotiating Agreements

It is imperative for asset managers to carefully review and negotiate each agreement to protect the rights of the hotel owner. It is important to not get lulled into a false sense of security and comfort by having the hotel owner use its form of agreement, or feel forced to start with the tenant's form of agreement because the tenant is a large national retailer or vendor. Attention to detail and care is always the best practice. In the following paragraphs we will use the terms "landlord" and "tenant" for readability, but these elements can be found in many types of agreements between the hotel owner or operator and an occupant.

Term

Asset managers should assess the term of the agreement and note any relationship between the opening date of the hotel and the commencement date of the agreement. Do not assume they are the same. It is often relevant to confirm the operating year under the agreement and compare it to the hotel's management agreement and/or franchise agreement. What happens at the end of the initial term? Assess not only whether there is an automatic or optional extension, but which party has the right to extend. The agreement will end at some point, either by reaching the end of its natural term or due to the actions of one of the parties. Assess the termination and surrender process, with particular attention to condition of the premises as well as the removal of a party's intellectual property, icons, decorations, signs, goods, and effects; and the removal of any machinery, trade fixtures, and equipment that are used in conducting the trade or business. There is likely to be some penalty if a party fails to depart and becomes a "hold-over."

Rent

The rent can take many forms and include many components. The assessment of rent must be mindful of the presence of the different rent components and how they work together. Base rent is easy to spot and typically is a stated annual amount paid monthly during the term. It might increase annually, as shown on a pre-negotiated chart, or based upon a percentage increase or similar formula. In the retail arena, there will commonly be variable or percentage rent (rent that is based on sales revenues). This is commonly a percentage of gross sales. The hotel owner should be very interested in the definition of gross sales. Here is one example of how gross sales might be defined in an agreement:

> As used in this agreement, "Gross Sales" means and refers to the total gross amount of all sales, income, receipts, revenues, monies, or other things of value received by or on behalf of Tenant, or any licensee, concessionaire, sublessee, or assignee of Tenant, for all goods or merchandise sold or delivered in, at, on, or from the Premises, all of the foregoing being exclusive of matters expressly excluded from Gross Sales, namely, each of the following: (1) returns and refunds; (2) sales by any valet for parking, coat check, or restroom service, or sales from any mechanical or vending device which is provided solely for the convenience and use of Tenant's employees or, with respect to any vending machine not operated by Tenant, revenues from such vending machine in excess of the amounts paid to Tenant; (3) sales where orders originate from or are accepted in the Premises but delivery or performance takes place else-

> where; (4) sales pursuant to mail, catalogue (unless the customer places the order from such catalogue at the Premises), telegraph, telephone, or other technology that are received or filled at or from the Premises; (5) sales of gift certificates (except upon redemption as set forth above); (6) discounts or charges of credit card issuers on sales made by credit card; (7) intercompany sales or transfers of merchandise between stores of Tenant (or its affiliates); (8) the amount of any sales tax, if any, which is both added to the sales price and paid by Tenant in respect of any tax imposed on Tenant (but not by any vendor of Tenant); (9) the net amount of discounts to customers or employees pursuant to Tenant's customary and reasonable policies; (10) sales of furniture, fixtures, equipment, or memorabilia outside of the normal course of Tenant's business, or other similar sales or transfers commonly considered capital in nature; (11) interest and dividend income; (12) proceeds of sales from charity events or special events, to the extent that such proceeds are donated by Tenant to charitable organizations within twelve (12) months from the event; (13) proceeds of insurance, condemnation, or indemnity for a loss or taking; (14) sales for credit which are charged off as "bad debt" in the ordinary course of business; (15) entries for complimentary services; or (16) discounts provided to Landlord pursuant to this agreement.

Percentage rent is determined from a written statement provided pursuant to the agreement, and it is usually verified and certified by a chief financial officer or another executive officer. Typically, both monthly statements and an annual statement will be required. The landlord or other party to the agreement will have the right to audit the books and records pertaining to gross sales to confirm the statements, and there will be penalties, including default, for uncured errors.

In some cases the percentage rent will be discussed in the terms of natural or artificial breakpoints. A natural breakpoint is defined as the volume of sales a tenant must generate to pay the fixed minimum rent. It is calculated by dividing the fixed minimum rent by the percentage used for the percentage rent calculations. For example, if you have a fixed rent of $50,000 per year, and were evaluating a percentage rent of 5 percent, the natural breakpoint would be $1 million. In this case, in a tenant agreement to percentage rent at a natural breakpoint, the percentage rent would commence after the breakpoint of $1 million revenue threshold has been achieved.

If using an artificial breakpoint, the fixed rent and percentage rent can be separated and discussed separately. Under this scenario, the percentage used calculating percentage rent will be defined separately from the revenue threshold used to trigger the percentage rent. Whether to use the natural breakpoint or artificial breakpoint must be determined by the asset manager, based on market considerations or ownership requirements.

"Rent commencement" is another term to evaluate carefully. The tenant may look to begin the rent term on the opening date, rather than the commencement date, which can have material impacts on the operation and financial projections, depending on the nature of the lease/license agreement.

Other rent terms and types may be encountered when negotiating a lease or license. Please refer to Exhibit 1 for more information about common rent terms and types.

Use of Premises

The nature and purpose of the occupancy and use should be specific and limited. If the asset is large and contains multiple tenants or users, it may be important to understand any exclusive uses granted to particular users. This part of the agreement may also include statements that the premises cannot be used for any unlawful conduct or purposes, and specify business hours and days as well as days that the premises can be closed for business.

Alterations

The limitations or obligations as to painting, decorating, and alterations should be very specific. There may be brand-related considerations and an obligation to achieve design and architectural consistency with the larger hotel facility. Certainly, any material structural alterations, additions, or changes in the premises should require prior approval. Additionally, all alterations must be performed by appropriately licensed and insured entities.

Liability of Parties

Assessment of the respective liabilities of the parties will be a legal analysis, but an asset manager may be called upon to initially identify the issues and risks. The tenant or occupant will bear the bulk of the risk, based upon its occupancy and use of the premises, but that does not mean that the owner or landlord will have no liabilities. For example, an owner or landlord will often be responsible for, and have the duty to defend, indemnify, and hold harmless the other party against and from any and all liability, claim of liability, or expense which arises out of or in connection with (i) any breach, by Landlord, of any representation or warranty of Landlord contained in the agreement; (ii) any failure to perform any covenant or agreement of Landlord contained in the agreement; (iii) any failure by Landlord to pay, perform, and discharge any liability or obligation of Landlord; (iv) all liabilities and obligations of Landlord other than those for which indemnification is provided by Tenant or occupant; or (v) the negligent or intentionally tortious act or omission of Landlord or its agents, officers, or employees. Then, except for those situations in which Landlord is obligated to indemnify and hold harmless the tenant or occupant, the tenant or occupant is responsible for, and shall defend, indemnify, and hold harmless Landlord against and from any and all liability, claim of liability, or expense arising out of (i) any breach by Tenant of any representation or warranty of Tenant contained in this Lease; (ii) any failure by Tenant to pay, perform, and discharge any liability or obligation of Tenant, owed to Landlord; (iii) any breach or default by Tenant in performing any of its obligations under the provisions of the agreement; or (iv) any negligent or intentionally tortious act or omission of Tenant or any of its agents and/or employees.

Design, Plans, and Specifications

The agreement will probably have extensive provisions concerning which party will be responsible for the design and development of the space and what, if any, allowances the owner or landlord might provide. This is often influenced by the larger project and what and where it is. Additionally, there may be design restrictions due to the hotel brand/brand manager. The owner or landlord may want to exert control over the entire process. Of course, this will be more of a negotiation when the other party is a branded nationally known vendor or retailer with its own specifications and requirements. Things to be very aware of include mandatory starting dates, completion dates, and penalties if the contractual date obligations are not met.

Maintenance

Once the premises improvements are complete and open to the public, the fundamental elements of maintenance will be crucial. The occupant or tenant will have significant maintenance responsibilities (other than building systems, which should always be the exclusive purview of the owner or landlord) and will usually be obligated to, at its own cost and expense, keep the premises in good order, condition, and repair as well as clean, orderly, sanitary, and safe.

Assignment

The owner or landlord will want to prohibit or limit assignment by the tenant/occupant. This element of the agreement should be analyzed in light of what is intended to be prohibited completely or merely restricted. The asset manager should be thinking in broad terms and consider not only assignment, but efforts to sublet, transfer, or encumber the agreement as well. Using the agreement as collateral security for a loan by the tenant or occupant may be prohibited or limited to borrowing capital for the development and improvement of the premises, and even then only with the written consent of the owner/landlord. It is important to also recognize that some changes in ownership will be deemed to constitute an assignment of the agreement. This would include a tenant or occupant engaging in: (a) the merger, consolidation, or reorganization of that party unless it is with a parent, subsidiary, or affiliate; and/or (b) the sale, issuance, or transfer of any voting stock by the party or the guarantor(s) of the party that results in a change in the voting control of the tenant or occupant, except for a transfer of stock in a public company or by public offering.

As the owner, it is critical to maintain flexibility should the owner need to assign the agreement due to a change in ownership or capital structure. The asset manager needs to make sure any agreement does not prevent or hinder the owner's rights with regard to the capital structure of the property, which could prevent or complicate a sale process. In an optimal case, tenant approval of an ownership transfer should not be required; however, some large organizations, such as national restaurant chains, will require that they be able to approve such a transfer. The asset manager should understand what the process is, and push for reasonable and responsive approval time frames for any assignment by the owner to another party.

Event of Default

Every agreement will specify events of default. Some of the more common and logical events of default will include: (i) failure to pay rent; (ii) failure to perform other non-monetary obligations under the provisions of the lease; (iii) sale of Tenant's interest in the premises under attachment, execution, or similar legal process, or if Tenant is adjudicated a bankrupt or insolvent under any state bankruptcy or insolvency law, or an order for relief is entered against Tenant under the Federal Bankruptcy Code; (iv) commencement of any action under any chapter of the Federal Bankruptcy Code by or against Tenant, or the filing of a voluntary or involuntary petition proposing the adjudication of Tenant as bankrupt or insolvent; (v) the appointment of a receiver or trustee for the business or property of Tenant; (vi) the making by Tenant of any general assignment for the benefit of its creditors; or (vii) the admission by Tenant of its inability to pay its debts when due.

Brand Loyalty Programs and Guest Matters

An agreement may contain very specific provisions with respect to honoring a hotel brand's loyalty program and permitting guests to charge the purchase of merchandise to the guests' account maintained at the hotel. These provisions should have reporting requirements and reimbursement requirements attached to them as well.

Information Technology Systems

The agreement may obligate the tenant to modify its point of sale computer system as necessary to interface with the landlord's property management system, such that (i) Tenant may fully participate in the rewards or point system; (ii) guests may redeem points to buy food, beverage, and merchandise from Tenant; (iii) guests may charge the purchase of merchandise to the guests' hotel account; and (iv) Landlord, from its computer system, and Tenant, from its computer system, can each independently run, on at least a daily basis, reports evidencing the actual amount of all food, beverage. and merchandise sold at or from the premises using points or charged to guest accounts.

Miscellaneous and Standard Clauses

Agreements will provide requirements for notice and various other standard clauses. Even the so-called boilerplate provisions should be read and understood. The general subject matters include several elements:

- A complete understanding/full integration clause, to state that the agreement represents the complete understanding between the parties without representations or warranties by either party.
- A no waivers clause, to state that the failure by a party to insist upon the strict performance of any covenant, agreement, term, or condition of the agree-

ment, or to exercise any right or remedy upon a default, does not constitute a waiver of the default, and no covenant, agreement, term, or condition of the agreement can be waived, altered, or modified except by written instrument signed by the party to be charged.

- A waiver of certain damages clause, to state that except for the indemnification obligations in the agreement, the parties waive (to the fullest extent permitted by law) any right to or claim for any punitive, exemplary, or multiple damages against the other, and agree that, in the event of a dispute between the parties, the party making a claim will be limited to equitable relief and to recovery of any actual damages it sustains.
- "Successors and assigns" provisions, to state that the agreement inures to the benefit of and is binding upon the parties and their respective successors and assigns.

These are just several of the general clauses that will be encountered in most leases or license agreements. When negotiating any agreement, it is critical for the asset manager to review each clause carefully to understand the obligations and implications of the language being presented. Making sure the lease/license language accurately reflects the business terms agreed to is critical to prevent unnecessary surprises.

Conclusion

Leases, licenses, and other related agreements can be terrific tools to further optimize a hotel's revenue performance. As with any tool, it is critical for the asset manager to carefully evaluate the pros and cons of each of these tools when looking to implement them in a hotel, remembering that all of these tools should help, not hinder, the hotel and its operations.

14

Key Legal Issues: The Battle for Control

By William M. Bosch and Anthony F. Cavanaugh

***William Bosch** is an accomplished trial lawyer whose practice is largely focused on the representation of real estate owners and developers, as well as high-end funds that invest in real estate projects. He co-leads the firm's interdisciplinary Hospitality Practice and regularly advises hotel owners and real estate joint venture parties in resolving disputes across the United States and internationally. Mr. Bosch has handled precedent-setting litigation and arbitration involving the enforcement and termination of hotel management agreements (including disputes involving most of the major hotel operators) and issues of fraud and racketeering, breach of contract, fiduciary duty, accounting, cost allocations, unfair trade practices, personal services, and agency. He also formulates and executes strategic plans to help clients navigate commercial and intellectual property challenges across a range of other industry sectors, including life sciences, IT, financial services and consumer products.*

***Anthony Cavanaugh** focuses on complex litigation in both state and federal courts, with an emphasis on counseling clients in the hospitality industry. He assists clients in the evaluation and, if necessary, litigation of disputes with management companies, franchisors, tenants, lenders or vendors. He has experience with the resolution of commercial disputes, including the negotiation and enforcement of management contracts, asset management, and evaluation of hotel operations. Mr. Cavanaugh also has handled cases involving toxic tort litigation, including the defense of a leading chemical manufacturer in a series of medical monitoring class actions. In addition, he has represented manufacturers and distributors of military supplies in commercial disputes.*

Mr. Cavanaugh graduated from the Georgetown University Law Center, where he was Editor of the Georgetown International Environmental Law Review.

"HOSPITALITY" BY NAME AND CONCEPT encompasses caring for guests and, across many cultures, embodies notions of safe refuge, respect, graciousness, and comfort. In our experience, some management companies use the sales process before the management agreement is signed to foster a false impression that hospitality will be extended to the owner as well as to the guest. This is not always the case, and for some managers, decidedly not. In short, *caveat emptor.*

Once a potential hotel investor closes on a transaction and becomes an owner, it bears the risks of diminution of property value common to all real estate, as well as on-going exposure to operating losses and liabilities arising from operating the hotel business. But investors can misunderstand and overestimate their ability to control or even influence these business risks. This "control risk" sometimes is lost amid the negotiation of the core economic terms, especially in connection with the selection and retention of a manager to operate the hotel business.

In this chapter, we build on prior publications describing the key legal issues confronting investors in hotels to highlight an emerging theme at the intersection of business and law: hotel managers proclaim that their interests are aligned with owners, but many prove otherwise in their contracts and performance. Owners dissatisfied with the manager too often have negotiated away control rights and find themselves with limited options to exert influence. This trend has increased as management companies have spent a lot of time, attention, and attorney fees developing form agreements favoring themselves with terms they claim to be non-negotiable.

A prudent investor therefore distinguishes the promises of the development teams selling the skills of a manager from the legal rights, duties, and obligations undertaken by the parties under the management agreement. It evaluates the operating model and the measure of control the investor desires to maintain over the duration of the term, regardless of its anticipated hold period. And such an investor wisely evaluates the positions management companies have taken in litigation, so that it can push back when it costs the least—at the negotiating stage.

Control under Different Operating Models

As an initial matter, the control risk varies with the type of operating model. This is not to say that one model is routinely better or worse than the next; they each have pros and cons. But the legal issues, including the key language in a management contract, should be evaluated by investors at the outset in the context of their appetite for control risk.

Accordingly, we outline below some general characteristics of the different operating models, so that investors can be sensitive to and negotiate the control risks when they're focused on more typical evaluation and allocation of economic risks.

Branded Hotel Management Company Model

Control risk arises foremost in the operator model where the authority to operate the hotel on a day-to-day basis is delegated to a branded management company. A branded management company typically does not own the hotel property, but rather manages the hotel business on behalf of the owner. The owner pays a fee in return for the branded management company's services, expertise, and use of the brand in marketing the hotel. Typically, that brand is incorporated in the name of the hotel.

Most branded hotel companies have a business model that primarily seeks fee income, with little equity invested in hotel real estate. As J. W. ("Bill") Marriott, Jr.

acknowledged in describing Marriott's growth, their goal was to reduce their proportion of ownership to one of every 100 hotels in Marriott's global system, instead focusing their business on management contracts.[1] Under this business model, in which the manager bears little to no investment risk and is compensated primarily by a percentage of hotel gross revenues, there is an inherent conflict of interest—the brand is incentivized to spend owner money in pursuit of revenues, regardless of overall profitability.[2]

As discussed further below, numerous disputes have arisen where the brand makes operational decisions that appear to promote brand interest ahead of owner interest. These decisions go well beyond territorial encroachment, where brands negatively affect one operation by operating affiliated properties in overlapping markets. They include, for example, evolving brand standards and decisions to move property-level services to "shared services" provided above property level by the operator's affiliates.

Some brand operators take the position that a rising tide lifts all boats—that what's good for the brand and its shareholders is necessarily good for the owners of individual hotels. But owners increasingly are questioning this proposition. The problem is exacerbated by the presumption of brand value, which is increasingly being challenged by research studies.[3] Lenders historically appeared to prefer branded operators, perhaps because of the perceived value of their reservations systems in driving revenue. But the most recent economic downturn had a dampening effect on how enamored lenders are of brands, especially as special servicers started looking more closely at expense structures.[4] The rise of third-party distribution services, such as OTAs and soft-branded reservations systems, as well as consumer access to rating sites, has further diminished the advantages that used to be associated with the larger brand operators.

This is not to say that all branded operators are bad, or that the branded model is inherently unfavorable to an investor. However, it is imperative that prudent investors more closely evaluate and distinguish between a branded manager's promises and what it is contractually committed to deliver. For example, when an investor asks for proof that brand initiatives are generating incremental returns for the owner, too often they're stonewalled by a branded management company that refuses to identify any obligation to respond to such inquiries. Then, when they look at the management contracts they have signed, some owners find that the operator has curtailed the scope of information it is contractually required to provide and/or circumscribes the owner's ability to object as part of the annual budget review. These control elements are best addressed at the operator selection stage.

The longer the term, the greater the control risk. The primary ownership risk under the branded hotel management model is the term of the agreements. Branded hotel operators typically insist on longer term contracts and press for "no cut" provisions that effectively commit the owner to bankroll the manager. They are known for negotiating so-called performance tests that are difficult (sometimes impossible) to fail, often relying on at least one "revenue index" prong that the operator knows presents no genuine performance termination risk.

Owners don't always understand that they're being asked to hand over the keys and surrender all control over how owner money is spent. The litigation positions taken by branded management companies reveal this is precisely their objective. Hence, when the relationship does not outlast the honeymoon following execution of the contract, disputes arise. In some instances, the owner is forced to seek judicial relief to regain control over its property, hotel business, and checkbook.

These control risk pressures are exacerbated in the context of a branded hotel management company model because they are influenced by operator culture. Operator culture is inherently difficult for investors to evaluate during the due diligence phase. Whereas some branded managers promote transparency and remain focused on generating returns for owners, others are less owner-friendly. Some are simply arrogant and litigious. Some promote their own interests, including their interest in developing and growing their brands, tapping into the public equity markets and, for public companies, pursuing shareholder interests even when those are at odds with owner interests. Sorting this out is difficult when investors are enamored with the property itself and with the pro formas promising a rosy future.

Managers that disclaim fiduciary duties increase control risk. Culturally, one bellwether of an owner's ability to control its investment is the manager's willingness to acknowledge and abide by its fiduciary duties to the owners for whom they operate. Fiduciary duties include the duties of loyalty, disclosure, and the obligation to put the interests of the owner ahead of the manager.[5] These duties, even if not expressly stated, are implicit in a relationship where the owner delegates the day-to-day authority and control over the operation of the hotel, funds that operation, and agrees to bear all risk of financial loss.[6]

Branded management companies can be less transparent. Some have used draft management contract language and legislative initiatives in an attempt to avoid well established legal authority that they act as fiduciaries on behalf of owners. For example, Marriott and Starwood successfully lobbied the Maryland state legislature to enact Title 23 of the Commercial Law section of the Maryland Code, which is applicable specifically to parties to hotel operating agreements. The statute subordinates common-law agency principles to the express terms of an operating agreement. Among other implications, the statute allows hotel managers to argue that there are no implied fiduciary duties, even where the terms of the management contract would suggest otherwise. And where Maryland law does not apply, some of these management companies have been unabashed in proclaiming that, in their view, they do not owe fiduciary duties to the owners for whose account they ostensibly are managing the hotel.

Pro forma and budget disclaimers by managers also portend increased control risk. Another cultural indicator is how the management company stands behind its financial forecasts after the management contract is signed. Given their size, branded operators tend to have development teams that engage investors and provide pro formas developed by in-house research departments. The pro formas typically have disclaimers by which the management company essentially says "do not rely on our forecasts." Often the management agreements will include a provision such as "Owner acknowledges that any written or oral projections, pro formas, or other similar information that has been (prior to execution of this agreement) or will (during the term) be provided by Manager ... is for information purposes only, and that manager ... does not guarantee that the hotel will achieve the results set forth in any such projection, pro formas, or other similar information...."

Given the unequal bargaining positions, especially as they relate to market conditions and hotel operating forecasts, investors and lenders typically have to rely on such forecasts. Legally, however, operators will be quick to point out that such reliance is misplaced, given their disclaimers. The issue is not merely one of "guarantee," but rather goes to the heart of the investor's due diligence. Owners confronted by a development team that will not stand behind the pro formas it offers to justify the owner's investment, at least during the initial budget years of the engagement, should be especially sensitive to control risk, as the trust owners necessarily must place with the manager is rooted on a very shaky foundation.

For most owners, control issues become evident only after a deal is signed, when the first budget is being evaluated. When the operating team, as distinguished from the brand management company's development team, assumes responsibility for presenting operating budgets and actual performance, the romance phase can rapidly move into a period of buyer's remorse. Branded operators increasingly are using the annual budget review process as the focal point for owner input and "control." But as with the pro formas, branded hotel management contracts typically provide that the budget is actually just aspirational. And when the operator fails to meet an approved budget or, more typically, unilaterally revises its "forecast" during the course of the budget year, owners sometimes find themselves with few concrete remedies under the contract. In short, a manager that will not stand behind its forecasts and refuses to provide the owner with concrete approval rights and access to information is grabbing perilous and potentially long-term control over the owner's property and bank account.

The Franchise Model

Control risk can be attenuated slightly but not completely where a non-branded management company operates pursuant to the system standards of a franchise flag. Under this model, the owner enters into a franchise agreement and license with a brand (the franchisor), by which it commits to employ certain franchise systems and comply with franchisor standards. In consideration, the franchisor receives a fee, typically a percentage of revenues. Day-to-day management, however, is undertaken by a third entity (i.e., an independent management company) or by an owner affiliate (i.e., an owner/operator). Obviously, an owner-operated franchise provides greater control. However, even an independently managed franchise can provide increased owner control, because investors typically have more leverage in negotiating shorter terms and otherwise more favorable control provisions with independents.

Even in an owner-operated situation, the investor cedes substantial control rights to the franchisor. The franchise agreement in most instances provides few (if any) options for owner termination without payment of liquidated damages. The brand, by contrast, typically retains several termination options and the ability to require costly owner investments to meet new system standards. As a general matter, the court decisions recognizing owner termination powers under agency or personal services theories (discussed further below) do not extend to a typical franchise relationship.

In many respects, the branded management and franchise models have started to merge. Several of the larger brands have moved essential management functions (like accounting, human resources, procurement, sales and marketing, and reservations) above property level. Hotel employees, whether working for a branded manager or a franchisee, are increasingly removed from the information and resources needed to manage the hotel on a day-to-day basis. But under a franchise model, at least, the franchisee has some control over which systems it agrees to use and over the fees it is willing to pay for such systems. In a branded management context, some managers unilaterally enroll properties in new systems and impose additional charges without owner input or approval—and without providing backup detail when requested. These are the types of managers a prudent hotel investor would do well to avoid.

The Independent Model

An independent hotel is usually managed directly by an owner affiliate or by a non-branded management company. Owner-operated independents obviously have the lowest control risk (assuming partnership equanimity), but many managed independents also offer control benefits. Shorter terms and broader owner termination rights, fewer system charges and hidden fees, increased owner access and input rights, and a culture focused more on the success of the individual property than on developing "brand equities" are the hallmarks of this model. The independent hotel also is free from brand standards so it can provide a unique experience, tailored to the market and more flexible in responding to changes in the competitive market landscape. Of course, under this model the absence of systems and brand equity portends longer ramp-up to stabilization, and success depends on the ability to hire and retain talent at the property level. But control risk is clearly reduced relative to the other prevailing models.

Control Rights in Management Contracts

The primary way investors in hotels can preserve control rights is through the terms of the management contract. The following are some exemplary provisions where prudent investors can and should push back when a manager tries to assert too much control.

Term and termination. The longer the term, the less control the owner has, absent a termination "without cause" provision. Owners also can negotiate for more control through a termination on sale provision and through a legitimate performance test. Managers unwilling to consider these provisions essentially are seeking to minimize the risks from their own non-performance, which should give any prudent investor pause. Of course, performance guarantees, fee stand-asides, and other similar provisions (e.g., fee caps) also can align owner/manager interests. But the owner's ability to terminate the manager is the ultimate control mechanism. Accordingly, when managers ask for disclaimers of any kind—disclaimers of agency, disclaimers of personal service relationships, or disclaimers of fiduciary duties—hotel investors should be especially vigilant.

Hiring and retention of employees, including the hotel's upper management team. Where the manager seeks the contractual right to hire, train and supervise employees, including the guidance team, the owner would do well to impose reasonable limitations. For example, even where hotel employees technically are employed by the manager (or an affiliate of the manager), the owner should secure the right to approve or disapprove of the selection or retention of key guidance team personnel (such as the General Manager, Director of Sales and Marketing and Controller). Some managers have whittled away at this control measure by inserting language that the manager has the ultimate discretion to hire and retain these employees, even if the owner objects. For example, owners cede some control when they allow the manager to insert language to the effect that "if owner disapproves of three (3) candidates for the position submitted in good faith by manager ... manager shall have the right to select the person to be offered the position, in its sole discretion ...."

Financial reporting. Most management agreements require that managers maintain financial statements reflecting hotel operations in accordance with the *Uniform System of Accounts for the Lodging Industry* and generally accepted accounting principles. Managers typically are required to provide periodic accountings to owners. But the agreements often do not specify the level of detail necessary to fulfill these obligations. And while there typically are outside audit provisions, they tend to be limited to audits of financial statements, which are provided in the first instance by the operator. Greater audit rights, including the right to audit the hotel operations (not merely the financial statements), would provide some added control benefit, although a preferable approach is manager transparency and more robust disclosures in the first instance.

Books and records. Most agreements also require managers to maintain and make available the hotel's books and records, but some leave vague what constitute "books and records." This is an essential control provision, because access to books and records permits the hotel investor to conduct its own evaluation of the manager's performance, without relying on selective materials or summary accountings provided by the manager.

Some branded managers now are trying to limit books and records just to "books of account," which they claim are merely the periodic profit and loss statements and nothing more. Others recognize a broader definition, extending to any books and records that "relate to the operation of the hotel." Even then, some branded managers try to limit owner access to books and records that are specific to that owner's hotel. Under this approach, the manager takes the position that the owner/investor is not entitled to any books and records relating to, by way of illustration, corporate-level charges and programs imposed on the hotel and paid for by the owner (e.g., chain service allocation materials, regional sales office data). Other managers go so far as to contend that they are entitled to withhold the owner's books and records on the grounds that they are proprietary to the operator, even refusing to turn over guest records, audit reports, and hotel standard operating procedures. Investors must be wary of managers unwilling to provide access to information necessary to confirm the manager's compliance with its obligations.

Fees and expenses. One area where some managers are less than forthcoming is regarding how much the owner will pay the manager for the day to day operation of the hotel. For these operators, management fees are the tip of the iceberg. "Corporate charges" (i.e., above-property-level fees, charges, expenses, assessments) can be many times the amount of management fees; however, these charges rarely appear in pro formas, nor are they spelled out clearly in management agreements. Some managers make these charges transparent, while others claim their methods for offloading corporate charges onto individual properties are too complicated for even the manager to explain. However, hotel investors must demand transparency. The longer the term of the agreement, the more transparency a good manager should be willing to provide into its fee structure.

Procurement. Purchasing and vendor selection is another area where the owner's rights to control the manager can be reasonably defined in the management agreement. Managers typically purchase hotel food and beverage, operating supplies, and capital goods for the owner's account, using the owner's credit. Investors need to be more wary of hotel managers that do not provide for competitive bidding requirements or other oversight, such as approval of vendor contracts generating purchases over a certain amount per year or access to vendor information.

Some larger branded operators offload purchasing responsibility to collective purchasing organizations (which themselves are sometimes related parties of the operators). These purchasing organizations ostensibly use the combined purchasing power of participating hotels to negotiate agreements. Prudent investors should inquire as to whether a manager using these procurement services will disclose the terms of the vendor agreements, and why a particular vendor was chosen. Owners should be aware, however, that managers sometimes themselves cannot identify net prices, because those prices may contain vendor rebates, allowances, and marketing dollars. A number of disputes have arisen where some or all of these fees have gone to benefit the purchasing organization or the manager, and not to the owner who paid for the purchases. Given the manager's ability to purchase on the owner's account, in this context it is hard for managers to justify any disclaimer of fiduciary duties with respect to procurement—and investors should not acquiesce.

Budget review and approval. One area where it may appear that the owner has negotiated for control is with respect to the approval of the budget. But looks can be deceiving. A good, transparent manager provides a detailed budget and gives whatever detail the owner needs to understand the manager's proposal. And the owner's ability to approve the budget, in total or in part, is another key control feature.

But even if the owner has an express contractual right to participate in the budget process, some managers press for language that limits that participation to making "comments," while reserving ultimate budget approval to the manager. For example, a management agreement may provide only that "manager shall meet with owner and shall in good faith discuss and consider all of owner's comments concerning the budget." A promise to consider comments in good faith may ring hollow after the ink is dried on the agreement.

Dispute resolution. Owners also need to be mindful of ceding control over how disputes get resolved. Increasingly, managers are trying to wrap all operational issues into the annual budget review process. One not so transparent reason for this move is to force contract disputes into the very limited "expert" dispute resolution mechanisms managers suggest for budget spats. For example, some managers provide that "in the event there is a disagreement pertaining to the budget that cannot be resolved by the parties ... all matters shall be determined by a panel of experts ..." One of the largest branded operating companies has gone so far as to assert that *all* disputes theoretically relate to the budget, and therefore must enter a circumscribed express resolution process. While alternative dispute resolution (e.g., arbitration) sounds reasonable, it actually tends to favor the manager. Limitations on discovery, minimal appeal rights, a dearth of qualified neutrals, and a host of other problems end up limiting the investor's control, which is one reason broad "arbitration provisions" are so widely promoted by management companies.

Miscellaneous control provisions. There are a number of other areas where the owner can exert (or cede) control. For example, the selection of the competitive set, the assignment provisions that may allow the operator to off-load its responsibilities to third parties or affiliates, and encroachment provisions that provide territorial restrictions preventing the operator from operating a competing hotel in the investor's market all need to be evaluated in this context.

Highlights of Recent Legal Disputes

Many of the disputes in the industry that grab the headlines reflect situations where the owner trusted the manager to deliver on promises not clearly expressed in the contract and to promote the owner's interests first and foremost—and then fought to regain control over its business. The less flexible (some might say, the more arrogant) the management company, the more likely that dispute ends up entailing a termination claim.

Whereas many of the owner/manager disputes over the last two decades focused on the existence of an agency relationship, the landscape has changed as managers have moved adeptly to reduce their agency termination risks and owners, in response, have had to adapt. The most recent trend has been recognition by the courts that management agreements are contracts for "personal services," which are always terminable at the will of either party (subject, as with a terminated agency, to damage claims for wrongful termination of contract). A personal services contract is generally recognized as one that requires the rendition of services that require the exercise of special skill and judgment.[7] In most jurisdictions, a court cannot compel specific performance of a personal services contract.[8]

Predictably, management companies already have started to inject "disclaimers of personal services" in their agreements, and other provisions reflecting their attempt to foreclose terminations. And perhaps just as predictably, some hotel investors are signing such agreements, either unwittingly or consciously counting on such disclaimers later being held unenforceable.

The Legacy of Prior Owner/Manager Lawsuits

Much has been written about the nature of the owner/operator relationship.[9] Decisions in the 1990s were largely pro-owner, recognizing that management contracts establish an agency relationship. The importance of this legal concept is two-fold.

First, an agency relationship necessarily is fiduciary in nature, meaning that the operator has duties of loyalty, disclosure, and not engaging in self-dealing (by way of illustration), even if the contract does not expressly spell this out. Second, in an agency relationship, the owner (the principal) always has the *power* to terminate the manager (the agent), even if it does not have the *right* under the contract. The seminal court decisions recognized that the only exception to this agency termination principal is where the manager has an "agency coupled with an interest."

Operators started injecting language into their draft contracts attempting to "create" an agency coupled with an interest merely by saying so. But that inartful attempt to avoid establishing an agency relationship soon was replaced by a more sophisticated effort to include disclaimers of agency and disclaimers of fiduciary duties. In some instances, brand operators pushed for legislative relief,[10] which militates against using Maryland in a choice of law provision. Some operators started inserting language characterizing the manager as being a mere "independent contractor," even though independent contractors can be agents.

The result has been an erosion of the legal foundation built by prior owners,[11] as some courts have been confused by the language inserted by operators. Some management companies even have seized on the broad delegation of authority to the operator to argue that no agency relationship exists, precisely because the owner has given up control over the day-to-day operation of the hotel.

For example, many hotel operators insisted on including language in their form operating agreements declaring that the operator is an "independent contractor." There is legal authority that an independent contractor also can be an agent, but the import of this language is clear – operators are setting up an argument that they are not agents, without expressly saying as much.

Some operators have been particularly clever, arguing that language disclaiming any relationship "like a partnership or joint venture" also disclaims an agency relationship and fiduciary duties, without expressly disclaiming agency or even mentioning fiduciary duties. While the language here was intended to address the parties' rights and obligations vis-à-vis third parties, operators instead have taken boilerplate language that most owners gloss over and used it to disclaim any duties of loyalty, care, or good faith in performing their obligations. In some instances, operators have buried express disclaimers of agency in this boilerplate. Some owners, for their part, have unwittingly allowed operators to use this clever drafting to create arguments that the parties "mutually intended" to allow the operator to walk away from the implied duties of loyalty, due care, diligence, and competence.

The Current Legal Landscape

Marriott International, Inc. v. Eden Roc, LLP/Eden Roc, LLP v. Marriott International, Inc., et al. (the Eden Roc case)

Eden Roc, LLP, the owner of the Eden Roc Renaissance Hotel in Miami Beach, Florida, brought a lawsuit in the New York Supreme Court against Renaissance Hotel Management Company and its parent company, Marriott International, for breach of the management agreement that installed Renaissance as the operator of the hotel.[12] Eden Roc sought to terminate the management agreement and remove Renaissance from the hotel. After a failed attempt to remove Renaissance from the hotel, Eden Roc sought an injunction from the court requiring Renaissance to leave the hotel, arguing that the management agreement was one for personal services. Eden Roc also argued in a footnote that Renaissance was Eden Roc's agent, but that the court need not reach the agency question for purposes of the motion before it.[13]

The trial court rejected Eden Roc's argument that the management agreement was a contract for personal services.[14] The court also rejected Eden Roc's argument that an agency relationship arose by virtue of the management agreement, noting "the parties specified the nature of their relationship in the Agreement, stating 'In the performance of this Agreement, [plaintiffs] shall act solely as an independent contractor.'"[15] Interestingly, no mention was made of the fact that the Restatement (Second) of Agency establishes that "[o]ne who contracts to act on behalf of another and subject to the other's control except with respect to his physical conduct *is an agent and also an independent contractor*." Restatement (Second) of Agency § 14N (1958) (emphasis added).

Eden Roc appealed on both the personal services and agency issues. The Appellate Division agreed with Eden Roc and reversed the lower court on the personal services argument, reasoning that the "detailed management agreement places full discretion with [Renaissance] to manage virtually every aspect of the hotel. Such an agreement, in which a party has discretion to execute tasks that cannot be objectively measured, is a classic example of a personal services contract that may not be enforced by injunction."[16]

The Appellate Division also held that, "[w]hile it is unnecessary to reach the question, we note that, contrary to [Eden Roc's] contention, the agreement is not an agency agreement. Defendant lacks control over plaintiff, the alleged agent, since the agreement provides for plaintiff to have unfettered discretion in managing the hotel's operations."[17] The court did not elaborate on the agency aspect of its decision.

In light of the Appellate Division's order, the lower court ruled that Eden Roc had the authority to terminate and eject Renaissance from the hotel as and when it wished, subject to damage claims for wrongful termination.[18] According to the court, "if Eden Roc tells Marriott/Renaissance to get out, Marriott/Renaissance must follow that directive."[19]

RC/PB, Inc. v. The Ritz-Carlton Hotel Company, L.L.C. et al. (the Ritz-Carlton Palm Beach case)

Almost concurrently, a Florida court tackling a similar dispute between a hotel owner and operator reached a parallel conclusion. RC/PB, Inc., the owner of what was formerly the Ritz-Carlton, Palm Beach, brought claims against the operator Ritz-Carlton and its parent company, Marriott, alleging breach of the operating agreement. RC/PB sought and received a declaration from the court that RC/PB had the power to terminate Ritz-Carlton as the operator, based on a personal services theory.[20]

The court's "examination of the Operating Agreement as a whole show[ed] a delegation to Ritz-Carlton of a broad range of discretionary authority" in operating the hotel, which "'undisputedly call[ed] for the rendition of services which require[d] the exercise of special skill and judgment.'"[21] The court rejected Ritz-Carlton's argument that a performance test in the contract provided an objective measure of its personal services, and also rejected the manager's contention that its limited rights of assignment were inconsistent with a personal services relationship. The owner subsequently exercised its power to terminate the operating agreement, which had more than six decades remaining, pursuant to the trial court's order.

FHR TB, LLC v. TB Isle Resort, L.P (the Turnberry Isle case)

In the case of *FHR TB, LLC v. TB Isle Resort, L.P ("Turnberry Isle"),* the United States District Court for the Southern District of Florida resolved both the agency and personal services issues in favor of the owner, which then paid a liquidated damages fee to the operator in consideration for the termination. In that case, the owner of the hotel formerly known as the Fairmont Turnberry Isle Resort and Club in Aventura, Florida, evicted the operator, Fairmont, from the hotel without any prior notice, on the ground that the relationship was an agency that was terminable at the will of the principal.[22] Fairmont sought an injunction from the court to reinstate it as operator.[23]

The *Turnberry Isle* court denied Fairmont's injunction, finding that the hotel management agreement created an agency relationship. The court stated "[t]he Restatement of Agency recognizes that hotel managers are agents of the owners of the properties they operate."[24] The court further held that "hotel management agreements are personal services contracts" because they call for "'the rendition of services which require the exercise of special skill and judgment ... managerial services [that were] wide-ranging and involve daily discretionary activities ... [including] hiring and firing managerial personnel and hundreds of other employees, contracting for ... services' and the like."[25]

M Waikiki LLC v. Marriott Hotel Servs. (the Waikiki Edition dispute)

In May 2011, the owner of the Waikiki Edition Hotel filed a lawsuit in New York State against the hotel's manager, Marriott, and boutique hotelier Ian Schrager claiming that Marriott failed to deliver pre-opening design and development assistance it promised prior to the hotel's opening and had mismanaged the hotel after opening. On August 28, 2011, the owner of the Waikiki Edition Hotel removed Marriott as the operator of the hotel and installed a new operator, despite a management agreement that allowed Marriott to operate the hotel for 30 years.[26]

Marriott filed a motion asking the court to reinstall it as the manager. Marriott argued that it was not the agent of the owner. The agreement in that instance stated that Marriott "shall act solely as an independent contractor" and that nothing will be construed "as making any party a partner, joint venturer with, <u>or agent of</u>, any other party." Marriott did not raise, and the court did not reach, the issue of personal services.[27] The court, troubled by the owner's self-help ouster after the complaint for Marriott's removal was already before the court for resolution, agreed with the manager that the status quo should not have been unilaterally altered and issued an order in August 2011 reinstalling Marriott pending a ruling on the merits. The owner filed for bankruptcy before that order could be executed.

In the chapter 11 case, Marriott fought to take over the debtor and propose its own plan. Ultimately the matter was settled for a compromised amount under a plan that enabled the owners to retain full ownership and management of the hotel.[28]

Lessons for Hotel Investors

Whether through the existence of an agency relationship or because a hotel management agreement is deemed a personal services contract, the courts are clear: owners have the power to terminate a hotel management relationship at will. While the recent decisions have been helpful to owners seeking to regain control over their investments, they do reflect that some courts are departing from what has been a well-accepted feature of the industry—the agency relationship between owner as principal and manager as agent.

Importantly, an agency relationship, unlike a personal services contract, necessarily imposes fiduciary duties.[29] Against their own interests, and perhaps unwittingly, owners have accepted language in management agreements (for example, the "independent contractor" language referenced above) that has laid the groundwork for managers' arguments that hotel management agreements do not create fiduciary duties. Now, some managers even are attempting to have owners sign disclaimers that state that the hotel management agreement is not a personal services agreement.

Owners also have accepted an erosion of control rights that later allows operators to claim that no agency relationship exists. The agency aspects of the *Eden Roc* decision, for example, show how some courts have used the owner's delegation of "unfettered discretion" over the day-to-day management of the hotel to find that one of the features of agency—control by the principal/owner—is not present. This control element is a vestige of the development of agency law in the context of vicarious liability claims by third parties (for example, when a bystander is harmed by the acts of an agent). The alleged "principal" in that instance reasonably would not be liable for the harm caused by the alleged "agent" if the principal had no control over the conduct of the agent. But this control element should not apply for purposes of establishing whether an agency relationship exists in determining the scope of liability between the principal and the agent themselves.[30] Until this issue is sorted out by the courts, prudent hotel investors should not accept a "broad delegation of authority" without at least reserving some control over how the agency exercises its duties.[31]

Notwithstanding the pro-owner court decisions in the recent *Eden Roc* and *RC/PB* cases, owners must be especially vigilant when negotiating management agreements to avoid control traps, and must continue to challenge managers' attempts to evade their fiduciary duties.

Emerging Legal Issues

The scope of legal issues facing hotel investors is vast. One emerging area that is certain to evolve further in the years ahead is cyber-security. In today's electronic data-driven world, hotel owners and operators must be aware of increasing threats to data security and also must address guest demands for safe and reliable access to the Internet. Two recent and ongoing legal disputes highlight the difficulty in balancing these two issues. As owners ultimately may bear the costs, these developments are worth watching.

Federal Trade Commission ("FTC") v. Wyndham. On three occasions between 2008 and 2010, hackers gained unauthorized access into Wyndham's computer network as well as the computer networks of several Wyndham-branded hotels. The hackers compromised payment-card information that Wyndham had collected from customers. Wyndham reported these hacking incidents to law-enforcement authorities.[32]

After a two-year investigation into Wyndham's data security practices, on June 26, 2012, the FTC filed a lawsuit in federal court alleging that Wyndham had engaged in "unfair ... acts or practices" in violation of the Federal Trade Commission Act 15 U.S.C. § 45(a), by failing to take "reasonable and appropriate" measures to protect the data stolen by the hackers.[33]

Wyndham moved to dismiss the case, arguing, among other things, that the FTC did not have the power to regulate cyber-security and, even if it did, Wyndham was not given proper notice of what cyber-security measures it was supposed to take. In April 2014, the federal judge presiding over the case rejected Wyndham's motion to dismiss the charges.[34]

In July 2014, a federal appeals court agreed to hear Wyndham's appeal of the lower court's refusal to dismiss the charges against Wyndham. Wyndham was joined in its appeal by a number of outside groups, including the United States Chamber of Commerce, the American Hotel & Lodging Association, and the National Federation of Independent Business. The FTC was joined in its opposition to Wyndham's appeal by a number of consumer advocacy groups such as Public Citizen, Center for Digital Democracy, Consumer Action, Center for Democracy & Technology, Electronic Frontier Foundation, and the Electronic Privacy Information Center.[35]

The briefing on the appeal was completed in December 2014 but the appeals court has not yet rendered a decision.

Marriott Agrees to Pay $600,000 Fine to Resolve Federal Communications Commission Investigation of Wi-Fi Blocking. The FCC recently took Marriott International to task for blocking guest access to personal Wi-Fi networks at some of its properties.[36]

In response to a complaint from a guest of a Marriott-managed hotel, in March 2013, the FCC launched an investigation into allegations that Marriott was "jamming" guests' personal Wi-Fi connections. In the course of its investigation, the FCC found that Marriott employees "had used features of a Wi-Fi monitoring system ... to contain and/or de-authenticate guest-created Wi-Fi hotspot access points in the conference facilities" while at the same time charging those guests from $250 to $1,000 per device to use the hotel's Wi-Fi service.[37]

In October 2014, Marriott admitted to the practice and agreed to pay a fine to the FCC of $600,000. Marriott also agreed to cease the practice and institute a compliance plan that includes periodic reporting to the FCC of its compliance.[38] Prior to its settlement with the FCC, Marriott and the American Hotel & Lodging Association had asked the FCC to condone and allow its hotels to jam personal Wi-Fi hotspots, arguing that such hotspots might be used to launch an attack on the hotel's Wi-Fi network, threaten other guests' privacy, or slow down Internet speeds for other customers. Technology giants such as Google and Microsoft have opposed such requests, arguing that jamming access is against the public interest.[39]

Conclusion

From minimum wage issues to management contract termination lawsuits, the scope of "key legal issues" facing hotel investors is vast. The ability to control that investment, and to exit if necessary, should be of paramount concern. Even investors with short hold periods have learned the hard way that plans often change, because the markets sometimes move in mysterious ways.

If there is one central lesson to be learned from the major lawsuits in the industry, it is that trust is a currency in short supply and of diminishing value. Trusting a manager that disclaims fiduciary duties, refuses to be transparent, requires a long-term agreement, limits termination options, and insists on unfettered discretion is a recipe for disenchantment. As is often the case, it is better to evaluate key control elements at the negotiating stage. When the key players are focused on pro formas of limited utility and fee structures that depend on revenues and profits that may never materialize, the savvy investor spends the mental capital on the control features of the management contract. It is, after all, the investor's money—and for too many managers, this fundamental feature of the owner/manager relationship is forgotten as soon as the deal has been won.

Endnotes

1. J. W. Marriott, *The Spirit to Serve: Marriott's Way* (New York: HarperCollins, 2001), p. 23.
2. The so-called "incentive fee," while intended to align owner and operator interests, is rarely a substantial part of the management company's overall compensation, and operators sometimes find it's more advantageous to bypass the incentive fee altogether by recouping company overhead through "operating expense" charges to the hotel in addition to the management fees.
3. See, e.g., O'Neill, J., et al., "Do brands matter? A comparison of branded and independent hotels' performance during a full economic cycle," *International Journal of Hospitality Management* 30 (2011) 515–521; HVS Rep. on Preferred Hotel Group, avail. at http://phgcdn.com/pdfs/uploads/ HVS_Study_Summary.pdf.
4. While some branded operators have spent considerable energy courting lenders and are trying to develop pro-operator language in subordination and non-disturbance agreements (SNDAs), the most sophisticated lenders are not being hoodwinked by mere promises of brand value without actual monetary contributions (e.g., performance guarantees, fee stand-asides, key money, etc.).
5. Restatement (Third) of Agency §§ 1.01, 8.01 cmt. b (2006).
6. *Woolley v. Embassy Suites, Inc,* 227 Cal. App. 3d 1520 (Cal. App. 1991); *2660 Woodley Rd. Joint Venture v. ITT Sheraton Corp.*, No. Civ. A. 97-450 JJF, 1998 WL 1469541, at *6 (D. Del. Feb. 4, 1998) (finding that a hotel management agreement created a terminable at-will agency).

7. See, e.g., *Woolley v. Embassy Suites, Inc.*, 227 Cal. App. 3d 1520, 1534 (1991) ("The management contracts here undisputedly call for the rendition of services which require the exercise of special skill and judgment. These managerial services, even by Embassy's own assessment, are wide ranging and involve daily discretionary activities. The manager's duties include: hiring and firing managerial personnel and hundreds of other employees, contracting for utility services, landscaping, maintenance and security, processing reservations, arranging for advertising and promotion, and filing legal actions on the owner's behalf to collect rent charges, cancel leases or dispossess guests. In other words, the contracts call for a series of complex and delicate business decisions and require mutual cooperation and trust, both of which have ceased to exist in the wake of rancorous litigation between the parties.").

8. See *Karrick v. Hannaman*, 168 U.S. 328, 336 (1897) (stating in a personal services contract "it is well settled that a court of equity cannot compel the performance of the service" "against the plaintiff, and will not be enforced against the defendant"); *Gov't Guar. Fund v. Hyatt Corp.*, 95 F.3d 291, 303 (3d Cir. 1996) (affirming district court's holding that "the management agreement was a personal services contract which cannot be specifically enforced") (quoting *Woolley*, 227 Cal. App. 3d at 727 (Cal. App. 1991)); *Weeks v. Pratt*, 43 F.2d 53, 57 (5th Cir. 1930) ("A contract for personal services will not be enforced in equity by compelling the rendition of the services.")

9. See e.g., Bosch, W. et al., "Key Legal Issues," in L. Raleigh & R. Roginsky (Eds.), *Hotel Investments: Issues & Perspectives*, 5th Ed (Lansing, Mich: American Hotel & Lodging Educational Institute, 2012).

10. Md. Stat. § 23-101 *et seq.*

11. A seminal case discussing the owner/operator relationship is *Woolley v. Embassy Suites, Inc.*, 227 Cal. App. 3d 1520 (Cal. App. 1991). Embassy Suites operated hotels for the plaintiff owners, who sought to terminate their management agreements with Embassy Suites for nine hotels. Embassy Suites obtained a court order enjoining the terminations, but the appellate court reversed the order. The California First District Court of Appeal explained that "a principal who employs an agent always retains the power to revoke the agency" and held that Embassy Suites was an agent of the owners. According to the court, "it should always be within the power of the principal to manage his own business and that includes the power of the principal to reassume the control over his own business which he has but delegated to his agent." Consistent with the *Woolley* decision, other courts, including the United States District Court for the District of Delaware in *Woodley Rd. Joint Venture v. ITT Sheraton Corp*, have found that the hotel management agreements create agency relationships that are terminable at will. See *Woodley Rd.*, 1998 WL 1469541, at *6 (D. Del. Feb. 4, 1998); see also *Pac. Landmark Hotel, Ltd. v. Marriott Hotels, Inc.*, 23 Cal. Rptr.2d. 555 (Cal. Ct. App. 1994.); *Gov't Guar. Fund v. Hyatt Corp.*, 95 F.3d 291, 297 (3d Cir. 1996) (recognizing the trial court's holding that a hotel management agreement "created a revocable agency that ended once [the owner] gave notice of its termination" (citation and quotations omitted).

12. First Amended Verified Complaint, *Eden Roc, LLLP v. Marriott Int'l, Inc.*, Index No. 651027/2012 (N.Y. Sup. June 29, 2012).

13. *Id.* at 11 n.2.

14. *Id.* at 4.
15. *Id.* at 6.
16. Order, at 1-2, *Marriott Int'l, Inc. v. Eden Roc, LLLP,* Index No. 653590/2012 (N.Y. App. Div. March 26, 2013).
17. *Id.* at 2.
18. Hearing Transcript on Order to Show Cause, at 8, *Marriott Int'l, Inc. v. Eden Roc, LLLP,* Index No. 653590/2012 (N.Y. Sup. May 21, 2013); see also Declaratory Judgment and Order, *Marriott Int'l, Inc. v. Eden Roc, LLLP,* Index No. 653590/2012 (N.Y. Sup. May 21, 2013).
19. *Id.* at 6-7.
20. Order on Plaintiff's Motion for Partial Summary Judgment Regarding the Power to Terminate, at 7-8, *RC/PB, Inc.*
21. *Id.* (quoting *Woolley v. Embassy Suites, Inc.*, 227 Cal. App. 3d 1520, 1534 [Cal. Ct. App. 1991]).
22. *Turnberry Isle,* No. 11-23115-CIV-Graham/Goodman, 2011 U.S. Dist. LEXIS 155742, at *5 (Sept. 26, 2011).
23. *Id.* at *8.
24. *Id.* at *78 (internal citations omitted).
25. *Id.* at 86 (internal citations omitted).
26. *M Waikiki LLC v. Marriott Hotel Servs.*, No. 651457/2011, slip op., (N.Y. Sup. Ct.N.Y. Cty. Aug. 30, 2011).
27. The day after the court ordered that Marriott be reinstalled as operator, the owner of the Waikiki Edition Hotel filed for bankruptcy. In that proceeding, Marriott claimed that it was owed damages for the owner's wrongful termination of the management agreement. As a part of the bankruptcy proceedings, the owner and Marriott entered into a confidential settlement agreement.
28. *In re M Waikiki LLC,* Case No. 11-02371.
29. These fiduciary duties include loyalty, care, and diligence and competence in actions taken pursuant to the agency relationship. In the hotel context, if the operating agreement vests broad discretion in the operator, fiduciary duties require that the operator competently exercise such discretion in good faith and with due care for the benefit of the owner.
30. The Restatement (Third) of Agency (2006) notes that "[a] principal's right to control the agent is a constant across relationships of agency, but the content or specific meaning of the right varies." *Id.* § 1.01 cmt. c. "Thus, a person may be an agent although the principal lacks the right to control the full range of the agent's activities, how the agent uses time, or the agent's exercise of professional judgment." *Id.*
31. "The power to give interim instructions distinguishes principals in agency relationships from those who contract to receive services provided by persons who are not agents." Restatement (Third) § 1.01 cmt. f(1).

32. *Federal Trade Commission v. Wyndham Worldwide Corp., et al.,* No. 14-3514 (3rd Cir. 2014) Appellant's Opening Brief.
33. *Id.*
34. *Id.*
35. *Federal Trade Commission v. Wyndham Worldwide Corp., et al.,* No. 14-3514 (3rd Cir. 2014) Appeals Court Docket.
36. http://www.fcc.gov/document/marriott-pay-600k-resolve-wifi-blocking-investigation
37. *Id.*
38. *Id.*
39. See http://money.cnn.com/2014/12/25/technology/marriott-wifi/

15

Risk versus Reward: A Lender's View of Hotel Investment Trends

By Michael H. Brown and Gregory J. Wolkom

***Michael H. Brown,** Vice President, Real Estate Syndicated Finance, Wells Fargo Securities, LLC, is the head of the Hospitality Real Estate Syndication desk for the United States at Wells Fargo Securities. Before joining the group, he served as a vice president and relationship manager for the Hospitality Finance group of Wells Fargo, where he was integral in building the group's Western United States lending platform since its creation in 2008. Mr. Brown's fifteen-year career has been dedicated to the hospitality industry, with prior positions including Vice President with Eastdil Secured's Hospitality Investment Sales division, as well as positions with KPMG's Gaming and Hospitality Consulting Group and Loews Hotels. Mr. Brown received his B.S. from Cornell University's School of Hotel Administration and holds series 79 and 63 securities licenses.*

***Gregory J. Wolkom,** Managing Director, Head of Real Estate Loan Syndications, San Francisco, is a managing director with Wells Fargo Securities and leads its real estate loan syndications practice within Wells Fargo Securities' Investment Banking and Capital Markets Division. As Head of Real Estate Loan Syndications, he oversees the syndication of commercial real estate transactions. With more than twenty-five years of experience in the field, Mr. Wolkom is a veteran of the real estate industry. He originally joined Wells Fargo in January 2011 to lead the hospitality finance group's West Coast office and public lodging coverage. In this role, he was responsible for a large portfolio of balance sheet loans on hotel and leisure assets, and publicly traded lodging REITs and C-Corps. Prior to joining Wells Fargo, he served as Executive Vice President and Chief Financial Officer of Kimpton Hotel & Restaurant Group. He began his career at Bank of America predecessor companies, where he held a variety of positions in both real estate lending and investment banking, including Global Head of Lodging and Leisure Investment Banking.*

Mr. Wolkom is a member of the Urban Land Institute, where he serves on the Hotel Development Council. He is also a member of the Board of Trustees of the Mercy Housing Corporation of California, the largest provider of affordable housing in the state of California. He is a frequent speaker on real estate lodging and leisure related topics on behalf of the Americas Lodging Investment

Summit and Urban Land Institute, among others. He has a B.S. degree in business administration with a major in finance from the University of South Carolina.

HOTELS ARE INDEED a special real estate asset class. Many of us have fond childhood memories of that first hotel we visited that featured a pool *and* waterslide or some other exotic amenity; maybe it's the themed hotel with access to an amusement park via a monorail; or it's the staple hotel that dutifully served for years as the annual family summer retreat. Either way, hotels have a unique ability to be part of our fondest memories or be the epicenter for much joy and excitement about upcoming trips. One may argue that an office building will never achieve the same emotional appeal that a great hotel experience can. Delivering on that great experience is what makes a hotel acquisition such an appealing investment, and plays a part in what drives investors, management companies, and brands to constantly redefine the hotel experience in order to draw more demand and create higher returns on their investment.

However, for lenders, hotels are actually categorized as a special asset class, and not in a good way. Lenders classify every hotel as a special purpose entity (SPE) because this particularly unique asset class represents significant underwriting and liquidity challenges. Hotels are purpose-built and extremely costly to reposition into other business ventures. For example, a traditional office or retail building has tall ceilings, limited plumbing, and floor plates that are fairly easy to reconfigure for different tenant uses. A hotel, however, is specifically designed, built, and engineered to deliver facilities to multiple guestrooms per floor and features uniquely configured public spaces and significant back-of-house support for business and social functions. In many instances, hotels are constructed and designed to a specific brand requirement, which often differs between brands and requires ongoing capital investments.

Further impacting a lender's underwriting of a hotel loan are the number of third parties involved in the operation of a hotel, which cloud and restrict a lender's access to its collateral. A typical hotel may involve a ground lessor and lessee, operating leases, a management agreement, a franchise agreement, an asset manager, and multiple/tiered equity investors, all of which have their hands in the operating cash flow. Hotels also require significant capital investment relative to other asset classes, both for deferred maintenance and value enhancements. Those continued capital investments, coupled with a significant level of fixed and variable expenses to manage, plus labor costs (which may include union labor) and licensing and marketing costs further impact a hotel's ability to generate strong and sustainable profits.

Unlike other real estate asset classes, hotels are a higher-beta operating business, with their leases reset nightly. In addition to a complicated investment team or high expense margins, hotels must sell and manage a perishable inventory: a room night's stay. By contrast, office buildings and retail facilities are able to sign up long-term tenants, which makes these assets easier to manage and their cash flows easier to underwrite (less risk equates to lower stabilized cap rates). Even multi-family and industrial investments benefit from longer leases and less capital investment than hotels. A hotel's nightly sales model requires significantly more coordination between the owner, manager, franchise personnel, and employees in order to properly market, sell, and accommodate a hotel's nightly perishable inventory. Therefore, a lender must underwrite and take comfort in a borrower's business strategy for a hotel operation, not just in the operation's intrinsic real estate value.

These factors make hotels a much riskier asset class for a lender to underwrite, originate, negotiate, manage, and exit. The overall driving decision in any real estate investment is "location, location, location," and hotel investments are primarily invested on the same premise. Unfortunately, hotels do require substantially more capital and operational expertise than other investments and are therefore deemed SPEs. As a result, hotel loans face a higher degree of compliance scrutiny, which in turn limits a lender's ability to issue loan proceeds and otherwise structure loan terms.

So why would a lender entertain making a loan for such a risky asset class and operating business? At some point in the capital markets cycle, hotels provide an attractive risk-adjusted-return on a lender's investment relative to other asset classes. For example, a stabilized urban office or multi-family property may obtain a loan at a 70 percent loan-to-cost (LTC) for a five-year term, with in-place cash flow that results in an 8 percent debt yield (Debt Yield = Net Operating Income/ Loan Amount) going in, and price at Libor+200 bps. By comparison, a stabilized hotel loan may be underwritten at a lower LTC of 60 percent, a higher 11 percent debt yield on in-place net operating income (NOI), and price at Libor+300 bps for a three-year initial term (along with more stringent performance covenants). The pricing for the hotel represents a 50 percent premium to the office building over a shorter term, lower LTC, higher cash flow coverage, and more stringent covenant requirements. All loan terms fluctuate depending on a variety of factors, and the spread premium between a hotel and an office building may compress and widen depending on various loan-sizing factors and points along the economic cycle. While a hotel typically offers investors a strategy to increase value through operational enhancements or capital investments, it also requires a higher cost of capital from lenders due to the risks associated with an investor's strategic plan.

With that in mind, in this chapter we will cover the key components a lender must evaluate and underwrite in order to provide a loan, discuss the various types of loans that can be made in the hotel space, and profile the various types of lenders in the industry.

People, Credit, and Real Estate

"Relationship lending" is a common phrase among commercial real estate lenders. As most buyers purchase commercial real estate with the hopes of increasing operating performance and exiting at a higher value, it is inherent to underwrite not just the real estate, but also the borrower itself, thus forming a relationship with your borrower. In terms of hotel lending, the relationships behind the real estate are magnified and underwritten to an even higher degree:

- *People.* You can't make a good loan to a bad person. At the end of the day, you lend to people, and those people need to be reputable, have a strong performance track record, and a high likelihood of supporting their real estate investments in good times and bad.

- *Credit.* Lenders will evaluate an individual's creditworthiness to make sure the individual has the financial wherewithal to repay the loan should the investment not play out according to plan. Pro formas may not achieve their projected performance due to internal or external factors, but a lender should always evaluate multiple sources of repayment, whether from the value of the real estate or the borrower's financial capabilities to repay the loan.
- *Real estate.* Does the transaction stand on its own? Does the business plan make sense? Lenders must conduct their own due diligence and leverage their knowledge of the marketplace to ensure an investment's likelihood of success and mitigate the loan's risks.

People

This is so important that it bears repeating: "There is no such thing as making a good loan to a bad person." This especially holds true in an operation-heavy investment like a hotel. Sometimes called the "Darling Stepchild of Real Estate Classes," hotels broaden their investment appeal at the wrong times of the economic cycle. Investors and lenders alike become more interested in a hotel's double-digit RevPAR growth late in an economic cycle. As a result, purchase prices per key increase, leverage levels increase, and financial covenants are loosened in an effort to benefit from unsustainable projected double-digit RevPAR percentage gains. When the music stops and the economic downturn hits, hotels tend to take the biggest decrease in valuation, because no one travels when economic times are difficult. They may still travel to work if they have a job; they will still shop at Walmart and Old Navy to buy clothes. But they won't take that trip to Disneyworld, and their company is unlikely to invest in business travel for a prospective sales meeting or industry conference.

While market influences and the competition to place capital always result in a boom/bust cycle, a lender's ability to maintain discipline and make loans to good people will aid in a bank's ability to manage troubled loans during a downturn. In order to maintain this discipline, a lender should evaluate a new borrower's "People Rating" with the following checklist:

- *Reputation.* Does the borrower have a good reputation in the industry? Does the borrower have a history of litigation or bankruptcy filings?
- *Expertise.* Is this the first hotel investment for the borrower, or does the borrower have a long history of successfully investing in hotels?
- *Cycle-proven.* What happened to the borrower's asset portfolio in previous downturns? Did the borrower simply give back hotels to lenders, or did it pay down the principal in order to modify terms?

These three principles should be the first questions a lender asks itself prior to investing in a hotel or engaging in a credit or real estate underwriting. As you may also conclude, borrowers who do fit these criteria will likely receive more favorable loan terms and pricing than those who don't.

Credit

The term "credit" is used to describe many elements of accounting and finance. In connection with this chapter, when we refer to a borrower's "credit," we are referring to a borrower's creditworthiness or ability to cover losses on a loan. First and foremost, a loan should be underwritten based on the merits of a property's specific operating performance or a borrower's property-specific business plan to increase operating cash flow. However, due to the cyclical nature of capital markets, outside economic factors may result in a distressed loan during the loan term. Signs of loan distress can be quickly assessed by a decrease in the hotel's debt yield and further validated by an increase in its third-party appraised "loan to value" (LTV). For example, if a loan was originated at an 11 percent debt yield and a 60 percent LTV, but at some later date in the loan term the fundamentals at the hotel or in the market caused the debt yield to decrease to 5 percent, a lender may require that a new appraisal be ordered to further test the hotel's implied valuation. Regardless if a borrower has invested 40 percent cash equity into the loan, during a negative economic event at the hotel or in the market, if the appraised LTV is north of 85 percent, then not only is the borrower's equity at risk, the loan position itself is in risk. If in the event the loan's LTV climbs north of 100 percent, then a lender will move quickly to modify the existing loan in an attempt to pay down the loan balance to an acceptable leverage level in order to protect itself from potential loan losses.

In order to properly mitigate a loan's risk of distress in the above scenario, a lender must underwrite a borrower's creditworthiness and financial resources to pay down a portion of the loan to regain an acceptable level of risk. Some key components in underwriting a borrower's creditworthiness are as follows:

- *Net worth.* Net worth is calculated by subtracting a borrower's liabilities from its assets. The important takeaway is that lenders typically look at both the cost basis and market value of a borrower's assets. In a bad economy, the market value may be less than a borrower's cost basis. In a good economy, the borrower may have refinanced out all of its cost equity and is borrowing based on implied/market equity. Lenders typically prefer the borrower's cost basis (i.e., cash equity) to be more than the market value (i.e., implied equity), as this points to the borrower's true equity tied up in the transaction and exposed, but both are examined in determining a borrower's overall net worth and creditworthiness. As such, a lender will typically require some minimum level of net worth as a condition to making a loan.

- *Liquidity.* Loosely defined as a borrower's cash and cash equivalents (including marketable securities), liquidity is the second most important factor in determining a borrower's creditworthiness. While a borrower may have substantial net worth in the form of other real estate assets, a borrower's cash accounts, stock investments, or other marketable and easily tradable securities represent a quick form of liquidity for a lender to underwrite. Again, in a down economic cycle, a lender will first approach a borrower's liquid assets as a source of repayment for a distressed loan. A borrower's liquid investments are much easier and faster to call upon than a borrower's equity in other long-term investments like real estate and hotels. As such, a lender will typically require some minimum level of liquidity as a condition to making a loan.

- *Contingent liabilities.* To further determine net worth and liquidity, a lender must underwrite a borrower's contingent liabilities, or its exposure and commitments to other investments. For example, if a lender requires a borrower to pledge $100 million of net worth and $25 million of liquidity for its subject loan, that same borrower may pledge the same net worth and liquidity requirements on other loans. If, for example, the borrower has an aggregate total of $200 million of debt in addition to the subject loan, and $100 million of net worth and $25 million in liquidity to those outside investments, then our subject loan may not be able to claim on the borrower's net worth and liquidity requirements if those other requirements were called on for those other loans. As a result, the loan will fail a performance test and fall into default, and our subject loan is exposed with no secondary source of repayment. Since borrowers are in the business of acquiring and leveraging their hotel investments, contingent liabilities are inevitable. However, a lender should evaluate and stress test those other contingent liabilities when sizing and structuring its proposed facility to the borrower. As such, a lender will typically try to limit or at least routinely evaluate a borrower's ability to take on future contingent liabilities.

Financial Review of Credit Profile. In order to evaluate and present a borrower's financial picture, a lender will put together a report detailing the borrower's general investment strategy, source of equity investment, and its existing hotel investment portfolio, as well as the contingent liabilities, in order to help determine the borrower's net worth, liquidity, and creditworthiness. Lenders will create these reports any time a borrower is a first-time borrower of the bank, and they are typically updated on an annual basis. These reports are produced with the active assistance of the borrower and typically involve an annual audited financial report. A lender must keep an accurate and up-to-date financial picture of the borrower in an effort to properly evaluate the bank's loan and credit exposure to any one borrower.

Borrower vs. Sponsor vs. Guarantor. Up until this point in the chapter, a hotel equity investor has been referred to as a "borrower." For simplicity's sake and unless otherwise noted, the chapter will continue to refer to the equity investor as a borrower. That said, it is important to note a significant legal distinction between a warm-body hotel equity investor and a type of entity that typically serves as a borrower. From a lender perspective, a sponsor is synonymous with our "people" definition above and represents the warm-body recipient of debt funds in order to invest in hotels. This is where the lending relationship is formed. The equity investor or sponsor may be a private individual, like an owner/developer, or it may be a public corporation like Marriott International Inc., or a private equity fund like The Blackstone Group. When lending at an institutional level, a lender will rarely get a sponsor to sign on as a borrower for a single-asset hotel loan. These large institutional sponsors must protect themselves financially from each of their investments, as there are a number of claims that may be made against the property and a sponsor would not want its substantial net worth and liquidity to be liable for any asset-level claims. As a result, a sponsor typically forms a single-purpose LLC as the borrower for each specific property investment. Should there be any legal or bank proceedings at the property level, those litigations would only go as far as that property's borrower for repayment or damages, thus insulating the sponsor's investment in other real estate transactions.

As illustrated in Exhibit 1, the borrowing entity typically is placed at the bottom of an ownership organizational chart. It is the borrowing entity that has a legal interaction with the management company and franchise company. Moving upstream from the borrower may be the guarantor. A guarantor may be the warm-body sponsor, but it may also be a downstream entity from the sponsor. In terms of real estate lending, a guarantor is an entity that serves to provide a lender some additional recourse should the primary collateral, or hotel real estate, not provide enough liquidity to pay off the loan. A sponsor may at times create a subsidiary guarantor that has financial capacity, further restricting a lender or legal claim from going further up to the ultimate sponsor. For example, The Blackstone Group may offer one of its investment funds as a guarantor, but wouldn't offer The Blackstone Group itself, which is the general managing partner of multiple investment funds.

Recourse vs. Non-Recourse. The distinction between a borrower, guarantor, and sponsor is further illustrated when discussing recourse vs. non-recourse lending. When a hotel is stabilized and generating underwritten NOI, it is typically structured as a non-recourse loan. A non-recourse loan means a lender may look only to the borrowing entity and hotel real estate collateral as a form of loan repayment. There is no liquid guarantor or upstream sponsor that can serve as an additional

Exhibit 1 Ownership Organizational Chart

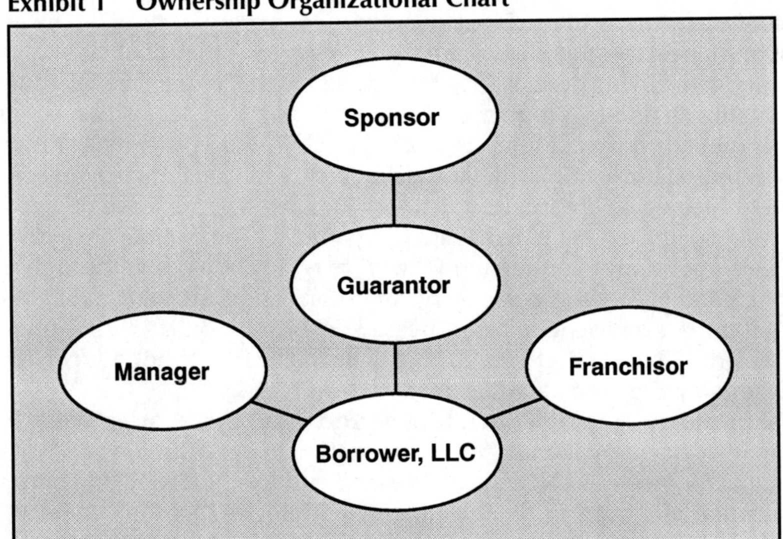

repayment source for a loan. A recourse loan implies just the opposite; a lender may look to a warm-body entity with financial capacity beyond the borrower and hotel real estate collateral as a source for repayment. Recourse loans are more typical in ground-up construction projects or deep renovation and repositioning investments, whereby the business plan is underwritten on creating substantial NOI growth, and the proposed loan amount can't be sustained or underwritten by an in-place concept or cash flow. Lenders look to additional recourse given the incremental risk associated with developing a hotel, versus a non-recourse loan that is supported by historical NOI performance.

Recourse or non-recourse, the ability of the borrower, guarantor, or sponsor to fund needed operating shortfalls or pay down the loan balance is critical in analyzing any loan's merits and the borrower's creditworthiness. If a lender is unable to mitigate potential loan losses with a loan pay-down from the borrower, then a loan will fall into a formal workout process, which is the precursor to a foreclosure. Lengthy workouts and foreclosures drain financial resources and impede on a future lending relationship with that borrower, so underwriting a borrower's creditworthiness and ability to support a loan through negative economic events is imperative.

Real Estate

A lender's primary source of repayment is through the borrower's successful execution of its business strategy. While understanding the people you are making a loan to and ensuring they maintain a level of creditworthiness is very important, underwriting the real estate and borrower's business strategy is also very important and is the most time-consuming element of the loan origination process. In the following sections, we will focus on the real estate due diligence and underwriting criteria that are critical to a lender.

Property-Level Underwriting. Location is the most important component to any real estate evaluation and what at the core will ultimately drive equity and debt investment, structure, and pricing. Lenders are even more focused on the inherent location and ancillary qualities of a hotel investment because of the heightened need to mitigate downside risk. A hotel located along Central Park Avenue South will ultimately maintain a higher percentage of its initial acquisition value in an economic downturn than a four-star resort in Hawaii or a three-star limited-service hotel in a suburb of Nashville. Location drives value and loan security. In addition to looking at the location, lenders look for a good sense of arrival, signage, visibility, and access when evaluating a hotel. The overall physical quality of a hotel is important to understand. Lenders typically require, through a Phase I environmental report and a property condition report, that any capital or environmental-impact deficiencies be addressed as a condition to closing the loan or be addressed within a short time frame of loan closing. If not addressed, these deficiencies may trigger a default under the loan terms.

Historical and projected operating performance. A borrower makes a larger return on investment by identifying and investing in opportunities that maximize the potential for increased NOI performance. Lenders underwrite the future operating potential of a hotel in determining exit strategies, but also underwrite the hotel's prior peak and trough NOI performance in order to mitigate downside risk. As shown by the summary historical and projected hotel income statement in Exhibit 2, a borrower may request a $100 million loan based on future renovation and operation enhancements, but a lender will evaluate how the hotel is performing at the most recent trailing twelve months (TTM) and through prior peak and trough performance.

In the example shown in Exhibit 2, while the hotel generates a strong 11 percent debt yield on TTM performance, it is projected to stabilize in one year at a 13 percent debt yield. The NOI as of the TTM period represents a 36 percent premium to the hotel's prior peak performance in 2007, and the NOI in 2009 and 2010 would result in a sub-1.00x DSCR (prior trough period). There is no cookie-cutter answer to how to properly size this loan, but this is a typical situation a lender must underwrite. The borrower is focused on how it can further improve cash flow, but what happens if there is a major accident at the hotel during renovation, a major labor dispute, or the broader economy crashes? A lender must manage a hotel's downside risk more than its upside potential and structure a loan in order to best mitigate any number of downside scenarios. Loan structuring mitigants may involve the following:

- *Lower loan amount.* If the loan facility is reduced to $86 million, a lender may get comfort that the hotel can generate enough cash flow, even in a down year, to cover debt service (an $86 million loan equals a 1.00x DSCR on 2010 NOI).
- *Structure an earn out.* The loan may provide for $86 million at closing, representing a 12.8 percent debt yield on the TTM NOI, and provide an earn out for the remaining $14 million of proceeds in conjunction with completion of the proposed renovation scope, or release the remaining $14 million upon the hotel achieving a 13 percent debt yield on the total commitment of $100 million (effectively a $13 million NOI).
- *Structure a senior and mezzanine loan.* The total facility can be bifurcated into a separate senior and mezzanine loan. The senior lender would reduce its LTC/LTV and increase its DSCR, but would be required to reduce its interest rate

Exhibit 2 Summary Historical and Projected Hotel Income Statement

300 Room Urban Hotel									
($000s)	2007	2008	2009	2010	2011	2012	2013	TTM 2014	2015
Occ.	80%	70%	65%	63%	67%	70%	78%	82%	83%
ADR	$300	$250	$190	$195	$197	$225	$250	$300	$315
RevPAR	$240	$175	$124	$123	$132	$158	$195	$246	$261
Room Revenue	$26,300	$19,200	$13,500	$13,500	$14,500	$17,200	$21,400	$26,900	$28,600
Total Revenue	$35,100	$24,000	$15,900	$15,500	$17,700	$21,500	$28,500	$37,400	$40,900
NOI	$8,100	$6,700	$4,500	$4,300	$5,000	$6,000	$8,000	$11,000	$13,000
Debt Yield **$100,000**	**8.1%**	**6.7%**	**4.5%**	**4.3%**	**5.0%**	**6.0%**	**8.0%**	**11.0%**	**13.0%**
DSCR @ L[(1)]+400	1.62	1.34	0.90	0.86	1.00	1.20	1.60	2.20	2.60

[(1)] "L" represents One-Month LIBOR and is fixed at 1.00% for the purpose of this analysis.

pricing in order to allow for the mezzanine facility to earn enough interest rate pricing to take on a thinly exposed piece of junior debt.

Management agreement. Referring back to the organization chart in Exhibit 1, you can see that there are other influences to a hotel's success and possible failure. A property manager will have the most direct impact on a hotel's day-to-day performance. Management may come in the form of a third-party operator associated with an international brand, like Marriott or Hilton, or it may be a third-party manager that operates hotels under independent or franchised concepts. Depending on who the property manager is, a lender will want to protect its loan collateral, which may result in certain rights or provisions to control a hotel's operating cash flow and restrict a manager's ability to earn a management fee (base or incentive fee). Conversely, a manager will want to protect its rights to manage the hotel if the manager is not in default of its management agreement, regardless of what may be in dispute between the property's lender and borrower (i.e., it's not the manager's fault that the borrower and the lender agreed to over-lever the hotel).

- *Scenario 1—the borrower of the hotel is also the manager.* In this instance, a lender will likely require the owner to subordinate its management fees and rights to manage the hotel to the lender's rights to get repaid on the hotel. This comes into effect during downturn periods when a hotel enters into monetary or non-monetary default. To the extent the borrower is in an event of default (i.e., hotel NOI can't cover debt service), then the lender may move to remove the borrower as the operator of the hotel and replace the borrower with a different operator of its choosing. A lender wouldn't typically enforce this action unless there is no way to negotiate repayment of the loan and the hotel is moving toward a foreclosure, whereby the lender wipes out the borrower's interest and assumes 100 percent control of its mortgage collateral.
- *Scenario 2—a third-party operator manages on behalf of the borrower.* In this scenario, if the third-party manager is not in default of its management agreement with the borrower, the manager will want to protect its right to manage and receive management fees at the hotel regardless of what the borrower and lender agree to do in an effort to cure a default on the loan. When there is a third-party operator, the lender will typically execute a subordination and non-disturbance agreement (SNDA) with the third-party operator as a condition to closing and funding the loan to the borrower. An SNDA stipulates that a manager agrees to subordinate its position to allow the lender to take control of the hotel in a default, foreclose it, assume the hotel as collateral, and assign its position through a sale to another investor with the current management agreement terms remaining intact. As an agreement to those lender rights, a lender will not disturb a manager's right to stay on as property operator in accordance with the previously agreed-to management agreement as executed between the manager and the borrower.

Franchise agreement. Many hotel investments employ both a third-party manager and a separate affiliation to a national brand. The franchise agreement between the borrower (franchisee) and the brand (franchisor) will trigger another set of requirements between the lender and franchisor, which are negotiated in a comfort letter. A comfort letter is designed to give a lender the comfort that, should a lender need to step into the equity ownership of the borrower (i.e., a foreclosure), the franchisor will not remove its flag affiliation from the hotel. It will, however, allow the lender to cure any potential franchisee/franchisor defaults and assume the franchise agreement on the same terms as originally agreed to between the borrower (as franchisee) and the franchisor.

Independent affiliation. Independent hotels (boutique hotels being one example of the types of hotels in this category) are widely accepted by travelers today, especially Millennial customers who value a unique hotel experience more than earning reward points at a branded hotel toward future travel. Independent hotels tend to be more successful as four- or five-star concepts in urban areas, but the overall growth and strength of independent hotels such as boutique hotels has forced the major brands to create similar branded concepts (for example, Marriott Edition, Starwood Luxury Collection, and Hilton Curio). From a lender perspective, an independent concept is a double-edged sword of credit risk. Typically, independent/boutique hotels have termination provisions on the management agreement, which provides broader optionality in an exit scenario like a foreclosure sale. Unfortunately, independent concepts also lack a strong reservation system to drive demand to the property, have a tendency to run at higher expense margins, and experience a bigger drop in operating performance in a down cycle. As such, a number of lenders won't lend on independent concepts as a rule. But those that do will focus more on the operator's performance history of similar concepts and more heavily rely on the hotel's location or further evaluate its business strategy. As a result of this further scrutiny, independent hotels tend to get sized and structured more conservatively than their nationally flagged competitors.

Business Strategy vs. Market Risks. A common theme developing in this chapter is the difference in perspective on an investment between a borrower and a lender. Where a borrower sees upside, a lender sees unproven performance; where a borrower sees a great local market, a lender may see a threat of new supply. A lender will invest time underwriting and conducting due diligence on a borrower's business plan that may include (1) a change in management; (2) branding strategy; (3) capital investment; and/or (4) cost savings and revenue enhancements; a lender will also focus on outside threats to that business plan. Outside market risks that lenders evaluate include:

- *Limited demand drivers or limited major employers.* A hotel is more defensible in a downturn if it benefits from multiple demand drivers. If a hotel is supported by one key demand driver or major employer to drive room-night demand, and that single demand driver no longer exists, then the hotel will suffer significantly.
- *Transportation issues.* Resort markets that may be fly-to only (Hawaii) or drive-to only (Santa Barbara) are a higher risk due to access restraints.
- *Competitive positioning.* A business plan to greatly enhance a hotel relative to all local comps may struggle to achieve its repositioned performance if the local market is inferior to that repositioning plan.

New supply. The most important market risk to any hotel loan is the threat of new supply. The relationship between demand and supply is the most consistent dynamic that mirrors economic up-cycles and down-cycles (see Exhibit 3). At the bottom of the cycle, most proposed hotel developments are scratched, as down-cycle performance precludes investment in development, and, more importantly, the cost to buy is significantly less than the cost to build. As a result, there is limited to no lender appetite to fund new construction. This allows the existing supply to benefit from a general economic recovery and an increase in occupancy levels and operating margins. The recovery period transitions to a period of economic growth, whereby occupancy sustains strong levels that then allow hotel managers and owners to increase ADR, flowing through to even stronger NOI growth. With increasing ADR levels generating impressive RevPAR gains and NOI growth, the gap between the cost to build and the cost to acquire shrinks and may even flip. At the same time, lending competition increases for stabilized hotels, providing alternative and attractive terms to lenders to provide construction loans. At this late point in the cycle, supply growth exceeds demand growth and a glut of supply is added to the market. Inevitably, borrowers miss their projections and competitively structured and over-levered loans begin to default, and foreclosures may occur. As a result, the cycle repeats itself.

Static demand analysis. Fortunately, today there are many information sources to access new supply pipeline data in a top-25 hotel market in the United States. Lenders should be able to analyze this data and do some local market due diligence to make their own analysis about the impact of potential new supply on a proposed hotel investment. A simple way for a lender to evaluate the new supply

Exhibit 3 Supply, Demand, and Economic Up-Cycles and Down-Cycles

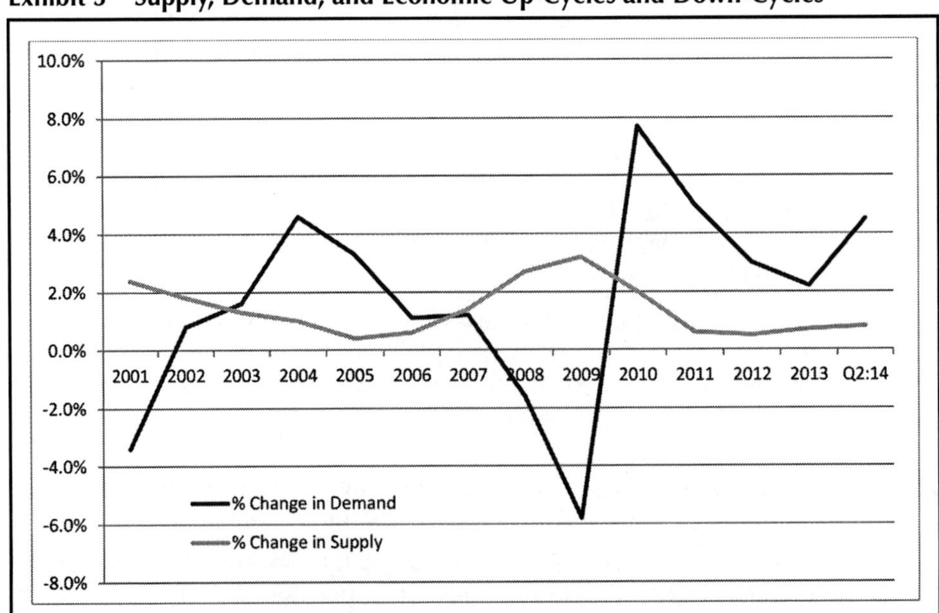

pipeline's impact on a specific investment is through a static demand analysis. As illustrated in Exhibit 4, by holding room night demand in a market at a constant rate, a lender can easily determine what impact new additions to supply may have on the overall performance of the local market and the subject hotel. The subject hotel's potential lower occupancy level inevitably results in a lower NOI and allows a lender to stress the hotel's cash flow in order to help reach a conclusion on how to properly structure and mitigate its potential loan exposure.

Key Hotel Loan Underwriting Principles

"People, credit, and real estate" remain the key fundamentals to underwriting any commercial real estate loan, hotels included. And while the introduction to this chapter stressed the difference between a hotel loan and other commercial real estate loans, the evaluation process and underwriting principals remain the same. The major considerations in making a hotel loan, like any investment, are to identify and analyze the key strengths and risks of a transaction. Inherent strengths may include the location and physical quality of the real estate itself. The sponsorship and operation team may also be a strength, in that the sponsor is a proven owner and operator with a track record of improving hotel operating performance. The sponsor's creditworthiness to support a proposed loan through renovation and ramp up can also be a loan evaluation's strength. Location, sponsorship, physical quality of an asset, loan to cost/value, and loan terms (structure and covenants) all may serve as loan strengths or at least risk mitigants for any given transaction. The goal in successfully underwriting a hotel loan is to fully understand both the inherent strengths and risks of a transaction and successfully mitigate the risks in an effort to properly size and structure a potential loan, as well as mitigate downside risk. And while all risks may not be mitigated, if they can be properly identified and limited, a loan may still be structured in order to accommodate the acceptability of those unmitigated risks.

Exhibit 4 Static Room Night Demand Analysis

Static Room Night Demand Analysis	
Number of Market Rooms	5,000
Market Annual Room Night Supply	1,825,000
Market Annual Room Night Demand	1,496,500
Market Occupancy	82%
Addition of a 500-Room Hotel	500
Addition to Annual Room Night Supply	182,500
New Market Annual Room Night Supply	2,007,500
Static Room Night Demand	1,496,500
New Market Occupancy	75%

Loan Sizing and Mitigating Risk

Loan terms are established to provide a lender some economic benefit and return on investment for making a loan, but the majority of the loan terms are put in place to manage and mitigate a lender's downside risk for making a loan. Prior to sizing a loan amount, a lender must clearly establish the capital structure of a transaction by creating a Sources and Uses Capitalization Chart. A Sources and Uses Capitalization Chart identifies the balance of equity and debt proposed to complete an investment. For example, Exhibit 5 references a typical acquisition capitalization, where the sources (debt and equity) are located on the left side of the chart and are equal to the sum of the uses on the right side of the chart. This level of detail provides a lender clarity on how loan dollars will be used and establishes a leverage point. In the scenario shown in Exhibit 5, the loan proceeds represent 60 percent of the total acquisition cost, which comprises the purchase price, an allocation to future capital investment needs, and closing costs.

Upon establishing the uses side of the capitalization chart, a lender can then focus on how to properly size the loan amount. The most important sizing tools in determining a proper loan amount are the loan to cost (LTC), loan to value (LTV), and a trailing debt yield. All three sizing metrics can be used when evaluating a loan's asset coverage and cash flow coverage. And while different lenders may see one element of loan sizing as more important than the other two, all three will be evaluated when making a loan.

Asset Coverage and Loan to Cost. Asset coverage describes the ratio between the loan amount and the all-in acquisition cost. In the example above, the loan amount is $60 million and the all-in acquisition cost is $100 million, resulting in a 60 percent LTC or 60 percent asset coverage. A lender can take comfort in its leverage risk, knowing that the borrower has 40 percent of real cash equity exposure in the capital stack in a first-loss position before the loan is exposed. This is an important concept to understand; a lender's view is that, in a downturn, a borrower with real cash equity at risk of being wiped out in a foreclosure will be more proactive in reaching a successful loan modification with a lender in order to protect the borrower's original investment.

Cash Flow Coverage and Debt Yield. In Exhibit 5, the borrower is investing $15,000,000 in capital expenditures to update the hotel; this is likely to make the hotel more competitive and improve its competitive positioning in the market-

Exhibit 5 A Typical Acquisition Capitalization

Sources			Uses		
	$	%		$	%
Debt	$60,000,000	60%	Purchase Price	$80,000,000	80%
Equity	$40,000,000	40%	CapEx	$15,000,000	15%
			Closing Costs	$5,000,000	5%
Total	**$100,000,000**	**100%**	Total	**$100,000,000**	**100%**

place. As a result of that capitalization, the NOI will be projected to increase to a new and higher stabilized level.

Let's assume the trailing NOI at the time of loan origination is $5 million, but per the borrower's investment plan, the NOI is projected to increase to $8 million in two years. The trailing NOI represents a low 8.3 percent debt yield on the $60 million loan amount ($5 million NOI divided by the $60 million loan amount), but also represents a 13.3 percent debt yield on its pro forma year 2/stabilized NOI. Traditionally a lender wants an in-place NOI north of a 10 percent debt yield, with a stabilized debt yield of 12 percent or greater. There are various reasons for this debt yield loan sizing, but the two most important factors are cash flow coverage and refinanceability. In a rising interest rate environment, which is imminent as this is being written, the in-place debt yield of 8.3 percent means interest rates can rise as high as 8.3 percent and the hotel's current NOI can cover debt service at a 1.00X DSCR. However, if the economy took a downturn tomorrow, that debt yield might drop to as low as 3 percent, by which time the hotel might no longer be able to cover debt service and the lender's loan amount could be exposed to being recovered at 100 percent of the original loan proceeds. By providing a loan at a 10 to 12 percent in-place debt yield, lenders are more confident that a hotel can take a substantial hit in an economic downturn and still cover debt service.

In terms of refinancing, a 10 to 12 percent debt yield remains a very attractive investment level for a new investor. While the borrower may be at risk of making a return on its investment, a lender can take comfort that even in a rising interest rate environment or down market, a lender's basis is safe at a 10 to 12 percent debt yield. So, while this investment scenario seems conservative from an LTC basis at 60 percent, the in-place debt yield of 8.3 percent represents a low debt-service coverage level and may preclude a lender from making a loan.

Loan to Value. The scenario just described presents an attractive LTC but a risky in-place debt yield. One mitigant to a low in-place debt yield would be the third sizing metric, a loan to value (LTV) requirement. The LTV is most commonly determined by a third-party appraisal, which can evaluate a hotel's as-is and as-stabilized value. The LTV test, which is usually determined by a separate third party with no vested interest in the transaction, can evaluate recent comparable transactions and underwrite the borrower's business plan and projected cash flow in order to determine and typically re-confirm the borrower's acquisition cost. If the appraised value is at or above the borrower's all-in cost of $100 million, then the LTV would be equal to or lower than the LTC (i.e., $115 million as-is value results in a 52.1 percent LTV). Typically, cash flow and debt yield are the driving sizing metric, but some lenders still look to LTV as the primary sizing metric.

As it pertains to the example above, the as-is appraisal value re-confirms that the borrower's investment strategy will increase NOI, which will allow the lender to make a case internally to approve the $60 million loan balance, even though the in-place debt yield is below 10 percent.

Price and Structure—the Asset vs. Cash Flow Gap. While most lenders rely on an LTC and LTV to help size their loans, the debt yield is becoming the most widely accepted and used sizing metric for an existing non-recourse loan, because it establishes a baseline of cash flow coverage and future ability to refinance.

How do we further mitigate the low debt yield in order to bridge the gap between asset coverage and cash flow coverage? In reality, the answer to this question is reflective of lending trends throughout the economic cycle, which will be covered later in the chapter. But there are various options that may work, depending on the competitive nature of the lending environment. A few solutions may be as follows:

- *Implement recourse.* Early in the hotel market economic recovery, lenders typically require a portion of guarantor recourse on the loan. A lender could structure a 25 percent repayment guaranty to the sponsor, reducing the lender's net-non-recourse leverage to $45 million (75 percent of $60 million) and achieving an 11.1 percent debt yield on a net-non-recourse loan amount of $45 million ($5 million NOI /$45 million net-non-recourse loan exposure).
- *Hold-back loan funds for renovation.* As the hotel market economy continues to recover and more lenders are competing for existing loans, a lender may no longer be able to obtain a repayment guaranty, but instead may structure a hold-back of $15 million of initial loan proceeds, which will only be funded upon completion (or in conjunction with completing) a renovation, subject to the lender's review and approval of the renovation plans. Now, the initial loan funding of $45 million represents an 11.1 percent debt yield. A lender may also require a completion guaranty from the sponsor, requiring the sponsor to complete the renovation in accordance with plans and funds approved by the lender or otherwise default on the loan. A completion guaranty is another structuring tool a lender can use to mitigate the potential risks associated with the renovation project.
- *Price the risk and bifurcate the loan.* This last example represents where the hotel lending market is in 2014/2015, now six to seven years removed from the last major economic downturn of 2008 (the Great Recession). At this time in the cycle, the competitive lender market has expanded significantly to where balance sheet lenders are competing with life insurance companies, debt funds, CMBSs, and other alternative sources of financing. And while we are long into the hotel recovery and growth phase of the current real estate economic cycle, lending underwriting standards are decreasing in an effort to place capital. In this scenario, if a lender is comfortable in taking on the low debt-yield risk, there is an opportunity to increase interest rate spreads to get paid for taking that incremental cash flow coverage risk. A lender then may decide to bifurcate the loan into senior and junior tranches (i.e., mortgage and mezzanine debt) in order to bifurcate the risk and earn better fee economics for the bank by originating and distributing pieces of the debt. For example, the senior facility may get sized to a $45 million A-Note (11.1 percent debt yield and 45 percent LTC), improving upon the senior lender's exposure risk, but the pricing for this senior debt will also decrease as a result. The remaining junior portion of the loan stack will have an exposed piece of debt at only 15 percent of the capital stack and will require a much higher interest rate spread to accommodate for that thin capital stack exposure (45 to 60 percent of capital stack) and a lower in-place debt yield (8.3 percent in-place). In this scenario, a borrower can make the decision to take less debt at better pricing in order to

protect itself in a downside scenario, or take on more debt at higher pricing in order to improve its internal rate of return (IRR).

When to Rely on Loan to Cost vs. Loan to Value. As a continuation of the three pricing and structuring mitigants above, it's worth revisiting when it may be more appropriate to rely more heavily on an LTC versus an LTV. In terms of a loan evaluation, the importance of an LTC and LTV tend to have an inverse relationship, depending on where we sit within the economic cycle. Early in the cycle and recovery phase, a lender may look at the LTV to validate the borrower's cost basis. Late in the hotel economic cycle, a lender will revert to requiring more cash equity to protect itself in the event of an imminent economic downturn.

Regardless of the cycle, lenders, like equity investors, are looking to place capital and will get more aggressive to win debt assignments as the economy continues to grow. Maintaining lending discipline throughout the lending cycles is difficult, but should be at the core of any loan evaluation. A good lender will evaluate the people, credit, and real estate as well as underwrite the investment's inherent strengths and structure to mitigate the potential risks.

Types of Hotel Loans

In the previous section, we discussed how lenders may bridge the gap between asset coverage and cash flow coverage in order to properly size and structure loans. This dynamic is at work in all hotel lending transactions, as lenders must evaluate the quality of the asset, location, and sponsor, as well as underwrite the historical and projected cash flow. The unique nature of a hotel's nightly perishable inventory and resulting high-beta operating cash flow as a primary source of repayment puts greater emphasis on the underwriting of a hotel's historical and projected cash flow.

The three most common types of loans made in the industry—standing/stabilized, opportunistic/repositioning, and construction/mini-perm—will be discussed in the following sections. It is important to note that each of these loans may fall in and out of favor with lenders, depending on where we sit in the hotel economic cycle, and the terms of each of these loans change as well. For example, at the time of this writing, the economic recovery is six to seven years removed from the last major market crash. Unlike with other economic recoveries, the general economy and GDP have been slower to regain steam this time around, but liquidity in capital markets ramped up faster due to low interest rates. Furthermore, the U.S. market is viewed as a safe haven and a preferred investment in comparison to international markets; therefore, loan terms and interest rate spreads are fairly aggressive relative to the middle-inning broader economic growth underway in the United States. As a result, please note that the loan discussions in the following sections reflect a snapshot in time of the lending appetite and structure in the United States in 2014/2015, and may change, depending on a change in the broader economic sentiment in the United States.

Standing/Stabilized Loan. The lowest-risk hotel loan to underwrite is a stabilized and cash-flowing hotel. That is also the most competitive loan to underwrite, resulting in a downward pressure on interest rate spreads, higher leverage, and looser covenants than other loan types. Key features of a cash-flowing, stabilized hotel loan are as follows:

- *Leverage/debt yield:* 50–65 percent LTV and LTC; debt yield between 9–12 percent on in-place TTM NOI on a senior loan basis.
- *Interest rate/coupon:* floating rate debt priced at (One-Month LIBOR) at L+225–350; fixed rate five-year debt prices range between 4.00–5.00 percent.
- *Term and extension:* floating rate debt terms are typically three–five years. Floating rate deals rarely surpass five years, due to lender cost-of-fund restrictions.
- *Amortization:* the loan may amortize over a twenty-five to thirty year term, even if the actual loan term is three–five years. Amortization provides lenders the ability to reduce their leverage over the term of the loan and serves as another mitigant to higher-levered loans with lower cash flow. If the loan is already low-levered and has a strong debt yield, amortization may not be required and would be interest-only throughout the term of the loan.
- *Recourse:* a stabilized and cash-flowing hotel loan at good leverage and cash flow coverage would be a non-recourse loan, whereby a lender's only collateral is the hotel real estate itself.
- *Covenants:* because of the non-recourse nature of the loan, lenders would look to institute various covenants in order to mitigate the non-recourse risk. Mitigants may include various performance tests that trigger a cash sweep or re-margin test if the hotel's NOI falls below a certain debt yield. A cash sweep may automatically take excess cash flow to pay down the loan balance (hyper-amortization), or may be held in an account which allows the hotel and borrower to earn back the excess cash flow if the hotel's performance improves. A re-margin test typically is based on a debt yield or appraisal test and would require the borrower to pay down the loan to suffice the re-margin test or otherwise would trigger a default.

Opportunistic/Repositioning Loan. An opportunistic or repositioning loan is also commonly referred to as a bridge loan. These types of loans are quite prevalent in hotel lending, as the new borrower's business plan calls for investing capital to achieve better operating efficiencies or reposition the hotel in order to achieve a higher operating profit. In a repositioning loan, a lender will more heavily weigh the sponsor's expertise than in a stabilized hotel loan, as this scenario may require a great deal of renovation and construction expertise and involve newly negotiated management and franchise agreements, changes to labor staffing and operational cost structures, and a disruption of the hotel's performance during the renovation. Key features of an opportunistic/repositioning loan are as follows:

- *Leverage/debt yield:* 60–70 percent LTV and LTC; debt yield between 8–10 percent on in-place TTM NOI.
- *Interest rate/coupon:* interest rates will widen, depending on the extent of the business plan and associated risk, but if a stabilized hotel next door is priced at L+250 at a 12 percent debt yield, the adjacent repositioning loan may size to an 8.5 percent debt yield and will price 75–150 bps wider (L+325–400). Fixed-

rate debt widens as well, but is likely provided because of more intrinsic qualities of the overall real estate, so the price differential to a stabilized hotel wouldn't be as significant as in a floating rate transaction.

- *Term and extension:* depending on how long a renovation will take (one–two years are common), the term for a repositioning loan would likely be a three-year initial term with two one-year extension options. Those extension options would require satisfying a performance test, such as an appraisal event and a minimum debt yield.
- *Amortization:* because a repositioned hotel should see an incremental increase in value beyond the dollars invested to create that value, a repositioning loan would likely get a one–three year period of interest-only debt, with amortization kicking in upon the projected stabilization or completion of the repositioning.
- *Recourse:* early in the cycle, a lender may be able to get partial to 100 percent recourse on a loan like this, but recourse will be negotiated away as more lender competition enters the market. The mitigant to offering a non-recourse repositioning loan is higher pricing and stiffer covenants. Again, sponsor expertise is vital in a non-recourse repositioning loan.
- *Covenants:* with an opportunistic/repositioning loan, cash sweep and re-margins are more likely to be implemented, as well as other forms of recourse, like a completion guaranty and interest guaranty, which a lender would like to hold the warm-body sponsor accountable for.

Construction/Mini-Perm Loan. A construction/mini-perm loan represents the highest risk for a lender. The major risks include the various circumstances that could delay or halt construction. A borrower may become embroiled in a lawsuit with its general contractor, causing the borrower to default on the construction loan. Now, the lender is in an extremely difficult scenario where its primary loan collateral is an unfinished construction project with competing claims and liens against the property. Lenders are not construction experts and are not in the business of owning real estate, let alone unfinished real estate. In addition to these hypothetical (but, unfortunately, all too real) scenarios, a lender must also deal with the unfortunate business of reserving 100 percent of loan proceeds for the construction project, without actually earning interest on that money until the project is complete and fully funded. In order to mitigate these severe risks, sponsorship is paramount, and interest rate pricing and associated fees widen, while leverage is lower than with a standing hotel loan. A borrower's expertise in successfully executing projects with a capable construction team (general contractor, architect, designer, project manager) is paramount. Inevitably, a senior-only construction loan will require the stiffest of covenants and recourse to the sponsor, which are highlighted as follows:

- *Leverage/debt yield:* 50–65 percent LTV and LTC; an as-stabilized appraised NOI of between 12–14 percent (three–four years from completion).
- *Interest rate/coupon:* pricing will fluctuate, depending on the strength of sponsorship and terms of recourse. If a lender received a 100 percent repayment

and completion guaranty from a strong sponsor and the leverage is below 60 percent, the interest rate pricing may be L+250 or lower. If there is a repayment guaranty as low as 25–50 percent, the pricing may be L+350 or higher. A larger loan ($100 million or more) will also drive higher pricing, as there are fewer lenders able to quote a loan that size and willing to invest substantial dollars in a single project, and they will need to be properly compensated for the risk.

- *Term and extension:* initial loans of three–five years, with extension options as far out as a six–seven year total term. In today's market, cost of funds/pricing increases substantially for a term outside of five years.
- *Amortization:* likely interest-only during construction, but typically amortization will kick in at the end of the initial term or upon completion.
- *Recourse:* early in the current economic cycle, construction loans were difficult to obtain, as lenders were focused on stabilized and repositioning loans. In 2013, construction loans were subject to a 100 percent re-payment guaranty. In 2014, re-payment guaranties dropped to approximately 50 percent, and are continuing to drop today. While other real estate construction loans today, like condominiums and multi-family, may be non-recourse, hotel construction loans for the most part maintain some level of re-payment guaranty. That said, a select number of debt funds provide non-recourse construction loans, but require interest rate spreads more than double or triple what a partial-recourse loan would require.
- *Covenants:* if a sponsor is providing a strong re-payment guaranty throughout construction and after completion, then a construction/mini-perm loan is light on performance covenants relative to the other two loan types just discussed. The only covenants may be an appraisal and debt yield test for each extension period and a possible cash sweep test at a later date, post completion/stabilization.

The Competitive Lending Landscape

Whether it is a CMBS or a balance sheet lender, a life insurance company or a debt fund, a domestic bank or an international bank, there are multiple lenders that actively lend in the hotel market. The number of lenders active in the market, however, ebbs and flows throughout the economic cycle. Each type of lender has unique characteristics and risk-mitigant check points, and all must manage how large their hotel loan portfolio is as a percentage of their overall real estate lending operation. In other words, none of these lenders wants to overweight its commercial real estate loan portfolio with too much hotel debt. In the following sections, we will briefly profile the major categories of lenders that issue hotel loans, with an emphasis on each lender's unique features and appetite for hotel loans. These sections present a general picture of lending at this point in the economic cycle; the terms below can and will change on a deal-by-deal basis.

Balance Sheet Lenders

Balance sheet lenders book and hold loans on their balance sheet. Typically a balance sheet lender forms a one-on-one relationship with its borrower, and both benefit from a direct dialogue on a loan or loan portfolio, should there need to be modifications or restructurings in a downturn, or should amendments need to be made to loan documents to adjust for revised business plans, or should changes in operating performance (good or bad) occur. The negative of dealing with balance sheet lenders is that they typically have a higher cost of capital (interest rate pricing) than the secondary market (e.g., CMBSs) and may have higher standards in underwriting and structuring than secondary market lenders. The following sections present a brief description of the various balance sheet lenders in the hotel market.

National Banks. National banks have a retail-branch footprint across the United States. The following are characteristics of national banks in regard to the hotel market:

- *Hotel appetite:* A national bank will be a sponsor focused on those borrowers that invest in hotels as a primary business or as an investment component to general real estate investing. In other words, national banks would not look to make a loan to smaller real estate investors that may only have one or two hotels in their investment portfolios. National banks' geographic appetite for hotel loans may be limited to the top coastal markets in the United States (New York City, San Francisco, Los Angeles, Washington, D.C., Miami, Boston), or may be as broad as the top 25 Metropolitan Statistical Areas (MSAs) in the United States, as there is quickly available market research on those MSAs.
- *General terms:* Senior leverage of 50–65 percent LTC/LTV; 9–12 percent trailing debt yields; non-recourse and recourse loans; heavier loan covenants in order to protect the balance sheet exposure; interest rate pricing between L+250–400. Loan terms are flexible and negotiable but vary by transaction.
- *Restrictions to hospitality:* The primary restriction is to only lend to those borrowers with a credible hotel investment portfolio. In terms of loan amounts, most national banks do not pursue hotel loans of less than $20 million, and have a hold appetite up to $75–$100 million. National banks will pursue hotel loans larger than $100 million, but will likely syndicate a percentage of the total loan in order to get to a target hold level. National banks are not likely to pursue a hotel loan (or hotel portfolio loan) north of $500 million, due to the limited syndication distribution for that much hotel debt on any single transaction. National banks tend to allocate between 10–30 percent of their overall commercial real estate loan portfolio to hospitality.

Regional Banks. Regional banks are banks with a regional-branch footprint within either a specific city or sub-region of the United States. The following are characteristics of regional banks in regard to the hotel market:

- *Hotel appetite:* Regional banks do not typically have a broad hotel appetite, but will pursue hotel loans if the sponsor and/or real estate is located proximate to their headquarters. A regional bank may have a broader commercial real estate or corporate lending relationship with a local hotel sponsor, or know the local hotel well and have a strong view of the local market's economic dynamics if the hotel is located near their headquarters.

- *General terms:* 60–70 percent LTC/LTV; 9–12 percent TTM debt yields; non-recourse and recourse loans; unpredictable on loan covenants, as regional banks will lend more on an emotional or intrinsic interest in the sponsor or real estate; interest rate pricing between L+225–300. Terms are likely to be inflexible, as their limited general hotel exposure restricts their ability to evaluate an individual deal's merits and strengths. Regional banks tend to be more selective on non-recourse loan opportunities.
- *Restrictions to hospitality:* Primarily a geographic restriction regarding both the sponsor and real estate. This dynamic restricts a regional bank's ability to form a lending relationship with a sponsor that invests in hotels on a national basis. Loan amounts are typically between $5–$15 million, and capped at $20–$25 million per loan. One $20 million hotel loan may represent a large percentage of that bank's overall exposure to hospitality relative to all of its commercial real estate loans, so interest in hospitality is limited.

International Banks. International banks attracted to U.S. hotel loans include various Asian banks in Japan, China, Korea, Taiwan, and Singapore; German banks; U.K. banks; and Canadian banks. For many of these banks, U.S. real estate provides a safe place and an attractive risk return on capital, relative to their local markets. The following are characteristics of international banks in regard to the hotel market:

- *Hotel appetite:* International banks, on average, can make big hotel investments in the United States but restrict themselves to top-tier markets like New York City, Los Angeles, and Miami, and focus on nationally branded luxury or full-service hotels. These top-tier markets are familiar to the home offices of these international banks and thus are easier to underwrite. In 2014/2015, international banks are attracted to hotel loans due to their attractive interest rate spread relative to other real estate classes; these banks are specifically attracted to marquee assets in top-tier markets.
- *General terms:* 50–65 percent LTC/LTV; 8–11 percent TTM debt yields; non-recourse and recourse loans; looser covenants than national banks due to the prominent locations and the physical quality of the hotel real estate. Interest rate pricing between L+200–300 (depending on the cost of capital to lend in the United States). Terms are flexible, depending on real estate and asset quality. International lenders are not as sophisticated on the structure and underwriting of hotel investments in the United States as are the national banks; thus, they rely more on easily identifiable real estate and internationally recognizable borrowers.
- *Restrictions to hospitality:* Primarily a geographic restriction and property-type restriction. Will likely not lend in secondary markets or on limited-service or independent hotel concepts. Well capitalized international banks may lend upward of $125–$200 million for a high-quality hotel asset in a highly desirable location.

Life Insurance Companies. Life insurance companies provide an attractive financing alternative for those borrowers seeking longer-term financing (five-, seven-, or ten-year fixed-rate loans). Life insurance companies are both lenders and equity investors in hospitality, providing them with a strong knowledge base for sizing, structuring, and pricing their loans. Life insurance companies also answer to a different set of regulations than traditional banks, allowing them to be more aggressive at times than their bank competitors. The following are characteristics of life insurance companies in regard to the hotel market:

- *Hotel appetite:* Not all life insurance companies are comfortable lending on hotels, but those that do lend are willing to source large loans at relatively more aggressive terms than balance sheet lenders. Life insurance companies are typically attracted to hotels of high-asset quality located in top-tier markets, but are also very aggressive in lending on high-end resorts and large group resorts. Traditionally, banks are not as aggressive on resorts; therefore, life insurance companies tend to be the dominant lender on high-quality resort transactions.
- *General terms:* 60–70 percent LTC/LTV; 7–11 percent TTM debt yields; non-recourse; looser covenants than national banks, due to the prominent locations and physical quality of the hotel real estate. Fixed interest rates typically in the 3.50–5.00 percent range. Some exposure to floating rate debt in the Libor + 200–500 range (transaction dependent). Terms and covenants are not flexible, and loan terms are typically fixed and locked out, restricting a borrower's exit strategy.
- *Restrictions to hospitality:* Life insurance companies are only restricted in the types of hotels they are interested in lending on, which tend to be high-quality assets in marquee urban and resort markets. Life insurance companies have the ability to issue debt up to $250–$500 million, and join with other life insurance companies to issue debt at $500 million or more. Life insurance companies tend to be more real estate focused, whereas traditional banks may be more relationship focused.

Secondary Market Lenders, Debt Funds/Mezzanine Lenders, and Alternate Funding Sources

Secondary Market Lenders. Secondary market lenders are those that originate single hotel loans and bundle them together with other general real estate loans in order to blend out the overall risk of the loan pool, and sell different tranches of credit-rated debt to bond buyers at varying interest rate spreads and exposure levels. Secondary market lenders are often referred to as "CMBS" lenders, as what they offer to bond buyers in the secondary market are Commercial Mortgage-Backed Securities. These securities can be freely traded in the open market. CMBS lenders fill a necessary void in commercial real estate lending by leveraging broad investor appetite for these real estate commodity securities and, as a result, are able to make both small and large loans on hotels. The negative with a CMBS loan is that there is no borrower/lender relationship that allows for amendments, adjustments, or "friendly modifications" throughout the economic cycle. The lender effectively becomes the end-user bond holders, and they are only intent to earn the coupon they purchased for the life of the pool. The following are characteristics of secondary market lenders in regard to the hotel market:

- *Hotel appetite:* CMBS loan appetite for hotels is limited to stabilized and cash-flowing hotels, rather than construction or deep repositionings. CMBS lenders can make small loans in amounts of $5–$20 million and up to $75 million and still place those loans in a larger general real estate CMBS pool. CMBS lenders can also originate and distribute single borrower issuances for an individual hotel or hotel portfolio and sell that in the market if the loan amount is greater than $200 million and up to $1 billion or more.
- *General terms*: 40–80 percent LTC/LTV; 7–14 percent TTM debt yields; non-recourse; looser covenants than those offered by national banks, but strict enforcement of a cash sweep, which can be punitive to a borrower's and operator's ability to manage the day-to-day demands of a hotel. Interest rate pricing between L+175–500.
- *Restrictions to hospitality:* CMBS lenders are limited to originating cash-flowing hotels, but will routinely underwrite the full debt stack risk and then parcel the loan up into senior and junior tranches, selling off both senior and junior mortgages and mezzanine debt. In an economic downturn, and when a hotel triggers a performance test or default, CMBS loans are extremely difficult to negotiate a successful loan modification. Thus, CMBS loans experience a significant foreclosure rate in down cycles relative to balance sheet–originated loans. CMBS loans are also exposed to broader capital market trends, as the end user is looking for the best return on capital on a liquid investment. As a result, bond buyers may at a moment's notice pursue other investments and cause a halt to CMBS placements and future originations.

Debt Funds/Mezzanine Lenders. Earlier, we evaluated how to bridge the gap between asset coverage and cash flow coverage, whereby the LTC may be 60 percent, but the debt yield is only 8.5 percent on a TTM basis. Debt funds and mezzanine lenders help fund that financial gap between a senior loan's desired exposure (50 percent and an 11 percent debt yield) and the remaining 10 percentage points of leverage required to meet a borrower's loan request. For taking that piece of exposed debt, a debt fund will look to get paid a much higher interest rate spread than the senior lender, say L+7–10 percent. Debt funds are successful in providing bridge financing for loans that are too aggressive for the senior bank market. However, when debt funds take on a mezzanine position, they are in a first-loss, highly exposed position, which is why they require pricing close to equity-like returns. The following are characteristics of debt funds/mezzanine lenders in regard to the hotel market:

- *Hotel appetite:* Debt funds have a broad appetite for existing hotel assets; a small subset of debt funds will also underwrite construction loans. Only a select number of debt funds will entertain construction lending, and it is quite expensive. Debt funds are more real estate and property-underwriting focused than sponsor focused, as they are investing in the riskiest piece of the debt stack and need to conduct thorough property-level due diligence to protect their investment. Debt funds are typically attracted to top-market and high-profiled hotels, as they have a higher intrinsic value to protect their basis. Debt funds will also look at broad hotel portfolios that offer geographic and local economic diversity.

- *General terms:* 50–85 percent LTC/LTV; 6–10 percent TTM debt yields; non-recourse; loose financial covenants are traded for clean and quick access to the UCC foreclosure process and the ability to replace the existing borrower if need be. Pricing between L+7–15 percent, which is all transaction- and leverage-related and unique to each deal. Typically, debt funds are seeking to provide a 10 percent IRR for their investors, but they have some flexibility, which means that deals can get priced above or below their general return threshold to investors.
- *Restrictions to hospitality:* No restrictions, other than self-imposed restrictions. Loan proceeds typically range from $10–$25 million and can go upwards of $50–$150 million, with larger mezzanine pieces getting preferential pricing treatment.

Alternative Funding Sources. The types of lenders just discussed represent the traditional competitive-lender landscape for hotels. While these lender types make up the majority of debt capital placed in the hotel industry, alternative funding sources will always exist. One popular form of alternative finance today is EB-5 funding. EB-5 represents a source of debt capital that comprises $500,000–$2,000,000 investments from foreign investors who make an investment in U.S. real estate developments in an effort to obtain a green card. These investors are granted a passive way to lend on projects, make a return on their investment, and obtain access to the United States. Terms of EB-5 financing can be lucrative to a U.S. borrower at low interest rates and passive loan terms, but arranging EB-5 debt is extremely labor-intensive, requires a broker to identify and recruit those foreign investors, and can take years to put together. Crowd funding is another in vogue form of capital raising; crowd funding utilizes the broad-reaching capabilities of the Internet and social media channels to promote and attract funding. This funding can be in the form of equity or debt capital. Payday lenders, micro-business lending, and other forms of high-interest rate capital exist as well. Traditional debt sources will be attracted to institutional-quality borrowers and hotel-asset collateral, but debt funds and alternative sources of capital will allow smaller and riskier projects to get capitalized.

Hotel Lending through the Economic Cycle

"Those who cannot remember the past are condemned to repeat it."—George Santayana. Hotel investing, more so than any other real estate investment class, is about timing the economic and investment cycle. In the world of hotel lending, you don't want to be late to the game. All too often, lenders turn to hotel lending in an effort to get a higher pricing yield for their real estate investment, without taking into consideration the inevitable decrease in performance that hotels experience during an economic downturn. Real estate performance and valuation is a lagging indicator in economic cycles, and hotels lag even further than other core real estate classes. A hotel experiences the strongest demand and ADR growth when the economy is accelerating. Once the economy crashes, hotels react the quickest and most violently, due to an immediate drop in both occupancy levels and ADR, while having to maintain a burdensome fixed cost load. Similarly, hotels have the highest exposure to event risk relative to other asset classes. Using 9/11 or the 2003 SARS epidemic as examples, hotel operating performance decreased significantly in the days, weeks, and months following those two events, due to the fear of traveling or contagion. As the general economy bottoms out and starts to grow, hotels are the slowest of real estate classes to recover, because of the lag to invest in travel (business or leisure). When an economy starts to recover, job growth starts to increase. Job growth eventually translates to increased demand for office space, which in turn drives increases in office real estate valuations. Job growth also leads to increased demand for residential real estate and increased consumer confidence and spending, which drives growth in retail and industrial real estate valuations. It's only once we are further along in the recovery that corporations, groups, and leisure travelers feel they have enough discretionary capital to expend it on travel, and thus hotels finally rebound. Of course, it isn't this simple, but hotel valuations typically lag other real estate classes and accelerate at the fastest pace (price per key and compressing cap rates) right before the next economic crash.

"Be greedy when others are fearful, and fearful when others are greedy."—Warren Buffett. It's worth repeating that uneducated lenders get burned when they enter the hotel lending business late in the cycle in search of higher pricing for their credit on a risk-adjusted basis, without considering proper covenants, and structure and sponsorship factors (as discussed earlier in the chapter). Conversely, savvy hotel lenders understand the opportunities to lend early in an economic and hotel recovery and ultimately will give up market share late in the market when their structure and covenants are not competitive. Unfortunately, those in the hotel lending business can't pull out entirely, so while some covenants and structure may give way to market forces, savvy lenders should maintain discipline in lending to strong sponsors who are cycle-proven. Exhibit 6 shows how major hotel lending terms may have changed between 2011 and 2014/2015 for a stabilized urban hotel with national brand/management affiliation and institutional sponsorship. The important takeaway from the variance of the terms shown in Exhibit 6 is that the same hotel, stabilized three to five years later in an economic cycle, is sized at a higher LTV and LTC, with looser covenants, and the interest rate spread is approximately 33 percent tighter. In addition, CMBS lenders, which do not actively manage their loans or lending relationships, are the winning bidders. Leverage on these types of loans may be as high as 75 percent, with debt yields as low as 7–8 percent, and require both senior and junior debt providers. This can further complicate an eventual loan modification that may ensue during the initial loan term if an economic downturn occurs during the next four years (2019).

Exhibit 7 shows the lending terms for a group resort hotel with national brand/management in place, in which the primary demand drivers to the hotel are groups and leisure guests. Sponsorship is a developer and a silent equity partner. The key takeaways from Exhibit 7 are that, while a balance sheet lender is likely the same lender both early and late in the cycle, the conditions under which the lender makes a construction loan are very different. Early in the cycle, a lender can be very selective about which construction loans it takes on. Frankly, a lender

Exhibit 6 Lending Terms for a Stabilized Urban Hotel

Terms	2011	2014/2015
Debt Yield:	12%	10%
LTV/LTC:	55%	65%
Recourse:	Non-Recourse	Non-Recourse
Interest Rate Spread:	L+375	L+250
Term:	3+1+1	4+1
Key Covenants:	Cash Sweep Test at an 11% Debt Yield. Remargin Test at a 10% Debt Yield.	Cash Sweep at a 9% Debt Yield on Senior. No remargin requirement.
Winning Lender Type:	Balance Sheet, Life Company	CMBS

Exhibit 7 Lending Terms for a Group Resort Hotel

Terms	2011	2014/2015
Appraised Stabilized Debt Yield:	15%	12%
LTV/LTC:	50%	65%
Recourse:	100% Joint & Several Completion and Repayment Guaranty	100% Joint & Several Completion; 50% Repayment Guaranty that reduces to 25% at completion & is eliminated upon achieving a 12% Debt Yield
Interest Rate Spread:	L+450	L+300
Term:	3+1+1	4+1+1+1
Key Covenants:	Cash Sweep implemented 1 year after opening at an 11% Debt Yield.	No Covenants other than recourse terms.
Winning Lender Type:	Balance Sheet Lender	Balance Sheet Lender

may not even provide construction financing for any hotel, let alone a group resort hotel. Any loan that is made in 2011 will be to the highest caliber borrower/sponsor. Three to four years later in the cycle, balance sheet lenders are forced to lend on more construction because their terms aren't competitive enough for stabilized assets and the borrowers/sponsors receiving loans at higher-risk terms are not of the same caliber required in 2011. And even though construction loans are riskier than existing hotel loans, balance sheet lenders are attracted to them because of the ability to obtain some level of recourse. By obtaining recourse, lenders often price construction loans as low as L+250. Lower levels of recourse, higher loan-to-cost/loan-to-value exposure, longer loan terms, and tighter interest rate pricing make construction lending extremely risky late in an economic cycle. Not only is there execution risk, but the return on investment is quite low, due to the fact that a lender must reserve 100 percent of loan proceeds for the subject construction loan, but isn't earning interest until loan draws are made, which are at the end of the construction timeline.

Conclusion

Inevitably, hesitation in real estate lending in a down market gives way to more aggressive lending behavior during an economic recovery, up until the point of correction. Due to their nightly perishable inventory, hotels react harder and faster in a downturn, making them one of the riskiest real estate classes to lend on. One focus of this chapter is to instill a guide and toolset to mitigate those inevitable and cyclical risks. The sponsor's creditworthiness, asset quality and coverage, recourse requirements, and other structural covenants serve to enhance and protect a lender's position. While interest rate pricing isn't a mitigant to loan risk, it should be viewed as an acceptable rate of return for taking on a certain degree of lending risk. The greater the risk, the higher the interest rate pricing.

Case Study: A Loan for the Heavenly Grand Hotel

ABC Private Equity Fund and Sky High Operating Partner (the sponsors) have recently won a widely brokered transaction for the Heavenly Grand Hotel, a 500-room, four-star independent hotel located in Santa Monica, California. The hotel features 20,000 square feet of indoor meeting space, a 100-seat three-meal restaurant, a deli café, a lobby bar, a pool bar, two pools (family and adult only), and a spa with fifteen treatment rooms. The hotel has an established reputation as a premier beachfront hotel but is in need of capital updates and is losing RevPAR market share to nearby competitors. The sponsors acquired a fee-simple interest in the hotel for $250 million (including closing costs) and plan to invest another $50 million to do a full guestroom and guest bathroom update, as well as reconfiguring the hotel's entrance, lobby, and public spaces; updating the spa; and repositioning the restaurant. The hotel will be closed for remodeling for five months during the offseason. While the majority of the construction will be finished upon the hotel's re-opening, approximately seventy guestrooms (one floor) will be offline for another seven months. The sponsors also plan to convert the signature restaurant into a high-end concept through a licensing agreement with a celebrity chef.

As a result of the capital investment, the sponsors expect to move the hotel into the five-star category.

In addition to investing significant capital, the sponsors will convert the hotel to the St. Regis brand and will hire Starwood to manage it. Sky High Operating Partner has acquired and disposed of several Starwood-managed properties over the last ten years, but this will be the first St. Regis brand and the first repositioning to a five-star asset that either sponsor has been involved in. ABC Private Equity Fund is a multi-billion-dollar investment fund with a twenty-year investment history. ABC Private Equity has a strong bank following, but this investment represents its first partnership with Sky High Operating Partner. ABC Private Equity owns nearby multi-family properties and is attracted to the collateral's long-term land value. ABC Private Equity represents 90 percent of the overall equity investment, but will not serve as guarantor due to various fund bylaw restrictions. Sky High Operating Partner will serve as the non-recourse carve-out guarantor. The majority of Sky High Operating Partner's capital is raised from friends and family and earned through asset management fees and promote structures on its various investments.

The hotel's current TTM NOI as of November 2014 was $20 million and its RevPAR penetration versus the competitive set was 95 percent. The hotel's prior peak NOI in 2008 was $18 million, with a RevPAR penetration of 110 percent. The hotel's NOI in 2010 was $10 million (100 percent RevPAR penetration), and the hotel is projected to achieve a $10 million NOI through 2015 because of the renovation disruption. The hotel's NOI is projected to increase to $25 million in 2016 (110 percent RevPAR penetration) and stabilize in 2017 at a $33 million NOI (130 percent RevPAR penetration).

There are no forecasted new additions to supply in the local market, but two of the hotel's four primary competitors have either completed or are undergoing significant renovations to improve their guests' experiences and increase their top-line performance.

The sponsors are requesting a $225 million loan—non-recourse, interest only—for a term of five years, with maximum prepayment flexibility.

Discussion Questions

1. What lender types would be viable candidates to provide financing to this hotel's sponsor?
2. Keeping in mind the three main principles in underwriting a hotel loan, identify the potential strengths and weaknesses of the proposed loan. How can the weaknesses be mitigated?
3. How should a lender structure the loan? What are the key loan terms that should be considered?

Suggested answers to these questions appear at the end of this book.

Part IV

Planning and Executing the Hotel Investment

16

Principles of Hotel Investment Ventures

By Sean Hennessey

Sean Hennessey *is a Clinical Assistant Professor at the Tisch Center for Hospitality and Tourism at New York University, teaching courses in finance, investment, and development. He also operates Lodging Advisors, a consultancy helping investors evaluate lodging opportunities. Mr. Hennessey has a culinary degree from Johnson & Wales and a hotel degree from Cornell. A past chairman of the International Society of Hospitality Consultants, Mr. Hennessey has many media citations and appearances. He has been referred to as "one of the country's top hotel consultants."*

FOR HOSPITALITY ASSETS, joint ventures have a special appeal because they recognize the two distinct—though interrelated—attributes necessary for a successful investment: the combination of a complex operating business with significant capital funds. The combination of an operating business within a specialized real estate asset has led to a common practice of bifurcating the ownership of hotels between an operating partner who deeply understands the hotel business and a capital partner whose job is to efficiently allocate capital.

The traditional model of hotel ownership has been the owner-operator, an entity that both owns and operates a hotel. Sometimes the owner is a sole proprietor, who enjoys complete control of the operation and all the benefits of ownership. More often, ownership is structured as either a partnership or a corporation, where a number of people or entities come together to invest in an asset. Whether structured as a partnership or a corporation, the venture will have someone in charge of the investment (the operating partner, but also referred to by other titles, including managing member or sponsor) and other participants who have defined roles, which can range from very limited to very active involvement.

Due to the scale of hotel investments, it is rare for owners today to be sole proprietors except for small properties. And while taking on partners may open the door to misunderstandings, reporting responsibilities, and the like, it undoubtedly has also opened the door to many opportunities for wealth creation. What manager hasn't felt, at some point, that his or her talents and experience were largely enriching someone else? Alternatively, what manager operating simply on a contract basis has not had a sleepless night wondering if an owner, who retains ultimate control over an asset, might try to terminate his or her services? Being part of the ownership team, despite potential challenges, holds broad appeal for many hotel management firms.

The following case study will describe a "sponsor/capital partner" investment structure for a stand-alone hotel investment. This will be followed by a discussion of more sophisticated forms of hotel investment ventures.

In this chapter, we will refer to the manager of the ownership venture as the operating partner or sponsor and the majority capital provider as the capital partner. In fact, these participants may be members of a corporation, but in common parlance they are normally referred to as partners. Similarly, the capital partner can consist of many capital providers coming together to fund an investment. For simplicity's sake in this chapter, both entities will be referred to as if there were only one operating partner and one capital partner.

A fundamental desire of many investors is to drive their financial returns as high as possible. Of course, there are trade-offs involving risk and return, and every investor should be comfortable with the risks undertaken. But more often than not, it is necessary for an investor to accept a healthy dose of risk in order to be an active player. Conservative investors who focus on protecting their downside are seldom the ones who successfully compete to acquire assets and grow their business platforms. Therefore, the ensuing model will show how an investor might look to enhance a deal to maximize yield.

Hotel Investment Case Study

The following case study will walk the reader through a potential hotel investment and several financial steps that the investor may take to enhance the total return. Consider a hotel that has an expected net operating income as presented in Exhibit 1. The projection shows ten years of ownership and an eleventh year ("Residual"), which is conventionally used as the basis for calculating an investment's residual, or resale, value (assumed to be realized on the last day of year ten). This property shows significant growth in net operating income during the holding period—which is unusual, but is used here to facilitate the presentation of the investment topic. The hotel in this case study shows strong potential appreciation by virtue of a repositioning.

Introduction to the Investment Opportunity

Assume that ownership sees an opportunity to hire a management company that can greatly enhance the hotel's operations. Ownership believes it can create value by negotiating the following ten-year management agreement: the hotel manager will earn base management fees of only 1 percent of total revenue; the manager can earn incentive management fees of 10 percent of cash flow after payment of first mortgage debt service, with a cap on total management compensation of 3.75 percent of hotel revenues. As can be seen in Exhibit 1, the management fee expense in the residual year steps up to $1,366,000—this represents a hypothetical market-based management fee of 3 percent of total revenues upon expiration of the management contract described above.

Exhibit 1 Projected Net Operating Income

projection year:	*1*	*1*	*2*	*3*	*4*	*5*	*6*	*7*	*8*	*9*	*10*	*Residual*
	2016	2017	2018	2019	2020	2021	2022	2023	2024	2025	2026	2027
Number of Rooms	300	300	300	300	300	300	300	300	300	300	300	300
Occupancy	77.0%	70.0%	73.0%	77.0%	77.0%	77.0%	77.0%	77.0%	77.0%	77.0%	77.0%	77.0%
Average Rate	$ 325.00	$ 334.75	$ 344.79	$ 355.14	$ 365.79	$ 376.76	$ 388.07	$ 399.71	$ 411.70	$ 424.05	$ 436.77	$ 449.88
Days Open	365	365	365	365	365	365	365	365	365	365	365	365
Rooms Occupied	84,315	76,650	79,935	84,315	84,315	84,315	84,315	84,315	84,315	84,315	84,315	84,315
Revenues	$(000)	$(000)	$(000)	$(000)	$(000)	$(000)	$(000)	$(000)	$(000)	$(000)	$(000)	$(000)
Rooms	$ 27,402	$ 25,659	$ 27,561	$ 29,943	$ 30,842	$ 31,767	$ 32,720	$ 33,701	$ 34,713	$ 35,754	$ 36,827	$ 37,931
Food & Beverage	$ 5,059	$ 4,855	$ 5,158	$ 5,528	$ 5,694	$ 5,865	$ 6,041	$ 6,222	$ 6,408	$ 6,601	$ 6,799	$ 7,003
Rentals and Other Income	$ 422	$ 414	$ 436	$ 461	$ 474	$ 489	$ 503	$ 518	$ 534	$ 550	$ 567	$ 584
Total Revenue	$ 32,883	$ 30,928	$ 33,155	$ 35,932	$ 37,010	$ 38,121	$ 39,264	$ 40,441	$ 41,655	$ 42,905	$ 44,193	$ 45,518
Departmental Expenses												
Rooms	$ 5,902	$ 5,858	$ 6,131	$ 6,449	$ 6,643	$ 6,842	$ 7,047	$ 7,259	$ 7,477	$ 7,701	$ 7,932	$ 8,170
Food & Beverages	$ 4,553	$ 4,546	$ 4,746	$ 4,975	$ 5,125	$ 5,278	$ 5,437	$ 5,600	$ 5,767	$ 5,941	$ 6,119	$ 6,303
Total Departmental Expenses	$ 10,455	$ 10,404	$ 10,877	$ 11,424	$ 11,768	$ 12,120	$ 12,484	$ 12,859	$ 13,244	$ 13,642	$ 14,051	$ 14,473
Departmental Income	$ 22,428	$ 20,524	$ 22,278	$ 24,508	$ 25,242	$ 26,001	$ 26,780	$ 27,582	$ 28,411	$ 29,263	$ 30,142	$ 31,045
Undistributed Operating Expenses												
Administrative & General	$ 2,100	$ 2,107	$ 2,195	$ 2,295	$ 2,364	$ 2,434	$ 2,508	$ 2,583	$ 2,660	$ 2,740	$ 2,822	$ 2,907
Marketing	$ 1,500	$ 1,505	$ 1,568	$ 1,639	$ 1,688	$ 1,739	$ 1,791	$ 1,845	$ 1,900	$ 1,957	$ 2,016	$ 2,076
Prop. Oper. & Maintenance	$ 1,200	$ 1,204	$ 1,254	$ 1,311	$ 1,351	$ 1,391	$ 1,433	$ 1,476	$ 1,520	$ 1,566	$ 1,613	$ 1,661
Energy Costs	$ 900	$ 919	$ 950	$ 983	$ 1,013	$ 1,043	$ 1,075	$ 1,107	$ 1,140	$ 1,174	$ 1,210	$ 1,246
Total UDOEs	$ 5,700	$ 5,735	$ 5,967	$ 6,228	$ 6,416	$ 6,607	$ 6,807	$ 7,011	$ 7,220	$ 7,437	$ 7,661	$ 7,890
Income Before Fixed Charges	$ 16,728	$ 14,789	$ 16,311	$ 18,280	$ 18,826	$ 19,394	$ 19,973	$ 20,571	$ 21,191	$ 21,826	$ 22,481	$ 23,155
Fixed Charges												
Management Fee	$ 329	$ 309	$ 332	$ 359	$ 370	$ 381	$ 393	$ 404	$ 417	$ 429	$ 442	1,366
Property Tax	$ 600	$ 618	$ 637	$ 656	$ 675	$ 696	$ 716	$ 738	$ 760	$ 783	$ 806	$ 831
Insurance	$ 300	$ 309	$ 318	$ 328	$ 338	$ 348	$ 358	$ 369	$ 380	$ 391	$ 403	$ 415
Reserve for Replacement	$ 1,315	$ 1,237	$ 1,326	$ 1,437	$ 1,480	$ 1,525	$ 1,571	$ 1,618	$ 1,666	$ 1,716	$ 1,768	$ 1,821
Total Fixed Charges	$ 2,544	$ 2,473	$ 2,613	$ 2,780	$ 2,863	$ 2,950	$ 3,038	$ 3,129	$ 3,223	$ 3,319	$ 3,419	$ 4,433
Net Operating Income	$ 14,184	$ 12,316	$ 13,698	$ 15,500	$ 15,963	$ 16,444	$ 16,935	$ 17,442	$ 17,968	$ 18,507	$ 19,062	$ 18,722

Direct Capitalization Analysis

Now let's take a look at how an investor might go about measuring and seeking to optimize his or her return from this opportunity. First let's assume a typical valuation of the hotel, using direct capitalization. We'll assume for purposes of this example that the investment market is weak, that financing is hard to find, and that an investment with similar risk characteristics merits a capitalization rate of 9.5 percent. The first year's net operating income is $12,316,000, which when capitalized at 9.5 percent indicates a market value of $129,642,000, which will be rounded to $130 million.[1]

Direct capitalization may be fine for valuing a stable property or submitting a preliminary offer to purchase the hotel, but it doesn't give a precise picture of what total yield an investor can expect from the opportunity. Specifically, the current return does not identify the appreciation component of an investor's yield. In this case, direct capitalization also doesn't make explicit what type of liability the owner may have to the hotel manager for incentive management fee payments as described above. Therefore, many investors prepare more detailed financial analyses.

Unleveraged Property Yield Analysis

The next step in the investment underwriting process is typically to prepare an internal rate of return (IRR) or discounted cash flow (DCF) analysis—both of which look at a property's total yield. Let's assume that the investor feels strongly that the market for real estate investments is likely to strengthen and that hotels can be acquired cheaply now, but that by the end of the holding period capitalization rates will return to a more traditional range—such that it is appropriate to use a residual capitalization rate of 8.5 percent (and selling costs of 2 percent of the residual sale price).[2] Consistent with the direct capitalization approach discussed above, we'll assume that the agreed-upon purchase price is $130 million. The IRR analysis is presented in Exhibit 2.

The IRR calculation shows a total yield on the investment of 15 percent. The yield is much higher than the capitalization rate because of the growth of the net income during the holding period and an optimistic view as to where capitalization rates will be when it's time to sell the property. This information is helpful, since it provides more detail about the key value drivers in the investment. However, the total property yield of 15 percent does not recognize that hotels are typically leveraged—and that incentive management fees would be payable to the extent there was cash flow available after the payment of debt service. Adding mortgage debt that is less expensive than equity capital will lower the total cost of capital and enhance the return on equity. Because hotels are typically mortgaged, that 15 percent yield is effectively the blended return received by the lender and the investor; we want to isolate the equity investor's position.

Leveraged Property Yield Analysis

To isolate the investor's potential yield, let's assume that a lender is willing to make a mortgage loan to support a $130 million hotel acquisition with the fol-

Exhibit 2 IRR Analysis

TOTAL PROPERTY YIELD BEFORE CONSIDERATION OF DEBT

ASSUMPTIONS		
Purchase Price		$ 130,000
Calculation of Residual Value		
11th Year Net Operating Income		$ 18,722
Residual Capitalization Rate	÷	8.5%
Residual Value		220,264
Disposition Cost %	x	2.0%
Disposition Cost	-	4,405
Net Residual Value		$ 215,859

Year		1	2	3	4	5	6	7	8	9	10
Net Operating Income		$ 12,316	$ 13,698	$ 15,500	$ 15,963	$ 16,444	$ 16,935	$ 17,442	$ 17,968	$ 18,507	$ 19,062
Residual Proceeds											215,859
Cash Flow After 1st Mortgage		12,316	13,698	15,500	15,963	16,444	16,935	17,442	17,968	18,507	19,062
Total Property Inflows/Outflows	$ (130,000)	$ 12,316	$ 13,698	$ 15,500	$ 15,963	$ 16,444	$ 16,935	$ 17,442	$ 17,968	$ 18,507	$ 234,921
Equity IRR, no leverage:	**15%**										

lowing terms: a loan-to-value ratio of 50 percent, an interest rate of 8.0 percent, and an amortization period of twenty years. So the initial mortgage amount would be $65 million (50 percent of the $130 million purchase price), with annual debt service of $6,524,000. At the end of the ten year holding period, there will be an outstanding balance of $44,811,000.[3] Exhibit 3 shows the payment of annual debt service from net operating income, the resultant cash flow to equity, the proceeds from disposition of the hotel, and the yield to the equity position. Also presented in Exhibit 3 is a supporting schedule showing the calculation of incentive management fees, consistent with the negotiated terms described previously.[4]

The leveraged equity yield of 19 percent represents the total expected investor return. Rational investors consider this expected rate of return, together with the risks involved, against alternative investment options. So now we are homing in on just how attractive this potential deal can be.

Leveraged Property Yield with Mezzanine Loan

Let's assume that the investor decides that the 19 percent equity yield is good but not great, given the risks of the investment. One alternative might be to layer on a mezzanine loan in addition to the first mortgage. As long as the rate of return required by the mezzanine lender is less than the equity yield rate, the addition of mezzanine finance will boost the equity investor's total return. An attractive attribute of mezzanine loans is that at some point the loan is repaid and the equity position is not diluted, whereas adding an additional equity investor means sharing the investment profits with others.[5] Normally, mezzanine loans are rather expensive, so they would only be used where a hotel is being repositioned or otherwise enhanced so that there is strong growth in net operating income. Fortunately, our hotel shows this strong earnings growth, so it meets this requirement. Let's now assume that the investor decides to use supplemental financing and that the mezzanine lender requires the following terms in exchange for a loan which would bring the total loan-to-value ratio (when combined with the first mortgage) up to 75 percent: a current pay (or "coupon") rate of 12 percent (interest only) with an additional payment at the end which will bring the mezzanine lender's total return up to 16 percent (often called a look-back IRR[6]). Exhibit 4 picks up where Exhibit 3 left off, layers in the mezzanine loan, and shows the resultant return to equity. Also presented at the bottom of Exhibit 4 is a schedule proving out the look-back yield of 16 percent earned by the mezzanine lender.

Now we're getting somewhere! What looked like a 9.5 percent return initially and then an 15 percent total yield became a 19 percent deal with the addition of a mortgage loan, and is now a 21 percent equity yield with the addition of a mezzanine loan. Certainly the risk is much greater, and a modest decline in cash flow might wipe out the equity position. It would be prudent and typical for an investor to run sensitivity analyses to measure the potential impact of various changes to the revenue and expense projections. But let's assume, for the purposes of this example, that the cash flow projections are reasonable, well supported, and the best basis for underwriting the investment.

Exhibit 3 Leveraged Property Yield Analysis

EQUITY YIELD, FIRST MORTGAGE ONLY

ASSUMPTIONS		Residual	
Purchase Price	$130,000	$215,859	Residual sale proceeds
First Mortgage	65,000	44,811	Outstanding mortgage balance
Equity Required	$ 65,000	$171,048	Residual proceeds to equity

Year		1	2	3	4	5	6	7	8	9	10
Net Operating Income		$ 12,316	$13,698	$ 15,500	$ 15,963	$16,444	$16,935	$17,442	$17,968	$18,507	$ 19,062
Residual Proceeds											
Mortgage Payment		6,524	6,524	6,524	6,524	6,524	6,524	6,524	6,524	6,524	6,524
Cash Flow After 1st Mortgage		5,792	7,174	8,976	9,439	9,920	10,411	10,918	11,444	11,983	12,538
Incentive Management Fees		579	717	898	944	992	1,041	1,092	1,144	1,180	1,215
Cash Flow after 1st Mortgage & Incentive Fees		5,213	6,456	8,078	8,495	8,928	9,370	9,826	10,299	10,803	11,323
Residual Proceeds to Equity											171,048
Equity Inflows/Outflows	$ (65,000)	$ 5,213	$ 6,456	$ 8,078	$ 8,495	$ 8,928	$ 9,370	$ 9,826	$10,299	$10,803	$182,370
Equity IRR, First Mortgage Only:	**19%**										

Incentive Management Fee Schedule	1	2	3	4	5	6	7	8	9	10
Base Fee	$ 309	$ 332	$ 359	$ 370	$ 381	$ 393	$ 404	$ 417	$ 429	$ 442
Incentive Fee %	10.0%	10.0%	10.0%	10.0%	10.0%	10.0%	10.0%	10.0%	10.0%	10.0%
Maximum Incentive Fee	579	717	898	944	992	1,041	1,092	1,144	1,198	1,254
Total Potential Mgt Fees	888	1,049	1,257	1,314	1,373	1,434	1,496	1,561	1,627	1,696
Total Revenues	$ 30,928	$33,155	$ 35,932	$ 37,010	$38,121	$39,264	$40,441	$41,655	$42,905	$ 44,193
Mgt Fee Cap %	3.75%	3.75%	3.75%	3.75%	3.75%	3.75%	3.75%	3.75%	3.75%	3.75%
Maximum Management Fees	1,160	1,243	1,347	1,388	1,430	1,472	1,517	1,562	1,609	1,657
Total Management Fees Payable	$ 888	$ 1,049	$ 1,257	$ 1,314	$ 1,373	$ 1,434	$ 1,496	$ 1,561	$ 1,609	$ 1,657
Less: Base Management Fee	309	332	359	370	381	393	404	417	429	442
Incentive Fee Payable	$ 579	$ 717	$ 898	$ 944	$ 992	$ 1,041	$ 1,092	$ 1,144	$ 1,180	$ 1,215

Exhibit 4 Leveraged Property Yield Analysis with a Mezzanine Loan

EQUITY YIELD, FIRST MORTGAGE AND MEZZ DEBT

ASSUMPTIONS		Mezz Loan		Residual	
Purchase Price	$130,000				
Mortgage	65,000	Amount:	32,500	$171,048	Residual proceeds to equity
Mezz Loan	32,500	Pay Rate:	12.0%	(32,500)	Outstanding Mezz Loan Balance
Equity Required	32,500	Lookback	16.0%	(27,718)	Mezz Loan Lookback Payment
				$110,829	Balance to Equity

Year		1	2	3	4	5	6	7	8	9	10
Cash Flow after 1st Mortgage & Incentive Fees		$ 5,213	$ 6,456	$ 8,078	$ 8,495	$ 8,928	$ 9,370	$ 9,826	$10,299	$10,803	$ 11,323
Mezz Loan Debt Service		(3,900)	(3,900)	(3,900)	(3,900)	(3,900)	(3,900)	(3,900)	(3,900)	(3,900)	(3,900)
Cash Flow after Mortgage and Mezz Debt		1,313	2,556	4,178	4,595	5,028	5,470	5,926	6,399	6,903	7,423
Residual Proceeds after Mortgage and Mezz Debt											110,829
Equity Inflows/Outflows	(32,500)	1,313	2,556	4,178	4,595	5,028	5,470	5,926	6,399	6,903	118,252
Equity IRR after 1st Mortgage and Mezz Debt	**21%**										

Proof of Mezz Loan Lookback Yield											
Initial Mezz Loan	$ 32,500										
Mezz Loan Annual Debt Service		(3,900)	(3,900)	(3,900)	(3,900)	(3,900)	(3,900)	(3,900)	(3,900)	(3,900)	(3,900)
Mezz Loan Mortgage Balance											(32,500)
Mezz Loan Lookback Payment											$(27,718)
Mezz Loan Inflows/Outflows	$ 32,500	$ (3,900)	$(3,900)	$(3,900)	$ (3,900)	$ (3,900)	$(3,900)	$(3,900)	$ (3,900)	$ (3,900)	$(64,118)
Mezz Loan IRR	16.0%										

Leveraged Property Yield with Mezzanine Loan and Capital Partner

At this point the investor has taken several steps to maximize his or her return. But let's assume that ownership is still not satisfied. A very likely option at this point would be to bring in a capital partner to the deal. Sometimes the sponsor brings in partners to reduce the total capital he or she needs to commit. Other times the sponsor may seek a partner who has lower return requirements than he or she does—in which case the addition of a capital partner will have the effect of raising the sponsor's yield.

The sponsor represents the "brains" behind the deal and will normally be the managing member of the investment venture. The sponsor will want to be compensated for coming up with the idea and for managing the investment. Sometimes sponsors are paid directly for these services—a finder's fee for sourcing the opportunity and an asset management fee for managing the investment. More often, though, the sponsor negotiates a disproportionately high claim on the cash flow to equity in return for his or her services. So while a sponsor might only contribute, say, 20 percent of the required equity for an investment, he or she would normally negotiate a greater than 20 percent claim on profits. This payment for the sponsor's "sweat equity" is one of the most fundamental elements of entrepreneurial activity in the real estate sector. This disproportionate claim on profits has traditionally been termed a "carried interest"; more recently it is frequently referred to as a "promote," as in: "The sponsor earned a promote on that deal because it was so successful." While there are some typical promote structures, an evaluation of these arrangements suggests that there is an almost infinite variety of ways that these payments can be structured.

Let's assume that the sponsor decides to bring in a capital partner—a pension fund advisor who is investing in real estate as part of a larger investment strategy. Now let's assume that the sponsor and the capital partner agree to the following joint venture deal: Equity required for the acquisition of the property will be contributed 90 percent by the capital partner and 10 percent by the sponsor. After debt service is paid, any remaining cash flow will be used first to pay a preferred return on equity of 6 percent of capital invested by the capital partner, followed by a 6 percent preferred return on the sponsor's capital; any amounts earned but unpaid simply accrue to a partner's capital account. If there is distributable cash left over after the payment of the preferred return, it will be used to reduce the partner's capital accounts, pari passu.[7] Thus, cash available for distribution at this point will go 90 percent to the capital partner and 10 percent to the sponsor, up to the point where all capital has been repaid. Once all capital has been repaid, remaining cash flow will be distributed 60 percent to the capital partner and 40 percent to the sponsor. The distribution schedule, or waterfall, is presented in Exhibit 5, which also shows the resultant yields achieved by the sponsor and the capital partner. For clarity's sake, supporting schedules have been included showing the IRRs for each of the investment partners and the repayment of partners' capital.

A Few Comments about Risk and Return

The prospective return for the sponsor from this investment opportunity has now jumped up substantially. By bringing in a capital partner (and negotiating a very

Exhibit 5 Leveraged Property Yield Analysis with a Mezzanine Loan and a Capital Partner

Year	0	1	2	3	4	5	6	7	8	9	10
Net Operating Income		$12,316	$13,698	$15,500	$15,963	$16,444	$16,935	$17,442	$17,968	$18,507	$ 19,062
1st Mortgage Payment		6,524	6,524	6,524	6,524	6,524	6,524	6,524	6,524	6,524	6,524
Subtotal		5,792	7,174	8,976	9,439	9,920	10,411	10,918	11,444	11,983	12,538
Incentive Management Fee		579	717	898	944	992	1,041	1,092	1,144	1,180	1,215
Subtotal		5,213	6,456	8,078	8,495	8,928	9,370	9,826	10,299	10,803	11,323
Mezz Loan Pay Rate		3,900	3,900	3,900	3,900	3,900	3,900	3,900	3,900	3,900	3,900
Cash Flow after Debt Service		1,313	2,556	4,178	4,595	5,028	5,470	5,926	6,399	6,903	7,423
Capital Partner Preferred Return		1,313	1,782	1,751	1,631	1,482	1,301	1,085	831	537	198
Subtotal		-	775	2,427	2,963	3,546	4,169	4,841	5,568	6,366	7,224
Sponsor Preferred Return		-	207	203	189	172	151	126	96	62	23
Subtotal		-	568	2,224	2,774	3,374	4,018	4,715	5,472	6,303	7,201
Distributions - Paydown of Capital Accounts											
Sponsor		-	59	231	288	351	418	490	569	655	384
Capital Partner		-	509	1,993	2,486	3,023	3,600	4,225	4,903	5,648	3,306
Subtotal		-	568	2,224	2,774	3,374	4,018	4,715	5,472	6,303	3,690
Remaining Cash Flow			-	-	-	-	-	-	-	-	3,511
Distributions: Promote											
Sponsor		-	-	-	-	-	-	-	-	-	1,405
Capital Partner		-	-	-	-	-	-	-	-	-	2,107
Sponsor IRR	**34.53%**										
Sponsor Outflow/Inflow	$ (3,250)	$ -	$ 266	$ 434	$ 478	$ 523	$ 569	$ 616	$ 665	$ 718	$ 46,143
Capital Partner IRR	**18.03%**										
Partner Outflow/Inflow	$ (29,250)	$ 1,313	$ 2,291	$ 3,744	$ 4,117	$ 4,505	$ 4,901	$ 5,310	$ 5,734	$ 6,185	$ 72,109
Entity Level IRR	**21.14%**										
Entity Outflow/Inflow	$ (32,500)	$ 1,313	$ 2,556	$ 4,178	$ 4,595	$ 5,028	$ 5,470	$ 5,926	$ 6,399	$ 6,903	$118,252
Capital Accounts											
Sponsor		10.0%	10.4%	10.4%	10.4%	10.4%	10.4%	10.4%	10.4%	10.4%	10.4%
Beginning Balance		$ 3,250	$ 3,445	$ 3,386	$ 3,155	$ 2,866	$ 2,516	$ 2,098	$ 1,608	$ 1,039	$ 384
Preferred return earned		195	207	203	189	172	151	126	96	62	23
Preferred return paid		-	207	203	189	172	151	126	96	62	23
Capital Distribution		-	59	231	288	351	418	490	569	655	384
Capital Partner		90.0%	89.6%	89.6%	89.6%	89.6%	89.6%	89.6%	89.6%	89.6%	89.6%
Beginning Balance		$29,250	$29,692	$29,183	$27,191	$24,705	$21,682	$18,082	$13,857	$ 8,954	$ 3,306
Preferred return earned		1,755	1,782	1,751	1,631	1,482	1,301	1,085	831	537	198
Preferred return paid		1,313	1,782	1,751	1,631	1,482	1,301	1,085	831	537	198
Capital Distribution		-	509	1,993	2,486	3,023	3,600	4,225	4,903	5,648	3,306

favorable promote) the sponsor's investment yield stepped up from 23 percent as shown in Exhibit 4 to 34.5 percent as shown in Exhibit 5. As you probably recognize, greater financial leverage comes with greater financial risk. Put another way, the risk-adjusted rate of return on the opportunity hasn't changed; the sponsor is simply taking on more risk in the hope of achieving a higher return. Bear in mind that this financial leverage is in addition to the high operating leverage inherent in hotel operations. The combination of high operating leverage and high financial leverage greatly magnify the success or failure an investment might otherwise demonstrate. Clearly, the type of investment structure used in this case study opportunity is not for the risk adverse!

But there is an interesting alternative perspective on this investment case. Not only does the projected return increase as the investment's capital structure becomes more aggressive, but the initial capital outlay required by the sponsor decreases, from $65,000,000 in Exhibit 3 to $32,500,000 in Exhibit 4 to $3,250,000 in Exhibit 5. While the deal as set forth in Exhibit 5 shows the highest equity yield, it is easily the riskiest of all the alternatives we've considered. But viewed from another angle, it also has the smallest downside in terms of the total dollars that the sponsor has at risk. If the sponsor had simply financed the investment with a first mortgage, the required equity would have been $65 million; but by the end of this financial engineering the sponsor only has $3,250,000 at risk.

Some Closing Thoughts on the Case Study

The preceding case study was designed to emphasize some of the financial attributes of a joint venture arrangement and the impact on investment returns resulting from leverage. However, this deal is not presented as typical or average. From the case study's simple conceptual model of how a deal might come together, there are many important potential financial permutations:

- Normally, the first claim on cash flow after paying debt service is to repay partner loans and other short-term contributions that have been made to cover short-term needs such as cost overruns, supplemental renovations funding, and other similar needs.
- In the preceding example, the preferred return that is earned by the sponsor in Year 1 but which is not fully paid accrues and is added to the sponsor's capital account, slightly changing the proportion of partners' accounts.
- In many cases, cash flow after debt service is used to pay down the partners' capital accounts first, while a preferred return on invested capital accrues, to be paid back after all equity capital has been repaid. Some capital providers, however, structure the preferred return to be paid before a return of capital (as is shown in this case study). In my experience, the preferred return might be paid first, because the capital provider is in fact getting its funds from somewhere else, and that funding source may expect or require a periodic return on its capital.
- Frequently there are different distribution schedules for operating income, refinancing proceeds, sales of partial interests, and the ultimate disposition of

the investment. Unlike the example presented in this chapter, it is rare for a sponsor to achieve a promoted return until after a capital event occurs, since operating cash flow alone is normally insufficient to fully amortize the partners' capital accounts.

- The promote structure in the example is a one-time step-up following the repayment of all capital. In actual practice, the sponsor's promote is often tiered into several levels keyed to the capital partner's return. For example, assuming the operating partner contributes 10 percent of the initial capital, the sponsor's share of profits may increase to 20 percent after the capital partner achieves an 18 percent total return, rising to 30 percent after the capital partner receives a 25 percent return, and so forth.
- When the sponsor is undertaking a new development project, the sponsor often commands a more favorable promote structure, consistent with the greater risk he or she is shouldering.
- Investment ventures normally have targeted horizons, setting forth the time by which the asset is to be monetized and all investment funds are to be returned to the partners. The joint venture agreement may provide incentives to encourage a foreshortened investment horizon if investment objectives can be achieved earlier than expected.
- An increasingly popular method of triggering the promote is to require a multi-part test: the returns must achieve a specified IRR and the profits must amount to a specified cash multiple (such as 1.5) of the original amount invested. While the IRR hurdle relates to the efficiency or speed at which the targeted performance is achieved, the cash multiple captures the magnitude of the profits achieved.
- Sponsors sometimes negotiate "catch-up" provisions in which the capital partner is entitled to a priority claim on cash flows. So while the capital partner may get the majority of cash flows early on, the sponsor would be entitled—once the capital partner has achieved some threshold amount—to take all subsequent cash flows until the sponsor catches up to a specified position.
- In some cases, a refinance of a property may be treated as a capital event, or as current income, or as a hybrid event.
- For simplicity's sake, this case study ignores income taxes. Obviously, taxes can have a sizable impact on the desirability of an investment.
- The distribution of net operating income is normally subject to a variety of legal documents. For instance, a hotel's mortgage note sets out that it has first claim on income after operating expense but before partner distributions. A management agreement may indicate that the hotel manager has the right to receive a portion of cash flow after debt service as an incentive management fee. And the partnership or joint venture documents of the owning venture specify how any remaining cash is distributed.

The case study used in this chapter presents a simple view of how net operating income is distributed and how returns are calculated. Be aware that small definitional changes can lead to meaningful movement in returns and yields. Significant resources are available to refine the concepts presented in this case study.[8]

A Closer Look at the Investment Outcomes for the Sponsor and Capital Partner

Now that we have set forth a model of financial performance, let's go on to explore two other important issues: (1) how would the venture perform under varying sensitivity analyses, and (2) how would you know if the structure was fair? Note that while the examples used in this chapter bear some similarities to actual joint venture structures, the terms are exaggerated to help explore various issues.

Sensitivity Analysis

Let's assume that you want to test the performance under some different assumptions. To keep the examples simple, we'll consider that the base case ADR of $325 used in Exhibits 1–5 rises to $375 in the upside case and falls to $274 in the downside case. The scenarios will use all of the same assumptions as the base case, other than for the anticipated ADR level; the following exhibits will summarize the calculations.

Let's look at the upside case first, since they are always more uplifting! The net operating income, mortgage payments, and partnership distributions are set forth in Exhibit 6. In this scenario, there is plenty of cash flow to provide a preferred return on invested capital and a complete return of invested capital during the ten-year holding period.

In the upside scenario presented in Exhibit 6, the project- or entity-level IRR increases from 21 percent to 33 percent. Notice as well that the return to the sponsor increases from 35 percent in the base case to 50 percent in the upside case, while the return to the capital partner increases as well, from 18 percent in the base case to 28 percent in the upside case. While both parties improve, the sponsor makes out much better, with a 15-percentage-point increase on his or her return while the capital partner has an increase on return of 10 percentage points. Although the sponsor does better in this case, both parties would be extremely happy with this investment.

Now let's look at the downside case, and here things become rather grim. The net operating income, mortgage payments, and distributions under the downside case are set forth in Exhibit 7. If you jump right to the heart of the matter, you'll see that the IRR at the entity level has slid from 20 percent to 5 percent; the sponsor's IRR is negative at -10 percent, while the IRR to the capital partner is limited to its preferred return of 6 percent. But let's look at this scenario in more detail to evaluate the various impacts of this downside case.

The first two years of the holding period show that there are not enough funds from operations to pay the first mortgage lender and the mezzanine lender. The shortfall in Year One of $2.131 million and in Year Two of $1.141 million are shown to be made up equally by the partners, with the sponsor providing additional equity to cover 10 percent of the shortfall and the capital partner picking up the other 90 percent of the shortfall. This continuation of the 90 percent/10 percent

Exhibit 6 Sensitivity Analysis: The Upside Case

Year	0	1	2	3	4	5	6	7	8	9	10
Net Operating Income		$16,066	$17,726	$19,876	$20,469	$21,087	$21,718	$22,368	$23,041	$23,732	$ 24,444
1st Mortgage Payment		6,524	6,524	6,524	6,524	6,524	6,524	6,524	6,524	6,524	6,524
Subtotal		9,542	11,202	13,352	13,945	14,563	15,194	15,844	16,517	17,208	17,920
Incentive Management Fee		954	1,028	1,115	1,148	1,183	1,218	1,255	1,292	1,331	1,371
Subtotal		8,588	10,173	12,237	12,797	13,380	13,976	14,589	15,224	15,877	16,549
Mezz Loan Pay Rate		3,900	3,900	3,900	3,900	3,900	3,900	3,900	3,900	3,900	3,900
Cash Flow after Debt Service		4,688	6,273	8,337	8,897	9,480	10,076	10,689	11,324	11,977	12,649
Capital Partner Preferred Return		1,755	1,607	1,365	997	576	99	-	-	-	-
Subtotal		2,933	4,666	6,972	7,900	8,904	9,977	10,689	11,324	11,977	12,649
Sponsor Preferred Return		195	179	152	111	64	11	-	-	-	-
Subtotal		2,738	4,488	6,820	7,790	8,840	9,966	10,689	11,324	11,977	12,649
Distributions - Paydown of Capital Accounts											
Sponsor		274	449	682	779	884	182	-	-	-	-
Capital Partner		2,464	4,039	6,138	7,011	7,956	1,642	-	-	-	-
Subtotal		2,738	4,488	6,820	7,790	8,840	1,825	-	-	-	-
Remaining Cash Flow			-	-	-	-	8,141	10,689	11,324	11,977	12,649
Distributions: Promote											
Sponsor		-	-	-	-	-	3,257	4,276	4,530	4,791	5,060
Capital Partner		-	-	-	-	-	4,885	6,413	6,795	7,186	7,589
Sponsor IRR	**50.23%**										
Sponsor Outflow/Inflow	$ (3,250)	$ 469	$ 627	$ 834	$ 890	$ 948	$ 3,450	$ 4,276	$ 4,530	$ 4,791	$ 74,424
Capital Partner IRR	**28.27%**										
Partner Outflow/Inflow	$ (29,250)	$ 4,219	$ 5,646	$ 7,503	$ 8,007	$ 8,532	$ 6,626	$ 6,413	$ 6,795	$ 7,186	$111,635
Entity Level IRR	**32.54%**										
Entity Outflow/Inflow	$ (32,500)	$ 4,688	$ 6,273	$ 8,337	$ 8,897	$ 9,480	$10,076	$10,689	$11,324	$11,977	$186,059
Capital Accounts											
Sponsor		10.0%	10.0%	10.0%	10.0%	10.0%	10.0%	0.0%	0.0%	0.0%	0.0%
Beginning Balance		$ 3,250	$ 2,976	$ 2,527	$ 1,845	$ 1,066	$ 182	$ -	$ -	$ -	$ -
Preferred return earned		195	179	152	111	64	11	-	-	-	-
Preferred return paid		195	179	152	111	64	11	-	-	-	-
Capital Distribution		274	449	682	779	884	182	-	-	-	-
Capital Partner		90.0%	90.0%	90.0%	90.0%	90.0%	90.0%	0.0%	0.0%	0.0%	0.0%
Beginning Balance		$29,250	$26,786	$22,747	$16,609	$ 9,598	$ 1,642	$ -	$ -	$ -	$ -
Preferred return earned		1,755	1,607	1,365	997	576	99	-	-	-	-
Preferred return paid		1,755	1,607	1,365	997	576	99	-	-	-	-
Capital Distribution		2,464	4,039	6,138	7,011	7,956	1,642	-	-	-	-

Exhibit 7 Sensitivity Analysis: The Downside Case

Year	0	1	2	3	4	5	6	7	8	9	10
Net Operating Income		$ 8,490	$ 9,590	$11,037	$11,364	$11,709	$12,058	$12,418	$12,793	$13,176	$13,572
1st Mortgage Payment		6,524	6,524	6,524	6,524	6,524	6,524	6,524	6,524	6,524	6,524
Subtotal		1,966	3,066	4,513	4,840	5,185	5,534	5,894	6,269	6,652	7,048
Incentive Management Fee		197	307	451	484	518	553	589	627	665	705
Subtotal		1,769	2,759	4,061	4,356	4,666	4,980	5,304	5,642	5,987	6,343
Mezz Loan Pay Rate		3,900	3,900	3,900	3,900	3,900	3,900	3,900	3,900	3,900	3,900
Cash Flow after Debt Service		(2,131)	(1,141)	161	456	766	1,080	1,404	1,742	2,087	2,443
Capital Partner Preferred Return		(1,918)	(1,027)	161	456	766	1,080	1,404	1,742	2,087	2,443
Subtotal		(213)	(114)	-	-	-	-	-	-	-	-
Sponsor Preferred Return		(213)	(114)	-	-	-	-	-	-	-	-
Subtotal		-	-	-	-	-	-	-	-	-	-
Distributions - Paydown of Capital Accounts											
Sponsor		-	-	-	-	-	-	-	-	-	-
Capital Partner		-	-	-	-	-	-	-	-	-	-
Subtotal		-	-	-	-	-	-	-	-	-	-
Remaining Cash Flow			-	-	-	-	-	-	-	-	-
Distributions: Promote											
Sponsor		-	-	-	-	-	-	-	-	-	-
Capital Partner		-	-	-	-	-	-	-	-	-	-
Sponsor IRR	**-9.65%**										
Sponsor Outflow/Inflow	$ (3,250)	$ (213)	$ (114)	$ -	$ -	$ -	$ -	$ -	$ -	$ -	$ 1,314
Capital Partner IRR	**6.00%**										
Partner Outflow/Inflow	$ (29,250)	$ (1,918)	$ (1,027)	$ 161	$ 456	$ 766	$ 1,080	$ 1,404	$ 1,742	$ 2,087	$48,138
Entity Level IRR	**5.07%**										
Entity Outflow/Inflow	$ (32,500)	$ (2,131)	$ (1,141)	$ 161	$ 456	$ 766	$ 1,080	$ 1,404	$ 1,742	$ 2,087	$49,452
Capital Accounts											
Sponsor		10.0%	10.0%	10.0%	10.0%	10.1%	10.3%	10.5%	10.8%	11.2%	11.7%
Beginning Balance		$ 3,250	$ 3,658	$ 3,992	$ 4,231	$ 4,485	$ 4,754	$ 5,039	$ 5,342	$ 5,662	$ 6,002
Preferred return earned		195	219	239	254	269	285	302	321	340	360
Preferred return paid		(213)	(114)	-	-	-	-	-	-	-	-
Capital Distribution		-	-	-	-	-	-	-	-	-	-
Capital Partner		90.0%	90.0%	90.0%	90.0%	89.9%	89.7%	89.5%	89.2%	88.8%	88.3%
Beginning Balance		$29,250	$32,923	$35,925	$37,919	$39,738	$41,356	$42,757	$43,918	$44,811	$45,413
Preferred return earned		1,755	1,975	2,155	2,275	2,384	2,481	2,565	2,635	2,689	2,725
Preferred return paid		(1,918)	(1,027)	161	456	766	1,080	1,404	1,742	2,087	2,443
Capital Distribution		-	-	-	-	-	-	-	-	-	-

arrangement would not necessarily be the case in many joint venture agreements. As an alternative, the parties may have agreed that any shortfalls would be made up through internal or external loans; typically, these loans would have priority over any payments to the joint venture partners. The joint venture agreement may call for the sponsor to pay a higher proportion—say 50 percent—of all shortfalls, with the reasoning being that the sponsor is responsible for oversight of hotel operations and thus must bear a greater burden if the performance doesn't meet expectations.[9]

If there are to be additional equity contributions to fund cash flow shortfalls, it opens additional concerns in structuring the joint venture agreement. What if the sponsor makes a cash call to the capital partner for additional funds and the capital partner refuses to provide them? In the chapter case study, with only two partners, the implications are fairly clear. However, in a partnership with many partners, the issues become more complicated. Oftentimes, a party that does not provide additional funds as required will have its interest diluted. One way to effect this is to grant the new equity a preferential, or greater than 1:1, status relative to the existing equity.

Another major attribute of the downside case shown in Exhibit 7 is that all of the cash flow after debt service for all ten years of the holding period goes to pay the capital partner's preferred return on its equity. Recall that earlier we established that the preferred return would be paid first to the capital partner and then any remaining funds would be used to pay a preferred return on the sponsor's equity. Only upon the sale of the hotel is there enough cash flow left over after paying the capital partner's preferred return to pay some, but not all, of the sponsor's preferred return.

This situation can be a double-edged sword. The capital partner may be happy that it at least has first dibs on any cash flow after the lenders have been paid. But if you are relying on the sponsor to actively oversee the property, and that sponsor has not been paid for nine years, it's hard to imagine that the sponsor will be putting much effort into the job. A capital partner wants to be able to hold the sponsor's feet to the fire but not completely incinerate him or her.

Another notable characteristic of Exhibit 7 is what happens when the hotel is sold at the end of the ten-year holding period. There are enough sale proceeds to pay off the lenders, but beyond that all funds go next to the capital partner in accordance with the provision that it receives a preferred return of 6 percent on its money. At the end of the day, as summarized in the IRR calculation, there was only enough cash flow to achieve a 6 percent return. So in fact the capital partner barely achieved its desired preferred return of 6 percent on its capital.

Balancing the Parties' Interests

In these upside and downside scenarios, we see interesting differences in the expected returns between the two investment partners, as summarized in Exhibit 8. The expected returns presented in Exhibit 8 show that the sponsor's position is much more volatile than that of the capital partner. And this is how it should be. The capital partner gets a priority claim on cash flow after debt service but then cedes a substantial portion of project profits to the sponsor (through the promote

Exhibit 8 Partners' Expected Returns

	Expected Return (Equity IRR)		
	Downside Case	Base Case	Upside Case
Sponsor	(9.65%)	34.53%	50.23%
Capital Partner	6.00%	18.03%	28.27%
Entity (blended)	5.07%	21.14%	32.54%

earned by the sponsor above defined financial hurdles). In simple terms, if the project is successful, the sponsor wins; if the project is not successful, the capital partner is in the best position.

So, does this joint venture structure provide for an equitable distribution of the risks and rewards of this investment? That is an exceptionally difficult question to answer. The terms of joint venture agreements are rarely made public. Similarly, the distributions between partners are almost never a matter of public record. There is no publicly available benchmark or published survey that sets forth the appropriate metrics. Thus, there is rarely a direct example of what an alternative investment would earn, particularly if the capital structure is complex and unique. And even if this data were available, they would not necessarily reflect the risks unique to a specific hotel investment. The real estate investment world often operates on the basis of past deals, suggestions of "best practices" learned from experience or proffered by advisors, and gut instinct.

One reasonable way to evaluate the fairness of a transaction is to assess the compensation each party (the sponsor and the capital partner in this case) receives under an expected range of outcomes. Such an analysis will measure the expected return, per unit of risk, ascribable to each partner. We can use the preceding sensitivity analysis as the basis for this calculation.

Exhibits 5, 6, and 7 set forth the base, upside, and downside cases assumed for our hotel investment. These various scenarios should reflect a reasonable and realistic expectation of the parties. In our example, only the ADR was modified, but more thorough changes to operating assumptions may well be called for in order to establish appropriate upside and downside cases. The changes to the operating assumptions flow through from the hotel's P&L to the distribution schedule of the partners.

From Exhibit 8 we note that the investment, at an entity level, is expected to achieve a 21.14 percent[10] return, with the return falling to 5.07 percent under the downside scenario and increasing to 32.54 percent in the upside scenario. As we've already mentioned, the sponsor sees a wider swing in total returns, out-yielding the capital partner on the upside and suffering more seriously on the downside.

The first step of this analysis is to establish the expected returns for each party. Because the rates of return established by the sensitivity analyses are nominal amounts, it is necessary to remove the risk-free rate of return from the achieved rates of return shown in Exhibit 8. For this analysis, I'll assume that the risk-free rate of return (typically measured as U.S. Treasury Bill yields) is 1.00 percent. This means that the risk premiums are 33.53 percent (34.53 percent less 1.00 percent) for the sponsor and 17.03 percent (18.03 percent less 1.00 percent) for the capital partner.

The next step is to measure the relative risk each party takes on in the investment. This can be measured by calculating the breadth, or range, of returns expected by both parties. This is measured as the difference between the upside and downside case returns. For the sponsor, this would be 59.88 percent (the difference between 50.23 percent and -9.65 percent), while for the capital partner this would be 22.27 percent (28.27 percent less 6.00). This calculation assumes that the upside and downside cases are the most reasonable scenarios envisioned by the parties. It also assumes the investment model accurately portrays how cash flow is distributed under significantly different cash flow levels.

Dividing the risk premiums calculated two paragraphs earlier by the anticipated range of risk calculated in the prior paragraph yields a "risk premium to risk" ratio that provides some context as to how well each party is compensated for the risk each is taking on. The "risk premium to risk" ratio is 0.56 (33.53 percent divided by 59.88 percent) for the sponsor and 0.76 (17.03 percent divided by 22.27 percent) for the capital partner.

All other things being equal, we would expect both parties to the transaction to be compensated similarly for the risk each is taking on. In this case, the sponsor is achieving less return for the level of risk he or she is taking on, relative to the capital partner.

To repeat, this analysis does not indicate whether either party to the joint venture is receiving an appropriate return relative to other alternative hotel investment opportunities. But this analysis can be useful for establishing a framework for evaluating the relative risk and reward between the two parties to the same investment venture. Thus, this analysis can help the partners establish negotiating positions. Each party can evaluate a proposed investment structure according to their own underwriting of a prospective investment and offer counter-proposals if a proposal proffered by the other party is considered detrimental—or, indeed, agree to a proposal which is favorable! Assuming that the example used in this chapter was a contemplated investment still in the negotiating phase, the sponsor might suggest alternatives to enhance its position. Some options might include to ask for all equity to be treated equally (thus avoiding standing behind the capital partner's first crack at distributable cash). Another option would be for the sponsor to ask for an ongoing asset management fee, which provides a form of compensation that might be superior to returns on invested capital. And certainly the sponsor could ask for different distribution percentages or an alternative distribution schedule. One's creativity is the only limit on how to deal with each unique investment opportunity. This is why so many investors love the "art of the deal."

The analysis set forth here is a starting point for gaining a deeper understanding of investment risk and return. For example, rather than using one upside and one downside case, an analyst may wish to develop multiple scenarios, with a probability assigned to each, in order to develop a more rigorous analysis. Another approach would be to use real options, a form of analysis which has been well-established in academia and is now becoming more visible in the day-to-day business world.

Conclusion

This chapter discussed several facets of hotel investment ventures. Sensitivity analysis was introduced, demonstrating how relatively small changes to operating assumptions can create relatively large changes to the expected investment returns to the parties to a venture. Finally, a model was presented showing how the sensitivity analysis can be used to measure the relative reward each party receives for the amount of risk it is taking on. This attribute of a sensitivity analysis is especially useful in establishing negotiating positions and evaluating counterproposals when considering hotel investment opportunities.

Endnotes

1. In the case study used throughout the chapter, annual amounts will generally be rounded to the nearest $1,000 and capital accounts will be rounded to the nearest $1 million for readability and simplicity.
2. Analysts typically use a residual capitalization rate that is slightly higher than the capitalization rate indicated at the onset of the investment. However, under certain circumstances, such as financial market disruptions, the conventional assumptions may be modified.
3. Calculation of mortgage balances is easily accomplished with a spreadsheet program or financial calculator.
4. In year 9, the hotel manager's incentive fee cap kicks in, as shown in the Management Fee supporting schedule in Exhibit 3. The incentive fee payment is the 10 percent of cash flow after debt service of $11,983,000—equaling $1,198,000—but this only is payable if, when combined with the base management fee, it does not exceed a maximum of 3.75 percent of total revenue. Total hotel revenue for year nine is $42,905,000 (as shown in Exhibit 1), so 3.75 percent of that amount is $1,609,000. Since this $1,609,000 is less than the sum of year nine base management fees and maximum incentive management fees, total hotel manager's fees are limited to the lesser amount. A base management fee of 1 percent of total revenue, $429,000, has already been paid, reducing the maximum hotel management incentive fee to $1,180,000.
5. Some mezzanine lenders require warrants that provide an opportunity to convert their loan to an equity stake in the venture. Consideration of this and other mezzanine loan terms is outside the scope of this chapter.
6. Calculation of a look-back IRR is readily handled with Microsoft Excel's Goal Seek or Solver functions.
7. This frequently used financial term in this context means "in proportion to the capital committed."
8. See, for instance, a series of articles on real estate JV promote calculations written by Stevens A. Carey and published in *The Real Estate Finance Journal*.
9. Note that the sponsor's invested capital, as a percentage of total capital, grows over the term of the investment. This is because the sponsor's earned but unpaid preferred

return is added to its capital account, while the capital partner is largely getting its preferred return paid out of annual distributions.

10. This return is the same as is calculated in Exhibit 4.

17

The Art of the Capital Structure

By Robert Stiles, Stephen O'Connor, and David Smith

Robert Stiles *is a Founding Principal of RobertDouglas and brings more than thirty years of domestic and international experience in structuring and executing capital solutions for hotel investors and owners as a partner with Sonnenblick-Goldman and a Founding Partner of Horwath Asia Pacific. He serves on the International Advisory Board of* Hotels' Investment Outlook *magazine; is the founder of HICAP, Asia's premiere hotel investment conference based in Hong Kong; and is a Co-Chairman of the International Lodging Finance Council (ILFC). Mr. Stiles has a Bachelor of Science degree with a focus in development and finance from Cornell University's School of Hotel Administration.*

Stephen O'Connor *is a Principal of RobertDouglas, based in Los Angeles, and brings ten years of investment banking and capital markets expertise to the firm, having previously held senior positions at Sonnenblick Goldman, Cushman & Wakefield, and HVS International. He is a regular speaker at industry events, including the Hospitality Asset Managers Association's annual meeting, and has contributed articles to the* Real Estate Finance Journal. *Mr. O'Connor has a Bachelor of Arts degree from Dartmouth College and a Master of Management in Hospitality degree from Cornell University.*

David Smith *is an Associate at RobertDouglas's New York City office. Prior to joining RobertDouglas in 2014, he spent three years with Macquarie Group, where he worked as a credit analyst with the firm's North America leveraged finance and balance sheet lending platforms. He previously worked with Horwath HTL, a leading hospitality consulting and advisory firm, in his hometown of Sydney, Australia, where he graduated from the University of Sydney. Mr. Smith also studied at the HKUST Business School in Hong Kong before obtaining a Master of Management in Hospitality degree from Cornell University.*

LIKE ALL CLASSES of commercial real estate, hotels are capital-intensive assets and are most commonly developed and owned using the financial resources of a number of different parties. In this chapter, we address the question of how a hotel investor can most effectively use money belonging to other individuals or organizations to best achieve its own investment goals.

We present our perspectives on this question primarily with the hotel's financial sponsor in mind. By "sponsor," we mean the investor who spends the time finding the property, structuring the deal, and (this is of crucial importance) finding other sources of capital to help fund the project. While the sponsor may not ultimately have the biggest financial stake in the deal, it is the party most responsible for designing a capital structure that artfully balances the risks and rewards inherent in using "other people's money." As this chapter will illustrate, finding such a balance is likely to be a major factor in determining the success or failure of the hotel investment overall.

The idea behind a capital structure is that the most efficient way to capitalize an asset is usually through a combination of different sources of money from different groups of investors. This is a simple idea that poses some intriguing questions:

- Why would an investor be willing to lend or invest his or her own money?
- Why are some sources of capital interested only in making low-risk loans while others are interested only in equity investments?
- Why don't all investors simply seek out the highest return possible?

The answer to these questions is that all investors, and therefore all sources of capital, have different degrees of risk tolerance. In other words, every dollar of available capital in the world can be thought of as seeking out a particular degree of risk and a commensurate level of return to compensate for taking that risk. Every tier of any hotel asset's capital structure—whether it is a senior loan, a mezzanine debt facility, or equity—carries a particular and unique level of risk and return profile. *The ideal capital structure is the one that matches each of these tiers with a source of capital that is seeking out that specific risk/return balance.* This is a fundamental concept that we will return to throughout the chapter.

This chapter is designed to give an overview of the issues that hotel sponsors must grapple with when designing a capital structure. At the time of this writing, the U.S. capital markets are at a period of heightened liquidity, affording hotel sponsors maximum flexibility in their ability to fine-tune the capital structure. While the availability of capital varies substantially throughout the economic cycle, the theory applies regardless of market timing.

The chapter is generally written from the perspective of the U.S. capital markets, which are broadly considered to be the world's most mature. In general, it may be harder to access some of the financial products discussed in this chapter outside of the United States (non-recourse financing, CMBS debt, and mezzanine financing are prominent examples), meaning that sponsors outside of the United States may need to rely on seller financing or use their own balance sheets or accept lower leverage debt structures.

Note that the discussions in this chapter will stick to a pre-tax viewpoint, as tax mitigation strategies are unique to each investor. Additionally, public incentives (ranging from property tax credits to outright equity grants and everything in between) are an important part of capital structure strategy that may be available for certain sponsors in certain markets; however, we will not include the public incentives variable in our discussions, as these programs are fundamentally local and vary widely. The complex topics of taxes and public incentives are deserving of their own chapters and are deliberately left outside the scope of this chapter.

Why Use the Capital Structure at All?

An important preliminary question to ask is: "Why would a hotel investor consider manipulating the capital structure in the first place?" Or, simply put: "What compels investors to use other people's money when they could use their own?" Aside from the obvious point that using external capital gives the sponsor additional financial resources and therefore more investment opportunities, there are a number of theoretical motivations behind these questions.

At the center of the idea of an optimal capital structure is the notion of financial leverage. Financial leverage is the way in which using fixed income capital, such as mortgage loans and bonds, multiplies returns to the sponsor:

- Whenever an investor's asset generates income that exceeds the cost of borrowing, it can be said that the borrower achieves *positive financial leverage*. In this situation, the leverage multiplier effect works in favor of the investor and creates returns to equity that are larger than would be achieved under an all-cash structure.
- Using debt also creates risk: if the rate of return on the asset is less than the borrower's interest rate, the sponsor's returns become *negatively levered*—and the return on equity is lower than the all-cash alternative.

This concept can be illustrated by the following example: imagine a hotel investor who purchases a small property for $10 million, holds it for five years, and then sells it at no capital gain for $10 million. The investor expects that during the hold period, the hotel will generate annual net operating income of $1 million. To finance the acquisition, the investor faces two alternatives:

1. Purchase the property entirely with cash available on the balance sheet; or
2. Contribute cash for 25 percent of the acquisition ($2.5 million) and arrange an interest-only loan providing the other 75 percent of the total acquisition cost ($7.5 million) priced at 5 percent per annum.

Imagine first that the hotel generates the predicted $1 million of annual returns. The calculations presented in Exhibit 1 show that in this scenario, the effect of the debt is to enhance the borrower's percentage returns on equity capital: by contributing less equity on day one, it achieves an internal rate of return of 25 percent and beats the all-cash alternative of 10 percent, which is simply the return on the asset. This is an example of positive financial leverage—and the investor achieved it because the rate of return on the asset (10 percent) exceeded the cost of servicing the debt (5 percent).

Real estate assets do not always perform as expected. Imagine an alternative scenario where the local market turns sour shortly after the investor buys the new hotel, and the property generates only $400,000 of net operating income each

Exhibit 1 Hotel Performs as Expected

Year	Unlevered Cash Flows	Debt Proceeds/ Debt Service	Levered Cash Flows
Investment	(10,000,000)	7,500,000	(2,500,000)
1	1,000,000	(375,000)	625,000
2	1,000,000	(375,000)	625,000
3	1,000,000	(375,000)	625,000
4	1,000,000	(375,000)	625,000
5	11,000,000	(7,875,000)	3,125,000
IRR	10.0%		25.0%

year—a 4 percent return on the asset. As the cash flow figures in Exhibit 2 show, this return leaves the investor with barely enough cash to service the $7.5 million loan, and after selling the hotel at the end of Year 5, the investor is left with an unimpressive return on equity of 1 percent. In this case, the use of debt *negatively levered* the investor's returns, because the asset's total return (4 percent) was less than the cost of debt service (5 percent).

There are two important implications from this example that are relevant to the art of constructing an optimal capital structure:

1. The ability to achieve positive leverage is dependent not only on the performance of the hotel, but also on the cost of the debt.
2. Adding debt to the mix of capital introduces the risk of the equity returns becoming negatively levered in the event of a market downtown—as well as the possibility of default and foreclosure.

In other words, while adding more debt to the capital structure increases the sponsor's *expected* return, it also creates risks that would otherwise not be relevant if the investment were made using all cash equity.

Exhibit 2 Hotel Underperforms

Year	Unlevered Cash Flows	Debt Proceeds/ Debt Service	Levered Cash Flows
Investment	(10,000,000)	7,500,000	(2,500,000)
1	400,000	(375,000)	25,000
2	400,000	(375,000)	25,000
3	400,000	(375,000)	25,000
4	400,000	(375,000)	25,000
5	10,400,000	(7,875,000)	2,525,000
IRR	4.0%		1.0%

Furthermore, this example implies that by adjusting the capital structure, sponsors can to some extent transform a prospective deal by pushing an investment opportunity up or down the risk-return spectrum. We regard this as the ultimate purpose of the capital structure, and therefore also the reason why an investor should consider manipulating it. *The thoughtful and creative use of capital allows sponsors of hotel assets to transform investment opportunities in such a way that they better fit their particular risk tolerance and set of objectives.*

Understanding Your Investment Objectives: A Starting Point for Capital Structure Strategy

Concluding that there are some advantages to a manipulated capital structure, the next relevant questions for the sponsor are how, where, and when to manipulate it. The sponsor's decision to commit some of its own equity to a deal is a given—so the question can more specifically be described as either, "How should I find and structure a joint venture equity partner?" or "How should I use leverage?"

We believe that these questions can only be answered by first building a thorough understanding of the sponsor's background and overall investment strategy. In essence, the capital structure should be tailor-made to suit the particular features of the investor:

- What are its goals and objectives?
- What level of returns is it targeting?
- What are the hot-button issues that it is unwilling or unable to negotiate on?
- What issues can it be flexible on?

The answers to all of these questions will ultimately determine which of a theoretically infinite number of capital solutions works best—they may also rule out entire categories of capital sources.

We consider the following to be the most important elements of the investor profile that are relevant to the capital structure:

- *Sponsor risk appetite.* In financial terms, risk is generally thought of as the potential for returns to vary from expectations. "Risk appetite" is simply the extent to which the investor is willing to tolerate deviations from those expectations. But there are many forms of risk, and using debt creates certain risks that do not exist for all-cash investors. Taking a high-level view, we think it is helpful to distinguish between operating risk and financial risk:
    - *Operating risk* is the normal threat of day-to-day cash flow volatility faced by all hotels and so applies to all investors. The hotel sector is so volatile because of the "one-night lease" nature of the business, which means that hotel assets are treated as being riskier than other classes of commercial real estate after controlling for other factors. However, even within the hotel sector, there are degrees of risk; urban properties tend to generate more stable returns than resorts, gateway markets tend to be more stable than secondary or tertiary markets, and so on.

- *Financial risk,* by contrast, is relevant only to deals financed by debt capital. As the previous example demonstrated, financial leverage amplifies the risk, and therefore the variance to the sponsor's returns, when market conditions change. But because real estate debt is typically "non-recourse" financing and is secured only by the sponsor's interest in the asset, the greatest financial risk is losing the investment via foreclosure.

Different investors tolerate different types of uncertainty. Opportunistic real estate funds, for example, are often backed by high-net-worth clients who are willing to accept the risk of loss in order to attain high potential profits. By contrast, pension funds have a longer-term investment horizon and are more focused on downside protection, and so may prefer to use more modest amounts of debt.

Between these two extremes lie a wide range of investor types, all distinguished from one another by their relative willingness and ability to accept different forms of risk as a means of achieving their objectives. See Exhibit 3 for basic information on three traditional real estate investor profiles.

- *Investment horizon and liquidity requirements.* Like most real estate investments, a hotel investment is an investment in a physical asset, not a financial security; a physical asset cannot be immediately sold and converted to cash and,

Exhibit 3 Traditional Real Estate Investor Profiles

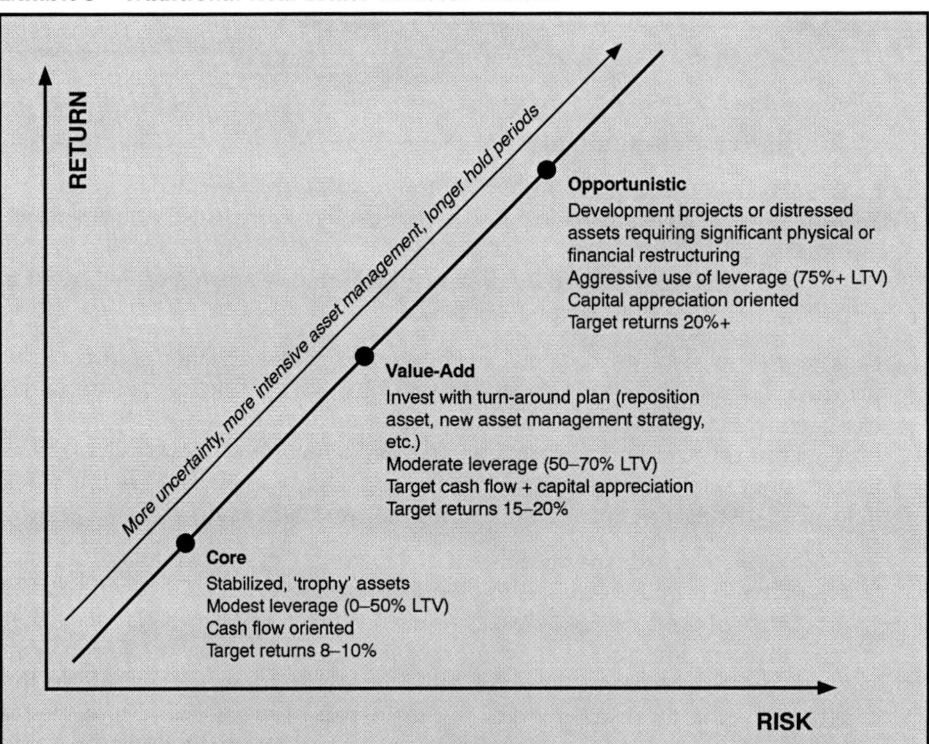

furthermore, an investor will incur significant fees and expenses on transfer. So, to some extent, all owners of lodging assets must be open to the possibility of a long-term hold.

But like risk tolerance, there are many degrees of targeted investment term or duration preferred by hotel investors. For example, some groups (e.g., private equity funds) that are obligated to return capital to their investors by a predetermined date consequently seek to add value and then sell their investments quickly, resulting in a relatively short-term holding period (less than five years). Other investors, such as real estate investment trusts, are more interested in "clipping a coupon" over a long-term holding period (greater than ten years). This distinction is important to the financing decision, because the sponsor's targeted exit date must be aligned with the targeted exit date of its lender and/or partner.

- *Desired level of control.* Control is important to some hotel investors but not to all. In fact, it is common for hotel investors to seek out arrangements under which they give up some control in order to gain the expertise of a well-qualified partner with special experience or knowledge of a given market. However, some investors may have a particular value-add plan that they need to be able to execute without any approval rights or limitations. Such an investor may not be willing to rely on the consent of its lender before making meaningful changes to strategy or management.
- *Willingness and ability to provide guarantees.* One of the strongest priorities for institutional owners of stabilized hotel assets is to secure non-recourse financing. "Recourse" is the ability of a lender to seek a judgment from a court allowing it to satisfy a debt by seizing assets owned by the borrower that are outside the loan's collateral pool, such as cash or other properties owned by the investor.

  Recourse lending means that the borrower's assets are on the hook in the event of a default. Even non-recourse loans require sponsors to show some ability to guarantee their obligations. Specifically, non-recourse lenders generally insist that the sponsor provide a further pledge of personal assets that can be seized as collateral to the loan in case a sponsor conducts certain bad acts such as fraud or misappropriation of funds from the asset; this is sometimes referred to as "springing" recourse.

  Therefore, the willingness and ability of the sponsor to provide financial guarantees helps guide the decision of what type of loan it should pursue—but to some degree it is also a binary issue that determines whether the sponsor will be able to access the institutional loan market at all. Borrowers who will not or cannot provide a conditional guarantee may need to rule out institutional debt as a source of financing for their assets.
- *Timing.* The sponsor's preferred timing for both the inflow (i.e., how and when it prefers to receive loan or equity proceeds) and outflow of capital (i.e., when those proceeds are returned) must be considered when constructing a capital structure. Timing requirements change with the nature of the hotel project. Specifically, projects with a staggered development or capital improvement

plan are best suited to a lender or partner who is willing to phase in capital. For the outflow and return of capital at the end of an investment, the key consideration is the costs associated with repaying debt ahead of its scheduled maturity date, thus allowing an investor the flexibility to exit early by selling the asset.

This is by no means an exhaustive list. In our opinion, the real art of the capital structure lies in two areas: First is in the ability of the financial advisor to process, consider, and balance the sponsor's goals and priorities; and, second, in the ability to create a financing solution that aligns with all or as many of these fundamental attributes as possible while also minimizing the overall cost of capital.

How to Use the Capital Structure: Key Concepts and Considerations for Investors

Matching a hotel sponsor to a particular financing strategy can be challenging because there is a wide variety of financial products available in modern capital markets. Finding, selecting, and structuring the most appropriate source of capital is generally a time-consuming process for hotel investors. Every deal is different, but there are broad categories of capital sources that can be thought of as building blocks for a capital structure. We discuss each of these broad categories in the sections that follow, working through the capital structure in the same top-to-bottom order that it would be presented on an investor's balance sheet.

Debt Capital

As with other classes of commercial real estate, the hotel industry commonly uses debt. The creation of a debt simply involves one party borrowing money from another, with an agreement to repay the money at a particular point in the future. As we discussed earlier, debt is a fundamental component of the artful use of the capital structure, because it allows the investor to create positive leverage and stretch its equity to access larger or more deals.

In this section, we provide an overview of the broad categories of debt before exploring some of the challenges and suitability issues that hotel sponsors must consider when using this type of capital. The starting objective of many sponsors with respect to their leverage strategy is often to simply achieve maximum possible financing proceeds at the lowest possible cost of capital. Our view is that this approach usually understates the complexity of most hotel investors' needs.

Primary Categories. Primary categories of debt capital include the following:

- *Senior loan.* The seniority of a loan instrument refers to the position of the lender's legal claim to the loan collateral, relative to other debt obligations of the borrower. As its name implies, a senior loan typically sits in a first-priority position with respect to interest payments and the return of capital in a liquidation scenario. For both development deals and stabilized assets, senior loans are usually secured by a mortgage and often constitute the largest part of the capital structure. An attractively priced and structured senior loan is therefore critical to the success of leveraged hotel sponsors' investment strategies.

During strong points in the investment cycle, we see a range of capital sources "open for business" for qualified hotel borrowers in the senior loan market. Participating groups range from balance sheet–style lenders (including banks, insurance companies, and loan funds) to specialty "conduit" groups, which originate loans for the purpose of creating securities for distribution in the commercial mortgage–backed securities (CMBS) market.

- *Subordinated debt.* Sitting below a senior loan in the hotel capital stack is subordinated debt, which may take on a range of different names, depending on the type of market it is issued into (e.g., private versus public) and how it ranks relative to other types of subordinated debt. Whether it is a simple second mortgage, a mezzanine loan (a subordinated loan with features of both debt and equity financing), or a "B-piece" (the junior tranche in a CMBS issuance), all forms of subordinated debt share a common feature: they allow the borrower to stretch to higher levels of leverage and therefore carry more credit risk to the lender than senior debt. As a result, pricing for this type of capital will always be higher than senior debt at a given property.

  Subordinated loans are also structured differently than senior debt financing. Senior lenders will prohibit junior debt from coming due for repayment, or maturing, before the first mortgage; therefore, the term length for junior debts is typically co-terminus with senior loans. Subordinated debt is usually non-amortizing and may even accrete as it approaches maturity, as it is common to divide the fixed debt service payment into cash that is paid current and the balance that is deferred, or paid in kind. The right to accrete interest (rather than pay it current with cash) may be granted as a way to meet the borrower's needs with temporary cash flow shortfalls (such as a hotel undergoing a renovation).

- *Hybrid financing.* As more and more structural features are added to a subordinated real estate loan, the facility may eventually begin to look more like equity than debt. As a common example, subordinated debt facilities might be packaged together with warrants that would allow the lender to share in the potential upside when the borrower exits the hotel investment. Warrants provide a boost to the lender's expected return that gives their overall position in the capital structure elements of both debt and equity.

  This is consistent with the idea that deeply subordinated debt may have risk characteristics that are also equity-like in nature (i.e., lower certainty of achieving an expected return and lower certainty of recovering principal in a liquidation). Loan facilities that blur the line between subordinated debt and preferred equity (which we will discuss later) are sometimes referred to as "hybrid financing."

The lender's decision of how much debt to extend to a borrower and on what terms is determined during the loan underwriting process. Loan underwriting refers to the process undertaken by lenders to analyze the creditworthiness of the borrower and its collateral, and to size and price the loan itself.

For hotel deals, the key component of the underwriting process is determining what adjustments the lenders are willing to make to the in-place performance to arrive at the underwritten net cash flow (UWNCF) of the asset. As a result, there is a natural source of tension between borrowers and lenders, and the deal sponsor is naturally inclined to focus on the upside, whereas lenders typically are more concerned about "stressed" results and how much they stand to lose in a downside situation.

Structural and Suitability Considerations for Borrowers. Structural and suitability considerations for borrowers include public versus private lenders, payment and repayment timing, and terms and conditions.

Public versus private lenders. It is important for borrowers to look beyond the terms of their loan and understand exactly who their ultimate lender is. This is particularly relevant for hotel deals, which tend to be highly structured and consequently are more likely to require lender consents or amendments during the life of the loan.

One critical dimension for borrowers to differentiate between is whether their loan is funded in the private or public debt markets. In this context, "private debt" refers to commercial loans originated and held on balance sheet by a single lending institution or by a small group of lenders. By contrast, "public debt" generally refers to the commercial mortgage–backed securities (CMBS) market, which consists of loans originated by "conduit" lender groups for securitization and sale to a pool of secondary buyers.

The CMBS market has become a critical source of debt capital for the hotel industry: in the first half of 2014, it accounted for more than half of the total balance of all new hotel loans. The primary advantage of public debt is the depth of liquidity it can offer during favorable points in the economic cycle. In strong markets, CMBS adds competition to the lending landscape and can provide borrowers with rates that are more favorable than those available in the private sector—particularly in secondary markets.

The downside for borrowers is that loans originated for securitization are rigorously structured and subject to complex servicing agreements that are designed to protect the interests of the diverse group of security holders who provide the liquidity. The administration of CMBS loans is managed by a designated third party (called a "master servicer"); these duties are transferred to a separate party (a "special servicer") in the event of a borrower default. Unlike under a privately issued loan, it can be difficult for a CMBS borrower to even identify the true decision-maker on the lender side in the event that it requests a modification or consent.

Fixed-rate loans from both balance sheet and CMBS sources can generally not be repaid ahead of maturity. Instead, they usually feature a hard lockout period followed by a defeasance right—which allows the borrower to replace the loan collateral with a portfolio of government securities that replicate the promised cash flows under the loan agreement. While defeasance allows the borrower to exit and repay its loan, it can be prohibitively expensive in a time of relatively low interest rates. The rigidity of fixed rate loans is a less attractive option for borrowers who anticipate a need for flexibility through the life of their loan.

Payment and repayment timing. One of the essential elements of the hotel sponsor profile is the anticipated or necessary timing for the inflow and outflow of investment capital. These timing requirements are usually tied to both the asset itself (What stage of the development cycle is the hotel in? Is the loan being used to fund construction?) and the sponsor (What is the targeted investment horizon? Is the investor obliged to liquidate and return capital to its partners at a certain point in time?).

It is critical that these questions be addressed by the sponsor's debt capital structure. For example, it is often more efficient for development and "value add" projects to be funded in stages rather than all at once in a regular term loan facility. Such a delayed-draw funding process offers advantages to both parties in a development deal by allowing the lender to "turn off the tap" and cap its exposure if the project does not progress as planned, while also minimizing the borrower's cost of capital by eliminating the payment of interest on any unused loan proceeds.

Hotel investors also must ensure that the timing features of their loan match their overall investment strategy. This is a key issue, because investment horizons vary greatly between different types of investors. For example, real estate investment trusts (REITs) are known as cash flow–oriented, "buy and hold" property owners. In general, REIT investments are better suited for long-term, fixed-rate financing. Private equity fund investors, on the other hand, tend to be more focused on short-term, "value add" opportunities and are often constrained by a requirement to return capital to their investors at the end of a stated fund life.

Sponsors interested in a short-term hold may not have the ability to ride out a cycle and so are more likely to focus on their ability to exit quickly in favorable market conditions. For these investors, fixed-rate loans are unlikely to be the best fit, since they tend to include prepayment lockouts and costly penalties if the borrower repays before maturity. Financing solutions do exist for sponsors who want the flexibility to exit in the short-term—but lenders willing to provide this flexibility will likely ask the borrower for something in exchange (for example, a higher interest rate or larger upfront fees).

Lastly, the timing of the sponsor's execution relative to the overall economic cycle may broaden or limit financing opportunities. The cyclical nature of the capital markets causes volatility in the cost of capital (interest rates)—but also in the outright availability of capital. The 2007–2008 credit crisis and subsequent macroeconomic downturn, for example, caused an extended closure of the CMBS market, with virtually no new issuance during most of 2008 and 2009 and only very limited activity in 2010. Cycle timing is also critical to the borrower's ability to refinance upon maturity of the debt. In the hotel industry, there have been many cases of hotel owners running into trouble upon refinancing in tight debt markets despite having easily serviced their loan for years prior.

Terms and conditions: the fine print. Debt financing deals usually require the hotel sponsor to sign a long-term agreement with multiple contractual obligations. These obligations include the headline terms that all owners focus on (amount of loan proceeds, interest rate and accrual features, term and extension options, and so on)—but also a host of other obligations that may significantly restrict the flexibility, control rights, and even the profitability of the sponsor. There are essentially no limits to the number of conditions or requirements a lender may impose before it is willing to close a deal. Moreover, hotel loans in particular are often highly structured because the operating nature of the hotel business creates risks for lenders not found in other real estate deals. We provide a few common examples of common hotel financing terms and conditions below:

- *Consent rights.* Loan documents often give the lender consent or veto rights for certain decisions that could affect the creditworthiness of the borrower. These rights can be attached to virtually any decision that the lender views as having a meaningful impact on the hotel's value. Lender consent is most commonly required before the sponsor can take out new debt, enter into leases, change management or branding, or make any significant changes to the hotel itself (such as a renovation project). Lenders almost always have the right to approve an assignment of the loan from one borrower to another (alternatively, they can usually call the debt immediately due on sale of the asset).
- *Franchise and hotel management agreement considerations.* Hotels are commonly operated under third-party agreements whereby the owner pays a percentage of hotel revenues to a specialist hotel management company in exchange for branding and/or management services. More so than in any other form of commercial real estate, these branding and management services are intrinsically tied into the asset's value. For many hotels, the brand of the property is more recognizable to consumers than the improved real estate itself.

  Because of this relationship, hotel lenders are particularly concerned about the borrower's ability to retain the services of a well-performing brand or operating partner or to terminate the services of a badly performing one in the event of a default and foreclosure. On the other side of the table, hotel operating companies often insist that they retain the right to continue branding and/or managing the property in the event of a default and foreclosure.

  To deal with these competing interests, hotel loans are usually coupled with a "Comfort Letter" (for franchised properties) or a "Subordination, Non-disturbance and Attornment Agreement" (or SNDA) for third-party managed properties. Among other things, these documents specify the rights of the lender and the existing operator after foreclosure. While these agreements may have no actual impact on the borrower so long as it continues to perform under the terms of the loan, they are a common prerequisite to securing debt financing. This means that the onus is on the hotel's owner to bring their lender and their operator to the table to negotiate an agreement as a precursor to closing a loan.
- *Positive, negative, and financial covenants.* Covenants are promises made by the borrower to the lender to do something (positive covenant), to not do something (negative covenant), or to commit to the hotel meeting some pre-determined financial hurdle (financial covenant). Because of the cyclical nature of the lodging industry, hotel borrowers must be particularly aware of their obligations under loan agreements to meet minimum thresholds of credit quality—which often take the form of either a leverage test (such as the ratio of trailing earnings to outstanding debt) or a debt service coverage test (such as the ratio of trailing earnings to current debt service payments).

- *Cash flow management.* Commonly, hotel loans require the borrower to direct all incoming cash flows to the property in a special lockbox account in which the lender has a security interest. These arrangements give the lender the ability to trap cash within the account under certain circumstances so that it can be used later to satisfy the debt, if needed. Lockbox arrangements can have significant practical impacts on the day-to-day operation of the hotel. They usually require owners to issue payment direction notices to their existing accounts to ensure that revenues flow to the appropriate lockbox account, and in some circumstances they effectively give the lender full control over the distribution of the hotel's cash flow.

  Most lenders also require borrowers to set up reserve accounts for the payment of insurance and property taxes; the periodic replacement of furniture, fixtures, and equipment (FF&E); and for future debt service payments under certain circumstances. Under typical hotel loan agreements, owners have an obligation to fund these accounts at a pre-determined level (e.g., 4 percent of gross revenues for FF&E) on a regular basis, using operating cash flow. Sponsors interested in accessing the institutional debt markets must ensure that they incorporate contributions to these accounts into their cash flow planning.

Equity Capital

Hotel sponsors use equity capital markets both as an alternative and as a complementary strategy to raising debt capital. Equity is simply an ownership interest: it represents the residual claim to the value in an asset after accounting for all outstanding liabilities. In practice, layering equity into a hotel's capital structure is a complex task akin to organizing a marriage between two (or more) parties. Equity can be structured in many ways to achieve the sponsor's investment goals. In this section, we summarize the advantages that equity capital offers to hotel sponsors before exploring a number of these structural considerations in depth.

Why Raise Equity? By definition, an investment of equity capital carries a higher risk than debt. Consequently, third-party equity investors generally demand more control rights and greater financial compensation (in the form of a higher expected rate of return) than lenders. This raises the question of why accessing third-party equity has any appeal to sponsors in the first place. We summarize two answers to this question below.

Stretch to diversification and bigger deals. Hotel real estate projects are generally highly capital-intensive. Even under favorable capital markets conditions, there are limits to the amount of debt capital that sponsors can reasonably expect to secure when capitalizing their property. Therefore, investors who seek to construct a portfolio without an equity partner may find that their financial resources quickly become tied up in a small number of investments. This introduces the risk of having a high degree of exposure to idiosyncratic problems at any one of the investment properties or their local markets.

By contrast, investors who commit to new projects with one or more capital partners can write smaller checks for each individual investment, thus allowing them to stretch their capital over a more diversified set of assets and also to bigger individual deals. Even well-capitalized investors may prefer to limit their exposure to individual assets if doing so allows them to spread their capital across more deals.

Access third-party expertise. Creating an equity partnership is sometimes less about accessing capital and more about accessing expertise. This concept is especially true in the market for hotel assets, which require more hands-on management and up-to-date market knowledge than other classes of real estate. While there are other ways of accessing third-party expertise (hotel management companies and asset management groups essentially provide this service for a fee), the equity approach is popular in the hotel industry because it gives the partner skin in the game and therefore better aligns its interests with the sponsor.

Structural Considerations for Sponsors. Structural considerations for sponsors include common equity versus preferred equity, operating partner/capital partner arrangements, and return sharing.

Common equity versus preferred equity. As in the debt markets, equity securities are stratified according to the seniority of claim to the cash flows of the asset and rights upon liquidation. The most prevalent distinction is between preferred and common equity:

- Strictly speaking, preferred equity refers to an ownership security with a more senior claim on the assets than the entity's common shareholders. While called "equity," this class of capital is debt-like in nature and is used most frequently by hotel sponsors as a means of stretching leverage through to a higher share of the capital structure than could be achieved with junior debt alone. Preferred equity securities typically do not have a fixed maturity date—but, like debt, they do carry a contractual interest rate that the hotel owner must pay before making any distributions of net cash flow to common equity holders.
- By contrast, common equity represents the true residual value in an asset once all other obligations and claims have been satisfied. When hotel sponsors raise third-party common equity to capitalize their asset, they are in a sense bringing in a true partner to the deal—this partnership is referred to as a "joint venture." More so than for any other type of capital, sponsors must carefully negotiate and memorialize their relationship with joint venture equity partners. We address some common features of these agreements below.

Operating partner/capital partner arrangements. A common approach to hotel ownership is the "operating partner" versus "capital partner" model, under which a passive capital partner deploys the majority of the equity (typically 80 to 95 per cent), but relinquishes most of its ability to control the asset. The general or operating partner (the sponsor), which likely has deeper expertise in hotel asset management, provides a minority stake but retains more significant control rights and is responsible for maximizing the investment's value.

The definition of control in this context is up to the parties negotiating the deal. In some deals, the general partner's "control" is simply a veto right over major decisions. In others, the sponsor outsources the asset management function to the partner, ceding responsibility for routine management decisions at the hotel. The details of the arrangements made between the joint venture parties should be recorded in writing and are usually found in a document called an "Operating Agreement."

Return sharing. Because joint venture investors often have distinct roles in their partnership, they also often receive uneven shares of the cash flows of the asset. Commonly, the operating agreement will even differentiate between cash flows from the operation of the hotel and proceeds received from the sale of the asset. Again, the details of return sharing arrangements are usually a highly negotiated element of the partnership agreement and vary widely from transaction to transaction.

Operating partner/general partner arrangements will often use the "preferred/promote" model of return sharing. This model provides the general partner with the potential to earn outsized returns (a promote) in the event that the asset performs beyond some threshold level (the preferred return). The rationale behind this approach is that it properly incentivizes the general partner to make decisions that maximize the hotel's value.

Preferred promote structures usually treat cash flows from operations and sale proceeds as a "waterfall," with the cash split between the two groups of partners in a certain manner until there is nothing left to distribute. The intent of the waterfall is to reward the general partner with increasingly outsized distributions as the investment clears higher and higher return thresholds. The following waterfall structure is common:

- *First:* distribute cash pro rata between the equity partners until the preferred return (e.g., 8 percent) is achieved.
- *Second:* distribute cash according to a certain split (e.g., 80/20—80 percent to the equity partners and 20 percent as a promote to the general partner) until the limited partner achieves a certain IRR (e.g., 12 percent). Note that the split is designed to give the general partner an outsized return relative to its capital investment.
- *Third:* distribute cash according to an even more outsized split (e.g., 70/30—70 percent to the equity partners and 30 percent as a promote to the general partner) until the limited partner achieves a higher IRR (e.g., 15 percent).
- *Fourth:* distribute all remaining cash according to a higher again outsized split (e.g., 60/40—60 percent to the equity partners and 40 percent as a promote to the general partner).

A hotel sponsor's approach to return sharing should be consistent with its strategy underpinning the overall equity partnership. The critical question is: how thoroughly is the sponsor prepared to asset-manage the investment and how much control is it willing to give up? The structural issues addressed in this section should be thought of as tools to formalize responsibilities and align interests; however, their use should ultimately be determined by the sponsor's experience, its asset management capabilities, its return targets, its relationship with the partner, and its ability to bear risk.

Case Study

We conclude our discussion with a simple, hypothetical case study designed to show how users and providers of hotel capital think about some of the concepts raised in the chapter.

Imagine that a 150-room hotel in Midtown Manhattan is currently for sale. The property is about twenty years old and was last renovated ten years ago. Since then, the owner has kept up with mechanical repairs and maintenance as needed, but the guestrooms and public areas have become clearly dated.

The hotel is franchised with a major hotel company under a well-known select-service brand. The franchise agreement expires in one year, and the franchisor is only willing to consider an extension on completion of a significant property improvement plan (PIP). The owner has estimated that the hotel will need renovations costing around $20,000 per room to bring it in line with brand standards.

The New York hotel market is strong and the asset has yielded steady cash flows throughout the last five years. However, with nearly a dozen brand-new select-service hotels having opened in the Midtown submarket in the last twenty-four months, the property is struggling to maintain rates and has lost five points of RevPAR penetration against its competitive set in the last year alone.

The hotel is owner-operated by a small real estate group that has shifted its strategy away from the hospitality sector. After losing focus on the asset in recent years, the group is unwilling to devote the capital needed to complete the PIP and have decided to sell.

After marketing the property, the owner receives bids from two groups that appear to have very different backgrounds and investment strategies. The following table provides a brief profile of each bidder:

	Investor A	Investor B
Investor Type	Publicly traded REIT focused specifically on U.S. select-service hotels.	Two local real estate partners with development expertise and extensive New York City connections.
General Investment Objectives	Invest in stable assets in primary gateway markets with in-place cash flow and long-term capital growth opportunities.	Identify underperforming assets with repositioning potential. Redevelop and flip to achieve short-term capital growth.
Strategy	Complete the PIP, renew the franchise agreement, and engage a well-known third-party management company to take over operations. Return the hotel to 100 percent RevPAR penetration and start harvesting cash flows.	Close the hotel, conduct an extensive "gut" renovation of the building and engage a well-known boutique hotel company to rebrand the property. Re-open after one year with new guestrooms, a rooftop bar, and an elaborate ground floor restaurant run by a New York celebrity chef.
Investment Horizon	Ten years +	No longer than three years—enough time to renovate, reopen, and stabilize the asset.

Target Levered Return	13–15%	20%+
Total Required Capital	Bid $75 million PIP $3 million Closing Costs $2 million **Total** **$80 million**	Bid $78 million Renovation $10 million Closing Costs $2.5 million **Total** **$90.5 million**
Capital Structure: Key Objective	Use leverage modestly (target 55% LTV) to enhance returns while protecting corporate-level credit rating.	Maximize proceeds to handle the limited financial resources of the sponsors.
Capital Structure: Design	**$** / **% of Value** Senior Loan $43 million 55% Equity $35 million 100% The REIT is extremely well-capitalized and plans to close the acquisition using all equity. It plans to lever the asset with a long-term, fixed-rate loan. After initial conversations, it has already received several indications of interest from life insurance companies and conduit lending groups for a ten-year, fixed-rate deal.	**$** / **% of Value** Senior Loan $57 million 65% Mezzanine $17.5 million 85% Equity $13.5 million 100% The sponsors have received tentative interest from a high-yield real estate fund to provide joint-venture equity financing. The joint venture would be arranged as a limited partnership. The sponsors plan to invest through a single LLC as general partner and provide 15% of the total equity ($2 million). The high-yield fund, a limited partner, would provide the remaining 85% ($11.5 million). They plan to use a combination of senior debt and a mezzanine loan to raise the incremental amount required to close the acquisition. They prefer a five-year floating rate facility and have received a term sheet from a local bank.

The owner is surprised that the two bidders have such divergent plans for the property, but, on further analysis, begins to understand how they are arriving at similar bids despite their significantly different underwriting assumptions.

In reality, it is unlikely to find two groups with such conflicting plans competing for the same property. Nevertheless, the investment strategies themselves are not unusual for buyers of hotel real estate. This example is designed to show that the most appropriate capital structure for a given hotel may look very different, depending on who the owner is. More than anything, it shows that an artful use of the capital structure ultimately needs to be tied back to the investment objectives and goals of the sponsor.

Discussion Questions

1. Which of the investors would you expect to have a higher cost of capital?
2. Specifically, what expenses might the closing costs incurred by both investors include?
3. Why might Investor A prefer a lower degree of financial leverage when it could in fact borrow more?
4. Why does Investor A prefer a ten-year fixed-rate loan while Investor B prefers a five-year floating-rate loan?
5. If you were the owner of the hotel, with which investor would you choose to enter into a Purchase and Sale Agreement?

Suggested answers to these questions appear at the end of this book.

18

Hospitality REITs and the Evolution of Lodging Ownership

By Joseph S. Bello and Barry A. N. Bloom

Joseph S. Bello, *CHA, CHAM, is Senior Vice President of Asset Management for Xenia Hotels & Resorts, Inc., and has held this position with Xenia or its affiliated entities since 2007. During his tenure with Xenia, Mr. Bello has had oversight responsibility for a portfolio of premium full-service, resort, boutique, and convention hotels throughout the United States. From 2003 to 2007, Mr. Bello was Director of Asset Management with CNL Hotels & Resorts, Inc., where he had responsibility for a diverse portfolio of hotels as well as involvement in key portfolio initiatives. Prior to his roles in asset management, from 1977 to 2003 Mr. Bello held regional manager, general manager, and property-level management positions in upscale branded hotels. Mr. Bello holds an Associate of Arts degree in Business Administration from Miami-Dade College, and has earned the CHA (Certified Hotel Administrator) and the CHAM (Certified Hotel Asset Manager) certifications from the American Hotel & Lodging Educational Institute.*

Barry A. N. Bloom, *Ph.D., has held the position of Executive Vice President and Chief Operating Officer of Xenia Hotels & Resorts, Inc., or its affiliated entities since July 2013. In this role, Mr. Bloom is responsible for direct oversight of the asset management and project management functions, as well as a variety of strategic and operational corporate functions of Xenia. From July 2011 to June 2013, Mr. Bloom served as an Associate Professor of the Practice in the School of Hospitality Administration at Boston University and from July 2010 to June 2011, Mr. Bloom served as an Instructor in the School of Hospitality Leadership at DePaul University. From 2008 to 2011, Mr. Bloom co-founded and was a Principal of Abacus Lodging Investors LLC, a hotel investment and advisory firm. Prior to pursuing an academic career, Mr. Bloom worked for a variety of leading hotel investment firms, most recently as Executive Vice President of Portfolio Management & Administration with CNL Hotels & Resorts, Inc., from 2003 to 2007, where he was responsible for oversight of the company's $6.6 billion portfolio. Prior to CNL, he served as Vice President—Investment Management for Hyatt Hotels Corporation from 2000 to 2003. In addition, Mr. Bloom has worked for Tishman Hotel & Realty, VMS Realty Partners, and Pannell Kerr Forster (now PKF Consulting). Mr. Bloom received his Bachelor of Science degree in Hotel and Restaurant Management as well as a Master of Business Administration degree from Cornell University and a Doctor of Philosophy degree in Hospitality Management from Iowa State University.*

IN 2008, THE YEAR *Hotel Asset Management Principles and Practices,* Second Edition, was written, the hotel industry and the economy of the United States in general were both struggling to work through an economic downcycle that began in late 2007. The five years that led up to the contraction was a period of high liquidity and record valuations that ultimately produced the largest hotel deal ever transacted to that point: CNL Hotels & Resorts, an Orlando-based Real Estate Investment Trust, or REIT, was acquired for $6.6 billion in April 2007.

This chapter will focus primarily on the hotel industry and its economic cycle from 2008 until present. Longer-term analysis of REIT performance as it relates to other investment vehicles is germane to the discussion as well. More specifically, we will explore how ownership entities, particularly REITs, have evolved to create greater value for owners and investors post-recovery. Additionally, we will take a closer look at recently executed industry transactions in the private and public arenas, including the mega-deal that dwarfed the record-setting CNL Hotels and Resorts, Inc., deal of 2007, with the purpose of discovering the effect on value and performance from these various transactions.

A Brief History of the Evolution of Hotel Ownership

The United States Congress passed the Real Estate Investment Trust Act in 1960 as a means for individuals to share in the benefits of owning real estate. Today, REITs have become a ubiquitous form of personal investment for income, long-term capital appreciation, and diversification that can be easily accessed through a variety of channels. Historically, the changes in types of hotel ownership and their various structures leading up to and including REITs can be described more as fits and starts rather than "evolution" in the scientific definition.

At one time, hotels were often seen as the crowning jewels in the life of successful entrepreneurs and titans of industry. An example of this is the Casa Marina hotel in Key West, Florida. At the onset of the twentieth century, railroad magnate Henry Flagler built the first rail system to connect the U.S. mainland with the Florida Keys and Key West. At that time, there were no roads and no way except by boat to travel from island to island or from key to key. Flagler conceived of a grand resort at the end of his rail line, where the affluent would vacation in splendor. The hotel opened in 1920, unfortunately just after Flagler's death. Over several decades, celebrities and the upper crust of society rode the rails to Key West, living Flagler's dream of luxury service and accommodations. Today, the Casa Marina has been restored to its original grandeur and is part of Hilton Worldwide's Waldorf Astoria collection, once again catering to visitors to an island that at one time was not accessible to the general public.

Americans' passion to "hit the road" in the 1950s and 1960s, spurred by the development of the interstate highway system, launched a different cycle in the hotel industry. Kemmons Wilson, founder of Holiday Inn, brilliantly conceived of a "motel" at which guests could literally drive up to and park directly outside of their room. Soon the American landscape was dotted with branded motels of consistent quality along all of its highways.

After the deregulation of airlines in the United States and many other parts of the world in the late 1970s, air travel became affordable to nearly anyone with modest resources and the desire to book a flight. Routes were expanded and new carriers such as Southwest Airlines were born to serve this new generation of leisure and business travelers. The country was on the move, and soon every airport in the United States had hotels with the big red Marriott sign on top. The formula for these hotels was so consistent that it was often hard to differentiate the city a business traveler was sleeping in that night. During this period of rapid supply expansion, the major brands for the most part were owner-operators, managing their business of guest service and bearing the risk and often complex nuances of real estate ownership.

In the late 1980s, there was a cleansing of sorts as it pertains to the financial viability of many hotels. The U.S. Tax Reform Act of 1986 negated the rights of passive real estate investors to reduce personal taxes by offsetting income with losses from real estate. This tax change caused an upheaval at many lending institutions that had underwritten projects that were basically tax shelters but were not viable on purely economic fundamentals. The resulting market correction was an auctioning off of many hotels by the Resolution Trust Corporation at highly discounted prices. Upside-down hotels were now right-sized from a valuation standpoint and the industry could move on. This also spurred the eventual disconnection between hotel management and hotel ownership, thereby creating not only the need for independent ownership entity structures such as REITs, but also the need for professional asset managers who would ensure that management companies kept ownership's objectives in mind.

The massive divestment of real estate by the major legacy brand operators freed them up to focus on a new model of hotel development with well-funded owners, customer-centric business practices, and a proliferation of new brands.

New Dynamics of an "Asset Lite" Environment

The divergence of ownership from operations that began in the early 1990s has now reached a pinnacle of success in our industry's evolution. We use the word success, because relieving company balance sheets of the capital intensity and related risk of being the owner of the asset remains a clearly stated objective by many major brands. The "asset lite" strategy and the evolution toward a fee-based model continue to accelerate for nearly all of the industry giants. Competing for franchise and management agreements and winning the battle of getting your brand name atop every new hotel in every market appear to be the benchmark and arguably the end game, albeit often to the dismay of owners encamped in already overbuilt markets. Additionally, there is heated competition to develop new brands within brands in an effort to target and win profitable new consumers (Millennials in particular), as evidenced by the seemingly endless barrage of annually announced new brands.

This dynamic shift, coupled with the continued popularity of sharing in the benefits of owning a sliver of real estate assets, has fueled the proliferation of REITs. As the major names shed assets and streamline balance sheets, their stock prices continue to move in a positive direction. Conversely, success continues for ownership groups as the deal market foments higher valuations, more transactions, and consistent dividends for investors looking for income. A key benefit to this divergence of owners and managers is a higher degree of leverage by owners in attaining management agreements that are more flexible and capital investment plans that have a more direct effect on the performance of individual hotels. When viewed with hindsight, many of the "legacy" management contracts that created encumbrances on properties for decades seem antiquated in their lopsidedness, favoring the managers' rights to a fault at times.

The current state of the industry, the owner plus manager scenario, seems to be a natural point in our industry's evolution. Professional asset management is a direct result and a critical component of that evolution, so it will continue to add further value to the equation in the future. As compared with other asset classes that generate a relatively predictable rate of return through long-term leases, it is important to understand and remember that hotels are ongoing business enterprises. As such, hotels are also where investors with a higher tolerance for risk often migrate. This differentiator poses a multitude of opportunities and risks for public company shareholders, private equity investors, and entrepreneurs who oftentimes decide to build a hotel in their hometown as a legacy to their success in some unrelated business. One can easily study decades of performance by the hotel industry and see that the business is extremely cyclical, often affected by major global and local events. The ability to maximize returns during upcycles through dynamic pricing, market share dominance, and yield management that is required in the hotel space is simply not in the DNA of many investors in other real estate asset classes.

Professional Asset Management Key to Increased Stakeholder Value

The asset manager was once the person who showed up periodically to drill through the P&L, take notes, and keep tabs on management. Before 1986, when the United States did away with the passive investment loss deduction, there was a clear lack of interest in improving that system. The owner/investor/asset manager often *was* the operator, with little or no compulsion or accountability to maintain the asset or optimize profitability.

To manage the myriad potential conflicts of interest between independent ownership and operator, today's professional asset manager needs a diversity of knowledge that includes, but is not limited to, operations, CapEx investment, sales and marketing, revenue management, social media and reputation analysis, and an understanding of real estate investment analysis to maximize short- and long-term returns. In today's environment, an "us versus them" relationship with the hotel brand or management company that is hired to operate a hotel or hotel portfolio is foolish. It will ultimately result in the unintended consequence of poor collaboration and less than optimal performance. Therefore, relationship building, clear communication, and negotiating skills are also extremely important aspects of the professional asset manager's toolkit.

Balancing the investment objectives, often tied to the projected hold period, for each type of ownership group is the charge and challenge of today's professional asset manager. Creating value for, and sharing in the financial success of, whichever ownership entity the asset manager represents is impossible without understanding the objectives and culture of the management company and brand associated with that asset. The professional asset manager will be fluent in the brand or brands of hotels in the portfolio and will participate in brand owner advisory councils, have ongoing communication with brand leaders, and continuously focus on initiatives that can have a financial effect on returns (positive and negative).

Recognizing that the profession of asset management is a key to the success of the hotel investment, the Certified Hotel Asset Manager (CHAM) designation was created through the collaborative efforts of HAMA (Hospitality Asset Managers Association), the American Hotel & Lodging Educational Institute (AH&LEI), and various members of academia. As in other professions (such as the CPA in accounting), rigorous experience standards, a deep knowledge base of the hotel industry, and successfully passing a comprehensive examination are required to secure the CHAM designation. As in other professions that offer certifications, designees have the ongoing responsibility of continuing education and industry participation to maintain their professional certifications.

Long-Term Value Creation Through Short-Term Opportunities

Hotels have the flexibility of great fluidity when it comes to price increases, which presents the opportunity to "yield manage" the revenue stream as market demand allows. This flexibility makes this asset class extremely popular with investors who are willing to take a measured degree of risk for above-average returns. The retail, industrial/office, and other real estate sectors that are primarily long-term lease driven cannot maximize pricing on a short-term basis (literally by the minute/hour/day) as hotels can when economic conditions become more optimal. Conversely, there are benefits to having a locked-in revenue stream during economic downturns, such as a leasing model provides. When demand begins to diminish, the hotel sector relatively quickly reflects the ebbing demand in occupancy, rate, or both, producing less profitable results. The successful hotel asset manager will have a strong understanding of this dynamic and its impact on his or her portfolio.

Controlling expenses and benchmarking efficiencies will always be a vital part of hotel asset management, but controlling expenses is a small part of a comprehensive asset management plan. Performance reviews cannot center solely on the P&L statement. There must be a strong focus and an abundance of energy and intellect dedicated to driving top-line revenue. The asset manager must have a deep knowledge of social media, e-commerce, direct sales strategies, and brand initiatives. The asset manager must ensure that all constituents (managers in particular) are focused and their hotel assets are positioned correctly. There are a multitude of tools available to measure not only financial success, but also market share, position, and social reputation across all media platforms. Additionally, capital investment must be prudent, designed either to enhance the hotel's current positioning or to move the asset to a more appropriate growth-oriented position.

CapEx Investment Strategies by Ownership Type

The degree to which CapEx funds are deployed and the timing thereof typically differ by ownership type. For example, CapEx decisions may directly affect the taxable income for individual partners in a limited or general partnership. CapEx funds deployed in the form of cyclical renovations, infrastructure upgrades, etc., within REIT hotel assets create a different dynamic, particularly given that REITs were created not as a legal entity, but rather a tax structure that pays no corporate taxes if a minimum of 90 percent of taxable income is redistributed back to shareholders. The following are some general nuances germane to a few of the more prevalent ownership structures related to the CapEx decision.

Partnerships. Of the three most common forms of partnership in the United States as described by the Internal Revenue Code (Limited Liability Company or LLC, Limited Partnership or LP, and General Partnership or GP), the LLC has become the most ubiquitous format. This is primarily due to the ease with which a person or persons desiring to have corporation-like protections can organize without the need to navigate the intricacies of corporate taxation. Although partnerships are not taxed, the various partners within the structure are individually taxed on income distributed by the partnership. Conversely, losses generated by the partnership become allocated losses to the partners. CapEx investment to hotels held within partnerships can have a direct effect on the performance and allocated income or losses to the partners. In a case where CapEx investments are made to the extent that the partnership realizes a loss, the partners may benefit from a taxation perspective. However, should the available cash flow of the business not be strong enough to fund the overall expenses of the enterprise outside of the CapEx funding, partners may need to provide incremental operating capital (a "cash call") to keep the hotel or hotels liquid. The buy, hold, or sell decision for hotels within these pass-through entities has a direct effect on whether the members are in it for the long term or plan to flip the asset or assets for short-term gains. Appropriate levels of CapEx reserves, subsidized by separate owner funding for major renovations and infrastructure needs, would be an appropriate strategy for a partnership planning to hold an asset or assets.

REITs. CapEx investment in the REIT world is in most cases a more straightforward process. As noted previously, REITs do not pay corporate taxes and distributions to shareholders are taxed individually as regular income. They do, however, incur a federal tax burden on capital gains from real estate transactions, unless the capital gains are distributed as well. From this perspective, additional owner investment in the form of CapEx would increase the basis of each hotel, thereby reducing future capital gains. Also, given that it is more common for a REIT to have a strategy of longer hold periods for core assets, a well-thought-out multi-year CapEx plan serves to ensure a quality portfolio. Short- and long-term planning for capital reserves and owner-provided capital funds would include, as an example:

- Brand initiatives.
- ROI projects such as adding keys, installing or redesigning a spa or restaurant, etc.

- Repositioning for enhanced ADR and market share, up to and including a PIP to move the asset to a higher-tiered brand.
- Major physical plant work (elevators, boilers, chillers, other HVAC, roof replacements, etc.).
- Normal wear and tear necessitating cyclical soft and case good replacements.

Most lodging REITs comprise multiple (in some cases hundreds of) assets. CapEx investments to the portfolio can often run into the tens of millions of dollars. A strict and deliberate process of deploying cash in the form of CapEx will mitigate "overspending" on an asset that has minimal chance of increasing in value or "missing the boat" on an opportunity to strategically allocate funds to maximize returns on an asset or assets within the portfolio.

C-Corporations. Specific differences in the CapEx methodology may be applied in the C-Corp environment, as protecting brand image tends to be a material consideration. This is admittedly both a necessity and good business. Marriott and Hilton present an interesting comparison in this regard. Hilton has a portfolio of owned, managed, and franchised hotels, whereas Marriott's move out of the real estate business created a new dynamic.

For brands with owned hotels as well as managed and franchised properties, there is a clearer path on the owned assets. CapEx planning for an owner-manager is an internal process often subjected to the same criteria used by third-party owners: current condition of property, competitive environment, and projected hold parameters. Large core assets that are strategic to the brand, usually within key markets throughout the world, often receive CapEx dollars intended to ensure that the hotel is a testament to the quality of that brand. In the case of third-party ownership, ownership interests and the investment horizon for individual hotels at times do not align with the brand's intentions. At the end of the day, it is simply a case of who has the checkbook and how much appetite the owner has for allocating funds to a particular hotel. In most cases where there is a strong alliance between an ownership group and the brand, a mutually acceptable CapEx plan can be agreed upon. In the rare case where the process seems likely to become contentious or litigious, often the franchise, management, or lender agreements contain language regarding such disputes.

In all cases of CapEx investment, it is important to reiterate that capital of all types, including human, cash, and time, will be wasted without detailed short- and long-term CapEx plans.

The Rise of Real Estate Investment Trusts

Over the past several decades, REITs have risen in public perception from relatively risky financial constructs to widely respected and highly regulated conduits for public participation in commercial real estate ownership. Advantages of the REIT structure for investors include strong liquidity, high current (dividend) yields relative to most stocks and mutual funds, and the avoidance of double taxation in most jurisdictions.

In the United States, to qualify for REIT status and avoid taxation at the parent entity level, corporations must comply with a number of strict rules, including but not limited to the following:

- Payout of at least 90 percent of taxable income as dividends.
- Ownership by 100 or more shareholders.
- Ownership of no more than 50 percent of shares by five or fewer individuals.
- At least 95 percent of income must be derived from "passive" financial investments, including rents, dividends, interest, and capital gains, as opposed to "active" income from business activities.
- At least 75 percent of income must be derived from real estate sources, including rents, mortgages, and capital gains on real estate.
- At least 75 percent of assets must be invested in real estate and cash.
- No more than 25 percent of assets may consist of non-qualifying securities of stock in taxable subsidiaries.

The last rule is of particular interest to lodging REITs as it touches on the requirement for REITs to maintain taxable REIT subsidiaries (TRS) to perform certain real estate-related services. The initial U.S. legislation in 1960 authorizing REITs prohibited them from providing virtually any services, but that prohibition was largely reversed under the REIT Modernization Act (RMA) of 1999, which took effect on January 1, 2001. Although lodging REITs are still required by law to lease the hotels they own to separate taxable entities that oversee operations, now hotel REITs can avoid the expense and hassle of coordinating leases with third-party companies, instead leasing their properties to operating companies that they own and control. Lodging REITs must still engage independent management companies to operate the hotels, but with the implementation of the RMA, lodging REITs could effectively perform asset management in-house.

REITs also typically report key financial metrics in a differentiated manner from other organizations. For example, REITs typically report: (1) Funds From Operations (FFO), which is a measure that reflects net income or loss (calculated in accordance with GAAP), excluding real estate depreciation and amortization, gains (losses) from sales of real estate, impairments of real estate assets, the cumulative effect of changes in accounting principles, and adjustments for unconsolidated partnerships and joint ventures; and (2) Adjusted Funds From Operations (AFFO), which is FFO adjusted for certain items such as hotel property acquisition and pursuit costs and other expenses that the company does not believe represent recurring operations. These are important metrics that allow investors to gain a better understanding of REIT performance without the impact of depreciation. Because these are also non-GAAP measures, different REITs may report these metrics differently, although most rely on the definition and guidance provided by the National Association of Real Estate Investment Trusts (NAREIT). These metrics are differentiated from earnings before interest, taxes, depreciation, and amortization (EBITDA) primarily by including the deduction of interest and taxes in their calculation.

As public REITs acquire new properties and reinvest in existing properties, these transactions are typically viewed by investors and Wall Street analysts with a view toward whether the transactions are "accretive" or "dilutive." Stated most simply, this can be both a pre- and post-investment analysis of whether the earnings per share (EPS) increases or decreases as a direct result of a particular transaction. Generally, an acquisition will be accretive when the price-earnings (P/E) ratio of the firm is greater than that of the target property and dilutive when the P/E ratio of the firm is less than that of the target property. Investors generally favor accretive transactions or slightly dilutive transactions that will become accretive within a short period of time.

Types of REITs

When referring to the REIT as an investment vehicle, it is important to understand some basic differences between the accessibility and liquidity of the most common types of REIT. First and foremost is the public equity REIT. Equity REITs can be either listed (primarily on the NYSE in the United States) or non-listed. In either case, they must be registered with the Securities and Exchange Commission (SEC). According to NAREIT, listed public equity REITs account for approximately 70 percent of all U.S. listed REIT assets. They offer the greatest level of liquidity, as shares of this type of REIT are traded on an exchange, but are also exposed to share-price fluctuations that add potential volatility. Exhibit 1 gives a breakdown of listed equity REITs by property sector.

Exhibit 1 Property Sectors for Listed Equity REITs

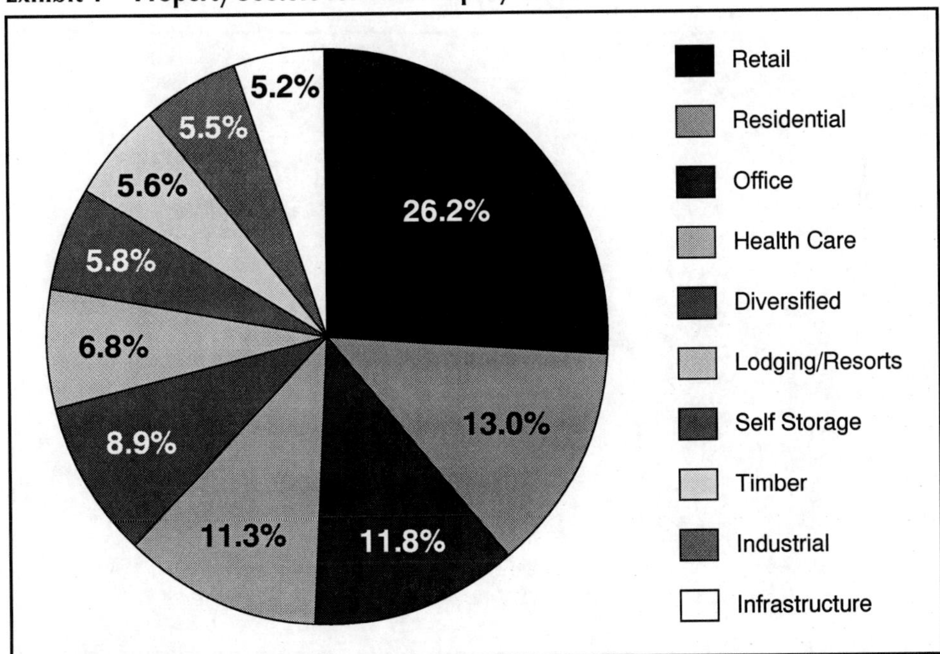

Source: NAREIT

Non-listed REITs, as well as privately held REITs, are less liquid by their nature. These investments are purchased primarily through the broker-dealer networks by individual investors who are primarily seeking income through dividends. Their share price has the potential to erode should the net asset value of the real estate held within the REIT decline, and shareholders may or may not have the opportunity to sell their shares at any given time.

Mortgage REITs are structurally the same as equity REITs, as relates to "listed/non-listed" and their requirement for conformance to the rules set out by the 1960 Act of Congress establishing today's REIT industry. As with equity REITs, they are required to regularly distribute the majority of their income to their shareholders. Mortgage REITs generate income from the interest earned on mortgages and mortgage-backed securities held in the REIT.

In this chapter, our focus is primarily on equity REITs. In particular, where does lodging as an asset class fit into the universe of this REIT type?

The REIT as an Investment: Follow the Money

As of 2015, REITs are solidly established and widely accepted as an excellent addition to a diversified investment portfolio. According to NAREIT, equity and mortgage REITs currently own more than $1.7 trillion dollars of debt and equity. Forty million Americans currently own REIT shares through pension and self-directed retirement plans such as IRAs and 401(k)s. More than 300 REITs are registered with the SEC. Listed REITs paid out approximately $34 billion in dividends in 2013. Exhibit 2 demonstrates the accretive nature of adding REITs to a portfolio strictly

Exhibit 2 Accretive Nature of Adding REITs

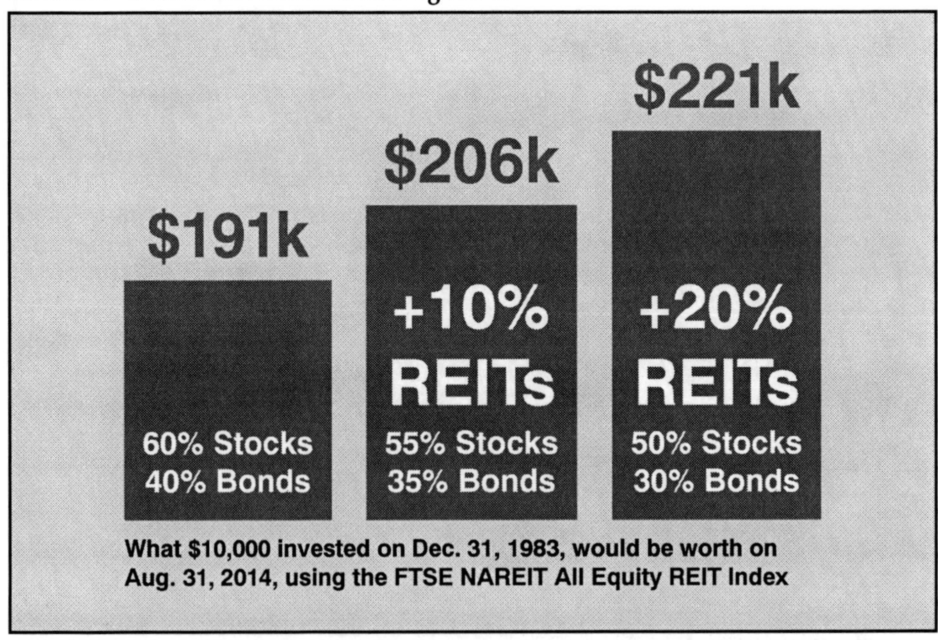

composed of stocks and bonds. According to NAREIT and SNL Financial, over the twenty-year period ending with 2013, U.S.-listed equity REITs delivered an annual average return of 11.16 percent, while the S&P returned 8.22 percent over the same period. As pertains to the recovery that began in early 2009, NAREIT also reports that U.S. equity REITs have returned 28.3 percent annually on average, as compared to 23.6 percent for the S&P 500.

For the individual investor, there are many ways to invest in REITs. More than 50 percent of the listed equity REITs are owned by mutual funds or exchange traded funds (ETFs). Investors can slice and dice the wide spectrum of offerings by region or sector (timberland or hotels, healthcare or self-storage, etc.) in order to achieve a customized portfolio of real estate holdings with the desired risk profile and product/geographical diversification. Listed shares can be purchased in the same manner that stock shares can be acquired. They may also be bundled into a low-fee ETF or mutual funds. One additional benefit to adding in REITs to a diversified portfolio is to create a hedge against inflation. According to SNL Financial as reported on REIT.com, the annual dividend growth rate of listed equity REITs exceeded inflation (measured by CPI) in eighteen of the past twenty years. For these and other reasons, it is easy to see why the popularity of REITs as an additional investment strategy continues to grow.

Lodging REITs Versus C-Corporations

As of December 2014, the SNL US EQUITY REIT Index contained 166 companies with a market cap on traded equity of $805 billion. The fifteen listed hotel REITs represented at that time had a market value of $54.4 billion, with Host Hotels & Resorts (HST) holding nearly a third of that value at $17.6 billion. Exhibit 3 shows their values as of February 17, 2015 (by which time there were seventeen). Another $83 billion in market capitalization is represented by Marriott, Hyatt, Hilton, and a variety of other publicly traded hotel industry companies. All ten of these are listed on the NYSE, except for Morgans Hotel Group (MHGC) and Marriott International, Inc. (MAR), which are both listed on the NASDAQ. Hilton and Marriott led the pack, at $25 billion and $22 billion in market capitalization, respectively.

Since 2009, the lodging/resorts sector has delivered large double digit returns in four of five years. This compares favorably with other property sectors (industrial/office, retail, residential, diversified, healthcare, and self-storage). Each REIT sector has inherent volatility, especially on a cyclical basis. Lodging REITs in particular may be hurt by interest rate fluctuations, as well as availability and cost of capital for acquisitions. Lodging REITs contain physical assets (hotels primarily) that are vulnerable to general real estate market influences. Portfolios and individual hotels that were acquired during market peaks at cap rates accretive to the overall portfolio valuation become dilutive in nature as NOI decreases during a down cycle.

The Globalization of the REIT Industry

For many of the same reasons that REITs have become vastly popular in the United States, so too have they continued to expand throughout developed and emerging markets. As of June 30, 2014, exchange-listed REITs and real estate

Exhibit 3 REIT Values as of 2/17/2015

Company	Trading Symbol	Type	Market Cap ($M)	Current Price ($)
Ashford Hospitality Prime Inc.	AHP	Hotel	415.9	17.14
Ashford Hospitality Trust	AHT	Full Service Hotel	1,076.2	10.75
Chatham Lodging Trust	CLDT	Hotel	1,176.0	30.74
Chesapeake Lodging Trust	CHSP	Full Service Hotel	2,028.9	36.97
DiamondRock Hospitality Co.	DRH	Hotel	2,841.8	14.52
FelCor Lodging Trust Inc.	FCH	Full Service Hotel	1,364.7	10.98
Hersha Hospitality Trust	HT	Limited Service Hotel	1,290.4	6.49
Hospitality Properties Trust	HPT	Limited Service Hotel	4,829.7	32.22
Host Hotels & Resorts	HST	Full Service Hotel	17,791.5	23.54
LaSalle Hotel Properties	LHO	Full Service Hotel	4,690.4	41.54
Pebblebrook Hotel Trust	PEB	Hotel	3,541.9	49.50
RLJ Lodging Trust	RLJ	Full Service Hotel	4,428.1	33.54
Ryman Hospitality Properties	RHP	Full Service Hotel	2,970.4	58.22
SoTHERLY Hotels Inc.	SOHO	Full Service Hotel	77.5	7.33
Strategic Hotels & Resorts Inc	BEE	Full Service Hotel	3,646.4	13.27
Summit Hotel Properties Inc.	INN	Limited Service Hotel	1,173.0	13.64
Sunstone Hotel Investors Inc.	SHO	Full Service Hotel	3,658.8	17.63

Source: SNL Financial Market pricing as of 2/18/2015.

firms from forty-seven different countries were represented in the FTSE EPRA/NAREIT Global Real Estate Index. An additional 150 publicly traded REITs and real estate companies from sixteen different emerging markets are represented in the FTSE EPRA/NAREIT Emerging Market Index. Thirty-one countries have listed publicly traded REITs as of June 2014, according to NAREIT.

It is important to expand one's perspective beyond the borders of the United States in order to grasp the global scope of the influence and market value of REITs. NAREIT, based in Washington, D.C., works through several global partners to represent the interests of both U.S. and international REITs and property ownership groups that have holdings in the United States. NAREIT partners in Asia, Europe, Australia, and Canada form an alliance that represents the interests and gives voice to hundreds of real estate ownership entities owning trillions of dollars of property across the globe.

The Global Real Estate Index Series, a combined index of developed and emerging market funds with REIT and non-listed holdings, is a key tool used by investors, fund managers, and others. These indices were created by FTSE, a global indexing company, in conjunction with NAREIT and the European Public Real

Estate Association (EPRA). The EPRA "Global REIT Survey 2014" is a detailed compendium of public REIT rules for all countries currently hosting REITs. While many of the basic structural components are the same or similar to the U.S. model, there are nuances in many that can be researched further in the EPRA Report.

As mentioned earlier, diversified portfolios that included domestic U.S. REIT holdings produced higher returns over various spans of time. The same metric has been shown to be true of global listed real estate. A long-term analysis by Ibbotson and Associates (purchased by Morningstar in 2006) demonstrated that between 1990 and 2007 portfolios consisting of various asset classes that included a 20 percent mix of global real estate generated more than a percentage point higher returns than those that did not. Interestingly, the same study concluded that U.S. real estate should be one- to two-thirds of the global holdings.

Notable Capitalization Events by Two Different Lodging Enterprises

Generating investment capital through the public markets can clearly be seen as the preferred direction in the lodging industry. Whether the business is structured as a REIT or listed as a C-Corp, lodging executive teams continue to organize their corporate structure to satisfy the requirements and "look" of a public entity. There are a myriad of reasons for achieving a listing on a major exchange and a wide spectrum of possible results. In this section, we will take a look at two different lodging companies and their activities and performance. Our first case study is the Blackstone/Hilton transaction whereby Blackstone took a public C-Corp (Hilton Worldwide) private and ultimately created the most valuable public lodging company in the world. The second case study looks at the REIT Pebblebrook Hotel Trust (NYSE:PEB), which had its IPO in December of 2009.

Case Study 1: The Hilton Revival

When we reflect upon the history and evolution of the company that Conrad Hilton launched in 1919 by purchasing his first hotel in Cisco, Texas, it is no wonder that at some point an unwieldy giant would need to be tamed. From the time that the first Hilton Hotel opened in Dallas, Texas, in 1925 to late 2007 when Blackstone acquired Hilton for an eye-popping (even by today's standards) $26 billion (debt and equity), the enterprise had left a circuitous trail of acquisitions that looked like a quilt of different cultures and business practices strewn across the lodging landscape.

In 1999, for instance, when Hilton acquired Promus Hotel Corporation, there were four separate brands wrapped into that acquisition. Hampton Inns, which opened its first hotel in Memphis, Tennessee, in 1984, was originally part of Holiday Inn. Doubletree, another brand in the Promus family, had merged with Promus just two years earlier in 1997. Homewood Suites and Embassy Suites were two additional Promus brands acquired in the 1999 acquisition. Hilton Garden Inns, originally launched as CrestHill by Hilton in the 1980s, never took flight as a brand but came back strong in the 1990s after the change to its current name. There are now well over 500 Hilton Garden Inns open. In 1991, Hilton Grand Vacations dived head first into the time share space, which now accounts for about 17.5 percent of the company's revenue and 12 percent of its adjusted EBITDA.

At the time of Blackstone's acquisition of Hilton in 2007, along with the concurrent appointment of Christopher J. Nassetta as President and CEO, the direction was to streamline and reinvigorate the organization. There were certainly opportunities to incorporate efficiencies and cost savings within what amounted to many tentacles of business units dating back to the Promus acquisition of 1999. A "reawakening" of the core Hilton brand within the corporate and group segments, vis-à-vis its peer group was also in the mix of potential benefits. Unfortunately, neither Blackstone nor Hilton could foresee the turbulence in the lodging industry that followed. The years 2008 and 2009 brought no end of second-guessing of the wisdom of such a large and risky transaction by Blackstone. The inordinate amount of debt added to Hilton's balance sheet would need to be addressed in rapid fashion, and it was. The story of the challenges, strategies, and sheer tenacity of the constituencies involved here during the economic downturn should be studied by anyone in our industry who is involved in the long-term viability of lodging organizations and assets.

Hilton International, which had been sold in 1967, was reacquired in 2006, a move that looks prescient in hindsight, as today Hilton is the leader in international pipeline room development. At approximately 5 percent of the global market share of room inventory, Hilton is the leader of a highly diversified (and wide-open) international development landscape. According to MarketRealist (derived from Hilton filings), 17.9 percent of the rooms under development outside of the United States are Hilton brands, a figure that has continued to accelerate since the 2007 acquisition of Hilton by Blackstone. This focus on Asia Pacific, the Middle East and Africa, and Europe is critical to the long-term growth of Hilton Worldwide. This pipeline reflects the company's stated focus on not just evolving internationally, but rather on holding the dominant position in global market share.

In December 2013, Blackstone took a reinvented, streamlined, more profitable Hilton Worldwide back to the public markets in an IPO that, like their $26 billion 2007 acquisition, was a record for the lodging industry. The initial offering of 117.6 million shares opened at $20 per share, raising $2.35 billion. Blackstone's shares of the newly listed Hilton Worldwide were valued at around $15 billion, creating a paper profit of $8.5 billion on their $6.5 billion initial investment. As of this writing, HLT (NYSE) closed at above $28 per share. Additionally, by taking advantage of the hunger for iconic properties by international investors, in early 2015 Hilton also sold the Waldorf Astoria in New York City for $1.95 billion, immediately beginning negotiations on new acquisitions to recycle the proceeds and mitigate the tax burden from the Waldorf Astoria sale. See Exhibit 4 for a comparison of Hilton Worldwide's actual and estimated EBITDA.

Consider the following questions.

1. What effect did Hilton's acquisitions strategy through the 1990s have on the operation of the company in the early 2000s? How did this strategy affect the sale of the company in 2007?
2. Compare and contrast the operating and capital markets environments Hilton faced pre-2007 and post-2007.

Exhibit 4 Hilton Worldwide: EBITDA (Actual vs. Estimates)

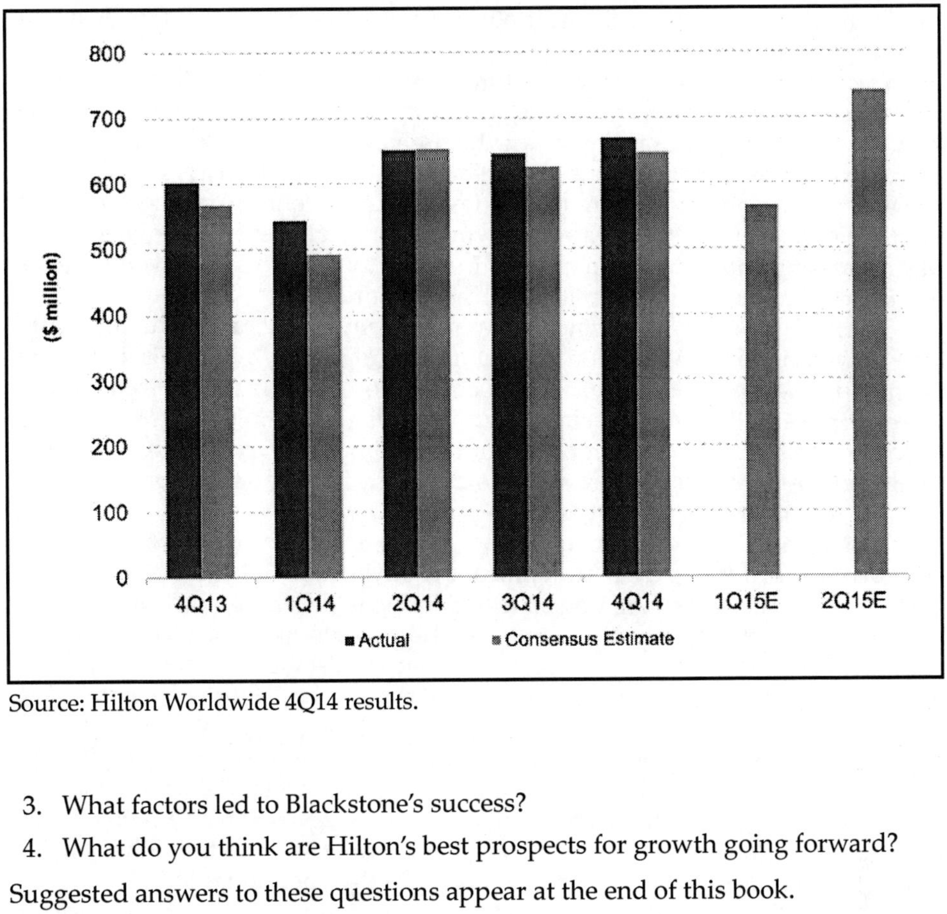

Source: Hilton Worldwide 4Q14 results.

3. What factors led to Blackstone's success?
4. What do you think are Hilton's best prospects for growth going forward?

Suggested answers to these questions appear at the end of this book.

Case Study 2: Pebblebrook Hotel Trust

After a very successful run as CEO of the company he founded, LaSalle Hotel Properties, from its IPO in 1998 until 2009, Jon E. Bortz decided to launch a new venture. The IPO of Pebblebrook Hotel Trust happened in December 2009. This transaction is unique in several ways and worthy of deeper study.

First and foremost, in 2009, the hotel industry was in a deep trough, having started its ugly descent in late 2007. The hotel REIT transactions that took place in 2006 and 2007 (capped by the CNL Hotels & Resorts sale for $6.6 billion in April of 2007) were executed at historically high valuations and unsustainable loan-to-value ratios fueled by the vaporous CMBS liquidity market. In any class of real estate, including residential, high valuations coupled with high LTVs always prove to be a recipe for disaster. It does not take much of a downdraft in property performance or market value to cause an implosion.

Between November 2008 and October 2009, the CMBS delinquency rate on hotels climbed from 0.5 percent to more than 8 percent. Between Q3 2008 and

Q4 2009, $5.25 billion dollars in CMBS loans above $25 million were outstanding, more than $4 billion transferring to special servicers. These loans contained over forty individual properties and nine hotel portfolios that were either upside down or in severe distress.

This was, of course, an excellent time to start a new fund with a mission to capitalize on the current state of the industry. Servicers and lenders would be thankful for the opportunity to divest themselves of toxic assets (better to start the hangover from untamed exuberance sooner rather than later). A selective purchaser would be able to acquire properties at high discount to replacement cost exactly where they saw the greatest growth potential. However, given that equity was decreasing and debt was nonexistent or unprofitably costly, it would take a special set of circumstances to pull off such a venture.

The deal Jon E. Bortz engineered was perfectly timed, and certainly could have only been done based upon the reputations of the key principals, including Raymond D. Martz. In December 2009, Pebblebrook Hotel Trust finalized its IPO. The enterprise held no assets, being basically a "blind" trust. There were no hotels to collateralize. In one of the most tumultuous times in our industry, *The Street* facilitated the startup of this new venture, primarily based upon the previous success and reputation of its principals.

Looking at the opportunity through a purely academic and market analytics lens, December 2009 was the perfect time for equity to jump into the fray. The existing lodging REITs were swimming in debt, EBITDA to debt ratios were horrendous, and singular asset values had plummeted. There would likely be plenty of prime assets available in key markets and segments that a well-funded owner of any structure might acquire. That was the goal of the PEB team as they launched their mission, fueled by a successful IPO and hindered by no legacy debt or balance sheet issues in building their new hotel portfolio. The objective was to acquire upper upscale properties in major U.S. cities and resort hotels located primarily in destination markets. Value would be extracted through an intense asset management plan, in conjunction with a diverse group of management companies that were hired through equitable contracts, which held them strictly accountable for their performance.

It is interesting now to look to the PEB investor presentation that was released in November 2014. In the five years since inception as an IPO, PEB seems to have achieved a number of key objectives:

- A high-quality diversified portfolio that includes thirty-one hotels (twenty-five wholly owned, fourteen of them unencumbered with debt, and six joint ventures)
- Twelve major urban markets; thirteen different operators
- 2014 adjusted EBITDA growth of 28–29 percent
- 2014 adjusted FFO per share growth of 26–28 percent
- Adjusted EBITDA per share growth from $1.62 in 2011 to $2.88 in 2014
- Between 2010 and 2014, 6,916 rooms acquired for $2.341 billion at an estimated discount to replacement value of 32 percent
- Enterprise value of $4.2 billion

Exhibit 5 clearly demonstrates the results of a plan of diversification both geographically and strategically (management expertise in the appropriate assets and locations).

Consider the following questions.

1. How important of a role does the founding CEO have in setting the tone and tenor of a company?
2. Looking at the capital markets landscape in the late 2000s, what are some of the factors (both pro and con) that you would consider in deciding whether or not to pursue a "blind" trust IPO?
3. Looking at the various performance metrics Pebblebrook has achieved through November of 2014, is there a particular metric or metrics that you think is most indicative of its success?
4. How important are geographic and operator diversification to a hotel REIT?

Suggested answers to these questions appear at the end of this book.

Conclusion

Between 2009 and 2013, the number of publicly traded lodging REITs (all exchanges combined) grew from thirteen to nineteen. FFO as a percentage of revenue has increased from 8.8 to 17.9 percent. From 2010 to 2013, FFO grew four consecutive years and finished 2013 at a peak 32.8 percent year-over-year growth. The overall Equity REIT Index tracked by SNL Financial has also experienced very strong growth, increasing from 117 listed companies in 2009 to 166 in 2013, reflecting double-digit FFO growth percentages over that four-year period. As the major

Exhibit 5 Geographic and Strategic Diversification

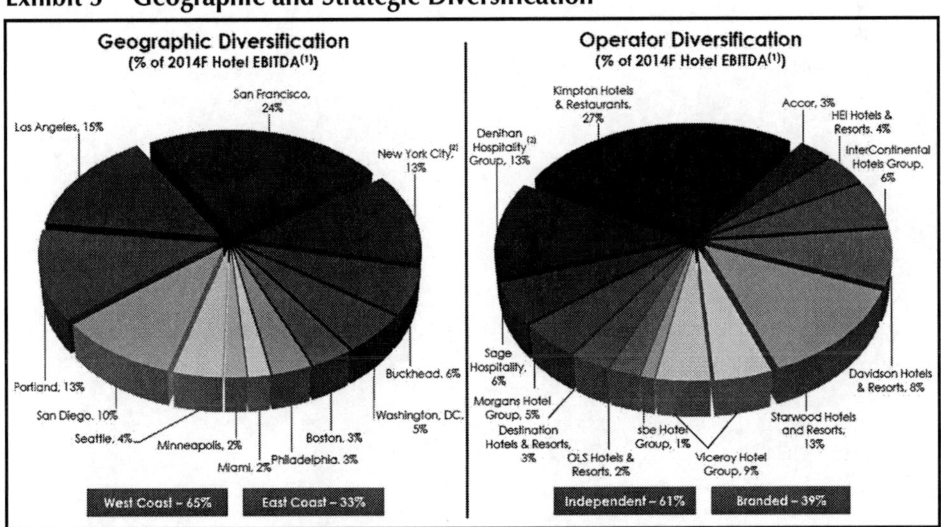

brand families continue to execute an asset-lite, fee-based model, it is highly probable that ownership of hotels will continue to transfer to REITs. This trend will further necessitate clearly defined ownership goals, coupled with brand "new-think" that will have the owner's interests supported within every decision and initiative. The role of a professional asset manager as the catalyst for maximizing results by orchestrating the performance of all constituencies will continue to become more critical in this evolving new environment.

19

Everything You Wanted to Know About Hospitality Valuation and Techniques, but Were Afraid to Ask

By Rachel J. Roginsky and Karen Johnson

***Rachel J. Roginsky, ISHC,** is the Owner and Principal of Pinnacle Advisory Group. She is based in the firm's Boston office. Ms. Roginsky has more than thirty years of experience in hospitality consulting. After graduating from Cornell School of Hotel Administration, she started her career in hospitality operations, then worked with the national accounting firm Pannell Kerr Forster, eventually becoming a Principal, overseeing the firm's Management Advisory Services practice in New England.*

In 1991, Ms. Roginsky founded Pinnacle Advisory Group. She provides operational, investment counseling, and advisory services to corporate, institutional, and individual hospitality clients concerning all facets of hospitality real estate. Additionally, Ms. Roginsky has participated in numerous litigation assignments, providing extensive experience for litigation support and expert testimony.

Ms. Roginsky is a board member of numerous hospitality-related organizations and societies, and is a regular guest lecturer at prestigious institutes of higher education. She is widely published and quoted and is the co-editor and an author of Hotel Investments: Issues and Perspectives, *a well-regarded book published by the American Hotel & Lodging Educational Institute. Ms. Roginsky is also certified as an arbitrator and mediator for Hospitality Alternative Dispute Resolution.*

***Karen Johnson,** MAI, CRE, ISHC, is President of Pinnacle Advisory Group West and supervises all of the consulting activities for that office. Ms. Johnson has been active as a hotel asset manager, consultant, and appraiser since 1981. Pinnacle is engaged in a wide range of hospitality consulting services. In 1998, Ms. Johnson led a survey of contract terms co-sponsored by HAMA that was later published in the* Cornell Hospitality Quarterly. *She was the author of the chapter on negotiating hotel management contracts in the Urban Land Institute's* Hotel Development Handbook. *Prior to opening the West Coast office of Pinnacle in 2011, Ms. Johnson was employed by Warnick + Company as a hotel asset manager and consultant. For more information on Ms. Johnson and Pinnacle Advisory Group, please visit Pinnacle's website at www.pinnacleadvisorygroup.com.*

WHEN WE WERE ASKED to write a chapter on hotel valuation, we looked at numerous industry publications that contained chapters or discussions prepared by hotel appraisers on hotel valuation techniques. We found that most of this literature was educational but dull, uninspiring, or not very practical. We also felt that most people who would read a book entitled *Hotel Asset Management: Principles & Practices* would already have a basic understanding of what a hotel appraisal is and would most certainly understand the basic concepts. We wanted this chapter on hotel valuation to be informative and useful for those individuals.

Over the past twenty-five years, our firm has prepared hundreds of hotel appraisals. As a result, we often receive phone calls from sophisticated hotel asset managers who ask questions, not about a specific appraisal, but about general issues they do not understand. Questions like: "How do you select a cap and discount rate?" or "I need an appraisal of a hotel, but I don't need one of those big reports; what can you suggest?" or "Do I need to hire an MAI, or can I hire a local appraiser who is state-certified, and what is the difference?" Given these types of questions and issues, we decided to write a valuation chapter that would be more practical and useful for hotel asset managers. The chapter first provides a basic framework for determining value. Second, it answers common questions that hotel asset managers have concerning hotel appraisals. Finally, the Chapter Appendix presents a glossary of some key appraisal terms.

The Basics: The Three Approaches to Value

Valuation is like a three-legged stool crafted from the income capitalization approach, the sales comparison approach, and the cost approach. Appraisals should *consider* all three approaches when estimating market value. However, the appraiser should also take into account the inherent strengths of each approach to determine which approach or approaches provide the most support for the value estimates. Unless a hotel is being bought to be operated as a religious retreat or for some other alternate use, the typical purchaser of a hotel will inevitably employ some variety of income analysis. As such, the income capitalization approach is typically well-suited for mirroring investor rationales across a wide spectrum of behaviors and is often the most heavily weighted approach in a hotel appraisal.

The Income Capitalization Approach

The Dictionary of Real Estate Appraisal defines the income capitalization approach as "a set of procedures through which an appraiser derives a value indication for an income-producing property by converting its anticipated benefits (cash flow and reversion) into property value." The most common income capitalization techniques are the capitalization of a single year's net operating income (a "direct cap") and a discounted cash flow analysis ("DCF") that reflects a specified income pattern, return on investment, and change in the value of the investment.

Hotels rent for twenty-four-hour periods. Even using a direct cap, the appraiser should conduct a comprehensive market supply-and-demand analysis to understand that dynamic and to pick a capitalization rate that reflects the pattern of trending and/or market risk. The DCF analysis requires forecasting both revenues and expenses for the subject property using a fixed and variable projection model. The projections of net operating income (NOI) are then converted into an indication of market value through discounting (to reflect the time value of money) and an assumed sale at the end of a holding period, employing a capitalization technique applied to the last year of the cash flow.

The Sales Comparison Approach

The sales comparison approach helps an appraiser come up with a value for a hotel through comparing the sales of similar properties to the subject hotel, with adjustments made for the differences among the properties, including location, quality, size, age, condition, income producing potential, and overall market appeal. This approach is driven by the economic principle of substitution, whereby no investor would pay more for the subject property than it would cost him or her to buy another hotel with similar income characteristics and functional utility.

During the sales comparison approach, local and regional hotel transactions are typically researched and analyzed. There are far fewer sales of hotels than houses, industrial buildings, or even office buildings. The appraisal industry has taken a position against the adjustment grids with percentage adjustments (called a quantitative analysis) unless the appraiser can produce an empirical analysis proving the percentage adjustment. The recommended analytical tool is a grid indicating whether the subject is better, the same as, or worse than the comparable—with no indication of percentage differentials. In many instances, the appraiser is unable to identify reasonably similar transactions or is unable to determine the income producing potential or the true buyer motivations. For these reasons, less emphasis may be placed on this approach to valuation.

The Cost Approach

The cost approach derives a value indication based on the cost to reproduce or replace the subject hotel's improvements. For a hotel that is even a few years old, or in a market in which supply and demand are out of balance, the cost approach must rely on an estimate of depreciation to produce a meaningful estimate of value. Depreciation is hard to empirically prove, so this becomes an exercise in circular logic that relies on the income or sales comparison approaches for the adjustments. The cost approach is most relevant in markets that are experiencing new construction, but is otherwise seldom employed by typical real estate investors when pricing properties. This means that the cost approach is not generally a meaningful indicator of value.

Appraisal theories have not undergone major changes over many years, and appraisal reports remain generally unchanged. The standards established by USPAP that guide the appraiser continue to provide the general framework within which a professional appraiser arrives at an estimate of value. What has changed is the complexity of the hotel industry and the ability of the appraiser to competently understand and estimate a value based on a myriad of variables. Understanding assumptions regarding hotel renovation costs, understanding economic downturns (or upturns) and their impact on hotel performance, pinpointing new supply, keeping abreast of the ever-evolving hotel brands, keeping track of the fixed and variable components of a financial projection, and analyzing the multitude of factors that influence risk rating a hotel are just a few factors that a hotel appraiser must consider. At the end of the day, a qualified appraiser can provide invaluable information to hotel managers, owners, investors, lenders, and hotel asset managers.

Common Appraisal Questions with Practical Answers

We asked HAMA members to submit questions they had regarding hotel appraisals, or questions covering appraisal issues they felt that other asset managers needed to know more about. The following are questions selected from those that they submitted, and our answers.

What are the three types of appraisal reports? Actually, effective January 1, 2014, there are only two appraisal report formats. The very long report (formerly called a "self-contained" report) was dropped in favor of a medium-size report that was formerly called a "summary" report. The new standard is called an "appraisal report," with the operative instructions being to summarize, summarize, and summarize. The short form alternative is a "restricted appraisal report" format, which can only be relied upon by the client of record. A restricted appraisal report may be as simple as a one-page statement of the value, with attached certifications, and assumptions and limiting conditions. The appraiser may not even feel compelled to attach cash flows, so if you want a very short report, make sure that you are clear on the supporting rationale you wish to see presented.

Is a feasibility study just an appraisal without a value conclusion? Even a fully developed feasibility study that compares probable value upon completion to the cost to complete is not as rigorous as an appraisal. Feasibility studies do not generally take into account sales or the market value of the land (versus the developer's basis in the land) or include a robust analysis to determine appropriate discount and capitalization rates. As such, the probable value upon completion in a feasibility study does not constitute an appraisal. The simpler market demand studies, which conclude at cash flows, are only a piece of the appraisal process—perhaps the most important part, but just a piece nonetheless.

How should you, the asset manager, prepare for an appraisal? The asset manager should gather all of the information that he or she would look at to price an asset and should be prepared to educate an appraiser on the local market. Many times, a generalist (appraiser) will respond to a bank's online bid system to complete the appraisal and may not be conversant on listings and pending transactions or even STR reports. The materials gathered should include an update of the hotel's year-end forecast, regardless of whether the appraiser asks for this. The asset manager should also provide the appraiser with sales leads, gossip on competitors or sales' PIP costs, brokers' names, etc. Finally, the asset manager should not put the appraiser in the presidential suite when the appraiser is inspecting the hotel—this could backfire on you.

Who at the property level should be involved in the process? This depends on how deep the organization is. At a large full-service hotel, the process involves an interview of roughly forty-five minutes each with the GM, DOS, and the controller. The chief engineer can lead the tour, since he or she is more likely to know the answers to questions about the age of the roof, the capacity of the domestic hot water heaters, and so on.

How do you intervene to educate an under-informed appraiser? Take a deep breath and gather the information that supports your point of view, such as sales, cap rates from other sales, PIPs associated with those sales, etc. Generalists might not understand how high the ratio of fixed costs in a hotel are and how quickly an NOI can double or triple. Give them lots of history to show past volatility, or show what happened at other hotels in your portfolio. If you have provided lots of information early on in the process, it should minimize the time spent trying to get an appraiser to change a number.

Why do appraisal firms request the terms of the purchase or sale of the subject property (including offers, options, and listings), terms required, price, date, financing, and a copy of the purchase and sale contract and the closing statement? This information tells the appraiser what the hotel sold for at a point in time; it does not tell the appraiser if the lender owns the hotel or what type of entity owns the hotel. First off, the Uniform Standards of Professional Appraisal Practice (USPAP) govern appraisals for any loan made with federally insured funds, and, under any circumstance, an MAI is compelled to abide by USPAP. USPAP compels an appraiser to report and analyze: (1) any sale of the subject property within the last three years, (2) any lapsed or pending sale, or (3) any current marketing efforts. Sales of the subject within that window under distressed circumstances or without the benefit of a professional marketing effort should be explained. The USPAP rule is to "analyze" and not merely to report. So do not waste any effort trying to withhold the information—explain it instead.

Provide non-binding letters of intent for the same reason. It is true that these agreements are not enforceable and may not be worth the paper they are written on, but virtually every consummated sale begins with a non-binding letter of intent. Accompany each letter with a short explanation of why you believe that transaction is or is not valid relative to the current circumstances.

The actual purchase and sale agreement might clear up some inconsistencies. For example, if a sale is predicated on retaining the seller as manager, it might explain what, in the context of the market sales, appears to be a low price. Likewise, if there is very favorable seller financing, it might explain what appears to be a high price. The reps and warranties section might alert an appraiser to an environmental issue, problematic title, or a pending legal decision that may have been factored into the price.

One last note: all appraised values are just estimates of value at a particular point in time. Unfortunately, there is no such thing as "intrinsic worth." Hotels have twenty-four-hour leases and practice highly dynamic pricing models. As of the writing of this book, the price of oil has fallen 50 percent over the previous six months. This has had a beneficial effect on the value of hotels in Hawaii (a long-haul destination, paid for with discretionary dollars) and a negative effect on hotels in oil-driven markets.

How do you develop growth rates for revenues? A well-thought-out appraisal will have forecast occupancy and ADR based on local market conditions. A competent hotel appraiser will have quantified the correlation between ancillary revenue items and increased or decreased occupancy. Expenses should be analyzed in the same manner and incorporated into a model that reflects fixed versus variable expenses. Pending changes should be considered (e.g., increases in wage rates, energy costs, etc.). In short, the income and expense forecasting process should be similar to, but less rigorous than, the annual budgeting process.

What is the basis for expense inflation rates? Why are they frequently listed at 3 percent growth? Is there historical data to support this? Inflation forecasts are consulted along with investor surveys to see what buyers are modeling for growth. Since the point of an appraisal is to mimic buyer behavior, appraisers aren't supposed to be "smarter than the market." Most buyers today are modeling increases in revenues and expenses that are above inflation rates.

Do appraisals factor in flow through or flex? The analysis within an appraisal *should* factor in flow through and flex. A competent hotel appraiser should understand fixed and variable ratios at the existing and projected occupancies. If you have doubts about the experience level of the appraiser, it wouldn't hurt to provide the appraiser with some of the recent studies on fixed and variable expenses. For example, Stephen Rushmore Jr. published research in 2012 that provides departmental estimates of fixed costs that range between 35 percent (food and beverage) and 52 percent (repairs and maintenance).[1]

Why do hotel appraisals show a ten-year cash flow forecast when, given the volatility of our industry, most investors look at the next five years? A five-year cash flow projection is probably a more intellectually honest approach, but doesn't match lender convention. Lenders expect ten-year projections and make the market for appraisers. The lender that rejected our trial five-year cash flow forecast told us that using shorter discounting periods made it difficult to benchmark discount rates and cap rates to the industry surveys. From the standpoint of theory, there is less risk estimating the reversionary value in five years than in ten years, so the discount and capitalization rates in a five-year DCF should be somewhat lower. If everything is properly calibrated, the value solutions should be the same. So, if you are using five-year projections and you are tempted to argue caps and discount rates with an appraiser working on a bank loan, think first about the risk differential between five years and ten years.

How do appraisers conclude on cap and discount rates? A savvy appraiser is estimating value both using a direct cap (based on one year's net operating income) and a discounted cash flow (DCF). It's important to understand that cap rates that are "extracted" from a comparable hotel sale may be wildly divergent from the metrics in a ten-year DCF, when everything has had time to stabilize. Those extracted rates belong in direct cap analyses, and not necessarily in DCFs.

When should you use a direct cap technique, and when should you do a DCF? A DCF is mandatory when there are likely to be changes in occupancy, real dollar growth, or expenses that escalate differently from inflation—for example, if a rent resets in year 4 or an incentive fee is likely to be earned in a latter year. Direct caps are perfectly adequate when the asset is fairly stable and the market is fairly stable. In a turnaround situation, they are pretty academic. The year selected in a direct cap can be historical or future. If the first year of the buyer's hold is capitalized, the rate used is called a "going-in" cap rate. Unless conditions are forecast to deteriorate, a going-in rate is generally higher than a rate applied to demonstrated historical net income. When you are talking about cap rates with a buyer or seller, it is important to confirm not just which year of income was used, but which expenses were deducted and whether the figure was calculated on the sales price only or the total investment (see Exhibit 1).

Cap rates from comparable sales should be recalculated after taking into account the planned renovation/PIP costs. Total investment value should be the base case from which the planned renovation is deducted.

"Low" cap rates imply substantial growth potential, especially when they are near or below the interest rate to be charged by the bank. Clearly, an investor does not anticipate a lower return than that of the lender. If someone "bought on a 5 cap," that purchaser believes that through market lift, repositioning, or asset management, they can dramatically increase the NOI. Either that or they want bragging rights or a really safe place to park money. So that 5 cap might be a good number to apply to the trailing-twelve-month income or even next year's income, but it probably isn't a good number to use as a terminal cap rate in a DCF going out ten years. What would that say about where commercial interest rates are anticipated to be?

What factors go into the decision? Trending and risk are the two most prominent factors to consider when selecting a cap or discount rate. Hotels that are

Exhibit 1 Illustration of Various Methods of Calculating and Quoting Cap Rates

	T-12	Year 1
Price Paid	$42,000,000	
PIP	$6,000,000	
Total Investment	$48,000,000	
Income before Management Fees & Reserves	$3,800,000	$5,000,000
Income before Reserve	$3,300,000	$4,400,000
Net Operating Income (Totally diluted income)	$2,800,000	$3,700,000
Cap Rates Quoted on Sales Price Only		
Buyer quoted Cap Rate (Income before mgt fees/reserves)	9.0%	11.9%
Wall Street Version of Cap Rate (Income before reserves)	7.9%	10.5%
Cap Rate on Net Operating Income	6.7%	8.8%
Cap Rates Quoted on Total Investment		
Buyer quoted Cap Rate (Income before mgt fees/reserves)	7.9%	10.4%
Wall Street Version of Cap Rate (Income before reserves)	6.9%	9.2%
Cap Rate on Sales Price Net Operating Income	5.8%	7.7%

showing consistent real growth or declines present different risk profiles. Where barriers to entry are high, cap rates are generally low. Hotels with clouds on their horizon (e.g., new supply entrants, local wage ordinances, etc.) will have higher cap rates to reflect the unknowns. Age is another important factor. A twenty-year-old hotel that will be thirty years old at the end of the cash flow period is due to have major mechanical systems replaced. It is important to note that all of the risk factors are embedded in a direct cap approach, but in a DCF, changes in occupancy, ADR, and costs of operation are discreetly modeled. Dialing occupancies down for new supply and then adding additional risk in the discount and terminal cap rates could be "double counting."

Does it depend on the type of interest being appraised? Absolutely, because of the different ways in which leasehold and fee simple interests affect ongoing operating risk and reversionary value. A ground rent payment is not usually subordinate to debt service, so there is, in effect, another investor in line ahead of both the bank and the hotel owner. A lender will be concerned about an investor's ability to refinance at the end of a mortgage. If there would only be a dozen years left on a ground lease at the end of a twenty-year term, it might not be possible for the next owner to refinance. Mortgages for leaseholds with relatively short remaining terms usually "hyper-amortize." Ground leases that have periodic wild-card rent adjustments to market value (sometimes with dueling appraisers) add risk. Finally, eternal cities such as London, New York, Paris, and Rome are perceived as very desirable places to own the land underneath an asset. Even condominium interests in a mixed-use development don't provide the latitude for heirs to redevelop a site that fee simple ownership permits.

Does a brand versus independent play a role? Yes, but brands can cut both ways. In the select-service property types, the ability to transfer a desired brand adds value to an asset (i.e., reduces the cap rate). However, as one moves up the quality spectrum, hotels are generally "worth more" (i.e., trade at lower caps) if they can be sold unencumbered. This affords a buyer the ability to change brands to better capitalize on market dynamics or to self-manage. Brokers hypothesize that a brand and management encumbrance can add fifty basis points to a cap rate. However, there are some hotel companies/brands that may buck this trend.

What reports should appraisals rely upon for cap rate and discount rate inputs? Capitalization rates to be applied to trailing-twelve-month and next year's income should be extracted from sales. A competent appraiser understands that those cap rates cannot be used interchangeably. The cap rates should be "totally diluted"—that is, after management fees and the reserve for replacement. There are frequently differences between cap rates and their obverse of multipliers because of the reserve for replacement. Cap rates deduct reserve for replacement; multipliers reported by publicly traded companies don't.

A great deal of information is available on cap rates in the REIT sales transactions disclosed in deal press releases, earnings calls, and investor presentations. Appraisers should be calling brokers, buyers, and sellers for the other information. If you get an appraisal in which the appraiser first estimated the NOI of a sale (based on industry norms) and then extracted a capitalization rate based on his or her own estimation, do the profession a favor and turn that appraiser in to Peer Review. Making up data to fill in all of the blanks in a table is not acceptable.

For the ten-year DCF analyses, the following sources may be useful:

- PwC (still referred to as "Korpacz")—published quarterly; provides national indicators (note that the hotel markets are covered in the first and third quarters only).
- CBRE/PKF (merged)—Hospitality Investment Survey, published annually.
- IRR Viewpoint—Published annually (based on prior-year data); provides both national and regional indicators.
- RERC—Published quarterly; provides both national and regional indicators.
- Realty Rates—Published quarterly; provides national indicators.
- USRC—Published in the summer and winter seasons; provides national indicators.

Should cap rate and discount rate inputs be sourced from regional reports, or are national figures adequate? For the ten-year DCFs, national reports are as good as it gets as long as the appraiser understands the relative risk profile of primary, secondary, and tertiary markets.

How do you land on capital needs for a hotel that does not have a long-term capital plan? And, to take this a step further, how do you deal with the underfunded nature of a reserve, since we all know 4 to 5 percent of revenue is insufficient? In a perfect world, your appraiser will specialize in hotels and will have knowledge of prevailing standards and renovation budgets. For example, the appraiser will know whether $30,000 per key is enough or merely a good start. Any diligent appraiser can gather information on planned renovations for each of the sales comparables and for the subject property's competitors.

Lenders require an "as is" value. The most common practice is to deduct a lump sum for the necessary near-term expenditures (necessary to achieve the cash flows projected) to arrive at the as is (i.e., net) value after concluding to the "as renovated" value. The industry norm typically requires a deduction of 4 percent of gross operating income as an FF&E reserve, unless the management contract calls for more. (Many contracts now step up to 5 percent reserve and stipulate that the reserve is to be used only for cosmetic items.)

Which leads us to the last part of the question: there is, in fact, a large body of evidence that indicates that 4 percent, or even 5 percent, is not adequate enough to sustain an asset over time. A savvy appraiser may increase the reserve to take into account the unknown but inevitable costs of maintaining a building envelope and its mechanical systems. However, that appraiser risks being "smarter than the market." The overriding consideration is to determine what the theoretical "prudent buyer" is doing. Right now, most appear to be content with a system whereby hotels undergo major renovations when they sell. It's one of the reasons that a terminal cap rate should be higher than a "stabilized" rate.

How relevant is replacement cost as a valuation methodology in markets where robust hotel income supports sale prices that are higher than replacement cost (e.g., Nashville currently)? There's an old adage that was discredited but will likely come back into vogue: "Excessive profits breed ruinous competition." Unless there are high barriers to entry or a very long lag time between the entrance of new competition, it is unwise to pay substantially more for an asset than its replacement cost plus a reasonable developer's profit. Yes, developers are entitled to make a profit for all of that risk; perhaps 15 or 20 percent.

How do you determine the reconciliation weighting that goes into the three approaches to value? The weighting is determined by the quality and relevance of the information going into each approach. If the sales were very comparable (competitors even) and the PIP information was available and credible, the sales comparison approach would be weighted more heavily than if the sales were in other cities/states or of older, lower-quality assets. In a foreclosure situation where there was no historical information, it may be the most reliable indicator of value. If the building is old, the cost approach may not be relevant at all.

Does this change based upon the economic cycle when the appraisal is being conducted, and, if so, why? Yes, when the market is over-supplied, the cost approach becomes less meaningful, even for a new building. In recessions, the pace of recovery is unknown. The sales comparison approach may be more reliable than the income approach.

When you consider how ownership of hotels has changed (for example, the growth of publicly traded REITs over the last 10–15 years), owners' willingness to accept lower returns (although they also seem to be buying prime assets), and the decline of insurance company ownership, how has this affected the way appraisals are perceived by owners and lenders? Said differently, has the use of appraisals changed over time? Market value is what prudent buyers will pay and knowledgeable sellers will accept at any given point in time. Asking an appraiser to determine how much an asset is worth versus what the "market value" of the asset is could yield two materially different answers. That is why in a competitive bid situation there are a range of bids. The high bidder, or the highest bidder with a track record of consummated transactions, wins a deal. The collective behavior of these bidders makes the market. Did that investor overpay? Only time will tell. Non-REIT investors did a great deal of handwringing in 2010 about the prices that REITs were paying for hotel assets, but 2010 turns out to have been a very smart time to buy.

If the pricing of a product is reflective of its perceived value, the public's perception of appraisals has deteriorated over time. The reports of the 1980s and 1990s had less historical trending information and a less rigorous analysis, but cost three times as much. We can only conclude that the transactional world regards standard bank appraisals as a compliance chore best addressed with a commodity product.

What proportion of hotel appraisers do you feel are completely objective and unswayed by their client's wishes/demands when they need more value? We wouldn't know and prefer not to think about it. There is a difference between an appraiser who reconsiders value based on new or better information and one who succumbs to pressure to submit a number that gets a deal done. The latter type of appraiser is committing an ethical breach.

What is the purpose of a "reliance letter?" It doesn't matter to an appraiser, since appraisers are prohibited from issuing reliance letters. The following question was taken from the Appraisal Institute's website:

> "Q7. Can I sign or issue a 'reliance letter' that says another party (not the identified in the report as the client or an intended user) can rely on a report I previously prepared?
>
> No. Such a letter would, in effect, add that party as an intended user after the completion of an assignment, and you cannot do that."

If a lender wants to rely on a document addressed to another lender, they may do so, but an appraiser has no (zero) liability to the second lender. Anyone who wants coverage from an appraiser's E&O policy must establish a new client relationship with that appraiser by receiving a new appraisal. The report may not be simply readdressed either. Also from the Appraisal Institute website:

> "Q4. Can I readdress a report, or change the name of the client, but otherwise give the same report to another client?
>
> No. It is improper to 'readdress' a report to another client for three significant reasons. First, simply changing the name of the client and then forwarding the 'readdressed' report to the second client does not change the first appraiser-client relationship. An appraiser-client relationship, once established, is cast in stone and cannot be changed. Typically, the reason the second party wants to be named as 'client' is that they want the appraiser-client relationship, and all the rights and obligations thereof, to be between *them* and the appraiser. The only way to accomplish this is for a new appraiser-client relationship to be established. In short, the only way to be named as 'client' in the report is to actually be a client. 'Client' is defined in the USPAP as the party (or parties) who engage an appraiser in a specific assignment."

To be named as the client in a report, one must have been the party who engaged the appraiser. A new contractual relationship must be established, and money should change hands. Think about it: that appraiser has just expanded his or her liability. The report must be re-dated and the prior assignment must be mentioned in the certification section of the report. Many appraisers insist on a new inspection or in updating some of the research.

Oftentimes the person who visits the property and writes the appraisal is a really young person fresh out of college, and then it is officially "reviewed" by an MAI; do you feel there are drawbacks to this process? Inexperienced people don't know what they don't know. Oftentimes, a comment will be made on a tour that opens a valuation issue or may explain the property's historical performance. (For example, the pool area and deck are not big enough at a resort hotel.) It is very dangerous to send neophytes out to do the only inspection of a property.

Do you think it makes a difference if an appraiser has significant experience in the hospitality industry when appraising hospitality assets? Hotels are the only form of real estate for which property taxes and insurance are minor operating expense items. Hotels are unique in that branding (in the form of franchise affiliations) is a major consideration in hotel appraisals. This is not a property type that should be dabbled in—so, yes, it does make a difference.

Summary

The questions presented in this chapter provide a good representation of all of the questions asked by surveyed HAMA members. Most asset managers believe that they know what an asset is worth; they talk to their colleagues, they read industry reports, they speak with buyers and sellers, and they understand the historical and projected income potential for the assets they are involved with. What we learned from our survey work is that most hotel asset managers have a reasonably good general grasp on appraisals, but they were less informed on the details. And frankly, the details can separate a good appraisal from a bad one.

Finally, while the opinions and methodologies expressed in this chapter represent standard practices, they are by no means universal, as each engagement presents its own set of unique facts and circumstances that may warrant a departure from such standard practices.

Please see the following Chapter Appendix for a glossary of some key appraisal terms.

Endnote

1. Stephen Rushmore Jr., "Time to Update Your Forecasting Models," *Lodging Hospitality*, July 2012.

Chapter Appendix

A Glossary of Key Appraisal Terms

The Dictionary of Real Estate Appraisal provides definitions for thousands of appraisal terms.* Listed below are a select number of terms that hotel asset managers should know and understand.

Absorption period: The actual or expected period required from the time a property is initially offered for lease, purchase, or use by its eventual users until all portions have been sold or stabilized occupancy has been achieved. Although marketing may begin before the completion of construction, most forecasters consider the absorption period to begin after the completion of construction.

Adjusted sale price: The figure produced when the transaction price of a comparable sale is adjusted for elements of comparison. When the appropriate sequence of adjustments is followed, several intermediate adjusted sale prices are calculated and used as the basis for subsequent adjustments.

Ad valorem tax: A tax levied in proportion to the value of the property being taxed.

Appraisal report: The written or oral communication of an appraisal; the document transmitted to the client upon completion of an appraisal assignment. Report requirements are set forth in the standards rules in Standard 2 of the Uniform Standards of Professional Appraisal Practice.

Assessed value (taxable value): A value set on real estate and personal property by a government as a basis for levying taxes.

Assessment ratio: The fractional relationship as assessed value bears to the market value of the property in question.

Band of investment: A technique in which the capitalization rates attributable to components of a capital investment are weighted and combined to derive a weighted-average rate attributable to the total investment.

Capitalization rate: Any rate used to convert income into value.

Cash on cash: The ratio of annual equity income to the equity investment; also called equity capitalization rate, cash flow rate, or equity dividend rate.

Conditions of sale: An element of comparison in the sales comparison approach; comparable properties can be adjusted for differences in the motivations of either the buyer or a seller in a transaction, e.g., when the comparable transaction is not an arm's length sale.

Definition of value: A written statement specifying the type of value to be estimated; must be included and/or referenced in every appraisal report.

---

* Source: Adapted from *The Dictionary of Real Estate Appraisal,* Sixth Edition (Chicago, Ill.: Appraisal Institute, 2015); ©2016 Reprinted with permission from the Appraisal Institute, Chicago, Illinois. All Rights Reserved.

Departure/rule: Specific requirements of the Uniform Standards of Professional Appraisal Practice that apply to an appraiser who performs an assignment that calls for something less than, or different from, the work that would otherwise be required. The appraiser must: (1) determine that the departure would not render the results of the assignment no longer credible; (2) advise the client that the assignment is less than, or different from, the work required by the specific guidelines, and that the resulting report will clearly identify and explain the departure(s); and (3) come to an agreement with the client that the performance of a limited appraisal service would be appropriate, given the intended use.

Direct capitalization: A method used to convert an estimate of a single year's income expectancy into an indication of value in one direct step, either by dividing the income estimate by an appropriate rate or by multiplying the income estimate by an appropriate factor.

Disposition value: The most probable price that a specified interest in real property is likely to bring under all of the following conditions:

a. Consummation of a sale will occur within a limited future marketing period specified by the client.
b. The actual market conditions currently prevailing are those to which the appraised property interest is subject.
c. The buyer and seller is each acting prudently and knowledgeably.
d. The seller is under compulsion to sell.
e. The buyer is typically motivated.
f. Both parties are acting in what they consider their best interests.
g. An adequate marketing effort will be made in the limited time allowed for the completion of a sale.
h. Payment will be made in cash in U.S. dollars or in terms of financial arrangements comparable thereto.
i. The price represents the normal consideration for the property sold, unaffected by special or creative financing or sales concessions granted by anyone with the sale.

This definition can also be modified to provide valuation with specific financing terms.

Easement: An interest in real property that conveys use, but not ownership, of a portion of an owner's property. Access or right of way easements may be acquired by private parties or public utilities. Governments dedicate conservation, open space, and preservation easements.

Economic life: The period over which improvements to real property contribute to property value.

Effective age: The age of property that is based on the amount of observed deterioration and obsolescence it has sustained, which may be different from its chronological age. (USPAP, 2002 ed.)

Entrepreneurial profit: A market-derived figure that represents the amount an entrepreneur receives for his or her contribution to a project and risk; the difference between the total cost of a property (cost of development) and its market value (property value after completion), which represents the entrepreneur's compensation for the risk and expertise associated with the development. In economics, the actual return on successful management practices, often identified with coordination, the fourth factor of production following land, labor, and capital; also called entrepreneurial return or entrepreneurial reward.

Excess land: In regard to an improved site, the land not needed to serve or support the existing improvement. In regard to a vacant site or a site considered as though vacant, the land not needed to accommodate the site's primary highest and best use. Such land may be separated from the larger site and have its own highest and best use, or it may allow for future expansion of the existing or anticipated improvement.

Exposure time:

a. The time a property remains on the market.

b. The estimated length of time the property interest being appraised would have been offered on the market prior to the hypothetical consummation of a sale at market value on the effective date of the appraisal; a retrospective estimate based on an analysis of past events, assuming a competitive and open market. Exposure time is always assumed to occur prior to the effective date of the appraisal. The overall concept of reasonable exposure encompasses not only adequate, sufficient, and reasonable time, but adequate, sufficient, and reasonable effort. Exposure time is different for various types of real estate and value ranges under various market conditions. (Appraisal Standards Board of The Appraisal Foundation, Statement on Appraisal Standards No. 6, "Reasonable Exposure Time in Real Property and Personal Property Market Value Opinions.") Market Value estimates imply that an adequate marketing effort and reasonable time for exposure occurred prior to the effective date of the appraisal. In the case of disposition value, the time frame allowed for marketing is somewhat limited, but the marketing effort is orderly and adequate. With liquidation value, the time frame for marketing the property rights is so severely limited that an adequate marketing program cannot be implemented. (The Report of the Appraisal Institute Special Task Force on Value Definitions qualifies exposure time in terms of the three above-mentioned values.)

External obsolescence: An element of depreciation; a defect, usually caused by negative influences outside a site and generally incurable on the part of the owner, landlord, or tenant.

Feasibility analysis:

a. A study of the cost-benefit relationship of an economic endeavor. (USPAP, 2002 ed.)

b. An analysis undertaken to investigate whether a project will fulfill the objectives of the investor. The profitability of a specific real estate project is analyzed in terms of the criteria of a specific market or investor.

c. Often interchangeable with investment analysis. Both studies forecast property revenues and expenses. Feasibility analysis is more often undertaken as part of a highest and best use study for a proposed property use. Also called highest and best use study, economic feasibility study, or financial projection study.

Fee simple estate: Absolute ownership unencumbered by any other interest or estate, subject only to the limitations imposed by the governmental powers of taxation, eminent domain, police power, and escheat.

Functional obsolescence: An element of depreciation resulting from deficiencies or super adequacies in the structure.

Going concern value:

a. The market value of all the tangible and intangible assets of an established and operating business with an indefinite life, as if sold in aggregate; also called value of the going concern.
b. Tangible and intangible elements of value in a business enterprise resulting from factors such as having a trained work force, an operational plant, and the necessary licenses, systems, and procedures in place.
c. The value of an operating business enterprise. Goodwill may be separately measured but is an integral component of going concern value. (USPAP, 2002 ed.)

Going-in capitalization rate: The overall capitalization rate obtained by dividing a property's net operating income for the first year after purchase by the present value of the property.

Highest and best use: The reasonably probable and legal use of vacant land or an improved property, which is physically possible, appropriately supported, financially feasible, and that results in the highest value. The four criteria the highest and best use must meet are legal permissibility, physical possibility, financial feasibility, and maximum productivity.

Hypothetical condition: That which is contrary to what exists but is supposed for the purpose of analysis. Hypothetical conditions assume conditions contrary to known facts about physical, legal, or economic characteristics of the subject property; or about conditions external to the property such as market conditions or trends; or about the integrity of data used in analysis. A hypothetical condition may be used in an assignment only if:

a. Use of the hypothetical condition is clearly required for legal purposes, for purposes of reasonable analysis, or for purposes of comparison;
b. Use of the hypothetical condition results in a credible analysis; and
c. The appraiser complies with the disclosure requirements set forth in USPAP for hypothetical conditions. (USPAP 2002 ed.)

Insurable value:

a. The value of an asset or asset group that is covered by an insurance policy; can be estimated by deducting costs of non-insurable items (e.g., land value) from market value.

b. Value used by insurance companies as the basis for insurance. Often considered to be replacement or reproduction cost plus allowances for debris removal or demolition less deterioration and non-insurable items. Sometimes cash value or market value, but often entirely a cost concept. (Marshall and Swift LP)

Intangible value: A value that cannot be imputed to any part of the physical property, e.g., the excess value attributable to a favorable lease or mortgage, or the value attributable to goodwill.

Intended use: The use or uses of an appraiser's reported appraisal, appraisal review, or appraisal consulting assignment opinions and conclusions, as identified by the appraiser based on communication with the client at the time of the assignments. (USPAP, 2002 ed.)

Internal rate of return (IRR): The annualized yield rate or rate of return on capital that is generated or capable of being generated within an investment or portfolio over a period of ownership. The IRR is the rate of discount that makes the net present value of the investment equal to zero. The IRR discounts all returns from the investment, including returns from its reversion, to equal the original capital outlay. This rate is similar to the equity yield rate. As a measure of investment performance, the IRR is the rate of discount that produces a profitability index of one and a net present value of zero. It may be used to measure profitability after taxes (i.e., the after-tax equity yield rate).

Investment value: The specific value of an investment to a particular investor or class of investors based on individual investment requirements; distinguished from market value, which is impersonal and detached.

Land utilization and marketability study: An analysis of the potential uses of a parcel of land that is to be acquired in an urban renewal project; considers the entire market to be served and the effect of the project on the area; used to determine what the highest and best use of the land will be when the development project is completed.

Leased fee interest: An ownership interest held by a landlord with the rights of use and occupancy conveyed by lease to others. The rights of the lessor (the leased fee owner) and the lessee are specified by contract terms contained within the lease.

Leasehold improvements: Improvements or additions to leased property that have been made by the lessee.

Leasehold interest: The interest held by the lessee (the tenant or renter) through a lease transferring the rights of use and occupancy for a stated term under certain conditions.

Legally nonconforming use: A use that was lawfully established and maintained, but no longer conforms to the use regulations of the current zoning in the zone where it is located.

Liquidation value: The most probable price that a specific interest in real property is likely to bring under all of the following conditions:

a. Consummation of a sale will occur within a severely limited future marketing period specified by the client.
b. The actual market conditions currently prevailing are those to which the appraised property interest is subject.
c. The buyer is acting prudently and knowledgeably.
d. The seller is under extreme compulsion to sell.
e. The buyer is typically motivated.
f. The buyer is acting in what he or she considers his or her best interest.
g. A limited marketing effort and time will be allowed for the completion of a sale.
h. Payment will be made in cash in U.S. dollars or in terms of financial arrangements comparable thereto.
i. The price represents the normal consideration for the property sold, unaffected by special or creative financing or sales concessions granted by anyone associated with the sale.

This definition can be modified to provide for valuation with specified financing terms.

Loan to value ratio: The ratio between a mortgage loan and the value of the property pledged as security, usually expressed as a percentage; also called loan ratio.

Overall capitalization rate: An income rate for a total real property interest that reflects the relationship between a single year's net operating income expectancy and the total property price or value; used to convert net operating income into an indication of overall property value.

Personal property: Identifiable tangible objects that are considered by the general public as being "personal," for example, furnishings, artwork, antiques, gems and jewelry, collectibles, machinery, and equipment; all tangible property that is not classified as real estate. (USPAP, 2002 ed.)

Prospective value opinion: A forecast of the value expected at a specified future date. A prospective value opinion is most frequently sought in connection with real estate projects that are proposed, under construction, or under conversion to a new use, or those that have not achieved sellout or a stabilized level of long-term occupancy at the time the appraisal report is written.

Stabilized value:

a. A value opinion that excludes from consideration any abnormal relationship between supply and demand, such as is experienced in boom periods, when cost and sale price may exceed the long-term value; or during periods of depression, when cost and sale price may fall short of long-term value.
b. A value opinion that excludes from consideration any transitory condition that may cause excessive construction costs (e.g., a bonus or premium for material, the abnormal inefficiency of labor, the cost of delay) or an excessive sale price (e.g., a premium paid due to a temporary shortage of supply).

Terminal capitalization rate: The rate used to convert income (e.g., NOI, cash flow) into an indication of the anticipated value of the subject real property at the end of an actual or anticipated holding period. The terminal capitalization rate is used to estimate the resale value of the property.

Uniform Standards of Professional Appraisal Practice (USPAP): Current standards of the appraisal profession, developed for appraisers and the users of appraisal services by the Appraisal Standards Board of the Appraisal Foundation. The Uniform Standards set forth the procedures to be followed in developing an appraisal, analysis, or opinion; and the manner in which an appraisal, analysis, or opinion is communicated. The Uniform Standards are endorsed by the Appraisal Institute and by other professional appraisal organizations.

20

The Hotel Investment Decision: Buy, Hold, and Sell Analyses

By Richard E. Musgrove

***Richard E. Musgrove,** CHAM, CHA, CPM, CCIM, RPA, is a thirty-year veteran and active investor in the hospitality and commercial real estate industries. His background includes senior leadership positions with investment advisory firms Hotel Asset Value Enhancement and Chartres Lodging Group, as well as public real estate investment trust Ashford Hospitality Trust, where he created the REITs asset management department while overseeing growth from a twelve-property portfolio to 120 properties within a three-year period. His additional asset management experience includes positions overseeing multiple classes of real estate with Host Marriott Corporation, The Estate of James Campbell, and the Trammell Crow Company.*

Mr. Musgrove is a long-time member of the Hospitality Asset Managers Association, through which he was instrumental in driving the creation of the Certified Hotel Asset Manager (CHAM) certification to recognize the preeminent practitioners of asset management within the hospitality space. He was the inaugural chairman of the CHAM Advisory Panel overseeing the designation program and was among the initial group of six individuals to obtain the certification.

Mr. Musgrove earned a Bachelor of Science degree from Cornell University's School of Hotel Administration and an MBA with a concentration in finance from the University of Chicago's Graduate School of Business. He holds numerous professional certifications, including the Certified Property Manager designation through the Institute of Real Estate Management, the Certified Hotel Administrator designation from the American Hotel & Lodging Educational Institute, the Commercial Investment Real Estate Member designation from the CCIM Institute, and the Real Property Administrator designation from the BOMI Institute. He is also a licensed real estate broker in Texas.

As a recent alumnus from a premier hospitality school graduate program, Bob was excited about his new position in asset management with growing private equity firm LOL Capital. With an undergraduate degree in accounting and several years of hotel feasibility experience, he was confident that his background was particularly well-suited for the financial orientation of his new post. When his initial portfolio assignment included a 600-room upper-upscale hotel near Times Square in midtown

Manhattan that was recently purchased for $250 million, he was thrilled with the idea of being responsible for such a high-profile asset.

At his second anniversary on the job, Bob was rethinking his initial assessment. The hotel's performance had failed to achieve pro forma, and the gap was growing wider by the month. The collective bargaining agreement for the majority of employees was set to expire soon, and the union was threatening to strike without major increases in wages and health benefits. Despite overall improvement in the economy and increased foot traffic in the neighborhood, cover counts had declined at both ground floor restaurants. New supply continued to pop up throughout the market, occupancy was on a steady decline, and Bob feared that things could get much worse before they started getting better. Reluctantly, he convinced the senior management of LOL to put his prize asset on the block. Within three months, the hotel was purchased by Great White Partners for $270 million, and Lou was just glad LOL had found a "greater fool."

Two years later, while skimming a trade periodical, Bob read that Great White had sold his former property to Urban Life Insurance Company and a local commercial real estate developer for $450 million. Bob was floored. How could he have been so far off-base? He had been through the numbers backwards and forwards. What did Great White know that he had not?

As he dug further into the article, Bob read that Great White had invested $50 million to bifurcate the hotel into complexed upscale brands, a move that would allow the property to maintain rates by significantly improving revenue management across all segments while also improving operating margins. Great White had also converted the project to a condominium structure, which had allowed separate ownership of the first floor for high-rent retail use and had facilitated a long-term lease of the building's façade for electronic signage. In short, the new owner had not based its purchase decision on what the hotel was; it had identified beforehand what the asset could and should become.

AVOIDING BOB'S EARLY-CAREER GAFFE is not a matter of luck or clairvoyance, but careful analysis. This chapter will discuss the investment-decision process for hotel owners. Although the universe of factors to consider in evaluating whether to invest in an asset could fill multiple volumes, the following pages will establish the basic framework for thoughtful evaluation.

The Hotel Acquisition Decision

Investors in real estate are motivated by a variety of factors. The benefits of owning hotel assets may include any or all of the following:

- Positive cash flow from operations
- Deferred taxation, providing enhanced cash flow
- Hedges against inflation
- Appreciation in property value
- Diversification from other investments offering different risk profiles

- The ability to apply positive leverage, enhancing equity returns
- Foreign residency benefits, resulting from job creation credits
- Psychological benefits (i.e., pride in owning a distinctive physical asset)

The first step in making any investment decision is establishing goals and objectives for that investment. In the case of hotel investments, determining the most appropriate path of ownership—developing new hotels, acquiring existing hotels of various performance profiles (e.g., stabilized, underperforming, renovation candidates), or converting buildings from other uses—is just one element an investor must contemplate. Capital availability or constraints, risk tolerance, cost of capital/required return, and the anticipated hold period for the investment must be established at the outset as well.

Once an investor has answered these questions, an exit strategy and acquisition criteria should be constructed. For a long-term investor, valuations at appropriate intervals may be prudent to ensure that returns are on target. For short-term investments, selling the asset at the targeted price is critical in generating the desired return. Faced with a shorter time window and greater volatility, investors with shorter intended holding periods must recognize that their exit strategy is just as important as their entry strategy. Investment discipline is the key to meeting acquisition goals and objectives. To this end, the critical factors of time window and viable acquirers, which are invariably linked, must be carefully studied and set before the acquisition trigger is pulled.

Acquisition criteria may vary widely among investors, but the common element is that the criteria should support the achievement of ownership's goals and objectives. Considerations include targeted hotel type (full-service, limited-service, convention, resort, etc.), size, potential brand affiliation, and location (e.g., airport, suburban, urban, international, domestic, etc.). An example of the investment criteria for a hotel investor could be the following:

- Acquire domestic luxury and upper-upscale full-service hotels with more than 300 rooms in growth markets with high barriers to new development.
- Target the top thirty hotel markets with subject submarkets comprising a hotel supply of at least 5,000 guestrooms.
- Invest at or below replacement cost, and provide ownership a return on investment to exceed a 14 percent internal rate of return (IRR), assuming no leverage and a ten-year investment horizon.
- Focus on fee-simple properties unencumbered by long-term management contracts and/or franchise agreements.

As investors set criteria for their lodging investments, they need to recognize that this necessarily creates certain limitations on the available assets that will meet their criteria. For example, the criterion that prospective acquisitions must be located in top-thirty Metropolitan Statistical Areas (MSAs) will eliminate many hotel investment opportunities, but honoring the constraint will simultaneously enable the investor to more quickly identify appropriate potential acquisition targets. Again, maintaining a disciplined approach is the key. In this instance, an asset that satisfies the top-thirty requirement carries the benefits of more restrictive barriers to entry (e.g., less available vacant land) and more efficient market pricing in a disposition, due to a larger pool of prospective buyers.

Acquisition Due Diligence

Once the acquisition criteria are established and target markets are identified, a number of steps must be undertaken before the transaction is completed. These steps, which center on the investment decision, are necessary if a successful transaction is to be completed. They are:

- Develop a list of potential targets, either through primary research in a market or through the use of intermediaries such as brokers and hotel network contacts.
- Screen potential candidates based on acquisition criteria and select target assets.
- Conduct a preliminary site visit to establish parameters in creating the framework for a strategic plan.
- Develop pricing for the asset.
- Develop a letter of intent that will establish the foundation of the transaction.
- Perform detailed market feasibility and property due diligence.
- Reassess whether the deal still fits the investment criteria.
- Negotiate final terms and close the transaction.

Detailed research of potential acquisitions will help ensure that new assets fit the investment strategy. The detailed research is accomplished through a comprehensive due diligence process before transaction closing that identifies the many investment risks and opportunities. An acquisition team of experts (either internal or third-party representatives) should be assembled to carry out the research and negotiations. While the team size may vary depending on the nature of the buyer or the asset to be acquired, necessary areas of expertise should include feasibility, asset management, accounting and tax, risk management, legal, engineering, design/architecture/construction, and operations management.

The primary function of the due diligence process is to conduct a complete investigation of any factors that may influence the return on investment and value of the asset. Those factors will include market considerations, product evaluation, risks and opportunities assessments, contractual considerations, and a financial review.

Evaluate Market Considerations

Regardless of investment criteria, the first step in an acquisition decision is analyzing the potential upside for a market, which is based on the supply and demand for lodging products. Possible overall market characteristics that may yield opportunities for hotel acquisitions include the following:

- Demand growth rates that are expected to exceed new supply.
- High barriers to entry for new hotel development.
- High costs of new development relative to valuations of existing inventory.
- Wide bases of employment that can hedge against demand risk from individual business sectors.
- Bottoming occupancy cycles that may offer significant upside if the acquirer buys into a depressed market (assuming an expectation of recovery).

Assessing Market-Wide Hotel Supply and Demand. Evaluating historical and future supply and demand growth is critical in determining the prospects of any potential acquisition. It is also extremely important to understand the equilibrium or disequilibrium of the supply-demand relationship in the market in order to accurately determine the upside potential for an acquisition candidate.

The evaluation of market trends should begin with a review of historical market-wide supply and demand statistics. STR is the standard data source for most North American markets and a growing number of international markets. STR presents useful data for a particular market—supply (total available room nights), demand (total occupied room nights), and hotel room pricing (total room sales). Studying the historical trends and patterns of occupancy and ADR will help an investor better understand how a market reacts to excess or tight supply. RevPAR statistics (occupancy × ADR) can provide smoother trend lines tracking overall rooms revenues in the market.

It is important to understand the dynamics of the overall market before drilling down to the various segments that compose total demand. A more detailed analysis focusing on the subsets of the market will reveal opportunities and challenges (e.g., continued growth or stagnant growth due to new supply) in individual segments. When dissecting a market, one can also look for segments that are underrepresented to identify opportunities for investment.

Determining the Competitive Set. The first step in analyzing the supply component of a market is to establish the competitive set for the acquisition target. This will help identify the market potential for an asset. If a property is performing below its proportional share (sometimes referred to as "fair share") in occupancy or rate, the acquisition team can then evaluate the property's location, physical attributes, brand affiliation, and management team to determine if changes are appropriate to improve the competitive position.

To evaluate the property's relative performance, a detailed competitive analysis is necessary. This will also serve as a basis in establishing a business plan to achieve investment goals. A thorough analysis of the strengths, weaknesses, opportunities, and threats (SWOT) for each competitor should be completed, including a property-by-property evaluation of market penetration for each demand segment. The SWOT analysis should include location, service quality, product quality, meeting space platform, scope of amenities, brand affiliation, management company, strength of ownership, rate structure by segment, mix of business, and occupancy patterns on both a weekday/weekend and a seasonal basis. This analysis reveals each hotel's main sources of demand and the key property characteristics that drive their success. If one product is dominating the market, can the target property exploit weaknesses or mitigate particular strengths by making changes? Without this information, it will be difficult to create a business strategy that will effectively position the acquisition target against the competition.

As part of the competitive analysis, future competition must be evaluated. Considerations include new products entering the market, as well as hotels that are potentially changing their competitive positioning by upgrading, expanding, or changing elements (e.g., adding a ballroom, feature restaurant, spa, or new room tower), or changing affiliations with management companies or brands.

Analyzing Market Dynamics of Demand Sources. After thoroughly evaluating the changes in supply that would have an impact on the market and the acquisition candidate, potential buyers must consider the demand component by studying the market dynamics of demand sources. Demand analysis could consist of a study of the local economy (for a transient market) or a review of feeder markets (for a destination market). It is important to review the historical growth of demand in the market, but to effectively estimate future demand, it is appropriate to look at growth in various sectors of the local economy to evaluate the correlation between those indicators and lodging demand. Some of the factors to study include the following:

- Population growth and characteristics
- Household income growth
- Employment growth
- Office building growth (supply and demand)
- Airport passenger traffic statistics
- Convention center growth (meetings, citywide conventions/conferences, attendance, or future expansion plans for the existing facility)
- Area attractions' growth (parks, museums, sports teams, festivals, etc.)
- Retail sales statistics
- Highway and rail traffic statistics
- Political trends affecting the economy and related lodging demand

To evaluate market demand further, potential buyers must understand the diversity within the marketplace. Is the economy driven by manufacturing or by financial services? Since certain industries generally create more lodging demand than others, it is imperative to understand work force characteristics and future prospects for various segments of the market. Understanding this relationship will help determine the level of risk for an investment. For example, a hotel that is located in a high tech corridor may have experienced substantial growth during a technology boom, but the lack of diversification in the economic base means greater volatility. The fortunes of a property in a sector-dependent market may follow a feast-or-famine cycle, as compared to a hotel that is located in a market with a broad diversification of demand.

When evaluating potential demand in the marketplace, feasibility experts will also evaluate two other types of demand—unaccommodated demand (due to lack of supply or product type) and induced demand (generated by a new area attraction, expanded convention center, aggressive marketing, or new brand representation in the market).

Determining Future Demand. After the data that will influence the demand of each lodging sector—business, leisure, group, and contract—are collected, they are used to forecast future demand for hotel room nights. For example, if the convention center will book 10 percent more business over the next three years, it is probably safe to assume that group business in the market will go up. Another important factor in determining the future growth of group demand is the extent to which a market's group business is dependent on the convention center. Similarly, projected growth in theme parks and other area attractions would be a reliable indicator of future leisure demand. It should be noted that the forecasting of both supply and demand becomes less accurate as the projection horizon increases, since many other influences outside of the area market, such as the state of the overall economy, can affect the market's future prospects.

Projecting Performance. After a thorough supply-and-demand analysis has been completed for the market, potential buyers can evaluate the acquisition candidate's potential performance by first applying historical penetration rates to future projections of market-wide occupancy. ADR levels are based on the supply-and-demand relationship and inflation. While not a hard-and-fast rule, when supply growth exceeds demand growth, ADR growth generally will be less than inflation; when supply growth is equal to demand growth, ADRs will more or less track with inflation; and when demand growth exceeds supply growth, ADR increases can be expected to exceed inflation.

Current occupancy levels in the market can be a good indicator of future growth potential. For example, a market with 53-percent market-wide occupancy may experience stronger demand growth than supply growth, with minimal gains in ADR. Conversely, a market with occupancies in the high 80-percent range may be able to sustain greater-than-inflation growth rates in ADR despite supply increases in excess of demand. In evaluating future ADR growth, buyers must look at the specific market segments in which a hotel is competing and determine if supply constraints will allow aggressive pricing. Once expectations for the overall market are determined, the acquisition target's rate potential can be estimated based on its competitive positioning as measured by such factors as its location, physical product, brand affiliation, management strength, and other factors. Proposed changes to these attributes will influence the forecasted penetration and yield assumed in the financial underwriting of the investment.

Evaluate the Lodging Asset

Once the acquisition target has been identified and market research indicates that the particular market meets the investment criteria, the hotel product must be evaluated to determine its current value, opportunities, and investment risks. Doing so will lead to developing a price that would be included in a letter of intent to purchase.

Location and Site Characteristics. The first step in understanding the hotel product is an evaluation of the property's location relative to major demand generators, its visibility and accessibility, and other physical site characteristics. "Location, location, location" is a familiar real estate mantra with good reason. Location is the primary determinant of success in any real estate investment. Hotels with locations providing a significant advantage over similar products in the market will often outperform their competition.

Site characteristics of a hotel should be evaluated to determine advantages or disadvantages in comparison to competitive properties in the market. For example, ease of ingress and egress and other traffic patterns are important factors to consider. If the visibility of the product is poor, would added signage (provided this is permitted under local zoning laws) improve the situation? Are changes planned for the neighborhood that will affect future demand? A good way to evaluate a site is to compile a map that lays out the location of supply (other hotels in the competitive set), both existing and proposed, and major demand generators. The map provides a visual representation of how the acquisition target's location compares to the locations of other hotels in the market, and also may indicate potential new demand sources for the hotel.

Regulatory and Legal Restrictions. Another aspect of site evaluation is a thorough review of regulatory and legal restrictions, including height restrictions; setback requirements; zoning ordinances (including grandfather clauses); land use restrictions in ground leases and any applicable covenants, conditions, and restrictions (CC&Rs); permit and licensing requirements; parking requirements; and maximum floor-to-area ratio (FAR or site density, defined as gross building area divided by total land area) utilization. Is the property fee simple or subject to a ground lease? If the property is subject to a ground lease, what are the rights and responsibilities of the lessee with respect to maintenance, change of use, or additions/deletions to the property? A comprehensive legal review should be performed on the site, which would include a complete analysis of the above-mentioned items as well as any deed restrictions, permit or code violations, air rights, easements, title search, whether the site is located within a flood plain, and any planned changes in zoning/land use for the neighborhood. Are any public works programs planned that may cause a condemnation of part of the property or potentially change the ingress/egress of the property? These questions are critical to understanding the potential value of any real estate asset.

Neighborhood Characteristics. Along with the site analysis, an investor must fully understand the subject property's neighborhood characteristics. Potential owners should understand the land uses of all properties located adjacent or near the subject property—including, but not limited to, the use, occupancy, tenancy, size, and condition of adjacent property improvements; proposed changes to their use or improvements; and the availability of vacant land available for future development. An understanding is also necessary of the history of the neighborhood, potential changes in land use or master plan, age of buildings and their image in the community, crime rates, trends in real estate pricing, economic profile of the people in the neighborhood or those that use the businesses in the neighborhood, and trends in the neighborhood. Is the neighborhood growing and becoming more affluent, or is it starting to decline? How does the neighborhood influence the demand for the hotel? Are there nearby restaurants and tourist attractions that can serve as amenities or demand generators? Do transportation systems facilitate access to the hotel? An understanding of all the characteristics of the neighborhood is necessary to evaluate fully the risks and opportunities the investment presents.

Physical Plant. The evaluation of the subject property's physical plant is often a critical juncture in the analytical process, determining whether the prospective purchaser goes forward with the acquisition or moves on to other opportunities. Evaluation of the hotel's physical plant starts with a complete inventory of the property's facilities, including an evaluation of the age, condition, and other characteristics of the following features:

- *Parking*—stand-alone or attached structure, surface, excess capacity, paid or free parking for guests, valet services, operator (managed, leased, or in-house)
- *Lobby*—layout, traffic flow, security
- *Guestrooms*—number; size; bathroom layout and number of fixtures; mix of suites, kings, double/doubles; amenities; style; balconies; heating/ventilation/ air conditioning (HVAC) system(s)
- *Food and beverage facilities*—description of each outlet, including style, décor, number of seats, hours of operation, managed or leased, price positioning
- *Meeting space*—total square footage, pre-function space, number and types of rooms, largest venue, flexibility of space, outdoor venues, technology in meeting rooms, ratio of meeting space to room count, comparison to market
- *Amenities*—retail services and management (third-party, in-house, or leased); transportation services; description of other possible services offered and their size or extent, including swimming pool(s), health club, spa, beach facilities, children's centers, game rooms, business centers, concierge services, concierge lounges, golf courses, marinas, stables, etc.
- *Building design*—architectural style, functionality, building and finish materials, fit with surrounding land use, curb appeal, compliance with current codes
- *Systems*—façade, roof, HVAC systems, plumbing systems, electrical systems, fire/life safety systems, kitchen/banquet facilities, structural systems, and grounds/landscaping materials
- *Technology*—property management system, sales and catering system, high-speed Internet access equipment, cabling in the meeting space and guestrooms, televisions, telephone switch/private board exchange system, computers and network servers, call accounting systems, property maintenance systems, energy management systems, etc. (many of these could change with a brand change or could be very expensive to replace if they are at the end of their useful lives)

Environmental History. Another important area that must be reviewed is the environmental condition of the site and building. A licensed environmental engineer should audit the property's history and conduct a thorough inspection of its current observable condition, generally termed a *phase I audit*. If prior existence of hazardous materials is confirmed through historical review or the current presence of hazardous materials is suspected through visual inspection, a more in-depth phase II audit will typically be conducted. A phase II audit includes physical sampling and laboratory testing of soils or building materials for the potential presence of asbestos, lead paint, PCBs, mold or soil contaminants resulting from an underground storage tank, or dry cleaning facility spills. If any of these issues affect the property, an operations and maintenance plan should be in place and employees must be certified to work with the applicable hazardous materials.

The property review should be conducted by many members of the acquisition team, including the acquisition officer, asset manager, architect, interior designer, engineers, feasibility analyst, and one or more representatives of the prospective property management company. Each member should observe the condition of the property, identifying any physical deficiencies and functional or economic obsolescence. This evaluation, along with myriad other inputs, contributes to the due diligence report assessing the opportunities and risks associated with the prospective investment.

Identify Upside Potential

When evaluating the upside potential for an asset, prospective buyers should start with a thorough financial and operational review. This review should include a detailed analysis of historical operating statements to reveal operational patterns and recent trends, as well as a comparison with similar properties to uncover areas where the hotel is underperforming. When benchmarking the subject hotel to comparable properties, the broad metrics helpful in identifying potential opportunities include departmental margins and sales and costs per occupied room (POR) and per available room (PAR). Many factors can affect an asset's upside potential, including the physical layout of its facilities, the current local labor market, the condition of the asset, the asset's location and brand affiliation, and its management team capabilities.

Specific reviews that can help an asset manager identify upside opportunities include the following:

- An operations audit that identifies departmental efficiencies and challenges, such as:
    - Staffing levels and services offered by each department in comparison to competitors.
    - Potential consolidation of management with other properties.
    - Food and beverage margins, menu engineering opportunities, hours of operation, and closure or repositioning of outlets.
    - Procurement—energy, food and beverage, and other supplies.
    - Leases and service contracts—at market rates? Opportunities to renegotiate or outsource?
    - Warranty enforcement.

  - Inventory adjustments.
  - New revenue potential—parking, new retail shops, and off-site catering.
  - Room mix—is there opportunity for increasing key count or adding premium rooms?
  - Guest satisfaction surveys to help identify product and service deficiencies.

- A sales audit that evaluates opportunities regarding:
  - Product positioning.
  - Sales strategy and implementation.
  - Effectiveness of the sales team in light of product attributes (physical plant, service, brand, and location) in comparison to competitors.
  - Future booked business and rate structure.
  - Penetration of major accounts in the market.
  - Characteristics of negotiated rates in place (term, rate discount, room night guaranties, last room availability, inclusion of meals or transportation, etc.).
  - Transient, group, and leisure markets (focus and strategy).
  - Availability of meeting space appropriate to market positioning.
  - Meeting planner satisfaction surveys to help identify product and service deficiencies.
- A labor audit that includes:
  - An evaluation of wage schedules by department and a comparison to wage surveys in the local market.
  - An evaluation of labor standards/staffing guidelines and productivity measures, benchmarked to appropriate comparable properties.
  - A benefits survey.
  - A turnover history.
  - A union activity or collective bargaining agreement review.
  - Opportunities to consolidate positions.
  - Opportunities to cross-train positions.
  - Opportunities to outsource or benefit from internal transfers.
  - Employee satisfaction surveys.
- A systems audit that includes:
  - An inventory of appropriate computer systems available to achieve staffing efficiencies.

- An energy audit to identify high return-on-investment capital expenditures or changes in operations with potential to reduce costs and improve investment returns.
- A building systems repairs-and-maintenance audit to determine if any individual system is absorbing an inordinate proportion of the property operations and maintenance budget.

Asset managers must look for opportunities to add revenue-producing space, such as additional guestrooms, incremental meeting space, or a new restaurant, retail pad, or condominium tower on the site. Opportunities also may exist to modify an existing use to one that allows the property to generate higher cash flow, including converting a restaurant to meeting space, changing a gift shop to a boardroom, or merely improving the flexibility of an existing space, which can be accomplished by changing the air wall system in meeting space or creating private dining rooms in restaurants that can double as small meeting rooms.

There also may be an opportunity to reposition the asset by upgrading the guestrooms and/or facilities to target a more lucrative segment of the market or to gain greater market share. This level of investment must be in line with the market potential and should be grounded in a thorough competitive and demand analysis. It is quite easy to over-invest in a property with the expectation that a superior product will be able to drive ADR. Since expectations do not always materialize, it is imperative to understand the true potential of the market.

A combination of operational changes and capital investments may yield a return on investment greater than the targeted return for the acquisition, thus enhancing the overall investment return. This in turn could justify paying more than a price based solely on historical operating performance.

Identify Downside Risks

Potential downside risks must be identified to accurately evaluate a property's current value and future growth potential. With planned dispositions, it is not uncommon for owners to cut operating costs to improve cash flow and justify a higher asking price. Operationally, these cuts might include:

- Reducing staffing to levels that fall below a brand standard, often resulting in poor guest service scores. Low staffing levels may also lead to employee dissatisfaction, potentially motivating employees to pursue collective bargaining in order to be heard by management.
- Offering wage scales significantly below market, which will also give rise to employee dissatisfaction and turnover.
- Cutting management, employee training, and/or employee recognition programs, all of which may increase turnover costs and employee dissatisfaction.
- Reducing inventory levels of food and beverage, laundry, and other operating supplies. Adequate inventory levels may need to be restored on acquisition, adding to costs. However, depleted inventories may also be identified as an opportunity for longer-term cost containment if inadequate inventories are negatively affecting operating efficiencies at the property.

- Reducing levels of maintenance or eliminating service contracts, thus shortening asset life cycles and increasing future expenditures for furniture, fixtures, equipment, and other capital items.
- Eliminating sales and marketing resources and/or failing to fill positions vacated once the sales team learns that a property is for sale. Good indicators of this possibility are weak booking pace trends.
- Reducing insurance coverage.
- Failing to pay appropriate occupancy and use taxes.

The due diligence team should also identify risks relating to the physical aspects of the property. Some of the areas requiring specific attention include:

- Evaluating the fire/life safety systems for compliance with applicable local codes and potentially more restrictive brand requirements.
- Determining any existing building code/zoning violations or accessibility deficiencies.
- Assessing the quality of the guest environment—guestrooms, food and beverage facilities, meeting space, and the lobby and other public areas.
- Evaluating the building envelope—condition and appearance of the façade and roof; condition and picket width of balcony railings, which in the case of older properties often do not meet current codes, brand standards, or insurance requirements.
- Evaluating the HVAC system's condition and adequacy to properly heat and cool the building.
- Evaluating the vertical transportation system's condition and adequacy to meet guest expectations and operational/housekeeping needs.
- Inspecting the grounds and site.

Each risk identified should be quantified to the extent possible and included in the investment analysis. Qualitative, less-tangible risks, such as guestroom sizes smaller than those of the competition, can be identified and factored into the analysis when determining the appropriate growth rate for the property RevPAR. Identification of all possible risks is beneficial in the negotiation of the final price for the hotel. Moreover, understanding the operational and physical opportunities and risks leads to the development of a comprehensive asset strategy that fully unlocks the value of the real estate.

Evaluate Contractual and Legal Obligations

Numerous legal documents should be reviewed before potential buyers can properly forecast the operating results of a hotel investment. Each contract should undergo a legal review, with an abstract prepared for the acquisition team. The asset manager should also read all legal documents to fully understand the rights and obligations of the property ownership group. Some of the essential documents and sections to review when preparing the underwriting analysis include the following:

- A hotel management agreement covering base and incentive management fees; sales, marketing, and reservation fees; chain services fees and caps; loyalty programs; procurement rights and requirements; budget submission guidelines and approval rights; capital expenditure requirements and control of any capital reserves; preferred returns for ownership on additional invested capital; termination and default provisions; requirements for property improvement plan (PIP) on sale; trade-area restrictions and definition of competitive set(s); conflict resolution provisions; employee control and approval/dismissal rights; insurance requirements; indemnification provisions; and relationship/agency definition.
- A franchise agreement covering fees and royalties; term, renewal options, and transfer/assignment provisions; loyalty programs; procurement requirements; and brand standards.
- Ground leases covering control provisions, lease term, renewal options, cost, approval rights on property changes of use, appearance or expansion, maintenance clauses, and other restrictions.
- Labor/collective bargaining agreements covering renewal term, escalation clauses, work rules, dispute resolutions, and termination of employees.
- Other leases and maintenance contracts describing term, costs, and termination provisions.
- Any pending litigation.

Understanding these documents and accurately reflecting the terms of these agreements in the financial analysis are critical steps in determining the value of the asset. Contracts that can be renegotiated or terminated should be reflected in the acquisition pro forma by using the market terms that the acquisition team believes it can negotiate in the future. Assumptions should include the timing of the new terms to be implemented, as well as any other cost that may result from a new contract. For example, if a management contract with a major brand is terminable and a new brand is to be introduced to the property, all costs of the conversion and remarketing of the asset should be included in the analysis. Assumptions should also include the loss of revenue when some or all of the property's services are unavailable during a projected renovation.

Evaluate Financial Information

As suggested in the previous discussion of techniques for identifying upside potential, a thorough review of the property's financial statements must be undertaken. This financial analysis is a critical aspect of the due diligence process, and should include a complete independent audit of the operating statements and balance sheets for the property. While a seller may offer audited statements, it is up to the buyer to fully understand the quality of the financials presented. The buyer can further protect him- or herself by requiring the seller to provide appropriate representations and warranties in the purchase and sales contract. A summary of the documents and areas to investigate as part of a thorough financial review includes the following:

- *A profit and loss statement*—review historical operating statements, including trend analysis; current operating statements, including variance analysis comparing actual/forecast to budget; and future-year forecasts or pro forma budgets.
- *A balance sheet*—review of all assets and liabilities.
- *A statement of working capital*—develop a history to determine if the property has too much or too little working capital to operate the hotel effectively.
- *Accounts receivable*—review aging of existing receivables and aging trends; determine party (buyer or seller) responsible for collection.
- *Accounts payable*—determine history and timeliness of payments to vendors; determine if any litigation or contract disputes are outstanding; investigate if any overpayments have occurred.
- *A statement of capital expenditures and escrow/reserve status*—thoroughly review historical expenditures for the property to determine if property operations and maintenance (POM) expenses are being paid from the capital reserves or, conversely, if capital items are being expensed to the POM department; evaluate the adequacy of the capital reserves to fund future projects and determine if additional owner's capital will be required above the projected contributions from operating cash flow.
- *Property tax and insurance report*—employ property tax and insurance specialists to evaluate the impact that the sale will have on future costs, including changes in insurance coverage if they differ from the previous owner's requirements.
- *Capital-structure evaluation*—review various considerations if you are creating a new capital structure or adjusting the existing capital structure, including target debt-to-equity ratio, cross-collateralization/debt pool implications, lender requirements and covenants, current debt characteristics (assumability, prepayment provisions, rates), etc.

Pulling the Acquisition Trigger

Once all of the areas identified in the preceding sections have been evaluated, it is time for the feasibility team to develop an acquisition pro forma, a capital expenditure plan, and an appropriate asset positioning strategy so that the investment valuation can be determined. This valuation should take into consideration any PIP required by the franchisor or management company and should specify the targeted exit window. Depending on their attendant risks, the valuation may or may not quantify the value of opportunities identified in the due diligence process. Including some opportunities that appear readily achievable may be appropriate if there is a strong level of interest from other potential buyers. If the acquisition pro forma indicates a value greater than the asking price of the seller, then the buyer is expecting returns from the investment to exceed his or her investment underwriting criteria. If the asking price exceeds the valuation, the acquisition team should either try to negotiate a reduced price or abandon the potential acquisition.

A potential buyer's determination to make the acquisition will sometimes affect how strictly that buyer adheres to previously defined underwriting criteria. Investors must be careful not to "push the envelope" when the acquisition valuation falls below the asking price. Absent a strong financial basis for making the investment at the asking price, acquisition teams may justify the purchase by resorting to a non-financial rationale, such as arguing the purchase is appropriate as a strategic move or by adjusting the pro forma to reflect more potential upside in the investment. These instances should be rare, however, if a buyer is intellectually honest in the acquisition due diligence process.

The Hold-Versus-Sell Decision

As with the initial purchase decision, the critical first step for an asset manager evaluating the options for an existing property is to thoroughly understand ownership's goals and objectives. Strategic plans evolve over time, and the prudent asset manager should not assume that the original investment criteria remain valid. Key factors affecting owners' objectives may include the holding entity's structure, the targeted holding period (particularly for private equity investors), capital structure, capital availability, risk tolerance, and investment-product preferences. To the extent any of these factors have changed since the time of acquisition, reevaluation of the investment plan is appropriate and necessary.

The "As-Is" Scenario

Upon confirmation of ownership's goals and objectives, the next task in the owner's investment decision process is to develop an "as-is" scenario reflecting the option of holding the asset in its current condition with no material changes. The as-is scenario will serve as the base case against which other options are measured. It may also be a proxy for market value, establishing for ownership the property's potential disposition proceeds. In developing an as-is valuation, asset managers must first discern whether the status quo is even an option. In many cases, a hotel will require some amount of remedial investment to stabilize performance or maintain an existing brand flag. In developing a valuation for useful comparison to alternative strategies, the as-is analysis should factor in any required capital to address the property's deferred maintenance needs and to account for any anticipated PIP likely to be imposed by the franchisor or manager to maintain an existing brand affiliation.

Redevelopment Scenarios

After the as-is scenario has been explored and an appropriate valuation established, the next step is to consider potential redevelopment scenarios. Redevelopment opportunities can be divided into two general classifications: (1) complete or "ground up" redevelopment and (2) partial redevelopment and/or adaptive reuse. The primary difference between the two is the extent of preservation of existing improvements. Although complete redevelopment tends to require greater investment, this is not always the case; conversion or expansion of an existing older facility can be extremely costly. Regardless of the scenario, however, the redevelopment process starts with the most basic real estate question: "What is the highest and best use of the property?"

Market Potential. To determine highest and best use, a number of elements must be considered, the first being the long-term market potential of the location. One good indicator of market potential is recent real estate development and transaction activity in the area. For example, if office projects are sprouting up all around the subject asset, hotel and office are likely to be attractive future uses for the subject property. Another important source of information is demographic growth data. Heavy population growth but few new jobs in the area could indicate that residential or retail use is most appropriate. A significant increase in the median age of the local population could signal an opportunity to convert the asset to a senior living facility. Typically, evaluation of overall market considerations will reveal several potential uses for the site and existing improvements.

Physical Aspects. A second element to consider in evaluating highest and best use is the physical nature of the site and improvements. Unusual topographical features, natural barriers (both real and perceived), and geotechnical (subsurface) conditions are examples of physical attributes of land that could influence redevelopment alternatives. Size of guest floors, ceiling heights, size of guestrooms, structural design, and mechanical plant design can similarly impact the technical or economic feasibility of reuse alternatives for existing facilities.

Entitlement Issues. A third element to consider in analyzing redevelopment options is the entitlement environment. The entitlement environment includes all of the statutory, regulatory, and private guidelines that govern or restrict land use, the most significant of which is zoning. Zoning ordinances will typically specify the allowed uses for a site, as well as maximum height, FAR, minimum setbacks, signage, and other criteria. Zoning alone may dictate the highest and best use for a property, and the flexibility to obtain variances or modify existing zoning varies widely by jurisdiction. Other factors that could affect development and property use are building codes, easements, shoreline/special use area restrictions, and private CC&Rs that may run with the land. Due to the wide array of possible factors, engagement of legal counsel is generally recommended to fully assess the entitlement environment.

Contractual Obligations. A fourth element to consider in evaluating redevelopment alternatives is existing contractual obligations. If the property is held under a ground lease rather than a fee simple interest, a change of use may be precluded outright. If not directly prohibited, onerous conversion terms or a short remaining lease duration could render any significant change or incremental investment economically infeasible.

Similar issues may arise when long-term management contracts or franchise agreements are in place. While most contracts are terminable at some cost, if the remaining term of an agreement is lengthy, termination may be prohibitively expensive. Other contracts that could affect the economics of redevelopment or reuse include space leases, concession agreements, rooftop leases or license agreements, service contracts, equipment leases, and sales/booking contracts.

Capital Structure and Availability. A final element to consider in evaluating redevelopment alternatives is capital structure and availability. The ability to pursue alternative directions for existing properties is often dependent on debt covenants under existing financing. Joint venture or partnership agreements can similarly constrain options. Capital structure can also affect tax considerations of redevelopment, such as the usability of potential tax credits that may be available for certain uses targeted by local jurisdictions. Even if the current capital structure is not an impediment to redeveloping an asset, lack of investment capital may still pose an insurmountable obstacle.

When all of the potentially feasible redevelopment and/or reuse alternatives have been identified, the various scenarios must be quantified for comparison to the as-is scenario. It may be desirable to use varying discount rates and exit-capitalization rates to adjust for the relative complexity and inherent risk of the options. While analyzing the array of opportunities for redevelopment is appropriate, complete redevelopment of productive assets is typically very difficult to justify purely on the numbers. Strategic factors or other non-financial rationales generally figure into the decision to redevelop as well.

As with initial acquisitions, major redevelopment should entail a comprehensive investment plan and exit strategy consistent with ownership's underlying goals and objectives.

Repositioning Scenarios

Once the as-is and feasible redevelopment scenarios have been established and quantified, the next step in the owner's investment decision process is to identify potential repositioning scenarios. To identify desirable repositioning alternatives, it is first necessary to establish the existing property's SWOT relative to the market. The primary focus in this effort should be on identifying the hotel's weaknesses and opportunities and potential solutions to address them. It is worth noting that some deficiencies, such as location or poor access, can be difficult or impossible to address. If the owner and asset manager are creative in their thinking, however, most weaknesses can be significantly mitigated.

Repositioning opportunities can be classified broadly as one or more of the following:

- *Repositioning through physical enhancement.* As examples, poorly performing food and beverage outlets could be outsourced or converted to alternative uses. To reposition a property to appeal more to groups, a full-service property with a poor meeting space/guestroom ratio could convert less-productive space to incremental meeting space. Conversely, to reposition a hotel with an excess of meeting space, ownership might consider a guestroom expansion or the conversion of some meeting space to retail or spa use.

  At this juncture, a point of clarification is necessary. While the term "repositioning" is sometimes used to refer to all renovation activity, in the author's view such usage is incorrect. Repositioning implies a significant change in a property's marketing direction. While such change usually is accompanied by significant capital investment, it need not be. Capital investment without a change in strategy is simply asset preservation, the costs of which should be incorporated in the as-is scenario for purposes of analysis.

- *Brand and/or management repositioning.* Of particular importance to the evaluation of brand repositioning alternatives is a thorough understanding of management and franchise agreements. The contracts largely determine the economic aspects and marketing direction of a hotel investment, and replacement of existing contracts represents one of the most common repositioning strategies pursued by owners.
- *Financial/capital repositioning.* Although not as obvious to the public as physical enhancements or brand changes, modification of the capital structure represents another category of investment repositioning. Refinancing or restructuring existing mortgages, renegotiating or buying out ground leases, adding mezzanine financing, and taking on additional equity partners are examples of financial repositioning opportunities that can significantly affect investment returns and ownership flexibility. It is worth noting that some financial repositioning options may not be viable for all owners. Since other potential investors may not have similar constraints, current ownership's restrictive capital structures or lack of available investment capital may result in a higher potential disposition value than the calculated as-is value of holding the asset.

All repositioning alternatives identified should be qualified using the same considerations used to evaluate potential redevelopment scenarios. To accurately gauge opportunities, the owner must be aware of market trends, including future supply additions, changes in market demand generation, and evolving guest expectations and preferences. Investment in additional guestrooms is unlikely to be profitable if market demand is insufficient or declining. A spa or additional retail space will be successful only if consistent with guest preferences and spending patterns (or those of potential local patrons). While it is possible to uncover latent demand in a market or to shift demand from other markets, such strategies are not for the risk-averse or those with a short-term investment time frame. Careful market research and a thorough familiarity with target market demographics are recommended to mitigate the risk of overestimating potential demand.

When all viable repositioning options have been fully vetted and quantified, the owner and asset manager should be able to compare the various options to the previously developed as-is and redevelopment scenarios. As noted earlier, risk-adjusted discount rates may be appropriate when comparing scenarios with substantially different risk profiles.

As a practical matter, repositioning pro formas developed by current or potential management companies should be evaluated critically. Operators generally take their fiduciary relationship with ownership seriously, but many operating company representatives charged with the responsibility of developing pro forma analyses are not accustomed to looking at investment decisions from the owner's perspective. It is therefore the responsibility of the asset manager to ensure that assumptions are reasonable and that projections account for all costs, including "below the line" items such as replacement reserves, corporate overhead charges, and incentive management fees.

The Disposition Decision

The final step in the owner's investment decision process is to evaluate the sale scenario. The as-is scenario and the sale scenario are closely linked, since the as-is valuation generally sets the baseline for potential proceeds on disposition. Whether the owner should entertain a sale depends on the degree to which the subject property continues to meet all of the goals and objectives of ownership. In economic terms, the owner needs to consider the opportunity cost of holding onto the asset; if the owner would not purchase the asset again at the as-is valuation, a recommendation for disposition is warranted.

An existing asset may fail to meet an owner's hold criteria for a number of different reasons. Anticipated cash flows or appreciation may not meet current investment standards, and ownership may have identified superior reinvestment alternatives. Portfolio strategy may have changed, and the asset may no longer fit targeted geographic or product parameters. Some owners have specific investment horizons and may need to liquidate a portfolio accordingly. Others may just need to raise cash to meet other operating needs. Still others may want to achieve a desired tax event (gain or loss). While a disposition to avoid taxes may be a valid objective, deferring a sale of a property solely to avoid tax gain usually is not. Rather than continuing to hold an undesired asset, owners should pursue other tax-efficient options, such as contributing property to a real estate investment trust for shares in a diversified "umbrella partnership" (UPREITs), or participating in a Section 1031 tax-free exchange in which property is traded for another comparably valued real estate asset. Regardless of the reason for disposition, owners need to ensure that the analysis of disposition proceeds and corresponding reinvestment basis reflects all transaction costs resulting from the sale.

The Post-Audit Process

As a wise individual once noted, "It's hard to know if you are winning if you don't keep score." Given the truth in that observation, it is surprising how few organizations bother to calculate the success or failure of discretionary investments over time. While nearly all owners calculate yield on total investment at disposition, many do not track the ongoing yields from individual ROI-driven investments or larger redevelopment/repositioning projects.

To a certain extent, omitting the post-audit function is understandable. Tracking a large number of projects can become time-consuming and tedious. If managed appropriately, however, the post audit can be a very effective tool in fine-tuning the ROI underwriting process. By regularly comparing actual results to pro forma, asset managers can validate their assumptions, an important step in developing credibility for future recommendations. In addition, building and documenting a base of experience improves future projections and decreases forecast risk (and potentially hurdle rates) associated with subsequent projects.

Assessing Costs and Benefits

As with the original pro forma, the development of a post-audit analysis requires two frequently challenging steps: (1) assessing all of the benefits of the investment and (2) assessing the true costs. Determining the costs is typically the easier of the two.

Elements of investment cost can generally be categorized as direct expenditures, indirect expenditures, and avoided expenditures. Direct expenditures are relatively straightforward, and they typically relate closely to the original project budget. Indirect expenditures are costs incurred as a result of pursuing the subject investment but absorbed into operations or other projects. Examples of indirect costs are additional housekeeping labor, contract cleaning, or POM expenses. It is worth noting that no in-house resources should be considered "free" to the project, with the arguable exception of management overtime; if not allocated to a specific project, hourly staff should be performing other necessary functions or hours should be reduced.

The third cost classification, avoided expenditures, reduces rather than increases the net investment allocable to a project. While this category has the potential for manipulation, it is nonetheless valid for consideration in assessing project return. The basis for reducing direct and indirect expenditures by avoided expenditures is the recognition that certain expenditures may be necessary only if a project does *not* occur. An example of avoided costs is the impending renovation of a dated food and beverage outlet that is converted instead to leased space. The cost of tenant improvements and any leasing commissions are direct expenditures, but the avoided refurbishment costs reduce the net project cost when performing the yield calculation.

Assessing all of the benefits of an investment tends to get more difficult as the complexity of the investment increases. For an energy savings ROI project such as a lighting retrofit or the addition of a plate-and-frame heat exchanger, calculation of the benefits can be as simple as quantifying reduced electrical costs and useful life extensions of equipment. For the conversion of a restaurant to meeting space, however, the benefits can include some or all of the following: meeting room rentals, catering revenue, incremental guestroom sales, and minor departmental revenues related to increased occupancy. Additionally, for purposes of calculating the net benefits of the project, cash flow generated by the meeting space should be reduced by projected cash flows lost from restaurant operations. Invariably, some assumptions will be necessary in analyzing complicated projects. Those assumptions are most defensible if based on firm numbers. For example, assumed incremental telephone revenue for the meeting room example above should reflect incremental guestrooms occupied multiplied by total telephone revenue POR.

One final point on post-audit technique is worthy of mention. For the post-audit analysis to be useful, it must reflect all expenses and deductions associated with the subject project, as well as the revenues. As when underwriting the initial pro forma, asset managers need to verify that information reported by the property includes all costs to the owner. Failure to account for the indirect costs of a project—such as incremental repairs and maintenance expenses, revenue-based chain service allocations, and "below the line" items such as ground rent and incentive management fees—will materially overstate the actual results.

When to Question (or Look Past) the Numbers

With good reason, this chapter has focused on quantifiable processes and techniques to support the investment decision. In the vast majority of cases, poor investment decisions are the result of insufficient or faulty underwriting. However, this chapter would be incomplete if it did not point out that in some situations, analysis of historical data can be pointless or even misleading:

- *Evolving markets.* In evaluating investments, it is sometimes difficult to anticipate the effect of changing guest preferences and product evolution. Sixty years ago, only a few visionaries foresaw the impact on the lodging industry from the development of the interstate highway system. The situation was similar thirty years ago when product tiering was in its infancy. The typical impact from market evolution is to accelerate economic or functional obsolescence, although in some circumstances changing markets can unexpectedly benefit an investment.
- *Changing technology.* As with evolving markets, rapid technological advancement can unexpectedly shorten the life of many investments. As an example, A/V equipment with a 30-percent annual yield may appear to be an attractive investment, but the payback may not materialize if most customers will be providing their own setups two years from now. Asset managers should be cautious and conservative in projecting the useful lives or holding periods for any investments featuring heavy technological elements, due to the potential for accelerated obsolescence.
- *Non-comparability.* Despite the best efforts to identify comparables, some investment opportunities are unique. The principal problem with any pro forma is its inherent reliance on assumptions; when one-of-a-kind investments require pro formas without established and quantifiable frames of reference, reliance on assumptions can become excessive to the point of losing relevance.

To some extent, the concerns raised by one-off investments can be mitigated through increased risk premiums (typically reflected in higher discount rates and hurdle rates), reduced holding periods, or diversification. Sensitivity modeling can also be a useful tool. Continued tweaking of assumptions, however, has been known to lead to "analysis paralysis" in which opportunities are lost due to the fear of making a decision. As with many things in life, investment decisions sometimes are not clear-cut. A decision not to buy or not to reinvest in an asset may appear to be the safer choice, but it fails to create value for ownership. Ultimately, the investment decision must be made based on the professional judgment of the asset manager and the team he or she has assembled, consistent with the strategic goals and risk-tolerance profile of ownership.

Conclusion

The choice to buy, sell, or reposition a property is the fundamental decision of real estate investment. Unlike other real estate forms, however, the hotel investment decision is complicated by the array of factors involved in operating the business. While no amount of analysis can eliminate investment risk, a thorough understanding of ownership's objectives along with consistent analytical processes can greatly reduce risk and render it manageable. The alternative—investing without a thoughtful plan and exit strategy—is little different from rolling the dice. It may be exciting and even profitable in the short term, but over time the odds are against you.

References

Baltin, Bruce, James R. Butler, Jr., and Peter Bernudiz. 1997. "The Hotel Acquisition Process." *Hotel Online.* (March 1997). http://hotel-online.com/Trends.

Commercial Investment Real Estate Institute. 1999. *Investment Analysis for Commercial Investment Real Estate.* Chicago: Commercial Investment Real Estate Institute.

Hotel Association of New York City, Inc. 2014. *Uniform System of Accounts for the Lodging Industry,* Eleventh Revised Edition. Lansing, Mich.: American Hotel & Lodging Educational Institute.

Raleigh, Lori E., and Rachel J. Roginsky, eds. 1999. *Hotel Investments: Issues & Perspectives,* Second Edition. Lansing, Mich.: American Hotel & Lodging Educational Institute.

Rushmore, Stephen. 1992. *Hotel Investments: A Guide for Lenders and Owners.* Boston: Research Institute of America.

Case Study 1: To Buy or Not to Buy

The head of real estate transactions at LOL Capital has identified an opportunity to acquire a fee simple, 350-key upper-upscale hotel in a direct "off-market" deal. The hotel carries a major flag (brand affiliation) under a long-term management agreement with the brand. A PIP that includes the renovation of public areas and all guestrooms by the end of year two has already been documented, at a cost projected by the brand of $6.825 million, or $19,500 per key. The hotel appears to meet all of LOL's established investment parameters, and the market, while not currently represented in the portfolio, easily meets the predetermined minimum market-size criterion. The seller's asking price is $76,500,000, reflecting a 7.1 percent capitalization rate on the most recent or "trailing" twelve months of earnings before interest, taxes, depreciation, and amortization (EBITDA) less replacement reserves ($218,571 per key).

The acquisition candidate is located in a large office park just outside the central business district of a Top Twenty MSA in the northeastern United States. Demographics are strong, the economic base is broad, and the local economy is growing at a healthy pace. Due to their distance from the convention center and decreasing city-wide activity, hotels in the office park do not participate directly in major convention events. The existing hotel stock is in fair to good condition, with most competitive full-service properties ten to twenty years old. Most, but not all, of the major brand flags are currently represented in the submarket. Even though barriers to entry are low to moderate in the office park, no new full-service hotels have been announced to date.

The fifteen-year-old subject hotel is currently achieving only a 93.5 percent RevPAR index against its competitive set. The property's physical plant has been reasonably well-maintained, but its guestrooms and overall décor have become dated. Most of the competitive set has recently renovated, contributing to the subject's 5 percent decline in market share over the past two years. The property's ingress, egress, and visibility are all good, and the overall property layout remains functional. SWOT analysis of the asset shows that it compares well to its competitive set in most respects, although its lack of a true junior ballroom highlights a relative deficiency in its meeting space/guestroom ratio.

As part of LOL's due diligence team, Bob toured the subject property's guestrooms, meeting space, and common areas, walked the hotels in the competitive set, and met with management to help identify potential upside and downside factors involved in the acquisition. Based on internal portfolio benchmarking metrics, staffing generally appeared appropriate and productivity was reasonable. The management team seemed competent and associate satisfaction, guest service, and product quality scores were all slightly above brand average. The sales team was energetic, and the group booking pace was ahead of the prior year. During his site visit, Bob did not find any significant downside potential with the property, but he did note an opportunity to convert an underutilized 4,000-square-foot sports lounge to additional meeting space. Conversion of the lounge to a much-needed junior ballroom would allow the property to eliminate a marginally profitable outlet while markedly increasing the hotel's group base, improving its segmentation balance, and allowing the property to better yield its transient demand. From a qualified local project manager, Bob obtained an estimate for the conversion work of $1,050,000, or $262.50 per square foot.

LOL's current targeted hold period for new acquisitions is four to six years. After sorting through all of the market and financial due diligence information, with Bob's assistance the feasibility team put together the acquisition analysis summary shown in Exhibit 1. The analysis indicates a 12.7 percent unleveraged IRR on a five-year hold of the acquisition versus a hurdle rate of 12.0 percent. Although initial cash-on-cash yields are relatively low, all years exceed the company's full-service-hotel minimum yield requirement of 6.5 percent. Assuming a reasonable comfort level with all inherent assumptions, the analysis supports the acquisition of the asset by LOL.

Discussion Questions

1. Have all significant market risks been identified and evaluated?
2. What areas of potential upside or downside may Bob have missed during his property visit and tours?
3. What are some potential risk factors in the assumptions behind the acquisition pro forma?
4. Under the existing management agreement, the manager benefits significantly through both base and incentive fees from owner-funded ROI projects, such as the sports lounge conversion, without bearing any risk. How might

Exhibit 1 Full-Service Property Acquisition Analysis Summary

Full Service Property
Acquisition Analysis Summary

Initial Investment		
Contract Price		$76,500,000
Add: Pursuit/Due Diligence Costs	0.75%	573,750
Less: PIP/Other Buyer Credits		-
Total Initial Investment		**$ 77,073,750**
Contract Price per Key		$218,571
Contract Price Trailing 12 Month Cap Rate		6.9%

Reference Data:	
Current Assessed Value	$71,255,000
Current Full Service Aquisition IRR Hurdle	12.0%
Current Full Service Aquisition COC Hurdle	6.5%

Return Analysis			Year 1	Year 2	Year 3	Year 4	Year 5
Initial Investment		(77,073,750)					
Additional Investment/Non-Reserve CapEx			(3,500,000)	(4,375,000)			
Pro Forma Cash Flow from Operations			5,285,004	6,008,949	7,536,439	8,182,188	8,650,226
Net Sale Proceeds (2.5% Costs), Yr 5 Exit Cap Rate	8.0%						107,583,927
Cash Flows		(77,073,750)	1,785,004	1,633,949	7,536,439	8,182,188	116,234,153
IRR			**12.7%**				
Discounted Cash Flow - Discount Rate of	12.0%		**$ 79,414,924**				
Net Present Value	12.0%		**$ 2,341,174**				
Cash on Cash Yields *			**6.7%**	**7.3%**	**8.9%**	**9.6%**	**10.2%**

* Assuming mid-year Additional Investment

	TTM Actual	%	Year 1 Pro Forma	%	Year 2 Pro Forma	%	Year 3 Pro Forma	%	Year 4 Pro Forma	%	Year 5 Pro Forma	%	Year 6 Pro Forma	%
Rooms Available:	127,750		127,750		127,750		127,750		127,750		127,750		127,750	
Rooms Sold:	98,368		95,813		95,813		99,645		99,645		99,645		99,645	
Occupancy:	77.0%		75.0%		75.0%		78.0%		78.0%		78.0%		78.0%	
ADR:	$158.00		$164.32		$174.18		$186.37		$198.49		$208.41		$214.66	
Rooms RevPAR:	$121.66		$123.24		$130.63		$145.37		$154.82		$162.56		$167.44	
Rooms RevPAR Growth:			1.3%		6.0%		11.3%		6.5%		5.0%		3.0%	
Total RevPAR:	$185.47		$182.35		$200.21		$233.29		$245.27		$255.63		$263.21	
Total RevPAR Growth:			-1.7%		9.8%		16.5%		5.1%		4.2%		3.0%	
Market Occupancy:	77.0%		77.0%		77.0%		77.0%		77.0%		77.0%		77.0%	
Market ADR:	$169.00		$174.07		$181.03		$190.08		$199.59		$207.57		$213.80	
Market Rooms RevPAR:	$130.13		$134.03		$139.40		$146.37		$153.68		$159.83		$164.63	
Market Rooms RevPAR Growth:			3.0%		4.0%		5.0%		5.0%		4.0%		3.0%	
Property RevPAR Index:	93.5%		91.9%		93.7%		99.3%		100.7%		101.7%		101.7%	
Operating Revenue														
Rooms	15,542,065	65.6%	15,743,910	67.6%	16,688,545	65.2%	18,571,012	62.3%	19,778,128	63.1%	20,767,035	63.6%	21,390,046	63.6%
Food & Beverage	7,869,400	33.2%	7,281,750	31.3%	8,623,125	33.7%	10,960,950	36.8%	11,289,779	36.0%	11,628,472	35.6%	11,977,326	35.6%
Other Operated Departments	183,947	0.8%	170,211	0.7%	161,700	0.6%	159,760	0.5%	151,772	0.5%	144,183	0.4%	136,974	0.4%
Miscellaneous Income	98,368	0.4%	99,645	0.4%	103,133	0.4%	110,476	0.4%	113,790	0.4%	117,204	0.4%	120,720	0.4%
Total Operating Revenue	23,693,780	100.0%	23,295,516	100.0%	25,576,503	100.0%	29,802,198	100.0%	31,333,469	100.0%	32,656,893	100.0%	33,625,066	100.0%

(continued)

Exhibit 1 *(continued)*

Departmental Profit														
Rooms	11,754,916	75.6%	11,907,578	75.6%	12,717,940	76.2%	14,317,701	77.1%	15,397,218	77.8%	16,254,697	78.3%	16,742,338	78.3%
Food & Beverage	2,124,738	27.0%	2,184,525	30.0%	2,673,169	31.0%	3,617,114	33.0%	3,725,627	33.0%	3,837,396	33.0%	3,952,518	33.0%
Other Operated Departments	21,154	11.5%	19,574	11.5%	16,170	10.0%	14,378	9.0%	12,142	8.0%	10,093	7.0%	8,218	6.0%
Miscellaneous Income	76,727	78.0%	77,723	78.0%	80,443	78.0%	86,171	78.0%	88,756	78.0%	91,419	78.0%	94,161	78.0%
Total Departmental Profit	13,977,535	59.0%	14,189,400	60.9%	15,487,723	60.6%	18,035,364	60.5%	19,223,743	61.4%	20,193,604	61.8%	20,797,235	61.9%
Undistributed Operating Expenses														
Administration & General	1,227,678	5.2%	1,276,785	5.5%	1,321,472	5.2%	1,361,116	4.6%	1,401,950	4.5%	1,444,008	4.4%	1,437,328	4.4%
Information & Telecom Systems	548,048	2.3%	569,969	2.4%	589,918	2.3%	607,616	2.0%	625,844	2.0%	644,620	2.0%	653,958	2.0%
Sales & Marketing	1,599,330	6.8%	1,572,447	6.8%	1,726,414	6.8%	2,011,648	6.8%	2,115,009	6.8%	2,204,340	6.8%	2,259,692	6.8%
Franchise Fees	-	0.0%	-	0.0%	-	0.0%	-	0.0%	-	0.0%	-	0.0%	-	0.0%
Property Operation & Maintenance	1,130,588	4.8%	1,175,811	5.0%	1,216,964	4.8%	1,253,473	4.2%	1,291,078	4.1%	1,329,810	4.1%	1,369,704	4.1%
Utilities	1,002,838	4.2%	1,103,121	4.7%	1,180,340	4.6%	1,262,964	4.2%	1,351,371	4.3%	1,445,967	4.4%	1,547,185	4.6%
Total Undistributed Expenses	5,508,480	23.2%	5,698,134	24.5%	6,035,108	23.6%	6,496,817	21.8%	6,785,252	21.7%	7,068,745	21.6%	7,337,867	21.8%
Gross Operating Profit	8,469,055	35.7%	8,491,266	36.5%	9,452,614	37.0%	11,538,547	38.7%	12,438,491	39.7%	13,124,859	40.2%	13,459,368	40.0%
Base Management Fees	710,813	3.0%	698,865	3.0%	767,295	3.0%	894,066	3.0%	940,004	3.0%	979,707	3.0%	1,008,752	3.0%
Incentive Mgmt Fees *	-	0.0%	-	0.0%	-	0.0%	164,448	0.6%	249,849	0.8%	314,515	1.0%	345,062	1.0%
Income Before Non-Oper Inc and Exp	7,758,241	32.7%	7,792,401	33.5%	8,685,319	34.0%	10,480,033	35.2%	11,248,638	35.9%	11,830,637	36.2%	12,105,554	36.0%
Non-Operating Income and Expenses														
Income	-	0.0%	-	0.0%	-	0.0%	-	0.0%	-	0.0%	-	0.0%	-	0.0%
Rent	-	0.0%	-	0.0%	-	0.0%	-	0.0%	-	0.0%	-	0.0%	-	0.0%
Property & Other Taxes	796,250	3.4%	854,861	3.7%	889,056	3.5%	924,618	3.1%	952,356	3.0%	980,927	3.0%	1,010,355	3.0%
Insurance	234,500	1.0%	243,880	1.0%	256,074	1.0%	268,878	0.9%	279,633	0.9%	290,818	0.9%	302,451	0.9%
Other	234,500	1.0%	243,880	1.0%	252,416	1.0%	259,988	0.9%	267,788	0.9%	275,822	0.8%	284,096	0.8%
Total Non-Operating Inc & Expenses	1,265,250	5.3%	1,342,621	5.8%	1,397,545	5.5%	1,453,484	4.9%	1,499,777	4.8%	1,547,567	4.7%	1,596,902	4.7%
Earnings Before Interest, Taxes, Depreciation and Amortization	6,492,991	27.4%	6,449,780	27.7%	7,287,774	28.5%	9,026,549	30.3%	9,748,861	31.1%	10,283,071	31.5%	10,508,652	31.3%
Replacement Reserve	1,184,689	5.0%	1,164,776	5.0%	1,278,825	5.0%	1,490,110	5.0%	1,566,673	5.0%	1,632,845	5.0%	1,681,253	5.0%
EBITDA Less Replacement Reserve	**$ 5,308,302**	**22.4%**	**$ 5,285,004**	**22.7%**	**$ 6,008,949**	**23.5%**	**$ 7,536,439**	**25.3%**	**$ 8,182,188**	**26.1%**	**$ 8,650,226**	**26.5%**	**$ 8,827,399**	**26.3%**

* Calculated at 10% of GOP Less Base Management Fees, in excess of $9 Million

the management agreement be modified to more fairly compensate LOL for its discretionary financial risk?

Suggested answers to these questions appear at the end of this book.

Case Study 2: Sell or Hold?

As part of its annual strategic planning process, LOL Capital is evaluating whether to sell or hold a 125-key limited-service hotel in its current portfolio. The property is located in a suburban submarket of a historically stable second-tier Sunbelt city in the United States. From a reputable broker, Bob has obtained an estimated sales price/valuation (otherwise known as a "Broker's Opinion of Value" or BOV) for the property of $11,875,000, reflecting $95,000 per key and an 8.1 percent capitalization rate on the trailing twelve months of Earnings Before Interest, Taxes, Depreciation, and Amortization (EBITDA) Less Replacement Reserves. As ownership recently invested to upgrade the property to meet all existing franchise standards, the brand representative has given an off-the-record opinion that the property should not be subject to any PIP on sale in order to transfer the existing franchise to new ownership.

In an effort to optimize the property's positioning, Bob has identified an opportunity to reflag the property to a stronger brand affiliation. Although the change would require an investment of approximately $10,000 per key, or $1,250,000, and an increase in franchise royalties from 5 percent to 6 percent of total room revenues, Bob projects that the new flag's improved distribution and quality perception will allow the property to improve its RevPAR penetration by 6.7 percent within three years. The replacement franchisor has tentatively approved the conversion upon completion of the required PIP work, to be documented after formal submittal of a franchise application. Based on preliminary conversations with the new franchisor's business development representative, Bob estimates that the necessary improvements will consist of guestroom soft goods and new flat-panel televisions, with project completion possible within six months. Bob's hold analysis summary, including a five-year hold pro forma, is presented in Exhibit 2.

Bob's analysis indicates a total discounted cash flow of $12.0 million from holding the asset, versus an estimate of current net sale proceeds of just over $11.5 million. The 13.0 percent IRR of implied reinvestment exceeds the acquisition IRR hurdle rate of 12.0 percent, and cash on cash yields of all years exceed the company's minimum yield requirement of 8.0 percent. Assuming a reasonable comfort level with all inherent assumptions, the analysis supports the position that a hold/repositioning scenario is preferable to a current sale for LOL.

Discussion Questions

1. What are some potential risk factors in the assumptions behind Bob's hold/repositioning pro forma?
2. How sensitive is the analysis to variations in the current market value assumptions? to the pro forma RevPAR growth assumptions?

Exhibit 2 Limited-Service Property Hold/Repositioning Analysis Summary

Limited Service Property
Acquisition Analysis Summary

Sale ["As Is"] Analysis		
Current Market Value		$ 11,875,000
Less: Transaction Costs	3.0%	(356,250)
Less: PIP/Other Buyer Credits		-
Total Initial Investment		**$ 11,518,750**
Current Market Value per Key		$ 95,000
Contract Price Trailing 12 Month Cap Rate		8.1%

Reference Data:	
Original Acquisition Cost	$ 9,500,000
Current Book Value	$ 9,195,000
Assessed Value	$ 10,525,000
Current Ltd Service Aquisition IRR Hurdle	12.0%
Current Full Service Aquisition COC Hurdle	8.0%

Hold ["Repositioning"] Analysis			Year 1	Year 2	Year 3	Year 4	Year 5
Implied Investment of Hold		(11,518,750)					
Additional Investment/Non-Reserve CapEx			(1,250,000)				
Pro Forma Cash Flow from Operations			991,062	1,081,836	1,223,305	1,348,102	1,413,319
Net Sale Proceeds (3.0% Costs), Yr 5 Exit Cap Rate	9.0%						15,586,092
Cash Flows		(11,518,750)	(258,938)	1,081,836	1,223,305	1,348,102	16,999,411
IRR on Implied Reinvestment			**13.0%**				
Discounted Cash Flow - Discount Rate of	12.0%		**$ 12,004,629**				
Net Present Value	12.0%		**$ 485,879**				
Cash on Cash Yields *			**8.2%**	**8.5%**	**9.6%**	**10.6%**	**11.1%**

* Assuming mid-year Additional Investment

	TTM Actual	%	Year 1 Pro Forma	%	Year 2 Pro Forma	%	Year 3 Pro Forma	%	Year 4 Pro Forma	%	Year 5 Pro Forma	%	Year 6 Pro Forma	%
Rooms Available:	45,625		45,625		45,625		45,625		45,625		45,625		45,625	
Rooms Sold:	33,306		33,534		34,219		34,675		35,131		35,131		35,131	
Occupancy:	73.0%		73.5%		75.0%		76.0%		77.0%		77.0%		77.0%	
ADR:	$102.50		$106.60		$111.93		$118.65		$124.58		$129.56		$133.45	
Rooms RevPAR:	$74.83		$78.35		$83.95		$90.17		$95.93		$99.76		$102.75	
Rooms RevPAR Growth:			4.7%		7.1%		7.4%		6.4%		4.0%		3.0%	
Total RevPAR:	$75.81		$79.36		$84.99		$91.24		$97.02		$100.88		$103.89	
Total RevPAR Growth:			4.7%		7.1%		7.4%		6.3%		4.0%		3.0%	
Market Occupancy:	73.0%		73.0%		74.0%		74.0%		75.0%		75.0%		75.0%	
Market ADR:	$102.50		$105.58		$109.80		$115.29		$119.90		$124.70		$128.44	
Market Rooms RevPAR:	$74.83		$77.07		$81.25		$85.31		$89.92		$93.52		$96.33	
Market Rooms RevPAR Growth:			3.0%		5.4%		5.0%		5.4%		4.0%		3.0%	
Property RevPAR Index:	100.0%		101.7%		103.3%		105.7%		106.7%		106.7%		106.7%	
Operating Revenue														
Rooms	3,413,891	98.7%	3,574,764	98.7%	3,830,105	98.8%	4,114,043	98.8%	4,376,584	98.9%	4,551,647	98.9%	4,688,197	98.9%
Food & Beverage	-	0.0%	-	0.0%	-	0.0%	-	0.0%	-	0.0%	-	0.0%	-	0.0%
Other Operated Departments	11,657	0.3%	11,150	0.3%	10,809	0.3%	10,405	0.2%	10,015	0.2%	9,514	0.2%	9,039	0.2%
Miscellaneous Income	33,306	1.0%	34,876	1.0%	36,833	0.9%	38,444	0.9%	40,118	0.9%	41,322	0.9%	42,561	0.9%
Total Operating Revenue	3,458,854	100.0%	3,620,790	100.0%	3,877,747	100.0%	4,162,892	100.0%	4,426,717	100.0%	4,602,484	100.0%	4,739,797	100.0%

Exhibit 2 *(continued)*

Departmental Expenses														
Rooms	699,431	20.5%	732,391	20.5%	773,494	20.2%	807,322	19.6%	842,483	19.2%	867,757	19.1%	893,790	19.1%
Food & Beverage	-	0.0%	-	0.0%	-	0.0%	-	0.0%	-	0.0%	-	0.0%	-	0.0%
Other Operated Departments	13,989	120.0%	13,380	120.0%	12,971	120.0%	12,486	120.0%	12,018	120.0%	11,417	120.0%	10,846	120.0%
Other	9,992	30.0%	10,463	30.0%	11,050	30.0%	11,533	30.0%	12,035	30.0%	12,397	30.0%	12,768	30.0%
Total Departmental Expenses	723,412	20.9%	756,234	20.9%	797,515	20.6%	831,341	20.0%	866,536	19.6%	891,571	19.4%	917,405	19.4%
Departmental Profit														
Rooms	2,714,459	79.5%	2,842,374	79.5%	3,056,610	79.8%	3,306,721	80.4%	3,534,101	80.8%	3,683,890	80.9%	3,794,407	80.9%
Food & Beverage	-	0.0%	-	0.0%	-	0.0%	-	0.0%	-	0.0%	-	0.0%	-	0.0%
Other Operated Departments	(2,331)	-20.0%	(2,230)	-20.0%	(2,162)	-20.0%	(2,081)	-20.0%	(2,003)	-20.0%	(1,903)	-20.0%	(1,808)	-20.0%
Miscellaneous Income	23,314	70.0%	24,413	70.0%	25,783	70.0%	26,911	70.0%	28,083	70.0%	28,925	70.0%	29,793	70.0%
Total Departmental Profit	2,735,442	79.1%	2,864,557	79.1%	3,080,232	79.4%	3,331,551	80.0%	3,560,181	80.4%	3,710,912	80.6%	3,822,392	80.6%
Undistributed Operating Expenses														
Administration & General	296,563	8.6%	308,425	8.5%	319,220	8.2%	328,796	7.9%	338,660	7.7%	348,820	7.6%	359,285	7.6%
Information & Telecom Systems	95,813	2.8%	99,645	2.8%	103,133	2.7%	106,227	2.6%	109,413	2.5%	112,696	2.4%	116,077	2.4%
Sales & Marketing	294,003	8.5%	307,767	8.5%	329,608	8.5%	353,846	8.5%	376,271	8.5%	391,211	8.5%	402,883	8.5%
Franchise Fees	170,695	4.9%	196,612	5.4%	229,806	5.9%	246,843	5.9%	262,595	5.9%	273,099	5.9%	281,292	5.9%
Property Operation & Maintenance	159,688	4.6%	166,075	4.6%	171,888	4.4%	177,044	4.3%	182,356	4.1%	187,826	4.1%	193,461	4.1%
Utilities	171,094	4.9%	188,203	5.2%	201,377	5.2%	215,474	5.2%	230,557	5.2%	246,696	5.4%	263,965	5.6%
Total Undistributed Expenses	1,187,853	34.3%	1,266,727	35.0%	1,355,032	34.9%	1,428,229	34.3%	1,499,852	33.9%	1,560,348	33.9%	1,616,962	34.1%
Gross Operating Profit	1,547,589	44.7%	1,597,829	44.1%	1,725,200	44.5%	1,903,322	45.7%	2,060,329	46.5%	2,150,564	46.7%	2,205,430	46.5%
Base Management Fees	121,060	3.5%	126,728	3.5%	135,721	3.5%	145,701	3.5%	154,935	3.5%	161,087	3.5%	165,893	3.5%
Incentive Mgmt Fees	-	0.0%	-	0.0%	-	0.0%	-	0.0%	-	0.0%	-	0.0%	-	0.0%
Income Before Non-Oper Inc and Exp	1,426,529	41.2%	1,471,102	40.6%	1,589,478	41.0%	1,757,620	42.2%	1,905,394	43.0%	1,989,478	43.2%	2,039,538	43.0%
Non-Operating Income and Expenses														
Income	-	0.0%	-	0.0%	-	0.0%	-	0.0%	-	0.0%	-	0.0%	-	0.0%
Rent	-	0.0%	-	0.0%	-	0.0%	-	0.0%	-	0.0%	-	0.0%	-	0.0%
Property & Other Taxes	168,750	4.9%	175,500	4.8%	184,275	4.8%	191,646	4.6%	197,395	4.5%	203,317	4.4%	209,417	4.4%
Insurance	106,250	3.1%	110,500	3.1%	116,025	3.0%	120,666	2.9%	124,286	2.8%	128,015	2.8%	131,855	2.8%
Other	12,500	0.4%	13,000	0.4%	13,455	0.3%	13,859	0.3%	14,274	0.3%	14,703	0.3%	15,144	0.3%
Total Non-Operating Inc & Expenses	287,500	8.3%	299,000	8.3%	313,755	8.1%	326,171	7.8%	335,956	7.6%	346,034	7.5%	356,415	7.5%
Earnings Before Interest, Taxes, Depreciation and Amortization	1,139,029	32.9%	1,172,102	32.4%	1,275,723	32.9%	1,431,450	34.4%	1,569,438	35.5%	1,643,443	35.7%	1,683,122	35.5%
Replacement Reserve	172,943	5.0%	181,040	5.0%	193,887	5.0%	208,145	5.0%	221,336	5.0%	230,124	5.0%	236,990	5.0%
EBITDA Less Replacement Reserve	**$ 966,086**	**27.9%**	**$ 991,062**	**27.4%**	**$ 1,081,836**	**27.9%**	**$ 1,223,305**	**29.4%**	**$ 1,348,102**	**30.5%**	**$ 1,413,319**	**30.7%**	**$ 1,446,132**	**30.5%**

3. Should Bob test the current market value assumption of $11,875,000 by listing the property to see if a higher price is obtainable? What are the advantages and disadvantages of doing so?
4. What other ownership considerations should be evaluated prior to recommending a current hold for the asset?

Suggested answers to these questions appear at the end of this book.

21

Hotel Investment Overview

By Richard Warnick

***Richard Warnick** is Co-Founder and a Managing Director of CHMWarnick (www.CHMWarnick.com), the leading provider of hospitality asset management and strategic advisory services to the hospitality industry. The company currently asset-manages fifty-eight hotels comprising approximately 24,000 rooms valued at more than $12 billion. CHMWarnick's advisory services cover virtually every aspect of the hospitality industry and all phases of a hotel's life cycle, including ground-up development and repositioning. CHMWarnick has offices in Boston, New York, Los Angeles, Phoenix, Fort Lauderdale, Denver, Minneapolis, and Honolulu. Before forming CHMWarnick, Mr. Warnick founded and was President of Warnick + Company, a leading provider of advisory and asset management services to many of the world's leading hotel and real estate companies, private investors, financial institutions, and government agencies.*

Mr. Warnick has been involved in virtually every aspect of the hotel industry, including operations, development, finance, brokerage, and brand and business strategy. Before forming Warnick + Company, he was a principal with Laventhol & Horwath (L&H), an international accounting firm known for its expertise in the hospitality and real estate industries. Prior to his time with L&H, he was a development executive for two international hotel companies. He began his career in hotel operations and held senior-level management positions with several noted hotel management companies.

Mr. Warnick is a partner and member of the board in Montage Hotels & Resorts, a luxury hotel company founded in 2002. He serves as a strategic advisor to the company and has represented Montage in acquisitions and development deals worth more than $2.5 billion in total asset value.

Mr. Warnick is a member and former co-chair of the Urban Land Institute Hotel Development Council and is past President and Chairman Emeritus of the International Society of Hospitality Consultants. He is also a member of the Hotel Asset Managers Association and a past member of the Arizona State University Council on Real Estate. Mr. Warnick is on the advisory board of Thayer Ventures, a technology venture capital firm focused on the hospitality and travel industries, and is a shareholder and board member of KEYPR, a cloud-based guest experience management system that includes mobile check-in, keyless entry, and back-office workflow management for hotels.

Mr. Warnick has written numerous articles on the hospitality industry and is a frequent speaker at real estate, finance, and hotel industry conferences and roundtables. He attended Pennsylvania State University and graduated from Western International University with a dual major in finance and marketing.

THIS CHAPTER is divided into two sections. The first section is an update and expansion of an article I wrote several years ago that was subsequently converted to a chapter entitled "Investor Lessons" in *Hotel Investments: Issues & Perspectives,*

Fifth Edition, published by the American Hotel & Lodging Educational Institute. Section 2 deals with macro trends that I believe will affect and shape hotel investment in the future.

The Immutable Laws of Lodging Investment

The Immutable Laws are based on the belief that most economic losses[1] in lodging real estate are self-inflicted. Stated differently, while recessions (especially bad ones like the Great Recession) and unpredictable events (like 9/11 and SARS) contribute in varying degrees to economic loss, the majority of the hardship felt in the lodging sector over the years has been caused by—or at least exacerbated by—questionable investment decisions and/or questionable lending practices. The patterns described in this section are not only clearly observable, but definitively predictive. All of the mistakes related in this section have been repeated multiple times in the past and will continue to be repeated in the future—regardless of admonitions such as those contained in this chapter—for a variety of reasons, including:

- Conscious or subconscious amnesia.
- Turnover among investment decision-makers and lenders, ensuring a continuous crop of the inexperienced and uninitiated.
- Misaligned incentives.
- The *it-won't-happen-to-me* syndrome.
- The ever-present "ances" of arrogance and ignorance.

The conditions existing years ago when the original Immutable Laws were conceived are very different from those that exist today and those that will likely exist in the future. Updating these laws for this chapter was a test of their basic premise: their immutability. While some of the accompanying descriptive/explanatory language has been modified to be more current, I'm happy to say that the sixteen original Immutable Laws still stand as originally written. So far, so good. For this publication, I have added four more laws that I hope will also stand the test of time.

Heeding these laws may not prevent financial hardship in the lodging sector, especially in an era where unexpected events like 9/11 can suddenly and radically disrupt normal economic cycles, nor will it completely insulate investors from severe downturns or the onslaught of new supply. Heeding these laws can, however, substantially reduce the likelihood of problems and mitigate adverse impacts if and when they occur.

In no particular order, let's consider the now twenty Immutable Laws of Lodging Investment.

1. With few exceptions, hotels are not an appropriate asset class for a long-term hold.

Hotels are not an appropriate asset class for a long-term hold because the lodging business: (1) is highly cyclical, (2) has high operating leverage (rapidly eroding profits during cyclical lows), (3) is vulnerable to uncontrollable and unpredictable external events (e.g., terrorist attacks, epidemics, oil spills), (4) is vulnerable to periodic (and unavoidable) spikes in supply, and (5) is subject to extreme irrationality by those who control pricing decisions. Hotels also require extensive reinvestment in capital over time in order to remain competitive. So, the highest yields will accrue to industry-savvy cyclical traders. The most recent manifestation of this phenomenon is what is occurring in the energy belt. Like Sinatra sang: "... you're ridin' high in April, shot down in May..."

2. Never fall in love with real estate.
It is all too easy for irrationality to quietly creep into decision-making when one becomes too attached to the allure of a particular site, building, concept, or opportunity. Emotional attachment has undone more investors than affairs of the heart have undone politicians. This may be one of the more insidious pitfalls, because it can happen without total awareness and is usually subject to vociferous self-denial. A related concept that was not included in the prior versions of Immutable Laws is: *Never fall in love with the hotel industry.* It's easy to do, especially in the luxury and lifestyle segments. Hotels are more fun than office buildings, industrial parks, or apartment complexes. There is a prestige factor. Like a sports franchise, hotels can be sexy to own. Unlike sports franchises, supply is not constrained. Cool, sexy, and prestigious are not necessarily words that mesh well with return on investment.

3. Location is and always will be the most important criterion differentiating real estate—and hotels are no exception.
This law applies at both the macro/destination level (general desirability, airlift, demand base, local economic drivers, labor market, seasonality, etc.) and the micro level (access, visibility, type and quality of surrounding uses, views, barriers to entry, proximity to demand generators and/or attractions, etc.). When markets are at their peak performance, compression will partially level the playing field. But market compression is no substitute for location—a lesson learned episodically when markets go through their inevitable declines.

4. Leave some chips on the table.
No one is smart enough to know precisely when the bottom or the top of a market cycle will occur. Those who catch it at exactly the right time are simply lucky. However, you do not need to be a first mover during cyclical lows to buy at a good price—and there are plenty of signs to indicate when the sector is nearing the top (i.e., still time to exit).

5. Easy construction credit is a leading indicator that the top is approaching.
Because lenders generally rely on the false security of well-established trends, one of the first signs that the market is becoming risky is when lenders deem it to be safe for construction financing. Ironically, that spigot generally opens at about the time it should be closing. When hotel construction financing becomes easy and plentiful, it may not *yet* be time to run for the exits—but the hairs on the back of your neck should be tingling. (Note: There are services that track hotel development and construction activity and are thus an excellent proxy for actual knowledge of construction lending activity.)

6. If you can't build a hotel so as to open in the early to mid-part of a growth cycle, you probably shouldn't build it at all.

The best time to commence new development is in the late stages of a downturn, because land is comparatively cheap, construction costs are at their most competitive, and the hotel will open with the maximum amount of time remaining in the ensuing up-cycle. In most instances, the only guaranteed winners of late-cycle new construction—especially for upscale and luxury full-service hotels and resorts—are (1) developers using other people's money ("OPM"), (2) brands bent on growth, and (3) the second or third owner (after the first one or two failed). This may be the most difficult of the laws to adhere to, because adherence requires debt financing to be obtained at the time when virtually every construction lender will be loath to provide it. Ironically, it is the best part of the cycle to lend on new construction.

7. Do not equate luck with skill or intellect.

Many lodging industry investors who made money because of cyclical good fortune have gone on to lose it in other deals because they could not distinguish that good fortune from the knowledge/experience necessary to develop and operate this complicated property type.

8. Cap rates should be viewed as a derivative of value rather than a determinant of value.

Viewed in the context of real estate cycles, cap rates are the inverse of what they should be. That is, they are at their lowest when the cycle is near the top, net operating income is peaking, and there is no place to go but down. They are at their highest when the market is at or near the bottom, net operating income is low, and the future holds the most opportunity for growth. (Note: Early cycle buyers often buy at low cap rates. However, at the bottom of the cycle, when net operating incomes are severely depressed, buyers are not pricing assets *based* on cap rates, but rather on some combination of discount to replacement cost, projected current yields, and overall yields, including reversion. Cap rates for such buyers are still, therefore, derivative values.)

9. There will always be a replacement source of irrational capital.

Every cycle manages to attract a source of capital that will over-value assets as the cycle matures. Indeed, these are the buyers every cyclical investor prays for. The trick is to take advantage of them—not become one of them.

10. Generally speaking, leverage of more than 60–70 percent loan-to-value is a high-risk proposition for hotels.

The degree to which a borrower chooses to lever lodging assets in excess of this level is inversely proportional to: (1) the number of cycles the borrower has experienced, (2) the amount of the borrower's "own" money in the deal (versus other people's money), and (3) the borrower's propensity to reduce risk. Even experienced cyclical investors can be affected by excess leverage because of unpredictable event–related downturns. An extension of this law is that if you are borrowing against the promise of future cash flow—as opposed to in-place demonstrated cash flow—you had better be prepared to provide out of pocket money to cover potential shortfalls or you might be handing the keys to your lender. A second extension of this law is that if you are borrowing against late-cycle (peak) cash flow, a debt service coverage ratio (DCF) of, say, 1.4, could easily become a .9 DCF or worse when the inevitable down cycle occurs.

Indeed, the only "safe" way to over-leverage (assuming the borrower doesn't care if the lender ends up owning the asset) is to go all the way. That is, have little or no equity in the deal with non-recourse financing. This is equivalent to getting paid (from current cash flow) for having a put option to a lender. The borrower clips coupons when times are good and hands back the keys when times are bad.

11. Understand the nature of various industry participants and diligently observe their behavior.

As Margaret Thatcher so aptly said, "Nothing is more obstinate than a fashionable consensus." It's easy to get swept up in excessive exuberance, especially when the entire market seems to be moving in the same direction. But most industry participants are self-serving entities that unwittingly or intentionally stoke the cyclical flames. After all, developers need to develop, managers/brands need to grow, lenders need to lend, brokers need to transact, etc. To borrow from an old saw: *Where there's a fee, there's a way*. The actions of entities that benefit from or rely on the upcycle are the least reliable indicators of cyclical downturns. The entities to pay closest attention to (through their actions) are industry-savvy agnostics—that is, those who are knowledgeable of the business and indifferent to advancing any agenda other than optimizing returns. They most likely have a return-maximizing strategy—and the discipline to stick with it. (Note: This category specifically excludes investment funds that have already raised their capital and need to place it.)

12. The degree to which asset pricing is rational is inversely proportional to the amount and cost of capital in the system.

When money is plentiful, competition for assets is high. This is especially true when so much hotel transaction activity is driven by public and private funds raised specifically for acquisitions (money raised must be spent). Heavy competition for assets drives prices up and yields down. In today's environment (2015/2016), this phenomenon is being exacerbated by international capital flows to safe-harbor locales.

The cost of money is also a significant factor—never more so than in this post–Great Recession cycle where debt is the closest we have ever seen to being free. Consider the illustration in Exhibit 1. To maintain a 12 percent levered equity yield for this hypothetical hotel, the supportable price would need to be roughly $8,000,000 less if interest rates were 7.5 percent instead of 4.5 percent. Arguably, the variance would be even greater, since equity yields would also rise in a higher interest rate environment.

The prospect of interest rates reverting to historical norms (eventually) also adds a layer of risk to the exit strategy. If interest rates remain low for the long term, the bets buyers are making on exit value are rational and support the higher prices being paid today. But what happens if (some would say when) interest rates rise. Prudent underwriting would suggest that exit cap rates should take into account the potential that debt will be more expensive for a new buyer than what it is in this current artificially suppressed interest rate environment.

(Note: There are those who believe that any increase in interest rates will be offset by a corresponding rise in ADR and, thus, EBITDA. This is based on the

Exhibit 1 Effect of Interest Rates on Value

	4.5% interest rate environment	7.5% interest rate environment
NOI	$5,000,000	$5,000,000
LTV	65%	65%
Debt	$38,076,305	$32,616,998
Equity	$20,502,626	$17,562,999
Interest	4.5%	7.5%
Debt service	($2,539,686)	($2,892,441)
Cash flow	$2,460,314	$2,107,559
Target Equity Yield (Cash on Cash)	12.0%	12.0%
Supportable Purchase Price	**$58,578,931**	**$50,179,997**

belief that interest rates wouldn't rise if the economy were not in a robust state, thereby supporting ADR increases as well as strong occupancy. This logic is flawed in two ways. First, rising interest rates do not always occur because of or even consistent with economic growth. If you are too young to remember the "stagflation" of the 1970s, look it up so you can understand its perverse consequences. Second, hotel pricing does not necessarily parallel inflation and, in fact, is often completely divorced from the underlying cost of product delivery, especially where there is excess supply. And even under stabile supply conditions, prices are susceptible to the dumbest competitor in the market and/or to the competitor with the lowest cost basis. Room rates reflect competitive market conditions far more than they reflect what it cost to build, maintain, and operate any given property.)

13. The first sign that a down cycle is nearing the end is when the vast majority of industry participants have joined in the funeral dirge.
Looking back on this latest cyclical nadir, for example, it was early in the fourth quarter of 2009 when the third movement of Chopin's Op. 35 became the background soundtrack for nearly every conversation about the lodging industry. That said, thinly capitalized investors should take heed of Immutable Law 4, because the only entities that can (read *should)* take advantage of the lowest cyclical pricing are those that can afford to guess wrong.

14. The liquidity of lodging real estate varies widely from market to market.
Liquidity in this sense refers to the ability to convert quickly from a hard asset to cash. Of course, "quickly" is relative, since real estate, by its very nature, is illiquid. Below, I have identified ten market factors that, when combined, have a material and measurable effect on the liquidity of lodging real estate:

- Depth of the buyer pool (i.e., number of investors likely to be interested in the market)

- A market's appeal to international investors
- A market's appeal to institutional capital
- Barriers to entry
- The variability from high to low of historical pricing within the market (obviously, less variability is better)
- Historical recovery time from a market's prior cyclical lows
- Degree of strategic importance to lodging brands
- Size (the larger the market, the less susceptible it is to the dilutive effects of any given number of new rooms)
- Demand diversity and demonstrated stability
- The degree to which the market depends on the old economy (e.g., traditional manufacturing) versus the new economy (e.g., technology)

The comparative liquidity of markets was particularly acute during the buying cycle that began in 2009. It was a case of the "haves" versus the "have nots." In the United States, the "have" markets are generally gateway cities on the east and west coasts (especially, New York City [which is in a category of its own], San Francisco, and Miami), and the "have nots," which to some degree are all the others (especially secondary and tertiary center-of-the-country markets). Of course, as economic cycles progress and pricing in the "have" markets becomes prohibitive, the "have not" markets become increasingly desirable. (Note: this law does not speak to where one might get the highest returns. Rather, it speaks to risk mitigation from the standpoint of where might an investor be able to exit within the narrowest range of time and, all other things being equal, with the least risk of loss.)

15. The liquidity of lodging real estate varies, depending on asset size and type. In addition to market factors, specific asset characteristics affect liquidity. This is generally related to the number of buyers for any given asset. For example, for the foreseeable future, there will be adequate buyers for:

- Top-tier branded select-service assets that have adequate remaining time under the license agreement
- Iconic assets in desirable markets
- Hotels in New York City (notwithstanding the surge in new supply)
- Hotels in desirable markets with high barriers to entry (e.g., San Francisco)
- Hotels that will look sexy on the cover of someone's annual report or equity offering memorandum

On the other hand, there are generally fewer buyers for:

- Generic resorts
- Small (less than 100 rooms) independent hotels, because they are not suitable for institutional buyers (though a number of REITs are now investing in the "lifestyle" hotel segment)

- Properties with some form of incurable obsolescence (e.g., exterior corridor mid-tier hotels)
- Management-intensive assets, such as those with an outsize reliance on food and beverage
- Hotels with a questionable branding future (e.g., an Embassy Suites nearing the end of its franchise term)
- Hotels with virtually no branding future (e.g., a thirty-year-old Days Inn)
- Hotels requiring a capital-intensive repositioning (unless the acquisition price justifies the repositioning investment)

16. Beware of "Star Trek" underwriting—boldly projecting that ADRs will go where they have never gone before.

This admonition applies at both the market level (projecting market ADRs well in excess of their inflation-adjusted historical highs) and the single asset level (projecting that a particular asset will achieve ADRs materially in excess of market comparables). This is a corollary to "if you build it, they will come"; that being, "if you build it, they will pay." A market's pricing and pricing power are, in fact, highly resistant to change. Therefore, in the absence of material and demonstrable changes in demand characteristics, the most reliable gauge of any given market's future cyclical ADR performance is its past cyclical ADR performance. Of course, there are exceptions. For instance:

- The rapid run up in rates in San Francisco in 2014 and 2015
- Markets with pent-up/unsatisfied higher-end demand without commensurate higher-end supply (Bentonville, Arkansas, before the introduction of 21C)
- Certain resort destinations where demand can be induced/created by brands like Aman, Four Seasons, and Montage
- Introducing a new generation select-service hotel (e.g., Hilton Garden, Marriott Courtyard) into a market with older/obsolete hotels

(The last three of these examples are not necessarily exceptions to Immutable Law 16, because they do not reflect the performance of true comparables in their respective markets.)

Investors would be wise to remember that gravity exists, both as a force of nature and a force of economics, and the lodging landscape is littered with the bones of those who believed they could ignore that reality.

17. You are more likely to make money on the buy side than you are on the sell side of lodging real estate.

Absent over-leveraging, under-capitalization, or simply bad execution, going-in price generally outweighs other factors affecting returns in lodging real estate, including re-branding, re-positioning, better management, and so on. Being in a hotel at the right basis is also the best hedge against downside market risks. The corollary is that every investor should take comfort in the fact that the only thing worse than losing a deal is winning it at the wrong price. Or, stated differently, the best deal you ever did may be the one you didn't do.

Readers will no doubt have observed numerous instances where an investor paid an aggressive price for a hotel only to sell it later in a frothy market for an insanely high price. However, this feels more like gambling than an investment strategy. Investors' propensity to pursue such an approach likely depends on the amount of their own money in the deal (versus OPM) and whether they have experienced a down cycle.

18. Replacement cost is an unreliable guide to value.
One of the factors most often used in gauging the value of a hotel asset—especially in down markets or periods of early recovery (when cash flows are not indicative of value)—is how the acquisition price compares to replacement cost. The basic assumption to this valuation methodology is that, at some point in the cycle, construction will recommence and that the asset will be worth at least what it would cost to reproduce it. The problem with this discount-to-replacement-cost theory is that it presumes that a hotel of the type and location being purchased is—or will be at some future date—economically viable at the cost it would take to build it. There are simply too many instances where that is not the case. This is especially true in the luxury tier, where development costs today typically range from $500,000 to $1 million per key (rarely less, and significantly more in some locations and with some product types). How many markets support the RevPARs necessary to justify that kind of investment without some other motive (e.g., the sale of branded residential, "place-making" for a resort community, or urban mixed-use)—benefits that will not generally accrue to a hotel buyer? Another danger in using replacement cost is underestimating the cost of CapEx for older hotels, which can run 8.0 percent to 10.0 percent of gross revenue—even after a renovation.

Replacement cost works best as an indicator of value on non-luxury mainstream hotels (not resorts). For other product types, an attractive discount to replacement cost should be nothing more than a starting point to warrant a closer look.

19. Industry fundamentals are not a proxy for hotel values.
One of the more frequent themes relating to hotel values (occurring at almost every industry conference) is, "Where we are in the cycle?" It is often expressed in terms of baseball innings ("What inning are we in?"). In early recovery periods, the question may be framed as follows: "When we will return to prior 'peak' performance?" The "fundamentals" generally referred to in these discussions is simply RevPAR (in real versus nominal dollars), because, thanks to STR, it is the most accurate publicly available data and it encompasses millions of hotel rooms.

Such discussions are interesting from the standpoint of cyclical supply and demand, but they can be quite misleading in terms of asset prices. The up-cycle prior to the Great Recession was a poster child for why this is true, because asset prices in 2006 and 2007 were driven by a confluence of favorable lodging fundamentals, low interest rates, high leverage, and plentiful capital. In order for prices to hit those same levels, all of these conditions must be repeated, or some must be strong enough to offset the laggards. Stated differently, there are many factors that influence asset pricing, and they do not always align with what most people consider to be industry fundamentals—even if one focuses on the only industry fundamental that really matters—namely, net operating income.

20. Barriers to entry are more of a speed bump than a stop sign.

Barriers to entry are highly touted (including by me) as an important investment criterion—but they are often transitory or based on conditions that can be altered. This does not diminish their importance, as they are and always will be a core determinant of successful lodging investment. Investors must realize, however, that not all barriers to entry are created equal; their effectiveness ranges from being merely an inconvenience for new development to giving properties a good head start over new development and to providing a sustainable supply-constrained market.

Barriers to entry are more effective for urban hotels than for resorts, because all individual business travelers and many individual leisure travelers are going to a specific destination for a specific purpose. That is, business travelers who have a meeting in New York City are not going to travel to Chicago instead because the rates are better there or they like a particular hotel there. That condition is not true for the meetings market segment, which accounts for a significant amount of the demand for most resorts. So, having high barriers to entry in a specific resort destination (Destination A) does not prevent someone from developing a competitive property in an alternate resort destination (Destination B) that can compete for groups and vacationers who may like, but are not locked into, Destination A. Take, for instance, the Coachella Valley in Southern California, which includes the desert cities of Palm Springs, Rancho Mirage, Palm Desert, and Indian Wells. Even though there has been a dearth of new supply in that area, the market has proven vulnerable to regional supply additions (e.g., the Southern California coast, Las Vegas, and Phoenix). This external vulnerability is particularly acute for destinations that are disadvantaged in terms of access, especially airlift.

Among barriers to entry, the least reliable is cost, because:

- Some public entity might use tax-free bond financing to build—or subsidize a private developer to build—a hotel in order to generate new transient occupancy taxes, support urban renewal, supply additional rooms for a convention center, etc.; or
- Some enterprising developer—or a brand hell-bent on expansion—might convince an equity capital source and a lender to finance an economically unsupportable deal; or
- Some high-net-worth individual might decide to build a monument to his/her ego irrespective of project economics; or
- A mixed-use component (probably residential) might sufficiently alter the economics of a hotel component to overcome the cost barrier;

... and so on.

Lack of entitlements is a more effective barrier, but the entities controlling entitlements may allow a re-zoning for a variety of reasons, including, but not limited to:

- A desire to generate tax revenue (municipalities love to tax visitors since they do not vote—except with their feet by choosing a different location).

- A change in the tenor of local politics (e.g., election of a new pro-growth city council).
- A successful lawsuit.
- Successful lobbying by a smart, well-capitalized developer.
- Urban redevelopment.

A lack of available land may also seem like an effective barrier. But public land (e.g., an old military base) may be privatized for development, or already developed private land might be converted to a higher and better use if the economics are compelling. The harder it is to find available development sites, the more likely it is that sub-optimized land will be repurposed.

NIMBYs (the "not-in-my-back-yard" crowd) can be a barrier to entry but, generally, only when combined with a required zoning change. Even then, there are countless examples of well-heeled, well-organized local citizenry losing a re-zoning battle to a committed municipality and a well-capitalized developer or land owner.

Ultimately, the most effective barrier to entry is really a combination of most or all of these factors (i.e., you need more than one). And, reflecting back on Immutable Law 3, location is the ultimate hedge against competition, regardless of the ebbs and flows of barriers to entry.

Economic, Demographic, and Industry Macro Trends Shaping Lodging Investment in the Foreseeable Future

At the risk of stating the obvious, the future is hard to predict. And in the lodging sector, it gets harder every day, because:

- The marketplace is complex and increasing in complexity.
- Change happens at a fast pace, and the pace is accelerating.
- The world is more integrated and interdependent—events in distant places can have far-reaching consequences on the lodging sector.
- There are rapid advances in technology and the application of technology, and the pace is accelerating.
- Economic and political volatility is extraordinarily high—"black cygnets" abound, and one or more may become a black swan.

For example: Who would have predicted in 2010 what has occurred with respect to Airbnb, a then two-year-old San Francisco–based startup? True, there was concept precedence (e.g., VRBO). But even if someone saw the potential growth for this concept in the sharing economy, who would have further predicted the size of this latent market or the speed at which it would grow to mainstream credibility? A mere six years from the introduction of Airbnb, the company's first major round of funding in April of 2014 valued the company at $10 billion. Subsequent rounds (one in June 2015 and another in November 2015) that raised more than $1.5 billion in additional capital pegs the company's valuation at $25.5 billion. To put this in perspective, as of January 2016, Hilton's market cap was $17.4

billion, Marriott's was $15.2 billion, Starwood's was $10.0 billion, and Hyatt's was $5.1 billion—and Airbnb does not own, operate, or franchise a single hotel room anywhere on the planet. Even founders Brian Chesky and Joe Gebbia must be pinching themselves to make sure this is not a dream.

A lot of Airbnb's value is related to its rapid growth and perceived potential for future growth. Still, think for a moment about comparative values. As of January 2016, an eight-year-old Internet distribution channel is worth:

- About 80 percent of the combined value of Hilton and Marriott
- Over two-and-a-half times the largest public hotel REIT (Host) and about the same as the top seven public hotel REITs combined[2]

Beside the value implications, Airbnb is changing the supply and demand equation in a very material way. In New York City, for instance, it is estimated[3] that Airbnb has over 30,000 listings and is believed to be one of the major factors limiting ADR growth in the market.

In spite of this general unpredictability, there are certain "transcendent" macro trends that are and will continue to affect lodging dynamics, and they should definitely be considered in evaluating lodging investments. It is worth noting that, for the most part, these trends are not investment-focused. However, hotel real estate is inextricably linked to the operation of hotels; what affects one will, directly or indirectly, affect the other. Listed below, in no particular order but numbered for ease of reference, are some of the more important of these macro trends. With apologies to international readers, they are decidedly U.S.-centric.

1. Continuing and escalating impacts on hotel investments by brands.
There are many ways in which brands influence asset pricing. Some of the more significant/prolific ones include the following.

Property Improvement Plans (PIPs) on change of ownership. Every time a branded asset is sold, the buyer is subject to an upgrade to the latest and greatest brand standards. The requirements can be eye-popping. Even when the initial PIP is negotiated down from the brand's wish list, buyers will likely be subject to future pressure to meet the latest standards. Investors need to obtain benchmarking guidance on typical PIPs at different stages of a product life cycle and factor this element into their acquisition underwriting (and exit strategy). While the buyer of the asset will pay for the PIP, the sales price of the asset will be affected. That is, the purchase price will equal the estimated asset value *less* the cost to meet brand PIP requirements and other required CapEx.

Cost escalation via centralized services. Operators (especially brands) have engaged in a gradual and systematic transfer of many services that were once part of their management fee to "centralized services" for which they are separately paid. Because most management agreements require centralized services to be provided "without profit," the operators providing such services do not mark up the cost of providing them. However, if a branded operator charges an owner "at cost" for something they used to include as part of a basic management fee, and if, as a result of doing so, more of the management fee flows to the brand's/operator's bottom line, it is a distinction without a difference. That is, it equates to more money to the operator, less money to the owner.

Brand outsourcing at the owner's expense. In addition to escalating centralized services costs, brands are outsourcing and relying on third parties for an increasing number of services and are passing these costs on to owners. Examples include commissionable group sales, online travel agency (OTA) "commissions," sales training, recruitment, purchasing, quality assurance inspections, energy studies, AAA/Forbes training, etc.

Short-term license agreements for purchased versus newly built hotels. If a franchise renewal is only awarded for, say, a ten-year period, what is the plan for the hotel post-expiration? How is exit value affected when there are only three to five years left on the license agreement for a desirable brand? What, for instance, is a thirty-year-old Embassy Suites worth if the license is not renewed on sale?

Same-brand impact issues. The big brands (mostly public companies) must grow. That means, given the opportunity, they will add as many hotels as they can to any given market. "Can" in this context is often determined by impact studies to determine "incremental" impact. That is, assuming the new hotel would enter the market in any event (and thus affect a given existing hotel regardless), how much additional impact would the existing hotel suffer if the new hotel bore the same brand as the existing hotel? A dip in revenue for an existing brand hotel that is recovered over a given time period (often, three years) is considered "acceptable" by most brands. Fees for impact studies are far less than for a traditional market study with financial projections, but the issues are easily as complex. Moreover, outcomes rely heavily on judgment calls—and the independence of third-party consultants conducting such studies is suspect, since they are beholden to the brands to be on an approved list.

Brand proliferation. There are many brands, and they vary wildly in terms of their value to a hotel owner. In the "lifestyle" segment alone, there are now about 100 brands (or wannabe brands).

Impact on a hotel from other brands within the same brand family. With the proliferation of brands within the same corporate entity, a frequent occurrence is for a brand holding company to enter the market with another competitive brand from their portfolio. Rarely does a management contract or franchise license agreement offer protection from such intra-brand cannibalization, even though these brands share all manner of systems, marketing intelligence, customer loyalty programs, and data (including customer data).

The brand attribute arms race. The Great Recession and a tepid recovery put a damper on brand initiatives (capital and operational). However, as the lodging sector strengthened, a steady increase in brand-mandated spending has occurred. Hotel owners should brace themselves, because that will continue into the foreseeable future. Increases in brand-mandated spending relate primarily to three areas:

- Enhanced services, especially to members of the respective guest loyalty programs which are financed by hotel owners (see next prediction).
- Increased CapEx costs as brands attempt to improve their product/image at the expense of hotel owners.
- Increased technology costs as brands try to leapfrog competitors—or play catch up—at the expense of hotel owners. (Please see additional comments under "6. Technology—the good, the bad, and the ugly" below.)

The bottom line is that, regardless of the cause, brands will have an outsized impact on lodging investment for the foreseeable future.

2. Increasing costs of brand loyalty programs.

> Dateline January 28, 2025 – Los Angeles
> Instant Hospitality News Network (IHNN)
>
> Hilltop Hotels & Resorts announced today at the International Lodging Investment Summit that it will roll out its latest Hilltop Honors program: "We'll pay you $50 to stay at any of our 47 Hilltop brands—and you'll get three free rooms at any Hilltop property worldwide."
>
> Not to be outdone, Marrionette Hotels vowed to match Hilltop's offer to Marrionette's 630 million Marrionette Reward members at any of their 62 brands—*and* include free breakfast.
>
> Hilltop's and Marrionette's latest offers appear to have been precipitated by the successful launch of a new program by Hyend Hotels & Resorts: "We'll Pay Your Transportation Costs to Our Hotel" available to all of their 300 million Gold Visa members.
>
> All three companies have stated they will impose a special assessment to hotel owners to cover the cost of the new programs, since the current 25 percent of total folio charge for each frequent guest stay has been insufficient to cover the escalating cost of their loyalty programs.
>
> The comments of frequent business traveler Juanita Perez exemplify those of most frequent travelers surveyed by IHNN staff for this story. Said Ms. Perez, who carries loyalty cards for seven hotel brands: "As long as they keep paying me, I'll keep staying at their hotels."

Though the preceding news release from the year 2025 was written with tongue solidly in cheek, it is not hyperbole to state that the offered benefits of the brands' guest frequency programs are increasing dramatically as hotel companies try to differentiate undifferentiated products with more benefits in order to "buy" the loyalty of their customers. I can't predict when the breaking point will be reached, but one thing is increasingly clear. As long as brand "loyalty" can be purchased with someone else's money, brands have no incentive to take their foot off the throttle.

One must also wonder about the long-term effectiveness of these programs, as OTAs and other intermediaries ramp up their own loyalty programs totally independent of any brand other than their own.

3. Continued escalation in the cost of guest acquisition.
The lodging industry has fought hard—to little or no effect—to reclaim pricing control over rooms inventory from OTAs. In 2007, 85 percent of all online bookings came directly from hotel brand websites (referred to generically as "brand.com"), with OTAs providing the remaining 15 percent. During the first half of 2015—the latest data available for this chapter—the allocation had shifted to 64 percent from brand.com and 36 percent from OTAs. To make matters worse, individual hotels and hotel companies have become more and more reliant on third-party intermediaries for group business as well, at a substantial incremental cost. It is common practice today to have local, regional, and national hotel sales teams dedicated to third-party group intermediaries—i.e., sellers focused on selling to sellers. The

industry's latest crack cocaine is Cvent, which currently offers relatively efficient access to meeting planners through sophisticated electronic RFP methodology. Do not be surprised if Cvent tries to shift to a merchant model based on a percentage of booked business sometime in the not-too-distant future.

Notwithstanding this massive shift in how business is sourced, owners still have to pay full brand marketing and group sales fees even if the brand is incidental to the purchase decision. This leaves only one party on the wrong side of rising customer acquisition costs: hotel owners. The industry's top expert on this topic, Cindy Estis Green, CEO of Kalibri Labs, has done significant research on the issue of third-party intermediary costs. Through its research, Kalibri Labs estimates that the U.S. hotel industry paid $14 billion in commissions and transaction fees in 2015, largely to the global distribution systems, travel agencies, and OTAs (not including most group commissions), and that number will continue to grow as more and more transactions are touched by more and more intermediaries. Preliminary numbers from the 2016 update of this Kalibri Labs report show that hotels' total customer acquisition costs are estimated to be between 15 to 25 percent of total guest-paid revenue. Another notable statistic from Kalibri Labs: commission costs in the U.S. market grew at *twice* the rate of revenue growth from 2011–2015.

All this is occurring against a backdrop of a new generation of middlemen bellying up to the trough with smartphone apps aimed at aggregating pricing data or simply becoming another fee-for-service purchase channel for consumers. Unless you are a hotel owner, these are great business models in that they get to price and sell inventory that they do not have to build, service, or maintain.

Adding insult to injury, the introduction of so many intermediaries into the booking equation means that there is a declining percentage of customers with whom hotels (and hotel companies) have a direct relationship.

Good strides have been made on the OTA front to correct this shrinking revenue problem, with certain big brands negotiating lower commissions, restrictions on last room availability, etc. Brands have also restricted or eliminated loyalty program points for business booked through OTAs. And consumers are finding that a room booked through an OTA is not afforded the same privileges and flexibility as a room booked directly. Many brands are introducing aggressive communication campaigns outlining the benefits to consumers of booking directly. Even the Federal Trade Commission, using data and examples compiled by the American Hotel & Lodging Association (AH&LA), has posted warnings to consumers about the high risk of booking through third parties. More work is being done by a group of owners and brands to level the playing field through AH&LA's Consumer Innovation Forum, which will be visible in the market later in 2016 and early 2017. Still, the concern is that there may not be enough fingers to plug all the revenue-leaking holes in the dike—and until the tide turns, hotel owners will continue to bear the brunt of revenue leakage.

4. Brand.com to the rescue—or not.

As noted above, a major effort has been underway by the major brands to take back lost ground from the OTAs by directing customers to their proprietary websites. Considering that OTAs have an effective "commission" rate of 15 percent to

25 percent, depending on each brand's negotiating strength/ability, owners have been rooting for the brands. What is not known to most owners (because it is obscured and difficult to assess) is that the cost of customer acquisition through the brands is now approaching the lower end of the OTA range (as high as 13 percent, according to in-house research performed by a large, highly sophisticated owner of many hotels across multiple brands).

5. The disruptors will get disrupted.

This topic brings to mind the 1969 movie classic, *Butch Cassidy and the Sundance Kid,* in which a pair of outlaws (Butch and Sundance) futilely attempt to escape a relentless posse that continues to find their trail. After a string of unsuccessful attempts to lose the posse, Butch says to Sundance: "I couldn't do that. Could *you* do that? Why can *they* do it? Who *are* those guys?" And thereafter, in growing frustration, he repeatedly asks Sundance, "Who *are* those guys?"

Now, the OTAs, companies that have devoured so much of the industry's revenue, profits, and wealth, are about to themselves be eaten. The posse in this case is Google (and perhaps Amazon). With enormous financial resources, first-in-line consumer contact, and a frightening amount of individual demographic and behavioral data, these behemoths will likely make Expedia and Priceline far less relevant in the coming ten years—notwithstanding the OTAs' efforts to morph and adapt through innovation and acquisitions of travel-related technology companies. Before popping the champagne cork, however, brands and hotel owners alike should note that it is only a matter of time before they also become part of the meal.

6. Technology—the good, the bad, and the ugly.

The hotel business has been woefully behind the curve in terms of developing or adopting technology. That is now changing so rapidly that the industry is going to be suffering from whiplash for the next decade. Here's a brief look at the coming technological changes—the good, the bad, and the ugly.

The Good. Technology is benefitting many aspects of the industry, including customer access, customer relations, marketing, revenue management, mobile check-in/keyless entry, service management, employee accountability, labor productivity, inventory management, real-time market intelligence, purchasing, data collection/management, and on and on. It seems that at least weekly there is a new application, system, or platform that promises material benefits to hotels. The emerging trend of hosted and cloud-based technology also affords the opportunity to deploy new systems without the need for costly on-site hardware, programming, and maintenance. Cloud computing has the added benefit of rapid deployment and inexpensive updates/upgrades. And while most consumer-facing applications are parasitic in terms of revenue, there are a few notable exceptions. For example, Nor1 is a technology that both improves hotel revenue and increases guest satisfaction by upselling underutilized premium rooms. Another recent example is HotelsByDay, which allows consumers to purchase hotel rooms for discreet periods of time during the day when rooms would otherwise sit idle (the equivalent of increasing inventory turnover in retail, or a chain like McDonald's adding breakfast to capitalize on an otherwise idle time period).

The Bad. Of course, new technologies are not free, and their adoption is generally not voluntary for hotels that are part of a brand. The rapid introduction of technology has become another competitive weapon in the fight for market share by the brands as they increasingly try to cater to the rising wave of tech-savvy consumers. Naturally, these costs are paid for directly or indirectly by hotel owners.

The Ugly. There are a number of scary aspects of technology that will affect the industry in profound ways in the foreseeable future. The ones I believe will be most impactful are listed below:

- *Pricing transparency.* Technology has introduced unprecedented pricing transparency and knowledge into the marketplace, providing consumers with virtually instantaneous and continuous knowledge of offered prices for rooms (and other services) on a real-time basis. These new technologies enable consumers to exploit the weaknesses in the industry's flawed pricing structure. Commoditization is bad for hotel ownership—and brands. Consider TripBAM, for instance. This clever tool gives consumers (both individuals and corporate travel departments) the ability to (1) book a room at a hotel of their choice far into the future, (2) identify other hotels in that destination that they would consider if their pricing was competitive, and then (3) allow TripBAM to automatically track pricing offers for that set of hotels on all electronic channels and automatically cancel their reservation and rebook it at a new hotel—*or at the same hotel*—any time a better price for the room is identified. The process is repeated over and over, all the way up to the date of arrival. Another relatively new rate-inhibiting technology is Rocketrip, which allows firms to reduce travel costs by providing a way for employees to share in the savings they generate by staying in less expensive hotels, flying during off hours, etc.
- *Third-party apps.* Advances in technology continue to allow new forms of intermediation, which is great for the consumer, but profit-eroding for the owners of the physical assets being intermediated. The introduction of third-party apps in the lodging space has become the latest disruptor to contend with, ultimately costing owners a lot of money. Historically, the introduction of new technologies by third parties was constrained by expensive research, development, and marketing costs. In today's world, it is much easier and far less expensive to develop, market, and distribute new platforms.
- *Technology obsolescence.* The shelf life or time between rollout and obsolescence of a given technology can be shorter than the expected amortization of its cost. While hosted and cloud-based solutions help mitigate this risk to owners, not all systems and applications are going to stand the test of time. Even those which seem "future proof" can become unexpectedly obsolete due to a market-disrupting advance or an unanticipated change in the way business is transacted. And there's no available source to tell us where the next world-changing innovation is coming from. Moreover, not all of the technologies being marketed will survive. Investing in a cool new technology may seem like a good idea, but not if it fails to get sufficient market traction before the venture capital funding runs out.

- *Airbnb.* This technology-driven platform is no longer just an option for adventurous leisure travelers and those willing to take risks in exchange for favorable pricing. More and more, it has edged into the mainstream, in spite of its drawbacks for the core travel marketplace (e.g., safety, sanitation, absence of services, inconsistency, the oddities of check-in, etc.). There are speed bumps, including regulatory agencies, homeowner associations, taxing authorities, AH&LA—but this "shadow inventory" is here to stay and it's growing. It is already having a serious impact on rate growth in certain major markets like New York City.
- *System integration.* The number of desired/needed/available systems is increasing, as is the number of vendors offering technology-driven solutions. System-to-system communication is a big issue—solvable, but at a price.
- *Brand proprietary systems.* Many brands are obsessed with developing and owning their own technology platforms (keyless entry, for instance). While it is understandable for a brand to want to have a system that no one else has, brands have not had a great track record of developing and operating leading-edge technology. Brand-owned legacy systems that do not run on an open platform also exacerbate the integration issue described in the point above.
- *Questionable brand pass-through costs.* Brand research and development expenditures are amortized by including those costs in centralized expenses and are, therefore, generally paid for by hotel owners. This may be justifiable in theory, but the investment pain is not shared by the brands. With few exceptions (e.g., Omni Hotels & Resorts), brands do not own much real estate. Those that still do are quickly divesting in pursuit of the so-called "asset light" capital strategy (largely a consequence of their public ownership—Wall Street does not like real estate on the balance sheet of the hotel brands). This situation is exacerbated by the issue in the point above.
- *Maintenance.* The cost of maintaining the various technology platforms can be quite high. These costs can also be difficult to measure/monitor, as they come in many forms: brand centralized services, vendor charges, IT consulting, software updates, and in-house payroll.

7. Evolving demographic influences.

There are at least three clear demographic trends that are affecting the lodging sector:

- While still influential, Baby Boomers are declining as a portion of active travelers. There were about seventy-six million births in the United States from 1946 to 1964, the nineteen-year period called the "Baby Boom." Of those seventy-six million boomers, nearly eleven million had died by 2012, leaving about sixty-five million survivors. When immigrants are included, the Baby Boomer number is still over seventy-six million. Every day, roughly 6,000 Baby Boomers turn sixty-five. Having retired or surpassed their peak earning years, their travel spending will both change (less business, more leisure) and decline over the next decade.

- The combined population of GenXers and Millennials (164 million) dwarfs the Baby Boomers. These consumers have different purchase criteria and spending habits than their predecessors.
- In addition to this shift in age demographics, the U.S. population has begun a transition from predominantly English-speaking Caucasians to predominantly non-Caucasians (66 percent Caucasian in 2009 to an estimated 46 percent in 2043). In the not-too-distant future, English may actually no longer be the first language of the majority of U.S. inhabitants. Even today, roughly fifty million Americans speak a language other than English in their homes.

8. Post–Baby Boomer travelers will continue to change the lodging landscape in profound ways.

As just mentioned, post–Baby Boom consumers are meaningfully different from their predecessors—at least so far. Their demands, desires, and behaviors are driving changes in hotel design, functionality, and even brand. Witness, for instance, the rush to so-called "lifestyle" product introductions across the industry, including by the big brands. At the time this chapter was written, there were about 100 lifestyle brands operating nationally or regionally in the United States, the majority of which were introduced to the market in the past five years.

The following are four significant ways that post–Baby Boomer consumers are different from Baby Boomers:

- Notwithstanding some notable exceptions (e.g., the iPhone), post–Baby Boomer consumers do not exhibit brand loyalty, at least in a traditional sense.
- Largely as a result of advances in technology and the post–Baby Boomers' natural embrace of it, the preferred purchase methods of post–Baby Boomer consumers differ radically from that of Baby Boomers.
- Post–Baby Boomers' method of product validation—that is, how they hear about products, whose opinions they trust, and from where those opinions emanate—also differ materially from Boomers (e.g., social media).
- Post–Baby Boomers distrust traditional advertising more than their predecessor generations. One possible reason is found in the following quote attributed to Shane Smith, founder of Vice Media: "Young people today have been marketed to since they were newborns, because cartoons are made to sell cereal. So, as a consequence, they have the most sophisticated B.S. detectors of all time." Whatever the reason, this distrust has serious implications in terms of how sellers communicate to this buyer pool.

9. Female travelers will continue to increase as a percentage of all business travelers.

According to a 2014 study by Judi Brownell, Ph.D., a professor at Cornell University in the Management and Organizational Behavior Program, women are the fastest-growing component of the business traveler market segment in the United States, and they already account for nearly half of all business travelers. Their needs and desires are different from those of male travelers, with implications that extend to hotel design, operating modalities, and marketing. Quite aside from the increasing importance of women to the business traveler market, Marybeth Bond, the creator of "The Gutsy Traveler" website and author of eleven travel books, asserts that 80 percent of *all* travel decisions are made by women.

10. Emerging demand sources.

According to the U.S. Travel Association, there are more than a billion potential travelers from Asia that will soon become lodging consumers outside their home country. Initially, their impact will be felt mostly in gateway markets. This surge in new travelers can have very positive impacts on owners and operators who understand their expectations in terms of physical plant, product offerings (F&B, amenities, etc.), and service (cultural sensitivity, translation services, and so on). Travel visas have been an impediment to this potential demand pool, but the United States is finally addressing this issue in the largest Asian market, mainland China. Growing internationalization does, however, increase vulnerability to currency fluctuations and international terrorism.

11. Continuing escalation in labor costs.

Notwithstanding advances in technology that improve measurement, accountability, and productivity, labor costs will continue to rise as a result of several inexorable factors:

- *Government intervention.* Government intervention takes many forms:
    - The Affordable Health Care Act is a costly burden on labor-intensive businesses like hotels and will materially and adversely impact operating costs.
    - Minimum wage increases (national, state, and local).
    - Living wage requirements imposed by a growing number of municipalities.
    - Mandated paid time off.
    - The Department of Labor's proposed amendments to the Fair Labor Standards Act (FLSA), which will dramatically increase the minimum salary required for employees to qualify for FLSA white-collar exemptions and substantially increase the minimum compensation required for employees to qualify for the Highly Compensated Employee exemption (from $23,660 in 2015 to $50,440 plus COLA adjustments in 2016 and beyond).
    - Changes at the NLRB that favor organized labor (see next point).
- *Organized labor.* Unions have placed a giant bull's-eye on the hotel industry. And why not? This labor-intensive business is geographically locked in place. That is, unlike most manufacturers, hotel owners cannot move their assets to right-to-work locales. Hotels are and will remain vulnerable to unions and the politicians who court them. This unholy alliance between unions and politicians is especially prevalent in situations where municipalities facilitate hotel development, either through subsidies or direct ownership. As for the impact on the bottom line, ask anyone who owns/operates a hotel in San Francisco or New York City what happens when hotel unions control wages, benefits, and

work rules. Even in less virulent locales, the adverse impact of unionization on a hotel's bottom line is significant.

- *Failed immigration reform.* The (misplaced) burden of immigration enforcement is a hidden cost on businesses that rely heavily on unskilled labor. It also depresses the labor pool for housekeeping, stewarding, and similar entry-level positions.

12. Increased government regulation (e.g., ADA).

Every business in the United States is affected by increasing regulation. A recent and notable example for the lodging industry was the pool lift regulation that increased the cost and litigation risk for every U.S. hotel with a swimming pool. While sensitivity to the disabled is a laudable objective, use of these unsightly and expensive devices has been astonishingly low. It is a virtual certainty that the next pool lift debacle is being cooked up in some government office right now.

Note: The aforementioned escalating cost factors bring to mind a very interesting (and disturbing) structural aspect of the lodging industry; namely, that increased costs cannot easily be passed on to the consumer in terms of higher prices. That is, like any business whose product inventory is fixed and highly perishable, prices of hotel rooms are market-based, not cost-based. Thus, pricing power is vulnerable to the dumbest or most desperate competitor in the market.

13. Increasing business complexity.

The goal of revenue management is to sell the right *product* to the right *customer* at the right *time* and for the right *length* of time at the right *price* with the *least intermediated cost* (net versus gross revenue). This is no small task, given the multitude of distribution channels, intermediaries, and technologies at play—and the speed and frequency at which changes in strategy need to occur. The human brain is incapable of managing a process this complicated. Even most automated revenue management systems fall short, including the ones used by the big brands.

Rapid advances in technology are not likely to abate, and new challenges will accompany those advancements. Take, for instance, how quickly Mobile Travel Chat (also known as Mobile Travel Concierge) broke into the market. Already boasting nearly a dozen entrants (e.g., HYPER, Lola, ETA, HelloGbye, GoHeroGo, Hello Scout), MTCs use artificial intelligence to personalize travel bookings for users by learning user preferences and remembering them to make suggestions for the next booking. They are creating a new form of commission-based OTA expected to be highly popular, especially with Millennials.

As a result of its increasing complexity and a recognition of just how important it has become, revenue management has evolved from:

- A part-time pursuit by existing hotel personnel holding other positions, to…
- Full-time clerical positions with little training and no corporate regional/support, to…
- Full-time clerical positions with strong regional/corporate support, to…
- Full-time revenue management professionals (often part of the hotel executive committee) *plus* corporate/regional support.

Yet, revenue management as a discipline is still sorely lacking at most hotels, especially at the strategic versus tactical level. For the foreseeable future, hotels are going to be playing catch up—or perhaps just holding on for dear life.

14. Reduced consumer spending power over the long term.

There is reason to believe that post–Baby Boomer generations in the United States will have declining purchasing power. The following are five factors that could cause such a decline, each of which has been raised publicly by various experts:

- *Declines in the lifetime earnings of younger generations.* Educational lapses and international competition are at the core of this problem, and even an optimist would have to conclude that it will take some time to turn this trend around. A number of recent studies have shown that the joblessness and/or underemployment experienced by many college graduates during the last seven years created a permanent decline in their future earning potential.
- *The shrinking middle class.* The shrinking middle class means reduced consumer spending power, which can't fail to have an impact on travel expenditures.
- *Entitlement burden.* The declining number of workers in the U.S. labor pool are earning less and paying more for a growing entitlement burden. When Social Security was introduced, the average U.S. male lived to the ripe old age of fifty. Not only has that increased to roughly seventy-nine (and women on average live even longer), but our aging population now believes that replacement of every conceivable body part is a matter of right. This is further exacerbated by extraordinary end-of-life care. According to a study by The Dartmouth Institute for Health Policy & Clinical Practice, the *average* Medicare cost of end-of-life care (the last six months) is $50,000. High medical bills for Medicare patients' final year of life now account for about a quarter of the program's total spending. All of this will be compounded by our national obesity crisis and the health care system's unaccountability, exacerbated by the Affordable Care Act.
- *Personal debt.* This factor is driven in particular by student loans.
- *National debt.* This ticking time bomb clouding our collective future brings to mind a line oft-stated by Wimpy the Moocher, a character in Popeye cartoons: "I'll gladly pay you Tuesday for a hamburger today." So it is with the national debt—consume today, pay tomorrow. But tomorrow must eventually arrive, and the tax dollars used to pay principal and interest on the national debt are not going to be spent on a vacation at the beach.

15. Collapse of traditional hotel product market segmentation.

Meaningful differentiation between limited-service/select-service/focused-service hotels and full-service hotels (excluding luxury) is disappearing, and this blurring of the lines will have serious implications with regard to the competitive nature of markets. Compare, for example, the early generation Marriott Courtyard or Hilton Garden Inn to their current offerings, and compare these newer offerings to full-service hotels (within the same brand family or otherwise). Or compare a current generation Hampton Inn with, say, any mid- to upscale full-service hotel built within the last ten years (e.g., a Holiday Inn). Except for meeting space and F&B, there is very little distinction.

There are numerous implications attending this collapse, not least of which is a brand's ability to oversaturate a market with products within the same brand family that are not covered by area of protection (AOP) clauses. Another example of how this blurring is impacting markets (or will impact markets in the future) is reflected in how the industry thinks about new supply. Part of the industry's euphoria over the past few years has been based on the fact that the supply pipeline is so small by historical standards. But the following are seven reasons owners of existing non-luxury full-service hotels should be concerned about new supply:

- The time to finance and develop the typical limited/select/focused-service hotel is far shorter than the time to entitle, finance, and construct the typical full-service hotel.
- The threat to existing hotel inventory is exacerbated by the age and condition of those existing full-service hotels.
- The product quality of the new generation of limited/select/focused-service products is much closer to the quality of full-service hotels than they were historically—and thus, more directly competitive.
- Increasingly, individual business and leisure travelers (i.e., non-group travelers) are not interested in or willing to pay for those components of a full-service hotel that define it as full-service (a restaurant and meeting space). This tradeoff is occurring despite the very narrow ADR gap that often exists between full-service and limited/select/focused-service hotels.
- Increasingly, limited/select/focused-service hotels have some type of food offering, further diminishing one of the historic differentiators.
- As every traveler knows, brand loyalty programs do not distinguish between sub-brands in the same family. If, for instance, there are six Marriott brands in any given market, travelers can get their Marriott Rewards at any one of them.
- Brands are on a tear in terms of portfolio growth and will jump at any opportunity to squeeze new hotels into markets (both new brands and existing ones).

Naturally, there are supply-constrained segments/areas—like destination resorts and markets with real barriers to entry (e.g., San Francisco). But the fact that there are few full-service hotels currently under construction should be cold comfort to owners of existing assets.

16. Year-round education and sports programs will have an impact on traditional family vacations.

The advent of a longer school year and unsynchronized schedules between different grades/schools will continue to challenge hotels that rely heavily on summer vacation travel. This is further exacerbated by sports programs that used to be seasonally focused but are now becoming year-round activities to elevate competitive performance.

17. The disparities between markets will increase.
Recall Immutable Law 14 regarding variations in liquidity. Notwithstanding the positive impact of compression on market by market performance, there will be continuing disparity between markets. Two of the most important characteristics that will drive this market disparity are: (1) appeal to international travelers and (2) the influence of the "new economy."

18. Continued growth in non-traditional lodging alternatives.
Whether it be cruise lines, vacation ownership properties, glamping, or any of a number of residential rental options (e.g., Airbnb, VRBO, FLIPKEY, Romorama, etc.), leisure travelers have a wide array of alternatives to traditional hotel rooms. Leakage is also occurring in the individual business traveler segment with a broadening appeal/acceptance of Airbnb and a rise in serviced apartments (especially with the consolidation occurring in that niche). As evidenced by the *Stratospheric Rise of Hospitality Alternatives* breakout panel session at the 2015 International Hotel Investment Forum in Berlin, this is not just a U.S. phenomenon. These hospitality interlopers have pretty much covered all the bases in terms of habitable real estate. And don't rule out the "virtual" vacation. With today's younger consumers living substantial parts of their lives within the confines of a 2" by 4" video display, it's not hard to imagine a not-so-distant future where these consumers enjoy a raft trip through the Grand Canyon or an elevator ride up the Eiffel Tower through a virtual reality device instead of a trip.

19. Brands will continue to propagate.
The growth in the number of brands in the past five years has been breathtaking, especially in the lifestyle segment. This is likely to continue because:

- Most of the large brands are public companies. Their share price depends in part on growth. There are only so many Brand X hotels that can fit into any given market, so brands have two choices: (1) move into international markets and/or (2) launch a new brand that has virtually unfettered expansion capabilities for the first ten to fifteen years of its existence.
- The big umbrella brands must continue to introduce products that have more appeal to the post–Baby Boomer traveler than do their legacy brands.

20. Eventual inflation.
According to Laurence J. Peter, "An economist is an expert who will know tomorrow why the things he predicted yesterday didn't happen today." I am not an economist, but, in spite of the continuing weak U.S. recovery, lots of excess labor capacity, and leaders who are loath to make necessary but politically unpopular decisions, it's hard to imagine a scenario where the mountain of currency pumped into the system in the past several years, coupled with our collective inability to live within our means, does not lead to higher inflation somewhere in the not-too-distant future. Happily, inflation has historically proven to be good for the lodging industry, except when it is coupled with excess supply.

21. Interest rate increases.
Out of fear for the adverse impact on a precarious economic recovery (and, perhaps, the impact on the government's ability to service its own debt), the Federal

Reserve's Open Market Committee has maintained near-zero interest rates since December of 2008. This is not sustainable, and, notwithstanding powerful inertial forces, rates will eventually go up. This will have profound impacts on hotel real estate. Please refer to Immutable Law 12 for details.

22. Continued hotel company consolidation.

There is a high probability that industry consolidation will continue to occur. From the perspective of the acquirer, the acquired, or the merged entity, the objectives are fairly obvious and include all or some combination of the following:

- Reductions in overhead and other efficiencies
- Increased negotiating power with vendors and intermediaries (e.g., OTAs)
- Greater global distribution
- Increased market share or "shelf space"
- Increased ability to grow in markets currently saturated with a holding company's other branded products
- Increased consumer reach and name recognition
- Increased membership in brand loyalty programs
- Increased ability to access expensive and ever-changing technological innovation
- Greater capital access

Regardless of the motives, the implications for hotel owners of these new Frankenbrands is not very appealing, to say the least:

- Less competition among brands for deals during acquisition and development (i.e., higher fees, higher reimbursables, and worse contract terms).
- More cannibalization in any given market (potentially offset in part by a greater pool of customers loyal to that brand).
- Reduced differentiation/competitiveness between similar hotels, with different owners operating under different brands within the same brand family. Think Marriott's *Sales Force One* representing Ritz-Carlton, Bulgari, St. Regis, Luxury Collection, JW Marriott, Westin, W, Edition, Le Méridien, Autograph, Marriott, Sheraton, Tribute, Four Points, and Delta—*all in the same market!* Then include all of their limited-service brands and overlay regional revenue management. Top this off with whatever rotation protocols the parent company employs for nonbrand-specific inquiries to their central reservation system and/or website searches.

When you consider the above factors, along with a shift in consumer psychographics and technology-enhanced market access, is it any wonder that more and more owners (even institutional ones) are considering independent/unaffiliated/non-branded options?

Endnotes

1. "Economic loss," as used here, means both an actual loss of income/value, but also a failure to fully capture income/value even though no actual loss has occurred.
2. Top seven publicly traded lodging REITs as of January 2016: HST, HPT, APLE, LHO, RLJ, SHO, PEB.
3. According to data from insideAirbnb.com.

Suggested Case Study Answers

THIS SECTION PROVIDES suggested answers for the questions that followed the case studies appearing in Chapters 15, 17, 18, and 20.

Chapter 15 Answers

1. **What lender types would be viable candidates to provide financing to this hotel's sponsor?**

A balance sheet lender (probably a national or international bank, due to the premier market) is a good lender fit for this loan. A CMBS would struggle with the prolonged turnaround story, as well as the hotel's closure and extensive renovation. A life insurance company might also be interested in this loan, given the location, and could likely offer an all-senior loan at a higher level than a traditional national balance sheet lender, but the loan request of 75 percent will likely require a loan combination of senior and mezzanine.

The reality is that a deal like this will get a lot of attention from national banks, international banks, life insurance companies, and mezzanine lenders willing to underwrite the entire capital stack—especially during a peak point of the economic cycle—because the hotel is high-quality collateral in a premier submarket of a top-five international market. A local/regional lender would not be a good option because of the size of the loan request. An international bank may have problems with the high LTC and could struggle in negotiating an inter-creditor agreement with a mezzanine lender. Ultimately, a team approach—a national balance sheet senior bank and an aggressive mezzanine lender—may be the best option.

2. **Keeping in mind the three main principles in underwriting a hotel loan, identify the potential strengths and weaknesses of the proposed loan. How can the weaknesses be mitigated?**

Strengths

- Location and strength of the market (beachfront in Santa Monica)
- Asset quality (amenities and capital investment)
- Conversion to an affiliation with an international luxury flag
- No projected additions to supply in the market
- Sponsorship with a major equity fund and knowledgeable opportunity partner

Weaknesses

- High LTC. Mitigate with a senior and mezzanine loan approach to bifurcate and properly price the risk.

- Downtime for renovation and execution risk. Mitigated by the strength of the sponsors in executing similar renovation plans and their success with other investments.
- Low in-place NOI on peak-cycle performance. Mitigated again by the success of the repositioning plan, sizing the senior and mezzanine loan, and properly pricing the risk. The senior lender will want a mezzanine lender it can be comfortable with in a first-loss piece, should the hotel default and the mezzanine lender assume the borrower and hotel collateral.

3. **How should a lender structure the loan? What are the key loan terms that should be considered?**

Again, the lender should set up a senior/mezzanine loan structure. The lender might cut the senior loan at a 60 percent LTC, which represents an 11.1 percent debt yield on TTM NOI, priced at L+250. The lender should hold back $50 million of the $180 million/60 percent LTC to fund a portion of the renovation. The lender should structure a completion guaranty. Allow the mezz to fund day one, or fund the renovation hold-back pari-passu with the mezz. It might be best to set up a three-year term with two one-year extensions, and set the extensions based on debt yield and appraisal tests. The lender should try to structure amortization during the extension periods and implement a cash sweep and potential remargin test set at, say, a 9 percent debt yield on the senior basis.

Chapter 17 Answers

1. **Which of the investors would you expect to have a higher cost of capital?**

Investor B: more leverage, less credit enhancement from sponsorship, needs to bring in an equity partner who will likely require a preferred return.

2. **Specifically, what expenses might the closing costs incurred by both investors include?**

Recording fees, fee title insurance, legal expenses, third-party reports, and mortgage origination costs (including recording taxes, brokerage, mortgage title insurance, etc.).

3. **Why might Investor A prefer a lower degree of financial leverage when it could in fact borrow more?**

REIT investors prefer a certain leverage target; REITs usually pay no or little tax at the corporate level, so less interest deductibility benefits; REITs often desire to maintain a minimum corporate credit rating to preserve their flexibility in accessing unsecured debt market.

4. **Why does Investor A prefer a ten-year fixed-rate loan while Investor B prefers a five-year floating-rate loan?**

Different investment horizons: fixed-rate deal allows Investor A to lock in long-term financing, while floating-rate facility gives Investor B flexibility to sell after the hotel's repositioning is complete.

5. If you were the owner of the hotel, with which investor would you choose to enter into a Purchase and Sale Agreement?

Investor B's bid is higher but comes with lower certainty of execution, given financing contingencies and less reputation/reliability.

Chapter 18 Answers

Case Study 1: The Hilton Revival

1. What effect did Hilton's acquisitions strategy through the 1990s have on the operation of the company in the early 2000s? How did this strategy affect the sale of the company in 2007?

Hilton acquired a multitude of brands in the interest of growth and market share, but lacking in identity and consistency. This aggressive growth gave Hilton a large, impressive collection of brands, but burdened it as well. While this large collection of brands may have earned Hilton a high valuation, it also created a level of disorganization that was in effect not efficient.

2. Compare and contrast the operating and capital markets environments Hilton faced pre-2007 and post-2007.

The pre-2007 hospitality industry had finally reached a solid bounce back from the challenges it faced post September 11, 2001. Room rates and occupancy were on the rise again. Hotels were hiring, and there were a record number of transactions leading up to the CNL Hotels & Resorts sale at $6.6 billion in April 2007.

Post-2007 budgets in all sectors were slimmed down at astonishing levels. Downsizing, restructuring, and reorganizing was the name of the game. Occupancy plummeted as every sector was hurting; rates hit rock bottom. For most hotel brands, nearly all capital projects were put on hold. One of the few pieces of good news was the fact that interest rates were essentially at an all-time low, easing the burden on debt and making it attractive for new REITs and investors to enter the field.

3. What factors led to Blackstone's success?

Most hotel companies in the period following 2007 were operating their properties with stringent cost-containment plans in place. At the time of the Hilton acquisition by Blackstone, the impending downturn in the industry was not foreseen. That event promulgated a need for a new strategy that hinged on retaining earnings and cost controls while immersed in a full reorganization of the company.

Blackstone and Nassetta also realized that Hilton presented opportunities for streamlining the organization from the top down, including how the regional management of various brands was organized. They worked to focus the company, including unifying its processes and structure. Finally, Blackstone sought to expand Hilton's global presence, which was recognized as an opportunity for faster growth.

4. What do you think are Hilton's best prospects for growth going forward?

The majority of Hilton's new rooms are being developed internationally. Hilton had strong brand recognition to build upon, which is working to its advantage. There might also be potential in selling off the time share portion of the business,

Hilton Grand Vacations Club. Marriott has already done so and Starwood is now heading in this direction as well.

Case Study 2: Pebblebrook Hotel Trust

1. How important of a role does the founding CEO have in setting the tone and tenor for a company?

As seen from the success of Pebblebrook, a founding CEO, along with other principals, sets the vision for the organization. In the case of Pebblebrook, Bortz was able to leverage his reputation to gain the trust of the investors in order to launch the IPO.

Pebblebrook set forth with a mission to acquire upper-upscale hotels and resorts in key markets. Their portfolio continues to stay focused in this area. While a company will evolve over time, the vision of the founding CEO often sets the foundation for the organization throughout its lifespan.

2. Looking at the capital markets landscape in the late 2000s, what are some of the factors (both pro and con) that you would consider in deciding whether or not to pursue a "blind" trust IPO?

Without any assets to examine and measure, a blind IPO is a leap of faith. The reputation and performance history of the organization's leadership are for the most part the only factors that can be examined deeply enough to value the organization. It would also be necessary to discuss the organization's business plan and understand what type of assets it hopes to acquire and how its leaders plan on doing so. Given the amount of bad debt in the marketplace during the late 2000s, a fresh new organization that is not highly leveraged would make an attractive option.

3. Looking at the various performance metrics Pebblebrook has achieved through November of 2014, is there a particular metric or metrics that you think is most indicative of their success?

One particular metric that tells of Pebblebrook's success is the fact that its portfolio contains fourteen hotels that are unencumbered by debt. This results in the desirable statistic of adjusted EBITDA growth of 28–29 percent in 2014. Pebblebrook came into existence when other REITs had balance sheets with inordinate debt to equity ratios. In order to maintain its reputation and strength, the Pebblebrook organization should continue pursuing the goal of minimal debt and high EBITDA growth.

4. How important are geographic and operator diversification to a hotel REIT?

While there may be some REITs that specialize in a particular brand or market, this is the exception to the rule. Most REITs will have a diverse portfolio both geographically and with operators. Diversification has the benefit of not putting all your eggs in one basket. Just like diversifying an investment portfolio, REITs should have an assortment of assets that are geographically positioned to absorb market fluctuations. If and when a particular market or management company faces challenges, the performance of other markets or other management companies will help offset any setbacks encountered.

Chapter 20 Answers

Case Study 1: To Buy or Not to Buy

1. **Have all significant market risks been identified and evaluated?**

Some additional market risks for potential consideration and evaluation include the following:

- The potential labor risk in the market. Despite the stated associate satisfaction being above brand average, larger markets in the northeastern United States tend to have heavier concentrations of union activity, and brand-managed properties represent notable targets for potential organization efforts.
- The potential for new supply. Before moving forward with a recommendation, Bob needs to complete a thorough market review, including identification of planned renovations and repositionings, rather than relying on a lack of announced new developments. He should also review trends and development activity in other submarkets that could be competitive with the subject's submarket, particularly as it relates to changes within the subject's brand family.
- Convention activity. Although the subject does not participate directly in citywide convention blocks, the decline in convention activity should be thoroughly reviewed, since continuing drops likely result in reduced market compression, which will affect the subject. The drop also could be symptomatic of other relevant market factors, such as reduced airlift into the market.

2. **What areas of potential upside or downside may Bob have missed during his property visit and tours?**

Some potential areas of upside or downside Bob may have missed include the following:

- Back-of-house and building system needs. Bob's tour did not appear to include a thorough inspection of the back-of-house spaces, roofs, and building/engineering systems. While some needs may have been identified on the brand PIP, it is ill-advised to rely on the brand reps to detail all of the mechanical and systems needs of a property as old as the subject property.
- Market interviews. Although Bob walked the competitive set, he apparently did not interview the management or sales teams of the competitors or anyone with the local convention and visitors bureau, forgoing the opportunity to glean valuable information on the subject's SWOT from the perspective of independent market experts.
- Meeting planner satisfaction and turndowns. As a large part of the identified upside centers on the potential for additional group business, Bob should review the meeting planner survey results and turndown reports to assess how well the subject property is servicing the groups, to identify any noted opportunities by the clients, and to help quantify the unmet group demand.

3. **What are some potential risk factors in the assumptions behind the acquisition pro forma?**

Some potential risk factors in Bob's pro forma assumptions include the following:

- The estimated PIP cost of $19,500 per key. Although the brand may issue "courtesy" estimates of the cost of PIPs, they typically are non-binding and the actual costs could be materially higher; Bob should have a qualified project management firm or similar organization independently price the PIP work.
- The assumption of only a 2 percent occupancy drop in Years 1 and 2. For a property with occupancy in the high 70s (see Exhibit 1 in Chapter 20), it would appear unreasonable to decrease occupancy only 2 percent during the renovation, particularly during highly disruptive work such as the sports lounge conversion.
- The assumption of rate growth throughout the renovation. Similar to the point above, it is typically very difficult to achieve rate growth during a highly disruptive renovation, notwithstanding the potential to better yield the reduced room inventory.
- The assumption driving A&G expenses. A&G growth is assumed to track inflation; however, due to the impact of credit card commissions in high revenue growth scenarios such as this, A&G expenses likely will exceed inflation unless offsetting cuts are made in other areas.
- The assumptions driving Real Property Taxes and Insurance. Although largely dependent on local/state jurisdictions and geographic/weather conditions, these expense lines both tend to have a variable component tracking profitability; as EBITDA growth is more than double the growth in these expenses over the pro forma horizon, Bob needs to validate the assumptions of significantly lower expense growth.

4. **Under the existing management agreement, the manager benefits significantly through both base and incentive fees from owner-funded ROI projects, such as the sports lounge conversion, without bearing any risk. How might the management agreement be modified to more fairly compensate LOL for its discretionary financial risk?**

To more fairly compensate ownership for its risk, the manager could agree to subordinate some portion of its fees to ensure that the owner gets a fair return on its discretionary capital before the manager benefits from incremental fees. A common example of this might include granting ownership a "priority" annual return deduction of some percentage of the investment, typically in the range of 10 to 15 percent, before calculating incentive management fees. Although not the case in the subject scenario, if incentive management fees are calculated after replacement reserves, another option could be to fund the discretionary investment from reserves.

Case Study 2: Sell or Hold?

1. **What are some potential risk factors in the assumptions behind Bob's hold/repositioning pro forma?**

Some potential risk factors in Bob's pro forma assumptions include the following:

- The assumption of increasing market share by 6.7 percent. While potentially reasonable with the expanded stronger brand lift, the penetration improvement should be substantiated with thorough market analysis, including a review of potential new supply, a review of area demand generators, and SWOT analysis of the competitive set.
- The estimated cost of improvements of $10,000 per key. It could be materially higher, and the capital requirement is hard to project in the absence of a formal PIP from the replacement brand.
- The assumption of improved occupancy in Year 1. It would appear unreasonable to increase occupancy in the first year, given the likelihood of renovation displacement and the initial loss of business that is typical on brand transition (even a transition to a significantly stronger brand).
- The assumption of rooms cost per occupied room (CPOR) rising at inflation. It may be reasonable, but Bob needs to get comfortable that the stronger brand will not also entail higher costs relating to enhanced brand standards.
- The assumptions driving A&G, Information & Telecom, and Sales & Marketing. As with the point above, Bob needs to get comfortable that the stronger brand will not also entail higher costs relating to enhanced brand standards and program costs.
- The assumptions driving Real Property Taxes and Insurance. Although largely dependent on local/state jurisdictions and geographic/weather conditions, these expense lines both tend to have a variable component tracking profitability; as EBITDA growth is roughly double the growth in these expenses over the pro forma horizon, Bob needs to validate the assumptions of significantly lower expense growth.

2. **How sensitive is the analysis to variations in the current market value assumptions? to the pro forma RevPAR growth assumptions?**

It is important for ownership that the analysis be highly sensitive to variations in the current market value assumption. The difference between net current value and the discounted cash flow under the hold scenario is less than $500,000, representing roughly 30 basis points of the capitalization rate on TTM EBITDA Less Replacement Reserves. Should ownership have other non-financial considerations factoring into the hold/sell decision, those considerations could outweigh the relatively small differential in the analysis.

3. **Should Bob test the current market value assumption of $11,875,000 by listing the property to see if a higher price is obtainable? What are the advantages and disadvantages of doing so?**

The primary advantage of actually taking the property to market is that ownership will obtain a true understanding of the market value of the asset (versus relying on a BOV from the broker or another method of estimating value). The disadvantages include disclosing proprietary information to the public, potential delays in decision-making given the time involved in marketing a property, and the potential negative impact on future transactions once the property is pulled back (future brokers and/or buyers could be reluctant to participate due to concerns of wasted time and effort).

4. **What other ownership considerations should be evaluated prior to recommending a current hold for the asset?**

Other considerations to be evaluated include whether the brand still meets ownership's geographic investment parameters; whether ownership has changed its investment allocation standards between full-service versus limited-service hotels, for hotels versus other classes of real estate, or for real estate versus other investment classes; whether ownership has an overriding need to generate cash for unrelated needs; and whether the subject asset has an upcoming loan maturity of other capital overriding capital considerations.